D1460681

THE

Aberdeenshire Library and Information Service
www.aberdeenshire.gov.uk/libraries
Renewals Hotline 01224 661511

14/1/19.
2 5 NOV 2019

2 6 FEB 2009

3 0 MAY 2009

2 7 APR 2011

HEADQUARTERS

- 9 FEB 2017

3 0 JUN 2017

1 5 DEC 2017

GUINN, Gilbert Sumter

The Arnold Scheme

THE
ARNOLD SCHEME

BRITISH PILOTS, THE AMERICAN SOUTH
AND THE ALLIES' DARING PLAN

GILBERT S. GUINN

History
PRESS   SPELLMOUNT

Published in the United States by The History Press
Charleston, SC 29403
www.historypress.net
and in Great Britain by Spellmount (Publishers) Ltd.
A Division of NPI Media Ltd.
Cirencester Road
Chalford, Stroud
Gloucestershire GL6 8PE
Tel: 0044 (0) 1285 760000
Fax: 0044 (0) 1285 760001
www.spellmount.com

First published 2007

Manufactured in the United Kingdom

ISBN (USA) 978.1.59629.042.6
ISBN (UK) 978.1.86227.446.4

Library of Congress Cataloging-in-Publication Data
Guinn, Gilbert Sumter, 1929-
  The Arnold scheme : British pilots, the American South and the Allies' daring plan / Gilbert S. Guinn.
    p. cm.
  Includes bibliographical references.
  ISBN 978-1-59629-042-6 (alk. paper)
  1. World War, 1939-1945--Aerial operations, British. 2. Airmen--Training of--United States. 3. Great Britain. Royal Air Force--Recruiting, enlistment, etc.--World War, 1939-1945. 4. Great Britain. Royal Air Force--Military life. 5. World War, 1939-1945--Personal narratives, British. 6. British--United States--Biography. 7. Airmen--Great Britain--Biography. I. Title.
  D786.G85 2007
  940.54'49410975--dc22

                              2007009402

British Library Cataloguing in Publication Data
A catalogue record for this book is available from the British Library

CONTENTS

Preface   6

Acknowledgements   21

Introduction   23

Chapter One. American, British and Canadian Flight Training, 1938–1941   26

Chapter Two. Setting Up Arnold Scheme Flight Training   44

Chapter Three. The Two Distant Primary Schools: Camden and Tuscaloosa   73

Chapter Four. The Two Georgia Primary Schools: Americus and Albany   106

Chapter Five. The Two Florida Primary Schools: Lakeland and Arcadia   145

Chapter Six. Background to Early Arnold Scheme Training
       and Responses from Britain, Canada and the United States   185

Chapter Seven. Final Classes of the Two Distant Primaries   217

Chapter Eight. Responses to the Washout Rate in the United States:
       The Four Georgia and Florida Primary Flight Schools   241

Chapter Nine. The Final Six RAF Classes in Georgia   274

Chapter Ten. The Final Six RAF Classes in Florida   293

Chapter Eleven. USAAF Basic Flying School: Gunter Field   304

Chapter Twelve. USAAF Basic Flying School: Cochran Field   342

Chapter Thirteen. Single-Engine Advanced Flying Schools: Craig and Napier   386

Chapter Fourteen. Twin-Engine Advanced Flying Schools:
       Maxwell, Turner and Moody   443

Chapter Fifteen. The Training of RAF Navigators   484

Epilogue   523

Appendix I. Arnold Scheme Statistics   529

Appendix II. War Brides   544

Sources   561

PREFACE

The airplane solved the problem of manned flight in heavier-than-air machines. Where dozens failed and a few would-be inventors had near successes, the Wright brothers achieved a major scientific and technological triumph. Their breakthrough created a new industry, but it was not yet apparent in 1903 that the airplane also constituted a revolutionary means of communication and transport, as well as a powerful weapon of war. The forty-two-year period of time between the flight at Kitty Hawk, North Carolina, in December 1903 and the end of World War II in August 1945 represented only a portion of the normal life span of a human being. In the realm of technology—the evolution from box-kite craft with limited power to the emergence of sleek and powerful fighters and massive bombers and transports—those forty-two years encompassed truly revolutionary changes.

The methods for training aviators and ground maintenance staff evolved in response to technological change. From the beginning, all such technical training was closely linked with aircraft design and manufacture. As aircraft designs changed, and as new controls, better instruments and more powerful engines were installed, special instruction was necessary for those using or maintaining the craft. The original *Federacion Aeronautique Internationale (FAI)* qualification standards for licensing required a pilot to take off, fly four figure eights and land. It was also deemed wise for pilots to gain sufficient knowledge of aircraft structures and engines to make minor emergency repairs.

In the United States, those who purchased aircraft from the Wright brothers and their licensees or from Glenn Curtiss and other manufacturers were provided with vocational apprenticeships as part of the purchase price. Every pilot trainee began work in an aircraft factory and spent more time learning about airplane structures, engines and maintenance than they spent flying. Providing prospective aviators with a grounding in the operation of controls and engines was a sound approach to pre-flight training and was continued in use for more than three decades in civilian airlines and army and naval air services. Aircraft manufacturers discovered that if they were to sell their machines, they had to expand their training facilities and provide year-round instruction. Since the open design of early airplanes and the exposed positions of pilots and passengers made favorable weather essential for operating the flimsy craft, the geographic location of air training was especially important.

Since flying was difficult or impossible during periods of high winds and inclement weather, and since the manufacturing firms were located in the north of the United States and in regions of most other countries where harsh weather conditions occurred regularly, flying periods were sharply restricted. Obviously, this restriction affected pilot training and consequently restricted sales. In pursuit of an improved climate, French and British pilots such as Louis Bleriot, Claude Grahame-

White and others followed the sun and their wealthy clientele to Pau in the south of France, where these early aviators operated winter flying schools.

During the winter of 1909, the Wright brothers also moved to Pau in order to demonstrate their aircraft and to sell manufacturing rights. When they returned to the United States, they followed that European example of moving southward. In February 1911, they established a winter flying school close by the Alabama River near Montgomery, Alabama, a site that later became Maxwell Air Force Base. During summer and autumn, their school was moved back to their Dayton, Ohio factory and flying field.

Similar patterns were followed by Glenn Hammond Curtiss at his factory in the lake district of New York. After expanding training as much as possible on and near Lake Keuka and at his factory in the small village of Hammondsport, Glenn Curtiss, the chief rival of the Wrights, was also compelled to branch out. Curtiss established winter flying operations on North Island at San Diego, California, and used that station as a center for training pilots to fly both land planes and flying boats.

During 1911, that magical year in which aviation enthusiasm knew no bounds, many nations began to seek military and naval applications for aviation. Each of them followed already well-established patterns of development. After assigning men to attend the flying schools of the major aircraft manufacturers, the armed services of the United States established their own small aviation sections. These tiny experimental stations housed several aircraft and were used by army or navy personnel or by men of both services to determine potential applications of aviation.

The United States Army and the United States Navy first jointly used Wright airplanes at a temporary hangar and airfield at College Park, Maryland, on what later became a part of the campus of the University of Maryland. Early on, the United States Navy withdrew from the Wright School at College Park and developed its own separate flying school on land and water courses adjacent to the U.S. Naval Academy at Annapolis, Maryland. During winter months, navy pilots sometimes left Annapolis and conducted flying exercises from Guantanamo Bay, Cuba.

Then in 1912, at Glenn Curtiss's invitation, the navy moved its winter flying operations to a leased site near Curtiss's winter base on North Island, San Diego, California. When in 1914 the U.S. Navy's attempt to purchase the island failed, it relinquished its lease on the California site to the U.S. Army, but continued to favor use of Curtiss Company aircraft. Before that year ended, the Navy Department purchased a large tract of land adjacent to Pensacola, Florida, and opened its own permanent aviation training center.

Army flying training also began in the Dayton, Ohio factory of the Wright brothers before being shifted to the joint-service airfield at College Park, Maryland. For some time, the army continued to use Wright Company aircraft at that airfield and at Fort Sam Houston in San Antonio, Texas. In 1912, the United States Army Signal Corps, which had been assigned control of army aviation, surveyed the United States in order to ascertain sites for conducting winter flying. After examining many potential sites, an army winter flying field was established at Barnes Farm on the Savannah River east of Augusta, Georgia. Then in late 1913, the U.S. Army established its first permanent air training center at North Island, San Diego. A year later, on 18 July 1914, the Aviation Section of the United States Army Signal Corps was officially established.

British aviation also began to expand. In April 1911, when the War Office decided to use aircraft for military purposes, a provision was made to form an air battalion of the Royal Engineers, which was composed of airship and airplane companies. The Royal Navy followed suit. Francis McLean persuaded the Royal Aero Club to make two airplanes available to four officers of the Royal Navy and to invite the officers to use the club's airfield and facilities at Eastchurch, Kent. The Royal Naval Air Service and Britain's naval flying school evolved from that arrangement.

In 1912, in an effort to reduce costs and avoid duplication, Great Britain's armed services consolidated air technology, maintenance and flying training. The air battalion was separated from the Royal Engineers and was re-designated the Royal Flying Corps (RFC). This new enlarged aviation establishment would control the Royal Aircraft Factory at Farnborough, Hampshire, and would operate separate army and navy wings. As with other regular service units, each of these wings would also maintain reserve units. The War Office was also authorized to form a central flying school (CFS). With an appropriation of £40,000 sterling (approximately $200,000), a large tract on top of a high hill near Upavon, Wiltshire, was purchased and developed into the CFS. Over time, the CFS staff would develop a common training syllabus for army and naval aviators and would regularly inspect all flying schools.

Through the development of standard course syllabi and inspection visits similar to those used in the British educational system, CFS staff would also supervise the training of air and ground crew. Course No. 1, which commenced training at Upavon on 17 August 1912 and completed written as well as flying examinations on 5 December 1912, was the beginning of the standardization of military flying instruction. As the Royal Flying Corps expanded, and aircraft became more complex, the CFS was instrumental in developing specialized schools for training RFC technicians at Halton, Berkshire.

Well before other nations paid very much attention to aviation, France promoted it. By 1914, French aviators had also developed flying training methods that were being observed and adopted by other air services. Following recruit training, French pilot trainees were put into under-powered aircraft with clipped wings. Use of these *rouleurs*, and basic instruction in aircraft, engines, traffic patterns, signals, etc., before they ever left the ground, taught trainees details of the airplane and how to maneuver it safely on the ground. The French flying training system was divided into twelve or more stages, each of which was taught by specialist instructors, often at separate airfields and using different types of aircraft. After some fifty hours of dual and solo flying, the pilot was deemed ready for assignment to further training in gunnery, pursuit, bombardment or observation schools before joining a combat squadron.

As civilian and armed services aviators throughout the world gained flying experience, each group sought to determine how to apply aviation to its mission or enterprise. Inevitably, the fliers of each nation and each branch of service developed distinctive syllabi, instructional methods and favorite aircraft. Even the names given to aircraft and squadrons reflected the culture and traditions of each nation and each branch of service. Military and naval attachés and other observers carefully followed new developments in aviation, and all nations borrowed from one another.

During the 1914–18 war, European airplane manufacturers enlarged their training facilities and continued research and development to meet or exceed every enemy advance. Changes also occurred in North America. When the simpler aileron system for lateral control of aircraft replaced the more complicated Wright wing-warping controls, and tractor-model (engines in front) airplanes gained popularity over pusher models, the influence of Wright Company aircraft faded and that of the Curtiss Company rose. The development of the Curtiss *Jenny* biplane trainer and its flying boats assured the Curtiss Company's emergence as the premier American aircraft designer and builder.

Other airplane manufacturers entered the field, and all competed to improve existing models and to develop new trainers, flying boats and aircraft engines for wartime domestic and foreign markets. As the demand for pilot training increased, American aircraft companies expanded existing schools and opened new ones. Hundreds of young men came to the United States from Britain and the Empire-Commonwealth and other nations for the express purpose of gaining pilot's credentials. Even with new equipment and enlarged training staffs, established American flying schools lacked the ability to provide for the increased numbers desiring flying training. As demand continued at a high level, more individuals gained qualifications in these manufacturers' schools and many of them, like the Stinson sisters and brother, purchased aircraft and opened their own flying schools.

During 1914–15, the air services of the Allied and Central powers sought to use aircraft effectively in war. At first, when patrols in slow pusher-type biplanes functioned as the eyes and ears of military ground formations in the traditional role of cavalry, the focus was on the training of pilots and observers (artillery spotters) and large numbers of maintenance and other support personnel. Laden with bombs and larger fuel tanks, the airplane evolved into long-range artillery, and because of its heavy load, slow speed and consequent vulnerability to attack, speedier armed fighter aircraft were needed to protect against bombers and aerial artillery spotters. Then, in order to defend their aircraft and crews, these flying observation posts were transformed into gun platforms and a greater amount of specialization followed. In 1916, by which time increasing numbers of armed fighter and bomber aircraft had assumed more aggressive roles, the training of airplane pilots and observers was modified to meet new demands.

In training pilots for service with bomber and fighter squadrons, the rigid curriculum emphasized the practical. Although there were significant variations, most nations followed a three-phase flying training system encompassing forty to fifty hours of flying. Initially, all students underwent eight weeks of ground school courses before learning elementary flying by imitating their instructors' movement of the controls and learning the "feel of the aircraft" in various attitudes of flight. That dual stage of flying instruction encompassed takeoffs, landings and elementary maneuvers. During these sessions with an instructor, the student gained familiarity with his aircraft, with local landmarks and with the danger of stalls and spins.

During the solo stage of flying training, the student repeated most of what he had learned and usually continued to fly for an additional twenty-four hours under an instructor's supervision. The goal of that phase of training was to gain mastery of basic maneuvers through repetition. The solo student was limited to two hours of flying per day in periods ranging from twenty to forty minutes. The repertoire of maneuvers that the student pilot was to master included circuits and bumps (takeoffs and landings), climbing, banking, figure eights, stalls, precision landings and different approaches to landing grounds. During the advanced stage of flying instruction, the student made two cross-country flights. He then made a triangular navigational flight of thirty miles, during which he was examined on landmarks. In three additional flights extending out from the main airdrome thirty miles, each student was examined on the effective use of maps and compass. After gaining basic qualifications, aircrew were introduced to tactical flying, which was designed to prepare them for active operations. The effective training of combat pilots and observers did not take place until they were assigned to active squadrons.

During 1916–17 at Gosport, Hampshire, on England's south coast, a revolution occurred in pilot training methods. Combat veteran Major Robert R. Smith-Barry of the Royal Flying Corps' 60 Squadron had analyzed the problems of many young airmen who arrived in France with from fifty to one hundred hours of flying. As a result of his experience, Smith-Barry determined to improve the existing training system. Using methods designed to make pilots more confident and more comfortable with their aircraft, he trained a number of experienced pilots in what he perceived to be the best techniques.

Smith-Barry first insisted that these experienced pilots improve their knowledge of both aircraft and engines, and then they spent much of their time flying and doing every conceivable kind of acrobatic maneuver at altitudes ranging from inches above the ground to around two thousand feet and above. Inspired by that knowledge and experience, they emerged from Smith-Barry's training school with greater confidence in themselves and their machines. This was the essence of what became the Gosport system of flying training. Gosport-trained and indoctrinated instructors were then posted to other training stations to teach the system, which came to dominate British pilot training in spirit and in reality.

At least one American flying training officer of the time was critical of the Gosport system because of its unusually high training fatality rate. From his perspective, the British system aimed to increase confidence and skill of the pilots by incurring risks and performing reckless feats. Men trained under the system were noted for their devil-may-care manner on the ground as well as in the air, and that image, which had borrowed heavily from British Guards Regiments, became the standard for all air services in the eyes of populations in need of romantic illusions during such a devastating and bloody war.

In 1917, although Americans had invented the airplane and had helped to prove its worth, the United States was far behind the rest of the world in flight training. At that time, many Europeans regarded the United States as an upstart emerging nation populated mainly by unfortunate working-class immigrants. The early twentieth-century stereotype accepted by too many British and European observers was that Americans were capable of copying the work of others and were geniuses at mass production but, outside the realm of commerce, it was felt that Americans lacked the organizational and planning abilities of Europeans. As a result of these attitudes, British, French and Italian interest in the United States focused on its immense resources, its industrial capacity and its manpower. By emphasizing the practical, by unashamedly inviting Allied missions and by sending American observers to study European experience, American officials unwittingly fed that assessment.

After 6 April 1917, when the Congress of the United States declared war, several American air missions were sent to Europe to learn about wartime aviation organization and manufacturing. Before the end of April 1917, both British and French air missions arrived in the United States and proved to be very effective lobbyists. They were convinced that if the United States could harness its mass production system and produce huge numbers of aircraft and aircrew, the Allied powers could gain air superiority and break the defensive stalemate in the trenches. They also convinced the Congress of the United States that air power would save lives. Congress quickly approved the expenditure of almost $640 million for aviation expansion, and on 24 July 1917 President Woodrow Wilson signed that appropriations bill into law.

The United States Army sought guidance in training matters from the British and French air missions, which had been welcomed to the United States within less than thirty days after the American entry into the war. Colonel John F. Curry, who served in the training section of the U.S. Army Air Service (USAAS) Headquarters in Washington, wrote of his experience in helping to direct the establishment of training schools in the United States:

> *Our actual knowledge in the office of what should be done and how schools should be run was very slight, and, to make matters worse, I could find no American in the office*

who knew any more than I did. As a result, we turned to the French and British Aviation Missions for recommendations and advice. The recommendations we received from these sources were so radically different—the French recommending extreme caution and, the British a rather reckless disregard for life and limb—that we did the only logical thing and followed a middle course, slowly evolving a training program of our own, by getting the advice of school commanders who commanded successful schools and any others upon whom we could depend.

   Though American officers did not accept all of the advice of the foreign air missions, many procedures were adapted for use. Among the accepted British and French recommendations were ideas concerning layout of airfields and buildings, ground and flying training syllabi, defense contracting procedures and dozens of other suggestions based on several years of wartime experience.

   Whether or not United States Army Air Service planners consulted the visiting missions about airfield designs or locations is unknown; either way, mistakes were made. The American officers adhered too closely to early patterns in developing air training camps and made a serious error. During the summer of 1917, training stations were rapidly built in a line extending across the United States from Long Island, New York, to Sacramento, California. During the autumn and winter of 1917, when heavy weather struck these airfields in Northern locales, training schedules were disrupted and pilot production declined. Having learned a valuable lesson, Air Service planners sought to rectify their errors.

   In 1918, these newly built airfields in Northern states were converted for use as technical training schools and operational airfields for the training of defensive air squadrons. In that year, the United States Army Air Service also hurriedly built some twenty new training airfields and depots, but this time the appointed boards of officers selected sites across the Southern tier of states. These air station sites extended southward from Virginia to Florida and westward across the nation to California.

   Although pilot and technical training had long existed in the United States, the military services had no experience in mass production of aircrew or of support personnel. There was no sufficient force of regulars or reservists to serve as cadre, so the American air service had to employ qualified civilians and to turn once more to European experience. When in 1917 the USAAS sought to develop its own wartime aircrew training system, its planners adopted from Canada the training syllabi of Britain's Royal Flying Corps. In exchange for that planning assistance and for agreement to train some American pilots and ground crew in established Canadian schools, the Royal Canadian Air Force was permitted to develop and use three flying fields near Fort Worth, Texas, for winter flying training.

   Lack of preparedness in 1917 forced the United States to turn to Europe for much of the aircrew training needed for creating an effective American air service. Since the shortage of trainers and service aircraft delayed the implementation of advanced flying training in the United States, the USAAS sent more than 10,000 partially trained pilots and other aircrew to European schools. Until a large enough number of American aircrew could be trained and organized into independent USAAS units, European-trained Americans would gain combat experience in active Allied combat squadrons. In addition to men sent from the United States for training in Europe, approximately 2,500 potential airmen were recruited for flying training from United States Army units in France.

In 1914 the United States Navy consolidated its air training at Pensacola, where it trained regular and reserve officers of the navy and marine corps as well as college and university graduates. It used a stage system of instruction similar to those of the air services of the French and British navies. By 1917, the U.S. Naval Air Service (USNAS) still possessed very few pilots, aircraft or airships, and its only air station was the one at Pensacola. As with the Army Air Service, the navy's wartime aviation expansion was hurried and chaotic.

The U.S. Navy used several universities for ground school training, as did the army, but its flying training followed a different pattern of development. At first, one group of navy pilots received their flying training at Yale University, then the navy contracted with the Curtiss Company to train pilots at one of its flying schools located near Newport News, Virginia. As an increased number of volunteers clamored for pilot training, the USNAS established flying schools at scattered locations along the Northeast coast.

In 1917, flying training continued at Pensacola, but was also instituted at three new naval air stations that were opened at Squantum, Massachusetts; Bayshore, Long Island, New York; and Newport News, Virginia. As equipment and flying boats were delivered for use by the newly trained aviators, units were organized for several coastal patrol air stations extending from Halifax, Nova Scotia, to Key West, Florida. Moreover, large numbers of American aviators and ratings were posted to Ireland, England, France and Italy with anti-submarine patrol squadrons. Preliminary training for a number of Marine and Naval Aviation Students was conducted in Canada, Britain, France and Italy, and advanced flying was completed in some of the Allied schools as well. In addition, a number of naval aviators were trained in United States Army Air Service schools in France, but in order to prepare them for combat, the navy established several of its own specialist schools in Europe.

As with army students, a majority of the several thousand naval aviators received their qualifying training in the United States and their operational training on active North American coastal stations and in Europe. During 1918, naval aviation was reorganized for maximum training. Pensacola was converted for use as the navy's advanced flying training station, and all elementary training was concentrated at several airfields around Key West and Miami in south Florida, and at other stations near Newport News and Bayshore, Long Island. Variations in statistical reports are confusing, so it is difficult to ascertain precise numbers of U.S. Naval Air Service pilots trained between 1917 and 1919, but the total was probably about seven thousand pilots and observers and about thirty-five thousand maintenance and other aviation ratings.

The similarity of the experience of American cadets in England in 1917–18 and that of British cadets under training in the United States more than two decades later is striking. One of the best records available of that American training experience in Britain is provided by the South Carolinian and former Princeton University student Elliott White Springs, who was trained in Britain and was credited with the destruction of twelve enemy aircraft, eight of them while serving in 85 Squadron of the Royal Air Force. According to Springs, the transport carrying 150 American cadets arrived in Liverpool Harbor and docked on 2 October 1917. The American cadets boarded train cars at dockside and traveled to Oxford.

Although Springs and others had already completed an American ground school course, they were told that everything they had learned was obsolete and were assigned to ground school at Oxford University. As they adjusted to their new surroundings, they found the local citizens and the Royal Flying Corps airmen friendly and helpful, but on occasion they also encountered hostility. Instead of their own war, some Britons seemed to think that they had been fighting the war for Americans, and they bluntly asked where Americans "had been for the last three years." Sooner than any of them realized, the eight-week ground school course at Oxford was over, and they were posted elsewhere for further training. Some of them moved directly to an elementary flying school, but others attended a gunnery course while awaiting a flying school intake. At preliminary flying schools, they flew Henri Farman Shorthorn and Avro 504 aircraft. On completion of that course, they spent a short leave in London, and several of them were posted to London Colney, Hertfordshire, for advanced flying training.

In the spirit of the Gosport training system, the American pilots spent a considerable number of hours learning to handle their aircraft in every conceivable flying attitude. They flew under bridges and sometimes bounced the aircraft's wheels on roads and the occasional building roof or chimney pot. Often they met the great and near great of the flying fraternity, but they also regularly received reports of colleagues and friends who died in training accidents or in combat. As they waited impatiently for their chance at the front, they also attended the funerals of comrades.

There are conflicting reports as to precise numbers of pilots, observers and ground crew trained in Britain, but a combination of two authoritative reports indicates that approximately 350 Americans entered flying training in Britain, and of that number 34 were killed in training accidents and 316 graduated, 309 as pilots and 7 as observers. Of the British flying school graduates, 214 American pilots flew with Royal Air Force combat squadrons. A few of them were reassigned, 95 of them were casualties and 102 transferred to squadrons of the United States Army Air Service. In addition to training American aircrew, Great Britain provided aircraft, equipment and other services.

Large numbers of American mechanics (fitters) and other support personnel were also trained in Britain during 1917–18. But it was not entirely a one-way proposition. Because of a British labor shortage, the United States furnished thousands of Americans for training as aircraft and engine mechanics in Britain and agreed to maintain at least 15,000 of them in British factories and schools until the end of the war. Almost 12,000 such technical ratings completed their training in Britain and were posted to France, while an additional 19,535 American maintenance ratings were still under training in the United Kingdom when the war ended.

During 1917–19, the United States government paid Britain $36 million for air service training. In connection with Britain's wartime labor shortage, the United States government entered into a contract with the Handley-Page Aircraft Company. Under that agreement, tons of building materials were purchased from the United States and nearly four thousand carpenters, brick masons and other craftsmen were recruited in the United States and sent to Britain to build facilities essential for American training. As the official history of the American Air Service recorded, the amounts paid to Britain for this assistance "were by no means disproportionate to the benefits received."

Shortly after Congress declared war on Germany, air cooperation with France commenced. American and French missions departed almost immediately for their assignments. On 25 April 1917 the French air mission headed by Major Tulasne arrived in Washington. In order to hasten the arrival of American aid in France, the French air officer proposed that Americans be sent to France for aircrew training. If a large American advanced flying school could also be built in France by American labor using materials shipped to France, the French government would provide the aircraft and engines to equip it. And if training could commence on 1 July 1917, it was believed that American pilots would be ready for combat in the autumn.

The United States Army Air Service Advanced Flying School proposed for construction in France was approved, funds were appropriated and an Air Service detachment was formed to man the school. On 16 July 1917, three cargo ships departed American ports loaded with materials for building the huge air training base. Three days later, Captain Lawrence S. Churchill embarked at New York with the first United States Army Air Service enlisted detachment. In August 1917, construction was begun on the American flying school, and on 15 September 1917 the USAAS opened its partially completed Third Air Instruction Center at Issoudun, near the geographic center of France.

In the meantime, approximately 500 American cadets commenced training in the French Elementary Flying School at Tours. Of that group, approximately 444 graduated as pilots and were posted to further training. Subsequently, France relinquished control of the Tours flying school to the United States, and elementary flying training was provided there for more than 1,200 additional American pilots. Most of the graduates of the school at Tours, as well as others who had completed elementary training in the United States, entered the advanced school at Issoudun. Before the war ended, the Third Air Instruction Center at Issoudun had been expanded into a complex of fourteen airfields, and the separate instructional staff at each field used French aircraft and the French "stage" system of instruction for training pilots.

Such a system could and did produce pilots rapidly, but since there had not been time to standardize instruction among so many different instructors and airfields scattered over a thirty-six-square-mile area, U.S. Army Air Service officers considered their training faulty. In addition to the instruction at Tours and the advanced training at Issoudun, other USAAS stations in France provided operational training for American pilots and observers. By 11 November 1918, flying schools in France had graduated more than three thousand American pilots and observers.

Between 15 and 27 July 1917, the Bolling Commission visited Italy, and the Italian government agreed to train 500 American pilots. On 28 September 1917, the first contingent of 47 American student pilots arrived at the Foggia flying school, which was located about 250 miles southeast of Rome. During the autumn, an American Air Service headquarters was established in Rome and newly promoted Major Fiorello LaGuardia (famous later as mayor of New York City) was assigned to the command. By the time the war ended in November 1918, approximately 450 American pilots had been trained at that Italian elementary flying school. While most of the Foggia graduates were posted to France for advanced training at Issoudun, almost 50 American pilots remained in Italy, received advanced and operational training on Caproni bombers and flew combat missions on the Italian front.

According to the official history of the United States Army Air Service, some 12,000 Americans entered flying training schools in France, 400 in Britain and almost 450 in Italy. Slightly more than 8,500 USAAS pilots and observers were graduated from European flying schools and more than 200 were killed in flying training accidents. In addition to training these aircrew, the Allied air services also trained more than 30,000 American mechanics and other support personnel.

Since American engineers had not yet developed combat aircraft of their own design, blueprints and sample models of British, French and Italian aircraft were brought to the United States. Work was begun on gathering raw materials and building aircraft and engines based on successful European models. On 11 November 1918, when the shooting stopped, the United States government quickly canceled production orders and left for disposal as war surplus partially completed airplanes, tons of aircraft parts, engines, stockpiled lumber and other raw materials. As a result, wartime American aircraft construction came to be associated in the public mind with terrible waste, and that view led to much grief and misunderstanding, which caused every administration during the twenty years between 1918 and 1938 to study and re-study every facet of aviation.

Failing to produce large numbers of aircraft as quickly as projected appeared worse than it was in reality. There had been errors, such as unrealistic production scheduling, but the practice that made that failure appear worse was the excessive and stupid braying over projected results and public news releases that led to false expectations. One significant American success was the Liberty aircraft engine, thousands of which were used in Allied aircraft. Most damaging in the eyes of many was that the United States failed to develop its own models of combat aircraft. This failure rankled in the minds of American aircraft manufacturers, airmen and the general public and left embarrassing questions to be resolved before and during World War II. Other errors that were brought on by haste, and that would be later embarrassments, included the selection of airfield sites, the layout of airfields and the organization and administration of aircrew training.

During the final nineteen months of the 1914–18 war, the United States Army and Navy trained large numbers of aircrew and ground staff, and that training was divided between North America and Europe. Five nations—the United States, Canada, Great Britain, France and Italy—trained American pilots, observers and maintenance staff. As a result of the internationalization of aircrew training during 1917–18, a great deal of administrative and technical knowledge was shared, but the United States paid its way. Between the wars, as aviation technology evolved and air services matured, the spirit of international cooperation that had developed during the war was replaced by competition.

During the 1920s and 1930s, a technological revolution in military aviation gradually unfolded, and the changes wrought were even greater than those that had occurred during the 1914–18 war. New records were set in speed, altitude, length of flight, distances and blind flying. New aircraft manufacturing companies appeared and hundreds of airports were established. Much of what had been learned from the war was retained, but the air services of each nation also developed distinctive organizations for the governance and administration of civil, military and naval aviation. They also developed aircrew training systems that reflected the values of the national culture. National and then international commercial passenger and freight airlines were established, and British, French, Dutch, American and later German airlines competed for international air routes.

Engines became more powerful and durable; aircraft range and airline passenger capacity increased dramatically; and aircraft were provided with special instruments to improve engine and personnel efficiency at higher altitudes and in varied weather conditions. Airframe designs were modified in order to make the changing of engines easier and more rapid, and to reduce the time the entire aircraft would be grounded for standard maintenance. Emphasis on safety brought about significant developments in communications. Flight plans were required for all departing aircraft, and a rectangular flight pattern was developed for aircraft landing or takeoff from airfields. All airfields were required to install windsocks or other devices so that pilots could easily determine wind direction for takeoffs and landings. Pre- and post-flight check procedures and rigid aircraft inspection regulations were also introduced.

Except in initial military flying training, powerful metal-framed and metal-skinned monoplanes displaced biplanes with wooden frames and fabric skins. Acknowledging and recording the direction of prevailing winds at different times of the year brought about the development of wind roses for each airfield, as this data was essential for use in modifying older fields and building new airports. The revolution in design, technology, maintenance, navigation and communication also contributed to the development of improved training methods and the use of synthetic training devices.

Air forces research and development organizations carefully observed, tested and assessed virtually every aviation innovation worldwide. If possible, improvements that had been developed for civil aviation were adapted to military use. By 1938, the airplane had become one of the major instruments of war whose power was being used to alter world conditions. Bomber raids on Guernica, Spain, and Shanghai, China, shockingly demonstrated the application of modern air power to warfare, underscoring the threat of air bombardment to urban populations. The nation that failed to develop an aviation industry and to link armed services aircrew training to innovations in the field might not survive a major war.

In 1937, in response to technological developments, the army air corps altered its pilot training syllabus. Division of the primary, basic and advanced phases of pilot training into three equal twelve-week periods (nine months total) and the use of improved equipment would provide not only better training than the standard twelve-month system, but would also help pilots adjust more readily to the sophisticated tactical aircraft being assigned to active squadrons. The net effect of the reform was to reduce training time from twelve months (forty-eight weeks of training plus four weeks' leave time) to nine months (thirty-six weeks of training plus four weeks' leave time). Pilots would still graduate from advanced flying schools with 225 or more hours' flying time.

It was felt that the acquisition of improved trainer aircraft would more than compensate for the reduction in pilot training time. In the American three-phase system of training, the most important period during which to screen out those students who might not become capable military pilots was the elementary or primary phase of training. Since the American student pilot's cockpit was not equipped with instruments, it was necessary for him to learn to feel the aircraft in various attitudes and to "fly by the seat of his pants." Because of customs of the parent services and the paucity of appropriations for the air arms, the army air corps had developed the habit of excluding all but the most select candidates.

Since student pilots were also candidates for officers' commissions, the minimum educational qualification was two years of college, but prewar candidates for pilot training were mostly civilian graduates of colleges and universities, army officer graduates of the United States Military Academy or the occasional reserve, national guard, navy or marine corps officers assigned to a course. Even with such stringent selection requirements, approximately 40 percent of each class failed, and the system produced about three hundred pilots annually. Unfortunately, this training philosophy, which excluded many well-qualified men, was maintained for much too long. Although most nations used some enlisted pilots, Great Britain continued that practice through the World War II years.

On 1 April 1918, Great Britain had created the Royal Air Force (RAF), an independent third branch of her armed services on an equal footing with the Royal Navy and the British Army. The Air Ministry was established as an equal of the Admiralty and the War Office. This new branch of the British forces nurtured a small coterie of airmen, carried on research and development, kept abreast of worldwide aviation developments, developed several professional schools and evolved policies for the governance of an ever-changing branch of military service. Although national debt levels were high and governments were unwilling or unable to appropriate sufficient funds, the RAF functioned well as an offensive and defensive force, and the Air Ministry developed into an outstanding agency for administering the nation's air force.

Prior to 1935, RAF flying schools produced about three hundred pilots a year who, according to the official history of flying training, had "the bare ability to fly an aeroplane." Pilot training lasted a year and was conducted in three distinct stages. As in the United States and elsewhere, only biplanes were available for training and tactical use, and most operational training took place in the active squadrons. Pilots were trained to use a circular pattern for landing or taking off from airfields. Little attention was paid to navigation, all-weather flying or night flying.

In response to increased concern about air expansion following the rearming of Germany, Air Commodore Arthur Tedder, director of flying training (DTF) in the Air Ministry, proposed an expandable system designed to increase pilot production. After the Tedder plan went into effect, students found qualified for pilot training were sent first to a civil contract elementary flying training school (EFTS), where their eight weeks of instruction included both navigation and instrument training. Student pilots underwent twenty-five hours of dual instruction and twenty-five hours of solo work while flying deHavilland (DH-82A) Tiger Moth biplane trainers. Having then received their wings and promotions, graduates of these short courses were directed to report for a period of two weeks to the RAF depot at Uxbridge. There, the breveted pilots were issued uniforms (uniform allowances, if commissioned) and underwent RAF military and administrative indoctrination.

At Uxbridge, the RAF pilots were divided into courses and were posted in forty-eight-man drafts to one of several flying training schools (FTSs) for nine months of flying—four and a half months of training on Harts, Oxfords and Masters, and an additional four and a half months of advanced flying exercises aimed at improving navigation and instrument flying and introducing gunnery and bombardment. In winter, owing to weather problems, schedules were significantly expanded at every stage. The Tedder plan, which may also have been labeled Expansion Scheme B, was an important step because it kept the flying training sequence within twelve months, cost less than earlier systems and, by shifting elementary flying to civilian contract schools, conserved experienced service personnel and paved the way for rapid expansion during a national emergency.

Meanwhile, planning continued. In May 1935, Air Ministry Expansion Scheme C was approved. This two-year plan spelled out the means by which the RAF might be increased in size. According to projections, expansion to 1,512 first-line aircraft by May 1937 would necessitate the training of more than 2,000 additional pilots. Such a rapid buildup would require an increase in the number of reserve as well as regular flying training schools. FTSs using RAF pilot instructors would have to be increased from six to eleven and, in order to staff them, large numbers of pilots would have to be assigned to instructional duties from active squadrons. As of 1 July 1936, RAF strength stood at 5,049 regular and reserve pilots, with 1,014 more under training.

Despite the best of intentions, the system did not work as planned. There were shortages of instructors and trainer aircraft. And although there was much excellent experience to draw on, official course syllabi had not yet been developed for every stage of training. And, but for one cross-country flight of some twenty miles, RAF night flying was restricted to six hours of mostly "circuits and bumps." Although pilots destined for service with Coastal Command and with the Fleet Air Arm were well trained in navigation, the RAF official history asserted that navigation training "remained very much where it had been since 1918."

The immense technological revolution in aviation during the 1930s put a special strain on both the equipment and flying training branches of the RAF. In 1937–38, RAF crew establishments were temporarily modified, and observers (navigators) were added to the squadron establishments

(Tables of Organization) of Bomber Command and Coastal Command. Until May 1938, some nine hundred general reconnaissance (GR) pilots destined for service with RAF Coastal Command had completed the ten-week navigation course taught by the School of Air Navigation, and some of them also completed a four-week astronavigation course. As with pilot training, there was a shortage of both navigation schools and qualified instructors.

Although the Royal Air Force was training hundreds of pilots and production appeared to be adequate, at least for the time being, there was still reason for concern. The greatest anxiety among Air Ministry planners concerned aircraft rather than aircrew production. Britain's limited population compelled the Air Ministry to recruit and train aircrew from the Empire-Commonwealth. However, genuine concern about design and production of aircraft, instruments and other equipment caused the Air Ministry to support the expansion of production by British aircraft designers and manufacturers. In order to take advantage of American mass production capabilities and its technological developments, British officials looked to experienced American manufacturers.

Given the crises emerging in Europe, American aircraft might well make the difference between disaster and survival for both Britain and France. Recognizing the problems encountered in manufacturing aircraft and the time delay between designing, developing and testing prototypes, producing approved models, air testing and receiving delivery, European nations sent air missions to the United States. These missions were authorized to place orders for American aircraft, engines and instruments. During May and June 1937, Canadian-born Air Commodore Robert Leckie, DSO, DSC, DFC, RAF director of training, traveled from London to the United States to survey aviation developments.

Leckie's packed itinerary carried him to numerous aircraft and components factories, to civil airports and to U.S. Army Air Corps and U.S. Naval Air Stations. Among those things on American airfields that interested Leckie were the sophisticated air traffic control systems in use on American civil and military airfields, as well as the mobile Lorenz Navigation System and Blind Landing equipment. Leckie also praised a runway lighting system and an apparatus for steam-cleaning aircraft.

The RAF director of training was impressed with two pilot training procedures: the use of the Link Trainer simulator for instrument training and the blind flying practice system, in which the pupil was placed under a hood during special training flights. The RAF officer also expressed interest in the North American AT-6 Harvard advanced trainer and was amazed at the rapidity with which its engine could be changed. As an experienced flying boat pilot, Leckie was impressed with the Consolidated Aircraft Company's PBV-2 Flying Boat, which he described as "better than any in service in the RAF." In addition, Leckie made note of the extent and efficiency of the meteorological service in the United States and of the large number of flying hours required annually of American military pilots assigned to general ground duties.

On returning to London and his Air Ministry offices in June 1937, he drafted a formal report of the visit and made a series of recommendations based on his observations. He called for a complete overhaul of the RAF "watch hut system," recommending establishment of American-type operations rooms that would unite wireless, chart and meteorological sections in a central location and would require registry of flight plans. Leckie called for the purchase of North American AT-6 Harvard advanced trainers, Link Trainers and the Lorenz Navigation and Blind Landing System. He also recommended trial of an American-type runway lighting system for a bomber station.

In line with American practice, the RAF director of training also called for a dramatic increase in the hours of annual flying practice required for RAF pilots on Air Ministry and other ground duty assignments. After seeing what the Americans were doing to improve the quality of pilot training, Leckie also recommended that the RAF increase its pilot training requirement from 150 to 200 flying hours. Despite his wish to borrow some American practices, Leckie was critical of some aspects of U.S. Army Air Corps and U.S. Navy pilot training curricula, especially the terrible waste in the systems and the lack of a central flying school.

The Royal Air Force director of training had come to the United States to observe, to share ideas and practices and to recommend Air Ministry purchase of American aircraft, instruments or other materials that might help to improve RAF effectiveness during the forthcoming critical months. Often the Air Ministry purchased samples of promising American equipment, aircraft, instruments and devices, examined and analyzed them closely in their research and development installations, copied or improved those features that they found useful and discarded the remainder.

Although all nations borrowed from one another, few acknowledged that indebtedness either immediately, prior to, during or after the war, ostensibly for security reasons. Air Commodore Robert Leckie's straightforward assessments of American aviation represent one of several kinds of attitudes that prevailed among professional airmen who visited the United States during the late 1930s.

In May 1938, RAF Expansion Scheme L was approved. It called for increasing pilot production from 1,500 to 2,500 per year and modifying the designations of its flying schools. Such a change meant that the output of the civil contract elementary flying training schools (EFTSs) would have to be increased, and at least eight more flying training schools (FTSs) would have to be added to the eleven already operating. Since such growth demanded the addition of about 4,000 officers and men to the more than 5,000 personnel already assigned to training duties, it was decided that Britain had sufficient men to properly staff only four new FTSs.

A full year after Air Commodore Leckie made his American visit and submitted his set of observations and recommendations, Air Commodore Arthur T. Harris, Air Force Cross, Royal Air Force director of plans, spent late May and early June 1938 in the United States. Ostensibly seeking assistance that might be useful to Bomber Command, Harris inspected virtually every aspect of American aviation. On completion of his visit Harris prefaced his account of what he saw with the remark that "I fear my report has come out on the facetious side—but there was much for laughter and little to learn." Despite either Harris's blindness or sarcasm, the report he submitted indicates that he did indeed learn a great deal.

In his report, Harris described observing all of the American practices and equipment that Leckie had observed the preceding year. Harris conceded that American aircraft "are kept cleaner in flight than ours" through the use of a compressed air steam cleaning system for engines and fuselages. He also praised the aircraft engine change system, the use of rubber joints in aircraft construction to lessen the effects of vibration and the engine test system that in a matter of minutes "can diagnose anything from a dirty sparking plug in an engine to appendicitis in its pilot."

Harris also conceded that the American air traffic control system—radio, weather reports, improved air charts and the mandatory registry of flight plans in a central operations room—that was used on both American civil airline and service airdromes was "remarkably efficient." "I am convinced," he wrote, "that it is thoroughly practical and indeed, so far as I can see, the only possible solution to the problem." However, the RAF officer was critical of American dependence on the Lorenz radio beam, beacon and radio compass for air navigation, a system that he felt "would not be of much use in wartime Europe."

Despite what he reported, Harris gave every evidence of being interested in evaluating American instruments for adoption or modification for use by the Royal Air Force. He examined radio sets for air traffic control, the RCA radio compass, the radio beam beacon and Bendix intercom radio sets, and he expressed more than mild interest in new and improved models of the Link Trainer, the Sperry Horizon and Drift Indicator, the Sperry Gyro Compass and the Fairchild Company's Maxson "Line of Position" Computer.

When Harris visited the Fairchild Aerial Camera and Instrument Company in New York, he was taken aback by the company's assertion that the Air Ministry had swindled it by copying the company's cine camera. Harris examined their Maxson Computer and received an exorbitant unit and quantity price quotation. Before returning home in June 1938, Harris placed orders for four hundred North American AT-6 Harvard trainers, two hundred Lockheed Hudson bombers, numerous American-made instruments and several thousand radial aircraft engines from the Pratt and Whitney and Curtiss-Wright companies.

Despite his interest in some features of American aviation technology, Harris was severely critical of United States Army aviation. In 1938, he was not alone in his views. Most American airmen would have agreed with his assertion that "neither the equipment nor the organization of the American Air Force are up to the standard of a first class air power. I am at a loss to understand where the myth of American air power and efficiency arose." Despite Harris's assertion that there was "little to learn," Air Vice Marshal W. Sholto Douglas, an Anglo-American and newly appointed deputy chief of air staff, noted in his penciled comment on Harris's report that "there is a lot of meat in this report which I would like to investigate thoroughly." Douglas apparently did so.

Leckie and Harris were properly critical of the lagging air strength of the United States compared with that of European countries, but whether they willingly admitted it or not, they both recrossed the Atlantic Ocean aware of specific developments of excellent American aircraft, engines and instruments and of a wide variety of innovations in both commercial and military aviation. However, they obviously doubted that the United States had the leadership essential to fuse these civil and military aviation advances and to produce an American air force strong enough to compete with other major powers.

ACKNOWLEDGEMENTS

As with all historical research, the details of British aircrew training in the Southeastern United States were derived from multiple sources: archives, libraries, books, manuscripts, documents and individual diaries and reminiscences in Britain, Canada and the United States. In the United Kingdom, staff members of the Public Record Office at Kew, Richmond, Surrey, proved especially helpful. Air Commodore Henry A. Probert and the staff at Air Historical Branch, Adastral House, London, provided valuable assistance. Several visits to the Imperial War Museum in London and to the Royal Air Force Museum and the Bomber Command Museum at Hendon were useful and inspiring.

In Canada, valuable assistance was obtained at every turn. Following the route taken by British under training aircrew forty years earlier, I intentionally avoided the voyage from Gourock or Liverpool to North America. However, I found valuable assistance at Halifax, Nova Scotia; Debert, Nova Scotia; Moncton, New Brunswick; and Toronto, Ontario. Greatest assistance came from the staffs of the National Library and Public Archives (NLPA) and from the History Directorate in the Ministry of Defence (MDHD) in Ottawa. Those persons who were most helpful included Ms. Barbara Wilson and Mr. David Smith of the National Library and Public Archives and Mr. J.D.F. Kealey and Mr. Paul Marshall of the History Directorate in the Ministry of Defence.

In the United States, several working trips to Washington, D.C., took me to the Library of Congress, the National Archives in the city and the branch archives in Suitland, Maryland, all of which were most helpful. Undoubtedly the most valuable archives were found at Maxwell Air Force Base, Montgomery, Alabama. Maxwell AFB was the wartime headquarters of the Southeast Air Corps Training Center (SEACTC), advanced flying school and acclimatization school for more than two thousand British cadets. It is now home of the Air War College, other USAF schools, USAAF/USAF archives and the Simpson USAF Historical Research Center (USAFHRC). Histories of almost all wartime USAAF training and operational units are held there, and the library nearby holds a massive number of books and magazines for use by researchers. The Alabama State Archives in Montgomery holds many papers and archives relating to Air Force history, including a complete file of Southeast Air Corps Training Center news.

My wife, Dr. Susan Hartley Guinn, has provided immense assistance over the years. She has joined me in research trips and in following the route of RAF cadets across half of Canada and to abandoned training airfields scattered over a vast region. In addition, she has provided comfort and constant encouragement. She has helped to entertain dozens of visiting former RAF cadets and their wives. She has also been a much-needed computer expert throughout my research and writing. Without her assistance, this book would never have appeared.

The award of a 1981 joint Fulbright teaching appointment in the United Kingdom paved the way for more extensive research. Assisting Norman Bate of Leicester in locating American friends of his RAF training days and in providing names and addresses of former RAF aircrew brought about a sort of reverse lend-lease system, which proved beneficial to both of us. For the remainder of his life, Norman's magnificent obsession was the Arnold Scheme Register, which he founded and led. Ultimately, Norman obtained the valuable assistance of George F. Pyle, Edgar L. Spridgeon, Owen Morgan, Arthur Asburey, Arthur Culff and many others too numerous to name. Their combined efforts to collect documentary and graphic evidence recording the fate of all Arnold Scheme RAF aircrew was probably impossible from the beginning, but they were successful beyond their wildest dreams. Before his death in August 2003, Norman Bate was awarded an MBE by Queen Elizabeth for his valuable work in promoting Anglo-American relations. His papers, which are held by his daughter, will long remain a valuable historical archive. Without his assistance and that of hundreds of other RAF aircrew who learned to fly in the United States or the dozens of Americans who either witnessed or were directly involved in training RAF aircrew, this book would not have been possible.

The late Air Vice Marshal Harry A.V. Hogan, senior Royal Air Force administrative officer at Maxwell Field from June 1941 to August 1942, and officer commanding UK training in the United States RAFDEL (RAF delegation), Washington, D.C., 1942–43, kindly read the original manuscript and rendered many valuable suggestions. Ronald A. Pickler (SE-42-H, Albany, and Dorval, Quebec, Canada) obtained a large plat of RAF 31 PDC at Moncton, New Brunswick, and mailed it to me, and a smaller drawing of that transit station was made. More than six hundred former RAF aircrew responded to advertisements in *Air Mail* and other publications, and many of them located other former Arnold Scheme aircrew and referred them to me and to Norman Bate and the Arnold Scheme Register. Norman generously kept me informed of contacts and documents of deceased airmen, which were held by relatives.

Many of the men of each of the thirteen RAF classes, which were trained in the fifteen flight schools of the Arnold Scheme, provided photographs from their American training days and gave permission for their use. In return for their assistance and the use of their photographs, all royalty proceeds from this book will be shared with the RAF Benevolent Fund.

Potted biographies of some esteemed airmen are appended to the chapters covering their primary flying schools under the heading "Where Have All the RAF Cadets Gone?" For expanded biographies of many more of the cadets, please visit www.historypress.net/arnold scheme.php.

INTRODUCTION

When war erupted in September 1939, Great Britain's war office called territorial and reserve units into active service and began to enlarge its army, navy and air forces. Units were quickly sent to France and Belgium, often to the same sites where thousands of men had been killed between 1914 and 1919. Since the British Empire and Commonwealth had lost almost one million men in the bloody trench warfare of 1914–18, there was great public anxiety against repeating the slaughter of land warfare. The Royal Navy, the British Army and the Royal Air Force would defend the British Isles against invasion. Since by summer 1940 Nazi and Fascist forces controlled much of Europe, the only means of taking the war directly to the enemy was by attacking with large numbers of aircraft. Aviation had come of age.

During the winter of 1939–40, British pilot production had declined because of harsh weather, and the Air Council recognized that it must pursue aircrew training outside the United Kingdom. Between July and November 1940, Luftwaffe bombers and fighters attacked Britain almost daily in what came to be called the Battle of Britain. RAF Fighter Command responded to the attacks using well-trained young pilots to destroy a phenomenal number of German bombers and fighters. When Germany decided against attempting to invade Britain, RAF fighter pilots were hailed as the saviors of Island Britain.

The Battle of Britain inspired many young men, who daydreamed of heroic acts while flying a Hurricane or a Spitfire in combat. Thousands of them rushed to volunteer for aircrew training. Since the skies of Britain became a war zone in 1940, much aircrew training was shifted to Canada, the nearest ally outside Europe.

Anxious to attract veteran American pilots, Canada and Britain recruited more experienced Americans for service as instructors and staff pilots with the RCAF and the RAF, including women pilots for service with the Air Transport Auxiliary (ATA) in Great Britain. There were two programs that trained experienced American pilots for service with Britain's Royal Air Force: the TWA Scheme at Albuquerque, New Mexico, which trained pilots to ferry multi-engine aircraft from American factories to Canada; and the Refresher Scheme, which operated four widely scattered civilian contract flying schools and prepared 598 American pilots for RAF service, many in the Eagle squadrons.

Later, British nationals were sent to the United States for aircrew training under the provisions of five plans or schemes. (1) Beginning in November 1940, the B-17 Scheme trained members of RAF 90 Squadron to fly multi-engine aircraft at Kansas City, Missouri, and provided conversion training to B-17-Cs at Mather Field, Sacramento, California. (2) On 24 March 1941, the Pan American Airways Scheme began to train RAF observers (navigators) in the Pan American Airways Navigation Training Section on the campus of the University of Miami at Coral Gables,

Florida. (3) In May 1941, the All Through Training Scheme (ATTS) established British flying training schools (BFTSs). Commanded by RAF officers, equipped with American trainer aircraft and staffed by American civilian instructors and civilian maintenance staff, the seven BFTSs trained more than 6,300 Royal Air Force pilots. (4) On 9 June 1941, the Arnold Scheme began to train RAF pilots alongside United States Army Air Corps Flying Cadets. (5) In July 1941, the Towers Scheme of the United States Navy began to train pilots, navigators and wireless operators/air gunners for the Royal Air Force and the Royal Navy's Fleet Air Arm. The U.S. Navy trained more than 2,500 pilots, 545 navigators, approximately 600 wireless operators and a small number of helicopter pilots and maintenance staff.

Arnold Scheme is a British label that refers to Major General Henry H. Arnold's April 1941 gift through lend-lease of training capacity for British pilots. British student pilots used some of the capacity of two USAAF replacement centers, six civilian contract primary flying schools, two USAAF basic flying schools and five USAAF advanced flying schools. Between 7 June 1941 and 26 March 1943, these fifteen separate USAAF stations trained American as well as British pilots. The USAAF also provided instructor training and additional flying experience for hundreds of USAAF pilots and almost 600 RAF pilot graduates. When British Arnold Scheme aircrew training ceased in March 1943, 4,370 RAF pilots had graduated, and the bases reverted to use by the expanding United States Army Air Forces.

As plans for implementation of RAF aircrew training in the United States developed, it was decided that British volunteers would be transported from Britain to Canada, where they would be documented (processed) for assignment to American training bases. Trainees of the first four Arnold Scheme drafts changed into issued civilian clothing and traveled by rail directly from Toronto, Canada, to their assigned primary flying training schools. The fifth draft, Class SE-42-E, was also dressed in civilian clothing, but it was posted from Toronto to an acclimatization course at Maxwell Field, Alabama, rather than directly to the six primary flying schools assigned to train British student pilots.

The subsequent eight drafts were documented at RAF No. 31 PDC at Moncton, New Brunswick, Canada, and entered the United States dressed in RAF blue uniforms. Classes SE-42-F and SE-42-G traveled by rail to Maxwell Field, Alabama for a four-week-long acclimatization course, and the final six drafts, Classes SE-42-H, SE-42-I, SE-42-J, SE-42-K, SE-43-A and SE-43-B, traveled to Turner Field, Albany, Georgia. On completion of the acclimatization course, each class was divided into smaller units for assignment to civilian contract primary flying schools. These young British airmen came from a long and proud military tradition, but most of their mechanical experience was limited to bicycles. In North America, they were thousands of miles from home and were about to commence training in one of the most technical branches of modern warfare. And their training was being conducted in a nation that most of the young British students knew only from newspapers, magazines and the cinema. In the words of Air Vice Marshal A.G.R. Garrod, air member for training, "they were strangers in a strange land."

The summer of 1941 was hot, and the United States was technically neutral, but war appeared to be coming closer. Plans were being developed in Britain to use massive air power as an offensive weapon, so the construction or purchase of numerous aircraft and the training of thousands of aircrew was essential. Facilities, materials and technicians for constructing the many aircraft and training the aircrew necessary to reach that goal required more aircraft and aircrew than Britain or her dominions could produce, so Britain reached out to the United States.

British flying training in the United States emerged from a complex of aims that stemmed from the political and military leadership in the United States, Canada and Great Britain. This study traces the establishment and development of Arnold Scheme flight training with an eye to its impact on British and American air forces, Anglo-American relations and communities near training airfields. In this example of international cooperation, there were errors and successes, and there was much borrowing of methods, whether or not the British, Canadian or American air forces acknowledged learning from others.

British cadet Gurth Addington of Class SE-42-G washed out of pilot training in an Arnold Scheme primary flying school as well as British Flying Training School No. 6 at Ponca City, Oklahoma, but was later qualified as an air bomber in Canada. Addington summed up British cadet attitudes and the consequences of the second global war in the twentieth century:

> *The relative positions of the United States and Britain in world affairs until about 1943 was that Britain was a world leader with a vast empire, but much of that great empire was on the verge of being swallowed up in global war not too long after the Japanese attack on Pearl Harbor. As with most of his fellow British students and staff serving within or in training in the United States, there was a habit of world leadership and a habit of thinking which always implied, if it did not state the point directly, that only Britain had the experience to handle such problems. Because of that world view, most British flying students training in the United States believed that they might be posted to the Far East "to help the Americans out of the mess they're sure to get into."*
>
> *That attitude represented the voice of experience in late December 1941, but soon there were to be disasters aplenty for everyone. The world of the pre-1939 years had crumbled, but the habit of thinking imperially, or in the case of Americans in racial terms, had not yet changed and was to be at the root of problems which developed between Britain and the United States later in the war. In the course of the war, Britain was toppled from the throne of world leadership, but few Britons recognized the change at the time; It was only after the passage of time and the end of the war that this fact was generally recognized.*

Addington's world view is an appropriate background against which to examine the training of British aircrew alongside American student pilots in the Southeastern United States from 1941 to 1943. The young men who came to America for training months before Pearl Harbor were products of an admired culture, were treated like royalty and proved to be outstanding ambassadors, but while enjoying the fabled Southern hospitality, they remained strangers in a strange land.

CHAPTER ONE

AMERICAN, BRITISH AND CANADIAN FLIGHT TRAINING, 1938–1941

The so-called United States Army Air Corps' Balanced Air Expansion Plan of 1937–38 advocated procurement of more airfields, aircraft and equipment and the training of greater numbers of aircrew and maintenance staff. In 1938, following much debate about training, air corps planners began to implement the revised twelve-month flying training syllabus to one of thirty-six weeks' duration. That reduction in pilot training time may have been influenced by Air Commodore Leckie's 1937 War Department lecture about the revised RAF training system. Unfortunately, the American plan was premature; air expansion plans coincided with a sharp downturn in the economy, a fact that led Congress to reduce military appropriations and thereby delay expansion. During the early months of 1938, President Franklin Roosevelt achieved only partial success in gaining congressional approval for a navy expansion plan.

Because of continuing economic problems and strong political opposition, the president was reluctant to push for army expansion. During the late evening hours of 13 October 1938, he met with William C. Bullitt, American ambassador to France. Although Bullitt's disturbing report of German air power later proved to be a Nazi exaggeration, it was true that aircraft production in France and Britain lagged behind that of Germany and Italy. In response to the reported expansion of German air power and the feelings of helplessness that compelled British and French leaders to sign the Munich Agreement of September 1938, the leaders of most countries felt that they had no choice but to modernize and expand their armed forces, especially their air forces. For Americans, developments in Europe and the Far East reconfirmed the necessity for neutrality, while also signaling the need to develop stronger defenses.

Although American political leaders had declared the United States neutral, leaders of Britain and the Empire-Commonwealth recognized that the United States was a friendly nation with vast resources and established production records in almost every field of manufacture. The cultural links between Britain and the United States were firm and, beginning in 1938, a stronger economic link was forged when the British and French air ministries placed orders for American aircraft, engines and instruments. As a result of the war scare and increased defense spending, the American economic depression slowly began to close. British, French and American orders for aircraft, equipment and ordnance would increase significantly after Germany invaded Poland in September 1939. The highly effective Nazi propaganda machine convinced world leaders that Germany had a huge air fleet capable of crushing any opponent.

Neither French nor British leaders believed that their nations were capable of launching aircraft development plans rapidly enough to provide for defense against the German air fleet. Since they were aware of American developments in civil and military aviation, a potential solution to their air defense dilemma lay in the purchase of selected American aviation technology. Friendly

European powers sent missions to the United States, but when they sought to purchase the latest tactical aircraft and other American war materiel, they encountered conflicting views. President Roosevelt was anxious for American factories to sell to Europeans in order to overcome the continuing American economic depression, but U.S. Army and Navy officers resisted the sale of their latest models of aircraft, weapons and instruments.

In November 1939, through successful lobbying efforts, British and French officials persuaded the government of the United States to modify the restrictive neutrality laws so as to permit a "cash and carry" system that would allow them to purchase defense-related materials.

During the winter of 1939–40, when Britain became a part of the European war zone, her leaders feared that their aircraft and engine factories might be bombed out of existence. In order to survive, it was necessary to make provision for the manufacture of both training and operational aircraft outside the British Isles. Some aircraft manufacture was transferred to key Commonwealth nations such as Canada, the Union of South Africa and Australia, all of which were encouraged to expand their aviation industries and to establish new ones in order to build British-designed aircraft.

A British Purchasing Commission (BPC) was established in Ottawa, which contained numerous missions representing virtually every branch of the British government, and it was charged with contracting for all purchases in North America. Equally important was an action of the United States government. On 6 December 1939, in order to monitor sales and to assist American companies with foreign orders, President Roosevelt appointed his Anglophile Secretary of Treasury Henry Morgenthau Jr. chairman of the Interdepartmental Committee for the Coordination of Foreign and Domestic Military Purchases.

Three days earlier on 3 December 1939, the Empire Air Training Scheme (EATS) Committee met at the Air Ministry in London with Commonwealth representatives and RAF officers. Since Britain might easily become a part of the European war zone, the Air Ministry was concerned that the training of aircrew might also be threatened. The committee proposed a cooperative system of aircrew training with Commonwealth nations, and Canada, Australia and New Zealand signed an agreement to train thousands of aircrew volunteers and to delay requests for payment of costs until the war ended. Canada would accept RAF training stations transferred from Britain and would also build and equip as many training airfields as needed for training Canadians and other aircrew volunteers.

Once the neutrality laws were revised, Britain began to purchase food, aircraft, munitions, ships, instruments, machine tools and other defense-related materials. The Morgenthau Committee became the official liaison between the United States and the Anglo-French Mission in supply matters. During early spring 1940, the BPC moved its offices from Ottawa to New York and immediately ordered hundreds of American products. When Depression-ridden American industries could not produce sufficient quantities of necessities quickly, the BPC encouraged the British government to invest in existing plants or to lend funds to American manufacturers so that production might be rapidly increased.

The United States government and American industries also encouraged such capital investment. Given the paucity of American defense contracts, these British investments and advances on contracts saved the American munitions and aircraft industries from financial collapse. Foreign orders and investments delivered many companies from the grips of economic depression. In military parlance, British investments were "education orders" that would stimulate many American factories to increase production of aircraft, engines and other materiel.

Peacetime aircraft manufacture normally required three years or more of lead time from the design stage to mass production, a system that involved designing and building a prototype, testing it, dismantling it, designing machine tools capable of mass producing its hundreds of parts and either making these parts or contracting to have them made.

The purchase of massive quantities of essential raw materials and engaging subcontractors to manufacture specific parts was time consuming, but essential. Finally, the manufacturer would build a massive assembly plant, then recruit and train a labor force capable of assembling finished aircraft. As a result of that set of practices and rigid inspection systems, delays were built into American contracting and production systems. Even so, American manufacturers were experts in these endeavors, and when provided with financial support, encouragement and clear goals could develop extraordinary levels of production.

Early 1938 and 1939 orders from Britain and France gave American manufacturers experience in expanding production before the demand increased dramatically with orders from the American armed services. The use of education orders was common to most countries and was followed with virtually every weapon model and type. For manufacturers engaged in selling aircraft and other equipment or components overseas, there were a significant number of laws, regulations, codes and licenses dealing with foreign sales. American aircraft and munitions manufacturers involved in such sales were glad to have Secretary Morgenthau's Interdepartmental Committee to smooth the way through the red tape for both the companies and the purchasers. Even so, many French orders were not completed in time to be of use, and many British orders for aircraft, engines and related aviation equipment were almost too late.

In order to replace the massive numbers of weapons lost in Belgium and France, Britain needed weapons and ammunition to furnish army and home guard units in preparation for an expected summer 1940 Nazi invasion. Under the recent "cash and carry" revision of the American neutrality act, the British Purchasing Commission spent almost $40 million for the secret purchase of surplus American weapons. Their staff also supervised the loading aboard British warships of these tons of rifles, pistols, machine guns, mortars, 75-millimeter artillery pieces and tons of ammunition for a fast run from Bayonne, New Jersey, to a British port.

As of mid-June 1940, most of Europe's industrial power was under Nazi domination; France was gone as an ally, and with her fall went her air force, airdromes, navy and facilities for producing armaments, aircraft and aircrew. Britons turned their eyes westward across the Atlantic. British scientists, who had extensive contacts among the American and Canadian scientific community, were sent to North America to consult with their counterparts, to describe new British technology and to interpret American attitudes concerning Britain's chances of survival. Among those representatives were Professors Henry Tizard and A.V. Hill. Tizard spent several months in the United States in 1940. Hill, a member of the Royal Society, served in Washington between February and mid-June 1940 as a scientific representative of the Air Ministry. During that time, he was critical of the "sticky and unimaginative" attitudes of British airmen and civil servants, and advocated the free exchange of technology between Britain and the United States. Initially, Hill had difficulty convincing his superiors, but that set of attitudes changed when the war became more threatening.

When France collapsed, the BPC acted very quickly. Without consultation, they assumed control over all undelivered French contracts for American war materiel, including those for a large number of aircraft, engines and aviation-related machine tools. These items, which American military purchasing agents had hoped to purchase and use for U.S. Army Air Corps expansion, had slipped through their fingers. Efforts by air corps officers to cancel the British takeover of French orders and to divert the undelivered materiel to USAAC use met with failure. When appeals to the Morgenthau Committee brought a ruling in favor of Britain, Major General Henry H. Arnold, chief of the U.S. Army Air Corps, was bitterly disappointed.

Much of that bitterness developed as a result of the conflicting priorities that had been established by American political and military leaders. Since the first priority of the president and his major advisors was to bring the economic Depression to a close by putting Americans to work, they favored selling American military hardware to friendly nations. Since they also believed that the defense of Great Britain was the first line of defense for the United States, they assumed that Britain's purchase of American technology would serve both economic and defense purposes.

Officers of the U.S. Army and Navy were pessimistic. They were responsible to the president for national defense, but as war materiel steadily flowed out of the country, they worried about what the United States would do if Britain also fell to Nazi aggression. War Department staff soon became convinced that agents of the president, especially Secretary Morgenthau and his Interdepartmental Committee, were permitting the sale of too many aircraft and great quantities of critical materials that were needed for developing effective American defenses.

Moreover, during the summer of 1940, as American mobilization began, the War Department found itself stripped of weapons. The critics who attacked the United States for delaying entry into the European war from November 1939 to December 1942 undoubtedly failed to realize that the United States had virtually disarmed itself for Britain in 1940. Under the Selective Service Act, the arming of American draftees and National Guard units with wooden rifles and conducting military maneuvers with "Quaker" artillery (wooden logs painted black) would prove embarrassing. Despite aiding Britain, perhaps there was yet time to provide real weapons and to produce sufficient tanks, aircraft and aircrew to develop an American army and air force.

In 1938, the United States had laid plans to embark upon a three-pronged system of civilian, army and navy aviation expansion, and these changes would ultimately attract the attention of the air forces of Canada and Great Britain. The newly created Civil Aeronautics Authority (CAA) was granted federal funds with which to train civilian pilots and other aviation personnel as reserves for army and naval air services. By teaching flying to these American university and college students, civilian proprietary flying schools, which had not received direct financial assistance before, would join with educational institutions to train pilots. As early as 1936, a number of U.S. Army Air Corps officers and several members of Congress had proposed using civilian flight schools to train a reserve force of pilots, but there had been no enabling legislation. In 1939, when it was discovered that legislation governing vocational education could be used to justify training pilots, the CAA instituted its Civilian Pilot Training Program (CPTP).

Not satisfied with gaining a promise of funds with which to implement its "balanced expansion plan" and short of sufficient flight instructors, army air corps officers borrowed from British, French and Canadian practice and launched a civilian contract flying training experiment as part of their plan to produce 4,500 pilots in two years. At the same time, the United States Navy, which had already begun to expand its air service, adopted plans to produce vast numbers of pilots by reducing training time from fifty-two to twenty-six weeks.

In time, the three American pilot training systems—the Civil Aeronautics Authority's Civilian Pilot Training Program (CPTP), the Navy's Air Pilot Program (NAP) and the U.S. Army Air Corps Flying Cadet Plan—were to complement each other. However, during the early phases of expansion, service rivalries and the mutual distrust between military and civilian planners limited cooperation to the borrowing of ideas and techniques and an occasional grudging approval. Experimental programs and further planning occupied the first six months of 1939; then, effective 1 July 1939, with the beginning of the new fiscal year, Congress appropriated sufficient money to cover the costs for implementing all three air expansion plans.

Civilian flight training, which complemented that of the navy and the army air corps, was offered by the United States Civil Aeronautics Authority (CAA). Between January and June 1939, the CPTP began for 330 students at thirteen colleges and universities. This initial project was funded with $150,000 from the National Youth Administration (NYA), a subsidiary agency of the Works Progress Administration (WPA). College and university science departments taught the required 240 hours of ground school courses in airplane structures, navigation and meteorology, while nearby CAA-approved fixed-base airport operators contracted to teach 35 to 50 hours flying in forty- to sixty-five-horsepower aircraft. The young men who completed such flying training were intended as a reserve of qualified pilots whose skills made them available for active service or qualified them for extra training to work as civilian flying instructors.

Institution heads and fixed-base airport operators alike were undoubtedly pleased to be a part of the new program, especially during the waning days of the Depression, when special programs were needed to attract students and to pay bills. The CAA paid the institutions $20 per student for ground school courses, and it paid the flight school operators $6 per student flying hour, a total of between $270 and $290 for each qualified pilot trained in the CPTP. Each enrolled student paid a laboratory fee of $40 for the semester course (fifteen weeks) to defray the cost of laboratory materials, life insurance and a standard flight physical examination. By June 1939, 313 of the 330 students enrolled in the experimental program had successfully completed the course and were awarded private pilot's certificates. That experimental program of spring 1939 led to a larger, more permanent one, which was funded by Congressional appropriations.

On 27 June 1939, Congress approved the Civilian Pilot Training Act, and ultimately more than four hundred American colleges and universities offered flight instruction. The educational institutions selected an affiliate civilian flying school nearby. In order to ensure safety of equipment and standardization of instructional methods, staff members of the Civil Aeronautics Authority inspected facilities and aircraft and certified the instructors. In essence, the CAA developed their own central flying school. Between 1 July 1939 and 30 June 1940, 9,885 private pilots were trained and licensed, and 1,925 qualified civilian pilots were given extra training and were certified as flight instructors.

The CAA elementary flying course was improved to include 240 hours of ground school in general aircraft, navigation and meteorology, plus 35 to 45 flying hours in light aircraft, half of that time solo. Graduates of the elementary course qualified for a private pilot's certificate and enrollment in the advanced course. The advanced controlled land plane course required 240 additional hours of ground school and another 40 to 50 hours flying a 225-horsepower airplane (half of the time solo). Graduates of CAA elementary and advanced courses had completed the equivalent of army air corps or navy primary flying courses, held CAA certificates as restricted commercial pilots and were qualified for further flying training.

During the autumn months of 1940, which coincided with the final stages of the Battle of Britain, the United States Civil Aeronautics Authority reached an early peak of expansion. Beginning on 1 July 1940, the CAA, armed with a $37 million budget, enrolled an additional 45,000 students in elementary flying courses at more than nine hundred institutions. An additional 8,000 licensed pilots entered advanced and flight instructor courses at ninety-three

CAA training centers. To assist the Civil Aeronautics Authority in meeting the rapidly increasing demand for pilots, Congress changed the enabling legislation to permit flying training for both college and non-college students.

In 1939, following British, French and Canadian examples, U.S. Army Air Corps staff enlarged and decentralized primary flight training. Eight proprietary flight schools were awarded contracts to train military pilots under air corps supervision. These civilian contract flying schools were scattered across the nation southward from Illinois and Nebraska to Alabama and westward to Texas and Oklahoma, Arizona and California. On 1 July 1939, 396 army air corps flying cadets entered these flying schools and were designated Class 40-A. In keeping with the 1937 balanced air expansion plan, the initial primary flight training courses lasted twelve weeks and provided 225 hours of ground school and 65 hours of flying. Primary flight instruction was conducted by civilian instructors, many of whom had logged thousands of hours of flight experience.

Having logged 215 hours of flying in progressively more powerful basic and advanced trainer aircraft, graduates received their wings and were commissioned second lieutenants. Following a short leave, they reported to tactical squadrons of the GHQ Air Force for training in operational aircraft. In anticipation of increased numbers of primary flying school graduates, army air corps officers began to plan expansion of military basic and advanced flying schools. Given time, an instructor shortage could be filled through training; the shortage of trainer aircraft was already being addressed.

American aircraft factories had sold large numbers of airplanes overseas, and they were then expanding production in order to fill new orders, foreign and domestic. Their designers were also working with army air corps staff to develop improved trainer aircraft. The North American AT-6 trainer had been available since 1938, and several models of Stearman (a Boeing Company subsidiary) biplanes, especially the PT-13, PT-17, PT-18 and PT-27, began to replace the old Consolidated PT-3 and PT-11D biplanes as tough, aerobatically sound, open-cockpit primary trainers. (The PT-27, used in Canada, had a closed cockpit.) The Fairchild and Ryan Companies also began to develop the army air corps' first monoplane primary trainers, the PT-19 and PT-22, many of which were used in American and Canadian flying schools. After ironing out some problems with the Vultee BT-13, that monoplane began to replace older basic trainers such as the Consolidated BT-9 and the North American BT-14. Thus, before mid-1940, a completely new series of single-engine trainers was being developed, and some of them were already arriving at flying schools as replacements for older models.

Deciding which models of aircraft to build presented problems. Because of the rapid development of twin-engine and multi-engine tactical aircraft, several twin-engine trainers were also being developed. However, since many army air corps officers believed that the North American AT-6 Harvard could serve as an all-purpose advanced trainer, the twin-engine building program was proceeding too slowly. As Beechcraft, Cessna and Curtiss Company twin-engine models became available, they were tested and were delivered to assigned schools, but none of them approached the AT-6 either in popularity or in training proficiency. Production of a sufficient number of the several twin-engine trainer models to supply the growing numbers of American, Canadian and British Commonwealth Air Training Plan (BCATP) flying schools and to replace those destroyed in accidents would continue to plague training officers into late 1942.

When war broke out in September 1939, a large part of Great Britain's projected training expansion had already been implemented. For that purpose, the RAF was then using fifty-six civilian contract elementary and reserve flying training schools (E & RFTSs) within the British

Isles. Sixteen of these schools were training pilots for entry into intermediate and advanced flying training schools, and the remaining forty E & RFTSs were training about five different categories of reserves, including men of the various university air squadrons.

As soon as war broke out, the Air Ministry's War Training Scheme was implemented. The production goal was raised from 2,500 to 5,600 pilots per year, and the size of flying training classes was increased at every level. In order to achieve the larger objective, thirty-seven reserve civil contract schools were closed, and their aircraft were transferred to other stations. Instructors and other civilian staff in the civil schools were commissioned in the RAF, and the nineteen schools that were to continue in use were now labeled elementary flying training schools (EFTSs). These nineteen EFTSs were classified according to maximum training capacity: A (96 students), B (72) and C (48), and their graduates would be fed into the RAF-operated advanced flying training schools (FTSs).

In late 1939, FTSs were re-labeled service flying training schools (SFTSs), by which time the fourteen schools had reached a combined capacity of 1,344 pilot trainees at any one time. As with the EFTSs, aircraft, equipment and personnel establishments varied according to type and size of the school, but the ultimate equipment establishment for each of the SFTSs was to be 108 aircraft. Owing to shortages of trainer aircraft, ground and flying instructors, as well as maintenance and administrative staffs, immediate standardization of intakes at every school was impossible. However, as staff and equipment became available, the numbers of trainees was gradually increased at each school.

The RAF's wartime training system, which was partially implemented during autumn 1939, reduced pilot training from twelve to eight months. Initial training wing (ITW) courses lasting eight weeks (later reduced to six) provided military indoctrination as well as intensive academic and physical training to qualified volunteers. Flying training in EFTSs lasted eight weeks, and that in the SFTSs encompassed sixteen weeks. During the winter months, owing to delays attributable to weather, the twenty-four-week RAF flying courses were extended to thirty weeks, so that the total RAF training period from ITW to wings standard consumed between thirty-two and thirty-eight weeks.

Other aircrew came to Britain's aid from the Empire-Commonwealth. In December 1939, the Air Ministry implemented the Empire Air Training Scheme (EATS), which the Air Ministry later labeled the British Commonwealth Air Training Plan (BCATP) and the Canadians referred to as the Joint Air Training Plan (JATP). Signatories to the documents creating the plan agreed to expand their air force recruiting and training efforts and to cooperate with Great Britain and other Commonwealth nations in training aircrew.

Canada's proximity to the mother country made it the kingpin in aircrew training. While training thousands of aircrew for war service in the Royal Canadian Air Force, Canada also began to receive into its expanding system American volunteers and partially trained aircrew from Australia and New Zealand and from the mother country. Initially, Air Ministry planners were confident that Great Britain and its Empire-Commonwealth could produce sufficient aircrew without assistance from other sources. In fact, during the seven-month-long "phony war" period, planners worried that pilot output might exceed real needs. Although Britain was rescued from that dilemma by formidable weather, some RAF personnel were still insisting in June 1941 that pilots were not needed.

As with training in U.S. Army Air Corps civilian contract schools in northern Illinois and Nebraska during the harsh winter of 1939–40, weather proved devastating to RAF pilot training in the United Kingdom as well. SFTSs in Britain normally logged 40,000 flying hours per month, but in December 1939, only 22,000 hours were documented; in January 1940, 29,000; and in February 1940, only 14,000 hours were flown. As a result of harsh winter weather, pilot output dropped by 550. Discussions about the impact of weather on flying training created worries for the future: if British winters proved so disruptive, perhaps the harsh climate of Canada might have a similar or even worse effect on all Canadian and Commonealth aircrew production.

On 25 May 1940, as the Dunkirk evacuation was beginning and German forces were pushing southward into France, planners in Britain and the United States reacted. U.S. Army Air Corps planners announced an increase from 4,500 pilots in two years to the annual production of 7,000 pilots and essential numbers of other aircrew and maintenance personnel. For pilot training, the USAAC Training Center (ACTC) would need more primary, basic and advanced flight schools, as well as tactical air stations, each with large allocations of aircraft, instructors and ground support staff. Such expansion would require much planning and massive appropriations. In order to continue pilot training year-round and to produce more aircrew per year, army air corps leaders shifted most flying training south of the thirty-seventh parallel latitude.

In the same month that the U.S. Army Air Corps announced its pilot expansion plan, the British Air Ministry implemented the so-called First Revize, a plan to produce 6,400 pilots per year. Although the elementary flying training schools (EFTSs) would continue to provide a minimum of fifty hours flying time, course lengths were cut from eight to seven weeks, but even that change was disrupted. During summer 1940, owing to active air operations over southern England and the Midlands, six EFTSs were moved to the north of England, and night flying was cut from the EFTS syllabus. Depending on whether they attended specialized fighter, bomber or mixed service flying training schools (SFTSs), the one-hundred-hour SFTS courses were reduced from sixteen to fourteen or twelve weeks. In some instances, pilots were sent to operational squadrons directly from SFTSs, after having been rushed through a modified syllabus totaling only slightly more than one hundred flying hours.

Because of Britain's limited land area and its small population, its air forces had no choice but to recruit and train volunteers from every potential source. Owing to their willingness and availability in increasing numbers, the Air Ministry sought a means for training the large numbers of Europeans who had fled to the United Kingdom. Refugees from Nazi-occupied European countries, many of whom were already qualified pilots, sought to join the RAF, but communication presented a major problem. Concern over language barriers led to the establishment of special flying schools that incorporated English language instruction into the flying training syllabus.

The experience that RAF officers gained by training Czechs, Poles, Yugoslavs, Belgian and French pilots in RAF procedures, communications and tactics laid the groundwork for the later creation of the British flying training schools (BFTSs) in the United States. In October 1940, a Franco-Belgian flying training school began operations at Odiham near Basingstoke, Hampshire. On that single airdrome, French and Belgian volunteers underwent both EFTS and SFTS training. During the next month, Polish Flying Training School No. 1 was established at Hucknall, Nottinghamshire, and it too combined EFTS and SFTS training on one airdrome. These double flying schools operated twenty-four-week pilot training courses for the emigrés. By June 1941, the Franco-Belgian school had completed its mission and was closed, and the Polish school was shifted from Hucknall to Peterborough.

In August 1940, during the Battle of Britain, the Air Ministry announced the Second Revize, and the Royal Air Force once again modified its pilot training program. Air Chief Marshal A.G.R. Garrod, the new air member for training (AMT), announced plans for the RAF to produce pilots at the rate of seven thousand per year. Courses in the EFTSs were again reduced, this time from seven to six weeks, and both single-engine and twin-engine SFTS courses were standardized at twelve weeks. Advanced and operational training were more closely coordinated, and training staffs worked hard to make the aircrew training system more efficient.

In September–October 1940, the RAF implemented its Third Revize. Owing to the discovery that aircrew attrition had been greater than expected during the first year of the war, RAF pilot production was further increased. Elementary flying courses remained at six weeks and 50 flying hours, but both single-engine and twin-engine SFTS courses were further reduced from twelve to ten weeks, with some variable hours permitted depending upon whether the pilot was to be assigned to a fighter or bomber operational training unit (OTU). Before RAF pilots of that time were assigned to an operational squadron, most of them had logged between 150 and 200 flying hours. By comparison, U.S. Army Air Corps pilots were required to log approximately 215 hours in order to earn their wings and to commence tactical training.

During the summer of 1940, as RAF attrition increased dramatically and as British airfields came under enemy air attack, flying training nearly ground to a halt in the British Isles. As a result, Air Ministry staff were convinced that a number of flying training schools and a large portion of the rapidly growing pool of aircrew candidates would have to be moved out of the British Isles to Canada and southern Africa for flying training. Among the men who were posted to Canada to be trained as aircrew were Poles, Czechs, Belgians, free French, Dutch, Norwegians and other European refugees who sought service with the RAF as a means of striking back at the common enemy.

If Britain was to meet the increasing demand for greater numbers of pilots, observers (navigators), wireless (radio) operators, gunners and radio technicians, she needed to find other sources of manpower. Canada might tap her own small population for men of experience, talent and technical skill, and the RCAF might well serve to channel American and other volunteers to Britain for war service. Although American neutrality laws prohibited advertising in an effort to attract American volunteers to serve in a foreign military service, Britain and Canada sought to entice younger Americans to volunteer for either the RAF or the RCAF.

Neither Britain nor Canada had a sufficient number of pilots and other aircrew to expand the RAF and the RCAF. Experienced American pilots were needed in Canada to serve as instructors for the increasing flow of aircrew candidates. Veteran American pilots, navigators and radiomen were also needed by the Atlantic Ferrying Organization (ATFERO) to deliver aircraft from American factories to modification centers and on to Canada and Great Britain. American men and women pilots and technicians were also needed in Britain to bolster the ranks of the Air Transport Auxiliary (ATA), which ferried aircraft from British factories and maintenance units to training and operational airfields. The need for experienced pilots, large numbers of aircraft and stable aircrew training would help to bring about closer cooperation than had ever existed among Great Britain, Canada and the United States.

Since officers in the government of Canadian Prime Minister McKenzie King did not appear overly anxious to encourage American pilots to volunteer for RCAF service, special arrangements were necessary to recruit them. RCAF Air Vice Marshal William Bishop, VC, Canada's top ace of the 1914–18 war, was worried about RCAF expansion and Canada's commitment to the

Empire Air Training Scheme, so he quietly contacted two former veterans of the air services, a Canadian and an American, to assist in locating and recruiting American pilots for RCAF and RAF service.

Royal Naval Air Service veteran F. Homer Smith, Canadian oil millionaire and a resident of New York and Palm Beach, joined Clayton Knight, an American artist-illustrator who had served with the RFC/RAF during 1917–18, and the two began to recruit American pilots. Unofficially, because of a desire to assist a friendly nation and to find employment for Americans during the final years of the Great Depression, United States government officials either turned a blind eye to Canada's recruiting efforts or provided quiet assistance and encouragement.

During spring 1940, Smith and Knight flew across the United States in order to ascertain the location and availability of qualified American aviators and the feasibility of recruiting them. At their different stops along the way, they met with aviation officials of several states. They also gathered lists of pilot prospects who might be willing to volunteer for service with the RCAF. Following this encouraging western excursion, the two erstwhile recruiters returned to Ottawa and met with the Canadian Air Council to present their findings and proposals.

Since Canada's need for qualified flying instructors was great and would increase as the British Commonwealth Air Training Plan was further expanded in the months ahead, the Air Council quickly approved Smith and Knight's proposals. Effective 1 June 1940, the Clayton Knight Committee became a civilian arm of the Royal Canadian Air Force (RCAF) and functioned as a recruiting agency and clearinghouse for American volunteers for the Canadian air services. Since Knight was a familiar figure in American aviation and journalistic circles, his name was used for the American branch of the Canadian recruiting organization. During that era of neutrality and isolationism, perhaps Knight's status and his public relations experience would help to steer the way through potential political and legal minefields.

The Canadian Air Council also authorized the establishment of the Dominion Aeronautical Association, Ltd., the legal entity that would act as liaison between the RCAF and the Clayton Knight Committee. The American-based committee would recruit qualified Americans, certify their physical and mental well-being, document their age and flying qualifications and arrange their transportation to Canada. When the pilots arrived in Ottawa, the Dominion Aeronautical Association would double-check their credentials and their health and arrange their entry into the RCAF. In order to ease relations between the two recruiting agencies, Canadian citizen F. Homer Smith was commissioned wing commander (lieutenant colonel) in the RCAF.

Before the Clayton Knight Committee began its recruiting work, its officers had to gain the approval of the American air services. In order to discuss their recruiting policies and plans, Smith and Knight wisely traveled to Washington to meet with officers of the United States Army Air Corps and the U.S. Naval Air Service. Since RCAF and RAF wartime physical standards and rules concerning age limits, vision and marital status were more liberal than those of the peacetime American air forces, Washington officials indicated a willingness to advise cadet eliminees from American flying schools that they might have an opportunity to continue flying if they would consult the Clayton Knight Committee.

For their part, Knight and Smith promised that they would not attempt to recruit men already in the American air services. Since Canadian qualifications for positions as RCAF flight instructors and service pilots were less strict than those in the U.S. air services, it might be possible to recruit older American pilots who could not qualify for army air corps service under the more strict American standards.

For flying instructor service, the committee was authorized to accept applications from American high school graduates, age eighteen to forty-five years, who possessed Civil Aeronautics Authority (CAA) licenses and a minimum of three hundred hours' flying time. The committee also accepted applications for RCAF aircrew schools and was especially anxious to contact those young men who had been eliminated from U.S. Navy and U.S. Army Air Corps flight programs or who held CAA-certified flight ratings.

Within a short time, central offices for the Clayton Knight Committee were established in a suite of New York's Waldorf-Astoria Hotel, and a staff was employed to process the files of many American fliers whose names and records had been collected earlier. Branch offices were also established in major hotels in twelve American cities. Arrangements were made in each locale for flight physical examinations to be carried out by CAA-approved physicians, flying ability testing by CAA inspectors and credit security clearances by a private agency. With committee approval and documents attesting to age, health and qualifications, applicants were channeled through the Waldorf-Astoria offices to those of the Dominion Aeronautical Association at the Chateau Laurier Hotel in Ottawa.

Close by this elegant and centrally located hotel in the Canadian capital, RCAF officials inducted the prospective American flight instructors. The candidates completed flight physical examinations, received their kit and underwent RCAF commissioning ceremonies. From Ottawa, the newly commissioned officer pilots were posted to RCAF stations to undergo another check flight and to familiarize themselves with RCAF administrative and training procedures. Following a brief instructional course with experienced Canadian pilots either at Trenton, Ontario, or at assigned elementary flying schools, they were assigned to RCAF flight schools scattered over the vast Canadian hinterlands. It was good that applicants were processed through several elegant hotels en route to their assignments, because Canadian flying training stations of that era were often lonely, isolated backwaters with few amenities.

As the Battle of Britain raged during the dark days of summer 1940, the British Air Ministry became increasingly anxious about pilot losses. Since the Clayton Knight Committee was already recruiting pilots for service in Canada, and since the British Air Ministry could not advertise for the services of American pilots, RAF staff engaged the Clayton Knight Committee to recruit and coordinate procurement of pilots for Britain as well. In order to move these pilots rapidly to operational duties, they were expected to have logged more than 250 flying hours. However, Clayton Knight Committee recruiters soon discovered that more men were being rejected than enrolled, because applicants lacked the requisite flying hours.

During the critical summer and early fall of 1940, the Clayton Knight Committee was still necessarily cautious and low-key. Dunkirk, the fall of France and the Battle of Britain undoubtedly stimulated recruitment, but the political realities in the United States were obvious: critical national elections would be held in November, and therefore caution was essential. Committee advertising was restricted to word of mouth and the placement of posters in major American airports. Staffs at the committee's twelve hotel regional offices were increased in number, but applicants were still channeled through New York to Ottawa.

Clayton Knight Committee recruiters were alarmed that too many American volunteers were being rejected because they lacked enough flying hours. They also quickly recognized that if a refresher flying course could be provided for pilot volunteers with less than 100 hours, a large number of otherwise qualified younger Americans could be recruited for RAF service. At that time, increasing numbers of American college students were enrolling in the Civil Aeronautics

Authority's advanced flying courses, and the Clayton Knight Committee was aware of this growing pool of young pilots. Most of the applicants for RAF service who had logged less than 100 flying hours had neither the time nor the money necessary to increase their flying time to 250 hours.

Members of the Clayton Knight Committee reasoned that if there was an arrangement whereby volunteers might join the RAF and receive the necessary further training, the committee could recruit from among already interviewed candidates large numbers of young men who had logged 80 hours of flying time. Since the RAF used 150 flying hours as the wings qualification, the committee argued that recruitment of Americans for RAF service would be much easier if the required number of flying hours was reduced from 250 to 150 hours.

As a result, Clayton Knight Committee officers also argued that if the Air Ministry could provide such partially qualified American pilots with seventy hours of "refresher" flying training, they could recruit a large number of these young pilots. Such training would cost about $1,000 per pilot for a relatively inexpensive, rapid accession of strength to the RAF. American pilots with a private pilot's license and eighty flying hours could be enrolled in American contract flying schools in order to complete a refresher course of seventy hours of specialized flying. British Air Attaché Group Captain George C. Pirie, DFC, recognized the validity of the Clayton Knight Committee argument and urged the Air Ministry to establish refresher training in order to qualify Americans for RAF service.

Air Ministry staff were obviously quite busy with the Battle of Britain, but it is likely that the proposed refresher training interested responsible officers, but caused them to worry about how Canada might react. That was undoubtedly a prime reason for sending Captain Harold H. Balfour, MP, MC, undersecretary of state for air, to Canada and the United States during August 1940, at the peak of the Battle of Britain. Balfour brought to North America the Air Ministry's endorsement of refresher training. He gained Canadian and U.S. Army Air Corps approval of the Refresher Scheme and concluded agreements with civilian fixed-base operaters who owned flying schools at Glendale, California; Dallas, Texas; and Tulsa, Oklahoma.

Applications already on file from American pilots would be reviewed by the Clayton Knight Committee, and because of the committee's experience and its links with the Civil Aeronautics Authority and the U.S. Army Air Corps it was authorized to handle future recruitment for the Refresher Scheme. The Canadian Air Council had created the Clayton Knight Committee and the Dominion Aeronautical Association in order to evade American neutrality laws. Similarly, the British Air Ministry created British Airways, Ltd., a dummy corporation, which was designed to serve as "employer" of the American pilots until they could officially enter RAF service.

Once pilots with a minimum of eighty hours were recruited, they would be assigned to a refresher school to gain fifteen hours of night flying experience, including ascent on instruments to twenty thousand feet, thirty cross-country instrument flying hours and a navigational flying standard of twenty-five hours. When the American pilots completed the seventy hours of refresher flying training, officers of British Airways, Ltd., provided them with transportation to Canada, where they were documented and commissioned as pilot officers (second lieutenants) in the Royal Air Force.

Included among the problems that plagued the Refresher Training Scheme from the outset were the prohibition against advertising for recruits into a foreign military service; the 1940 United States Selective Service Law, which required registrants to notify local boards of any change of address; and the lack of service-type advanced trainer aircraft at the refresher schools located in Dallas, Texas; Tulsa, Oklahoma; and Glendale, California. Even with these problems, the scheme was implemented as rapidly as possible because it promised to be inexpensive, and the British need for pilots was perceived as critical.

An organization that disturbed RCAF and RAF officials, and that competed with the Clayton Knight Committee's recruiting efforts, had been undertaken by Colonel Charles Sweeney, an American who had resided in Paris for a number of years. In order to form another LaFayette Escadrille, similar to the one for which he was partially responsible during World War I, Sweeney had begun to recruit experienced American pilots for service in France's Armee de L'Air. The fall of France in June 1940 put a halt to Sweeney's recruiting efforts, and the American volunteer pilots already in France escaped to Britain, where seven of them were absorbed into the RAF in time to fight in the Battle of Britain.

Without consulting British or Canadian Air Ministry authorities beforehand, Sweeney switched his recruiting efforts to Britain's Royal Air Force. By October 1940, Sweeney's recruiting efforts began to interfere with the quieter, more effective and broader recruiting efforts of the Clayton Knight Committee. Although glad to accept qualified airmen, the British Air Ministry and the Foreign Office were disturbed about reports of Sweeney's flamboyant and noisy recruiting methods, and were worried about the effect Sweeney's efforts might have on larger plans. They might attract criticism and create political problems that could interfere with Britain's active pursuit of direct American aid. According to at least one source, concern over Sweeney's activities resulted in his being persuaded to visit England and to accept a commission as acting group captain in the Royal Air Force. Sweeney was thus neutralized by British service regulations and censorship, and his recruiting efforts in the United States were then absorbed by the Clayton Knight Committee.

The Clayton Knight Committee still experienced difficulties because of the American ban on advertising, but it now had a clearer field for recruiting American citizens to RCAF and RAF service. By working closely with the Civil Aeronautics Authority, the committee expanded and intensified recruiting by sending interviewers out regularly from regional offices to meet with prospective volunteers and to process applications. In order to reduce excessive transportation costs, applicants, instead of being channeled through the Waldorf-Astoria Hotel as before, were sent to Canada by more direct routes and were transported by the Canadian National Railway to Ottawa for processing and induction.

In order to evaluate the effectiveness of the Refresher Scheme and to remove any additional burden from the shoulders of the British air attaché in Washington, the Air Ministry arranged to send him an assistant. Early in 1941, Squadron Leader R. Stuart Mills, DFC, a highly qualified RAF flying officer fresh from 263 Gladiator Squadron and combat in the 1940 Norwegian campaign, was assigned to work with the newly promoted Air Commodore George C. Pirie. With bandages still on his arms and hands from burns received in a Norwegian crash, Mills reported for duty at the British Embassy in Washington.

Since President Roosevelt had asked to meet an RAF combat veteran, Pirie took Mills to the White House to meet the president. Here was an air officer direct from combat who could answer questions and could reaffirm RAF needs. The RAF squadron leader was amazed at the attention given him by President and Mrs. Roosevelt. Initially Mills was assigned to administrative duties in Washington, but in early March 1941 he was sent to inspect the four refresher schools (in February, the fourth school had been added at Bakersfield, California). The Clayton Knight Committee continued to recruit barely qualified American pilots for the four Refresher Scheme schools. Some of them had been trained in the Civilian Pilot Training Program, and others had been eliminated from air corps or navy flight schools.

Concerned about training sufficient observers (navigators) for the expanded air force, Air Ministry officers sought information about such training in the United States. Whether the London officials learned of the Pan American Airways Navigation School through Air Commodore Pirie, the CAA or the Clayton Knight Committee is unknown. In October 1940, when the Air Ministry queried U.S. Army Air Corps officers about the possibility of training RAF observers alongside American navigator cadets, the American officers did not object to the British government's making an arrangement with Pan American Airways (PAA) for the training of a proposed ten RAF observers with each American navigator course at that facility.

On 5 November 1940, in response to that offer, RAF Group Captain Mackworth of the British Air Commission made an "unofficial" visit to the PAA School in Coral Gables, Florida. At that time, Class 41-A, the first fifty-man U.S. Army Air Corps navigation course, was nearing graduation at the school and was scheduled to undergo an additional six months of training in practical navigation aboard aircraft on long-distance flights. Following discussions with army air corps and Pan American Airways staff and a critical examination of the curriculum, Mackworth opposed RAF participation in the school's aerial navigation courses. Mackworth's objections were legion, but his primary concern was that the course was too short, its students did not get enough personal attention or flying experience and the syllabus contained no armaments training.

Since Air Ministry staff were campaigning to establish British pilot training schools in the United States and were also lobbying for more extensive American economic and military aid, it was concluded that Britain should not reject observer training for fear of jeopardizing other efforts. Mackworth's opposition to the American school was overruled, and the Air Ministry agreed to send ten RAF student observers to Coral Gables, Florida, in time for the February 1941 intake. The pressure of time caused the intake date to be pushed forward a month, so it was agreed that ten RAF student observers would be expected for the 24 March 1941 intake. A second ten-man draft would arrive in May.

In February 1941, as the American, British and Canadian (A-B-C) Conversations were drawing to a close and the Lend-Lease Bill was being debated in Congress and the news media, American public opinion was strongly pro-British. In order to prepare for a massive increase in armaments manufacture, a supremely confident President Roosevelt, having been elected to an unprecedented third term, sent Harry Hopkins on a hurried trip to London to persuade the British government to prepare requests for all of the materiel it wished. Once projected British needs were on record, costs could be calculated and budget requests could be drafted, which might be defended more easily before committees of Congress. Such British requests, coupled with those of the armed services of the United States, might also be useful in persuading members of Congress to approve the Lend-Lease Bill.

In response to Hopkins's prodding, and evidently without consulting responsible ministers, Prime Minister Churchill resorted to a somewhat faulty memory and requested "American pilots to ferry planes to England," veteran American pilots for duty on British bombers and "five training schools for pilots." In the future, delivery of specific types of American aircraft would "be determined by a joint military mission stationed in London." In the meantime, the Lend-Lease debates and other events would hasten the establishment of British flying schools in the United States.

On 6 March 1941, Air Attaché Pirie cabled the Air Ministry that the president had ordered General Arnold to render assistance by providing primary and advanced trainers for six British flying training facilities in the United States. As a result of the Hopkins memorandum and the news from Pirie that trainers were to be allocated, discussions concerning British aircrew training in the United States were officially resumed and Pirie was given discretionary authority to negotiate with both the United States government and the civilian flying school operators.

At the Air Ministry in London, Air Vice Marshal A.G.R. Garrod, member of the Air Council for training (AMT), described to the council his earlier efforts to establish RAF aircrew training in the United States. "We have been hammering at everyone in the U.S.A. from the President downward," he wrote, "trying to get additional advanced trainer aircraft, so that we could develop ready-made facilities in the United States." Garrod also described the beginning of the Refresher Scheme and FDR's recent order for the army air corps to divert almost six hundred elementary and advanced trainers from its own orders to the six British flying training schools that were to be established as commercial operations in the United States.

Now that these decisions had been made, much planning was necessary. The British flying training directorate began to develop a modified syllabus for use by the British flying training schools in the neutral United States. Officers who would staff a British training organization in the United States were also selected. Pilot training courses to be offered at the six schools to be built in the United States would include ground school and 150 flying hours, of which 70 would be elementary and 80 advanced. It was hoped that two of the six schools would be used exclusively for training American volunteers for RAF service, while the other four schools would receive British pupils from the United Kingdom.

For American volunteers entering these RAF schools, the course would run twenty-four weeks and would encompass a four-week-long initial training wing (ITW) course as well as completion of the elementary flying training school (EFTS) syllabus and the service flying training (SFTS) syllabus. Since they would already have completed ITW (pre-flight) courses, UK or Commonwealth students would undergo eighteen to twenty weeks of flying training in the neutral United States. Upon receipt of the Air Ministry proposals, members of the Empire Air Training Scheme (EATS) Committee were elated.

Perhaps the pending Lend-Lease Bill, which promised greater American assistance, led Garrod to propose that the RAF seek to locate nine additional SFTSs in the Texas-Oklahoma area of the neutral United States, in addition to the six all through training schools (ATTSs or BFTSs) already approved. Garrod believed that it would be possible to establish in the United States the six SFTSs not yet transferred from Britain as well as the three new SFTSs deemed necessary to reach the RAF goal of fifty-six such advanced flying schools. In reporting to the chief of air staff, Garrod asserted, "Personally, I believe the USA is ready for us to ask for everything that we require." Even so, Garrod's larger training proposal was vetoed by the Empire Air Training Scheme Committee.

The sequence of events, which opened the way for greater cooperation among Britain, the United States and Canada, followed a circuitous route during the months in which the Battle of Britain was fought. British air missions to the United States and American air missions to Britain helped to open and maintain communications. The Battle of Britain and Air Commodore John Slessor's mission to the United States helped to nullify critical reports that had been made by some American observers. Slessor focused attention on enemy bombing raids, which had ripped apart British airfields, factories and dwellings, and on Britain's dollar shortage.

When during the course of the A-B-C Conversations it was revealed that Britain was short of dollars and needed financial assistance if it was to continue to purchase American war materiel, President Roosevelt and Secretary Morgenthau were anxious to resolve that crisis. On 13 February 1941, the American treasury secretary's Special Committee met and developed plans for the United States government to assume all outstanding British loans and investments in the United States, including British defense contracts, through 28 February 1941. Such action would relieve Great Britain of a heavy financial burden of capital investment in American defense industries. For the United States, such action would consolidate war costs and make accounting less complicated.

The assumption by the United States government of these British obligations amounting to $2 billion was in keeping with established practices. The construction or expansion of most American defense industries, including building and equipping civilian contract flying schools, had been financed with funds borrowed by the civilian contractors and guaranteed by the Reconstruction Finance Corporation (RFC), a New Deal agency that made low-interest loans to strengthen the domestic economy.

Beginning in 1940, the RFC guaranteed loans for contractors who undertook national defense contracts, and in 1941 the Defense Plant Corporation (DPC), a newly formed subsidiary of the RFC, began to assume control over all earlier defense-related RFC loan guarantees. The formation of the DPC marks the division between Depression-related and war-related expenditures. By March 1941, the DPC assumed responsibility for the British investments in American defense industries, as well as for funds due on yet undelivered British orders.

As collateral for the assumption of contracts, the British government conveyed British-owned stock certificates to the RFC, and that American agency agreed to hold the certificates until the postwar accounting. The United States Treasury also repaid the British Treasury some $781 million cash, which Britain might need to meet obligations falling outside the scope of Lend-Lease funding. Some British capital expenditures for the expansion of American factories and for designing and constructing machine tools, and those debts could not legally be assumed by the Reconstruction Finance Corporation and might later become Lend-Lease obligations, if and when that legislation became law.

Other events fell into place. Internal crises in both Britain and the United States were resolved, and the way was opened for greater cooperation. President Roosevelt had won a third term, and Treasury Secretary Morgenthau's Committee on Domestic and Foreign Military Purchases was first strengthened and then replaced by a broader agreement. The A-B-C Conversations of January and February 1941 focused attention on Britain's procurement of American aircraft and on joint planning. Until the United States went to war, it was agreed that the British and American governments would share American aircraft production fifty-fifty. The agreement to share technical secrets as well as lessons learned from air operations would help Americans to develop their own air forces more rapidly. Undersecretary Balfour and Air Attaché Pirie were also able to convince the Air Ministry to proceed with the All Through Training Scheme (ATTS or BFTS) for training British nationals as pilots in the United States.

On 11 March 1941, Congress passed the Lend-Lease Bill and President Roosevelt signed it into law. Under its provisions and later amendments, Britain and other nations would receive from the United States food, ships, tanks, aircraft, weapons, ammunition and other necessities. As in the December 1939 aircrew training agreement among Britain, Canada and other Commonwealth countries, payment would be deferred until the end of the war. Many goods and services provided by Britain and other Allies to the United States would be regarded as "reverse lend-lease," and a final accounting of costs would await a postwar settlement. Heretofore, Secretary Morgenthau had carefully guarded British orders against raids by the American military; now he found the United States armed services much more cooperative and himself in the peculiar position of assuming control over some $2 billion worth of outstanding British defense orders.

The sequence of events leading to greater, more direct assistance to Britain followed closely on passage of the Lend-Lease Bill. On 5 April 1941, the British Air Commission submitted requisitions for Defense Articles 88 and 89 to cover expenses for training pilots in Refresher Scheme schools and in six British flying training schools at an estimated cost of $21,337,165.62. On being informed of the British request, Major General George Brett, newly appointed chief of the air corps, approved the requisitions and indicated that the army air corps would provide "285 basic or advanced airplanes and 260 primary trainers" for use in the six BFTSs. These 545 trainers would be delivered to the six schools in time for the arrival of the first intakes from the United Kingdom.

Early in April 1941, when Air Attaché Pirie received Brett's assurance that trainer aircraft would be available, he recommended to Garrod that RAF staff officers be selected immediately and that they be sent to the United States so as to be on hand for posting to the six RAF flying schools as they opened. His remarks concerning the qualifications essential for RAF officers assigned for service in the United States deserve quotation in full, because they underscore basic problems already existing in relations between Great Britain and the United States:

> *They must be able to get on well with the American, possess considerable tact, discretion and patience, and still be very strong minded as to what we want in the way of training. The latter is very important to my mind, because the standard in flying training in this country is not as good as ours by a long way. I am confident, however, that with good people from England in charge it can be made so, especially if our representatives show clearly but tactfully that they know their business. Our people have to realise however that the American thinks that everything in America is superior to everything in any other country and one has to play up to this form of vanity—or is it inferiority complex?*

As with so many generalizations, Pirie's assumption of British superiority was apparently based on limited knowledge of his host country and on an obvious belief in the superiority of the British Empire. Since he had served as air attaché in Washington's British Embassy for several years, his qualifications as an observer appear questionable. This would be neither the first nor the last time in which British assumptions of American inferiority were expressed.

Since during early spring 1941 the time had not yet arrived when Congress anxiously approved virtually every War or Navy Department budget request, the Lend-Lease Law was important to both departments as a means of assuring the rapid expansion of all defense industries. Passage of the Lend-Lease Bill and the simultaneous submission of huge American and British aircraft orders made it possible for the United States government to build all of the factories and assembly plants deemed necessary to assure maximum expansion of American production. And that industrial expansion ought to prove extensive enough to supply the needs of the American, British, Canadian and other Allied air forces.

By mid-March 1941, everything seemed to be going well: American pilots were being trained for RAF service in four Refresher Scheme schools; ten selected RAF observer students had arrived in Canada and would soon be en route to Coral Gables, Florida, where on 24 March they would commence training in the Pan American Airways Navigation Section at the University of Miami. Since four of the six BFTSs were expected to be ready to train RAF students early in June, three hundred student pilots (fifty men for each school) would have to be indoctrinated and transported from Britain to the schools in time to commence training as scheduled. That initial intake, plus others that were scheduled to enroll each seven weeks thereafter, compelled the Air Ministry to increase its recruitment efforts and to expand preliminary aircrew training in Britain.

Generals Marshall and Arnold and War Department planners were alarmed at the course of events. A number of American pilots who volunteered for service in Britain or China had already been given temporary releases from active or reserve duty and were en route to their assigned posts, but the transfer of greater numbers of experienced pilots to Britain was blocked. When Marshall asserted that Britain should receive as many combat aircraft "as can be efficiently manned by the trained British Commonwealth personnel available in the British Isles," he reconfirmed provisions of the A-B-C Conversations, but was determined to prevent the stockpiling of American aircraft in the British Isles, as had happened during summer 1940 when the British Purchasing Commission assumed control over French aircraft orders.

Realizing that the British request for greater assistance would affect army air corps strength, General Marshall urged General Arnold to act quickly. When the Hopkins memo was referred to the War Plans Division, American analysts asserted that Britain's most critical need for assistance would occur during the months of 1941, after which the United States should have on hand "54 combat groups, plus the necessary personnel and facilities to undertake an immediate expansion to one hundred combat groups." [American groups were the equivalent of RAF wings.] As a result, General Arnold evidently decided that if the army air corps should train four thousand Royal Air Force pilots alongside American flying cadets, the airfields, facilities and equipment used for that purpose could later be used to expand American air power.

Arnold flew to London in April 1941 and met with RAF officers at the Air Ministry. In that meeting, the chief of the army air corps proposed to train four thousand British pilots alongside American aviation cadets. The British Air Council gratefully accepted the generous American offer and began to develop plans for establishing a personnel pipeline from British pre-flight training schools via Canada to and from the neutral United States. Ultimately, this American system for training British pilots would be labeled the Arnold Scheme. The Air Council also recognized that a Royal Air Force administrative organization, similar to that which had been established in Canada, was needed in the United States immediately.

CHAPTER TWO

SETTING UP ARNOLD SCHEME FLIGHT TRAINING

ORGANIZING

During May and early June 1941, Group Captain D.V. Carnegie, who had been appointed director of UK training in the United States, flew to America. Carnegie was authorized to assign an RAF administrative officer to each of the three USAAF Flying Training Center headquarters and to each of the six Arnold Scheme primary schools. Initially, there was a delay in assigning RAF officers to the staff at the Pan American Airways Navigation Section in Coral Gables, Florida. However, on 1 July 1941, when RAF intakes at that school climbed from ten to one hundred, several staff officers and noncommissioned officers were ultimately assigned there.

Most of the RAF officers scheduled to be assigned to schools in the United States had reported to Ottawa from duty at flying schools in Canada. Following an interview with Air Vice Marshal Lionel D.D. McKean, air officer commanding (AOC) the United Kingdom Air Liaison Mission, those who held a lower rank were advanced to acting flight lieutenant (captain). They were then ordered to report to the director of UK training at the British Embassy in the Washington, D.C. offices of the air attaché. After undergoing further interviews and briefing sessions, each new RAF administrative officer (RAFAO) was provided vouchers with which to reach the station to which he was assigned, and most of them arrived there during the first week of June 1941.

Initial assignment of RAF staff officers for Arnold Scheme primary schools were as follows: Flight Lieutenant John Garthwaite was posted to the Alabama Institute of Aeronautics, Tuscaloosa, Alabama; Flight Lieutenant J. Leonard Keith, OBE, was posted to Camden, South Carolina; Flight Lieutenant Maurice O'Callaghan went to Carlstrom Field, Arcadia, Florida; Flight Lieutenant W.W. Watson reported to the Lakeland School of Aeronautics at Lakeland, Florida; Flight Lieutenant Alfred G. Hill was posted to Darr Aero Tech, Albany, Georgia; and Flight Lieutenant Leonard Speck reported to Souther Field, Americus, Georgia.

The orientation of these RAFAOs was as thorough as early experience permitted. When the command organization was explained to them, they learned that they would regularly file written reports to Wing Commander H.A.V. Hogan, DFC, senior RAF administrative officer (SRAFAO) at Maxwell Field. They were also informed that a draft of 550 RAF students had arrived in Canada and would begin training at the schools on 9 June 1941. Similar intakes would arrive every five weeks, each constituting a separate Arnold Scheme course.

Although the U.S. Army Air Corps civil contract schools were likened to elementary flying training schools (EFTSs) in Britain, it was explained that primary training was only the beginning. Each of the three phases of American pilot training—primary, basic and advanced—was a separate ten-week-long course, conducted on different flying fields, often in a different state. More specifically, in conjunction with the American officer commanding each training detachment, the RAFAOs were directed to be generally responsible for the discipline of UK students and for disbursement of pay and the preparation and submission of records and reports. "At all times, he will act in close cooperation with the C.O., who is in direct command of all students whether U.S. or U.K." was the specific order that was emphasized to these subordinate RAF officers.

The directives to the RAFAOs were also careful to define student responsibilities and duties, and are important to clarify, especially because so many former student pilots were later critical of many aspects of their Arnold Scheme training. Particularly disturbing to the RAF students were restrictions on their time, the army air corps cadet system of organization and discipline and the imposition of U.S. Army drill. However many may have later deemed these practices an error, the original orders, which were transmitted through the Air Ministry to the RAF administrative officers, were specific and allowed very little latitude.

Since British student pilots were to attend American flight schools alongside American aviation cadets, training officers believed that it was imperative that there be uniformity in discipline and practice. Since they deemed the learning and use of American-style drill and ceremonies essential for success alongside American classmates in the basic and advanced flying schools, the American form of drill would be required of all RAF students, even in the primary schools. In carrying out their own duties, the RAFAOs served on the staff of detachment commanding officers, advised the cadets concerning RAF policy and sat on numerous committees and boards. Initially, these junior RAF officers were required to submit weekly written reports to the SRAFAO at Maxwell Field, Alabama.

For a brief period before his assignment to Maxwell Field, Alabama, as liaison officer for all of the Arnold Scheme schools, Wing Commander Harry A.V. Hogan had served in the Washington office with Carnegie. As SRAFAO, Hogan was appointed to serve at Maxwell Field, Alabama, in two capacities. His prime responsibilities were to represent the RAF and to supervise RAF Arnold Scheme aircrew training within the Southeastern United States. In carrying out these duties, Hogan had to become thoroughly familiar with the U.S. Army Air Corps training system and to coordinate with air corps staff and training officers. Brigadier General Walter R. Weaver, commanding general, Southeast Air Corps Training Center (SEACTC) at Maxwell Field, Montgomery, Alabama, assigned Hogan to his staff, thus paving the way for greater cooperation than might otherwise have developed.

Born in 1909 in India, Hogan was educated at Malvern College and RAF College, Cranwell, and was commissioned in 1930. Over the next decade, he became a highly skilled pilot while serving in several squadrons of the RAF and the Fleet Air Arm. In 1936–37, he had served as a flying instructor at the central flying school in Upavon, Wiltshire, and in 1938, he was engaged in a long-distance record-setting flight from Egypt to Australia. During the 1940 Battle of Britain, Squadron Leader Hogan commanded the 501 (County of Gloucester) Squadron of fighters (Hawker Hurricanes) and served most of that critical period in sectors of 11 Group, Fighter Command, defending the approaches to London and other population centers. For this service, in which he was credited with destroying five enemy aircraft, Hogan was awarded the Distinguished Flying Cross and promotion to wing commander (lieutenant colonel).

When Group Captain (Colonel) D.V. Carnegie was assigned to a higher post than that at Maxwell Field, which he had originally thought himself best qualified to undertake, he selected Hogan to serve in that post. Hogan proved to be an ideal choice for the sensitive position at Maxwell Field, and he carried out his extensive duties with great skill. Quarters and office facilities were provided, and Hogan's wife, Venetia, was able to join him there. Since the Hogans were unable to transport household goods from Britain for their use, USAAF wives gave them a "shower" consisting of linens, pots and pans and other essentials not provided with post housing. The young British couple was very popular with the USAAF set, as well as with local political and business people in the Alabama state capital. They proved to be very effective ambassadors.

On 6 June 1941, as he assumed his post, Wing Commander Hogan understood that he was to act as advisor to Brigadier General Walter R. Weaver, commanding general of the SEACTC, in all matters relating to British students under training (u/t) within the command. In addition, Hogan was to have responsibility for a formidable set of tasks. He would supervise the RAF administrative officers (RAFAOs) assigned to the schools at which British students were under training. In that connection, Hogan received regular reports from these RAFAOs and compiled weekly (later fortnightly) summaries and training progress reports for Group Captain David V. Carnegie, director of UK training, in Washington, D.C. And Carnegie, in turn, kept the Air Ministry Training Directorate in London closely advised of training progress and problems.

Other duties to which Hogan was assigned at Maxwell Field included service on the academic board to review progress of British students and to deal with any serious disciplinary cases arising among them. During the first sixty days, Hogan also reviewed the records of student failures and interviewed many of them in order to decide the alternate aircrew training for which they appeared best suited. Evidently, Air Ministry officers hoped that the SRAFAO would act in a capacity similar to that of an RAF central flying school instructor and would visit all training airfields in order to personally check the proficiency of civilian flying instructors. However, such an assignment could not be diplomatically carried out without possibly offending the host U.S. Army Air Corps detachment commanding officers who had already checked records and flown with each civilian instructor.

While on duty at Maxwell Field, Hogan served at the operating staff level and at first had limited influence in the development of policy. Policy remained in the hands of higher authority in London and Washington. In the course of his normal duties, Hogan's prime daily concern was for the problems of several thousand students undergoing training in a foreign land. Only after he was absolutely inundated with work at Maxwell Field was he given significant assistance with which to carry out his varied duties. As will be seen, he was provided with an aircraft to visit the six primary flying schools when the first draft arrived in the United States.

THE FIRST FOUR RAF ARNOLD SCHEME COURSES TRAVEL TO CANADA

Transporting large numbers of men round-trip through the dangerous waters of the North Atlantic from Britain to Canada and back was not a simple process. In an effort to avoid long-range Nazi reconnaissance aircraft and U-boats, troop ships embarked from ports on the west coast of Britain, mostly from Glasgow (Greenock or Gourock) or Liverpool, but occasionally from Avonmouth or Milford Haven. More than fifty westbound ships laden with RAF aircrew pupils destined for Canada or the United States sailed across the North Atlantic to Canadian or American ports. Some large and fast former ocean liners zig-zagged alone across the North Atlantic at speeds of fifteen knots or more, while other transports and "armed merchant cruisers" traveled in small groups or in convoys protected by armed escorts.

For a time during the early months of the war, many passenger ships and troop transports departing from or arriving in Canada did so through the port of Montreal. However, after the mouth of Canada's St. Lawrence River increasingly attracted enemy U-boats, Montreal ceased to be used as a major port of entry or embarkation. On occasion, St. John, New Brunswick, may have been used as an alternate port for shipping cargo, but the Bay of Fundy's fierce thirty-foot tides made sustained use of that harbor and bay too risky. Most of the early large drafts of British aircrew trainees traveled to Canada aboard former ocean liners.

Members of Class SE-42-A traveled aboard the former Cunard-White Star Liner *Britannic*, now a 27,000-ton troop transport capable of a speed of eighteen knots. On 29 May 1941, as members of Arnold Scheme Class SE-42-A disembarked from HMT *Britannic*, a freakish winter-like storm, under the power of gale-force winds, dropped temperatures into the thirties (Fahrenheit) and pushed snow flurries across Canada's Maritime Provinces. Upon disembarking onto the cold and windy docks of Halifax, Nova Scotia, the men hurried and immediately boarded train cars for the thirty-hour trip to Toronto.

Members of that first RAF Arnold Scheme draft were not provided with Canadian money. Before they could purchase any of the food, cigarettes or other items that they saw in abundance for the first time in months, they had to wait until they reached Toronto to receive an advance on their meager pay. The unheated train cars irritated the airmen; that no food was available until the train made a brief stop in Truro, Nova Scotia, was unforgivable. To say that the young aircrew students were "cheesed" or "browned off" is a vast understatement.

Loud complaints about such conditions undoubtedly reached the proper authorities and resulted in plans for solving several problems related to the transportation of westbound aircrew candidates from Halifax. In the future, so as to be sure that every man had sufficient pocket money for small expenses incurred during travel, each airman, on disembarking from a ship, would be provided with an advance on his monthly pay of ten Canadian dollars. Better handling of the money problem might improve morale, but there still remained the larger question of where and how to accommodate such increasingly large numbers.

A large part of Class SE-42-B sailed to Halifax aboard the *Chitral*, a former Pacific & Orient Liner, now a 15,000-ton Armed Merchant Cruiser capable of a speed of seventeen knots. Concurrently, around 20 June 1941, several small RAF and FAA drafts traveled by rail from their tent encampment at RAF Wilmslow to Glasgow. Next day, they boarded three tiny, barely seaworthy Irish Sea steamers, the *Manxman*, *Royal Ulsterman* and the *Ulster Monarch*, and, escorted by two old American destroyers, sailed for Iceland. They complained of the crowded boats and the extreme cold, but two days later, the little ships docked in Reykjavik harbor. On disembarking, the men boarded trucks to Helgafell, some twelve miles away.

LAC Douglas Coxhead (Albany, 42-B) recorded his views in his diary:

> We lived in Nissen huts sans furniture—we slept in all our clothes & just 2 blankets. No pillows or beds, just got down on the floor boards—very hard. Lived on canned stew, beans & butter, doughie bread & biscuits. No bogs or washing—so we washed in a mountain stream & bathed in one of the hot mountain lakes—about 90 degrees F with steam rising from it. Did a lot of walking, climbing, & swimming & enjoyed the stay immensely…
>
> On 3 July, sighted a ship in the harbour from "our" mountain; packed up & went down by trucks & aboard her—AMC Wolfe, ex CPR Liner Montcalm. Sailed in the evening—lots of fog outside—going dead slow…Had cinema shows & concert aboard—did gun watches also by day & night. Had a good trip, met & joined main convoy of about 50 odd vessels, then left them somewhere in the fog as we sloped off into Halifax.

Other Iceland drafts boarded armed merchant cruisers, including the *Ranpura*, the *Circassia* and the *Maloja*, and joined a convoy destined for Halifax.

LAC Norman Cass (Albany, 42-B) had slightly different memories of the RAF experience in the camp at Helgafell, Iceland:

> *We slept on "biscuit" mattresses on the wooden floors of the huts, and since the "dark" only lasted 4/5 hours, it was not the most restful of situations. I recollect the local inhabitants showed a complete disinterest in our "invading" presence—no hostility but no welcome either. I also remember that the C.O. of this camp was an RAF officer of advanced age, reputedly ex-Indian Army and as nutty as a fruitcake. He spent his time riding 'round the camp on a white horse, and solemnly taking the salute on a small cliff near the camp whenever we returned from our route marches or other physical training exercises.*

Experience while aboard ship remained essentially the same: lower decks were often awash in vomit, and Halifax remained their Canadian port of entry.

That port city was the first sight of Canada for most British aircrew students, and they were curious about the port. The sights and sounds of that time, when these men were young and had just arrived in one of the busiest seaports in the world, were etched into their memories for a lifetime. Francis W. Preston (Arcadia, SE-42-D) spoke for hundreds of men when he recalled, "What a contrast to England—lights at night—plenty of food—no rationing. We went mad on bacon and eggs, bananas, etc., and tried to see everything possible." They would always recall the sounds of the city and of sea birds, buoys, the wind and ships' foghorns and bells, and some of them would experience the blistering effect of frigid gale-force winds.

Many of the drafts arrived at night, and if they did, what really fascinated them, as Preston and others indicated, were the lights. Accustomed to blackout conditions at home, the British trainees saw lights, filtered by rain or mist and fog, twinkling from both the Halifax and Dartmouth shores like an ethereal fairyland. Since daylight revealed rusty derricks, tanks and the flotsam of a busy seaport and thrust the ship-weary aircrew trainees into another form of disillusioning realism, memories of that arrival and the lights remained all the more compelling. Their ITW training in signals and in navigation and meteorology sensitized them to things not obvious to the casual observer.

Their recent training also forced them to question and attempt analysis of everything they saw. The clouds, the wind direction and velocity, the sun, moon and stars, the sight of pilot boats and lighters, the debris of the busy dock area were all of interest. Of greater concern was the sight of small boats running from ship to ship, of ferries plying the harbor waters between Halifax and Dartmouth and of ships gliding past in preparation to depart for unknown ports. These were some of the sights that the young wartime airmen observed, but did not truly see. As with most young men of their training and time, their minds were occupied with flying and girls and food and music and tomorrow.

Since huge drafts were only the beginning of enlarged training schemes in both Canada and the United States, the citizens of Halifax and other ports were already in danger. The deadly 1918 influenza epidemic and the polio epidemic of 1940–41 provided sufficient warnings to the medical profession that the mix of large numbers of people from different parts of the world increased chances for spreading disease. The traditional means of dealing with such emergencies was to quarantine incoming passengers who had been exposed to one or more communicable diseases.

However, in early summer 1941, the nearest camp capable of accommodating large numbers was located far into the interior at Toronto, Ontario. Insufficient train cars, the necessity for quarantine and other potential hazards no doubt worried Movements Group officers. They knew that the day might soon come when large numbers of men might need to be fed and provided with temporary quarters for extended periods.

On 24 May 1941, RAF Flight Lieutenant Paul Goldsmith had arrived at Toronto's RCAF No. 1 Manning Depot as the first commander of the RAF detachment in Toronto. By 19 June, three other British officers had arrived. The unit was now called the RAF Transit Section, and its commander was Squadron Leader J.F. Houchin, a veteran pilot of the 1914–18 war and of the 1940 Battle of France. Houchin, who had recently been stationed at a training base in Saskatchewan, arrived in Toronto in time to meet a flood of RAF aircrew students bound for flight training in both Canada and the United States.

The Toronto facility's usefulness for housing troops was enhanced by its central location and its spacious buildings, which were easily altered to house and feed numerous transient aircrew. The RCAF No. 1 Manning Depot was located on the grounds of the Canadian National Exhibition on the south side of Toronto. It served as a RCAF recruit depot for that part of Canada, and as an aircrew processing station for British Commonwealth Air Training Plan (BCATP) personnel as well as for separate units of the RAF and the Fleet Air Arm. The mission of the small fifty-man British detachment at that RCAF station was to provide shelter and food and to handle records and schedule transport. The RAF detachment also maintained liaison between the RCAF, the newly arrived RAF students, the United Kingdom Air Liaison Mission in Ottawa and the British air mission (later the RAF delegation) in Washington.

In describing the documentation of an Arnold Scheme draft, Norman Cass (Albany, 42-B) recalled that "everyone was photographed and fingerprinted for a Non-Immigrant Visa Card which was to be carried in one's wallet. We were also fitted with gray flannel suits which had been brought from the U.K.—some of them required drastic modification to be worn at all." As these various tasks were undertaken, a few transient aircrew students were regularly assigned to assist the RAF staff in preparing documents for each draft.

Class SE-42-C sailed for Halifax aboard the Cunard-White Star Liner *Stratheden*, now an 18,700-ton troop transport capable of a speed of sixteen knots. As LAC Roger F. Pye (Camden, 42-C) of Oporto, Portugal, described it,

> *ITW completed, we were promoted from AC2* [air craftsman second class] *to LAC* [leading air craftsman] *and went on 2 week's leave. That over, I was posted to #2 PDC* [personnel dispersal center] *at Wilmslow, Cheshire* [just outside Manchester] *to await embarkation. About 10 days later, in early August, I embarked with some thousands of others, on the Liner Stratheden for a 6-day dash across the Atlantic without escort, from the Clyde to Halifax, Nova Scotia.*
>
> *The ship had been stripped to make her into a transport, and the other ranks (or enlisted men, as you would say) were accommodated in messes of about 200 men each. The space in each mess was almost entirely taken up by a large table at which they ate; sleeping at night in hammocks slung above them from hooks in the beams (remarkably comfortable). The troops were confined below for certain fixed hours of the day, as well*

as at night, and had the ship been torpedoed during one of these periods, the loss of life would undoubtedly have been heavy.

The only major year-round eastern Canadian ports with adequate safe anchorages and docking facilities were Halifax, Nova Scotia, and St. John's, Newfoundland. St. John's was used primarily by eastbound drafts, which could be safely transported from Halifax to Newfoundland aboard small vessels.

Since plans called for a large increase in the size of westbound aircrew student drafts, the Canadian government chose Halifax as the port for entry and embarkation for most troops. Regardless of the time of year, when westbound ships arrived in the vicinity of Newfoundland, they usually encountered fog. Often, transports sailed westward out of the fog into clear blue skies and sunshine. After the aircrew students had stowed their hammocks and lined ship's rails, they saw the gulls and rocky green hills and headlands of either Newfoundland or Nova Scotia and knew that their transport would soon make port.

Occasionally, they heard or saw patrolling aircraft and little else until their ship was gliding through offshore waters, stopping to take on a harbor pilot, then moving ahead more slowly past the boom at the entrance to the Halifax harbor. From their positions along the railings of the transports, they could usually make out McNab's Island and George's Island, and a great number of ships anchored about the harbor.

Prior to docking, care was taken to ensure compliance with currency regulations; British pounds sterling were remitted and amounts were registered, so that each student might later be reimbursed in Canadian money. Although they were often assigned to cleaning and polishing or watch assignments aboard ship, the aircrew trainees usually observed the activities of the ship's crew and the pilot and often read the messages of semaphore and blinker light signals, excitedly anticipating landfall.

Since most of the aircrew trainees had never traveled by sea, most of them suffered from seasickness aboard ship and tried to hide it for fear of being rejected for aircrew training, so large numbers of them hardly ate anything during their voyage across the North Atlantic. As a result, many of them were very weak on arrival in Halifax, and when local newspapers reported that one of them had fainted, rumors circulated that the people in Britain were starving. Whether or not people in Canada believed that rumor, they knew from other sources that Britons had been deprived of many food items and that most consumer goods were rationed. They could not know about conditions aboard troop ships.

Halifax was not only the closest mainland Canadian port to Britain for ships plying the North Atlantic, but it also provided one of the safest natural harbors along the North American coast. With its vast docks, warehouses and transport, and its huge Bedford Basin for forming, protecting and dispatching convoys, Halifax was well equipped to handle maritime traffic. Another advantage for Halifax was that the Canadian rail network joined its docks to the rest of Canada and connected at several points with lines running to all parts of the United States. When one considers the great distances from Halifax to training airfields in western Canada and to those scattered about the United States, the potential for administrative problems is readily apparent. Coordinating the transportation of large drafts of men the approximately 1,800 miles from Halifax to Toronto was difficult at best.

The journey from Halifax to Toronto consumed approximately thirty hours for each draft and was obviously wearing on men who had already been at sea for ten days or more. To send them westward beyond Toronto to the Prairie Provinces, or across the Canadian Rockies to British Columbia, or southward to the Southeastern states, or southwestward to Oklahoma, Texas, Arizona or California, would require more than just train cars and food. Transient quarters and other facilities located at Halifax or along the main lines of transport into the interior of Canada constituted the greatest need.

As a temporary measure, provision had already been made for groups of citizens to board the troop trains at Truro, some sixty miles west of Halifax, and to distribute sandwiches, milk and fresh fruit to each group of aircrew candidates passing through. After Truro, the trains turned northwestward across New Brunswick and a small slice of Quebec on the southeast side of the St. Lawrence River, then they ran southwestward along the river, crossing through Montreal into Ontario, and continuing southwestward along the north shore of Lake Ontario. The rail journey carried the British aircrew students through some of the most beautiful lake and forest areas in North America.

Along the railway were occasional brightly painted wooden houses, tiny villages, farms and grazing lands, granite knobs, hills and mountains, quick flowing streams, broad and sluggish rivers and many varieties of maple, birch, ash, pine and beech trees. However enticing the scenery and the pull of history, however fascinating the huge rail cars and their massive engines, the thrill to the RAF students only increased. The clicking rails, the mournful sounds of the train whistle and the sporadic ringing of bells at crossings were memories to be retained for a lifetime. The excitement of the aircrew students was continuous and was diminished only by hunger pangs. The sights and sounds of that long wartime rail journey would live on in their memories, as would memories of their voyage and arrival in North America.

Initially, the transportation of RAF aircrew was coordinated from Montreal by the RCAF No. 1 Movements Group. Since Montreal was the location of the central offices and shops of the Canadian National and the Canadian Pacific Railroads, that city was an ideal location for RCAF Movements Group Headquarters during the early months of the war, and it remained so until October 1941. The arrival of the ten men for each of the March and May 1941 RAF observer drafts destined for training at Coral Gables, Florida, could hardly have created a ripple of concern for RCAF Movements Group staff. The same could be said of the one-hundred-man draft that was divided between Numbers 1 and 2 British flying training schools in Texas and California, but the arrival of larger drafts during subsequent months would demonstrate that Movements officers needed to pay greater attention to apparent small details.

In a letter home, LAC John A. "Jack" Cook (PAA 42-1) exaggerated only slightly in describing the duties for which he volunteered at RCAF No. 1 Manning Depot:

> *I've just finished the typing I had to do for today. You see, last Monday, the Flight Sergeant asked for volunteers to type out forms, and told us that we should get special privileges for it…As we are going into the States, we have to fill in quite a number of forms for passports, visas, fingerprints, and practically sign our lives away. Well, we've been pretty busy all day. The privileges are that we are allowed out every night until 2 a.m., whereas the others have to be in at 10.30 every night except Wed. and Sat., and we also get a weekend every week.*

Although visas were necessary and passports were not, the members of each draft had to be properly documented and clothed before departing for their various flying schools in the United

States. Cook also neglected to say that he and other "volunteers" were probably too tired at the end of the day to enjoy a late night pass. In addition to documenting RAF personnel passing through Canada to and from American flying schools, there were others to be processed as well. As indicated earlier, the Canadian government had agreed to the transfer of a large number of RAF schools to Canada.

These transferred RAF schools covered the entire flying training spectrum from initial training wings (ITWs) for RAF volunteers from the western hemisphere, elementary flying training schools (EFTSs), service flying training schools (SFTSs), operational training units (OTUs), bombing and general reconaissance schools (B&GRs) and air observer and navigation schools (AONSs). Many British aircrew students brought along addresses of relatives and neighbors who had immigrated to Canada years before, and during their evenings and weekends off the station they visited those relatives or family friends. Their welcome by the people of Toronto and vicinity was warm and friendly.

On 1 June 1941, the *Toronto Star* reported the comments of some of the RAF trainees. "If our reception last night is a sample of Canada's war effort," Reginald Levy (Albany, SE-42-A) is reported to have said, "you don't need to worry on that score. We arrived here and within an hour all of us had been fed, showered, and were in our bunks. They even had a band out to greet us." "We get so many invitations to dinner or supper or to come for a ride in their cars or to spend the weekend at their places," wrote Jack Cook (PAA, 42-1), "that we begin to feel somewhat embarrassed!" As representatives of Great Britain's Royal Air Force, which had won the Battle of Britain, they had absorbed the reflected glory, and were treated like royalty wherever they went. However, the Arnold Scheme students had seen nothing yet; they would soon experience the celebrated Southern hospitality.

Generous and hospitable though the Canadians were, Toronto was not London, and it was impossible to please everyone, especially those who were beginning to feel homesick. In terms of geography, language, customs and outlook, Canada was neither British nor quite American. For too many of the young RAF transients, it was only halfway between Britain and the many flying schools in the United States. Critical minds and personalities perceived it as definitely not Britain, and therefore strange. To the more sophisticated, "Canadian liquor laws were medieval, and the city of Toronto was dull and too Presbyterian." To the majority, their Canadian interlude was a great experience.

Of the five large RAF drafts that traveled westward from Halifax to Toronto, only the one, which included the men destined for Class SE-42-C, was delayed in Halifax and was billeted in the incomplete RCAF No. 1 Y Depot. That camp, sometimes referred to as the Air Embarkation Depot, was hurriedly built during the summer of 1941 and was to prove especially useful for quarantined arrivals or for eastbound drafts awaiting a ship. The depot was located on the northern outskirts of Halifax at Windsor Street and Bayers Road adjacent to the Canadian National Railroad (CNR) lines and about halfway between the Halifax dock area and Bedford Basin, the deep anchorage where convoys formed up. The camp began as a small facility and was to grow more than double its original size during the course of the war. One of the gates of the RCAF installation opened onto Conolly Street, and the nearest trolley line was four blocks away, probably at Oxford Street and Bayers Road.

In a letter written over a period of several days, and finally completed and mailed in mid-August 1941, LAC Richard F.H. Martin of North Devon (Americus, 42-C) described his experiences and observations in great detail, often contrasting conditions with those in Britain and aboard ship. Martin also provided a description of the care and concern of staff at the newly finished RCAF No. 1 Y Depot in Halifax:

> *We arrived at the camp* [RCAF No. 1 Y Depot] *and it looked like another of the usual type. However, once inside we were greeted by a Sergeant who told us to hurry as there was a meal waiting. It is a new half-built camp with no proper roads so plenty of mud. We went into a marvelous hut, which had double deck beds with spring mattresses! Also pillows!! Then to the mess where we had our first proper meal since rationing, and you could have as much as you wanted of everything. We then went to a film at the YMCA and then to bed on those lovely beds to sleep off that meal.*
>
> **Sunday, 17 August 1941.** *Up at 7:30 a.m. (great after the 6:15 on that awful troopship). Breakfast consisted of jam and honey, bacon, beans, bread and also about half a pound of butter. We are to be paid $10 today, and tomorrow we should get the equivalent of English money we gave in on the ship. If what they say about our final destination is right, then all the discomfort of the troopship will have been worth it…*
>
> **21 August 1941.** *I have now been in this disembarkation camp nearly a week. We have not had much to do but have been split up into groups of about five to go on different drafts to different flying schools. Lloyd has been lucky and got the best one somewhere in Florida. I got the last one on the list. We were told that it is a good school and has good instructors but is some way from a town. I leave here on Friday for Toronto where we stop for a bit. We all hope to go to the Exhibition there, which is just starting. I have bought a camera to take photos of this tour.*
>
> *We have been into the town every afternoon and evening; it is not much to look at, but the food is good. It is a seaport full of Navy, but they have not seen the RAF here before and are a bit surprised to see so many of us. The trams are called streetcars and the chemists, drug stores. Today is our last whole day here and we had to go for a route march around the town and back under command of Canadian officers.*

Martin's draft was held in Halifax's No. 1 Y Depot for a week, ostensibly because the Canadian National Exhibition (national fair) had opened in the massive facilities at Lakeside in Toronto. Even without the fair, the RCAF No. 1 Manning Depot at Toronto was already becoming overcrowded.

In early August, Class SE-42-D originally boarded the twenty-ton Canadian Pacific Liner *Duchess of Atholl*, but when her engines malfunctioned they returned to Glasgow, entrained for Liverpool and there, after considerable waiting, boarded the *Stratheden*, which had recently returned from North America. For this trip to Canada, LAC Denys R. Ding (Tuscaloosa, 42-D) was appointed flight leader for his mess deck. Later, at Tuscaloosa, in a written report to the commander of No. 10 ITW at Scarborough, Yorkshire, he made some important recommendations. Ding warned against listening to rumors, and suggested that all postings be warned "that the journey, traveling troop deck, is anything but comfortable." Continuing, he asserted that "the advantages of training in this country [the USA], and the amenities which go with it (when compared to Great Britain under present conditions), far outweigh the marked differences which are experienced in discipline and the extra ground work involved."

For a few months between about 1 June and 15 October 1941, the flow of RAF aircrew trainees between Halifax and Toronto increased, and the Manning Depot was the equivalent of a Royal

Air Force Times Square. There was much truth in the application of a description of the famous New York City landmark to the transient station in Toronto. Of New York's Times Square, it has been said that if visitors remain there very long, they are sure to encounter someone they know. To confirm the Times Square comparison with Toronto's No. 1 Manning Depot, many RAF students described encountering various friends, schoolmates and even relatives in this, only one of many RAF crossroads worldwide.

Basic accommodation included the provision of shelter, bedding and food. Several hundred double-tiered bunks were set up in the huge covered animal show arena of the Canadian National Exhibition Building. Depending on the attitudes of particular RAF aircrew students, the building was referred to as the bull pens or sheep pens, and it was here that the transients slept, ate and mustered for assignment, documentation and shipment. As might be expected, men of the various RAF drafts reacted differently to each new experience. "The gigantic room we occupied contained 600 double-decker beds," wrote Leslie Rosser (Lakeland, 42-B), "so sleep was quite an achievement." Former schoolmaster Frederick G. Higson (PAA, 41-7) asserted that his draft was "bedded down between the Holsteins and the Hogs."

The significance of the Toronto location of the RAF Depot in the bull, sheep or hog pens was not lost on the aircrew students. They could and did laugh and sing a great deal—usually bawdy songs of the time—and the city dwellers among the students were introduced to experiences totally new to them. In American GI parlance, a doctor's inspection of men's bodies for evidence of venereal disease was called a "short arm"; in British service terminology, an FFI meant "free from infection." Depending upon the tolerance of the medical officer (MO), there was usually a flurry of lewd banter preceding and following such an inspection. Since modesty promoted nervousness, it was necessary to divert attention away from the nervousness in order to maintain a macho image. Even the toughest of men never becomes accustomed to such leveling treatment.

As an expression of their view of things, a humorous incident was said to have occurred during a medical inspection. As the story made the rounds among several RAF drafts moving through the Toronto bullpens, it grew in the telling. One version insisted that during the Canadian National Exhibition in late August or early September one or more young ladies (Canadian farm girls with show animals) led one or more bulls into the area occupied by RAF student aircrew. The precise moment of their arrival occurred while medical officers (MOs) were conducting the medical inspection of a RAF draft. The embellished variety of the story was that the bulls were being presented for an FFI.

If there was only occasionally reason for laughter within RAF territory on the grounds of the Canadian National Exhibition, it could often be found in the sarcasm and good-natured exchange of insults between inhabitants of different parts of the British Isles. Such banter between members of the ever-changing population of the crowded transient camp was a common occurrence. When His Royal Highness the Duke of Kent, brother of King George VI, visited Toronto on an inspection tour, airmen from the Manning Depot were assigned to line the streets along his route through the city. How large numbers of RAF aircrew students felt about their billets and their experiences in Toronto is little known, but there was apparent unanimity in praise of the food.

In a long letter to his parents, John A. "Jack" Cook (PAA, 42-1) was specific in his description of the food:

They certainly feed us well here, and there are second helpings for anyone who can eat them. Their usual breakfast consists of porridge, bacon and egg, toast, as much butter as you want, coffee and jam. Dinner is something like this: soup (usually tomato), roast pork or beef, two veg., followed by sweet, and tea or coffee. There is also bread and butter and cheese on the table! Every tea time, there are apples on the table, and it is always a cooked tea [supper]. So you can imagine I'm in my paradise…the food is always well cooked, in fact, I haven't had such good grub since I was at home.

After getting the men settled into their unusual billets, procedures were straightforward and were much more relaxed than comparable processing in the American armed forces. Assignment to a flying school might be described as almost casual.

Unless flying school assignments had already been made in Britain or at the No. 1 Y Depot in Halifax, as happened with members of Class SE-42-C, the young trainees were assembled in the depot, and students selected their own school assignments. At this all-important parade (formation), the RAF Transit Section staff usually hung huge placards that were clearly marked with the name and location of the school and the size of the expected draft. The students then selected the flying school they thought they wanted and stood under the placard representing their choice.

Except for grousing by disgruntled cadets who had "washed out" of American or Canadian flying schools, other students derived information from American films and very rough ideas of American geography, and only the rare British cadet had enough information on which to judge the merits of any flying school. Efforts would be made to keep friends or brothers together, and to give students the flying school assignment of their choice. The two Florida schools always filled quickly, as did the British flying training school (BFTS) at Miami, Oklahoma, but those who chose the latter were to discover that they were not going to Florida. The leftover students were assigned to a school that had vacancies. Staff NCOs would then count draft members to assure correct numbers for each school and prepare official nominal rolls.

Officially, little was said to incoming students about what happened if one failed a flying course, but the grapevine provided more than enough information. When aircrew students failed their courses, they were returned to the RCAF No. 1 Manning Depot at Toronto until they could be posted to RCAF Trenton, a flying boat station some fifty miles northeast of Toronto. At Trenton, they would be interviewed by RCAF officers and would be remustered to other duties. As of September 1941, more than one thousand RAF aircrew u/t (under training) had been eliminated from pilot training in the United States alone and, because of their numbers, no one knew what to do with them. The Toronto Manning Depot did not have enough space available to absorb all of the washouts as well as regular new drafts arriving from Britain. By 15 September, the large numbers of men overwhelmed the two Canadian depots and both stations became bottlenecks, which slowed movement through the training pipeline.

According to men who were there, westbound students met large numbers of embittered washouts who were impatiently waiting to be remustered. Tempers flared, men "gave tongue" to their feelings and a minor rebellion was in the making. Letters home to parents and to officers in initial training wings (ITWs) described chaos. Military censors of personal mail, ever mindful of rules to report morale problems, regularly reported discontent to commanding officers and, inevitably, the complaints made their way up, or evaded, the chain of command. Most reports that reached political leaders came from influential parents. Some washouts were reported as being quartered in a flying boat hangar at RCAF Trenton, where men were reported to be sleeping on a hangar floor. Moreover, a near-riot was reported to have occurred among eliminated airmen at the RCAF No. 1 Manning Depot in Toronto. In order to resolve the problems, high-ranking staff officers traveled from London to Toronto and to other Canadian and American air bases to inspect and sort out the problems.

The fifty-one-year-old Canadian-born Air Commodore A.C. Critchley, CGM, DSO, officer commanding 54 Group, ostensibly arrived "to inspect RAF training in Canada." Critchley was responsible for the recruitment and training of instructional staffs, and for organizing and administering aircrew receiving wings (ACRCWs) and ITWs. He and his staff had handled formidable problems common to the rapid expansion of all military services. The RAF officer may well have inspected, but he also met in Toronto with a large assembly of disgruntled airmen in efforts to sort out remustering and other problems. He arrived in Toronto during the evening of 16 September 1941 to tour "No. 1 Air Training Command."

In a brief article in the *Toronto Star* with a picture that showed a grim, stocky figure in uniform, Air Commodore Critchley is reported to have said, "The men I have talked with, men sent from overseas after their initial training, can't speak too highly of the training they get here." If the aircrew students who were in the Toronto Manning Depot at the time are to be believed, their reaction was not quite as simple as the newspaper reported, and as Critchley might have wished.

Though these may not have been the precise orders given by Critchley or staff officers to the "bolshie" airmen, the effect of their directives was the same: "break 'em down into smaller groups, move 'em, send them to air stations and get them off their duffs...keep 'em busy!" Washed out airmen at Toronto were quickly separated from aircrew students newly arrived from Britain. The failed aircrew trainees were divided into smaller groups and were posted on general duties assignments to air bases scattered about Canada. Their arrival at these stations occurred just in time to pack or remove a few thousand tons of snow from runways and airdrome streets and to peel a few tons of potatoes. Inevitably, many of these "washed out" airmen were forgotten or "lost," or at least they believed that RAF staff had done so.

Since all Canadian aircrew training schools at the time were crowded, and the training pipeline was plugged at Toronto and Trenton, those who were "lost" wondered if their transfer had been done accidentally or on purpose. Given the distances and complexities of wartime travel, the record-keeping and the loss of ships, mail and documents to U-boats, some such dislocations were perhaps inevitable. Regardless of cause, such administrative ills were beyond either the interest or the concern of the young airmen. They wanted to fly, and many of them demanded another opportunity to do so.

Air Commodore Critchley's official report of these developments could not be found, and his autobiography oddly fails to even mention his September 1941 sojourn in Canada (his birthplace). However, there is no doubt that he and other RAF officers were there and were trying desperately to solve the problems that had created embarrassing bottlenecks in Canada and elsewhere. By autumn 1941, the major culprit appeared to be American aircrew training, which was much more rigid than that of the RAF. Significant problems were also uncovered in the existing system of Canadian transient camps, and steps were taken to remove the bottlenecks and reduce aircrew wastage.

In order to address problems within the American system, other high-ranking RAF officers would inspect training stations in the United States and meet with American air officers in training conferences. As a result of Air Commodore Critchley's mission to Canada and Air Vice Marshal A.G.R. Garrod's visit to Canada and the United States, the officers of all three nations learned much about the early experiences of British aircrew students. In the United States, agreement was reached whereby some of the best RAF pilots to be graduated in 1942 from Arnold Scheme and British flying training schools would be posted to regional instructors' schools for later assignment as flight instructors in many primary, basic and advanced USAAF flying schools. In addition, hazing was stopped, the curriculum in each phase of flight training was reviewed and improved and regular training conferences were instituted. In addition, a drive began for the standardization of aircrew training, and the amount and quality of supervision was significantly improved.

Ships and trains were of central importance to the efficient operation and administration of Movements Groups in both Britain and North America. The more central location of Heaton Park, Manchester, near major rail lines provided slightly more comfortable space and improved the transport of trainees to ports of embarkation. In Canada, better scheduling of trains, the availability of strategically located shops and roundhouses and the connecting links with American railroads, the Canadian National Railway and the Canadian Pacific Railway systems were adequate for the assigned tasks. Even so, coordination of ship and train schedules was difficult under the best of circumstances. When Nazi U-boats began to take a heavier shipping toll among vessels plying the North Atlantic, train and ship schedules became closely guarded secrets. Delays caused by ships arriving late or not at all focused greater attention on the need for sufficient bed and board facilities, as well as improved currency exchange and pay advances for transient aircrew.

With the movement of large and small drafts through Halifax during the summer and early fall of 1941, it soon became obvious that the RCAF No. 1 Movements Group could not continue to coordinate mass transport and accommodation from Montreal, several hundred miles away. An embarrassing incident in mid-September 1941 confirmed the need to improve the administration of transportation and caused the Canadian Air Ministry to act. On 15 September 1941, some 270 personnel from Australia and New Zealand, mostly trained aircrew, boarded the *Empress of Asia* in preparation for sailing to Britain. When they found the ship filthy, they unequivocally refused to accept accommodation and marched off the "stinking tub" and back onto the Halifax docks, no doubt giving loud voice to their objections. As a result, the RCAF established a cardinal rule that ships would be thoroughly cleaned and deodorized, inspected and approved before passengers boarded. Effective 1 October 1941, RCAF No. 2 Movements Group (later designated No. 11) was formed in Halifax with headquarters at RCAF No. 1 Y Depot. The rationale for change was clearly stated in the establishment order:

> *The number of personnel, both proceeding overseas and arriving in Canada for duty on the North American continent, has now reached such proportions that it has become desirable to relieve Eastern Air Command of the responsibility for the flow of personnel through the "Y" Depots now in, or later to be established in Eastern Canada, and for all matters directly connected with embarkation and disembarkation. It has accordingly been decided to establish a Movements Group under Eastern Air Command, which will be directly responsible to Air Force Headquarters for all matters relating to movements of personnel in Eastern Canada.*

The changed status and increased responsibilities of the new Movements Group at Halifax came just two weeks after the incident involving the *Empress of Asia* and one month after RCAF No. 1 Y Depot opened in Halifax.

Group Captain Frank S. Magill of Montreal, forty-six-year-old former director of postings and records in RCAF headquarters, was appointed commanding officer of the Movements Group. From the No. 1 Y Depot in Halifax, Magill directed an enlarged staff to inspect facilities, including ships and trains, and to analyze the details involved in transporting troops by land and sea. Within one month, major problems had been identified and solutions had been proposed and implemented. No. 1 Port Transit Unit was created, and this subordinate unit, with its two detachments, refined the process of embarking and disembarking air forces personnel and equipment in Halifax and, when necessary, in Boston or New York. By 15 October 1941, Magill moved his offices from No. 1 Y Depot to 203 South Park Street in the United Service Corporation Building, opposite the Public Gardens at the foot of Citadel Hill in downtown Halifax. This new central location permitted close coordination of movements by land and sea.

What remained to be done in Halifax was the establishment of tougher administrative policies and the recruitment and training of able personnel to carry them out. Group Captain Magill and his staff had quickly reorganized RCAF No. 2 Movements Group and laid down rules necessary for efficient operation. Other port transit units were established, and officers from nations involved in the British Commonwealth Air Training Plan (BCATP) were assigned to the RCAF Movements Group staff. These additions included one squadron leader each from the Royal Air Force (RAF), the Royal Australian Air Force (RAAF) and the Royal New Zealand Air Force (RNZAF) and these officers, in turn, kept their respective liaison missions in Ottawa apprised of developments. Two of the plans for Canadian improvements had been implemented; the third, completion of two more Y depots and construction of RAF and RCAF personnel depots at Moncton, New Brunswick, remained to be completed.

In April 1941, the RCAF had opened No. 3 (temporary) Y Depot, which was located adjacent to the massive Canadian army camp at Debert, Nova Scotia. During late summer 1941, No. 1 Y Depot, where Class SE-42-C was held for a week, opened within the city of Halifax. However, even when completed, these small transient camps would be inadequate for the accommodation of thousands of airmen. It was necessary to design and build a larger facility capable of accommodating vast numbers of westbound as well as eastbound airmen. As a result, RAF and RCAF authorities agreed that two huge depots should be built accessible to railroads at Moncton, New Brunswick.

On 2 August 1941, construction on "Special Accommodations, Moncton," was begun. Originally designed to house eight thousand air force trainees, it was referred to by one of the local newspapers as "a town within a city." A large tract of bush-covered land adjacent to the Canadian National Railway shops in northwest Moncton was the location of this defense installation. During late August and early September, new streets had been cut, and employees of Contractor Carter, Halls and Aldinger, Ltd., had laid out sites for buildings, roadways, utilities, waterlines, etc.

On the construction site, activity increased rapidly. A lumberyard and building materials site was developed, and more than six hundred construction workers were brought onto the job. The local newspaper exclaimed that a "street has been cut through from Wilbur Street near the John Street intersection to Essex Street. One side of that new street is already lined with buildings." On 11 October 1941, Flight Lieutenant E.A. Goodwright arrived in Moncton with thirteen airmen of the 108th Mobile Advance Party to open the new RAF depot, which was still under construction.

Within a few days, other personnel arrived, as did all equipment and materiel essential for a military post. Equipment, food supplies, kitchen and dining implements, office furnishings, desks, typewriters, supplies of mimeograph machines, official forms, paper and dozens of other items were put into place. Normal maintenance and operating services were implemented, inspections were made, procedures were established and street and building signs were installed. By 18 October, four barrack blocks, which could sleep eight hundred men, were ready for occupancy, but other barracks, classrooms, warehouses and drill halls were still under construction. On 18 October 1941, RAF Squadron Leader J.F. Houchin arrived from Toronto to assume temporary command of the new station.

At almost the same time, a group of 146 eastbound RAF observers (navigators) of Class 41-G arrived in Moncton from the Pan American Airways Navigation Section in Florida. They were "attired in light tweed suits" and became the first RAF students to occupy some of the completed facilities. Tragically, on that same day, death came to a carpenter riding his bicycle to work on the massive construction project. He was struck and killed on the site by an automobile driven by another carpenter.

On 20 October, by Secret Organization Order No. 22, dated 3 October 1941, RAF No. 31 Personnel Depot was formed with the establishment of "personnel and mechanical transport" on the site. By 25 October, the temporary RAF Transit Unit, which had been established as part of the Royal Canadian Air Force's No. 1 Manning Depot at Toronto's Canadian National Exhibition, had closed, and on that date, fifty-six airmen arrived at the new station to continue their duties. Perhaps some effort should have been made to establish a large, more permanent RAF depot sooner, but events during the preceding ten months had moved too rapidly for anyone to anticipate the need. Even so, the new arrangement was not a Catch-22.

THE FIRST FOUR RAF STUDENT PILOT COURSES TRAVEL FROM CANADA TO SIX AMERICAN CIVILIAN CONTRACT PRIMARY FLIGHT SCHOOLS

While construction on the new RAF personnel depot proceeded rapidly at Moncton, New Brunswick, members of the first four Arnold Scheme courses had traveled directly to American flight schools in the United States. During the first week of June 1941, the initial draft of Arnold Scheme student pilots had been fingerprinted, photographed and issued temporary American visas. Contrary to the views of many British student pilots, they had not been discharged by the RAF. In preparing to enter the neutral United States, they donned their issue gray flannel or pin-striped worsted suits, and added black shoes, socks, blue shirts and black ties from their regular uniforms. As they boarded cars of the Canadian Pacific Railroad on a siding within the grounds of the Canadian National Exhibition, each student was issued two blankets.

That initial draft and succeeding ones were accompanied on their journey by a Royal Canadian Air Force (RCAF) escort officer assigned by the RCAF No. 1 Movements Group. These officers would carry with them route schedules and special travel requisitions and would handle the administrative details, including meal and luggage vouchers, and supervise document checks by American immigration officers and delivery of the men to their respective destinations. The RCAF escort officers would also deliver accurate nominal rolls and other documents to the appropriate flying school staff.

The train cars departed Toronto's Canadian National Exhibition grounds and entered the United States by two different routes. The RAF contingents destined for Camden, South Carolina, traveled southward via Black Rock and Buffalo directly across the states of New York and Pennsylvania to Washington, D.C., and points south. Those destined for schools in Alabama, Georgia and Florida traveled by way of Detroit, Cincinnati and Chattanooga. At Chattanooga, the draft destined for Tuscaloosa, Alabama, changed trains and continued southward, while the RAF contingents destined for four separate flying schools in Georgia and Florida continued their journey via Atlanta.

On Friday, 6 June 1941, sixty-six British pilot candidates (one corporal and sixty-five leading aircraftmen or LACs) were issued blankets and boarded a single waiting train car within the Canadian National Exhibition Grounds. They were joined by RCAF Flying Officer J.P. Morris, the conducting officer, and the train departed the grounds at 5:30 p.m., stopped briefly at Toronto's Union Station some minutes later and left there at 6:15 p.m. The train crossed the international boundary at Black Rock at 9:15 p.m.

During the stop at Buffalo, the baggage car was switched to a southbound train, and the conducting officer called the roll to be sure that all of his charges left the Canadian Pacific Railway car and boarded cars of a waiting train of the Pennsylvania Railroad. Having arrived on one crowded Canadian coach, the sixty-six men were able to divide into two groups for their southward journey. For the overnight run to Washington, D.C., they would have space in two cars to spread out in the coach seats and to make use of the assigned blankets in an effort to get some sleep.

At Washington's Union Station, the British airmen and their baggage were switched to a Seaboard Railway train. To the British students, their travels appeared to be endless, but in reality they had not lasted very long. Around twenty-eight hours after leaving Toronto, sixty-six disheveled men of Class SE-42-A, and their RCAF conducting officer, arrived in Camden, South Carolina. When they filed off the train at the tiny Seaboard Railway station, they were still dressed in their wrinkled, gray flannel woolen suits. It was 9:30 p.m. 7 June 1941, a hot and muggy Saturday evening. They were the first Arnold Scheme contingent of RAF pilot trainees to arrive at an American flying school, and they were the first of five such groups to train at Camden. Since the flying school lacked the means for transporting the new arrivals to the airfield in one group, civilian instructors and townspeople formed a welcoming committee and lined their automobiles along the railway station driveway to provide transportation for the five miles through and beyond the town to Woodward Airport.

Early in the morning of Saturday, 7 June 1941, at about the time student pilots of the sixty-six-member Camden, South Carolina RAF contingent were having breakfast in the dining cars while the train raced toward Washington, D.C., a larger RAF draft was preparing to leave Toronto. Nine Canadian Pacific Railway coaches, two baggage cars and four dining cars had been cleaned and rolled onto the siding within the grounds of the Canadian National Exhibition.

At 6:30 a.m., a working party began to load the baggage cars in proper reverse order for the five separate destinations. One baggage car would contain only the bags of the 190 men traveling the greatest distance and destined for schools at Lakeland and Arcadia, Florida. Another car would contain the baggage of men destined for the Tuscaloosa, Americus and Albany schools, and that baggage would have to be kept separate so as to expedite unloading at different points en route.

Then, according to a pre-set schedule, the RAF student pilots were issued two blankets each and, accompanied by commissioned RCAF conducting officers, boarded assigned railroad coaches standing on the siding. The fifteen-car Canadian Pacific Special train departed the National Exhibition grounds at 7:45 a.m. Saturday morning, 7 June 1941, sped across western Ontario and crossed the river into Detroit. Before arriving at "automobile city," later "Motown," at about 1:30 p.m., the men ate lunch aboard the train.

At Detroit, as they filed off the Canadian Pacific Train and onto nine coaches of the New York Central Railway, their two baggage cars were shunted onto nearby tracks to be joined with the train for the trip southward. Some six hours later, about 8:00 p.m., the train rolled into Cincinnati, Ohio. At Cincinnati, the men changed trains once more, this time boarding coaches of the Southern Railroad for the trip southward to Chattanooga and Atlanta.

At around 4:30 a.m., Sunday, 8 June 1941, the train rolled into Chattanooga, Tennessee, late. It had failed to arrive there in time for the RAF contingent to join Southern Railway Train No. 43 bound for Birmingham and Tuscaloosa. With some difficulty and minor delay, their baggage was finally off-loaded, but they were compelled to wait about four hours in Chattanooga for another southbound train. The headlines of the *Tuscaloosa News* of Sunday, 8 June 1941, proclaimed, "RAF CADETS WILL ARRIVE HERE TODAY FOR TRAINING." Small groups of people hung about the railway station and Wing Commander H.A.V. Hogan, who had flown in from Maxwell Field, waited impatiently. Instead of 8:30 a.m., the draft arrived in Tuscaloosa around 12:45 p.m.

The Tuscaloosa intake, escorted by RCAF Flying Officer J.D. Murray, was supposed to contain seventy men, but nineteen-year-old LAC James Hatfield of Ripley, Derbyshire, became ill in Toronto and had been sent to a hospital there. As a result, he did not travel to Alabama with other members of the first RAF intake. A few days after his classmates left Toronto, Hatfield was provided with vouchers and traveled southward alone. Other members of the RAF intake commenced flying training on Monday, 9 June 1941, but Hatfield was apparently able to make up the training he had missed and to catch up with other members of the course.

When the train rolled into the Tuscaloosa rail station early Sunday afternoon, the young men were undoubtedly embarrassed. Dressed in their gray, woolen issue suits, rumpled and sweaty from a two-thousand-mile, twenty-eight-hour journey, they came off the train into the heat, humidity and bright Alabama sunlight. A Royal Air Force officer and a large crowd of citizens and local dignitaries met them. Their rumpled condition apparently disturbed no one but themselves. Once their baggage was off-loaded onto a waiting truck, the student pilots were rushed to the airport in a fleet of civilian cars, and after they had stowed their baggage, thirty-two-year-old Wing Commander Hogan gave a brief welcome address. Before rushing to the showers, the British students also listened to words of welcome from First Lieutenant Robert E. Burnham, officer commanding the army air corps detachment, and from Walter Thorpe, vice-president and general manager of the Alabama Institute of Aeronautics.

At Chattanooga, Tennessee, the twelve coaches of the Southern Railway train were supposed to be hitched to an express train, but for some reason that did not happen. Instead, following a thirty-minute stop for off-loading the baggage destined for Tuscaloosa, Alabama, the Southern Railway train sped southeastward toward Atlanta with the larger group of RAF student pilots and their baggage. Some four hours later, at about 8:30 a.m., Sunday, 8 June 1941, the train rolled into Union Station in Atlanta, Georgia, a city that, because they had seen the motion picture *Gone with the Wind*, many of the British students felt they knew well.

While the largest group remained aboard the Southern Railway train standing at the station in Atlanta, RCAF Flying Officer S.C. Foster led the RAF contingent destined for Americus and Albany, Georgia, off the train onto the station platform. Their baggage car was detached and shunted onto a siding, and after it was joined to the waiting four coaches of the Central of Georgia train, the British students boarded. Within thirty minutes, the train jerked and rattled, and then began to glide slowly out of the rail yard and through the outskirts of Atlanta, en route to Macon, Americus and Albany. In Macon, the train was delayed until just after noon, Sunday, 8 June, and finally, at around 12:45 p.m., it rolled southward out of Macon.

Following a brief stop at the Central of Georgia Railway station in Americus, where the fifty-three-man RAF contingent disembarked and their luggage was off-loaded, the train continued southward with the RAF draft destined for Albany, Georgia. As at Camden and Tuscaloosa, men of the initial RAF draft assigned to Souther Field were transported that Sunday afternoon from the railway station northward some nine miles to Souther Field in automobiles provided by flying school staff and citizens of the small town.

Reporters and a photographer from the Americus *Times-Record*, an afternoon daily, descended on the British cadets. Photographs were taken and articles were written, and page one of the issue of Thursday, 12 June 1941 preserved for posterity a picture of the fifty-three Britons in formation wearing new ill-fitting, Canadian-issue khaki uniforms and northwest Indian frontier sun helmets. In providing such inadequate clothing for the early RAF drafts sent to the United States for training, RAF equipment officers demonstrated a total lack of knowledge of the climate of the American South. However, the mixture of woolen civilian clothing, heavy khakis and pukka sahib sun helmets brought out the "musical hall comedian" imbedded in many of the RAF student pilots.

At 7:20 p.m. that same Sunday evening, 8 June, the southbound Central of Georgia train reached the Albany railroad station. As at the other towns with primary flying schools, the RAF student pilots were greeted by a large crowd of civilians who had been awaiting their arrival for several hours. Although RCAF Flying Officer S.C. Foster, the conducting officer, had accompanied the RAF student pilots, several RAF officers were in Albany in time to welcome them at the railroad station. Group Captains D.V. Carnegie, AFC, and F.W. Trott, OBE, MC, from the British air mission in Washington; Wing Commander H.A.V. Hogan, DFC, from Maxwell Field; and Flight Lieutenant Alfred G. Hill, the RAF administrative officer newly assigned to the Albany school constituted an impressive welcoming committee.

The 119 assigned RAF student pilots boarded buses and were transported to the primary flying school, four miles southwest of Albany. The RAF students, having arrived late, were rushed to the dining hall at Darr Aero Tech for a sumptuous meal with plenty of milk, white bread and butter. They were then issued blankets and sheets and assigned to their billets. There, they quickly removed the rumpled, dirty and hot woolen suits, showered, made their bunks and fell into them for much-needed rest. Since Darr Aero Tech was equipped to train 172 British students in each class, 53 more cadets were needed to raise the enrollment to capacity.

At Atlanta's Union Station on Sunday morning, 8 June 1941, RCAF Flying Officer J.A. Grant had escorted the remaining 189 RAF students who remained aboard their Southern Railway cars, and within an hour left Atlanta destined for Jacksonville, Florida. Following an all-day ride from Atlanta diagonally across Georgia and a small portion of Florida, they arrived in Jacksonville a few minutes after 7:00 p.m. There, the baggage car and the four Southern Railway coaches were switched to the Atlantic Coast Line Railroad for the journey southward to Lakeland and Arcadia. For some reason, the train was delayed en route, and the men did not arrive as scheduled.

On Monday, 9 June 1941, just before daylight, the Seaboard Railway train bearing a ninety-man RAF draft rolled to a stop at the rail station in Lakeland, Florida. The train had been expected at 11:30 p.m., Sunday, and was some six hours late. For some unknown reason, heat had poured into the passenger car during most of the journey southward from Jacksonville, so the men who disembarked at Lakeland had had little rest. They already knew what hell must be like. An hour earlier, at Lake Alfred, the Lakeland draft gained a respite from the heat when their cars had been shifted to the Tampa line of the Seaboard Railway.

At around 5:00 a.m., disheveled, hot and sweaty, the RAF contingent, escorted by RCAF Flying Officer J.A. Grant, assembled for roll call on Lakeland's Railway Station platform. Among those who greeted them was a crowd of some fifty citizens, including three young ladies who handed out oranges. Local dignitaries among the welcoming party included Albert I. Lodwick—a co-owner of the recently renamed Lakeland (formerly Lincoln) School of Aeronautics—and several civilian and military staff members from the school, including Flight Lieutenant W.W. Watson, RAF administrative officer, who had arrived two days earlier.

The men of that first RAF class were quickly transported to the nearby airfield and were shown to their billets. At about 5:30 a.m., they walked to the dining hall and were provided with hot coffee and doughnuts. Later in the day, before beginning the long process of physical examinations and the issue of equipment, they took cooling showers, ate a more nourishing breakfast and were allowed some time to unpack their bags and straighten their kit. For most of them, the respite on the first day would be one of few they would have during the next ten weeks of tightly organized schedules. Before they could get settled, they were summoned to undergo a cursory physical examination (FFI), and later in the afternoon, they were greeted by Group Captains D.V. Carnegie and F.W. Trott, who had flown to Lakeland from Albany, Georgia.

Meanwhile, the newly arrived and worn RAF cadets of Class SE-42-A were getting settled in. They soon discovered that special care had been taken to provide them with English tea and familiar foods. In the recreation hall, they found dart games and a large number of British phonograph records. They also discovered that schedules were tightly adhered to at the school. At "lights out" that evening, they were more than ready to collapse into their comfortable double-tiered bunks with clean white sheets and mosquito netting, but they were not ready to rise at the required 5:30 a.m. on Tuesday, 10 June 1941.

After leaving the Lakeland flying school RAF draft at Lake Alfred, Florida, in the wee hours of Monday morning, 9 June 1941, the Atlantic Coast Line Railway train continued southward to Arcadia, Florida. With an occasional blast of its horn and continuous bell clanging as it entered the town limits, the giant train rolled slowly past citrus groves and street crossings toward the station in Arcadia, Florida. At 6:15 a.m. that Monday, 9 June 1941, it was cool and bright, but the sun had not yet disturbed the peace of the small southwest Florida town. The train was supposed to have arrived in Arcadia at around 1:00 a.m., but for some unknown reason had been delayed more than five hours.

The outside air was cool, but that within the two train cars on which the ninety-nine Royal Air Force student pilots rode into Arcadia was unbelievably hot. Evidently, the train crew had turned the heat on either in Jacksonville or en route southward and, despite complaints and efforts to increase the ventilation in the two rail coaches, nothing helped very much. Already sweaty feet were swollen because hot air seemed to flow from every vent in the cars.

Even after they opened as many windows as could be opened, the cars were still hotter than the proverbial "hinges of hell." Perspiring heavily in the heat, the men were exhausted and reeked of body odor. Having removed coats, ties and other impediments to coolness, and having turned in every direction possible in efforts to get some rest, they were disheveled beyond belief. They were dressed in lightweight gray woolen suits, but these items of clothing were not light enough for the climate south of Cincinnati, Ohio.

The small town they saw from the train's windows was a pleasant place. A few automobiles were parked along neat tree-lined streets. Although some townspeople had been up for hours preparing for the arrival of the train and its passengers, the only vehicle about was a bicycle that raced along the streets and walkways as the newsboy tossed papers onto the steps or porches of neatly painted houses surrounded by shrubbery. Close by the houses, businesses and public buildings were beds of annuals, roses, oleander, hibiscus, hydrangea and other flowers. There was pride of place here.

In the lobby of the Arcadia House, three attractive teenage girls of about fifteen years of age, and dressed in cowgirl outfits, yawned and preened as they stood nervously shifting from one foot to another listening to the distant approach of the train. The long tresses of the three girls hung down from under their wide-brimmed hats, which were held firmly in place with thin leather straps; one girl was blonde, another brunette and the third had auburn hair. Around and past them, older women hurried to and from the hotel's dining room and several large cloth-covered tables on the hotel lawn.

With the girls were members of the Trinity Methodist Church Ladies Auxiliary and several of the hotel's employees, and all were hurriedly preparing refreshments. Chilled orange juice was being poured into large glass pitchers, and fresh doughnuts were being stacked on platters, baskets and trays. Paper cups for juice, tea and coffee were set out. From the door of the Arcadia House came a voice warning that the train had stopped and that the British cadets should be along soon.

The ninety-nine RAF student pilots filed down the train steps in their gray woolen suits with their sun helmets (topees) unbuckled, ear flaps hanging down and radio plug connectors much in evidence. If it was said that they conspired aboard the hot train to shock their American hosts, that was a fabrication of many years later. It is likely that RCAF Flying Officer J.A. Grant had directed the British students to remove their topees from where they were attached atop kit bags and to carry them separately. By doing so, the sun helmets would not be crushed or otherwise lost when their heavy baggage was thrown onto trucks for the seven-mile journey to Carlstrom Field. As they left the train and assembled in a group at the station, they were embarrassed at their own "scruffy" appearance.

Most of the British students had shaved (if necessary) and brushed, and many had donned their coats and ties before filing down the steps of the railroad coaches. Some had not bothered, as they perhaps concluded that without a bath, they could do little to improve either their feelings or their appearance. Former Mayor Stonebreaker; Nate Reece Jr., business manager of the local newspaper, the *Arcadian*; John Paul Riddle, president of the Embry-Riddle Company; and Charlie Ebbetts, company photographer, constituted the welcoming committee.

After about an hour, a fleet of private automobiles driven by instructors, staff and townspeople arrived at the hotel, and the drivers aligned their vehicles behind others already there. The British trainees were divided among the vehicles and were driven the seven miles to Carlstrom Field. Since school staff already knew the number of new students to expect, dormitory rooms at the school had been prepared to receive them. The RAF trainees were quickly assigned to quarters, and were given time to take showers and change into lighter clothing before being served a more substantial breakfast in the attractive dining hall.

In his initial written report dated Tuesday, 10 June 1941, Wing Commander Hogan urged Group Captain Carnegie and Air Commodore George C. Pirie to attend a reception being given by General Weaver at Maxwell Field on Sunday, 14 June. Hogan then reported that he had visited schools in Alabama, Georgia and South Carolina. During these visits, the RAF officer had been embarrassed at the appearance of a large number of the khaki uniforms, which had been issued to the RAF students in Canada. It appeared that the universal military service joke that "one size fits all" was apparently not a joke at all and, no doubt, some of the uniforms gave the appearance of having almost swallowed the students.

In order to pay for the necessary alterations for the worst uniforms, Hogan made immediate financial arrangements for the RAFAOs at the various schools. One RAF student felt that he and his course mates in their Canadian-issue khaki "tents" looked like orphans in comparison to American aviation cadets in their neat, pressed khakis. Evidently, the Americans thought so as well, because within a brief period, the army air corps began to supply American-issue fitted khaki uniforms and summer flying kit for the RAF students.

After the first RAF class became settled at the six Arnold Scheme primary schools, Hogan's labors really began. First, he sought to coordinate the air corps flying training syllabus with the subjects that British aircrew students had already studied in ITWs. Shortly after his arrival, Hogan met with Major Luke Smith, SEACTC director of training, and reviewed the ground school curriculum that was used in all primary schools. Since RAF students had already studied a great deal of navigation and mathematics in their initial training wing courses, Smith agreed to a number of changes in the primary ground school courses.

Syllabus changes for RAF students included the omission of mathematics, a reduction in navigation instruction to twenty-two hours and in meteorology to twenty-one hours. The thirty-four hours of ground school omitted would be replaced by ten hours of aircraft recognition, ten hours of current events, five hours of RAF organization, four hours on the Aldis signal lamp and five hours on RAF procedures and extra study. Owing to the high level of academic work that the British students had already done, if they had indeed completed an ITW course, that syllabus change was undoubtedly a good one.

No sooner had the change been made for RAF students in the ground school syllabus of the six primary schools than Group Captain Carnegie notified Hogan that RAF students arriving between July and September 1941 (Classes SE-42-B and SE-42-C) would have covered only about 70 percent of the ITW syllabus. "In navigation," Carnegie wrote, "they may not have done any map reading, instruments, or meteorology." If the USAAF ground school syllabus had already been changed in the primary schools, these omissions in the ITW syllabus for the 1,100 students of these two courses may well have contributed to the increased number of men eliminated from primary flying training. At the time, there were other, more pressing concerns.

During his survey of the schools, Hogan took great care to ascertain how the six RAF administrative officers were able to function in their new environments. He discovered that only Darr Aero Tech at Albany, Georgia, and Carlstrom Field at Arcadia, Florida, were providing on-post accommodation for the RAFAOs, and they were doing so only out of kindness. Hogan recognized that the administrative officers would need automobiles in order to travel to and from where they lived in neighboring towns and their duty stations, and he was determined that these officers should receive "board and lodging at government expense."

For the RAF administrative officers, there were many pressing problems much closer and more disturbing than concern about their own comfort. In the Arnold Scheme primary flying schools, they were in a most difficult position. They had their orders from Maxwell Field as well as official policy directives from Washington and London, and often they had within their jurisdiction a large number of rebellious students who condemned them for all of the problems the students themselves encountered and often helped to create. In addition to their normal duties, when changes were made in the USAAF ground school syllabus, the RAFAOs found themselves teaching RAF procedures and leading public affairs discussions.

In order to prevent future problems, Hogan advised of the misinformation that RAF students had absorbed at some point before arrival in the United States. He asserted that RAF students were grossly misinformed about the laxity of discipline in American primary schools. Having been given that wrong information, they objected to the discipline they encountered and this "caused some dissension between them and the school authorities." Hogan felt that if the RAF students "had known what they were coming to, these incidents and minor upheavals would not have occurred." Despite some problems, the Arnold Scheme training program was succeeding beyond everyone's wildest dreams.

Hogan pointed out how the students "rise at 5:20 a.m., and go to flights from 7:00 to 11:00 a.m., then after a large lunch they are given a lecture in a language which they have difficulty in understanding, and it is no wonder that they get sleepy." In that first report, the senior RAF administrative officer was generally pleased with conditions in the schools and in the training, but imbedded in much of what was reported was a concern that the RAF students behave themselves. Perhaps such concern was natural, as the RAF officers and men were guests in the United States and were expected to conduct themselves properly at all times.

Months before the arrival of either American or British student pilots, army air corps personnel were trying to adjust to civilian contract flying schools. Air corps and civilian personnel were wary of each other in the beginning. The flying school operators and the army air corps officers were anxious to prove the effectiveness of using civilian flight and ground instructors and civilian maintenance personnel to train army air corps pilots. Although civil flying schools had been used extensively to train army and navy pilots during World War I, the practice had died out in the United States, but continued in most European countries. Such contract training of pilots for the military services had been proposed and re-proposed many times since 1919, but was quietly adopted from European examples in 1938, and was implemented on 1 July 1939.

The experience these operators and schools gained in the first two years of operations led to such wartime expansion that before mid-1944, seventy-two such contract schools had existed, and about 20,000 employees of these schools had provided initial training for more than 200,000 cadets. Even before the Japanese attack on Pearl Harbor in December 1941, American civilian schools had not only trained thousands of pilots, but some schools trained aircraft and engine (A&E) mechanics as well. In addition, several of the schools were also training pilots for China and Great Britain.

The United States Army Air Corps was unsure of continuing its contract arrangement with the civil schools and had inserted a provision into each early contract to the effect that it could be cancelled at any time by giving a thirty-day notice. This ultra-conservative contract system was unfortunate, but necessary, because of American neutrality and the tentative nature of congressional appropriations. The War Department's contract arrangements spoke volumes about its experience in gaining funds. However, the contracts eventually created problems, because the civil schools became anxious about their future and formed a lobbying agency in an effort to protect their financial interests. Perhaps their action is understandable in the light of the Depression years and the risks being taken in expanding training facilities without any guarantee of future contracts.

The system of War Department contracts is interesting and reveals how charges were modified over a period of time. Since this kind of civilian contract work had not been done for the military services since World War I, no one knew or was able to calculate what the actual costs were or should be. The initial War Department contract with the flight schools stipulated that cadets would enter training by classes every six weeks beginning 1 July 1939, and that the contract period would terminate on 17 June 1940. Each class would contain a maximum of seventy students, no more than five per trainer aircraft. The army air corps would furnish the airplanes, parts, the overhaul of engines, parachutes, flight clothing for the students and a small staff of officers who would supervise training, and would provide administrative support and medical service.

The multiple duties of these small detachments of four or five army air corps officers caused each of them to wear many hats. Usually, the commanding officers of these army air corps detachments had been trained at West Point and Randolph Field and were regular army air corps flying officers (rated pilots and usually first lieutenants) who had total responsibility for supervising the contracts, and ably performed the myriad duties involved. On the administrative side, they were assisted by an adjutant or administrative officer (usually non-rated transfers from Arms and Services duties), and one or two civil service secretaries. On the training side, the commanding officers were assisted by a small staff of military pilots, some regular and some reserve officers, who were designated assistant air corps supervisors and who monitored the training program to determine that civilian instructors were adhering to the air corps syllabus.

When air corps officers gave elimination check rides at ten to twelve hours, or check rides at twenty, forty and sixty hours, their concern was whether the student had learned the maneuvers and the precision prescribed in the USAAC syllabus. These check rides with students not only measured student progress, but also provided insight into the effectiveness of the various civil instructors, a fact that made it possible for the air corps supervisor to call student deficiencies or errors to the attention of civil contractors and their managers. And since all army air corps training emphasized safety first, the detachment staff had as a prime duty the monitoring of aircraft maintenance. It was in these critical areas of aircraft maintenance and flying instruction that the greatest conflict occurred between army air corps supervisors and civilian contractors and their personnel.

In addition, military leadership demanded a concern for everything affecting student morale, such as food, housing, sanitation, physical training and recreation. In the small civil contract primary schools of the period 1939 to 1941, recreation was virtually ignored because small classes of USAAC flying cadets usually had ample leisure time, wore civilian clothing off the stations and sought recreation in nearby towns and cities. The military portion of the training was also neglected because the limited military staff simply lacked the time. Moreover, there was a general feeling that, since the civil contract primary flying schools were experimental operations, it was better to emphasize teaching men how to fly an airplane safely. The rationale for this action was that military courtesy, discipline and leadership training could best be handled in the basic flying schools, which were operated by the army air corps, and which were organized, equipped and staffed to provide military training along with its flying training.

By conserving the supply of military instructors and using them in the air corps operated basic and advanced flying training schools, the job could still be done efficiently; or at least that is what army air corps leaders and civil contractors thought. Under the original War Department contracts, which were later modified significantly, the civilian schools were allocated army air corps biplane trainers at a ratio of four students to each trainer aircraft. Before the United States entered the war in December 1941, the contractors were expected to provide the gasoline and oil, the flying and ground instructors, as well as aircraft and building maintenance and adequate ground staffs essential for the smooth operation of the school.

Originally, each civil contract flying school would be training from 100 to 120 flying cadets in two classes (50 to 60 students would commence training, and when they were halfway through the twelve-week course, a new class would arrive). The upper class, as part of its training, assumed some leadership responsibility in handling the indoctrination and military training of the lower class. Each six weeks thereafter, if the contract continued, additional classes would arrive and depart every six weeks, thus maintaining a steady flow of flying cadets into each school and out at the end of twelve weeks. Flying schedules would be rotated to provide both morning and afternoon flying experience for new student pilots, as well as for upper-level students.

The army air corps syllabus for twelve weeks of primary flying training encompassed 65 hours of flight training and 225 hours of ground school. Before the school opened, the air corps furnished from the inventory of its training center at Randolph Field, Texas, Consolidated PT-3A biplane trainers (Model 1928), which had neither tail wheels nor instruments. Staffing of the school would be based on student capacity. Perhaps from British or French experience, the USAAC determined that the ideal enrollment per class was 50 or 60 students, so total school capacity should not exceed 100 to 120 students for each two classes enrolled at one time.

From army air corps training experience, 40 percent wastage for each class was considered about normal, so a small school enrolling 120 students would maintain a rather small civilian staff. As a result of these calculations, each civil contract primary school would employ from 20 to 30 experienced pilots as instructors and 3 or 4 flight commanders. In order for the army air corps to standardize instructional techniques, many civilian flight instructors at each school were sent through the USAAC central instructors' school at Randolph Field northeast of San Antonio, Texas.

The small flight schools were also required to maintain additional staff to handle the details of training, administration and maintenance. Other school staff included three or four ground school instructors, a flight dispatcher, a parachute packer, twelve to fifteen qualified mechanics and five general assistants who cleaned hangars and aircraft and serviced airplanes with gasoline and oil. At the beginning of operations, the total school staff, all civilian employees of the contractor, was limited to about eighty to one hundred people. Later, as schools expanded, sometimes increasing student capacity to six hundred or more cadets, the number of contractor employees expanded as well, and school civilian staffs sometimes numbered five hundred or more.

Since financial charges were later to become a bone of contention between school operators, War Department contracting officers and air corps supervisors, the subject deserves some attention. Flight and ground instructors' salaries, as well as those of maintenance and administrative personnel, are difficult to generalize, but it is important to remember that between 1939 and 1942, twenty-five to fifty dollars per week was considered a very good salary. The areas in which the civil contract flying schools were located or new schools were to be built were essentially rural farming communities that had been devastated and their people demoralized by an agricultural depression of twenty years' duration. Land was cheap, wages were low and opportunities were limited. Civil contractors often took advantage of these conditions to employ flight and ground instructors and mechanics at the lowest possible wage levels and to keep wages low for much too long.

The result of this short-sightedness was that, as the demand increased, many of these experienced and highly competent people were embittered and left to join other companies, even when their employers belatedly offered to increase their compensation to hold them. Some of these American civil pilots and ground crewmen expressed their dissatisfaction by taking higher-paying jobs with private industry. Many others gravitated to Canada after September 1939 to gain British or Canadian ferrying contracts or RCAF commissions as instructors and operations officers with much higher pay and fringe benefits. Hundreds of civilian instructors received direct commissions in the expanding U.S. Naval Air Service. Others, who held army air corps reserve commissions, were called to active duty as air corps expansion dictated.

The constant turnover of flying and ground personnel in many of the civil contract schools, which affected the quality of training and maintenance services, often resulted from morale problems brought on by low pay, limited fringe benefits and inadequate housing. Although all contractors had considerable employee turnover, some of them developed excellent personnel policies, paid their employees well and were still able to make sizeable profits, something that remained a bone of contention among many army air corps contracting officers as well as American and British flying officers. Contractor profits came from a variety of sources. Charges for cadet housing at seventy-five cents per day and food at one dollar per day were stipulated in the contracts.

Flying cadets, later termed aviation cadets, were paid $127.50 monthly. This amount included $75 monthly base pay, plus $52.50 quarters and food allowance, but the cadets received only their base pay at each monthly pay formation; the remainder was deducted from their pay and was remitted to the contractor for food and housing. The purchase of food, the preparation of three nutritious meals per day and the payment of salaries for the dining hall workforce undoubtedly absorbed most of the monthly deductions from cadet pay and allowed only slim profits, if any at all, from that source.

Housing was different. Initial investment for building and furnishing a sixty-man barracks with all of the essentials might have cost a maximum of $12,000 during that era. Assuming even a regular population of forty students at a charge of $22.50 ($.75 times 30) per month, yield to the contractor for twelve months ($900 times 12) would be around $10,000. As a result of this rapid return on his investment, dormitory costs could be retired in one year or less, and dormitory income after that time would cover fixed costs, such as insurance and basic maintenance, and would still yield sizeable profits to the contractor.

As the curriculum changed and more experience was gained, the contracting system was modified. Reimbursement to the company for the initial contract period beginning 1 July 1939 included $1,170 for each student graduated and $18 per flying hour for each student who was eliminated from training. Under that initial contract and for seven classes averaging fifty flying cadets each to be trained between 1 July 1939 and 17 June 1940, income for a contract school was estimated to have totaled $270,900.

With flying and ground instructors receiving $50 to $60 per week, mechanics $25 to $35 and most secretarial and administrative workers receiving salaries quite similar to or below amounts paid mechanics, wages for civil contractors probably averaged $150 per employee per month for one hundred employees. Using the estimated salaries for that first year (12 months times 100 times $150) gives a total of $180,000. Lease charges for hangar space in a town or county municipal airport were either nonexistent or at a very low level. Both gasoline and oil were purchased for about 10 cents per gallon. Since auxiliary enterprises such as dining hall, barracks and canteen yielded additional returns on a relatively small investment, profits were considerable.

On 25 May 1940, at a meeting held in the Munitions Building in Washington, the army air corps announced its second expansion plan to the eight original civilian flight school contractors. The second army air corps contract, which extended from 17 June 1940 to 15 March 1941, reduced the air corps primary school flying hours from sixty-five to sixty flying hours and the training period for each class from twelve to ten weeks. However, the contract rates were reduced only very slightly from $1,170 to $1,050 per graduate and from $18 to $17.50 per flying hour for those students who failed. These reduced flying hours and standard fees remained the same until the United States entered the war.

BFTS and Arnold Scheme civil schools, which had gained an excellent reputation for efficient and rapid aircraft maintenance, were allowed under their second and subsequent contracts to overhaul trainer aircraft, and reimbursement for this labor was made through flying hour charges. The primary flying hours and the contract rates remained the same until January 1942. For training in a contractor-overhauled aircraft, pay was $1,386 per graduate instead of the standard $1,050, and $23.10 was the rate charged per flying hour for eliminated students, instead of the usual $17.50 per flying hour. Since many BFTS and Arnold Scheme contractors also did aircraft overhaul work, calculation of precise income is difficult without documentation, but some idea of profits can be discerned from the information provided.

ARNOLD SCHEME PRIMARY FLYING TRAINING

The six civil contract flying schools that were assigned to train British student pilots were located in the Southeast Air Corps Training Center (SEACTC), later designated the Eastern Flying Training Command. The entire system of using civilian companies to train army pilots that the United States Army Air Corps instituted in July 1939 had not been used in the United States since World War I. Since the British student pilots were to train alongside army air corps officer cadets, the use of American military organization, drill, ceremonies and discipline created problems, even in the beginning. Most of the civilian flying instructors had logged hundreds of flying hours and enjoyed their work.

This excerpt from the "Syllabus For USAAF Primary Flying Training" and the following table detail the skills that were being taught to the Arnold Scheme participants:

> *First day. Preliminary phase. Assignment to Instructors; check flying equipment, explanation of instruments, location and function of controls and starting and stopping the engine. Effect of controls; straight and level flying, gentle and medium turns, confidence maneuvers, climbs, climbing turns, glides and gliding turns, rectangular courses, taxying, use of brakes, parking the airplane. Dual: 5 periods of approximately 30 minutes.*

Week	Dual	Solo	Total	Description of Lessons
1	1:50		1:50	
2	3:20 (five periods of forty minutes)		3:20	"S" across roads, stalls, power-on and -off, spins, landings and takeoffs.
Cumulative	5:10		5:10	
3	3:00 (four periods of forty-five minutes)	1:30 (three periods of thirty minutes)	4:30	Supervised solo. Instructor to supervise solo flights on three separate days. Beginning of solo stage and traffic flying. Students to be graded daily on landings, takeoffs and traffic by an instructor who supervises stage and gives dual to students whose flying indicates a need for it.
Cumulative	8:10	1:30	9:40	
4	2:30 (five periods of thirty minutes)	2:30 (five periods of thirty minutes)	5:00	Same as for third week.
Cumulative	10:40	4:00	14:40	
5	3:00 (four periods of forty-five minutes)	3:20 (five periods of forty minutes)	6:20	Spot landings, using ninety-degree approach from five hundred feet, students approach the field and land for a designated spot. Dual to consist of forced landings, lazy eights and chandelles.
Cumulative	13:40	7:20	21:00	
6	3:45 (five periods of forty-five minutes)	5:00 (five periods of one hour)	8:45	180-degree side approach from eight hundred feet. Dual and solo practice to be concluded with stage check off as in spot landing stage. Dual to include forced landings, lazy eights and chandelles.
Cumulative	17:45	12:20	29:45	
7	2:30 (five periods of thirty minutes)	5:00 (five periods of one hour)	7:30	180-degree overhead approach. Dual and solo practice to be concluded with stage check off as in 180-degree side approach. Additional dual on lazy eights, chandelles and pylon eights.
Cumulative	19:55	17:20	37:15	
8	3:00 (four periods of forty-five minutes)	5:00 (five periods of one hour)	8:00	360-degree overhead approach. Dual and solo practice to be concluded with stage check off as in 180-degree side approach. Additional dual on lazy eights, pylon eights and chandelles.
Cumulative	22:55	17:20	37:15	
9	2:30 (five periods of thirty minutes)	5:00 (five periods of one hour)	7:30	Review of chandelles, pylon eights and lazy eights. Loops, vertical reverses, half rolls.
Cumulative	25:20	27:20	52:45	
10	2:15	5:00	7:15	Review of chandelles, pylon eights and lazy eights. Advanced aerobatics consisting of snap rolls, slow rolls and Immelman turns. Final check.
Cumulative	27:40	32:20	60:00	

Learning to be a pilot in tough and reliable open cockpit Stearman biplanes and being treated like royalty by an adoring public was about as great a set of memories as one could ever hope for. Little wonder that many British cadets think of their aircrew training in America as one of their most memorable lifetime experiences.

Although some student pilots failed when they continued to become ill from motion sickness or other health problems, most early washouts came when students did not solo within the allotted twelve hours. The large number of washouts among British students stemmed from their lack of mechanical experience. These early eliminees believed that they would have qualified as pilots if they had had sufficient time to develop their coordination, and that was undoubtedly true in some cases.

The two main training checkpoints were the twenty- and forty-hour checks, and at each of these checks a number of students were "washed out" of the course. At the five-week halfway point in the course, the senior class departed and a new junior class arrived, and it was rush! rush! rush! The British and American cadets were rushed about everywhere, because aside from flying, there was academic work as well as physical and military training.

The first five courses of Arnold Scheme student pilots, Classes SE-42-A, SE-42-B, SE-42-C, SE-42-D and SE-42-E, disembarked at Halifax, Nova Scotia, and traveled by rail to RCAF Manning Depot No. 1 at Toronto. After being documented, the first four courses traveled by rail directly from Toronto to their assigned civilian contract flight schools in South Carolina, Alabama, Georgia and Florida.

Class SE-42-E was the final course to be documented at the RCAF Manning Depot at Toronto and the first to complete an acclimatization course at Maxwell Field, Alabama, before being assigned to a primary school. Classes SE-42-F and SE-42-G were documented at RAF No. 31 Depot at Moncton, New Brunswick, and also completed acclimatization at Maxwell Field. The final six Arnold Scheme courses were also documented at Moncton before traveling by rail to an acclimatization course at Turner Field, Georgia.

CHAPTER THREE

THE TWO DISTANT PRIMARY SCHOOLS

CAMDEN AND TUSCALOOSA

SOUTHERN AVIATION SCHOOL
CAMDEN, SOUTH CAROLINA, 42-A–42-D

Southern Aviation School, Woodward Airport, Camden, South Carolina, was probably the least important of the Arnold Scheme primary flying schools. The main airdrome of the flying school was located 2.9 miles northeast of Camden at an elevation of three hundred feet. Its specific location was at thirty-four degrees, seventeen minutes north latitude, eighty degrees, thirty-four minutes, thirty seconds west longitude. During 1941, as the Sixty-fourth U.S. Army Air Forces Flying Training Detachment, it enrolled five classes of British student pilots and graduated slightly fewer than three hundred. Its elimination rate was relatively high in comparison with other schools, but its historical importance lies not in its training record, but in the availability of records describing its early activities. Since four of the five classes containing RAF student pilots published classbooks with pictures, the *Camden Chronicle* regularly reported aviation developments within the town and county, and two former company officers preserved a smattering of early records and documents.

By 1938, largely as a result of the labor of New Deal agencies, the Depression was slowly waning, and except for the establishment of the Civil Aeronautics Authority (CAA), the aviation industry had been neglected. In that year, evidently at the behest of the CAA, the Works Progress Administration (WPA) launched a concerted national drive and offered financial assistance in efforts to persuade state and local authorities to develop airports or to improve existing ones. Dexter C. Martin, director of the South Carolina Aeronautical Commission, traveled about the state seeking statewide airport expansion. The recently created Camden and Kershaw County Airport Commission agreed to use county equipment and WPA funds to resurrect and maintain Camden's derelict Woodward Airport.

However, even when cosmetic work was performed on the sod airfield and its small brick hangar, such improvements proved to be temporary. In May 1939, a year after those initial repairs, the local newspaper announced that the airport was "being cleaned, grass and weeds cut, and ruts caused by the wheels of automobiles in the hands of inebriated drivers on joyrides have been leveled." Cuts in fences were repaired, a telephone and lights were installed and No Trespassing signs were erected. The changes wrought at the Camden airport were evidently completed just in time. On 21 June 1939, one hundred aircraft of the "Cavalcade of the Air" stopped at Woodward Field. The flight, which originated in Tampa, Florida, was sponsored by the Gulf Oil Corporation.

By the summer of 1939, Earl Friedell had leased the airport and its hangar from the Camden and Kershaw County Airport Commission and was managing it. As a fixed-base airport operator, Friedell made a living by providing flight instruction, selling gasoline to the few local and transient aircraft owners and providing minor repairs and inspections. Friedell owned or rented several aircraft and maintained them at the airport for the purpose of instructing his twelve pupils. At the end of the year, on 30–31 December 1939, another of Gulf Oil's promotional flights landed at Camden. With a small staff, Friedell serviced 250 aircraft in two days. The single brick hangar needed some major repairs, and there was a strong need for a paved apron in front of the hangar as well as a parking area for automobiles.

On 1 July 1939, following the practice employed by Great Britain and other European countries, the United States Army Air Corps decentralized its flying training in order to expand its pilot training system. A select group of fixed-base flying school operators signed contracts with the War Department to provide primary ground and flying instruction to air corps flying cadets. These contractors employed experienced civilian instructors.

Simultaneously, in an effort to assist civilian pilots and fixed-base airport operators, the CAA established college pilot training program courses in ten colleges and universities. In November 1939, when war erupted in Europe, men who could gain sufficient financial support to form pilot training schools were in an excellent position. Frank Wilson Hulse, who was born in North Augusta, South Carolina, in 1912, had learned to fly at nearby Augusta, Georgia, and had organized with Ike F. Jones of Augusta a fixed-base operation at a small airfield near that city's famous Master's Golf Course. Hulse and Jones had expanded their sales, service and flight instruction operations rapidly, and by mid-1940 their company maintained offices at Augusta and Atlanta, Georgia; Birmingham and Muscle Shoals, Alabama; and Greenville, South Carolina. Jones operated the Greenville office.

Because of their successful experience in operating CPTP programs, the U.S. Army Air Corps (USAAC) offered the company a contract to develop one of the USAAC's contract primary schools for the twelve-thousand-pilot training expansion program. In June 1940, Hulse was given assurances of a contract with the War Department to build and operate a primary flying school that would provide the initial sixty hours of flight instruction for USAAC flying cadets. First, Hulse had to locate an appropriate site for such a school. Initially, he intended to expand his flight operations in Alabama, but the site amid Gulf coastal swamps near Mobile was rejected by USAAC site selection officers, ostensibly for health reasons. The real reason for the rejection was probably that the air corps already planned to locate a huge air depot near Mobile and did not want the heavy traffic of the depot disturbed by trainer planes.

Finally, in August and September 1940, Dexter C. Martin, director of the South Carolina Aeronautical Commission, contacted Hulse and persuaded him to examine potential flight school sites in South Carolina. Quietly and unobtrusively, Hulse surveyed several potential sites within the state. Though they spoke of several sites, Martin urged Hulse to select Camden's Woodward Airport as an ideal location for his pilot-training venture. Following an inspection of the premises and discussions with city and county leaders, Hulse traveled to Wright Field near Dayton, Ohio, and requested army air corps contracting officers to approve the Camden site. There were other details to be arranged, and economies were essential.

Since it is difficult for outside interests to move into a small community and purchase or lease a large block of property, it is always good practice to have the purchasing or leasing done by someone locally. If that local person can be a government entity, landowners might more easily be persuaded to part with their property for the common good. Since the Camden and Kershaw County Airport Commission was willing to lease the airport for nothing, perhaps they might be willing to purchase contiguous acreage and lease that land to Hulse as well.

The airport commission agreed to purchase the land required for the flying school, and did so with alacrity. Almost nineteen acres of land adjacent to Woodward Airport was purchased for $2,420—5 acres from Julian Burns cost $650 and 13.2 acres bought from Pauline S. Trotter cost $1,420—and both deeds were executed on 11 December 1940. On that same day, four key corner lots (approximately .5 acre), which were located near the Woodward Airport brick hangar and along the original post road, were purchased from Annie S. Davidson for $350. The Camden and Kershaw County Airport Commission conveyed the 18.7 acres of land to the Southern Aviation School in fee simple title for the duration of the school. Thus, the land, which cost the flight school nothing, was of value not only as the site for the proposed flying school, but also as collateral in the pending loan from the Atlanta offices of the Trust Company of Georgia and the Reconstruction Finance Corporation (RFC).

Before being advised of the rejection of the Mobile, Alabama site, Frank Hulse had been quite busy. Aware of Oliver L. Parks's school at Tuscaloosa, Alabama, Hulse visited and inspected that school and gained a variety of tips (probably too many) that would be helpful in developing his own flying schools. Architect Henry Sprott Long of Tuscaloosa was engaged to design the buildings essential to fulfill the contract at Camden. For that initial contract, Hulse needed a barracks to house 112 cadets, a dining hall, classrooms and an additional hangar for maintenance of army-owned training aircraft, as well as an administration building plus water, sewerage, electrical service and transportation. Architect Long provided the drawings and specifications for each building, and suggestions as to the amount of land necessary for the domestic site of the miniature military town.

With these arrangements completed, the officers of Southern Aviation School could breathe a sigh of relief, but not for long. The timetable imposed by War Department Contract W535 (AC) 17326 stipulated that Southern Aviation School would train no fewer than fifty-six USAAC pilots between 22 March and 30 June 1941. It was now winter, almost Christmas 1940; the loan was not yet approved, no buildings had been built and the deadline for the arrival of the first class of flying cadets was ninety cold, short days away—the worst possible time for construction projects.

On 9 January 1941, while the A-B-C Conversations were taking place in Washington and preparations were underway to debate the Lend-Lease Bill, officers of the N.C. Morgan Construction Company of Tuscaloosa, Alabama, signed contracts with Frank W. Hulse for building the Southern Aviation School. Four separate contracts provided for the construction of an administration building, a two-story barracks, a dining hall and a classroom building, all to be completed within sixty-eight days.

The aggregate cost of the initial buildings was almost $59,000. The administration building would include offices for civilian school officers and USAAC supervisory officers, as well as space for a small recreation room and a snack bar. The initial barracks building was to be a two-story bay-type facility designed to house 150 students. The classroom building would contain offices for civilian ground school instructors as well as three large classrooms for instruction in meteorology, navigation, theory of flight, aircraft engines and mathematics. The mess hall (dining hall) was to be a separate facility designed to feed at least 110 persons at one time.

As had been done at other primary flying schools in the region, a well was drilled in order to get a supply of water. However, the Virginia Machinery and Well Company, which had been engaged to drill a well and construct a water system for the school, was unable to reach an adequate flow of water at 320 feet, and therefore found it necessary to continue drilling. The company had planned to build a huge water tower and tank to provide a gravity pressure system, but the search for an adequate flow for the anticipated population of the school proved elusive. It was probably just as well that the school avoided the construction of a huge water tower and tank, which would undoubtedly have become a flying hazard. Ultimately, when the well failed and the tank project was abandoned, a more than adequate supply of potable water was supplied by running a six-inch water main from the Camden waterworks to the school.

By 31 January 1941, the *Camden Chronicle* reported that buildings at the flying school "were going up like magic." The steel arrived for the erection of two huge steel hangars measuring 100 feet by 184 feet each. It was expected that these structures would be erected in two weeks' time. Reid Able Company of Asheville, North Carolina, was preparing the concrete hangar foundations, and contracts were being let for the mess hall, administration building and other facilities. By 21 February, the two new steel hangars were nearing completion, as were the green-roofed, white asbestos-shingled buildings in the nearby pine grove.

Although some school staff had been visiting Camden since early January in efforts to locate housing, both military and civilian personnel began to arrive in February to take up residence. Captain Roy T. Wright, who had commanded the contract primary schools at Lincoln, Nebraska, and Lakeland, Florida, arrived and activated the Sixty-fourth Army Air Corps Flying Training Detachment, which would supervise training at the new contract school. Initially, he checked the credentials of the growing number of civilian flying instructors and flew with each of them on check rides. Wright also reviewed the ten-week USAAC primary school curriculum with both flying and ground school instructors. Wright also served as a semi-official project officer for the purpose of determining the appropriateness of the new school's facilities.

Wright was assisted in his organizational duties by First Lieutenant Henry Huglin, newly arrived from instructional duties at Kelly Field, Texas. Huglin, a graduate of the U.S. Military Academy at West Point, New York, would serve as air corps supervisor, commanding the Sixty-fourth AAC Flying Training Detachment at the Southern Aviation School. Lieutenant Jesse Brown, a native of Selma, North Carolina, and formerly of the field artillery, arrived to assume his duties as adjutant at the school. Other military personnel, recent graduates of an army air corps advanced flying school, arrived in the following months. They were Lieutenants Leonard Hauprich, John H. Foregger and Oliver L. Duncan, all of whom would serve as assistant air corps supervisors or army check pilots; Lieutenant Winfred R. Fahs, commandant of cadets; Captain Isadore S. Edelstein, MD, and Captain C.A. Pigford, MD, who served as station medical officers between February and October 1941; and Lieutenant Sidney Maislen, MD, who served after October 1941.

In the beginning, the civilian staff of the school was very small, but highly competent. B.M. Cornell, graduate of the United States Naval Academy and professor of aeronautics at Auburn University in Alabama, assumed his duties as general manager and director of the ground school. Laurie Hill was promoted from the company's Greenville, South Carolina operations as director of maintenance at Camden. C.S. Syer was the very popular teacher of meteorology; J.W. Hoover taught aircraft structures and engines; C.V. Walton taught navigation; and J.H. McDaniel taught theory of flight.

A few months later, Cornell, Syer and Hill were transferred to Hulse's new primary school at Decatur, Alabama, and company Vice President Ike F. Jones moved from Greenville to become general manager at Camden. William Fishburne came from Columbia to assume his duties as business manager, and Jack Nettles of Camden became airport manager or superintendent of the school's buildings and grounds. Harbin Lawson came from Snead Junior College in Alabama to direct the flying school's physical training program, and Mrs. Gertrude Zemp and Mrs. Rhetta Blakeney of Camden served as dieticians.

Although the school was not yet complete, Class SE-41-H, the first class of army air corps aviation cadets, began to arrive during the evening of 19 March 1941. Most of the young men hailed from the New England states. Flying training and ground school began immediately. Aviation Cadet R.D. Smith of Fairfield, Connecticut, was the first cadet to solo one of the glossy blue-and-yellow Stearman (Boeing) PT-17 *Kaydet* trainers. In early April, Brigadier General Walter R. Weaver, commanding general of the Southeast Air Corps Training Center, arrived from Maxwell Field to inspect the new primary flying school. And on 7 April 1941, the airfield was opened to the general public for the day. As a result of General Weaver's visit and his announcement of plans for further air corps expansion, Southern Aviation School officers implemented plans to enlarge the flying school.

U.S. Highway Number 1 ran in a north-south direction parallel to Camden's Woodward Airport, about five hundred yards east of the main brick hangar, and was connected to the airfield from three directions. One could reach the airport via the Old Post Road, which departed from the paved No. 1 Highway about one mile south, where the new highway intersected with the Old Telegraph Road or Old Wire Road, which ran northeastward past Adams' Mill Pond toward Hartsville, South Carolina. It was also possible to reach the airport via the Post Road by turning onto a well-worn dirt track from the No. 1 Highway about a mile north of the airport at the so-called five mile bottom. The nearest and most direct route to the airport was westward from Highway No. 1 just north of Dymock's Tourist Cabins and small auto service station and grocery store.

Along the quiet Old Post Road, which in 1941 no longer suffered extensive automobile, bus and truck traffic, were numerous houses that had been built several years earlier in the pine and hardwood groves along that route. Across the road from the landing field and the apron on which aircraft were lined up for flying, and within two hundred yards of other school buildings, were several tenant farm houses that, despite being in various states of disrepair, were occupied by impoverished black families. Their unpainted weathered boards stood out in sharp contrast to the new white buildings with green roofs situated in the nearby pleasant pine grove. When the Southern Aviation School commenced training, these tenant houses were situated just to the rear of the school's dining hall, and served as awful reminders of the grinding poverty of the region and the racial problem that would not go away.

There were other reminders. Westward, along a sandy and little-used trail, just beyond the newly constructed shiny metal hangars, was an old black school that stood among the blackjack oaks and scattered pines. In the interest of developing the flying school to its fullest potential, all of these trees had to be removed. The land on which the tenant houses and school were located was purchased. The offending members were removed, and the airport was enlarged. All of the land along the west side of U.S. No.1 Highway, north of Dymock's Tourist Cabins for about five hundred yards, was also purchased by the Camden and Kershaw County Airport Commission.

Removal of some pine trees and the tenant farm shacks, and closure of that segment of the Old Post Road that ran northward past Woodward Field's brick hangar, doubled the size of the main airport and made it possible for aircraft to land and take off in east-west as well as north-south directions. An argument for removal of the black school was that such removal made it possible to add an additional hangar at the main airfield, thereby doubling the school's training capacity. And though the airfield fence ultimately enclosed part of that site, it was never used for buildings or airfield. During spring 1941, Daniel Construction Company of Greenville, South Carolina, was given the contract to build an operations building, three additional barracks, a hospital (infirmary), an academic building and a recreation building with post exchange and snack bar. By autumn 1941, the flying school had also added a swimming pool with other athletic facilities, and had doubled the size of the dining hall.

The area around the Southern Aviation School was a study in contrasts. The western boundary of a large part of Kershaw County was the Wateree River. That great river, which gathered waters from numerous tributaries and bisected the ancient Catawba lands, began in the mountains of North Carolina as the Catawba River, and its name changed to Wateree some miles northwest of Camden. It flowed past Charlotte, North Carolina, southward a few miles west of Camden, and meandered through a vast swamp (west and south of Shaw Field, a basic flying school) into the Congaree River, where both rivers combined about seventy-five miles south of Camden to form the Santee River. The history of that river system has been well described in Henry Savage's *The Santee*, an excellent contribution to the *Rivers of America* series. Savage, an attorney and longtime mayor of Camden, also served as secretary of the Southern Aviation School.

The Hardaway Dam, seventy-eight feet high and a half-mile long, had been completed in 1919 and drove the turbines of Duke Power Company's hydroelectric generating plant. It was located five miles northwest of the town and held back a lake more than a mile wide in places and some twenty miles long. Even with the volume of water somewhat controlled by the dam, there were days, sometimes weeks, every year when water flowed several feet above the high dam and flooded the low-lying areas along the river and on the western and southern outskirts of Camden. Other bodies of water in the vicinity were not nearly so damaging.

The Hermitage Lake, covering approximately 1,200 acres, was located directly east of Camden a few hundred yards below a high ridge or precipice running in a northeast-southwest direction. A portion of the precipice was called Paint Hill because during the eighteenth century, vari-colored clay dug from a section of its base was said to have been a prime source of paint for the Catawba of the district. The lake, which during the nineteenth century had been enlarged, dammed and channeled by a mile-long canal to provide waterpower for a textile factory, was by 1941 very popular among town residents as a place for swimming, boating, fishing and building summer cottages. These lakes and other landmarks served as good reference points for students flying solo exercises, and their buzzing the lake got a few of them, like RAF Cadet Richard Guthrie of Class SE-42-B, in trouble.

Another small lake had been formed in the nineteenth century by damming the chill waters of Pine Tree Creek. In 1941, the small dam, located on the northeast edge of the town, served as a source of power for yet another textile factory, the Wateree Cotton Mill, a division of the Kendall Company. Its contiguous village, which was owned at the time by the company, consisted of about one hundred wooden bungalows neatly aligned along paved streets with a community building and a playground for children. The small three-hundred-acre lake, technically an elongated pond or reservoir, boasted a swimming area on its northwest side and also provided facilities for boating. Since the lake was surrounded by tall pine and hardwood trees and was situated only about one mile southwest of the main airdrome, student pilots on solo flights were aware of two reasons, proximity to the airfield and the tallness of the trees, not to "buzz" or "dive bomb" it.

The soil of Kershaw County varied from sand or sandy loam, with clay or chalk underlying it, to red clay hills northwestward along the Wateree River toward and beyond the Hardaway

Dam. In 1941, the sandhill region of the northeastern section of the county had been used for more than a century and a half for the production of cotton and tobacco, and much of it was now so devoid of nutrients that every crop required the liberal use of fertilizers. To the north and northwest of the town, most of the sand and red clay hills were eroded almost beyond redemption. When flight school officials began to lease land in order to develop auxiliary airfields, the soil, which had a clay base, was excellent, but large patches of deep sand created problems, and in 1942 the company abandoned Pritchard Field (formerly Funderburk Field), an auxiliary landing ground located near the village of Lugoff on the west side of the Wateree River.

Although rich soil in the southern part of the county produced much corn and cotton, that area was dominated by swamp lands that were covered by a wide variety of hardwood and cypress trees and a morass of vines. Moreover, since during late 1941 and early 1942 Shaw Field, an army air forces basic flying school, was built on a plateau east of the Wateree River and about twenty-five miles south of Camden, the flying of primary trainers in that region was prohibited. Similar restrictions applied to the enlarged Fort Jackson military reservation, which trained two infantry divisions at one time. That huge tract stretched for about thirty miles from the city limits of Columbia eastward to U.S. Highway 601, within a mile of the Wateree River and its massive swamp, which claimed at least one American aviation cadet from Shaw Field. His wrecked aircraft was found within a fortnight, but his remains were not found until 1947.

In 1941, the population of Camden was officially listed as 7,312, and may well have had that many people, if it incorporated into its population the whites who resided in two contiguous textile mill villages located on the eastern edge of the town and the African Americans who lived just beyond the town limits on the southern, western and northern outskirts of the town. The black population constituted about half of the total and was concentrated in pockets on the periphery of the town. Based on a unique eighteenth-century town plan, Camden's main thoroughfares, DeKalb and Broad Streets, divided and bisected the town. DeKalb Street carried U.S. Highway No. 1 directly through the town westward to Columbia, and northeastward past the airport to Cheraw and points north. Broad Street ran north-south and carried U.S. Highway 521 through Camden, bisecting DeKalb Street and connecting Camden with Shaw Field and Sumter to the south and Lancaster and Charlotte, North Carolina, to the north.

Near the intersection of these two main thoroughfares, along Broad Street in the northwestern quadrant of the town, were a bookstore, several offices, the courthouse and the First Baptist Church. The area westward from the intersection along DeKalb Street contained a variety of businesses and institutions including an automobile dealership, at least two automobile service stations, several black churches, a funeral home, the segregated black elementary and high schools, the Mather Academy (a private institution for black students) and a few modest dwellings.

Northward along Broad Street from DeKalb beyond the post office and the First Baptist Church were some huge mansions, a large number of smaller dwellings and several tiny parks. The sprawling Kirkwood Hotel with its high ceilings and vast porches had been a tourist haven since about 1890. Its tennis courts and the nearby polo grounds attracted regular winter visitors and permanent residents as well. Northwest of Hobkirk Hill in the direction of the Hardaway Dam and the village of Liberty Hill was the Springdale Race Course, on which steeplechase races were run every year. Horses were also boarded and trained there by several well-known trainers and their legions of assistants. Hobkirk Inn, another attractive tourist hotel with wide porches across its front on two levels, tastefully furnished rooms and well-designed gardens, was located nearby between North Main and Lyttleton Streets.

Much of the remainder of the northeastern quadrant of the town contained some of the town's most elegant antebellum homes, its public schools for whites and its large established churches, including the Presbyterian church on DeKalb Street, the Methodist church, Grace Episcopal Church, a small Jewish synagogue and the tiny but magnificent stuccoed Spanish-style Our Lady of Perpetual Help Catholic Church, all located along Lyttleton Street. The musical Father Burke, who presided over the church, the local Catholic flock and many visitors, was very popular with citizens, school staff and cadets.

Two large parks that occupied entire blocks in this section of the town were much appreciated by local citizens. One park, which occupied a block between Fair and Lyttleton Streets, served as a memorial to the six Confederate states general officers who were born in the district and later served during the Civil War. Another park bordered by DeKalb, Lyttleton and Fair Streets honored CSA General and former Governor and U.S. Senator Wade Hampton. Along the shaded streets between the various churches and parks, the Camden Hospital and the white public elementary and high schools were residences of the town's doctors, lawyers, merchants, managers and teachers.

Northward from DeKalb Street along Mill Street was the sprawling and elegant Court Inn, another tourist hotel dating from the turn of the century. During the Carolina maneuvers, Secretary of Treasury Henry Morgenthau stayed at the Court Inn with his army officer son for several days, as did many high-ranking army officers. By 1942, rental property quickly found occupants, and the resulting housing shortage created morale problems among the military and civilian staff of Southern Aviation School. In order to deal with that problem, the town fathers applied for and received a federal grant that permitted the construction of some thirty small rental houses, which were built on a tract located in the triangle formed by Haile and Mill Streets.

A few blocks north of the Court Inn on Mill Street was the much-appreciated Sarsfield Club, a private institution that maintained a bar and sponsored regular dances and other social events for its members and their guests, including graduation parties for RAF and USAAF cadet classes that trained at the Woodward Airport. In late 1941, Southern Aviation School officials leased the DeSaussure House, a huge antebellum house on the corner of Mill and Haile Streets, and converted it into a Cadet Club. In 1942, the Southern Aviation School also leased a large house on Greene Street and established an instructor's club.

The section south of DeKalb Street constituted the "old" town of Camden and was truly "the other half." Although a few shops, a drugstore, two restaurants, two automobile dealerships and garages were located along DeKalb Street, and a few small shops, a seed and feed store and a farm implement dealership could be found along other side streets, most of Camden's compact business district aligned both sides of Broad Street between DeKalb and Rutledge Streets. That district also included two banks, three drugstores, two large grocery stores, three small department stores, two hardware stores, two furniture stores, a photo shop and two five-and-ten-cent stores. Others of the town's retail businesses included two cinemas, one located on the corner of Broad and Rutledge Streets, the other on DeKalb Street near the Presbyterian church. Unfortunately, one of the most historic spots in Camden, the site of the former British headquarters during two critical years of the American Revolutionary period (1780–81), had become the city dump.

In 1941, following fifteen long and dreary years of an agricultural depression, the town began to take on new life. A number of stores and storefronts were refurbished. Included among eight new shops that opened during early 1941 were a dairy bar and a milk pasteurizing plant. Strategically located automobile service stations and garages served motorists entering or leaving the town. On the west side of the town, the new national guard armory was being built with federal funds. For much of the war period, while its regular occupant, Company M, 118th Infantry Regiment, 30th Division, was serving on active duty in Iceland, Northern Ireland, southwest England, France and Germany, the armory would be used for weekend dances and home guard drills.

For many local citizens, the balance sheet was very important. They had supported establishment of the flying school at the town's airport for business as well as patriotic reasons. The Southern Aviation School was an industry that pumped money into the local economy through the purchase of goods and services and the employment of local people. Its instructional, maintenance and other support personnel and its student pilots expended money regularly and stimulated the local economy, which, in turn, fed people, paid bills, kept children in school and provided revenues for essential public services. In early May 1941 when Class SE-41-I, the second class of USAAC cadets, arrived at Southern Aviation School to commence training, the flying school was beginning to affect the community. In an effort to determine the economic impact of Southern Aviation School, its personnel were paid in $2 bills during the month of June 1941. The flying school's payroll was calculated at $30,000 per month, and workers were paid every two weeks, so it was easy to observe the flow of Jefferson $2 bills through the local economy. Many other contract flying schools used the $2 payroll scheme to measure their local economic impact.

The service and sacrifice of some Southern Aviation School graduates was a far more important measure of the school's influence on the war, the nation and the town, but in most instances the general public would rarely hear of that service. Dozens of the school's graduates made their mark during war service in the southwest Pacific and in every theater of operations in the worldwide conflict. Two years after he left Camden, Robert K. Morgan of Class 41-I became one of the school's most famous graduates when he completed twenty-five combat missions as pilot of the Eighth Air Force Boeing B-17 bomber *Memphis Belle*. Morgan revisited the Southern Aviation School in 1943, and subsequently commanded the first B-29 to bomb Tokyo. Dale Davenport, who had flown on the Doolittle Tokyo raid in May 1942, also came back to Camden and demonstrated in front of a huge crowd how a B-25 could take off in less than five hundred feet.

For instructors and other school staff, working at the Camden school was a job, but it was also great fun. Since the Lindbergh transatlantic flight in 1927, aviators had occupied a special place in the romantic view of the universe. From the perspective of many people, there was almost as much satisfaction in the status accorded fliers as in the flying itself. They were young, the job was pleasant and although instructing could sometimes be a drag, all of it constituted a great adventure! They loved the Stearman PT-17 and enjoyed seeing their students succeed.

Perceptive student pilots who were assigned to the Southern Aviation School for flight training were primarily interested in flying, but most of them learned something of the town and its people. For many students from different parts of the United States, and especially for those from Britain and the Empire-Commonwealth, this was their first visit to the Southern United States, and they were curious about the land and its people. However, since their stay in primary, basic and advanced flying schools spanned only thirty weeks or less, their impressions were limited.

What the young student pilots probably could not discern at the time was that the Southern states and the nation were being rapidly transformed by World War II. The nature of modern warfare, American rearmament, the 1940 Selective Service Act, mobilization of national guard units, emergency aid to Britain and the Lend-Lease program created the need for rapid expansion of defense and other industries. In 1940–41, the United States began to disperse its food processing and defense industries. New edible developments included dehydrated eggs, potatoes and milk, Spam, canned butter, bacon and amazing troop rations, which included chocolate and cigarettes. In addition to building ships in virtually every port along the Atlantic, Gulf and Pacific Coasts and many of the nation's rivers, the United States built numerous training camps and developed dozens of airfields and petroleum pipelines. These changes brought about the beginning of a revival of the national economy. The changes that could be observed in Camden, South Carolina, were transforming other towns, states and regions, but their impact was especially great in the cotton states. As the USAAF surgeon general wrote, "Anywhere you can grow cotton, you can grow aviators."

The *Camden Chronicle* used several pages to describe activities at the Southern Aviation School, and a large part of the May 1941 issue of *Dixie Air News* was devoted to pictures and narrative descriptions of the facilities and training. The hyperbole used in describing the initial barracks building as "situated in a growth of young pine trees that cool the hot summer air and make sleeping as comfortable as a mountain top cottage or a seashore home" no doubt produced much laughter from the flying cadets of Class 41-H and those of later classes. Most of them had never traveled in the Southern states and, when they had free time, they became tourists, anxiously observing everything in the vicinity.

Escorted by RCAF Flying Officer J.P. Morris, the sixty-six men of Class SE-42-A arrived in Camden on Saturday, 7 June 1941. They were the first British servicemen to arrive in Camden in 160 years. They commenced flying training on Monday, 9 June 1941, some thirty-six hours after their arrival. On that day, the class was divided, half to fly in the morning, the other half to attend ground school classes. The RAF students assigned to report to the flight line entered into a conspiracy that demonstrated their sense of humor. Deadpanning most of the time, even in the terrible humidity of a Southern summer morning, the assigned students marched off smartly and "reported" to the flight line dressed in RAF flight regalia with boots and flying topees (cork sun helmets with chin straps and radio plugs). Apparently, USAAC officers, civilian flight commanders and flying instructors lost their studied calm immediately and rushed away, doubled over, trying desperately and unsuccessfully not to laugh. This antic by the RAF students broke the ice and called attention to the fact that RAF flying togs were totally inadequate for the climate.

The students assigned to attend ground school that first morning were also able to use the inadequacy of their issue khaki uniforms to demonstrate their sense of humor. The khakis that the British students had been issued in Canada were of excellent quality, but they were somewhat large and hot, and there had not been sufficient time in Toronto to have them tailored. As a result, RAF students joined ground school formations in rumpled, heavy oversize khaki uniforms. American khaki slacks and shirts (tunics) for parades (formations) of all kinds were quickly issued from air corps stocks, and steps were taken to have the RCAF-issue khakis tailored and laundered. Air corps fatigue overalls were the equivalent of semi-porous tents and, until laundered perhaps a dozen times, provided a sandpaper-type fit at the neck, underarms and other sensitive areas. Their redeeming qualities were that they had many pockets and provided a measure of comfort in the chill air above five hundred feet in the open-cockpit Stearman trainers.

Among the natural RAF comedians at Camden were RAF Corporal Arthur D. Moore and LAC Michael J.S. Mycroft. The comedy team of "Moore and Mycroft," which had been formed while they underwent ITW training in England, often used articles of their uniforms to provide many hours of entertainment with their zany "music hall" routines. The "joke uniform" in the American military services was and may still be "jock straps and helmet liners," but such garb was as nothing when compared to "jock straps and topees." A plain old RAF forage cap (with or without badge) worn at a rakish angle merely elicited wonder about defiance of the laws of gravity, but the topee brought out the fourteen-year-old hidden away within most RAF students. With a coin to screw into one eye as a monocle, a moustache real or fake and an exaggerated accent, class comedians could don a topee and have one or fifty people rolling with laughter almost instantly. Like the boater of the song-and-dance man in music hall shows, the topee could be tilted to one side, parked squarely on the head or turned at a dozen different angles to extract different characters and personalities from its wearer.

On 1 August 1941, *PM* magazine provided an excellent pictorial coverage of RAF Class SE-42-A at the Southern Aviation School. Arthur Leighton-Porter was shown with three other LACs hauling a student to the showers after he had soloed. Men were also shown standing before lavatories shaving, but failed to show the line of loos on the opposite side of the bathroom. This open arrangement contributed to much constipation among arrivals, until they adjusted to the lack of privacy. The publication also failed to photograph the "community showers."

On Saturday, 14 June, their first free day off-post, the British cadets were entertained at a tea in Richardson Hall adjacent to Grace Episcopal Church. A group of ladies led by Mrs. Roland Goodale organized the tea, and Mrs. Maurice Clark, British-born wife of the church's rector, presided over the occasion. Forty-eight of the sixty-six RAF cadets of Class SE-42-A were members of the Church of England, and they all attended Grace Episcopal Church on Sunday, 15 June. On that occasion, twelve of them donned robes and sang in the choir, and that practice continued with each successive class as long as British cadets were trained at the Southern Aviation School. It is not recorded that very much singing occurred, but on 21 June, Peter G. "Admiral" Nelson of Bristol celebrated his twenty-first birthday at the Sarsfield Club and, strangely, did not remember leaving. When orders came for student pilots to shave off mustaches, twenty-nine-year-old LAC Arthur Leighton-Porter and others were most unhappy.

Bernard Victor Anthony Thompson of Derby, England, was just nineteen years old when he commenced flying training in the United States. More than forty years later from his home in Derby, England, Thompson remembered Camden with affection, and his early training experience with appreciation:

> *I remember the upper classmen, American Aviation Cadets, who were taller than most of us and were well disciplined. I liked the "hazing" system. We grumbled about it, but this was the "done thing"; it was not too dissimilar to that practiced at school in Britain. This is perhaps why some of us thought it a little "off." But generally, it was well accepted and we, in turn, practiced it upon our lower classmen, though perhaps not with the same enthusiasm as our American upper classmen. Recreation was essentially of a sporting nature. Mostly swimming in Adams' Pond and in the Hermitage Lake. Sometimes we were invited to share someone's boat for a ride on the lake. We took to softball, archery, and clay pigeon shooting.*
>
> *I cannot ever remember having a "date" with a girl, nor can I remember other chaps "dating" girls. On Saturdays, the families I have mentioned would take us for trips around the town to see the main points of interest. Dances on Saturday evenings were usually organized affairs with daughters well chaperoned. We were made to feel very welcome,*

and we sincerely appreciated the efforts that were made to make us feel at home. We were discouraged from hiring cars, but in 1941 that was not as very well known an activity as it is today and was difficult to do without a driver's license which very few of us had. Generally, we rode the bus to town on Saturday afternoons and on Sundays to church, or we were picked up at the main gate into the camp by friends with automobiles.

Food was a great experience! After rationing in Britain, the abundance and variety was astounding—Southern Fried Chicken (long before the finger licking Colonel had been heard of), T-bone steaks, and iced lemon tea were all new to us. The size and excellence of the dishes may have gotten exaggerated a little by the time we got back to England. Generally, for me and for many others, weekends at that time were a necessary break to be gotten over with as soon as possible so that we could get back to flying—flying was the be-all and end-all of everything! We would've flown 7 days per week without any worry.

Most of us were in the 18-to-22 age bracket, but there were one or two very ancient chaps of round about 30 who, for all of their advanced years, seemed to get through all of the tests and exams very well. First solos were, of course, a major event, and most of the failures came at that point. I went solo after 9 hours, and, as I remember, between 7 and 10 hours of dual instruction before going solo was the norm. During my 10 weeks at Camden, there were no fatal accidents, but quite a number of aeroplanes got "bent" and the official enquiry which followed was another avenue for departure of men who were deemed better suited for other jobs.

Unfortunately, the Moore and Mycroft comedy team was eliminated from pilot training during the first six weeks at Camden; Corporal Moore was posted to Canada for reassignment, but Mycroft, who was washed out with fifteen flying hours, was assigned by Wing Commander Hogan to British Flying Training School (BFTS) No. 3 at Miami, Oklahoma, where he continued pilot training and succeeded.

In the ensuing weeks, many other adjustments were to be made. The summer heat increased, no rain fell and the dust became an even greater problem. To make matters worse, the school did not yet have a swimming pool. Harbin Lawson, the civilian physical training instructor, made every effort to tailor his program and to avoid extremes of heat. The school bought a bus, and the cadets were regularly transported to Adams' Pond or the Hermitage Lake to enjoy a cooling swim. Unfortunately, several men contracted a fungus condition in their ears, and at least two of them were grounded. Swimming in lakes and ponds continued with precautions, but efforts were redoubled to complete the school's swimming pool. Despite hurried efforts, it was not completed soon enough to be used by members of the first two RAF classes. In addition to swimming, Lawson promoted a number of sports and a game that combined soccer and volleyball.

Before the students of Class SE-42-A completed their training, they published a mimeographed (cyclo-styled) class magazine entitled *Contacts*. The magazine was dedicated to the staff of the Southern Aviation School and included tributes to citizens of Camden and numerous musings by cadets. The stalwart and handsome Cadet Captain Frederick H. Bradford was teased unmercifully. One couplet entry in *Contacts* alluded to an embarrassing landing: "Student Captain and ship twenty-nine Do ground loops and somersault mighty fine," but Bradford apparently took the ribbing in his stride. Bradford, who earned the nickname "Mother," became cadet captain at Cochran Field as well, and went on to another outstanding record at Craig Field, Selma, Alabama, and later in RAF 65 Squadron.

Around 15 July, after the British students of Class SE-42-A had completed five weeks of training, during which they had soloed and had begun to practice maneuvers and aerobatics, the American cadets of Class SE-41-I graduated and were posted to a basic flying school. The British cadets of Class SE-42-A became upperclassmen, and a few days later on 18 July, the British students of Class SE-42-B arrived and, for a brief period, the school became all-RAF. During the ten-week-long flying course, the thirty-six eliminees of Class SE-42-A departed in ones and twos or larger groups, usually traveling via Maxwell Field, Alabama. From Maxwell Field, a few, like Harry Hepplewhite and Michael Mycroft, were assigned elsewhere to continue pilot training, while others were posted to Canada either to continue pilot training there or to be remustered to other duties. By 10 August 1941, the two LACs who had contracted an ear fungus were held over to Class SE-42-B to complete their training, and the twenty-eight SE-42-A graduates departed for the USAAF basic flying school at Cochran Field near Macon, Georgia.

The RAF students who left the cool of Toronto arrived in South Carolina in the midst of a heat wave. Everyone suffered considerably from heat and dust. At night, there was a general cooling, but often because of the heat and lack of ventilation except from open screened windows, it was impossible for the students to get to sleep before 11:00 p.m. or midnight, and they had to rise shortly after 5:00 a.m. to begin another crowded day of activities. Visiting RAF and USAAF staff officers expressed concern about heat and dust and the absence of ramps, aprons and runways. Despite the attractiveness of the domestic facilities and the excellent quality of food, RAF staff objected to the school because of the heat, dust and washout rate, but they were willing to suspend judgment temporarily in order to see how successful the school would be in training RAF student pilots.

Construction for expansion continued; the six-inch water line from the Camden waterworks to the airport was completed, and the company let contracts for improving the airport by extending the paved ramp and flying field and adding another hangar and an operations building. On the domestic side, contracts were approved for enlarging the dining hall and the classroom building and adding three additional single-story barracks and a fifteen-bed infirmary. School officials also asked the building contractors to rush to completion the swimming pool and the new pine-paneled recreation hall.

In addition to enlarging the main airdrome, the company leased or purchased several more auxiliary airfields. Since the arrival of the second class of American cadets in late April 1941, flying had been divided between the main airdrome and Bateman Field, an auxiliary field located a few miles northwest of the main airdrome, near the site of the 1780 Battle of Camden. Funderburk Auxiliary Airfield, which was located west of the Wateree River and south of U.S. Highway No. 1 near the village of Lugoff, continued in use as a temporary landing ground.

Before the heat wave was broken by heavy rain and dazzling thunderstorms, citizens as well as newcomers to the region suffered with the British student pilots. Besides some flying instructors from colder states to the North, there were other British visitors who experienced the smothering heat. During August, the RAF cadets at Camden received two weekend visits from large groups of Royal Navy men whose damaged warships were being repaired in the Charleston and Portsmouth, Virginia navy yards. Until the repairs could be completed, the tars had been sent on R&R (rest and recreation) assignment to the Cheraw State Park, which was located on a lake in the middle of a pine forest some forty miles north of Woodward Field.

In September, other visitors from cooler climates included many American soldiers and some Russian and other military observers of the United States Army's Carolina maneuvers. During this "invasion" by ground, armored and air forces, Camden served as headquarters for one of the two opposing forces. While tank, infantry and airborne units "seized" strategic points and "fought" in the pine forests, sand hills and swamps of the central portion of the state, reconnaissance and transport aircraft occasionally landed at the Southern Aviation School. Combat pilots from the United Kingdom came to the United States in order to fly different models of fighters and to assess their combat value.

LAC Albert Victor Dorman, reputed to be the shortest member of Class SE-42-B, was a native of Port Talbot, Glamorgan, South Wales. In 1941, he was nineteen years old and in love with life. Forty years later, as the retired fire chief of a huge industrial complex in north Wales, he recalled his training days at Camden and his solo flight:

> My flying instructor was a civilian by the name of Harry Howton. We got on fine right from the start and were never at cross purposes like some cadets were later with Army instructors. The expressed aim of some Army instructors was declared to be, "we are here to make you officers' and gentlemen and teaching you to fly is purely secondary." This was not the case with civilian instructors; most of them had hundreds of hours flying and loved it.
>
> Harry Howten was one of the best, and after 10 hours of teaching me every trick in flying the Stearman PT-17, we took off one morning and headed for the auxiliary field North of Camden which we had often used for "circuits and bumps" (take off and landing practice). After two landings, Harry told me to taxi to a corner of the field as he wanted to smoke. He got out and turned to me saying, "It's all yours!" What a strange feeling taking off alone on your first solo, twice around the field and in for the first solo landing. It must have been a good one as Harry said, "Go around again; I haven't finished my cigarette yet!" (it must have been a king size).
>
> Our stay at Camden was made much happier by the hospitable families which adopted us for the duration of our stay. The Mayer Family (he was City Fire Chief) were very kind; they introduced several of us to watermelon and pecan nuts which we had never before tasted. We also enjoyed swimming at Hermitage Lake until several cadets came down with an ear fungus. After 10 weeks at Camden, the last function I remember was a dinner dance at the Sarsfield Club. Next morning, we carted our kit down the drive to the red brick Gulf Service Station where a Greyhound Coach waited to take us to Macon, Georgia for basic flying school.

Dorman, who had a talent for drawing, did not mention that the giant pair of wooden RAF wings that he drew, cut out of plywood and painted was affixed to the front of the bus that carried the graduates to Macon, Georgia.

Virtually every British cadet who trained in the United States was astounded at two strange cadet regulations: the enforcement of restrictions against cadets' moustaches was a painful loss, and the cost of a lowly haircut and a shoeshine was perceived as downright robbery. Even more traumatic for British men, who still resist perfumed scents with a passion, was the American barber's practice of applying (with permission) hair tonic as well as an astringent followed by powder to shaved areas of the neck, face and temples, all aimed at inhibiting heat rash, but misunderstood by the British students.

In *Goggles*, the SE-42-B class magazine, LAC Eddie Castle recorded for posterity the traumatic collision of an RAF cadet with an American barbershop. Castle's article undoubtedly struck responsive chords in the entire RAF contingent and was appropriately entitled "My first visit to an American Barber."

Upon leaving England, I resolved to put behind me the days of short hair "a la I.T.W." and to allow my locks to grow again to their previous civilian splendour. However, on reaching Camden, I found that the short hair practice was still to continue, so on my first Saturday afternoon here, I "melted" my way to the local barber's.

I was greeted profusely and told to "Take a seat." No sooner was I seated, than I was conscious of a pair of enquiring eyes on my shoes, and I hurriedly dusted them on the backs of my trousers. Being uninitiated, I said "yes" to the two enquiring eyes of the shoe shine boy, administered by the expert slap-slapping of a duster wielded by the shoe-shiner. The cry of "Next, Please" released me from the exuberant clutches of the black wizard and before I realized it, I was sitting on the barber's chair feeling very much like a king on his throne.

First, I was spun into position (1½ turns precision spin) ready for "Sweeney Todd" to perform, and then yards of white gauze were wrapped round my neck and a white smock completely enveloped me. I felt as if I was going to operate on someone instead of being operated upon. Next, the clippers buzzed into action, followed by scissors at hair-raising (?) speed. Within a short space of time, my hair was duly cropped, short enough to pass any inspection and my shorn locks were in a heap at my feet.

Anticipating a quick get-away, I saw (to my surprise), a razor appear and before I could protest, my neck was lathered; I began to wonder if I was in Fleet Street after all, but I was very relieved to find it was only a neck shave. The cry of "Something on the hair, Sir?" rang through my ears, and no sooner had I nodded my head than my hair was drenched in hair tonic. As I looked in the mirror, I could see that all my initial hopes of allowing my hair to regain its normal length had been dashed to the ground.

To finish off this elaborate performance, dusting powder was applied to the nape of my neck, and I stepped down from the chair, exuding perfume. My shoe shiner dashed up flourishing a huge brass brush and proceeded vigorously to remove imaginary specks of dust from my clothing. Being unfamiliar with American currency, I gave the barber a dollar bill and received 45 cents in return. This "shook" me considerably, for at home, a hair cut, pure and simple, costs only 8d. or 14 cents, and I emerged from the Barber's after my first American hair cut, a poorer but a wiser man.

With the advent of public television and *Masterpiece Theater*, Eddie Castle's "inside" jokes about "Sweeney Todd" and Fleet Street "toughs" need not be as remote as they undoubtedly were for Americans during the summer of 1941.

A few days after Class SE-42-A departed for basic flying at Cochran Field, Class SE-42-C arrived. Owing to overcrowding at the Toronto manning depot, it was the only westbound draft that was held for a week at the RCAF No. 1 Y Depot at Halifax. The seventy-six men assigned to the class at the Southern Aviation School finally arrived at Camden on 25 August 1941 and joined Class SE-42-B, then in its fifth week of training. For a brief period of about five weeks, student enrollment at the school was entirely British, and LAC Peter Morgan served as cadet captain of Class SE-42-B.

Just as Class SE-42-A departed for a basic flying school and Class SE-42-B completed half of the primary flying course, Class SE-42-C arrived at Camden. Most of the RAF students were around twenty years of age, but several of them ranged from twenty-seven to thirty; a few of them were British army veterans. RAF cadet experiences ranged from student to schoolmaster and included such occupations as engineer, civil servant, printer, bank clerk and accountant. Roger F. Pye of Class SE-42-C was born to British parents in Oporto, Portugal. Although he was critical of the requirement that British students abandon their RAF-style drill and adopt the American style, Pye was very positive about his Arnold Scheme flying training.

After indicating his "great good fortune" to have the quiet and competent J.W. Rush as his flying instructor, Pye provided a more personal assessment.

> *The Stearman PT-17 was, of course, the perfect aircraft to fly. With absolutely no vices, unlike the D.H. Tiger Moth on which most British pilots began their training at this time and which, as I immediately realised when I first flew one 7 years later, was an absolute bitch that would have had me eliminated in less time than it takes to tell. In fact, all my American instructors turned out to be patient, conscientious men, whereas, possibly, one hopes, by some extraordinary coincidence, almost all my subsequent RAF flying instructors turned out to be exceedingly impatient hectoring tyrants who seemed to think that the only way to teach someone to fly was to shout at them.*

In describing unpopular barracks inspections at Camden, Pye expressed the view that they "kept us on our toes," and that was "extremely good for us."

During the five weeks before the end of September and the departure of Class SE-42-B, the members of Class SE-42-C followed the normal course of training, and eliminees departed for Maxwell Field singly or in small groups. Among the members who washed out of pilot training at Camden were Eric Harrison of Sunderland, County Durham; Ian B. Brown, a civil engineer from Bridge of Weir, Scotland; and Allan Grant of London. Allan Grant's wife and child had been bombed out of their apartment in London, so they came to the United States and joined him at Camden. When Grant was eliminated from pilot training, he and the others returned to Canada for reassignment to training as navigators.

After his arrival in Canada, Grant penned a short poem for the SE-42-C class magazine *Relax*, and mailed it back to the editors. In that verse entitled "To the Departed," the stoic Grant, who was obviously suffering as a result of having failed to qualify as a pilot, registered for posterity how it felt to an RAF student pilot to fail:

> *Unhappy we, and lack-a-day,*
> *Sackcloth and ashes scatter*
> *An ode I give you here, to us*
> *Whose dreams are all a-shatter.*
>
> *4000 miles to fail a course,*
> *Is surely fate most bitter,*
> *It is enough to shake and shock,*
> *Or paralize a "critter."*
>
> *"Relax," "Nose Down!" "Co-ordinate,"*
> *"Use rudder when you turn"*

"Keep looking round," "Fly with the tee"
"Oh will you never learn?"

We thank the noble band of men,
Our ever patient tutors,
Who truly worked like men possessed
To aviate our futures.

We tried our best to make the grade,
But it was not to be,
And now we've gone to learn,
To guide you home from Germany.

And so cheer-ho! to all you blokes,
We'll meet soon never fear,
And yours will be the privilege
Of paying for the beer!

It is presumed that Mrs. Grant and their three-year-old son joined Grant in Canada. When Class SE-42-C was elevated to senior-class status, LAC John H. Bracewell became cadet captain. Bracewell successfully completed pilot training, spent a year in the United States as an instructor at Cochran and Turner Fields and married a Florida girl. In 1944, Flight Lieutenant Bracewell died over Berlin.

The dispatcher at the Southern Aviation School registered stars by the names of students who were guilty of infractions on the flight line. The "awarding of stars" was a means of enforcing flight line regulations, and the ten-cent (later twenty-five-cent) "fines" for each infraction were pooled and used to supplement funds allocated by the company for each class's graduation party at Camden's Sarsfield Club.

In the course of the final five weeks of training, a few more RAF cadets departed, and other class members began to prepare their class magazine, which they entitled *Relax*. When the editors were gathering materials for their magazine, they thoughtfully asked the Reverend Maurice Clark, rector of Camden's Grace Episcopal Church, to write an afterword. In complying, the kindly rector wrote from the heart: "You have been in our homes and made us all the richer for your friendship. And the special word of ending is this—God be with you in all the days to come—and give you strength and courage equal to your mighty task."

In late September 1941, after Class SE-42-B graduates had departed Camden for Cochran Field, the surviving students of Class SE-42-C were joined by Class SE-42-D, which contained fifty UK students and thirty American aviation cadets.

In the style of the ancients, twenty-one-year-old LAC Kenneth Ord of SE-42-C, a geography graduate of Sheffield University, produced a clever and amusing "parable." In language reminiscent of the King James version of the Bible, he described the advent of war and detailed a few of the problems of adjusting to army air corps primary flying training. Travel from small-town Camden to the city of Columbia, South Carolina, the state capital, and its Jefferson Hotel is typical of similar travels from other small towns to the nearest cities:

Now it came to pass that the land of Germ did stir up strife on the earth and went to war with the land of Brit. And the leader of the Germites was Hit and the leader of the Brittites was Chur who was famed in all the world for he did smoke expensive weeds.

And the leader of the Brittites chose Raf to be one of his three chief warriors. And behold! Raf was given a blue mantel adorned with many brass buttons, at which people did marvel, saying, "Ho, this truly is to be a great tribe!"

And because of the strength of the warriors of Hit, Chur did send the children of Raf to the land of Usa, which was across the great waters, that they might learn to fly even as the birds of the air, in great numbers.

In the land of Usa, the children of Raf did many wondrous feats known as solo and ground loop, but in days to come some fell by the wayside and were sent back to the land of Can, there to become droppers of bombs or sweepers of hangars.

But many of the Raffittes flourished and grew strong in the city of Cam in the county of Carol, and did often visit the city of Colum, there to feast and dance at the house of Jeff who was a rich man.

Yet there were days when the Raffites did commit great sins called dustonlocker and dustunderbed, for which they were punished by long journeys in the small land known as Ramp.

And it came to pass that an evil king named Schof or Despat held much sway in the village of the Raffites, and many there were who called him Starmaker, because of the marvelous design he made of stars on a tablet, for which he taxed the Raffites heavily, calling out from his throne "a dime a time."

On the sabbath, in order to escape the wrath of the four overlords whom men called Hut, Two, Three, and Four, many of the Raffites visited the temple where the food served by the High Priest was famous through all the land.

But despite the trials and tribulations the hardy children of Raf finally returned to the country of Brit bearing with them silver wings on their robes that men might see that they were of the mighty tribe.

Then there was much rejoicing and feasting in the land, and the Raffites were glorified in the words of the scribes for many years.

Although Class SE-42-A had received its first five weeks of training alongside American Cadet Class SE-41-I, this new arrangement at Camden intentionally mixed British and American cadets and trained them to live and fly alongside each other.

In early November, when Class SE-42-C completed its primary flying course, thirty of its number had been eliminated or washed out of training and had returned to Canada via Maxwell Field for remustering to other duties. As with the two previous courses, the forty-seven surviving graduates boarded Greyhound buses and were transported to Cochran Field, Georgia.

In 1982, Joe Crossman of Coventry (SE-42-D) recalled his days at Camden and his initiation to flying:

We mixed well with the American boys and enjoyed our games periods where we taught the Americans our Rugby football, and they taught us theirs. There was one very black day [Wednesday, 29 October 1941] at Camden. We were standing on parade in front of the hangar watching one plane taking off, whilst another was coming in to land close by. They almost touched, and the plane taking off pulled away into a stall, dived into the ground, and burst into flames. The pilot, LAC George James Pritchard, died later in hospital. He was buried in the local cemetery and a large gathering of the townsfolk attended the funeral.

We were invited out at weekends, usually to church and lunch afterwards, then a drive out somewhere, on one occasion to a polo match. Towards the end of the course, Japan attacked Pearl Harbor. America was now at war themselves, and we could now wear our RAF uniforms.

The death of LAC Pritchard (SE-42-D) in Camden Hospital at 3:00 a.m. on Thursday, 30 October 1941, was the first death of a student pilot at the Southern Aviation School, and the tragedy had a traumatic effect on the students as well as the community.

The reaction of the people of Camden, spurred on by well-meaning individuals and by the local newspaper, was disturbing to many RAF staff officers and to students at Southern Aviation School. For some of the British visitors, the events surrounding the tragedy of Wednesday morning, 29 October 1941, at Woodward Airport was their first introduction to what British writer Jessica Mitford later described in *The American Way of Death*. Dr. Maurice Clarke, rector of Camden's Grace Episcopal Church, conducted the burial service with dignity, but virtually everything else surrounding the funeral took on the aspects of a staged production.

Excerpts from the *Camden Chronicle* of 31 October 1941, indicate how the tragedy and the plans for interment were reported:

> *The British lad...of Ashford, Kent, England will rest in ground hallowed by the dust of American heroes of the Revolution, the War Between the States, and the last world war.*
>
> *A guard of honor of twenty British cadets will accompany the body to its final resting place. A squad of American soldiers from Battery E, First Army, will fire a salute over the grave while the Field Artillery band from the Public Relations headquarters of the First Army will play the funeral dirge.*
>
> *The rites at the grave will be closed with the sounding of "taps" by a bugler from the First Army Public Relations Headquarters.*
>
> *Overhead, a formation of five planes, with the sixth, that of the dead cadet, missing, will fly [over] during the final rites.*
>
> *The entire personnel of the Southern Aviation School including the officers, clerical staff, instructors, mechanics, and cadets will attend the funeral services at the church and at the grave.*
>
> *The death of Cadet Pritchard cast a deep gloom over the school personnel and extended throughout the community. The British cadets by their fine personality and gentlemanly qualities, their intense devotion to their country and gracious acceptance of American ideas have won the deep respect, admiration, and affection of all Camden peoples.*
>
> *The news of the tragedy of Wednesday morning spread like wildfire through the city and community, and through the afternoon and evening the ever-recurrent inquiry on the streets was as to how Cadet Pritchard was faring. News of his death Thursday cast a pall of gloom over the city.*

The *Camden Chronicle*, which was issued on Friday, 7 November, confirmed that the ceremonies did indeed take place as described in the issue of the preceding week. When they learned of it later, the parents and relatives of the dead student undoubtedly appreciated the tribute to their son. British officials saw things differently.

There is no question that the editor and writers meant well and intended to express their respect not only for the dead youth but for Britain, the RAF and the British cause. However, overlooking the numerous type-setting and factual errors in the story, such emotionalism was alien to British culture and contrary to standard practice of the military services. From the perspective of American and British administrative officers, it may also have caused students still in training considerable anguish at a time when they needed to concentrate on their training. Some of the anxiety of British staff stemmed from embarrassment and from concern about too much publicity.

From experience, Royal Air Force officers and NCOs expected casualties (wastage) in flying training. In order to ease the pain of the loss of a loved one, it was at that time, and remains today, the British custom to pay one's respects briefly, adequately and finally, and to push on with stoic resolve. The British habit of reserve dictated that public emotional outpourings were to be avoided, that grief and other emotions are closely guarded and private. RAF staff were less than pleased because they feared excessive publicity about the RAF presence months before the United States entered the war. Publicity concerning British military training in the neutral United States before Pearl Harbor might touch off an isolationist reaction, which could damage the British cause and impair relations between the two countries.

In early December 1941, as Class SE-42-D made preparations to graduate, its members produced a mimeographed class book entitled *Primary Log*, and since theirs was a combined Anglo-American class, staff assignments were shared as equally as possible. Near the time for its graduation, when the Japanese attacked Pearl Harbor, the appropriateness of such a combined class project was underscored and resulted in a true alliance in common cause. Sounding the alliance theme firmly and solidly was Flight Lieutenant H. Edmund Taggart, RAF administrative officer who, in November 1941, had replaced Flight Lieutenant J. Leonard Keith, OBE. Keith had been transferred to the basic flying school at Macon, Georgia. LAC Walter Reginald "Mac" McEvoy, cadet captain, conveyed a similar message, as did the American civilian and military officers at the school. It was an appropriate time as well to recognize the new insignia of the Southeast Air Corps Training Center (SEACTC) with its motto, "Prepare for Combat."

Each of the three preceding RAF classes had been posted to Cochran Field, Georgia, for basic flying training. Most Camden-trained cadets successfully completed the basic flying course, and a Camden graduate was selected to serve as cadet major for each of the first three classes at Cochran Field. In an effort to assess the quality of training at the Georgia basic school and Gunter Field, Alabama, the only two Arnold Scheme basic flying schools that trained British cadets, Camden's Class SE-42-D graduates were posted to Gunter Field for their basic flying training. Of the Camden primary school's net intake of forty-six RAF cadets, thirteen were eliminated, one was killed in an accident, five were held over and twenty-seven graduated.

THE ALABAMA INSTITUTE OF AERONAUTICS
HARGROVE VAN DE GRAAF FIELD, TUSCALOOSA, ALABAMA, 42-A-42-D

The Alabama Institute of Aeronautics, the U.S. Army Air Forces Fifty-first Flying Training Detachment, was the oldest of the Arnold Scheme primary flying schools. It was established first as part of a national experiment in pilot training. Early in 1939, the Civil Aeronautics Authority (CAA) announced plans for implementing an experimental Civilian Pilot Training Program (CPTP) at ten widely scattered universities. When W.H. Nicol, president of the Tuscaloosa Chamber of Commerce, read of the plan, he contacted Oliver Parks, owner and proprietor of Parks Air College at East St. Louis, Illinois. Nicol asked Parks to establish a CPTP school for students of the University of Alabama at Tuscaloosa's municipal airport. Parks agreed to open such a flight school at the Tuscaloosa airdrome, and the CAA approved both the contractor and the airfield. Thus, the University of Alabama became the only university among many in the Southeastern United States selected at that time for a CPTP school.

In late February 1939, when Parks Air College staff arrived in the Alabama town, the Hargrove van de Graaf Airport was under construction on a large tract of land four and a half miles west of Tuscaloosa between the Black Warrior River and U.S. Highway 82. One large brick hangar was being built by the Works Progress Administration (WPA) on the edge of the landing ground. Within that single large building were facilities for offices, aircraft maintenance and operations, but the small special program for teaching university students to fly did not require very much space. By May 1939, the hangar was complete, and most of the young men who had enrolled in the trial CPTP had already become licensed pilots.

The success of the Civil Aeronautics Authority experiment led to an expanded pilot training program for civilian students. A large number of small colleges and universities were added to the CAA program, and pilot training was offered at small airports scattered over the United States. Impressed by the CAA's success, training officers of the army air corps identified and contacted the owners of the strongest and most financially stable proprietary flying schools in different regions of the country. Eight of these school operators were persuaded to sign contracts to train army air corps flying cadets.

Oliver Parks was one of the most well-known flying school operators in the United States. He had opened Parks Air College at East St. Louis, Illinois, in 1927 and had continued successful flying school operations even during the very lean years of the Great Depression. Within a brief time following the army air corps decision, Parks had signed contracts to operate two such pilot training schools, one as part of his Parks Air College at East St. Louis and the other at Tuscaloosa. However, unlike most other civil contractors, Park refused financial assistance from the Defense Plant Corporation and handled building and other costs in his own way. When Parks designated the latter school the Alabama Institute of Aeronautics and began to expand it into a larger contract flying school, he and his staff learned much about the Alabama town.

Tuscaloosa had two primary claims to fame: it had served for two decades—from 1826 to 1846—as the capital of the state of Alabama, and since 1831 it had been the location of the University of Alabama. In 1940, the town had a population of about 25,000, and the university enrolled approximately 5,000 students and employed around 350 faculty. The town itself lay concentrated on a plateau a few hundred yards east of the Black Warrior River. Contemporary maps show that the town's transportation needs were served by three railroad lines (Louisville & Nashville, Gulf & Mississippi and Southern), two state highways (6 and 13) and three United States Highways (11, 43 and 82). Although some coke furnaces, which were vital to war production, were soon to reopen nearby on the Black Warrior River, Tuscaloosa served primarily as an educational center and as a market town for the citizens of a vast farming and lumber district.

U.S. Highway 11 arched through the town from Birmingham, 55 miles to the northeast, and became University Boulevard. People traveling the 135 miles from Montgomery to Tuscaloosa in 1941–42 usually traveled northward via U.S. Highway 31 and westward on secondary roads via Montevallo or Helena to U.S. Highway 11, and then turned southwestward to Tuscaloosa. 1940 maps show that the main part of the town and the University of Alabama lay west of McFarland Boulevard, close by the river. Apparently, its streets were counted eastward from the river and its avenues southward from the university. U.S. Highway 82 ran through Tuscaloosa, and as it crossed over the Black Warrior River, it curved westward through and beyond the town of Northport and passed the entrance gates to the municipal airport.

As with other Southern market towns, Tuscaloosa's compact business district contained several hotels and restaurants, small department stores, five-and-ten-cent stores, specialty men's and women's clothing stores, drugstores, jewelry stores, photograph studios, seed and feed stores, automobile and insurance agencies and professional offices. The university was the town's cultural affairs center. Large numbers of wooden and brick Greek Revival houses with massive columns and other more modest dwellings with wide porches stood along the tree-lined streets of the town and among the brick buildings of the university. And in each district of the town small parks and the grounds of public and private buildings were landscaped with a variety of plants and trees, which produced a profusion of color during each season.

At Tuscaloosa's municipal airport, the contractor was apparently less concerned with beauty of surroundings than with profits. As a result of experiences during some very lean years, Parks and his staff were accustomed to deriving maximum value from every dollar expended. Parks and several other civilian contractors emphasized flying training and placed minimum emphasis on the quality of quarters and other amenities. Since the whole system of civilian contractors offering introductory flying to U.S. Army Air Corps flying cadets was new and experimental, officers of the Air Corps Training Center (ACTC) at Randolph Field, Texas, had given little thought to anything but flying instruction. During the early stages, these shortcomings did considerable harm to the training program, but other more serious problems emerged when flying training was expanded.

The lack of specific guidance from the ACTC, when combined with the contractor's compulsion for closely monitoring expenditures, ultimately led to conflict. The design and administrative shortcomings of the Alabama contract flying school resulted in its remaining very small in comparison with other schools whose contractors were more cooperative and built better facilities. In the long term, the conflict did greater harm to the reputation of the contractor than to the general program of civil contract training, but long before its operations became history, administrators of the civil contract school at Tuscaloosa gave headaches to numerous young army air corps supervisors.

Flying training at the Alabama Institute of Aeronautics commenced on 1 July 1939, and as more students were added, the contractor was compelled to build more facilities. Barracks No. 1 consisted of eighteen rooms measuring ten by twenty feet, and each room was equipped to house four men. Large rooms measuring twenty-one by twenty-five feet were located at each end of the barracks, and these were intended to house an additional ten men each, thus giving the barracks a capacity of ninety-two students. Since early classes were very tiny (thirty-five men each), the two end rooms were used for lectures and for recreation. Except for that single barracks near the flight line, which was completed on 1 July 1939, the day on which army air corps flying cadets arrived, the entire school was housed in the one huge brick hangar.

In the first-floor rooms located in the four corner towers and along the sides of the massive WPA-built hangar were offices for the contractor, army air corps officers, a stock room and two classrooms. At the rear of the hangar were two offices, one of which was used for civilian instructors, the other as a cadet ready room and a large supply room. The dining hall, medical detachment and one classroom were situated on the second floor of the hangar. In 1939, these small rooms in the hangar were barely adequate, and there was concern that the hangar itself might not be adequate for maintaining the military trainer aircraft.

When army air corps Lieutenant Colonel George W. Hastey of the Inspector General's Department visited the field for an inspection tour, he cited numerous deficiencies. Since the airfield was too narrow and congested for use as a two-stage airfield, he believed it to be unsafe for student use, and the one auxiliary field inadequate and unused. Although he was able to praise one hangar classroom equipped with chairs, Hastey found others either devoid of proper equipment or too small. The inspecting officer was also critical of the crowded conditions in the barracks and the inadequate furniture. Indicating that the dormitory had cost $13,000 to build and that the students paid $20 per month for a room, Colonel Hastey calculated that with four students per room in fourteen rooms, the annual rent would be $13,440 on an investment of $13,000, a sizeable return.

Inspection of the dining hall also revealed a series of inadequacies. Hastey considered both the kitchen and dining room too small. In addition, the kitchen did not have adequate refrigeration, it had no dishwasher or other "labor-saving devices" and the food was "inadequate as to quality and quantity." The colonel also found the school short of supplies and in need of an additional flying instructor.

Hastey insisted that the WPA-built permanent brick hangar could not continue to serve the complete needs of the school. As a result, the contractor developed plans for building additional wooden buildings with asbestos siding and linoleum floors and aligning them with the first separate barracks building along a semicircular drive approaching the flight line from Highway 82. The new kitchen/dining hall was completed in September 1939, and the contractor's staff was able to prove itself. One night after dinner was served, stoves, equipment and tables and chairs were moved overnight from the second-floor rooms of the hangar and were installed in the new dining hall in time for breakfast to be cooked and served next morning.

Before that demonstration of efficiency took place, a disaster befell the school. In August 1939, the water system at the Alabama Institute of Aeronautics was analyzed as contaminated. When the contractors were indefinite about when the proper repairs would be completed, the air corps supervisor acted quickly. He ordered the students moved to hotels and boardinghouses in Tuscaloosa. Most of the army air corps flying cadets were housed in the Burchfield Hotel in Tuscaloosa, while thirty were billeted in five boardinghouses.

The cadets continued to take their meals, ground and flight training at the airfield. They paid their own housing costs with army air corps allowances, and the school provided transportation to and from the airfield. Since the contractor was losing money with this arrangement, he was spurred to have the water system at the flying school brought up to standard. Later that same month, air corps supervising officers cited the contractor for failing to provide a much-needed auxiliary field. With two classes in training, if both used only the main airdrome, safety standards would be compromised, and confusion would result. An auxiliary field would allow instructors to separate early familiarization flying training from the later precision and solo stages.

In May 1940, when the army air corps increased its pilot production goal to seven thousand pilots annually, planning projections indicated that in order to train that many pilots, the USAAC had to double the number of civil contract primary schools. Civilian contractors were asked to double the size of their existing schools and to open an additional school the same size. Despite problems at its two contract schools, the Parks organization had a very good flying training record. Therefore, Parks was permitted to enlarge its two original schools (the ones in Alabama and Illinois) and to develop two more, one in Mississippi and another in Missouri.

During 1940, construction at the Tuscaloosa school included Barracks No. 2, additions to the dining hall and a separate academic building. Barracks No. 2 was a two-bay structure, each of which measured forty-six by fifty feet and housed forty-four men per bay. The academic building, which included several classrooms and offices, was completed in sixty days. Once these new buildings were in place, only the medical detachment remained on the second floor of the brick hangar. The tower rooms of that edifice were now taken over by the instructors, and the former instructor ready room at the rear of the hangar was relinquished to the maintenance department.

Despite the efforts of army air corps supervisors to enforce the provisions of successive government contracts at the Alabama Institute of Aeronautics, higher authority would not support their recommendations. Apparently, when frequent conflicts occurred between civil and military authority, they normally resulted in the transfer of the air corps supervisor rather than in any punitive action against the civilian contractor. With few exceptions, the physical facilities of the Alabama Institute of Aeronautics never really measured up to most of the other civil contract schools. However, the school was partially able to compensate for such shortcomings by employing many first-rate flying and ground instructors and maintenance personnel, most of whom were graduates of Parks Air College in East St. Louis, Illinois.

However slow in doing so, the flying school administrators did eventually make many improvements to the main airdrome. They also developed three auxiliary fields and one satellite airfield. Auxiliary Field No. 1, later called Moody Field (not to be confused with the USAAF advanced flying school at Valdosta, Georgia), was located four miles east of the main airdrome, and had been completed shortly after the August 1939 inspector general's (IG) inspection. Auxiliary Field No. 2 (Rice Field), located west of the main airdrome, was added in March 1940. In January 1941, a third auxiliary field was developed four miles southeast of the main airdrome (it was later called Knauer Field in honor of Carl Knauer, a civilian instructor who was killed in an aircraft accident).

In 1942, a dual-purpose auxiliary field was added. Not only was it the fourth auxiliary field, but it was also a satellite airfield that was equipped with a hangar, a stage house and an operations building. It was well equipped so that a short flying course could be provided for members of the University of Alabama's Fifty-seventh College Training Detachment (CTD), the equivalent of Britain's later established flight grading schools. The CAA-controlled detachments used Piper Cubs or other small aircraft to provide fifteen to twenty-five hours of flight instruction for potential U.S. Army and U.S. Navy student pilots attending colleges or universities. Hundreds of these units existed nationwide; they helped to reduce the number of washouts among American cadets, and they also encouraged the training of thousands of primary flying instructors among men and women who could not qualify for active service. Although the American practice probably caused or encouraged the RAF to establish flight-grading courses in the United Kingdom, the American schools did not grade pupils pilot, navigator or bomb aimer (PNB) as the RAF did.

From the beginning of operations in 1939, air corps officers had rated the quality of the Tuscaloosa school's flying instruction as excellent, and the cooperation of the school's civil administration as miserable. Early air corps complaints had centered on contamination of the water supply, a poorly equipped kitchen, overcrowded conditions in barracks and inadequate toilet facilities. By June 1941, most of these problems had been at least partially addressed and, except for sparse recreation facilities, army air corps inspectors rated the Alabama Institute of Aeronautics as "adequate" or "barely adequate." Even though the Alabama school was thus damned with faint praise, the facilities of the Alabama Institute of Aeronautics were considered superior to similar ones developed and used for aircrew training by most other air forces of the world.

Between July 1939 and spring 1941, primary training lasted twelve weeks, and the Alabama Institute of Aeronautics enrolled 287 army air corps flying cadets and 33 student officers in eight classes (Classes 40-A through 40-H). In 1940–41, the school enrolled 508 army air corps flying cadets and 48 student officers in nine classes (41-A through 41-I). Only the last two classes (41-H and 41-I) were trained under the reduced ten-week primary flying training syllabus. Although precise records could not be found to indicate attrition, it is assumed that the school followed the same standards as others and graduated approximately 60 percent of the numbers enrolled.

That local people took little interest in "goings on" at the airport during the first two years of its operation may well reveal that, despite its university, Tuscaloosa remained a closed society with all of the faults that description implies. However, the flying school's administration, which was composed mostly of Yankees from the East St. Louis school, either did little to develop good public relations or failed in their efforts. Between July 1941 and August 1944, the Alabama Institute of Aeronautics was assigned to train British and French student pilots exclusively. That assignment may have resulted from failure of the Parks organization to cooperate fully with USAAF supervisors.

Escorted by RCAF Flying Officer J.D. Murray, sixty-nine of the seventy members of Class SE-42-A arrived in Tuscaloosa on Sunday, 8 June 1941. With the arrival of British student pilots, public interest in AIA and its personnel changed dramatically. RAF students were very positive in their comments about school facilities; USAAF officers were less so. Since most white people in the region could trace at least one line of their ancestry to the British Isles, they were anxious to meet the British cadets. The RAF lads who came among them were just "kids" far from home and in need of kind words, good food and hospitality. In addition to citizens of Tuscaloosa and Birmingham, and those of Boliger, Moundville and other nearby towns, families of faculty and staff members at the University of Alabama opened their hearts and doors to the young Britons.

Although many ill-informed people believed erroneously that the British people were starving to death under wartime privation, they were sincere in their concern and their desire to help in any way possible. Although they could not directly assist their distant "British cousins" except through Bundles for Britain or other similar organizations or means, they could make life more comfortable for the young men who had come so far to train in that most dangerous of occupations, flying airplanes. The Littles, the Wilsons and dozens of other Tuscaloosa families "adopted" British cadets and wrote to their parents, wives or girlfriends.

In most instances, the young Britons were simply accepted as family members—they attended to chores when they visited, went with the family to church or other activities and often attended high school, college or university graduation ceremonies of family members. Local citizens also learned that the "British boys" had little money and, in the case of the school and airfield located several miles west of Tuscaloosa, there were very few facilities for recreation, and limited transportation to and from the city.

Regularly, parents drove out or their sons or daughters were sent in the family automobile to pick up the young men at the entrance roadway to the airfield. Gruff, taciturn fathers often handed over the keys to the family auto or quietly and without fanfare tucked into a gray or blue coat pocket the occasional five-dollar bill that might be useful for some purpose. Officers of the University of Alabama also made the institution's swimming pool and other facilities available to the young visitors.

Most of all, despite considerable jealousy on the part of local young men, the less shy British cadets enjoyed meeting the "smashing young ladies" who were either college students or seniors in high school. Although there may have been an occasional doting mother who daydreamed that a mature daughter might capture one of the young Britons as a husband, that was not even a consideration of most local people who shared their homes, time and food with the British cadets. In the spirit of the renowned Southern hospitality, American families were anxious to make the young men feel at home.

All features of training proceeded steadily; LAC Donald D. Knott of Redhill, Surrey, was the first British student to solo at Tuscaloosa. Although the RAF student pilots were accustomed to greater freedom, and many of them felt that training consumed too much of their time, most did have sufficient time and money to visit Tuscaloosa, Birmingham and other neighboring towns. These limited travels stimulated further interest in activities at the Tuscaloosa airport, which citizens of the region had not indicated before.

Although further confirmation was unavailable, the USAAF unit history of the school indicated that a conflict developed on the school's flight line between the British students and civilian instructors. According to that document, the clash proved difficult to resolve until Flight Lieutenant John G. Garthwaite, the first RAF administrative officer at the station, was replaced by Flight Lieutenant Arthur T. Grime. The unit history indicates that Garthwaite, who had arrived in Tuscaloosa in June 1941, was accused of siding with the British students in rejecting American training methods. It may be, however, that he was shifted to another station primarily because it was standard practice to reassign RAF liaison officers every six months or on being promoted.

Another clash that the members of RAF Class SE-42-A could not avoid was with the American aviation cadets of Class SE-41-I. As David Munson of Harrow, Middlesex, described it, "We were all very accustomed to, and expected, discipline, but not submission to petty college foibles and deference to fellow cadets who wished to impose their upper class status on us." Following serious clashes, Brigadier General Weaver was said to have visited Tuscaloosa to address the cadets, and "both sides gave a little and peace was restored." As Munson summarized the series of incidents, "we learned to respect and enjoy each other—very valuable." Of course, there would be other clashes, but communications were improving with time and experience.

Communication problems between American cadets and flight instructors on the one hand, and British students on the other, appear to have been resolved by patience, time, the assignment of RAF officers to the school and the introduction of many RAF manuals and posters. Other means of bringing about better relations at the Tuscaloosa school included after-hours debates and discussions that compared American and British methods and equipment. Discussions of the war and other current events were also introduced, and proved especially effective after the addition of a shortwave radio set that allowed the students to listen to BBC broadcasts.

Class SE-42-A shared the first five weeks of its ten-week course with Class SE-41-I. Around 15 July, Class SE-41-I graduated and departed for a basic flying school. Three days later, Class

SE-42-B arrived, and the school became totally British for a while. Class SE-42-A now became the senior class, and cadet officers were appointed. LAC Ernest R. Whincup of Bishop Auckland, County Durham, and a veteran RAF fitter, became first captain; Peter S. Kyd of Essex became captain of one flight; and Kenneth Watkins of Swansea, South Wales, was promoted to captain of the second flight.

In addition, other men who were named cadet lieutenants included Bruce R. Lucas of Buckingham, a veteran RAF clerk and an ideal adjutant; and Henry P. Lee Warner of Dorset, who had attended Oxford University and had been employed by Imperial Airways. The remaining cadet lieutenants included P. Norman Sayer of Leeds; Thomas Lowe of Essex, who had been educated in the United States; and Stanley Holden from Harrow, a former teacher.

Near the end of the course, the members of Class SE-42-A published a student magazine entitled *Fins and Flippers*. In that thin mimeographed volume, they paid tribute to the officers and instructors, to the school and to Southern hospitality. "See Sub-Ell," the ground instructor who often referred to the coefficient of lift (C/L), came in for some good-natured ribbing. In expressing appreciation for kindness, the people of Tuscaloosa were listed first for opening "their homes to us." Thanks were also extended to the University of Alabama, which "extended the use of its swimming pool" and arranged dances and parties especially for the RAF. The town of Columbus, Mississippi, was singled out for providing "a very pleasant weekend for us." In describing off-post hospitality, they listed a catalogue of memorable foods such as fried chicken, watermelon, ice cream, barbecue and peaches.

When the staff of *Fins and Flippers* wrote potted biographies of class members, they took great care to use the maximum amount of sarcasm so as to elicit the greatest number of laughs. LAC Leonard G. Peacock was said to have "spent twice as long on the telephone as on the flight line." LAC John Pratt was said to be "passionately fond of Chamber music and dive bombing anglers." There were rumors about local infatuations and about farmers, fishermen and drivers along country roads suddenly finding themselves being dived on by the yellow-and-blue Stearman biplanes.

In his "Odd Ode to A.I.A.," LAC David Munson described a Sunday visit to Tuscaloosa, the evening after and the following day. In doing so, he does battle with the oft-heard admonition to "Get on the ball, Mister!" After reading Munson's clever *Fins and Flippers* account of student antics on the ground and in the air, it is clear why this admonition was heard so often by most student pilots undergoing training. It also becomes clear why primary ground and flying instructors led such hectic lives. In ones and twos or larger groups, they usually traveled via Maxwell Field, Alabama, to Canada to be remustered to other duties or to continue pilot training. At the end of Class 42-A's primary flying course at Tuscaloosa, nineteen students had been eliminated from pilot training, three students were held over to a subsequent class and forty-eight students graduated and were posted to the USAAF basic flying course at Gunter Field, near Montgomery, Alabama.

Class SE-42-B, another seventy-member class, arrived at the Tuscaloosa railway station on Sunday, 18 July 1941. One week after their arrival, the students saw some distinguished visitors. Major General George H. Brett, new air corps chief, and Air Commodore George C. Pirie, MC, DFC, British air attaché, accompanied Captain Harold Balfour, MC, MP, British undersecretary of state for air, in his rapid tour of flying schools. These officers inspected the station, and Balfour spoke to the students, assuring them of a British victory.

Within a few days after the visitors left, Robert W. Johnson of Liverpool became the first member of that second RAF class to solo. Johnson later gained a reputation for low flying over

Alabama farms. In his class potted biography in the September 1941 issue of *Fins and Flippers*, he was reported to have originally intended "to become a trader on the African coast, but he came to Tuscaloosa and commenced farming in a P.T. 17." In that same issue of the student magazine, Johnson wrote an article entitled "Forty Years On," in which he confirmed his "farming" practices and anticipated looking back after four decades to his own primary flying experience and that of his classmates.

After undergoing ten weeks of flying training, the surviving members of Class SE-42-A departed for basic flying school, and Class SE-42-B was elevated to senior-class status. Cadet officers appointed from that second RAF class included Cadet First Captain Keith Higham of Blackburn, Lancashire, and Cadet Second Captain or Adjutant William K. Ashley of Wallesey, Cheshire. Cadet lieutenants included Ralph Brown of Bishop Auckland, County Durham; Robert A. Appleby of New Allerton; Eric Eastwood of Blackburn, Lancashire and Haileybury College; and Michael L.B. Frankson of London.

In *Fins and Flippers*, the staff took amusing and sarcastic shots in describing each other in terse biographies. Thin Henry Brown of Leeds was described as "seen when not looked at sideways." Heftier John F. Cunningham of Surbiton, Surrey, was said to have stood upon a "Speak Your Weight" machine, which responded, "One at a time, please!" Douglas Crowther of Darlington and South Africa was said to have worked in the Air Ministry, after which "he decided to enter the practical side of the business, so he joined the RAF." Frank S. Higginbottom of rainy Manchester was said to like Alabama—"the rain reminds him of home."

The practice of administering multiple choice quizzes in virtually every ground school subject was a baffling practice and one of the great mysteries to British student pilots. Unless they were asked to write an essay on a given subject, most of them did not feel that they had been "examined." By way of explaining the system while at the same time expressing his true feelings about such quizzes and other irritants, LAC Humphrey R. Green produced a multiple choice quiz in the class magazine. "For the best results," he wrote, "we continue to recommend the well known pin-sticking or pencil-jabbing system." Author Green, formerly of the CID Branch of the Metropolitan Police (Scotland Yard), undoubtedly had a great deal of fun in the process.

In that same magazine issue, John T. Evans of Class SE-42-B recorded for posterity a "slightly" exaggerated account of a check ride with Nelson Reavis, chief pilot at Tuscaloosa. Evans's delightful, humorous account in verse indicated how it was possible to be eliminated from pilot training. At about the time Evans was concerned with washing out of pilot training, Class SE-42-C arrived at the Tuscaloosa train station from RCAF No. 1 Manning Depot at Toronto. Since additional barracks had been added at the Alabama school, instead of the usual seventy class members, the Class SE-42-C intake rose to ninety-one, a 30 percent increase.

William Andrew Coffee of Wallesey in the Wirral Peninsula of Cheshire, Ronald Furness of Lancashire and Kenneth I. Pearson from Finchley, London, were among the members of Class SE-42-C who arrived at Alabama Institute of Aeronautics around 25 August 1941. Reflecting on his American experience, Pearson described the close ties that developed between American hosts and the British cadets. They were maintained over the years, "in my own case by the correspondence which was maintained between Mrs. Annie Evans, a widow of Montgomery, Alabama, and my family for over thirty years, until she died at age 87."

On 10 September, LAC William Natrass, a native of Newcastle-on-Tyne and former master at the Gosforth School, was injured when his trainer crashed at Foster Field, but he survived the accident. Natrass was restored to pilot training and completed it successfully with Class SE-42-D.

In late September 1941, when Class SE-42-B's forty-seven graduates departed for Gunter Field, Class SE-42-C moved to senior-class status and the ninety-five members of Class SE-42-D arrived in early October and commenced training as the junior class at Tuscaloosa. In November 1941, when SE-42-C completed primary flying training, thirty-five of their number had been eliminated, three were held over and fifty-five graduated to basic flying school.

Upon arrival from Canada in early October 1941, members of Class SE-42-D immediately commenced flying training. As soon as they were able to leave the station on weekends, they were introduced to the civilian population. Naturally drawn by the city, many men gravitated to Birmingham and the hospitality of families there, while others enjoyed Tuscaloosa and the small towns of the area. Many RAF men had their first introduction to American college sports competition when they were able to attend some of the games played by the University of Alabama's Crimson Tide football team.

When they discovered the sorority girls in the Western Annex and other girls in the University's Tutwiler Hall and Colonial Hall, many others preferred to ignore football. On station, members of the new class were caught up in the training regimen and concern about surviving and winning their wings. They quickly discovered that discipline was fairly strict, and that inspections could result in their being penalized with mind- and foot-deadening tours on the ramp. However, in October, conditions changed. The wounds resulting from clashes between earlier classes and the RAF students had healed, and hazing was minimal.

In recalling his own days in training at Tuscaloosa, LAC Denys Ding of Class SE-42-D, who had almost traveled around the world to be trained as an RAF pilot, made some telling points:

> *The impact of America on some of the RAF boys was quite stunning. It was I think in inverse proportion to the amount of time they had spent outside their own tight little environment back home. Not unnatural and in anyway confined to a very small minority. They just wanted to get back to the U.K. A large number were shaken by the peacetime approach to training in the Army Air Corps though some of this "bull" had been worn away by previous RAF classes by the time we got to Tuscaloosa. And we wore away a bit more. Open toilets kept quite a few constipated for awhile. Lower Class customs were resented as entirely unnecessary—we had a serious job to do—what was all this school boy nonsense?*
>
> *Seriously resented by some who knew little of local problems was being instructed on how to treat "Negras." This was too much of a challenge for some of the fellows, and the first thing they did as a result was to frat[ernize] like mad. And they made some good friends as a result. In the overall picture, these things all became very minor matters. We soon settled in and the vast majority of us thoroughly enjoyed ourselves, and I can't overemphasize that. It was a great experience.*

As with members of each RAF pilot trainee class, most of the British students were pleased by the reasonableness of the AIA staff's Notes Preliminary to Beginning of Flying Training and irritated by USAAF aviation cadet regulations and rules for each arriving new class.

Among the rules set forth as required of all lower classmen at the Alabama Institute of Aeronautics (during their first five weeks of flight training), and often referred to as "bullshit" by British student pilots, were contained in Memorandum No. 2 of 13 September 1941, entitled Lower Class Customs:

1. Lower Classmen will use the expression "No Excuse, Sir," in explaining an offense or delinquency in case there was no relevant reason. The expression will not be used, however, when some explanation is necessary in order that the matter in question may be understood.

2. Lower Classmen will address Upper Classmen as "Mr.," and refer to Lower Classmen as "Mr.," when speaking to an Upper Classman or an officer. In no case will the RAF rank be used as a title. Title or rank of officers and non-commissioned officers of the Army will always be used.

3. Lower Classmen will not converse in the Mess Hall. They will sit "At Ease" during the meal. This position will be one which is without strain, but does not permit gazing about the Mess Hall or placing the elbows or arms on the table. Lower Classmen will leave Mess Hall in pairs.

4. Lower Classmen will not talk in the barracks area or Mess Hall area when going to or returning from formation.

5. Lower Classmen will walk in a military manner at all times and will not loiter in the hallways or area.

6. Lower Classmen will salute Senior Flying Cadet Officer of the Day and all other Flying Cadet Officers.

7. Lower Classmen will wear goggles around their necks at flight formation and at the line until they have soloed.

8. Lower Classmen, when leaving their barracks, will be in proper uniform at all times, except when participating in athletics.

9. Lower Classmen will leave their barracks in police inspection at all times.

10. Lower Classmen will not speak above a conversational tone in the barracks.

Learning to fly was the goal of every cadet, British or American, so they learned quickly to tolerate almost anything to attain that goal, but they did not have to like it. The redeeming feature of American training for RAF student pilots was that they made numerous great friends among civilians in towns near airfields where they trained.

In October, the Tuscaloosa flying school received a visit by another group of RAF and USAAF officials. Concerned over the very high wastage among members of the first four Arnold Scheme classes, Air Marshal A.G.R. Garrod, air member for training (AMT), visited Canada and several Arnold Scheme schools prior to attending a training conference at Maxwell Field. Garrod and the other officers were impressed with the 150 students at Tuscaloosa, dressed in their RAF blue uniforms, marching snappily past a line of Stearman PT-17 trainers and the reviewing stand. In addressing the large group of British students, Air Marshal Garrod "reminded us that the training we were receiving in the States by far exceeded anything we could have hoped to receive in England." Following an inspection of the flying school, the party flew to Maxwell Field to examine numerous questions as to how to reduce the number of RAF student washouts in the primary flying schools.

When in late October orders came down from Washington and Maxwell Field that all student pilots would be called "cadets," and the British students could wear their blue RAF uniforms off-post, it was a happy day at all six of the Arnold Scheme primary flying schools. At Tuscaloosa, lifting the uniform ban was regarded as a special event that resulted in a tremendous boost in morale. The cadets were proud of their distinctive and well-tailored blue woolen uniforms, and they enjoyed the swagger of RAF foot drill. As a result, when the entire student population was invited to participate in Tuscaloosa's Armistice Day Parade, the British cadets were delighted to be able to demonstrate their "spit and polish" to friends and acquaintances.

On Tuesday morning, 11 November at 9:00 a.m., a fleet of taxis began to transport the two hundred RAF cadets to the parade rendezvous point on University Avenue. At 10:30, the Tuscaloosa High School band stepped out and began the march. Just behind them in the place of honor as the first marching unit was the RAF contingent. Despite the fact that the runaway beat of the high school band climbed to about 150 steps per minute, the steel-tapped RAF-issue boots made it possible for the British students to hold their formation.

With arms swinging to the front at shoulder level and to the rear at waist level, they marched proudly, and their precision met with cheers from civilians along the parade route. The parade marched quickly down University Avenue to the center of town, turned off Broad Street around the flagpole and continued along Greensboro Avenue. Shortly before 11:00 a.m., the marching units turned right onto Eighth Street and halted before a church for the traditional period of silence. It was a solemn occasion, and it also marked a Royal Air Force triumph.

Cadets Ronald H. Simmons and Kenneth Green described meeting and having Sunday dinner with the Reverend R.S. Watson, rector of the Tuscaloosa Episcopal church. They described how Reverend Watson wanted to establish a club in Tuscaloosa in which the RAF cadets might find relaxation and entertainment instead of wandering the city streets. Simmons and Green spoke with their colleagues at the flying school, and the RAF students approved of the club wholeheartedly. Shortly thereafter, the British Cadet Club was established behind the 'Bama Theater, and remained active and busy until the final British cadets of Class SE-43-B graduated in February 1943.

When Class SE-42-D reached senior-class status, appointed cadet officers included Cadet Captain Robert G.H. Weighell of Cheshire and Cadet Lieutenants Denys Ding of China and Clifford J.C. "Johnnie" Manning of Barbados. Among other members of Class SE-42-D were Albert E.H. Ayres of London, who had been a meat importer, and Harold H. "Sonny" Lawrence from Shanghai, China, who was said to speak four Chinese dialects and who was described as "a member of the Corn Cutters Club." Lawrence was also reputed to have made "a real forced landing 23 miles away" and "still talks about the farmer's daughter."

The class could claim several distinctions. Stan Kirtley, Laurence Davies, G.N. Stephenson and Denis Steeper were the four men who had served as aircrew wireless operators and were considered among the wilder members of the class. Kenneth Chivers of Harrow, former Junior Boxing Champion, was married, and since his wife was expecting their first baby in England, his classmates always knew when he received a letter from her. (Later, while Chivers was undergoing basic flying training at Gunter Field, his wife gave birth to twins.) Among the RAF cadets who had resided outside the United Kingdom, P. Chillcott, Bryan Robinson and Edward Lindsell had lived and worked in Argentina before joining the RAF.

Near the end of their course, the members of Class SE-42-D organized an editorial board to publish their edition of the class magazine. K.E. Layton-Bennett of Barnet, Hertfordshire, served as editor and publicity manager; the popular pianist and former wireless operator Stan Kirtley of Bournemouth was assistant editor and business manager; and Denis Steeper of Liverpool, another of the four wireless operators in the class, served as photographic editor.

Regardless of criticisms leveled at the administration of the Alabama Institute of Aeronautics, its flying department was deemed excellent because of the quality of its flying instruction.

Conscientious efforts were made to assist the school's instructors to examine their instructional techniques and to seek to improve them. When unit histories were being prepared in 1942 and subsequent years, flying instructors were urged to talk about their jobs and their students.

These experienced pilots were generally critical of the lack of mechanical sense displayed by many British students. Joe Sierra, the popular flight commander, and other instructors felt that the British cadets "lacked judgement of speed, distance, and depth. It was difficult to explain why a carburetor did not work while flying in an inverted position, why the wing might come off in too steep a dive; or what made planes fly. They had to learn most of these things in practice." The instructors also learned that because of the British students' "disregard for rules," it was necessary to fly dual during the last two hours of flying at the end of the course.

In describing the RAF students' disregard for rules, the unit history was specific:

> British cadets also lacked air discipline. One buzzed a highway and caused two trucks to collide. One flew so low over a Tuscaloosa swimming pool that swimmers had to submerge to avoid being hit by the propeller. There were tales of flying under bridges, dog-fighting over Tuscaloosa, losing upper wings through buzzing in an inverted position, and numerous incidents of bouncing their wheels on the highway in front of vehicles. Not all of them were eccentric—on the whole, they were good flyers. They had nerve and a certain calmness, which made them great once they got into combat. They had no standing rules, as does the American Air Corps, and did not learn as quickly as an equal group of American cadets, but once they settled down, they learned quickly.

Apparently, the practices that Major Robert Smith-Barry and his Gosport School had instilled in RAF pilots during 1917–18 were still alive within RAF students in 1941. Since very few members of the early Arnold Scheme classes had been near an airplane, and few had ever ridden in one, the question remains as to where the RAF cadets learned to perform such "violations" of air discipline?

A possible answer to this question was provided by former Cadet Laurence Davies of Weymouth, England, and Class SE-42-D:

> The flying instructors were civilian pilots, although the testing was carried out by Air Corps officers. My instructor was a real character of a man. Apparently, he had been a circus pilot and there were stories of him flying under bridges, riding on the wings of planes and other hair-raising exploits. His name was Jimmy Sproule, and his face had a perpetual twitch. I remember clearly his reaction when we were introduced and he learned, in response to his inquiry, that I had never been off the ground and could not even drive a car. "Horseshit," he exclaimed (that was his favourite expression), "well, I guess you can at least ride a bicycle?" Anyway we got along quite well, and I was allowed to fly solo in a Stearman PT-17 after ten hours instruction.

Davies continued flying until he was given a final primary school flight check after having logged fifty-six hours. Unfortunately, the check pilot felt that he lacked sufficient mechanical ability to fly military aircraft, so he was eliminated from pilot training. Subsequently, Davies joined one of his Weymouth friends, Clifford Austin, in Canada, and they both remustered for training in Florida as wireless operators/air gunners.

In each of the class books at the Tuscaloosa school, light references are made to the Ground Looper's Club and the Corn Cutter's Club and to serious airplane accidents as well. From these references, it is possible to understand why the accident and elimination rates climbed at Tuscaloosa and at other Arnold Scheme primary schools. Since Stearman PT-17 No. 200, later No. 300, was used by the USAAF officers for the final sixty-hour flight check, that aircraft was called the "washing machine" and became an institution at the Tuscaloosa primary school. In that same issue of *Fins and Flippers*, Stanley Whitehead of Middleton, Lancashire, provided a verse description of the check aircraft in action.

Ultimately, 38 members of SE-42-D were eliminated, 3 were held over for further training and 57 graduated and were posted to a basic flying school. Of a net intake of 323 RAF pilot trainees in the first four RAF classes at the Alabama Institute of Aeronautics, 207 pilots graduated and 116 were eliminated and sent via Maxwell Field to Canada to be remustered to other duties.

Several of the outstanding RAF pilots trained at Tuscaloosa were asked to serve as flying instructor/check pilots. There were others from earlier courses, but Class 42-D graduates who were commissioned and ultimately served as flight instructors were cadet officers Weighell, Manning and Ding. All three of the pilot officers served six months in American primary schools as check pilots. Ding and Manning were assigned to their primary alma mater, Alabama Institute of Aeronautics, and Weighell was posted to Darr Aero Tech, Albany, Georgia. As a form of reverse lend-lease, outstanding British graduates of the South Carolina, Georgia and Florida primary schools also furnished instructor/check pilots for service in USAAF flight schools beginning in February 1942.

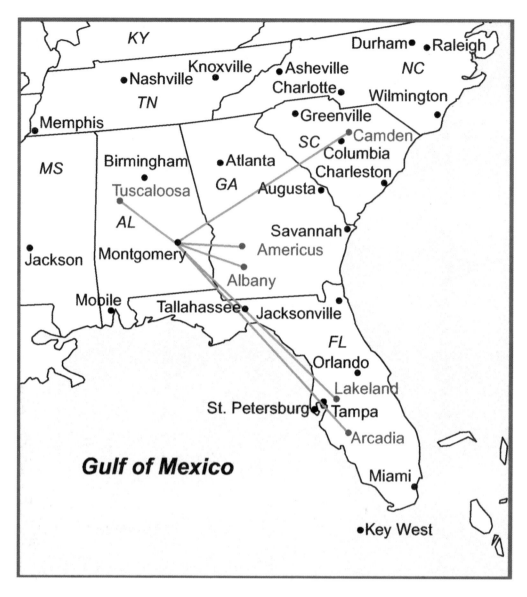

Map of acclimatization training at Maxwell Field, Alabama, to six primary flying schools. *Courtesy of C.D. Guinn.*

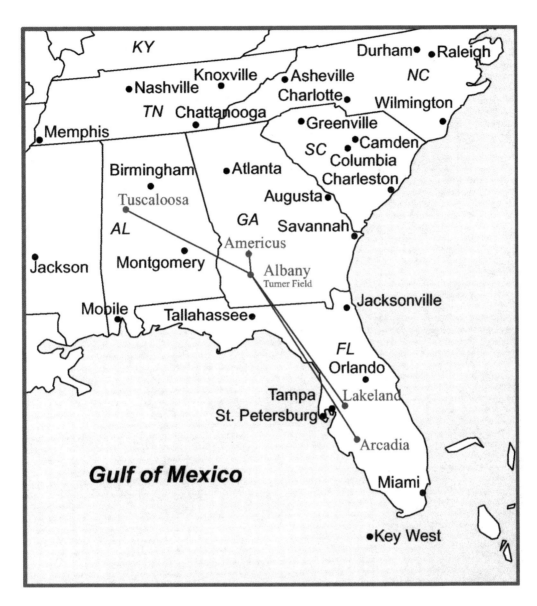

Map of acclimatization training at Turner Field, Albany, Georgia, to five primary flying schools. *Courtesy of C.D. Guinn.*

RAF funeral procession at Oakwood Cemetery Annex, Montgomery, Alabama. *Courtesy of the SEACTC.*

RAF cadets boarding the bus at Maxwell Field, Alabama, 1941. *Courtesy of R. Farrow.*

RAF and French graves in Oakwood Cemetery Annex, Montgomery, Alabama. *Courtesy of the SEACTC.*

Aerial photo of Pan American flying boat base, Dinner Key, Coral Gables, Florida. *Courtesy of Arthur Morris.*

Sikorski four-engine amphibian flying boat at Dinner Key, Florida. *Courtesy of W.G. Bailey.*

42/4 CLASS CADETS

Request the Pleasure of the Company of

at their

GRADUATION DANCE
(Formal)
Country Club   =   Coral Gables
Tuesday, June 30th, 1942   .   .   .   10 p. m. = 2 a. m.

Pan American navigation class's invitation to graduation, 1942. *Courtesy of D. Howell.*

Alabama State Capitol, Goat Hill, Montgomery, Alabama. *Courtesy of Jean Clark.*

RAF cadet formation, Maxwell Field, Alabama. *Courtesy of J. Clark.*

Wing Commander H.A.V. Hogan, DFC, SRAFAO, 1941–42. *Courtesy of V. Hogan.*

John and Jean Clark, Montgomery, Alabama, 1943. *Courtesy of Jean Clark.*

Vultee BT-13 and Stearman PT-17 trainer before hangar, Lakeland, Florida. *Courtesy of F.N. Plum.*

Helen Keller, Major Cumming, MO, and RAF cadets, Lakeland, Florida. *Courtesy of G.G.A. Whitehead.*

Barracks at Lakeland, Florida. *Courtesy of F.N. Plum.*

RAF cadets in blue uniforms marching in a downtown parade, Albany, Georgia. *Courtesy of G.G.A. Whitehead.*

Accuracy and Acrobatics

Student.......... .... Date

Instructor......... .... Grade .....

	Grade			Gr:
1. Steep Banks	....	11. S Across Rd.	....
2. Chandelles	....	12. Loops	....
3. Lazy 8s	....	13. Half Rolls	....
4. 180° Side	....	14. Slow Roll	....
5. 180° Overh'd	....	15. Snap Rolls	....
6. 360° Overh'd	....	16. Vert. Rev.	....
7. Stalls	....	17. Immelmans	....
8. Spins	....	18. Coordination	....
9. Forced Land.	....	19. Progress	....
10. Pylon 8s	....	20. Judgment	....

Remarks

Flying instructor's grade sheet used in primary flying schools. *Courtesy of F.N. Bate.*

Boxer Jack Dempsey seated in a trainer at Napier Field. *Courtesy of J. Cook.*

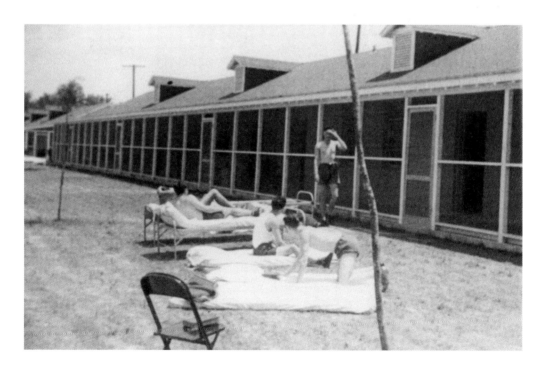

Sunbathing behind the barracks, Craig Field. *Courtesy of F.N. Bate.*

Pettus Bridge, leading out of Tuscaloosa toward Craig Field. *Courtesy of F.N. Bate.*

Cadets preparing to get some sun. *Courtesy of F.N. Bate.*

Squadron Leader R.T. Bowring, AFC (with mustache), and colleagues, Berlin Air Lift. *Courtesy of R.T. Bowring.*

Hawker Typhoon. *Courtesy of W. Freshwater.*

Vultee BT-13 basic trainer. *Courtesy of F.N. Bate.*

RAF pilot graduates (42-B) dine on a train bound for Canada. *Courtesy of D. Coxhead.*

Vultee BT-13 basic trainers in formation, Gunter Field, Alabama. *Courtesy of J. Cook.*

Calisthenics at Turner Field, Albany, Georgia. *Courtesy of D. Coxhead.*

Skeet shooting at advanced flying school, Dothan, Alabama. *Courtesy of D. Coxhead.*

Group Captain D.V. Carnegie, AFC, and Flight Lieutenant J. Leonard Keith, MBE. *Courtesy of
J.L. Keith.*

RAF cadet quarters, ready for inspection. *Courtesy of G.F. Pyle.*

Main brick hangar, Tuscaloosa, Alabama. *Courtesy of R.R. Farrow.*

Canadian train in Toronto, 1941. *Courtesy of R. Levy.*

Cadet beds in "bull pen," RCAF Manning Depot, Toronto, 1941. *Courtesy of W.C. Warner.*

Departing RAF aircrew waiting at train, Babbacombe. *Courtesy of W.C. Warner.*

DeHavilland Tiger Moth (DH82-A) used in all flight grading courses. *Courtesy of D. Coxhead.*

Aircrew posing on front of Canadian train. *Courtesy of W.C. Warner.*

RAF cadets march proudly in Heroes Parade, Montgomery, Alabama. *Courtesy of J.R. Johnson.*

A large draft of RAF u/t pilots in civilian clothing await transportation, Toronto, 1941. *Courtesy of R. Levy.*

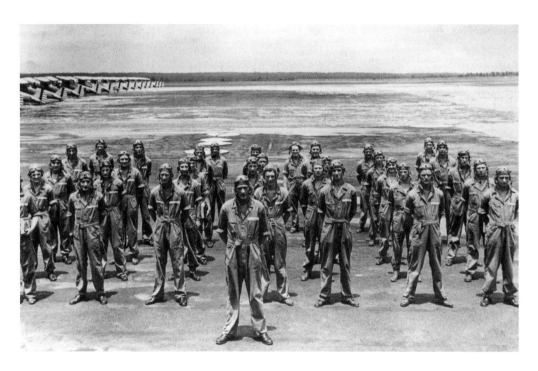

RAF Class 42-A in flying coveralls, Southern Aviation School, Camden, South Carolina. *Courtesy of H. Howton.*

Three RAF Class 42-A cadets deliver a cadet to the showers, Camden, South Carolina. *Courtesy of* PM *magazine.*

CHAPTER FOUR

THE TWO GEORGIA PRIMARY SCHOOLS

AMERICUS AND ALBANY

SOUTHER FIELD
AMERICUS, GEORGIA, 42-A-42-D

The Fifty-sixth U.S. Army Air Forces flying training detachment at Souther Field was isolated on the edge of a vast plateau close by rolling hill country. The contractor for the civilian contract primary school was William J. Graham of Pittsburgh and Butler, Pennsylvania. The airfield was located some seventy miles from Fort Benning and approximately two hundred miles from Savannah. Eight and a half miles south of the airfield was the town of Americus, which was connected to other towns and cities by several highways and two railroads. The Central of Georgia line began in Atlanta and, after reaching Macon, cut directly southward about a mile west of Souther Field and ran on to cut across the north-northwest section of the town to Americus's railway station at the foot of a hill west of the business district. A long spur line of this railroad ran alongside Souther Field Road to provide a rail connection to the airfield and its adjacent packing case industry.

The area between the airport and the town offered a variety of attractions. Along Souther Field Road were several peach orchards, and just at the edge of town along North Lee Street was a district of small wooden houses, many of them presenting a sad picture of poverty and neglect. Lee Street, which ran north-south, divided the town roughly in half, and all cross-streets and avenues were designated east and west of Lee. Lamar Street was evidently intended as the main east-west thoroughfare, and though there was little consistency in such labeling, many streets had their names changed as they crossed Lamar or were designated north or south at that street. Since there appeared to be great confusion even in 1941 as to which of the east-west streets was the main thoroughfare, there may have been some truth in the chamber of commerce brochure's assertion that the town's name may have come from some "merry cusses" who laid out the town and named it.

The compact business district of Americus was clustered along several streets including Jefferson, Lamar, Lee, Jackson, Prince, Hampton and Forsyth. East of Lamar Street, a massive cemetery halted 1940s business expansion in that direction. South of Lamar Street along tree-shaded Church, Felder, College and other streets was the more affluent residential district. In 1941, that section of the town also contained the tiny two-year Georgia Southwestern College, a number of modest as well as elegant and beautiful old houses and a large number of the town's churches. On the southern edge of the town were extensive pine and hardwood forests, beyond which lay the Seaboard Railway line. Beyond the railroad lay wooded hills and rich farmland.

The Seaboard Railroad cut across Sumter County from the southeast, entered the town's limits and ran through the southwestern section of Americus to join the Central of Georgia line near the railway station. Whereas the Central of Georgia line followed U.S. Highway 19 southward to Albany and other towns, the Seaboard Rail line ran alongside U.S. Highway 280 west of the town to and beyond the village of Plains, Georgia. Radiating out from Americus were approximately nine Georgia state roads, most of which in 1940 were either unpaved red clay and hard-packed gravel or were freshly paved with a relatively thin layer of macadam.

Main paved thoroughfares were United States Highways 280 and 19, which cut through the region linking Americus with other towns and cities. Some three miles northwest of Souther Field, near the highway leading to Atlanta, was the 148-acre Bill Graham Field, or Auxiliary Field No. 1. The location of Souther Field in relation to distance from the town of Americus and from its No. 1 Auxiliary Field was comparable to that of Camden, South Carolina, the Southern Aviation School and its main auxiliary field.

Unlike South Carolina's sand hill region, land that was appropriate for landing fields in this rich Georgia farm belt could neither be leased nor purchased easily. Despite apparently moderate efforts by city and county officials and officers of the Graham Company to acquire a more appropriate landing field, Bill Graham Field remained in use until it was replaced in June 1942 by Auxiliary Field No. 2 or Plains Auxiliary Field, almost fourteen miles west of the main airdrome.

With a 1940 population of approximately ten thousand people, Americus was a delightful, small Southern town. It was a market town for a large agricultural region and contained Georgia Southwestern College, at that time a two-year institution, and it had all of the strengths and weaknesses of dozens of similar small Southern towns. Much of the economy of Americus was based on service industries, which included small railroad shops, large lumberyards, packing sheds and warehouses for local agricultural products.

As befit a market town amid a rich farming region, the fringes of the business district of Americus held stores that dealt in seed, feed and fertilizer, as well as shops that sold farm implements, automobiles and trucks. In the heart of the town along the paved, hilly streets were two large multi-storied hotels, a tall brick water storage tank, a single movie theatre, city and county offices, public schools, the courthouse, a small hospital, the local newspaper, professional offices, chain stores, drugstores, department stores, churches and a large variety of houses indicating extremes of wealth and poverty.

For those brought to Americus by global war, the weather was another matter, and its variety brought both pleasure and many surprises. Visitors and citizens enjoyed the cool of spring and autumn, and the mild winters were a delight, even when it rained. The cadets were never there long enough, but Souther Field's civilian and military staff members learned to look forward to the hunting, fishing and other outdoor activities in season.

During spring and summer, the cadets never ceased to be amazed at the almost technicolor quality of strange and quiet mornings when atmospheric conditions were right. They also quickly learned to respect the heat of the sun, to consume salt and, if not flying, to find shelter in the smothering middle hours of summer days. They quickly adopted the Southern practice of relishing the early hours of quiet summer evenings from the coolness of a porch or verandah or a quiet walk along tree-lined residential streets.

As these normal and everyday events proceeded as they had each year for decades in Americus and Sumter County, the people at Souther Field were caught up with their regimen as well. For students, instructors and maintenance staff alike, it was constantly airplanes, flying and war news that captured and held their attention. As long as the school operated, citizens recalled seeing aircraft being shifted about on the ramp for servicing, or being landed or flying from the extensive airfield or its auxiliary fields.

Before the United States Army Air Service built Souther Field in 1918 and operated it as a flying training station until 1922, the site was reputed to be one of the largest peach orchards in the world. The World War I training base consisted of barracks and quarters for two thousand men, fifteen small wooden hangars, paved macadam roadways and other support facilities for an active military airfield that provided primary flying training on the Curtiss JN-4D Jenny for U.S. Army Air Service student pilots. The airfield was bounded on the north and west by unpaved red clay roads, on the east by fields of cotton, peanuts, corn and peach orchards and on the south by an extensive forest of pine and hardwoods and more peach orchards.

Notable landmarks in the vicinity included scattered lakes, creeks and ponds, and some fifteen miles directly east of Souther Field was the Flint River, which formed the eastern boundary of Sumter County. Initially, 1918 War Department contracting officers signed a lease for the land, which also provided the government an option to purchase the property later. Although several hundred pilots were trained at the primary school while it was under construction, the airfield and school were hardly completed before World War I ended.

Since it had proved to be a successful primary flying training station and had been developed at considerable expense, War Department officers purchased the site on 5 July 1919 for $32,534.50, converted its facilities into a general supply depot and brought in a considerable number of surplus aircraft, engines and equipment from other former training airfields. During the years between 1919 and 1922, while the United States Army was disposing of surplus aircraft and equipment, a limited amount of flying training continued at Souther Field.

One of the purchasers of a Jenny at the Souther Field Aircraft Depot was Charles A. Lindbergh who, having had minimal dual instruction at the Lincoln Airplane and Flying School at Lincoln, Nebraska, came to Americus, bought his first aircraft there, soloed it and then flew it to his home in Wisconsin. In the years following the purchase of one of Souther Field's surplus aircraft, Lindbergh went on to fame and beyond. By the time Lindbergh's reputation was established for his famous flight to Paris, Souther Field had been reduced to nothing. By 1925, most of the wartime buildings had been sold, dismantled and moved, leaving behind several warehouses near the railroad, scattered concrete pads, storm drains and a water tank. As in most cases where man has halted maintenance on discarded works, grass and weeds soon covered up the evidence of his having been there.

Three years later, in 1928, War Department planners indicated that the airfield site was no longer needed, so title to the 400-acre Souther Field was conveyed to Sumter County, Georgia. Since the county had no immediate use for the large airfield, a tract of 64 acres along the Central of Georgia Railway was sold to the Dayton Veneer and Lumber Company, manufacturers of produce crates and baskets to serve the region's agricultural marketing needs. Souther Field, minus that industrial tract, still totaled some 350 acres for future industrial development or other uses. In November 1940, the Graham Aviation Company of Butler, Pennsylvania, leased the tract.

Between December 1940 and October 1944, Souther Field was identified closely with the Graham Aviation Company and specifically with William J. Graham of Pittsburgh and Butler, Pennsylvania. Graham had established his Pennsylvania company in 1938, and during the next two years he built a solid reputation as a fixed-base operator for eight large airports in western Pennsylvania. During 1939–40, the Graham Company expanded its operations under the auspices of the Civil Aeronautics Authority (CAA) and the College Pilot Training Program (CPTP).

While operating these programs, Graham and his staff gained vital experience, so in the summer of 1940 when the army air corps began to seek additional civil contractors to operate primary schools for the proposed twelve-thousand-pilot expansion plan, his company was recommended by officers of the Civil Aeronautics Authority. When interviewed for the USAAF unit history of Souther Field, Graham, rarely one to give much credit to USAAF staff, asserted that Souther Field was recommended to him by a pilot who had been trained there in 1918.

From his perspective, Graham's assertion may well have been true, but the development of airdromes was hardly a product of chance conversation. Several state and federal agencies kept records of available sites, and had Graham not been given the contract to develop Souther Field, someone else would have. The Civil Aeronautics Authority, the Works Progress Administration, the army air corps, the Georgia Aeronautics Commission and local government officials were all well aware of semi-developed airports that might be leased, developed and used for different phases of aircrew training.

Whatever the source of his information, Graham visited Americus and, after talking with city and county officials, confirmed that the old World War I airfield site was indeed available and could be leased. Since a flying school was the equivalent of a small industry and would provide a boost to the economically depressed area, local officials were anxious to have a flying school in the county. In December 1940, officials of the City of Americus and Sumter Country leased Souther Field to Graham, and construction was begun as quickly as possible.

As was true of many Yankees who came South during that period, Graham gave evidence of having a well-developed ego, which made relations with Georgians somewhat difficult. He and some of his Northern staff often mistook the politeness of many native Georgians as a sign of weakness, and their own brusque manners alienated many local people. In the words of the unit historian, "The contractor's close [stingy?] business policies emphasized profits, and relations became more unpleasant as time passed." The WPA paid the labor costs, and Sumter County provided the equipment necessary to grade the airfield, remove the concrete slab foundations of World War I buildings and perform a large number of tasks in preparing the airfield proper. William J. Graham was president of the company and his father, John Graham, was general manager. Architect for the school was Sherley S. Hudson of Americus, but supervision of the building project was in the hands of John Graham, who was reputed to have had extensive business experience.

At the northwestern edge of the landing field, builders moved rapidly to complete a wooden maintenance hangar measuring 80 feet wide by 93 feet long and a steel hangar 138 feet wide by 204 feet long. Nearby domestic facilities included a gigantic two-story barracks measuring 50 feet wide by 235 feet long and a dining hall and kitchen building that was 60 feet wide by 120 feet long. Apparently, the War Department and the army air corps provided only minimal guidance in either location, design or interior layout of buildings.

Why the Graham Company constructed such huge barracks and other buildings at Souther Field is unknown. John Graham's experience in the North, where snow and ice were common for several months of the year, may have dictated that it was cheaper to build large buildings, and to put as many activities under one roof as possible. By persuading Sumter County to use WPA funding to do as much construction as possible at the airfield, and by using every inch of space in all of the buildings until it was absolutely necessary to construct others, Graham himself did not have to spend much of his own money.

By early February 1941, the first stage of construction at the new school was complete, and at that time, a refresher instructor program was implemented with five old and worn PT-15 biplane trainers. The PT-15s, which had been built by the St. Louis, Missouri Street Car Company, were evidently the last of the breed, for there were no parts with which to keep them flying. As a result, two were cannibalized to keep three of them serviceable. On being assigned such relics for refresher flying, Souther Field instructors must have thought of themselves as "red-headed stepchildren." Fortunately, these airplanes were furnished to the school by the army air corps for temporary use only, and were replaced within the month by bright factory-issue Stearman (Boeing) PT-17 biplane trainers with blue fuselages and yellow wings.

Although all contractors adapted their operations to existing facilities and did not build other buildings until compelled to do so by the assignment of additional students, only Oliver Parks's Alabama Institute of Aeronautics at Tuscaloosa, Alabama, equalled the Graham Aviation Company for stinginess and making maximum use of available space. At first, the ground-floor rooms of the huge barracks provided space for civil and military offices, the infirmary, a classroom, a parachute room, canteen, recreation room and a barbershop. As a result of the contractor's unwillingness to spend money, air corps supervisors, without backing from superiors, gingerly deemed the school's facilities "almost inadequate."

Although some contract flying schools located in relatively isolated areas, like those of the Embry-Riddle Company at Arcadia and Clewiston, Florida, were careful to develop facilities for student and staff recreation and physical training, the Graham Company did not do so until compelled by a USAAC threat to limit enrollment. The problem of adequate facilities at Souther Field was never resolved to everyone's satisfaction. As at Camden, South Carolina's Southern Aviation School, early physical training at Souther Field included mostly hiking, cross-country running and, if there was equipment available, student-organized intramural sports. By 1941, Souther Field's physical training facilities included a softball diamond, two volleyball courts and little else but the promise of adequate space for the later development of playing fields and other necessities.

Before training began on 22 March 1941, the maintenance staff thoroughly checked and serviced all aircraft, prepared individual aircraft records and organized maintenance and servicing schedules. At the same time, administrative, supervisory and instructional staffs also made last-minute preparations to receive students. Between 17 and 20 March 1941, Class SE-41-H, the first class of army air corps flying cadets, arrived at Souther Field individually and in small groups. They commenced training immediately.

The Graham Aviation Company commenced operations with approximately eighty-seven staff members, which included twenty-six flying and ground instructors, fifteen dining hall staff members, five office employees and thirty-five maintenance personnel. On 5 February 1941, Captain James W. Gurr, a native of Shellman, Georgia, and 1932 graduate of the United States Military Academy, arrived in Americus and assumed command of Souther Field. Gurr had previously served as a flying instructor at Randolph Field and had also served as the first commanding officer of the Alabama Institute of Aeronautics at Tuscaloosa. Gurr was promoted to major and was reassigned after 15 October 1941.

Other officers assigned to the new primary school included First Lieutenant Littleton J. Pardue, adjutant; First Lieutenant Leslie L. Rood, commandant of cadets; Second Lieutenant

Ernest F. Baldwin, assistant air corps supervisor; and Captain Joseph Rose, MD, station flight surgeon. On 1 June, RAF Flight Lieutenant Leonard Gordon Speck arrived to serve as the first RAF administrative officer (RAFAO), a position he filled until 1 November 1941, when he was posted to Canada. Between 1 November 1941 and 9 October 1942, Flight Lieutenant D. Easton Smith served as RAFAO at Souther Field. After 15 November 1941, Second Lieutenant Hiram K. Undercofler arrived to serve as assistant air corps supervisor.

Since during its early months of operation no more than two small pilot training classes, totaling fifty-three flying cadets each, were under training at any one time, the students were assigned to quarters on the second floor of the huge barracks. Early in May 1941, when Class SE-41-I, the second American cadet class, arrived, the parachute room was moved from the lower floor of the barracks to one of the hangars, and that move made space for an additional classroom. Until larger classes were assigned to the school in August 1941, the ground floor of the barracks also continued to house most of the domestic service facilities of the Graham Aviation School.

On Sunday afternoon, 8 June 1941, escorted by RCAF Flying Officer S.C. Foster, the fifty-three members of Class SE-42-A arrived in Americus, Georgia, on a Central of Georgia train. They were transported the few miles northward to Souther Field in automobiles provided by school staff and citizens of the small town, and Flying Officer Foster continued southward by rail with the remaining RAF student pilots. Shortly after moving into the barracks, the young men were able to get out of their rumpled gray woolen suits, shower, shave and clean up in time for supper in the dining hall. As part of settling in, they were disconcerted to learn that they would be subject to the formidable rules and procedures described in the new U.S. Army Air Corps Aviation Cadet Manual.

Since most of the RAF student pilots did not at that time aspire to commissioned status, and the whole idea was alien to them, many perceived officer cadet training as unnecessary and tedious. They viewed the West Point–style hazing as juvenile bullying. Others felt that such discipline and hazing were a small price to pay in order to qualify as a pilot. As the British student pilots were adjusting to their new surroundings, reporters and a photographer from the Americus *Times-Record* descended on them, and articles and photographs adorned the pages of that afternoon daily newspaper for many weeks. In the issue of Thursday, 12 June 1941, the front page preserved for posterity a picture of the fifty-three Britons in formation wearing new, ill-fitting Canadian-issue khaki uniforms and Northwest Frontier pukka sahib sun helmets.

The unfortunate set of circumstances that provided these proud young RAF volunteers with inadequate uniforms at that critical juncture probably did both damage and good. Before there was time for any but the most confirmed curmudgeons to become bitter, the young men were provided with American-issue khaki uniforms and cotton twill coveralls. The issue of clothing more suitable to the climate probably did not help the RAF men to overcome the image of "poor cousins," but that image may well have encouraged the civilian population to adopt the "orphans" from Britain.

As with other contingents of British student pilots, the young men were required to wear civilian clothing when off-post. The long, hot rail journey from Canada, while dressed in the gray woolen RAF-issued suits, had been most uncomfortable. Off-post in a Georgia summer made the heavy clothing even more uncomfortable. After being regularly invited to homes, local churches, dances and picnics, rather than suffer extreme embarrassment and discomfort, many of the young men spent some of their limited cash on cooler civilian wear.

As the British cadets went about the town and county, the people they met were aware that these polite and very young visitors would, on completion of their training, be returning home to an uncertain future, and those Americans were anxious to show them around and to give them a sampling of true Southern hospitality. As the RAF cadets traveled about Americus and Sumter County, they were treated like royalty. Each time members of the earlier RAF classes were permitted to leave the confines of the airfield, they found cars lined up near the airfield gate awaiting them. Business and professional people in Americus readily "adopted" them and introduced them to Southern life. The young men were amazed with everything they saw. There was so much space and sunshine, and so many trees and plants. However, visits to the site of the infamous Confederate prison and its very large cemetery near Andersonville, some fourteen miles northeast of Americus, were sobering experiences.

The wives, mothers and daughters of Americus and Sumter County were anxious to demonstrate what Southern hospitality meant. Wherever the RAF students went, they sat down to sumptuous meals including a wide variety of dishes that they had either never sampled in the form presented, had not seen for some time in Britain or had never heard of before. Soon they were perfectly familiar with iced tea, large servings of Southern fried chicken, corn on the cob, creamed corn, fried okra, fresh tomatoes, Spanish rice, peach cobbler and pecan pie. Among the fresh melons and fruits they enjoyed were peaches, cantaloupes, strawberries and watermelons.

In the school dining hall and in the drugstores of Americus, they enjoyed ice cream, milkshakes, banana splits and a wide variety of sundaes. For their part, the cadets discovered that everyone appeared anxious for information to supplement the limited war news they received from newspapers, radio and magazines. On and off Souther Field, RAF Administrative Officer Flight Lieutenant Leonard G. Speck proved to be very effective. Speck's early arrival allowed him to meet people and to pave the way for the RAF student pilots who were due a week later. Speck found quarters in Americus and introduced himself to a large number of business and professional people in Americus and Sumter County.

During his tenure, he was in a very difficult position as a guest officer among American civilians and United States Army Air Forces officers (after 20 June 1941, USAAC became USAAF). He served on the school's academic board, counseled with and paid RAF cadets and handled problems of liaison concerning supply, morale, discipline and other problems affecting the RAF students.

As with RAFAOs at other Arnold Scheme primary flying schools, Speck found himself invited to speak to various civic and garden clubs in Americus and nearby towns, and to a June encampment of Boy Scouts. The RAF officer took a strong interest in ground school classes and obtained a considerable number of maps, charts and other instructional aids from Canada. Apparently, Speck enjoyed his liaison and public relations duties during his stay in Americus, and appears to have been very popular with civilians and military personnel alike.

Among the students in that first class was Raymond William Stanley, a former railway clerk from Nottingham. Stanley, who enlisted in the Royal Air Force in December 1940, was eliminated from pilot training at Souther Field, but his case was reviewed by Wing Commander Hogan at Maxwell Field and he was permitted to reenter pilot training with Course No. 3 at British Flying Training School (BFTS) No. 1 at Terrell, Texas. Stanley successfully completed pilot training and survived the war as pilot of Spitfires, later 247 Squadron Hawker Typhoons.

From his home in Nottingham, more than forty years afterward, Stanley recalled his training experience:

My first flight was 10 June 1941 (Instructor Lou Hemmer), and I went solo in the Stearman PT-17 after 10 hours, 38 minutes dual instruction. At Americus, we had a fellow student, Paddy Rogan, from the Irish Free State, who was not doing too well on the course. He just disappeared one day, and although we were sent out to look for him, we did not find him or ever hear what became of him. [Officially, Rogan was the only RAF cadet listed as having deserted.]

I was taken off this course at the beginning of August after some 50 flying hours, and only about a week from completion of the course. The reason appeared to be due to a rather hairy landing when I disappeared below a hangar on final approach, but did open up, climbed over it and landed O.K. the other side. However, this was not to be the end of my flying career, although at the time I was certain it was. I was then posted to Montgomery, Alabama to await a decision as to my future.

I would add that during my stay at Americus, accommodation, food, and hospitality were very good. The local people were very kind, often invited us into their homes, and I remember attending church with some of them who became our friends. They were less reserved than us (but remember our average age was about 20 years), and this helped break the ice.

The climate was a big problem for us. It was summer and very humid. I can well remember that in ground school classes, many of us would just fall asleep because we were not acclimatised, and had to be awakened by our instructor. This was a big factor in lack of progress in ground subjects, and we were made to make up for it by being confined to camp at week-ends on occasion.

Generally, we flew from very early in the morning and attended ground school in the afternoon [alternating weekly]. *So far as flying was concerned, we were taught to fly "by the seat of our pants." We could not speak to the instructor in the air, and we had no air speed indicator in our cockpit (the instructor had one in his). The accent was on circuits and landings, and this invariably meant glide landings. Once the throttle had been cut, it was a sign to open up again, but the crafty ones would give a quick burst on pretext of keeping the engine warm. We did no cross country flights and no night flying at primary school.*

These methods were interesting when compared with later experiences, and I believe it was a mistake not to have two-way communication in the aircraft. The instructor could speak to the pupil, but no provision was made for the pupil to speak to the instructor. Consequently, there was only one-way communication in the air. After about three weeks at Montgomery, I was more than delighted to be posted to No. 1 B.F.T.S. at Dallas, Texas to start all over again. I did not fly from Dallas, as we were moved to Terrell, some 50 miles away soon after arrival.

Stanley's second chance at one of the British flying training schools (BFTSs) was an experience that only slightly more than fifty Arnold Scheme eliminees shared.

Another member of that Souther Field class who was among the twenty-one eliminees of Class SE-42-A was Reginald G. McCadden, a former merchant seaman from Belfast, Northern Ireland, and one of the older RAF students on the course. McCadden was provided a different and unique kind of second chance shared by only a few RAF student pilots. Many years later from his home near Belfast, McCadden recalled those wartime training days at Souther Field:

I was probably one of the oldest members of my class (27 years) which included a few 18 year olds. These latter took to the air more easily than those in the mid-twenties and upwards; but overall, there was a high failure rate within the first 4 to 6 weeks. The civilian contractor who operated the school at Souther Field was William Graham of Butler, Pennsylvania. Mr. Graham was friendly with Wing Commander Harry Hogan, DFC, who was the Senior RAF Administrative Officer in charge of the Arnold Scheme schools, and whose office was located at Maxwell Field, Montgomery, Alabama.

Five of us left Souther Field after about 12 hours instruction, and spent 4 weeks (From 31 July to 2 September 1941) at Butler, Pennsylvania with several more RAF students from other Arnold Scheme schools. We received instruction from Mr. Graham's Chief Flying Instructor there, flew in Piper Cubs and a Waco biplane, and soloed successfully after a few hours of dual instruction. All of us benefitted from the more temperate weather, and the relaxed atmosphere. Three of the group—Jennings, Hepplewhite, and me—were posted from Butler to Souther Field to join incoming members of Class 42-C (42-B, an all RAF class, was the "upper class," so that only RAF personnel were under training at the field).

As indicated in describing the Southern Aviation School at Camden, South Carolina, LAC Harry Hepplewhite was sent from Camden, and the other four subjects of the CPTP training experiment at Butler, Pennsylvania (including the two who failed), were evidently transferred from Souther Field.

On 24 June, Lieutenant Colonel J.I. Grisham of the Inspector General's Department in Washington, D.C., visited Souther Field. In his report of 3 July, Grisham cited the Graham Aviation Company for failure to provide sufficient facilities. Grisham cited overcrowded housing conditions and the lack of a swimming pool, tennis courts, general athletic facilities and only a fair basketball court. Hangar facilities were also considered inadequate. The inspector general (IG) felt that the contractor was much too dependent on the county and the WPA for construction at the airfield, and should do much of it himself. Since the construction was being done so slowly by these outside agencies, the IG felt that the resulting dust and confusion hampered training. As a result, Colonel Grisham recommended that the number of students undergoing training at the Graham contract school not be increased until sufficient facilities were available to warrant it.

On 11 July, Captain James Gurr was able to forward the IG report through channels, with a long and detailed endorsement indicating that the contractor was still too dependent on others for construction. A further inspection that month confirmed Gurr's assessment when the inspector asserted that the Americus school "has the least adequate facilities of any school visited." Graham had in July begun to build an administration building so as to remove offices from the barracks, thereby providing room for an increased enrollment. The Grahams also quickly constructed basic athletic facilities at Souther Field. Although it is doubtful that there was ever any real danger of contract cancellation, Gurr underscored that possibility when he indicated that the region and the airdrome had great potential for flying training and recommended that the contract not be canceled.

Before they departed for assignment to a basic flying school, members of Class SE-42-A wrote and produced their issue of the class magazine, the *Souther Cadet*. The editor's duties were shared by LAC Richard A. Wise, a former journalist from London, and LAC Joseph G.W. Foster, a journalist from Barrow, while artwork was done by LAC Jack Hartley, a salesman from Leeds, and J.W. Thornborrow, a Landsdale cinema operator.

In an article entitled "To The People of Americus," author Norman L."Paul" Jones paid special tribute to their Americus hosts:

> *You Americus people have been kind.*
> *You've given us untold joys.*
> *You've provided a home from home*
> *For a gang of British boys.*
>
> *You've taken us here, you've taken us there—*
> *Luxury mixed with pleasure,*
> *We owe you all a vote of thanks,*
> *In no uncertain measure.*
>
> *We appreciate your kindness,*
> *You've taken our hearts by storm,*
> *With your Southern hospitality,*
> *Your smiles sincere and warm.*
>
> *We should have been quite lonely,*
> *But for your timely aid.*
> *You threw your homes wide open—*
> *'Twas thus good friends were made.*
>
> *We'll have to leave you shortly—*
> *We've heard the bugle call,*
> *And for all the things you've done for us,*
> *We want to thank you all.*
>
> *And when this war is over,*
> *With all its grief and pain,*
> *We'll come back to Americus,*
> *And meet you all again.*

Unfortunately for many members of Class SE-42-A, those happy times were much too short, and the promise of a safe return was not to be.

Of the fifty-three RAF students enrolled in Class SE-42-A at Souther Field, two were held over for further training, twenty-one were eliminated and thirty graduated from the primary flying school on or about 15 August 1941. The RAF LAC who is mentioned by Ray Stanley as having disappeared was reported to have deserted. He could not be traced, but it is suspected that he was listed officially in Class SE-42-A statistics as the one RAF class member who was eliminated for "reasons other than flying."

Since the initial intake of RAF students had experienced difficulty in adjusting to USAAF cadet discipline, the British students were pleased when the fifty-three RAF students of Class

SE-42-B arrived on Saturday, 19 July 1941. Their arrival made Americus an all-RAF school. Members of the new class were not able to settle into their new surroundings before invitations from local citizens began. On Sunday, 20 July, the entire fifty-three-member class attended the First Presbyterian Church as special guests, after which they were guests for Sunday dinner in the homes of church members.

With their late arrival and attempts to adjust to the July heat, the invitations must have created panic. The necessity to clean and press the rumpled gray suits they had worn on the long rail trip from Canada undoubtedly created special problems, but the young men rose to the occasion and apparently enjoyed meeting and dining with their American hosts. During the next several days, they also got to know members of the senior class and learned much from them.

Perhaps it was because the school was now all-British, for when Class SE-42-A came to write the first edition of the *Souther Cadet*, the two classes cooperated. Within the covers of that mimeographed (cyclostyled) class book were expressions of gratitude to their instructors as well as numerous reminiscences of their training days.

Leslie Hastings, a member of the junior class, wrote "A Prayer of Young England," which appeared in the *Souther Cadet* and was reprinted by several newspapers. It deserves quoting for the sentiments it expresses:

> *To us who stand*
> *On the threshold of life*
> *Youth of a land*
> *Now tortured in strife,*
>
> *Grant, Lord, a love*
> *Of all that is good*
> *And strength from above*
> *To do as Thou would.*
>
> *Faith in the things*
> *Unseen, yet so dear;*
> *Vision that brings*
> *Their presence more near;*
>
> *Remembrance of friends*
> *Now far from our sight;*
> *Affection that lends*
> *Glad stars to their night;*
>
> *Power to pursue*
> *Trying tasks with a smile;*
> *Patience to do*
> *Without peace for awhile*
>
> *Courage to fight*
> *With vast throngs—or alone*

For all that is right:
Country, comrades, and home.

And may the reward
Which our faithfulness bears
Be defeat of the sword,
End of trials, tears and cares;

Last painful path trod,
Love proved in the test,
Our hearts nearer God
And souls calmed in rest.

But all was not seriousness. The students printed an imaginary alternative daily training schedule that included numerous discussions, debates and breaks for Coca-Colas.

In addition to the (hoped for) revised schedule, LAC Wilfred Pugh invented, selected or modified the titles of specific hymns to fit the occasion that, if sung by some "Georgia Peaches," would brighten each stage of the daily schedule. Pugh's selections were:

First Formation	*"Art Thou Weary, Art Thou Languid?"*
Breakfast	*"Meekly Wait and Murmur Not"*
C.O.'s Parade	*"When He Cometh—When He Cometh"*
Marching to Flying line	*"Flight the Good Flight"*
Taking off	*"Oft in Danger, Oft in Woe"*
Barrack's inspection	*"All Things Bright and Beautiful"*
Calistenics	*"Here We Suffer Grief and Pain"*
Dinner	*"O Come All Ye Faithful"*
Study Hall	*"Go Labour On"*
Lecture	*"Tell Me the Old, Old Story"*
Supper	*"What Means This Eager Anxious Throng"*
Taps	*"All Are Safely Gathered In"*
Lights out	*"Peace, Perfect Peace!"*

However amusing and witty the desired schedule and its proposed musical accompaniment, training continued according to a very different schedule.

For Class SE-42-B, training proceeded according to the established schedule during the following weeks. Members of the new class were soon formed into flights and were assigned to instructors. In order to provide maximum flying experience, they, like students in all other flying schools, alternated their training regimen weekly. As they slowly adjusted to very long daily schedules, strange accents, inspection of quarters, clothing and equipment and the noise of aircraft, morning ground school and afternoon flying shifted about to morning flying and afternoon ground school. By the end of the third week for the new class, the senior class were veterans who were now flying "stages" while a few members of the new class were beginning to take the big Stearman PT-17s on solo flights.

Unfortunately, many men found flying training a frightening and very difficult business. Some of them had never ridden or operated anything more complicated than a bicycle, and found it very difficult to judge distance from the ground. The most common occurrence in this lack of depth perception was for students to attempt to land fifty feet or more in the air. Another major problem was that in landing the Stearman trainers, it was necessary to hold the aircraft on course while applying the brakes with the greatest of ease. Excessive speed, over-correction with the rudder or heavy-handedness with the brakes could result in a ground loop or a nose over, and until students became accustomed to technique, most of them either experienced a ground loop or barely missed one.

Every student was given eight or more hours of dual instruction, but some of them failed at about the eight-hour level because they were either afraid of flying, became airsick or lacked sufficient mechanical ability to coordinate hands and feet for smooth rather than jerky maneuvers. Those men who failed to demonstrate significant progress before logging twelve hours of dual instruction were scheduled for a check ride with one of the USAAF officers, and if his assessment confirmed that of the civilian instructor, the student was eliminated from pilot training. Many members of Class SE-42-B departed for Maxwell Field and Canada in small groups.

Before they too parted for Canada and reassignment or to a basic flying school, the members of Class SE-42-B published their edition of the *Souther Cadet*. R.W. Findlay served as editor; V.E. Dawson as assistant editor; Douglas Lowe as photographic editor; and H.M. Lynes was responsible for the artwork in the publication. In several serious and amusing articles, their writers described class experiences such as laundry day. In "McFlying," LAC J. McCallum of Benenden, Kent, wittily described some problems with a solo flight, which included the dropping of a Coke bottle into the Flint River as a means of determining altitude, checking wind direction by holding a wet finger over the side of the cockpit and close encounters with other aircraft that resulted from landing without checking the Tee setting.

Among the members of that second RAF class were Maurice J. Latham, John Douglas Blackburn and Douglas Charles Lowe. Since he was a former air gunner and survivor of Dunkirk, Latham's experience captured the attention of newsmen, and his story appeared in the local paper and was picked up by other newspapers. Apparently, Latham was one of seven survivors of a large group of RAF men who had served on airfields at St. Quentin and Amiens before withdrawing to Dunkirk's beaches. On the crowded beach, he was slightly wounded by shrapnel but, as with so many others who survived that ordeal, Latham and several of his comrades waded into the surf, swam a half-mile to waiting boats and were finally delivered to safety in England. What happened to Latham after his time in Americus is unknown.

However, LACs Blackburn and Lowe survived the war. Douglas Charles Lowe of Woodley, Berkshire, was described in the *Souther Cadet* as a person with "only two passions—the Hut Sut Song and snapshots." During the war, Lowe developed an outstanding record, gained a permanent commission and became a career officer. Following a distinguished career of ever-increasing responsibilities, he retired as Air Chief Marshal Sir Douglas Lowe, GCB, DFC, AFC and ADC, the highest-ranking RAF graduate of the primary flying school at Americus, Georgia.

When Class SE-42-B was halfway through its primary training, the surviving thirty members of Class SE-42-A departed for the USAAF basic flying school at Cochran Field, Macon, Georgia. After their departure on 15 August, only Class SE-42-B was in training for about two weeks; its junior class was late. Because of overcrowding at the Canadian National Exhibition, the huge RAF draft, which included members of Class SE-42-C, was held for about ten days in No. 1 Y Depot at Halifax, Nova Scotia. Even though steps were taken so as to be able to rush the entire

550-man draft through Toronto to the waiting American primary schools, they were two weeks behind schedule, and civilian contractors and air corps officers were understandably alarmed.

Finally, on 31 August, the new fifty-man RAF intake arrived at Americus and were joined by the three men from an earlier class who were being given a second chance. Joining that tardy RAF intake at Souther Field were Reginald G. McCadden of Belfast and James Thomas Jennings of Liverpool (both formerly of SE-42-A at Americus) and Harry Hepplewhite of Yorkshire (formerly SE-42-A at Camden), the three survivors of the five who had attended an experimental flying course at Butler, Pennsylvania. Designated Class SE-42-C, the fifty-three RAF students commenced training immediately.

Among the new students of the class were Richard F.H. Martin of Tavistock, North Devonshire; Donald Ogilvie and Peter George Hills, both of Kent; Harold Norman Evans of Wolverhampton; Cecil Arthur Tardie of Guernsey, Channel Islands; and Basil Bonakis of London. Tardie had transferred from the British army to the RAF and, despite removing the lower wings from a Stearman, managed to graduate and ultimately to fly Spitfires in a photo reconnaissance unit. Bonakis was held over one class owing to health problems, but later graduated as a pilot and ultimately served as a flying instructor before returning to the United Kingdom. Ogilvie washed out and was trained as an air gunner in Canada. Hills and Evans completed the course, but unfortunately drowned while swimming at Jacksonville Beach during the short leave before entering a basic flying school.

Richard F.H. Martin, whom the reader encountered earlier at No. 1 Y Depot, Halifax, Nova Scotia, wrote to his parents regularly while absent from the United Kingdom and graciously lent copies of his letters for this work. Excerpts from them provide an excellent account of the concerns, experiences and thoughts of a typical RAF student at Americus in the late summer and early autumn of 1941.

> *1 September 1941. This is just to tell you that I arrived here just after midnight yesterday after a thirty-hour train journey from Toronto. We had to change trains in the middle of the night at the border and did not get much sleep due to this and the heat. Souther Field is a nice station and very comfortable. There is one RAF officer; all the rest are U.S. Army.*
>
> *We live and eat under the Stars and Stripes, use the American salute, their military law and cadet system. We are given demerit marks if we break the rules; if you get five of them, you have to walk up and down the parade ground in the sun for an hour. This system seems to be the cause of all the friction between the British and Americans training over here.*
>
> *The food is very good, though I survive on ice cream and iced drinks in this heat. We all are suffering from the heat and all our RAF clothes are too thick, so we have had to buy thin clothing here. I hope to fly for the first time today when we have been issued with flying kit; our RAF kit is fit for Iceland rather than here. The local people ask questions just to hear our English accent. I had a good time in Toronto and saw Niagara Falls and the Canadian National Exhibition.*
>
> *2 September 1941. The thing that worries us here is that we are on a peacetime course for training American cadets as pilots in their Army Air Corps, like our Cranwell. We are here because we are at war, but on this course, we have to learn the American method of navigation which is different from ours, as are the weather charts and the maps.*

None of them will be of use to us in England or over enemy territory. Also, there is nothing on armaments or signals which we need. Otherwise, the course seems fine.

It is very hot here and we just wear a pair of pants and flying overalls and no more. I have met my flying instructor, a Mr. Bishop, who seems a nice person. The airfield here was a last war training school for Americans. It is the place that trained Lindbergh, and the locals are very proud of him. I have just had my first flight and did some turns, glides and climbs. Since then, I have been flying again and have not felt sick at all; some RAF students were and they had to clean up the ship afterwards. Our daily programme here is as follows:

05:30   Get up
05:45   Parade (formation) then wash, etc.
06:00   Breakfast parade
06:50   "A" Flight flying; "B" Flight classes and study hall.
09:20   "B" Flight flying; "A" Flight classes and study.

This morning schedule is followed by lunch and a rest period of half an hour in which we have to rest. In the afternoon, we have lectures and then Physical Training (calisthenics) for one and a half hours.

19:00–21:00   Study period
21:30   Bedtime

The people here all seem very pro-British, however, they are still fighting the Civil War, and one has to be careful what one says on that subject. The failure rate on the previous course seems to be a lot higher than the rate in England.

8 September 1941. *I have been flying every day and yesterday tried four landings; I like flying very much. Here they have check rides after so much flying, and then, if they do not think you are good enough, you get an Army check which it seems not many pass and they then are washed out, that is "failed." In the class which preceded us 50 came here and 27 have already had the "washing machine" and have gone.*

The town here is about the size of Tavistock and has one cinema. The population seems to be three black to one white, and the blacks have to make way for the whites and travel in separate street cars. On Sunday, to further relations with the local people, we were divided up into groups and each group went to a different church in the town; some were lucky and got invited out to lunch. In the afternoon, we went swimming and were given a lift back.

On the way, we were shown a place full of memorials to Northern prisoners who had died in a prison camp here during the Civil War. [It was the site of the infamous Andersonville Prison, about six miles north of Souther Field.] *The senior class is going to give a dance in our honour. This is done by each class before they leave, so as to introduce the new boys to the local girls.*

16 September 1941. *We have been ordered to have our hair cut U.S. Army style, and that is very short. No moustaches are allowed, so there is an uproar from the many with moustaches! Souther Field is a private concern owned by Mr. Graham, a pleasant chap who runs the flying and the servicing of the planes and looks after the buildings. The lot is rented by the Army and we have a Major Gurr in command, and he has four lieutenants and a number of soldiers under him. Then there are the flying instructors, all civilians and very friendly and anxious to help us with any problems we may have.*

At last the wind has dropped a bit; it has been too strong for any of us to be allowed off for our solo flights, but now I have at last done it! I did three landings without any difficulty, but on the fourth, I ground looped and scraped a wing tip. When you do your first solo, you are expected to buy all in view a soft drink; that is a Coca Cola or orange drink at 5 cents each. The Parachute Man gave a demonstration jump after we each gave him a quarter (25 cents) to do it. The Army has introduced a stricter system of demerits, so there is not a thing we do or not do that is free from getting demerits.

***22 September 1941.** The dance was a success; there was an Army band from Fort Benning at nearby Columbus, Georgia. We were briefed before it started on the system of cutting in that is used here. It seems that a girl here expects to change her partner at least twice in each dance. It means you can dance with anyone. I enjoyed it a lot!*

***25 September 1941.** Yesterday, we had a small hurricane. It got very dark and very strong winds blew, followed by a curtain of sand which hung over the field making it impossible to land. Three managed to land in a nearby field, and to get them out again, the hedge had to be cut down. I had my check ride with Army Lieutenant Roper. I did my best for him, and he seemed satisfied as he then did a lot of aerobatics which I enjoyed, so he did some more. I made a pretty rough landing at the end, but passed O.K. My instructor was pleased, as ten have failed this week. I have now, with others, collected 8 demerits, enough for three hours walking on the parade ground in the sun. What a way to run an Air Force!!*

For Martin and his classmates, the first week in October 1941 marked the midpoint in their primary flying training and the departure of the surviving members of Class SE-42-B. Of Class SE-42-B's fifty-five-member total enrollment, thirty-one students were eliminated or washed out, three were held over and twenty-one successfully completed the course. Around 4 October, Class SE-42-C was elevated to senior-class status, and Class SE-42-D arrived and became the junior class.

In further excerpts from his letters of October, Martin describes the final weeks of primary training and experiences off-post during early Autumn 1941.

***6 October 1941.** I have now done about 30 hours flying so far. I am "Officer of the Day" today and have to answer the telephone, see that all cadets are in class and in bed at night, change money, and generally fetch people for the different offices here. The duty runs from noon one day to noon the next and includes sounding the Klaxon at 0530 to wake everyone up. I do not have to go on parades but still fly. We have been flying twice a day, dual in the morning and solo in the afternoon. I have just completed an accuracy stage which consists of making seven landings on a line marked on the ground.*

***12 October 1941.** I went to another football game—Americus High School against another school. Americus lost as usual. On Saturday, John Butson and I went to supper with two girls and then to the dance—RAF and girls from the high school. We have been told we can wear our uniform, but it is much too hot to wear that thick blue uniform. It is strange in a neutral country to be told to wear it. Some have gone to church in it to see what effect it has on the local population. The lower class [Class SE-42-D, which arrived on 4 October] all went to a Barbecue given by the people of Ellaville, and they had a marvellous time. We should have had one when we arrived here, but it seems* *we were unlucky as few knew that we had arrived since we were a week late. I am now due for a 40-hour check with the Army.*

19 October 1941. *We get paid 25 dollars every two weeks, and every so often, they deduct 5 dollars for British income tax!! We had our second crash. Someone turned over on landing; the previous one was when someone went through the hedge on take off and ruined the ship. No one was hurt in either accident. Friday night we all had to wear RAF uniforms to go to a football game in Americus.*

28 October 1941. *This week we have all been flying hard to complete the 60 hours required before we leave here. So far, I have done 54 hours. I still await the 40-hour check, so when I get it, that will be the last check. One Lieutenant who does the check has failed so many that some say he works for Hitler! There are now 37 left out of the original 50. We have held our Class Dance and it was a great success.*

4 November 1941. *Last Wednesday night, we had a formal Instructor's Dinner. We all had to wear uniform and drink the President's and the King's health in Coca Cola! I have finished the course, done my 60 hours, and am now on leave. We said goodbye to Mr. Bishop, our instructor, and gave him an electric razor from the four of us. We have leave till Monday and can go within a radius of 250 miles from here. John and I are staying with the Holstons in Americus. They have two sons about my age and one daughter. We have just heard that Peter Hills and Harry Evans were drowned at Jacksonville; very sad especially since they had completed the course. Peter had the same instructor I had—Mr. Bishop. We leave here this morning to go to Cochran Field for basic training.*

The death of LACs Hills and Evans shocked the close-knit British contingent at Souther Field and served as a cruel reminder of the soldiers' own mortality. The tragedy strongly affected their classmates. During what was intended to be a happy leave time following ten weeks of training, Harold A. Newland of London, Peter George Hills of Faversham, Kent, and Harry Norman Evans of Woverhampton, Staffordshire, traveled to Jacksonville Beach, Florida. There, on Sunday afternoon, 2 November, while Newland sat on the beach, Hills and Evans went swimming. Apparently, the two nineteen-year-old cadets went out into the surf too far, and either had cramps from the cold water or were caught by a terrific undercurrent or riptide. Before help could be summoned to the scene, both young men drowned. Evans's body was recovered by lifeguards that afternoon, and burial services were held a few days later in south Jacksonville's Oaklawn Cemetery.

Hills's body was not found immediately. It was swept out to sea and was not returned to shore by the tide until 28 November. Hills was laid to rest beside Evans in the Oaklawn Cemetery. Except for the tiny mortuary signs, the graves remained unmarked for several months. Residents of Americus, cadets at Souther Field and members of the Daughters of the British Empire were joined by RAF students at the U.S. Naval Air Station, Jacksonville, in collecting funds with which to install more suitable markers until the Commonwealth War Graves Commission could place its own permanent grave markers after the war.

As if these two tragedies were not enough, in mid-November, LAC Jack Hartley, one of the most popular young men of Class SE-42-A, was killed while undergoing advanced flying training. Hartley had been "adopted" by the family of Dr. Herschel A. Smith of Americus, and even after he was transferred elsewhere to continue his pilot training he had returned to Americus virtually every weekend. Almost exactly three months after his class finished primary training at Americus and departed for Cochran Field, Hartley was killed in a flying accident at Turner Field. When his funeral was held in Albany and interment took place at Albany's Crown Hill Cemetery, a large number of saddened Americus citizens attended.

A Class SE-42-C classmate, Reginald G. McCadden, was twenty-seven when he entered primary flying training. His experience was probably unique in Arnold Scheme annals. McCadden, ex-merchant navy man and former cadet captain of Class SE-42-A at Souther Field, was also appointed cadet captain of SE-42-C at the same primary flying school. That third RAF class also included a number of ex-army men who had remustered to the RAF. McCadden recalled his second tour at Americus and asserted, "I cannot speak too highly of the treatment accorded RAF students by the citizens of Americus. They housed and entertained us in their homes each weekend."

In the lead article of Class SE-42-C's issue of the *Souther Cadet*, McCadden was more eloquent and more specific:

> *To Georgia and Americus! A toast this, to which every man in Class 42-C will subscribe with fullest heart! To have this opportunity of setting out our gratitude to the "Warm South" is something that cannot be passed by lightly; and should our pen fail to do the duty that justice which it deserves, it will certainly not be due to lack of sincerity or deep-felt appreciation.*
>
> *In our first few days spent under your blazing summer skies, it required Herculean efforts to suppress the feeling that "we could never get used to this!" The first week-end came as a welcome relief to all. Donning our well known flannel suits we wandered forth—strangers in a strange land—to accept with mixed feelings the invitations sent us by those who had heard of the arrival of "some British boys."*
>
> *Members of the Upper Class had warned us of what to expect from these visits, and there were few who did not feel like the famous British statesman who was wont to counsel "wait and see." We waited, and we saw! The reunion of that Sunday evening gave sufficient evidence of the truth attaching to your world-wide reputation for hospitality. The Georgia of song and story was no mythical place. It was real, and red, and warm, and peopled by a proud race of self-styled "Crackers" to describe whom, the terms "warm hearted, kindly, and hospitable" are totally inadequate.*
>
> *We try here, to offer our humble thanks to "you-all" for the way in which we have been treated during our ten weeks at Souther Field. Tribute has already been paid to those who have worked with, and tended us in our main work here; but, this is dedicated to all those people of Americus and other Georgia towns who have so ably helped to make our stay the real joy it has been to all of us.*
>
> *We are due to move on from here in a few days time and, to the new work that lies ahead, we shall be able to apply ourselves with the new vigour and purpose which your inspiration and encouragement have given us. The common task which has brought us together and which has cemented more firmly the bonds existing between our two great nations, will be tackled as resolutely in the future as in the past. From whatever share we might be permitted to take in the final victory, we trust that you will be able to draw something of that gratitude which these present words are trying to express.*

Other articles in that issue of the cadet magazine were devoted to tweaking the noses of authorities about the various flying and non-flying rules that hampered the life of free spirits among the RAF students. Perhaps the most amusing dealt with the newly enforced rule that moustaches were to be shaved off.

It is not recorded how many members of Class SE-42-C lost moustaches, but the class's fifty-one-man net intake was diminished by sixteen eliminees, fourteen of whom were washed out for non-flying reasons, the largest number of such eliminees of any Arnold Scheme class. Despite efforts to discover why the class had so many eliminees "for reasons other than flying," there was no success. Although official reports allude to students having been eliminated at other Arnold Scheme schools on charges of cheating on ground school examinations, no evidence could be found to indicate that such a breach occurred at Souther Field. It is likely that medical and/or disciplinary problems accounted for the large number of non-flying washouts among members of Class SE-42-C.

On 1 October 1941, Class SE-42-D, ninety RAF students strong, arrived at Souther Field from Toronto. There, they joined the forty-two students of Class SE-42-C, now at the end of their fifth week of primary. Within a few days of their arrival, a powerful hurricane developed near the Bahamas, swept across those islands, crossed Florida into the Gulf of Mexico and then turned northeastward through the Florida panhandle and diagonally through Georgia, exiting into the Atlantic Ocean between Savannah and Charleston, South Carolina. On Tuesday, 7 October, as the now weakened hurricane approached Souther Field, the Stearman trainers were grounded and closed up in the hangars to prevent their being damaged. During that afternoon and evening, high winds and heavy rain swept through Sumter County doing minimal damage.

A week later, amid heavy rain from the fringes of yet another hurricane that struck south of Jacksonville, Florida, Major James W. Gurr, the first commanding officer of Souther Field, departed to assume the post of director of flying at Shaw Field, South Carolina. Captain Littleton Pardue, a 1938 graduate of the United States Military Academy, replaced Gurr as commanding officer at Souther Field, and Pardue remained in that post until 1 June 1942, when he was transferred to the primary flying school at Lafayette, Louisiana. From 1 June to 28 December 1942, the commanding officer at Souther Field was Captain Ernest F. Baldwin, who was viewed by many RAF cadets as the "washout king."

Among the new RAF students who arrived at Souther Field were William D. Parker and E.M.H. Relton. Later, Relton served as editor for the class's edition of the cadet magazine. In his editorial, Relton asserted that "regret at leaving is mingled with pride in having travelled at least a third, perhaps the thorniest part, of the road to our 'Wings,' and if we part from our friends and various tutors now, it is with the assurance that we are not, yet, going far, and shall return from time to time to visit them." In closing his editorial, Relton paid tribute to Peter George Hills and Harold Norman Evans, the two members of Class SE-42-C who were drowned after they had completed their primary training.

William David Parker, another member of Class SE-42-D, was nineteen on 19 August 1941 and completed primary successfully, but was washed out of pilot training at Cochran Field, Georgia. He served as a navigator in Coastal Command, survived the war and stayed in the RAF until his retirement in 1977. From his home in Leicester, Parker recalled his American experience of more than forty years earlier:

We arrived at Americus late evening, were taken to the barrack block and just told to find an empty bed space. We knew Course 42-C would already be in residence. I wandered up to the 1ˢᵗ floor, picked out one of the bays and found an empty bed space. A voice from the next (occupied) bed said, "Hello, Dave." It was from a friend, and he and I had been in the same form at school (at Leiston, Suffolk). I hadn't seen him since he left school in 1938, nor did I know he had joined the R.A.F. What a fantastic coincidence! My school friend's name was A[lbert] Clouting. He went on to graduate as a Sergeant Pilot at Alabama. Unfortunately, he was killed in a flying accident (in the U.K.) in December 1942.

The course was of 10 weeks duration with 2 courses in residence at one time (42-C had been there 5 weeks when we arrived). Both courses in training were accommodated in one large wooden 2-storey barrack block with bunk beds in an open bay system. Everything was immaculately clean and polished. Discipline was very strict American officer training with a demerit system for offenses. The climate was warm to hot and dry. Our "uniform" was solely cotton khaki-type overalls of olive drab colour. We had no problems adapting to the climate because our course started flying on 6 October 1941, and those who survived completed the 60 hours flying around 9 December 1941.

The mess hall was civilian run and served American-style food which was plentiful and palatable. The physical training program included involvement in American-type games such as softball, netball, etc. We also made 2 or 3 visits to some local lake for swimming. The hospitality and generosity of the local citizens of Americus and the surrounding area was marvellous. Streams of cars used to arrive at the camp at noon on Saturdays to take us to their homes for the weekend. We just got "adopted" for the duration of the course.

By the time Class SE-42-D was halfway through primary training, Class SE-42-C departed, and at about that same time, Flight Lieutenant Leonard Speck was transferred and replaced by Flight Lieutenant D. Easton Smith.

DARR AERO TECH
ALBANY, GEORGIA, 42-A-42-D

The Fifty-second U.S. Army Air Forces Flying Training Detachment was established at the municipal airport of Albany, Georgia. Harold S. Darr of Evanston, Illinois, was the civilian contractor for this large primary flight school. The region around Albany in southwest Georgia was made up of a vast plain with few hills, so most of it was about three hundred feet above sea level. Since the plain encompassed eleven Georgia counties and Albany was located on the Flint River at the very center of that rich agricultural region, growth of the settlement was assured. Early in its history, the large number of artesian wells and springs of the region that gushed water from subterranean streams attracted attention. By the 1890s and the first decade of the twentieth century, railroads brought to Albany and Thomasville people who envisioned building recreation and resort facilities that might attract tourists and winter residents.

Since the region had an annual mean temperature of sixty-seven degrees, an average rainfall of fifty inches and very rarely any snow, that prospect appeared bright. Lodges and resort complexes, such as the one at Radium Springs and others at Thomasville and in neighboring counties and towns, catered to sportsmen and winter residents and did indeed attract them in increasing numbers. As a result of the popularity of these recreation facilities and the availability of fresh water from numerous springs, Albany came to be referred to as the Artesian City.

Albany's location on the Flint River in the heart of a rich agricultural district undoubtedly contributed to its early growth, but the fact that it became a junction for seven railroad lines assured its status as a market town and distribution center. Although by 1941 the Flint River was no longer important as a transportation route, it provided other, different benefits. The dams and generating plants built along its course in the 1930s produced immense quantities of electricity for industries and homes. Early in the 1940s, electric cooperatives formed under the aegis of the Rural Electrification Administration began to push transmission lines to farms in the countryside. And the reservoirs created by the dams opened up recreation and sports facilities for a growing population.

By 1936, when Albany celebrated its centennial year, its development had followed patterns established in the evolution of many other small American towns. Except for Front Street, which meandered along the flood plain of the Flint River, the town's layout followed an orderly grid system: streets ran north-south, avenues east-west. Scattered among substantial houses along the tree-lined thoroughfares were several parks, schools, a hospital, the Carnegie Library, an 1,800-seat auditorium, a sports stadium and a compact business district.

As with most other towns, a close examination of a map of Albany and tracing out street names reveals much about its history and evolution. The town's founders and early settlers named Albany's original streets after presidents of the United States. And even though they used the name Jackson (president when the town was incorporated in 1836), the town fathers demonstrated a distinct Virginia bias by naming Washington Street the main north-south artery, and following west of Jackson Street with Jefferson, Monroe and Madison Streets.

Located along Washington Street were the railroad passenger and freight terminals on the north end and Riverside Cemetery on the south end. During 1941–45, the middle section of the town, stretching westward between Washington and Jefferson Streets and along Washington and three adjacent streets between Cotton Avenue on the south and Residence Avenue on the north, was the main business district. However, since residences as well as business and professional offices were interspersed, it was not exclusively a business district.

By 1940, most of the town's major streets and avenues were paved, but many were not. Both United States highways and Georgia state highways joined with Albany's major streets and avenues and connected the town with neighboring towns and cities. Broad Avenue, the main east-west artery, also served as U.S. Highway 82 and cut directly through the center of Albany, linking thoroughfares on both sides of the Flint River. Eastward, it crossed the Flint River Bridge and connected the town with eastward-bound roads to Cordele and Sylvester (U.S. Highway 82) and the southbound Radium Springs Road (Georgia Highway 3).

The latter highway served the Albany State College, an excellent African American college. Westward, Broad Avenue carried U.S. Highway 82 to Dawson and joined other streets, avenues and highways leading northward to Leesburg and southward to Newton and Thomasville. U.S. Highway 19 followed a north-south route. North of Albany it was known as the Leesburg Road; south of town, it was the Camilla Road. Several Georgia state highways served Albany in 1940, and these state roads were also, though not always, labeled according to their destinations.

Although the larger railroad companies maintained separate rail yards and service facilities, their seven rail routes converged at the Albany depot between Washington and Front Streets. While some routes crossed the river to rail yards there, most of the lines cut through and across Albany, linking other towns at different points of the compass. United States highways and state and county roads generally followed the rail lines so, since Albany was established on the west bank of the Flint River, railroad lines, highways and roads connecting it with neighboring towns roughly divided the town and its outskirts into triangular tracts.

With a population of around 24,000 in 1940, Albany had become the major market town for the vast agricultural region. It was a cotton center with a huge gin or cotton compress, a textile mill and a cottonseed oil mill. It also had railroad shops, several wholesale distributors, automobile and farm implement dealerships and marketing facilities and warehouses for the agricultural products of the region, which included cotton, tobacco, pecans, livestock and peanuts. The town's merchants operated hotels, drugstores, local and chain grocery stores, fertilizer and seed stores, cafes and restaurants, motion picture theatres and a variety of service shops such as laundries, taxi service, beautician's shops, barbershops and shoe repair shops. Surprisingly, until about 1942 Albany also had a red-light district called Ragsdale.

As with other Southern towns, Albany's population was divided into five distinct and identifiable elements—people who resided in town, those who lived on farms, those who lived in a nearby mill village, blacks (who were of one category regardless of where they lived) and those from outside the state and region. Despite these class divisions, the bulk of Albany's population perceived themselves as middle class. Most of them were honest, hardworking churchgoers who took care of their obligations and were proud of their town, state and country. They were also inveterate hero worshippers who, if they had no heroes of the moment, were not beyond accepting those proposed by others.

Since the natives of a Balkan country were more properly called "Albanians," citizens of Albany, Georgia, were undoubtedly sensitive about having that label used to describe them, even by their own local newspapers. The state and the region in which they lived was a stronghold of the Democratic Party, but pride in the nation and its leaders caused some of the town's citizens to put aside partisan politics long enough to honor several Republican presidents by naming streets after them.

In February 1940, three months before Nazi forces crushed all opposition as they swept across Western Europe, disaster befell Albany, Georgia. A tornado with a wind velocity that was said to exceed 250 miles per hour ripped a path through twenty-eight blocks in the heart of the town, killing eighteen people and injuring dozens. The storm inflicted heavy damage on commercial and private property, amounting to more than $2 million. That disaster brought great trauma to many of the town's citizens, but it undoubtedly made them more sensitive to calamities suffered by the people of Western Europe and Britain. During the summer and autumn of 1940, while British citizens were enduring repeated crises, the people of Albany, Georgia, made the necessary repairs to their tornado-ravaged town and identified closely with the British cause. The townspeople also watched with great interest as United States Army Air Corps site selection teams chose southwest Georgia for a number of major air stations.

For Harold S. Darr, an Evanston, Illinois banker, aviator and government contractor, Albany was a particularly attractive prospect for developing a flying school. Harold S. Darr was born in Iowa in 1893, and had learned to fly in the United States Army Air Service in 1917–18. Darr had gained a commission and served as a flight instructor at Kelly and Brooks Fields near San Antonio, Texas, and at Carlstrom Field near Arcadia, Florida. During the late 1920s and early 1930s, he had been employed by the Curtiss Company and American Airlines. In 1935, he had leased facilities at Curtiss Field near Glenview, Illinois, and had opened the Chicago School of Aeronautics.

In 1939, Darr's company also operated from Palwaukee Airport near Chicago and trained students from Northwestern University and other colleges and universities in the government-sponsored Civilian Pilot Training Program (CPTP). Darr aided in the training of black pilots in the Chicago area and strongly supported the establishment of the Tuskegee, Alabama contract school. His former air service and CPTP experience placed him in an excellent position to become a flying school contractor. During spring 1939, Darr and seven other flying school operators obtained the first of a series of War Department contracts to provide primary flying training to army air corps flying cadets. On 1 July 1939, Darr's Chicago School of Aeronautics commenced training members of Class 40-A at the Curtiss Airport in Glenview.

In late May 1940, when army air corps officers announced the seven-thousand-pilot training plan, the eight civil contractors were asked to establish an additional school with the same training capacity in the Southern region of the United States. The purpose of seeking sites in warmer regions to the South was at the urging of air corps officers who were anxious to ensure that contractors might conduct flying training year-round with minimal disruption owing to adverse weather conditions. Except for Harold S. Darr and the Reverend Ernest J. Sias, who operated the northernmost flying schools, the other six civilian contractors were urged to double the size and capacity of their existing schools.

Since the Reverend Sias's Lincoln Airplane and Flying School at Lincoln, Nebraska, and Darr's Chicago School of Aeronautics at Glenview, Illinois, had encountered severe weather problems during the winter of 1939–40 and lost much training time, they were urged to locate sites in the sunbelt states to which they might move their schools. Sias reluctantly moved his flying school to Lakeland, Florida. However, Harold Darr was able to convince army air corps officers that since the U.S. Navy had indicated its intention to acquire the Glenview airport for its own use, both Darr and the army air corps would profit by continuing flying training as long as possible at Glenview.

In June 1940, while flying continued at Glenview, Harold Darr visited Albany. After seeing the town and the large airport site, he concluded that, if an arrangement could be reached with Albany and Dougherty County officials, it could be mutually beneficial. Darr and the army air corps would get a large and excellent site for a flying school, and at war's end, the city and county could assume control of a fully developed airport. Because of the drain on financial resources caused by the Great Depression and by the repair work and rebuilding undertaken by the city of Albany and Dougherty County following the February tornado, town and county officials were understandably anxious to develop a new municipal airport at minimal expense to the public treasury.

As a result, negotiations were rapidly completed, a contract was signed and Darr leased the unfinished new municipal airport, a very large site of slightly more than six hundred acres some four miles southwest of Albany on the Newton Road (Georgia State Highway 91). In order to develop the airport, city and county officials agreed to seek WPA funds and United States government grants. In addition to leasing the airport, Darr purchased a tract of approximately thirty-five acres directly across the highway east of the airfield and quickly developed plans to use WPA labor as much as possible to build both domestic and ground instructional facilities on that site.

When completed, the administration building, which contained offices for civilian and military officers, dominated the east side of the school. Nearby were several two-story barrack blocks capable of accommodating 230 cadets each and a dining hall large enough to seat the entire student population. In addition, the area east of Newton Road also contained a recreation building that housed a canteen, barbershop and library. One end of the domestic site held complete physical training facilities, including a large swimming pool, an obstacle course and playing fields. On the west side of the Newton Road, where flight instruction was to take place, two large hangars, an operations building and a control tower and beacon were erected. Earth was hauled in to fill and level a huge depression in the middle of the airfield. Sod runways were laid out, grass was planted and the Stearman PT-17 aircraft were maintained in the open until sufficient hangar space, shops and a paint shop could be completed.

As indicated, the civil contract primary flying school was being developed on the southwest side of Albany. A few months later, an army air corps site selection team chose a huge site on the opposite (northeast) side of Albany on which to build a new army air corps training station. The new airdrome, Turner Field, became a major army air corps advanced flying school for training pilots and navigators. Beginning in January 1942, a portion of Turner Field also housed the RAF Reception Center, much of it under canvas, for its four-week-long acclimatization course. Except for payroll, a hospital and other support services, Turner Field had little to do with the civil contract primary flying school on the opposite side of Albany.

Between 8 and 12 August 1940, the first army air corps flying cadets arrived at Albany, and since Darr Aero Tech's barracks were not yet ready, they were housed and fed temporarily in the Georgian Hotel. When the primary flying school commenced operations, Darr had already transferred some of his Glenview, Illinois employees to Georgia. Many others who continued to work at the Illinois school until it closed in March 1941 were later transferred to Albany or to one of Darr's other contract flying schools at Augusta, Georgia, and Lakeland, Florida. Although the older name, Chicago School of Aeronautics, continued in use at Albany for a time, the school's official name was changed to Darr Aero Tech, Incorporated. By autumn 1940, when the primary flying school commenced full operations with Classes SE-41-E and SE-41-F in residence, the town was whole again, and the municipal airport was no longer a financial drain on local government.

The name change was undoubtedly necessary to comply with its Georgia corporate charter, but it was also a good idea to remove the name "Chicago" from the company name if it was to do business in southwest Georgia. A good reason for the change was that the American Civil War was still being fought verbally, and nowhere more spiritedly than within the state of Georgia during the years immediately following the appearance of the popular motion picture *Gone With The Wind*.

Civilian staff at Darr Aero Tech included a number of men with many years' experience in aviation. D'Ross Ellis, a former army air corps officer, combined the jobs of general manager and director of flying. When Ellis was sent to the Darr school at Ponca City, Oklahoma, he was replaced by Gordon Matthews as general manager and by John H. Armstrong as director of flying. F.K. Savage, formerly chief pilot at Glenview, Illinois, directed the instructors' school at Albany. William H. Teufort, who had been chief of maintenance at Glenview, transferred to Albany in that same capacity. As with other contract schools, Darr Aero Tech organized training flights and appointed flight commanders and instructors for each of them. Every twelve weeks, each instructor received a new contingent of flying cadets.

During the early months of operation, the military staff included as commanding officer and army air corps supervisor the highly experienced Captain Andrew J. McVea, 1931 West Point graduate, who had served in Panama and as an instructor at Randolph Field. When in May 1941 McVea left

Darr Aero Tech, he was replaced by the equally experienced and tough Captain William M. Brown. Captain Marshall Groover served as flight surgeon at the school and with his staff maintained a small infirmary. Years later, Dr. Groover was appointed surgeon general of the USAAF.

Others of the military staff included several assistant army air corps supervisors who wore many hats, but who served primarily as military check pilots. Lieutenant Francis K. Wood Jr. of Taunton, Massachusetts, a member of Darr Class 41-E, won his wings in May 1941 and was assigned to duty at the Albany school. For several months, Wood held a variety of jobs, including commandant of cadets, until he was replaced by Captain Gordon Wheeler, a native of Vermont and graduate of Northeastern University. In March 1943, Wood was promoted to major and commanding officer of the school. As with other primary flying schools, Darr Aero Tech initially employed a civilian director of physical training. Between August 1940 and June 1941, more than six hundred U.S. Army Air Corps flying cadets entered training at the Albany school.

In early June 1941, British student pilots arrived in Albany. Each contingent was accompanied by RCAF officers on assignment from the No. 1 Movements Group as escort officers. These officers brought with them route schedules and special travel requisitions for use in handling administrative details, including changing trains, meal and luggage vouchers and physical checks by American immigration officers. Once they reached their destination, the escort officer would call the roll and provide accurate nominal rolls to the appropriate American officer and the RAF staff administrative officer (RAFAO).

The brief period at Toronto had been one of relative relaxation. Now, before the harsh and demanding grind of flying training, came long train journeys for each draft. Some of the trips on the huge Canadian and American trains would be of almost epic proportions, conveying their young British passengers southward. American music and the Hollywood cinema had given them a particular view of the United States, but even these impressions could not convey the excitement at glimpsing for oneself many of the places only vaguely seen before in films or learned about from magazines, books or music.

Actual entry into the United States was a first for most of them. The initial five drafts were properly "disguised" as civilians for entry into the neutral United States. As one RAF cadet wrote, "their civilian 'uniforms' made them look like a convention of insurance salesmen."

At around 7:20 p.m., Sunday, 8 June 1941, Flying Officer S.C. Foster delivered the 140-member Class SE-42-A, the first class of British cadets, to RAF and army air corps officers in Albany. The students were greeted by a large crowd of civilians who had been waiting several hours for their arrival. They immediately boarded buses and were transported to the primary flying school four miles southwest of Albany. Darr Aero Tech at Albany, Georgia, was the largest of the Arnold Scheme primary pilot training schools.

For fear of a reaction by American isolationists, efforts had been made in Washington and London to prevent publicity being given to the movements of the British student pilots. RCAF conducting officers were ordered not to allow either photographs to be taken or publicity to be given out about their drafts, but most such efforts proved useless. Once publicity about the British cadets proved beneficial and their worries unfounded, RAF officials were glad that the press did not cooperate.

A lead article on the front page of the *Albany Herald* of Monday, 9 June 1941, captured the public mood before and during the arrival on Sunday of the first RAF contingent in that small American town:

In spite of the fact that no definite information was forthcoming from either Darr Tech or railroad officials as to the time of the boys' arrival, a good-sized crowd had gathered at the Terminal Station by the time the boys' special train came in, for public interest was keen, and many persons haunted the station throughout the afternoon. A number of these had cameras, but no pictures were permitted to be taken by any other than The Herald *photographer.*

A majority of the young men were dressed almost exactly alike, in severely plain gray sack suits. Speculation arose as to the reason for this, one opinion being that this was a patriotic measure adopted generally throughout Britain. It was explained by one of the officers, however, that the gray flannel suits worn by most of the boys conformed to the usual summer dress in England. Spontaneous applause burst from the crowd as one youth passed by with an apparently improvised flag with the initials RAF painted in red.

Having arrived late, the RAF students were rushed to the school dining hall for a sumptuous meal with plenty of milk, white bread and butter. The cadets were then issued blankets and sheets and were assigned to their billets. There, they quickly removed the rumpled, dirty and hot woolen suits, showered, made their bunks and fell into them for much-needed rest.

The large draft of RAF students of Class 42-A brought together young men from virtually every county in England and Northern Ireland and small representation from Wales and Scotland. It also included a few volunteers from Eire. Several of them had attended prestigious public schools; others had been trained in architecture, medicine and engineering; a majority of them had left school early and had gained jobs in government or business; and a few were farmers. Several of the students were sons of parents who had left England for South Africa, India, Canada, Chile or Brazil. Although the RAF students were accompanied by an RCAF escort officer, other officers arrived in Albany in time to welcome them.

Among them were Group Captains D.V. Carnegie and F.W. Trott, and Wing Commander Harry A.V. Hogan. Though most of the officers were dressed in the distinctive summer RAF uniforms, Flight Lieutenant Alfred G. Hill, the newly assigned RAF administrative officer (RAFAO) at Darr Aero Tech, arrived dressed in a civilian suit. Carnegie, the senior UK training officer in the United States, was interviewed by reporters. The interview gave him an opportunity to express his appreciation for the reception given UK students and such obvious support for the British cause. He also publicly expressed his concern that the British cadets might receive so much American hospitality that it would interfere with their flying training. That was a refrain that would be repeated to no avail by virtually every RAF officer who visited the flying schools.

In the meantime, Flying Officer S.C. Foster, RCAF conducting officer, turned over the students and nominal rolls to air corps officers listing their charges by name and serial number. The next day, if he had received them, he left individual pay and equipment books with Flight Lieutenant Alfred G. Hill. Any RCAF blankets on consignment for the journey were collected from the men and packed for shipment back to Toronto. After a few days' leave, Foster returned to Canada by rail to join another draft destined for assignment to a flying school.

The first full day on the Georgia station proved to be a rude awakening for the RAF men. Immediately, indoctrination began, as did ground and flying classes; everyone and everything seemed to be in a terrible rush. When the British cadets removed their ill-fitting RAF or Canadian-issue khaki uniforms from their kit bags, donned them and formed up in front of their barracks, they looked like victims of a disaster. Not only were the uniforms new and wrinkled, but most of the khakis were also "one size fits all," and some of them might easily accommodate more than one student.

In order to avoid further embarrassment, Flight Lieutenant Hill quickly appealed to Wing Commander Hogan at Maxwell Field for funds with which to meet the expenses necessary for the RAF students to make a presentable appearance. In a few instances, cadets modified their own uniforms, but most of them were sent out and the cost of tailoring was paid from RAF imprest funds. As with their American classmates, the British students were also provided with a laundry allowance.

On the day their training commenced, the British student pilots were formed into flights and assigned first either to ground school or to flying. When cadets scheduled to report to the flight line donned the heavily lined RAF-issue flying suits and formed up in front of their barracks with pukka sahib flying pith helmets, which were equipped with ear flaps and radio plugs, the effect was predictably amusing, especially given the heat of a June day in south Georgia. In place of the cumbersome RAF winter flying suits, the army air corps quickly issued their own loose version of one size fits all cotton drill coveralls (in blue or olive drab), which doubled as fatigue and flying outfits until proper khaki slacks and shirts could also be issued from air corps stocks for wear while on the station.

Although some of the later classes were also issued a different style of sun helmet, the early contingents had been issued cloth-covered cork pith helmets that had evidently come from RAF stocks left over from operations on India's northwest frontier. From an interview with Flight Lieutenant Hill and several cadets, an *Albany Herald* news reporter was impressed with their sincere expressions of appreciation for the hospitable reception, fresh fruit and plenty of food. The reporter also drew out their responses concerning adjustment to the heat and dust of summer 1941. In the course of the interview, it was learned that Coca-Colas were entirely new to the British cadets, and that they were drinking the carbonated beverages (five cents each) at a terrific rate; the record for one cadet was sixteen in one day.

In an effort to keep cool, some of them were also taking as many as six showers per day. Further adjustment to the heat and humidity, and to strange but plentiful food, would take some time, but Nelson, Speedy, Snowball and Walter, the cheerful young black waiters in the dining hall, helped to make adjustment to strange food easier. Adjustment to unusual accents and to rigid regulations about nearly everything imaginable would take longer. American aviation cadet Class SE-41-I was the senior or upper class, and it had the responsibility for introducing the incoming lower class of British student pilots to the mysteries of cadet life. Hazing in its many forms took place, and was accepted for the most part in the spirit in which it was intended.

Once the British cadets learned the "form," they began to adjust to the school, to American customs and to Albany. Close by their barracks, they enjoyed the swimming pool, horseshoe pitching and assorted sports. Their first opportunity to leave the school occurred at noon on Saturday, 14 June, and lasted to 4:00 p.m. on Sunday, 15 June. Normally, they would not have been allowed to leave the station for two weeks, but within five days of their arrival they were permitted to go off-post, in the commanding officer's words, "principally so they could shed their long underwear in favor of garments more suited to the climate."

Although their limited pay could never be stretched far enough, the British cadets were compelled to purchase some items of clothing in order to survive the heat. They also purchased cameras, film, snacks and gifts for their loved ones at home. Many of them roamed Albany's wide sidewalks, struck up acquaintances at random and had a "bit of a look," while others joined the benefit golf tournament at the American Legion course. Within the coolness of the Gordon Hotel, many of them quickly found themselves welcome in such clubs as Freddie's Office and the Cadet Club while others went to the Marine Room at the New Albany Hotel.

Long before Britain's Boots Company and other chemists' shops in Britain modified their marketing systems, there was the American drugstore, which to the young British student pilots was one of the marvels of their lives. They quickly discovered the Lee Drug Store at the corner of Broad and Jackson Streets and several others in the city. Within these unusual shops, they bought malted milkshakes, film, pens and paper, sandwiches and a wide variety of other items. Nearby in downtown Albany were all of the other necessities of life including movie theatres, cafes and restaurants, milk bars, men's shops, Spielberger's and Collum's Photo Shops, laundries, shoe repair shops, department stores, taxi stands, barbershops and jewelry stores.

They also found within the town the American Legion Club and the Centennial Bowling Lanes on Washington Street. Across the Flint River and a few miles to the south were two additional recreation centers. The magnificent Radium Springs Country Club with its hotel, swimming pool, golf course, beautiful grounds and walks was an ideal summer spot, while farther south, Riverbend Park offered similar recreation in addition to roller skating. In the course of their training at Albany, many of the British cadets would be taken by American hosts on picnics, and a few undoubtedly dined and danced at such nearby night spots as the Paramount Club in adjoining Lee County and, after July 1, the Hangar Club on Radium Springs Road.

The newspaper reporter recorded citizens' impressions of the British newcomers: "Albany liked them, liked their grins, and liked the way they chop off words just before you think they're going to end. Most of all, it liked their friendliness." On Saturday evening, 14 June, American Legion Post 30 paired one group of twenty-five cadets with a group of young ladies of the Hospital League and treated them to a dinner-dance at their club. Understandably, members of each of the RAF drafts had difficulty adjusting to the adulation and overwhelming hospitality that they encountered.

LAC Reginald Levy, who arrived in Albany on Sunday afternoon, 8 June 1941, could not have known when he arrived in that sleepy south Georgia town that he was launching a distinguished career in aviation, nor could he have known that his friend, Kenneth Barlass, would die in a flying accident at an advanced flying school about six months hence. More than forty years and 25,000 flying hours later, Levy, a retired airline pilot, recalled the difficulty of adjusting to army air corps cadet discipline, inspections, gigs and walking tours. Levy also remembered with warmth and affection Leslie H. Freye and "Kinky" Gunn, his two highly experienced civilian instructors at Darr. He remembered that Freye was "a veritable 'father' to me," and that H.F. "Kinky" Gunn, who was unfortunately killed in an Oklahoma flying accident on 3 November 1942, had been a Hollywood stunt pilot.

Flight Lieutenant Alfred G. Hill, the RAFAO who was perceived by many cadets as having a "cushy" job, was busy cultivating good public relations. In the course of his service at several Arnold Scheme flying schools, Hill probably spoke more often to small town civic clubs than any other RAF officer serving in the United States during World War II. Virtually every week, a local newspaper reported his having addressed some civic group such as the Kiwanis, Lions, Rotary or Exchange Clubs. Regularly, Hill conveyed to grass-roots Georgia community and business leaders Prime Minister Churchill's message of defiance and hope, which helped to seal American affection and sentiments to their cause.

Paraphrasing one of the prime minister's famous deliveries and adhering to instructions from Washington as to the approval of statements released to the public, Hill told one Lions Club audience, "We have the pilots; all we need is the tools to do the job, and the U.S. is giving them to us." Although the point was not picked up by the *Albany Herald* reporter, nor evidently by an audience intent upon how it was said, rather than what was being said, no one apparently raised the obvious question: if Britain has the pilots, why are more being trained in the United States?

Hill's remark was not a slip; it was the honest assertion of what British officials had been saying for some time in London as well as in Washington. What Britain wanted from the United States was food, arms, tanks, airplanes and related equipment. The Air Ministry was also recruiting experienced American volunteer pilots for RAF and RCAF service either directly or through the four Refresher Scheme schools. It now also had the Arnold Scheme pilot training program.

General Arnold's offer to train four thousand British pilots alongside American cadets was sincere and generous, but the American general's apparent ulterior motive was to remove himself from President Roosevelt's doghouse. His early opposition to the president's policy of selling American tactical aircraft to friendly foreign powers had placed him under a cloud and caused the president to hint that perhaps he should retire. Arnold was saved by General George C. Marshall's support and the air corps chief's timely aid to Britain.

Since the Air Ministry did not, and never would, completely trust any other pilot training system, it had gained permission to establish six RAF-controlled British flying training schools in the United States. These BFTSs would use the RAF training syllabus, a small number of experienced British officer-supervisors, American aircraft, American civilian flying instructors and American maintenance and support staff to train additional British pilots. And all charges would be paid from Lend-Lease funds.

Use of American flying schools would not drain large numbers of British pilots from active squadrons to serve as instructors; use of American aircraft and American personnel would not diminish active RAF strength. Although Britain was training large numbers of pilots in Canada and elsewhere in the empire, these American-staffed aircrew training schools would serve as insurance to maintain RAF pilot production levels, especially in the event of problems with Canadian weather, and would, Air Ministry officers hoped, also allow the recruiting and training of aircrew in the neutral United States.

There was nothing wrong that Air Ministry officials and such subordinate officers as Flight Lieutenant Hill were telling the truth, nor, despite minor carping by a few tiny elements of American society, was there anything amiss in having RAF training in the United States. During the summer of 1941, the United States was at peace, but the war appeared to be coming ever closer. In order to prevent such horrible slaughter as had occurred in the static trench warfare of 1914–18, plans had already been developed by British leaders to use massive air power as an offensive weapon. Facilities, materials and technicians for constructing the thousands of aircraft necessary to make such plans realities, as has been stated earlier, required more aircraft than Britain or her dominions could build, so Great Britain wanted American aid primarily for the purpose of obtaining aircraft.

On 10 July 1941, Hill spoke to the Albany Rotary Club meeting at the Gordon Hotel and told his audience that United States aid was not only necessary and appreciated, but was essential to Great Britain's survival. "We once had one great song that rang in our hearts," said the rotary speaker, "and that was 'There'll always be an England.' Now we have two, for we have added,

'God Bless America.'" However corny the remarks might sound several decades after the war, they brought cheers from those present. Hill was doing a superb public relations job.

As the days rolled past into July 1941, the UK cadets watched their numbers dwindle rapidly as many of their fellow students were eliminated from pilot training and moved to a special barracks at Darr Aero Tech designated for those awaiting reassignment. Before American aviation cadet Class SE-41-I departed and abandoned the Darr Glee Club, Class 42-A's LAC Eric W. "Stonewall" Jones organized a new glee club. Those who were persuaded to join him included LACs Clifford Goodwin, Ted Headington ("gig" champion), Harold "Kipper" Stripp, George T. Shaw, Herbert J. "Randy" Anderson and Rycharde H.W. Hogarth, who had attended the Christchurch Cathedral Choir School at Oxford and had sung in that choir for four years. Lieutenant W.T. Smith served as sponsor of the new choral group. Within a brief time, they were making regular weekly broadcasts on Albany's radio station, WALB.

In July, Julian "Tarzan" Burkness, who was remembered by the RAF cadets as "of mighty physique," arrived on the station. Within a short time, the flying school had a full-fledged athletic and physical training program, and the British cadets learned American games such as volleyball (net ball), basketball and also the meaning of the word "calisthenics." *Albany Herald* reporter Kenneth Pryse, later an employee of Darr Aero Tech, reported these activities in an article entitled "Ambitious Plans Made For Physical Training of British Cadets Here."

Between 11 and 15 July, the American cadets of Class SE-41-I graduated and departed for basic flying training, and preparations began immediately to receive a second RAF draft, Class SE-42-B. On 20 July 1941, 85 men of a 170-man second RAF intake arrived at Albany. Five days later, an additional 85 men arrived to complete Class SE-42-B and to make the school completely British. As seniors, Class SE-42-A elected student officers. LAC Guy E.C. Pease, a tall cadet from Yorkshire, was elevated to the rank of cadet major, while blond and debonair Anthony Notley of Sutton, Surrey, became cadet captain and former medical student Nigel L. Bottome of Bromley, Kent, became cadet captain-adjutant. As was common practice, other men from Class SE-42-A were appointed cadet officer flight leaders and noncommissioned officers.

The lateness of the RAF drafts was an irritant to army air corps as well as civilian contractor staffs. When students arrived late, it was often necessary to double up and hurry them through portions of their training syllabus in order to meet output schedules imposed by higher headquarters. Although half of the class arrived late, everything appeared to be going smoothly at the flying school, for during its ten months of operation, there had not even been a serious accident. In Albany, the auxiliary guild of St. Paul's Episcopal Church opened recreation rooms in the parish house on Flint Avenue.

On Friday morning, 25 July 1941, that spotless record was broken when an RAF student going on a solo flight from the main airdrome plowed into a PT-17 waiting to take off. A Darr Aero Tech mechanic received a broken leg in the accident, and nineteen-year-old LAC D'Arcy H. Wilson of Windermere, Westmoreland, in England's stunningly beautiful Lake District, became the first fatality of the Arnold Scheme training program. The Reverend Harry S. Cobey conducted funeral services for Wilson at St. Paul's Episcopal Church. Just after noon on Saturday, 26 July, a twenty-man honor guard led by Flight Lieutenant Hill escorted the body to the church and to the Crown Hill Cemetery west of Albany on the north side of Dawson Road.

American practice for men killed while serving their country within the United States was and is to ship their remains home for burial. If killed overseas during wartime, most servicemen of all nations were buried in temporary graves. At the end of the war, in order to ensure perpetual care, remains were moved to permanent and beautifully designed military cemeteries. At the time of the relocation, American families were given the option of returning their loved ones to their homeland for permanent burial or consigning them to space in the nearest overseas military cemetery. Although British practice was similar, standard procedure borne out of custom was to bury their dead where they fell and leave them there.

The death of the nineteen-year-old British youth so far from home and loved ones produced an outpouring of emotion from many people of Albany, Dougherty County and the state of Georgia. Since such tragedies were to be expected as a cost of war, RAF staff and some of the older, more hardened RAF cadets were offended by all of the "bother." As was to become standard practice wherever such tragedies occurred in the United States, heartbroken mothers and fathers in Britain quietly and politely wrote letters expressing their appreciation for kindnesses shown to their young men in life and death.

Some people handled the tragedy well; others gushed. A poem appeared in an Atlanta newspaper; some well-meaning people sought out the address of survivors, and their sentiments were undoubtedly conveyed to the dead student pilot's mother in Britain. Some weeks later, her sad letter arrived and was duly published. After the war, she expressed a desire to "see the place my D'Arcy lies." Although during the next forty years many British mothers and fathers did arrive in the Southeastern United States on such sad missions, it is not known whether that particular wish was ever fulfilled.

On 15 August 1941, Class SE-42-A completed its primary flying course and began preparation for departure. Of its original 172 cadets, the class suffered 1 fatality, 85 of its members were eliminated and 86, or 50 percent of that first RAF class, graduated. As the primary school graduates departed on 17 August, Courtney Hayter-Preston, former reporter for the London *Evening Standard* and editor of the Class SE-42-A edition of the cadet magazine *Pee Tee*, spoke for the entire class in thanking the people of Albany for their "hospitality, kindness, and sympathy with the British cause." In 1942, Pilot Officer Hayter-Preston died in an air collision near Sacramento, California, where he was undergoing training to be a flight instructor. His remains and those of 4 other RAF pilot officers were interred in a Sacramento cemetery.

Since Darr Aero Tech had extra billets early on, large numbers of RAF eliminees had been held at the school until they could be transferred to Canada, but with three hundred British cadets on the station, there were no longer any extra beds, so eliminees were being sent directly to Maxwell Field to await reassignment. Although a few of the original military and civilian staff members had been transferred to duties elsewhere, the school staff had been expanded considerably. Within a few weeks, amidst the heat and thunderstorms of midsummer in southwest Georgia, members of Class SE-42-B also watched their numbers dwindle as many of their classmates were eliminated from pilot training.

During that time, many of these young eliminees were interviewed, and some of them were posted to other primary schools in order to be allowed a few extra hours of instruction. One such student from Darr Aero Tech was Fred Fish of Nottingham, who was posted to the primary school at Camden, South Carolina. Other eliminees were posted from Albany to other Arnold Scheme primary schools or to one of the British flying training schools to continue pilot training. Some of them succeeded, and others were again eliminated. In a number of instances, after British student pilots were denied further opportunities for training in the United States, they continued a pilot's course in Canada, Britain or South Africa.

One such member of Class SE-42-B was Norman Cass. Writing forty-two years later from his home in Scotland, Cass recalled that his class drank "lots of Coca Colas at 5 cents each from the revolutionary new ice machine (it was new to us at that time, and it could be 'fiddled' by a sharp kick, sometimes)." Cass and some of his fellow classmates were disturbed at observing "a chain gang of convicts walking along the roadside—truly a sobering experience." Told by someone in Albany that a village called Ragsdale, which was reported to be inhabited by prostitutes, existed a few miles from the training field, Cass and several classmates decided to have a look.

Norman Cass described that experience:

> To a crowd of 18 year old British boys, mainly from the "sticks," this represented "sophisticated sin," which we declared would not be sampled. On the first Saturday night, we sampled the bars of Albany—then four of us succumbed to a taxi trip to "Ragsdale" merely to "case the joint!" We agreed to keep a low profile for the good name of our contingent. We were taken aback as the taxi drove into "Ragsdale" and the headlights picked up more gray flannel suited figures slipping around bungalows than I'd had hot breakfasts! It seemed a well-organized community.

Unfortunately, about three weeks after his arrival at the Albany flying school, Cass was eliminated from pilot training.

On 28 August 1941, within a few days of Cass's departure, a Darr cadet on a solo flight created a local stir when he landed his airplane in a peanut field five miles north of Donalsonville, Georgia. Although the Stearman PT-17 flipped over onto its back, neither the airplane nor the RAF student was hurt. Later, such events would hardly be noticed, but so soon after the accidental death of LAC D'Arcy Wilson of Class SE-42-A, even a forced landing attracted newspaper attention.

LAC John C. Bliss, a twenty-eight-year-old former detective inspector with the London Metropolitan Police, was one of the older RAF students on the course. From retirement some forty-two years later, he recalled how the American people adopted them. "We were treated superbly," Bliss wrote, "welcomed into every home and looked after with great affection and also with great tolerance." Since he later served as a flying instructor on single-engine aircraft in a USAAF advanced flying school, his assessment of the training at Darr Aero Tech is particularly valuable.

As John Bliss recalled:

> We did not realise that the system was geared very rightly to callow youths from High School who knew everything and had to be re-moulded. A metropolitan police officer of some years standing and with a good deal of experience of death and destruction was not always very cooperative, but experience modified both attitudes, especially as a result of the wonderful flying instructors—civilians at Darr and Army Air Forces at Basic and Advanced.
>
> These men were excellent and put up with a lot of very clumsy piloting, but were wise enough to see that even if some of us were rather old (in my case, 28), we were at least keen and interested and might be of some use because of our reliability. They must have been excellent; otherwise they would never have taught me to fly.

Life continued for Class SE-42-B as it had for its predecessors. There were adjustments to be made, and there was fun as well.

To the British student pilots, the bright sunlight and summer temperatures of ninety-five to one hundred degrees Fahrenheit were unbelievable, but there were pools and ponds and lakes to swim in, even if, owing to the terrible drought that swept most of the entire Southeast, the water levels were unusually low. There were also people to meet and picnics to enjoy. During off-duty hours, many of the young men were able to use the new recreation center that had been established in the parish house of the Episcopal church.

The dietician at the primary school and the wives and mothers of host families were delighted to receive instruction in the mysteries of making Yorkshire pudding and a "proper" cup of tea. Whether or not any of the RAF students at Darr were able to attend the performance of Count Basie and his band in the Albany Municipal Auditorium on Thursday evening, 4 September, is unknown, but there were undoubtedly many who certainly would have enjoyed the opportunity to do so.

As with Reginald Levy of Class SE-42-A, Stanley N. Freestone of Class SE-42-B was learning to fly for the RAF and was launching a career as well. More than forty years later, Captain Freestone, DFC, MiD, veteran of twenty-seven years and thousands of flying hours as an airline pilot, recalled his Georgia days and described one of many incidents that undoubtedly caused some American staff members to mutter on occasion such words as "mad dogs and Englishmen!!" and the British students suffering from hazing to retort with "mad dogs and Americans!!"

As Freestone remembered,

> Darr Aero Tech was a beautifully equipped modern school just a short distance outside Albany, Georgia. The summer was very hot upon arrival and our first three weeks was in almost drought conditions. I remember one evening a very heavy storm came in from the Gulf of Mexico, as they were wont to do. Torrential rain fell with an immediate drop in temperature of some 20 degrees F. The barracks were not air conditioned in those days, and all of the pupils raced out onto the drill square in the scantiest of clothing, prancing about in the cooling deluge. Within minutes, large puddles formed which served as excellent water splashes as we all raced about shouting.

The shouting continued, but it was of a different kind. Class SE-42-B was introduced to United States Army aviation cadet discipline, and it was not a pleasant experience for some of the British students. From the vantage point of many years of experience, Norman Cass wrote that he "still bristled" at the thought of the hazing. No doubt both Cass and Stanley Freestone knew the reason for the hazing, and both admitted reacting against the practice.

In reminiscing about differences between the two services, Freestone recognized that there were logical reasons for the tightly organized schedules and for each demand placed on the student pilots.

> Senior cadet officers were the immediate disciplinarians. The American term, "hazing," was used to describe a form of harrassment which in the American mind kept recruits on their toes; it did not appear to be designed to suit the average Anglo-Saxon. Such things as eating a "square" meal were ordered by a senior cadet. The victim had to move the hand that he was feeding with through 90 degrees for each movement to the mouth, and each one away from it. One would be challenged anywhere anytime to recite "Fuzzy

Wuzzy," and if unable to perform what I regarded as a completely childish exercise, one was awarded a demerit. Three demerits made a tour, and a tour consisted of half an hour's walking up and down a ramp on the square in the hot sun during one's off duty time, which was pretty scarce.

The general system seemed to be designed to run you off your feet throughout the waking day. Reveille was at 0530 and Lights Out at 2115, and you were certainly ready for it. With daytime temperatures often in the nineties, plus humidity during high summer, British cadets found the whole exercise most enervating. Food was excellent, that is, if you were given enough time to eat it. All senior cadets had to be served first, and when they decided the meal was finished, it was, and if you had just got your soup—hard luck.

Remonstrations to the RAF Liaison Officer were of no avail, because he was informed by the US Army Air Corps that that was the system for their cadets and that was how it was going to stay. Opposition to this system by the more "hard headed" Anglo-Saxon produced what the Americans called an "attitude" case. If not controlled, this "attitude," after a time, was enough to get you back on the train to Canada—washed out. However, to be fair to the United States Army, this was their system to put pressure upon men when they were learning something quite complicated like learning to fly. The rationale being that we wish to find the "weaker" characters who will break under battle conditions.

The school was equipped with a fine swimming pool and we also played volleyball and baseball. Our American PT instructor could never understand how we could play a game without needing a referee. When we told him we all played "cricket," he still did not understand, saying that American lads when left alone would have some pretty furious arguments within minutes. Here must be one of the basic differing characteristics of the Britisher and the American.

Freestone and his classmates were primarily concerned with flying, and it was on the flight line and in the skies over southwest Georgia that they came to feel more at home.

His flying instructor was Mr. C. Ebert, who was born in Germany and had immigrated with his parents to Milwaukee when he was a boy. In American aviation parlance of the time, Ebert was a "hamburger pilot," which meant that he earned his living from flying. He had a commercial license and lots of experience flying passengers and cargoes and dusting crops with pesticides. Freestone, who was the first of his particular group to solo, remembered Mr. Ebert as a "first class instructor" who was "a tanned fair-haired man of 'ample girth' and some 5'7" tall."

When his students were not "performing quite up to standard," Ebert's remark was usually, "If I have to wash you out, Hitler will send me another Iron Cross!" Unfortunately, some RAF students believed Mr. Ebert's little joke and similar expressions made by other American instructors of German descent. Years later, several former British students even expressed the view that a conspiracy existed among German Americans to wash out as many British students as possible so as to aid the Nazi cause. Freestone expressed no such views. He was concerned about the wastage problem and was sympathetic with students who washed out and returned to Canada for remustering, but he understood the reasons for such standards.

Stanley Freestone enjoyed flying the Stearman PT-17 and was impressed with the efficiency of school maintenance and training personnel. As he expressed it,

Superb is the best word to describe the equipment and the standard to which it was maintained. Something like 30 Stearmans were on the tarmac and ALL were washed down and "leathered" off first thing in the morning. Servicing equipment and standards were also first class, as was everything issued to us by the U.S. authorities. This standard was also required in the flying training. No border line performances were tolerated. The final washout rate at Primary School at Albany was something in the region of 45% [actually 46.4 percent].

The Stearman was built with quite a narrow track undercarriage, the purpose, I believe, to demand concentration on direction when taking off or landing. A narrow track meant little or no inherent directional stability and this feature was to be the "cross" of many pupil pilots. The consequent incident, when not coping with this characteristic, was called the "ground loop." This meant that the aircraft slewed off line in an ever-decreasing radius until it tipped over on to its wing tip. Two or perhaps three of these incidents and one was "on the way home," i.e., washed out.

Although at later schools, the washout rate decreased considerably, as the primary school had weeded out the really doubtful ones, finally at advanced school, only about 50% of the original intake got their wings. One of my colleagues was scrubbed at advanced school with only 6 hours to go to get his wings; the reason: formation flying not up to standard. When the RAFAO pointed out that this pilot was almost certain to go to heavy night bombers, the answer, I understand, was quite to the point—"He does not leave here with Air Corps Wings!!"

I can still recall the depression and sadness witnessed when the unhappy student was finally scrubbed from further training. We used to work in pairs and my own partner, after ground loop problems and a seeming inability to know how far he was from the ground when landing, finally had what was known as the "kiss of death." This was a progress "check" ride with the Flight Commander who gave the final verdict. The next day, I helped this unfortunate to pack his things for his return to Canada and possibly another chance at pilot training or re-mustering to a navigator's course.

As with most of the British cadets at Darr Aero Tech and other primary schools, Freestone had no difficulty meeting American civilians. While his own experience might at first appear to be unique, it was indeed typical.

As in many other similar but unrecorded instances, Stanley Freestone's chance encounter at the main gate to the Albany primary school resulted in a lifelong friendship. On his first weekend pass, he was short of money, so he wandered to the main gate, intending to catch a ride into Albany. At the highway, he met a farm family who had driven thirty miles from Bridgeboro for the purpose of meeting and offering hospitality to some British cadets.

Initially, they invited Freestone to their home for lunch, but after that weekend their home became his own "home away from home" whenever he could leave the post during the remainder of his stay in Albany. He was allowed to drive the family automobile, he did chores around the farm and became "one of the family." As Freestone recalled, "I met local girls and went to local dances; I was expected to join the family at church on Sundays and this I also did." Until the old folks died some twenty-five years later, Stanley Freestone corresponded with the family.

On 17 August 1941, after Class SE-42-B had been in training for five weeks, Class SE-42-A departed. Almost two weeks later, on 31 August, Class SE-42-C arrived to commence training.

As with the two preceding classes, it too was late in arriving, and because of its tardiness, the contract school staff was no doubt irritated. Finally, the 170-man intake was complete and was joined by the 5 men held over from the preceding class. Training commenced on 2 September 1941, and no sooner had Class SE-42-C begun its training than Darr Aero Tech celebrated its first anniversary. Since its inception in August 1940, the flight school had graduated 559 pilots (473 Americans and 86 British) and had expanded considerably. Additional airplanes, another huge barracks block, a separate administrative building and a classroom building had been added. The instructional staff had grown from 11 flying instructors to 78, and the ground and military staffs had also expanded.

During their final five weeks of training, the members of Class SE-42-C selected an editorial board for the purpose of producing their edition of *Pee Tee*, the class magazine. Thomas W. Good was designated editor; F.T. Keeping, assistant editor; David E. Cooke, advertising manager; and Enoch Booth, photographer. In addition, Peter Chapman, Arnold Shrimpton, Maurice Andrews, Thomas G. Eyre and Robert Broughton solicited advertising, and B.B. Wood and H. Bletcher were responsible for the magazine's artwork. The editors and staff produced a series of serious and light articles and sketches including "Flying Instructor's Lament" and "The Ghost of a Solo." On behalf of the class, the editors also expressed their appreciation for the treatment accorded them while they were undergoing training at Darr.

As the early days of September passed, young people in Albany and neighboring towns were preparing to return to schools, colleges and universities. Swimming pools began to close, and the number of outdoor picnics diminished rapidly. Stores and shops were displaying goods for the autumn season and were already planning Christmas and post–New Year orders. Homeowners were beginning to rake leaves. Furnaces were being inspected and tested, orders were being placed for coal, wood and fuel oil. On 30 September 1941, the Class SE-42-B graduates departed. Of the 171 British student pilots enrolled in that course, 5 were held over for further training, 77 were eliminated and 89 graduated.

Baseball season closed with the playing of the World Series, and football season opened for universities, colleges and high schools. Football games between area high schools were played virtually every Thursday and Friday night from mid-September to mid-December, and townspeople turned out in droves as boosters of the home team. Avid golfers were enjoying the sunny and relatively cool links as often as possible. Bowling leagues and roller skating clubs were preparing teams and schedules for fall and winter competitions. Social clubs and resort facilities were planning their autumn and winter entertainment. Hunt clubs were organizing field trials and preparing guns and dogs for the forthcoming hunting season.

Southwest Georgia was rich farming country. However, except in a few scattered, irrigated fields, many crops had failed to mature because of the prolonged drought. Plants were smaller, and yields were diminished. Reduced crops of wheat, oats and other grains had already been harvested. Hay had been cut and most of it had been brought in from the hot, dry fields. Instead of tall, green corn (maize) just beginning to turn brown for harvest, most of it was already browned off. When the wind blew, the long brown leaves of corn fodder made an eerie rustling noise not unlike that of small animals rustling over dead leaves or through tall, dry grass.

Cotton was ripening and a first picking had begun. Peanuts (ground nuts) were being dug and draped over poles to dry before removing the nuts from vines, filling the bulbous one-hundred-pound sacks and hauling them to market. Tobacco was ripe and its leathery yellow leaves were being harvested and placed in barns for flue-curing. Although the crop was smaller because of the summer drought, the tremendous pecan groves that were scattered throughout the region were hanging partially full of ripening nuts.

On 1 October, Class SE-42-D, 165 men strong, arrived at Darr Aero Tech, and with the addition of the 1 cadet held over from the preceding class, its enrollment rose to 166. As that fourth RAF class began its instruction at Albany and at other primary flying schools in the Southeastern United States, autumn was slowly creeping in. Though daytime temperatures occasionally reached eighty degrees, they remained mostly in the seventies. Nights were becoming chill, and leaves on the hardwood trees throughout the region were beginning to show some bright colors.

During the first week in October, a hurricane threatened all of south Florida, and people of neighboring states were alerted to the possibility that its heavy rain and one-hundred-plus-mile-per-hour winds might affect them. On 4 October, the storm churned out of the Atlantic, crossed the Bahamas and then swept westward across south Florida into the Gulf of Mexico. It then turned northeastward, regained strength and swept across northwest Florida. Movement over land slowed the storm, but it continued its course and cut diagonally northeastward through Georgia, reentering the Atlantic Ocean near Charleston, South Carolina.

On Tuesday, 7 October, flying was suspended as the huge storm with winds estimated at seventy miles per hour passed directly over Albany and caused damage in the city estimated at $50,000. Aircraft that would not fit into hangars had been flown northward out of the storm's path. When the relative calm of the eye of the storm passed over Albany, and the winds then reversed direction, the British students experienced an eerie feeling. During a twenty-four-hour period, almost seven inches of rain fell in the city and county. Along the storm's path, torrential rains soaked and damaged all crops not gathered and under shelter, and the high winds blew loads of pecans to the ground. As a result of the hurricane, three people died in the Bahamas, five in Florida and one in Georgia.

In Albany, glass windows and doors of shops and other buildings were shattered and strewn over walks and streets. In residential areas, storm drains were clogged and downed trees and limbs covered sidewalks and streets. Water stood three feet deep in many streets and was reported to be two feet deep in the bowl of Albany's municipal stadium. Occasional stalled automobiles, farm and delivery trucks partially blocked streets, bridges and highways.

On most thoroughfares leading out of town and farther south on the Radium Springs Road, huge trees lay across the roads, splintered limbs were ripped away from giant trunks, arcing electric power lines were down and their poles were leaning in every direction. At Albany's old municipal airport, one tethered aircraft was blown against a hangar and tipped on its nose, and at Darr Aero Tech two hangars and the classroom building suffered some damage, but there were no injuries to students or staff.

For more than a week afterward, the Flint River and its tributaries, as well as creeks, ponds and lakes throughout the region, were colored an orange-yellow from the Georgia clay that the heavy rains had washed into them. The hurricane damage was reminiscent of the February 1940 tornado that had brought disaster to the town and region. Maintenance crews began to cut and remove fallen trees and limbs, repair power lines and damaged buildings and clean up debris. Hardly had the vast cleanup begun in Albany and in neighboring towns and counties than a new tropical storm descended on the region.

On Sunday, 19 October 1941, almost exactly two weeks after the first hurricane struck south Florida, another storm swirled out of the Atlantic and came ashore just south of Jacksonville,

Florida, approximately 140 miles southeast of Albany. The latest storm broke all rainfall records for northern Florida and spread over the entire region extending from Tampa, Florida, to Savannah, Georgia. Between Sunday, 19 October and Tuesday, 21 October, 12.37 inches of rain were recorded by the University of Florida at Gainesville, 9.93 inches of which fell in the twenty-four-hour period extending from 8:00 a.m. Monday to 8:00 a.m. Tuesday. Georgia red clay continued to discolor streams, ponds and lakes. And although Albany was just on the fringes of that second storm line, it received its share of rain for about three days, during which flying in the open-cockpit Stearman trainers was again suspended.

Earlier heavy winds and rain had already devastated many farms and pecan groves. More trees were uprooted and more pecans littered the ground. Despite concern over storm damage, past and present, life had to go on. At the airfield southwest of Albany, the training of Classes SE-42-C and SE-42-D resumed. The noises of marching men, calisthentics on the PT field and aircraft landing and taking off replaced the noises of the storm and provided yet another unusual experience for the British student pilots. Raymond George Spear, nineteen-year-old member of Class SE-42-D, recalled the second storm when "a hangar roof was lifted and dropped on aircraft below. Ground school buildings were badly damaged, and bungalows were flooded, so all students were quartered in barrack blocks for safety."

On his first visit to Albany, Spear and several classmates attended St. Paul's Episcopal Church and met the rector and his family and were, in turn, introduced to "Mr. and Mrs. W.M. Furlow, who became our adoptive parents for the whole of our stay in the USA." Spear thought the training excellent, and was unsympathetic with those who were washed out. "Failures," he wrote, "were due to personal ineptitude not to school standards." George R. Billany, another successful member of Class SE-42-D, especially remembered his final sixty-hour check. "I had a check in the 'washing machine' at the end of my course," he wrote, "as I had an 'off' period with my flying, but the gremlins smiled on me and I flew as well as I had ever done on the day of the test."

Apparently Reginald W. Everson of Croydon, Surrey, another member of Class SE-42-D, did not have such a close call with the "washing machine." He and his classmates thought their first multiple choice examinations amusing because "the Chief Ground Instructor had a strong sense of humour." He and others were also amused by the theory of flight instructor who taught them about the coefficient of lift (C/L, or "See Sub Ell") and used the expression "little biddy." "They were a great crowd of instructors," Everson wrote, "both flying and ground, who made an introduction to aviation enjoyable as well as efficient." Off-post, Everson enjoyed getting to know a number of people at a Baptist church in Albany. On one occasion, Everson and a large group of other RAF cadets traveled to Atlanta as guests of the English Speaking Union for a sightseeing tour of *Gone With the Wind* country.

Unfortunately, as it had with Class SE-42-A, disaster also struck Class SE-42-D. On 30 October, just after noon, civilian instructor Joe Frank Machamer of Knoxville, Tennessee, and nineteen-year-old LAC Eric N.G.N. Furze of Plympton, Devonshire, England, were killed instantly when their aircraft collided with that of LAC Kenneth Archibald. Both aircraft crashed in flames at the northeast edge of Darr Field. Furze's remains were interred close by the grave of LAC D'Arcy Wilson in the American Legion section of Crown Hill Cemetery. The aircraft of twenty-year-old Archibald of Southall, Middlesex, crashed nearby. Archibald was seriously injured and would spend several months in the U.S. Army's Lawson General Hospital in Atlanta.

On 6 November 1941, Class SE-42-C completed its primary flying training. Of the original 175-man intake, 1 was held over, 55 were eliminated and 119 graduated and were posted to a basic flying school. Several weeks before Class SE-42-D completed its primary training, an editorial staff was chosen to produce the class's edition of *Pee Tee*. LAC William E. Sawdy was editor; Robert A. Chorley, R.W. Kerr and Arthur H. Radbourne served as associate editors; George E. McLean and E.W.A. Jefferies were the art editors; and Eric Parsons was advertising and business manager, and was assisted by Leslie F. Axby, Raymond V. Rendall, George B. McCormack, Denys Channing and J.P. McGarry.

Unfortunately, most of the staff who worked so hard to finish the Christmas edition of the magazine were eliminated from pilot training before the magazine was published. Of the original 166 members of Class SE-42-D, 1 student was killed, 3 were held over for further training, 72 were eliminated and 90 graduated on 9 December 1941.

CHAPTER FIVE

THE TWO FLORIDA PRIMARY SCHOOLS

LAKELAND AND ARCADIA

THE LAKELAND (LODWICK) SCHOOL OF AERONAUTICS
LAKELAND, FLORIDA, 42-A-42-D

The Fifty-first U.S. Army Air Forces flying training detachment was the second civil contract primary flying school to be established within the Southeast Air Corps Training Center. Its roots lay in a distinguished record within the early history of American aviation. The parent company of the Lakeland School of Aeronautics was the Lincoln Auto and Tractor School. It had been organized in 1910 in Lincoln, Nebraska, to train automobile and tractor mechanics. In 1917, Reverend Ernest Jeremiah Sias, a well-known minister, lecturer on the Chautauqua Circuit and business agent, aided in reorganizing the company. As part of its reorganization, and in an effort to gain an army contract to train auto and truck mechanics, the company built a huge warehouse-like building on the corner of Twenty-fourth and C Streets in Lincoln.

Early in 1920, the company leased the lower floor of the building to Mr. Ray Page, who had bought numerous surplus military airplanes, engines and parts and was assembling aircraft for sale. Page called the aircraft he assembled and sold the Lincoln Standard and Jenny Airplane. Ray Page also built the Lincoln Primary Trainer, established a flying school and operated Page's Flying Circus, a popular team of barnstormer exhibition pilots who were in demand for air shows and fairs throughout the Midwest.

With Page's success so apparent, owners of the Lincoln Auto and Tractor School decided to enter the field of aviation as well. Surplus army and navy aviation engines, tools, equipment and parts were bought by the company, and an aviation mechanics course was added to their second-floor enterprises in the building at Twenty-fourth and C Street. In 1920, the opportunity arose to expand, so the company bought Page's flying school, hired a larger staff and began to train both airplane mechanics and pilots.

The Lincoln Airplane and Flying School was established at Union Airport, southeast of Lincoln, and it was at that school on 11 April 1922 that young Charles A. Lindbergh presented himself for some dual flight lessons. Young Lindbergh had ridden a motorcycle from his home in Madison, Wisconsin. From its inception, the school offered courses in automobile and aircraft engine mechanics and in piloting to hundreds of students from different parts of the world. From 1929, the president of the school was the Reverend Ernest J. Sias and executive vice-president was C. Fred Bowers, both of Lincoln.

In May 1939, the school entered into a contract with the War Department to train United States Army Air Corps flying cadets under army supervision. In 1940, the school also began to train army air corps aircraft and engine mechanics at its downtown Lincoln facility. Initially, the training of flying cadets was relatively easy. Union airport, which was used by the Lincoln Airplane and Flying School for flight operations, had one hangar, two paved runways and two taxi strips. There were no classrooms or locker room facilities for either the cadets or the instructors. Ground school shared the shop in a lean-to addition to one side of the hangar. Since it was so close to the flight line, an effort was made to soundproof the room against aircraft and shop noises.

The cadets at the Lincoln school were accommodated and fed in somewhat cramped quarters some three and a half miles from the airfield. Forty-four cadets lived in an old three-storied college fraternity house with kitchen and dining room in the basement. An additional fourteen cadets were accommodated nearby in a former sorority house. Both of these buildings were leased by the Lincoln Airplane and Flying School from Wesleyan University in Union, Nebraska, a town located in the suburbs of Lincoln.

Reverend Ernest Jeremiah Sias (1878–1955) and his wife Alma Demerest Sias (1882–1974) had experienced many economic recessions during their long lives, and they brought to their labors in this new technology a conservatism rooted in an older agrarian society. They also had a sincere and vital concern for the welfare of their charges. According to the USAAF unit history, the army air corps flying cadets who attended the contract primary school at Lincoln lived the lives of college and university students and were "mothered" by the Siases.

The Union airport was adequate in size for two-way traffic so that the upper and lower classes could fly from the airfield at the same time. The surrounding region was flat enough to permit safe landings, but winter flying was almost impossible, and flights in summer and autumn were often made in the face of turbulent air currents. To illustrate the problems encountered by civil instructors and cadets in training at the Lincoln school because of cold and gale-force winds, there were only eleven days in September 1939 when flying was possible, and five of these flying days were on Saturdays and Sundays.

According to the unit history, the remaining months of the year read like a catalogue of disasters for any kind of flying schedule: in October, there were fourteen flying days; in November, sixteen days; in December, fifteen days; and in January 1940, there were only seven and a half flying days. In the winter of 1939–40, the training of one class at Union airport was delayed for six weeks, so that the training progress of two classes was affected. Although winter temperatures were often below zero, the main thief of flying hours was the eternal wind of the high plains, which normally blew between sixteen and twenty-nine miles an hour, occasionally reaching as high as thirty-six miles an hour. Such gales were simply too great for inexperienced student pilots to cope with in the light trainer aircraft of that day.

The director of training at headquarters of the Army Air Corps Training Center at Randolph Field, Texas, had no choice but to cancel one intake of students at the Nebraska school and redesignate the cadet classes undergoing training there. Class 40-D became 40-E, and Class 40-E became 40-F. Perhaps more than at any other school, it was the experience of air corps supervisory officers at the Lincoln Airplane and Flying School that convinced United States Army Air Corps officers to move all flying training in the United States to the region south of the thirty-seventh parallel latitude.

On 25 May 1940, army air corps staff officers announced that decision at a Washington, D.C., training conference. Contractors for the nine existing civil contract primary schools were asked to double the capacity of their existing schools and to build an additional school of the same size. In order to assure year-round flying training and the successful training of seven thousand pilots annually, army air corps headquarters established some new rules. The school at Lincoln and two more of the nine original civil contract primary schools were to be relocated. All future flying schools were to be built in the region south of the Pacific Coastal rainbelt and south of the thirty-seventh paralled latitude in other regions of the country. The weather in these more southerly states would permit year-round flying training.

Army Air Corps Training Center headquarters at Randolph Field, Texas, informed the Reverend Mr. Sias that his school in Nebraska would receive no further army flying cadets after 25 November 1940. If Sias wished to retain his air corps contract beyond that date, he would have to relocate his school southward. Lakeland, Florida, had been seeking a flying school, so Sias was encouraged to visit that town to discuss relocating his school there. He did so, but he really did not like the idea of being so far from a business enterprise, and he had no intention of personally moving to Lakeland.

In 1940, Lakeland was an attractive town that was noted for its tourist, citrus and pebble phosphate industries. Located near the center of the Florida peninsula amidst that state's lake and citrus district, it had a normal population of 25,000, which was almost doubled by an influx of tourists between about 1 November and 15 April each year. Lakeland also served as the winter training camp for the Detroit Tigers, a popular and powerful American Major League baseball team. It was served by United States and Florida state highways, by the Atlantic Coast Line Railway and by coach and airline services.

Because of its service as a tourist center, the small town abounded in hotels and recreational facilities. As might be expected from sixteen lakes within the city limits and the hot climate, much of the recreation was related to water sports. In addition to fishing, sailing and water-skiing centered around the city's yacht and country club, the municipal swimming pool attracted large numbers regularly. Other recreational facilities within the city included two eighteen-hole golf courses, a social center, bowling greens, tennis and shuffleboard courts. In the downtown area, the city provided a civic center, four cinemas, two bowling alleys and a huge city park with baseball and football fields. Lakeland was also the home of Florida Southern College, a four-year Methodist college whose buildings had been designed by Frank Lloyd Wright, the famous American architect.

When Lincoln Airplane and Flying School officials negotiated the contract with town officials, the site selected for the airfield was located on the northeast edge of Lakeland on the western shore of Lake Parker. It was a small municipal airport situated within the town limits, two and a half miles from its center. Lakeland officials agreed to lease to the school the town's steel hangar, which was located on the west side of the airfield adjacent to the east-west runway.

Regardless of the climate and potential of the Florida city, Reverend Sias was no longer a young man in 1940 and, ironically, had never flown in an airplane before. He also gave little indication of ever intending to fly. His interest was aviation training as a business enterprise. If he should agree with the army air corps suggestion and move his flying school to Lakeland, Florida, he would have to depend on others to operate it. Since he refused to fly, he would also have to travel across a large part of the country several times a year by rail.

Ultimately, Reverend Sias decided that he could not leave Lincoln, Nebraska, so after arranging for the development of the school at Lakeland and transferring much of the Lincoln school's equipment and many members of the ground and flying instructional staff from southeastern Nebraska to central Florida, Ernest Jeremiah Sias sold his school's assets and the army contract for $80,000 to Harold S. Darr of Chicago and Albert I. Lodwick of New York.

Although he was still operating a flying school at Glenview, Illinois, and was building another at Albany, Georgia, Darr flew into Lakeland in early August 1940 to rush construction on the flying school he had just purchased. Since the air corps contract assigned to the Lincoln Airplane and Flying School indicated that training was scheduled to begin on 15 September 1940, it was essential that construction begin immediately. While the building contractor rushed his work, most of the experienced flying and maintenance staff of the Lincoln school joined the Darr school and made preparations to begin the training of Class SE-41-C shortly after its arrival in mid-September 1940.

But for the runway and the old city hangar, the flying school site, which nestled between a palm and a citrus grove along the west side of Lake Parker, was empty. During the late summer of 1940, a massive construction project commenced there and continued through the autumn of 1940. It resumed again and again between 1941 and 1945. The City of Lakeland's utilities departments provided adequate potable water and extended to the school electrical services from its oil-fired steam generating plant.

At the airport, the building of the flying school was proceeding rapidly. Construction was being rushed on two steel hangars, two two-storied barracks, a small dispensary, a twelve-bed infirmary and a dining hall. On completion of that initial construction, Lakeland officials agreed to disassemble and move the original hangar to a new site specified by the contractor. Arrangements were also made to lease three auxiliary landing fields. At a cost not to exceed $6,000, Lakeland officials agreed to lease and improve the three fields and to allow the school to reimburse the town government with twenty-four equal installment payments.

Flying training was being conducted in Stearman PT-17 biplane trainers from the main airfield and from available auxiliary fields. Initially, the contractor's offices were located in the basement of the New Florida Hotel, and ground school classes were conducted at a third site, the Lakeland National Guard Armory. On the northwest side of the municipal airfield, opposite the school construction site, the city hangar provided shelter for numerous civil aircraft and shared available space temporarily with army air corps staff and the contractor's flight department. Flying cadets were billeted in the Thelma Hotel in downtown Lakeland, which also housed the dispensary and the medical detachment.

Until the school's administrative and domestic facilities were completed in December 1940 and all four separate elements of the flying school could be brought together at the airfield on the shores of Lake Parker, transportation and other problems plagued school personnel as well as the first three student intakes at the school. Buses and private automobiles were used to transport cadets, instructors and other staff to and from the airfield, the national guard armory and hotels, as necessary. Even then, however, the ground school and some offices had to remain for a time in temporary quarters.

According to the USAAF unit history of the school, neither Mr. Darr nor Lodwick took a great initial interest in the school, with the result that its first manager was said to have brought about bad relations between the school and townspeople. In January 1941, that manager was replaced, and H.D. Copeland, the new manager, restored good relations. At about the same time, Lodwick moved to Florida for his health. As a result, the partial owner began to take a direct interest in the school.

As with Harold Darr and the Reverend Ernest J. Sias, Albert I. Lodwick was a native of Iowa. He had received a bachelor of arts (AB) degree at Iowa Wesleyan College and a masters of business administration (MBA) degree from Harvard University. In 1929, he had joined the Curtiss-Wright Company as a statistician, and in 1931 he had moved to the public relations division with the same company. Later he had served as president of Stinson Aircraft Company and had then joined Howard Hughes's operations. Lodwick had managed Hughes's "around the world" flight and other noteworthy flights as well.

Lodwick's arrival in Lakeland and his taking up residence there evidently generated considerable activity. Expansion of the school continued. At the main airdrome, a two-story administration building was built, and the upper floor provided space for offices of the civil contractor and army air corps and other service personnel, while lower-floor rooms served as the ground school. In addition, earlier problems appear to have faded, and officials of the town of Lakeland were apparently more cooperative.

As promised, the original municipal hangar was disassembled and reerected on the opposite side of the airfield beside the other two hangars that had been built in the interim. This February 1941 change removed civil aircraft from the field and provided more airfield and hangar space. When the lease agreement on the Winter Haven airport ended later that same year, two new auxiliary fields were leased, cleared, leveled and sodded, and the Haldeman-Elder Airport, which was located several miles directly east of Lakeland, was doubled in size and became a satellite airfield.

Before the first intake of RAF students arrived in June 1941, the Lakeland School of Aeronautics was in superb condition, and the quality of its training had already attracted notice. Six classes of army air corps flying cadets (SE-41-C through SE-41-H) had completed their training at the Lakeland school. In July 1941, when Class SE-41-I, the seventh American cadet class, departed for basic flying school, the school at Lakeland, Florida, had yielded more than five hundred primary school pilots for service with the army air corps.

On Tuesday, 10 June, half of Class SE-42-A reported to the flight line and the other half reported to ground school. LAC John Staples was the first to fly when he took off with M.D. "Doc" Holman, director of flying. On Saturday afternoon, 14 June, the RAF cadets were invited to a huge party laid on at the city park by Lakeland's Junior Chamber of Commerce. Wearing sportshirts with cards attached indicating their names and hometowns, the cadets were driven away in a fleet of cars to their first American picnic. There they played a cricket match that was "not a little unusual both in technique and in its lack of respect for the rules." They also learned softball and enjoyed the swimming pool, palm trees, newly made friends and enormous quantities of food, including potato salad and other vegetables, hot dogs, hamburgers and plenty of freshly squeezed juice as well as oranges brought in from nearby citrus groves.

Following the picnic, the British cadets were taken to the national guard armory, where they enjoyed musical entertainment and a radio broadcast. That picnic and radio broadcast served to introduce the young men to many people from Lakeland and the vicinity and resulted in invitations and hospitality during their remaining nine weeks of primary training. On 6 July, the cadets traveled to Winter Haven for a cricket match and picnic there. Around that same time, ten members of Class SE-42-A were selected as weekend guests of the director of Cyprus Gardens. One of those guests at the Winter Haven resort was Rossiter Gregory of Purley, Surrey, who was later eliminated from pilot training at Lakeland and went on to qualify as one of the wartime pioneers in the developing new field of air traffic control.

Although he was compelled to shave off his moustache while in training at Lakeland, Gregory enjoyed himself. More than forty years later, he recalled that early service experience:

> *American drill and discipline was a bit much! 0520 in the morning—last one out got*
> *one gig. There was another R.E. Gregory and we swapped gigs to avoid walking. We*

were issued khaki uniforms in Canada—RCAF buttons and red tabs, but they never fit anybody. I did my first instructional flight on 10 June 1941, went solo 3 July, and had my last flight on 23 July. I had flown 19 hours, 12 minutes when I washed out. I wasn't all that sad about it; I did try, but I felt the plane was flying me rather than my flying the plane.

Training of the RAF cadets was proceeding steadily. LAC William Hume of Edinburgh, Scotland, was the first to solo on 23 June 1941. On 3 July, an instructor was injured and LAC Steward escaped injury in the first serious accident that occurred at the school. The Stearman trainer in which they were practicing forced landings "struck a tall pine tree, sending the plane spinning to earth."

While the RAF students were continuing their training and whenever possible were also enjoying the hospitality of people within the area, Flight Lieutenant William W. Watson, RAFVR, carried out his administrative duties. Watson, a Canadian, had apparently worked his way across to the United Kingdom aboard a cargo ship and had come back to North America as an RAF officer. As RAF administrative officer (RAFAO) at Lakeland, he wore many hats. His regular duties included serving on the academic board, reviewing the records of student eliminees, handling disciplinary cases, maintaining records, paying the British cadets and keeping his senior officers informed of training progress.

Outside the station, Watson represented the Royal Air Force to the general public. As with other RAFAOs, a part of Watson's representation of the RAF to the general public included addresses before civic clubs in Lakeland and nearby towns. Watson's work undoubtedly stimulated great public interest in everything about the RAF cadets and resulted in the publication of an essay with photographs in the feature section in the Sunday, 13 July edition of the *Lakeland Ledger*. Evidently, the reporter-photographer followed the British students "around the clock" for a typical rushed twenty-four-hour schedule.

In mid-July, Class SE-41-I departed for Gunter Field, Alabama. Class SE-42-A became the senior class and within a few days, the second contingent of British student pilots arrived. Before RCAF Conducting Officer RCAF Pilot Officer H. Moffat delivered his charges to Lakeland at 5:35 on Thursday morning, 17 July 1941, Cadet Captain Hall traveled to Lake Alfred, boarded the train and accompanied the new class on to Lakeland. It was the responsibility of the senior class to indoctrinate the incoming junior class and to maintain discipline among the students of what was now, with one exception, an all-British school.

As they were getting settled into their quarters that first day on the training station, they were joined by American flying Cadet Fred J. Eisert of Astoria, Long Island, New York. Eisert, formerly a member of Class SE-41-I, had injured his ankle before completing the course, so he was held over to continue training with Class SE-42-A. Although USAAF Generals Weaver and Brett had visited the school earlier, as had Group Captains Carnegie and Trott and Wing Commander Hogan, that was only the beginning of a steady stream of visitors to the Florida school. On 18 April, Major General Davenport Johnson, director of the training and operations section in the office of the chief of the air corps, accompanied by Colonel Harry Johnson, visited and inspected the school.

During 21 July and succeeding days as Class SE-42-B was being introduced to the regimen of the flying school, the surviving members of Class SE-42-A began to alternate dual and solo flying in the process of learning aerobatics and precision flying. However, a large group of British visitors descended on the Lakeland school on Saturday, 26 July. Major General George H. Brett, newly appointed chief of the army air corps, escorted a large group of distinguished British visitors from Washington and Maxwell Field, Alabama, and on to Lakeland and several other schools where RAF personnel were under training.

Among the visitors to Lakeland were Captain Harold H. Balfour, undersecretary of state for air; W.W. Wakefield, parliamentary secretary to Balfour; Air Commodore George C. Pirie, air attaché to the British Embassy in Washington; Group Captain D.V. Carnegie, director of training of the newly established RAF Delegation in Washington; and Wing Commander H.A.V. Hogan, RAF administrative officer for the Southeast Air Corps Training Center. A few days later, on 6 August, Noel Monks, correspondent for the *Daily Mail* and author of *Squadrons Up*, a book about RAF combat operations, visited Lakeland, observed training and talked with the students.

As the weeks passed, members of Classes SE-42-A and SE-42-B jointly compiled a record of their class that was published in the school magazine, *Sololand*. Students of each of the classes were identified by short paragraphs alluding to their past or to activities while undergoing flying training. E.R. Robertson was described as "one of the most prominent noises about the barracks," F. Barnes was said to be a "terrible snorer" and D.G.L. Jenkins was described as a Welshman "still learning to speak English." Thirteen students, each of whom had ground looped or otherwise damaged a Stearman trainer, were named members of the RIP (Rest in Peace) Club.

Skinny nineteen-year-old David N. Ellis of Aylsford, Kent, who appeared to be much younger than he really was, was accused of having discovered "the Elixir of Life." Instead, Ellis found a near equivalent of himself in the Lakeland dining hall. Recalling almost forty-five years later, Ellis indicated that there was a table for overweight cadets at one end of the dining hall and one for underweight cadets at the other. "I was a skinny lad and was delighted to be allocated to the 'underweights' table where we were fed extra proteins and encouraged to eat as much as possible…I had a good appetite, but did not increase my weight by an ounce." Owing to physical exercise, regular hours and good food, most of the British cadets, excluding Ellis, emerged from the ten weeks at primary school bronzed, several pounds heavier and tougher.

One of the great shocks that the RAF cadets encountered at the American primary flying schools was the USAAF discipline and hazing associated with officer cadet training. Though some objected, many enjoyed the experience and joined in the spirit of the hazing. However, unknown to them, the American training was doing exactly what was intended: it was building individual pride, confidence and an *esprit de corps* that none of the RAF cadets emphasized in their normal relations. However, the American training had tested their mettle and had often aggravated them, so they wanted to prove what was in them.

Shortly before their primary training ended, the British cadets at Lakeland put on a polished demonstration of RAF drill, which apparently surprised them as much as it did the American cadets. "Drilled by our own cadet officers," wrote David Ellis, "we performed for the first and probably the only time in our service lives like the Brigade of Guards." Although they may not have known it at the time, this assertion of nationality was an expected result of the training and discipline they had received as a unit and was not a surprise to the West Point officers.

At 11:00 a.m., Saturday, 16 August, the surviving members of Class SE-42-A were joined by visiting dignitaries and cameramen from several newsreel companies and assembled in the school's dining hall. There amid popping flashbulbs, they listened to brief addresses from Florida Governor Spessard Holland, a decorated United States Army Air Service flier who served in France in 1918, and from other officers and visitors, including Group Captain Carnegie and

Wing Commander Hogan. That afternoon, the graduates of that first RAF class at Lakeland departed for the USAAF basic flying school at Gunter Field, Alabama.

The crowning tribute to the British students came in the form of two editorials that appeared in the *Lakeland Ledger* during their final week of training. That of 13 August 1941 closed with the following tribute:

> *Lakeland reluctantly gives up these first British lads and wishes them unending good fortune as they do their valuable bit for democracy.*
>
> *They will be remembered by the citizens of this community as likeable, hard-working young men who conducted themselves as gentlemen and represented their native land with great credit. They have set a high standard for the young Britons who are to succeed them here.*
>
> *We feel confident they are not preparing themselves in vain and that they eventually will see Hitlerism defeated and democracy again secure.*
>
> GOD SAVE THE KING.

Of Class SE-42-A's original enrollment of ninety men, one student was held over for further training, thirty-two were eliminated and fifty-seven successfully completed their training.

Ten weeks later, some thirteen or more members of Class SE-42-A returned to the nest that they had left in mid-August. All of them had just completed basic flying school at Gunter Field, Alabama, and had a few days' leave before reporting to a USAAF advanced flying school. In order to get to Lakeland, one group of them pooled resources and bought a jalopy that they drove; another group rented a car, while still others hitchhiked to Florida.

As David N. Ellis recalled that experience,

> *Towards the end of our period at Gunter, we had a week's leave. Some of us decided to return to Lakeland for a visit. I and two friends hitch-hiked and wore our RAF uniforms although we were not really authorised to do so. But it had the anticipated effect. People were curious about the unfamiliar uniform, and we had no trouble getting lifts. One family who picked us up in the evening offered us beds at their home for the night and gave us breakfast the next morning before setting us on our way. A typical instance of the friendliness and hospitality shown to us throughout our training.*

In Lakeland, Ellis had gotten to know the Johnson family, the Starnes family and the Lodwicks. On that occasion, although he stayed with the Johnsons, he undoubtedly saw the others. As with so many RAF students, Ellis and his SE-42-A classmates returned to the towns of their primary flying schools because that is where they were made to feel most at home.

On 18 July 1941, the members of Class SE-42-B joined Class SE-42-A and commenced training within a few days. Michael Aldridge, a member of the new class, was eliminated after a few weeks of training. Aldridge had already had significant experience in the London theatre, and in the years after 1945 he would become a distinguished stage and television actor. Aldridge returned to Canada by way of Maxwell Field and was "messed about" a great deal before being sent back to the United Kingdom as a charter member of the "319 Club." Later trained as an observer (navigator) in South Africa, Aldridge served as a group navigator and operations briefing officer.

More than forty years after his RAF experience in North America, Aldridge reminisced about his experiences at Lakeland:

> *The classes on navigation, etc, were O.K., except that they differed greatly with what we had learned in the UK. Barrack room inspections were dreaded by one and all. Writing this—looking back—I think we were a rather "bolshie" lot probably because we wanted to retain our national identities and traditions. I think also that we felt that there was far too much time given to "Bullshit" and not enough to the actual business of making us pilots (we had a tremendous urgency to get back to the U.K. and fight!). There was also the question of money. We were on RAF Airman's pay which was pitifully small compared to that of the American Airmen. They got about three times as much.*
>
> *The flying I enjoyed very much (we all did), but I was aware that I wasn't ever going to be any good. I tried very hard and was bitterly disappointed when I was "washed out" together with quite a few of my colleagues. My instructor was a delightful fellow from Texas, and we were great friends. The Americans we met outside the camp were very friendly and incredibly generous, almost to our embarrassment, as we didn't have enough money to repay any hospitality.*
>
> *I must have washed out in August 1941 because I remember I was on a train travelling to Maxwell Field at Montgomery, Alabama when I had my 21st birthday. None of us had much money, but we clubbed together and bought a bottle of Bourbon with which to celebrate. At Maxwell Field, we were left more or less to our own devices. We played cards a lot, and got along very well with the American GIs and Sergeants. They seemed to accept us with a good deal of tolerance, and we joined in with their sports—baseball, football, etc. We even gave a display of RAF drill in what remained of our grey suits.*

Aldridge soon entrained for Toronto with other pilot eliminees from Arnold Scheme schools. Another member of that second RAF class was LAC Leslie Rosser, who reminisced about his Florida training days many years later.

> *The weather at Lakeland in July was a little too warm for comfort, but the food was excellent. Flying commenced a few days later, and a few cadets were eliminated almost immediately. We really felt flattered that the flying instructors were civilians with so much and such varied flying experience. Of course, we were well aware that military discipline prevailed though we were under the direction of a different organization and under officers with very different standards. I think the officers and ourselves coped quite well with a difficult situation. We took the rather larger number of demerits awarded with pride. Those with the largest number of demerits were regarded as "top of the class."*
>
> *The hospitality of the local people was exceptional and we soon made some good friends. It was very surprising to find the attitude of some of the older "Southerners" was quite hostile to people from the North. My instructor was a Mr. Lettico who had been instructing at a college in the Chicago area. I went solo after 12 hours, though of course quite a large number of cadets were eliminated because they had not gone solo in the required time. At age 25, I was one of the oldest to finish the course at Lakeland.*
>
> *One incident is perhaps worth mention which shows the political background to the Arnold and other related schemes. A train was due to leave Lakeland one afternoon*

taking a number of cadets who had been "washed out" and were returning to Canada. The section of cadets who were flying in the afternoon, one half of the course being on lectures, decided to give the train a good send-off with some rather hair-raising low flying and aerobatics. An instructor with a pupil having strayed into that area, five or six of the cadets involved were caught by the instructor's taking the numbers from the side of the planes. They were placed under close arrest and packed off back to Canada.

We did understand that any publicity which may have reached the "Hearst" press would have been a serious matter, but such wholesale eliminations were shocking. Some years later in North Africa, I met one of the culprits and he was flying a Mustang (P-51). At the time of the incident with the train at Lakeland, he was 18 years of age and did "flick" or "barrel" rolls in his Stearman PT-17 alongside the train at about 200 feet.

Since USAAF training regulations and training officers took a dim view of dangerous and low flying that endangered the student pilot, aircraft and others, the students of the class who were caught and eliminated for "buzzing" the train were sent packing for disciplinary reasons and as an example to others in training.

James Cook, a British army veteran of Dunkirk whose experience in France has been described during his stay in Toronto, was also a member of that second RAF class at Lakeland. Many years later, after having retired from his position with the Electricity Generating Board, Cook recalled his training days in Florida:

We were very favourably impressed with the school at Lakeland. Quarters were excellent—the beds were complete with mosquito nets. The training programme entailed staying at the School Monday through Friday with weekends off. We had a standing invitation by a retired couple who had a beach cottage down on the Gulf of Mexico at Bradenton; three or four of us went there on a coach nearly every weekend. My flying instructor was W.N. Baxter; very few, if any, of Class 42-B had any flying experience. We lost about 6 in the first weeks through air sickness and inability to come to terms with flying. They went back to Canada, but I don't know what happened then.

Later courses had about 10 hours flying in the UK before being sent overseas so as to cut out this waste. I had no problems with accent or the American way of life and got on very well with my instructor. I would say that the Army Air Corps doctor who was in charge really looked after us in every possible way—there was extra food for underweights and prompt care of the sweat rash we all suffered from in the hot and humid climate of South Florida in summertime. He was really approachable at any time.

But the weather was not always just hot and humid. Just after 4:00 p.m. on Sunday afternoon, 3 August 1941, the RAF students received their introduction to the fury of a Southern summer electrical storm. As happens in the region after several very hot days, dark clouds began to appear first, then moderate winds that were followed by high winds and very heavy rain. These storm features were accompanied by rolling dark clouds, heavy thunder and the almost simultaneous sight of wild stabs of lightning and the cracking sound of its striking nearby.

In Lakeland that afternoon, 2.61 inches of rain fell within a short time, and lightning struck seven places in the city, contributing to the outbreak of fires at most of the sites. In addition to fire damage, debris from shrubbery and trees littered streets and walks, awnings were blown down, roofs of some houses and businesses were damaged and many huge shade trees were uprooted. Aside from the damage, the display of nature's power was awesome, especially to those who had never witnessed such an occurrence. However, for many of the RAF cadets, the sights and sounds of the storm must have been strong reminders of the Luftwaffe raids on British cities.

When Class SE-42-A departed for basic flying school in mid-August, Class SE-42-B became the senior class. In preparation for the arrival of a junior class, several men were appointed to serve as cadet officers and NCOs. During the preceding five weeks, while the school had been all-RAF, south Florida had been plagued with weather problems. Because of a drought, the remainder of the month of August was very dry, and it was reported that temperatures appeared to be greater than they actually were. Even so, the month was recorded as the hottest and driest on record.

On 29 August 1941, the *Lakeland Ledger* announced that Albert I. Lodwick, who had recently moved from New York to Lakeland for health reasons, had purchased the shares of his partner, Harold Darr. Despite the change in ownership, it was indicated that all civilian staff would continue as in the past. From that day until the school was closed in 1945, Lodwick took an active role in the operation of the school. In fact, the very next day, Saturday, 30 August 1941, at 6:35 a.m., Lodwick joined Lieutenant Lemon, commanding officer of the USAAF detachment, and Flight Lieutenant Watson at the Lakeland Railway Station to welcome the third RAF class. Almost two weeks late, Class SE-42-C joined Class SE-42-B as the junior class.

Since the new class arrived on Saturday of the Labor Day weekend and received physical examinations that day, they were able to spend the remainder of the day unpacking their bags and straightening their kit. On Sunday and Monday, they were allowed to relax for two full days before commencing training. Despite a dangerous polio epidemic that was then raging over all of North America from Canada to Mexico and had afflicted more than a dozen people in Lakeland, the new arrivals were allowed to go swimming.

On Tuesday, 2 September, while the new class was becoming familiar with the huge Stearman biplanes, some members of Class SE-42-B were undergoing dual instruction while others were doing solo practice of maneuvers. Within a short time after flying commenced that day, a storm was reported to be approaching from the southwest, and signals were raised to notify aircraft to return to station. Instructors and army officers hurried about the skies of the various training zones signaling all aircraft to land as quickly as possible. One Stearman trainer could not be found, and the dispatcher's records indicated that LAC Robert Arthur Gordon Cleave of Class SE-42-B had signed for the aircraft and was observed taking off at around 10:00 a.m. in a northerly direction for the purpose of doing solo practice of maneuvers.

As the storm passed through with its wind, clouds and heavy rain, flares were shot into the air, but without results. James Cook, one of Cleave's classmates, recalled the tragedy that followed:

> *The Stearman biplanes were always in the pink of condition and viceless. I soloed in 5 hours. The course had its few overshoots, flip overs, and ground loops, but no student was seriously hurt. However, we did have one fatality which was particularly disturbing. From what I recall of the circumstances, the Stearman trainers had no radios, and to get students down in an emergency such as bad weather, flares were sent up.*
>
> *The country to the east of Lakeland was all swamps and was reputed to be full of snakes and alligators and consequently out of bounds for flying. Most of the flying*

activities took place between Lakeland and the Gulf. We did not have sea survival equipment, so there was no flying over the Gulf itself. With a sudden tropical storm approaching one day, Robert Gordon Cleave went missing. Officially, Gordon was listed as "killed in action" or "killed on active service" on 2 September 1941; evidently he lost direction in fog or storm and went down in the Gulf of Mexico. We heard later, when in Basic Flying School, that parts of the plane had been washed up and traced to Gordon.

Many aircraft, including Stearman trainers from Lakeland and Carlstrom Fields and planes from USAAF airbases at Tampa and Orlando, criss-crossed the entire region looking for the bright blue-and-yellow Stearman biplane bearing the number three. Fearing that the aircraft might have crashed in a lake and the young RAF cadet might have bailed out and come down in remote and dangerous swamplands, volunteer ground search parties of civilians and servicemen canvassed the thick scrub and swampy regions around Lakeland in an effort to find the missing airman.

On 4 September 1941, in an editorial entitled "The Missing British Student," the editors of the *Lakeland Ledger* captured the feelings of citizens and trainees alike:

A 20-year old lad from England, in training at the Lakeland School of Aeronautics for RAF duty, goes up on a routine flight and fails to return.

Forty planes go in search of him, Army fliers from Tampa and Orlando joining in the search. News that the young flier is missing quickly spreads through Lakeland. Citizens who have never seen the young man nor heard his name make anxious inquiry from hour to hour. "Have they found the British flier yet?" "No word yet." "Oh, that's too bad."

Why such interest in a young man they do not know? Because tragedy makes the whole world kin. Robert A.G. Cleave is somebody's son, somebody's brother, somebody's sweetheart.

Has that young man who had recently come to a strange land to train for a war not of his making lost his life in a Florida swamp? Of course not, the public feels, such a thing just ought not to happen.

Let's hope the public is right. Maybe there'll be some good news soon.

Although the search continued for some time on the ground and in the air, no good news was forthcoming.

As the members of Class SE-42-B prepared their part of the joint issue of *Sololand*, they too identified each class member. As with the preceding class, it included bank and insurance clerks, civil servants and many men who had already seen service with British army units. They also poked fun at each other and chided "professional" Welshmen and Irishmen among their group. In seeking to impart to others some of the knowledge they had gained, one of their members wrote a parody of Rudyard Kipling's "If" that traces training experiences at the Lakeland school:

If you can match the upper class for Virtue,
Be Yankified, yet keep the British touch,
If you can walk your Gigs, nor let them hurt you,
Just half an hour a Gig,—that's not much;

If you can make a guess at all your Quizzes,
Not doing any work each weekday night,
And pass, in spite of all the dismal dizzes,
Who prophesied you'd fail with huge delight.
And If you can bring your plane down at Plant City,
And know which way the wind is blowing too;
If you can make your patterns very pretty,
And estimate your Key position true;
If you can spin, and not make spins your master,
And fix your glides, and use the rudder well;
If you can make your rolls a trifle faster,
Your stages will be absolutely swell.

If you can keep your head when your Instructor
Is losing his, and blaming it on you,
And watch him glaring through his darn'd reflector,
And make allowance for his glaring too;
If you can fix Form One up to the minute,
With no mistake, when solo has been done,
Yours is the sky, and all the thrill that's in it,
And, what is more, You'll pass your checks, My Son.

Of the ninety-one-member net intake for Class SE-42-B, one was listed as killed (Cleave, actually missing for several months before he was assumed to have crashed in the Gulf of Mexico), twenty-nine were eliminated for flying deficiencies, five were eliminated for reasons other than flying and fifty-six graduated on 27 September 1941 and were posted to a basic flying school.

The students who buzzed the train bearing eliminated classmates northward to Maxwell Field were themselves washed out for disciplinary reasons. Undoubtedly, they were the five men listed in Class SE-42-B statistics as eliminated for "other than flying" reasons. However, as indicated by Leslie Rosser above, there is reason to believe that these men were permitted to continue pilot training in Canada or elsewhere.

One hundred members of Class SE-42-C arrived at Lakeland directly from Toronto around 21 August 1941 and commenced flying training a few days later. As the class was just beginning its flying training, the excitement and worry about the fate of LAC Cleave was at its peak. Daily reports were given on the radio and in the local newspaper. The official air search had been called off. However, every rumor and suggestion was still being followed up by school officials and USAAF training supervisors, and both instructors and cadets from the Lakeland school continued to scan every area of the countryside.

During the week beginning Monday, 8 September, since there had been no success in locating either plane or pilot from the air, final efforts were made to find either the twenty-year-old British cadet's remains or his aircraft. As they swept through the large, swampy, thickly wooded and dense "Polk County scrub section," members of the Polk County Defense Company, the Florida Highway Patrol and other volunteers donned wet gear and old clothes and carried weapons to ward off snakes. The Florida Cattlemen's Association also met and asked that cowboys checking cattle and range fences be on the watch for the aircraft and its pilot.

After exhausting all possibilities, the conclusion was inevitably made that Stearman Trainer No. 3 and its pilot were missing forever. Despite rumors that Cleave had been picked up by a German submarine and made a prisoner of war (a scenario that many accepted as late as 1985), the truth was that LAC Cleave's luck had run out. In December 1941, three months after he disappeared, the local newspaper indicated that an aircraft wheel had been discovered by a fisherman off the coast of Louisiana, and there was speculation that it came from the missing Stearman aircraft. As far as is known, the wheel retrieved from the Gulf of Mexico was never officially linked with the aircraft missing from Lakeland, Florida.

Far to the north in Ottawa, Canada, is a strikingly beautiful ten-foot-high bronze globe that rests on stone, is surmounted by a bronze eagle and is supported at the base by bronze beavers. Nearby are benches and bronze panels mounted along curved stone walls. The Ottawa memorial commemorates the sacrifice of 6 women, 19 civilians and 773 airmen from Canada and Great Britain and from other nations of the British Commonwealth and Empire who lost "their lives in Canada, in the United States of America, and in neighbouring lands and seas, and who have no known grave." The memorial sits on Green Island, in a small and lovely setting high on a hill near where the northern branch of the twin falls of the Rideau River drop forty or more feet to join the Ottawa River. Inscribed on one of the bronze panels beneath the year 1941 is the name of LAC Cleave, R.A.G.

Among the members of Class SE-42-C were a number of men from every part of Great Britain and different parts of the world. Erwin J. Lischke, a Czechoslovakian, probably had the most exciting and dangerous past. He had left his home in October 1938 after having gained sixteen hours of flying time as a Czechoslovakian Air Force cadet. The class also included Kenneth R. Waugh of Sao Paulo, Brazil; Peter Ready of Argentina; Richard N. Emmett from India; A.G.R. "George" Ashley of South Africa; and class artist Jimmy O'Hara from Dublin, Ireland. Among other members of the new class were nine former policemen and Albert and Harry Sorensen, twins from Manchester, England.

While training continued at the school, the citizens of Lakeland and other towns in the vicinity sought to provide entertainment for the British students, and they reciprocated. The Women's Club of Lakeland organized regular tea dances, which were enjoyed by Lakeland girls and members of the RAF contingent. The British cadets put on skits, singsongs and dramatic readings whenever possible and thus entertained each other as well as civic club members and other townspeople.

As the seasons were changing in central Florida, there came a personality who was to have a dramatic effect (literally) on the Lakeland primary school. Captain (later Major) Richard C. Cumming was assigned as flight surgeon at Lakeland School of Aeronautics in September 1941. Not only did Dr. Cumming administer to the health needs of the men and regularly provide the stringent Form 64 flight physical examination on cadets and military staff at Lakeland and on civilian instructors at several Florida flying schools, but he was also an excellent morale officer. Immediately after his arrival, as he probed throats and examined tonsils, he was looking for other evidence. He capitalized on the talent he found and formed choral groups from among the students of each class. It is no wonder that LAC James Cook of SE-42-B and many others described Dr. Cumming as a caring and conscientious "M.O."

During October, the first group of Dr. Cumming's choosing began to present singsongs over radio station WLAK in Lakeland and later over radio station WFLA in Tampa. In addition to presentations over the airwaves, many British cadets sang in church choirs, played various musical instruments (including LAC MacKinnon's bagpipes), presented shows and generally contributed to community cultural and social events. In addition, in a program no doubt instigated by high school girls, several RAF cadets were persuaded to appear at the high school to lecture on geography and answer questions from students.

On September 25, the *Lakeland Ledger* reprinted Noel Monks's article from the *Daily Mail*. Monks, who had visited the Lakeland school early in the summer of 1941, had described for British readers the schedule of the British cadets undergoing training in an American flying school and, echoing Group Captain Carnegie, indicated that they were in danger of being spoiled by the hospitality of Americans. Families in Lakeland and other nearby towns regularly entertained the RAF students, and there may well have been some spoiling.

The hospitality continued, and other visitors also arrived at the flying school. On Sunday, 28 September, Wing Commander Hogan brought to the station Air Vice Marshal S.P.C. Maltby, air officer commanding, the Royal Air Force's Army Cooperation Command. Maltby, who had spent a month exchanging ideas with air and ground commanders during the United States Army's Louisiana maneuvers, inspected the station and the British cadets. Shortly after he completed his inspection and flew on to Fort Benning, Georgia, with Wing Commander Hogan, the graduating members of Class SE-42-B were escorted to Gunter Field by Flight Lieutenant William W. Watson.

Class SE-42-C had been in training for five weeks and now became the senior class. Its officers included Thomas M. Horsfall, a Metropolitan Police inspector, cadet captain; J.B. "Jack" McConway of Newcastle, cadet lieutenant adjutant; Geoffrey H. Rowson of Nottingham, lieutenant of A flight and class editor of *Sololand*; Geoffrey C. Robinson of Liverpool, lieutenant of B flight; Kenneth R. Waugh of Sao Paulo, Brazil, lieutenant of C flight; and Jimmy O'Hara of Dublin, Ireland, lieutenant of D flight.

Several students were singled out in *Sololand*, the class magazine, for special mention. Alan O. Wakefield, a former bank clerk, apparently held "the School record for thirteen wing ups and an undercarriage," and it was suggested that it was untrue that he was "working on commission" for the Boeing (Stearman) Company. Alluding to the famous Devonshire clotted cream and LAC Andrews's propensity for frightening cattle while "practicing" forced landings, the cadet magazine suggested that Frank Andrews, a former bank clerk from Truro, Cornwall, was "an indirect manufacturer of clotted cream." Londoner G.E. "Graham" Jackson, an articled surveyor whose nickname was likely derived from the famous American jazz musician, was the class cartoonist and was described as a former commissioned Link Trainer instructor before he became a pilot candidate.

In the early morning hours of Thursday, 2 October 1941, the one hundred members of Class SE-42-D arrived from Toronto. LAC Kenneth G. Dale of Portsmouth, Hampshire, recalled how at each change of trains on the trip southward, the RAF students must have presented an incongruous picture as, dressed in gray civilian suits, they formed up into stiff military formations to the tunes of a bagpipe played by ex-Pipe Major Duncan MacKinnon. As with earlier classes, their numbers diminished as they traveled southward and small RAF drafts were diverted to different trains and routes, and the final numbers were destined for Lakeland and Arcadia in south Florida.

Hardly had the class arrived at the Lakeland primary school and unpacked their bags and straightened their kit than their training commenced. However, it also ceased just as abruptly as it had begun. Eastward at sea beyond the Bahamas, a tropical storm formed up on Saturday,

4 October, and rain began to fall within a 250-mile radius of the storm's center. On Sunday, it turned westward, killed three people and was cause for concern about the safety of several missing Bahamian fishermen, as its 100-mile-per-hour winds sped full force across the islands.

As it rushed on westward, the storm continued to gain strength. As the hurricane approached south Florida on Sunday, all aircraft that could not be battened down in hangars at flying schools were flown northward to other airfields by instructors and army officers. When the hurricane slammed into the coast of south Florida Sunday night, its wind velocity was reported by the Pan American Airways Training Station at Dinner Key, south of Miami, as being 123 miles per hour. By early Monday morning, 6 October, as the storm surged into the Gulf of Mexico and turned northward, rain continued to come down in torrents.

At the Lakeland school and others in south Florida, the men remained in quarters as winds and rain swept the region. Limbs and leaves and a large amount of fruit were blown down from trees of the orange grove adjacent to the airfield. As the storm swept northeastward out of the Gulf of Mexico on Monday night, it struck St. Marks and Tallahassee, and with diminishing force continued northeastward diagonally across Georgia, reentering the Atlantic Ocean a day later between Savannah, Georgia, and Charleston, South Carolina.

By that time, the aircraft had been returned to Lakeland, and training resumed. Slightly more than a week later, another storm struck the Florida coast south of Jacksonville, and though it did not inflict damage on the Lakeland area, it brought heavier rains than the preceding storm. But these were only minor inconveniences; the sun came out again, and the training schedule was modified. In order to make up for lost time and to complete the course on schedule, flying training continued seven days per week for a while.

The lost time was quickly made up, and on 3 November when Class SE-42-C completed the primary flying course, sixty-two men graduated, thirty-eight had been eliminated and the graduates were posted to the basic flying school at Gunter Field, Alabama. Class SE-42-D became the senior class and cadet officers were appointed. Among members of the class were J.A. Jones of Aberystwyth, Wales, who "breaks into Welsh if English isn't sufficiently expressive"; Kenneth G. Dale, a newspaper clerk of Portsmouth, Hampshire, who "thinks that 'Column Right' is a call for 750 words"; James "Jimmy" Thain of London; J.A. "Tony" Mason of Weston-Super Mare, Somerset; Duncan MacKinnon of Glasgow, Scotland; two suburban Londoners, Raymond L. "Ray" Rowett and William E. "Bill" Pearce; Ronald J.H. Pile of Biarritz, France; and Kenneth J. Trelfer of Sunderland, County Durham.

Following very active war service and postwar career, Trelfer recalled his training days from his retirement home in the Yorkshire Dales:

> We eventually left Toronto at 5 p.m. on 30th September and arrived at Lakeland, Florida at 7 a.m., 2nd October, travelling by train via Buffalo…Lakeland, Florida was the home of Lakeland School of Aeronautics. This was a private flying school with civilian Flying Instructors (Military Check Pilots) flying Stearman PT-17s. I was assigned to Class 42-D and had my first flight on 7th October 1941. My instructor for my entire sojourn at Lakeland was Mr. M.R. Bell, a veteran pilot who sent me on my first solo flight after 5 hrs., 26 minutes dual instruction.
>
> I have a note in my log book to the effect that the washout rate for my particular course was 45%, but I don't know how I arrived at that figure or even how accurate it is. For some strange reason, the thought of being washed out never actually entered my head. In

my ignorance, I always assumed that I would pass without any difficulties. Maybe I was blind to my faults, and my instructors managed to eradicate them without my being aware of it. Either way, I was never conscious of having any problems.

The two things which had the greatest impact on the British cadets were, in my opinion, a) the food and b) the reception by the local civilian population. After two years of strict food rationing in England, the vast quantities available in Lakeland were a revelation. Not one egg per week, but unlimited numbers for breakfast! I have never, either before or since, been welcomed to any place with the friendliness and enthusiasm accorded to us by the citizens of Lakeland and surrounding district. We were feted, entertained, and invited into people's homes literally every weekend. One of my main regrets of the war years is that I have lost touch completely with all the very good friends I made in Florida.

The quality of the flying instruction was excellent. As I became a flying instructor myself at a later date with an "above average" assessment, I feel that I am competent to pass a valid judgement. The type of flying I was taught by Mr. Bell belonged to a bygone age. He taught me to fly by the "seat of your pants" and not by instruments. Although this type of flying clearly belongs to the open cockpit biplane era, it nevertheless provided me with a firm basis from which to progress.

According to my logbook, I was rated as an "above average" bomber captain, flying instructor, and transport command captain. A great deal of the credit for this undoubtedly belongs to Lakeland School of Aeronautics and to Mr. Bell in particular for the firm grounding they gave me. I graduated from Lakeland after 60 hrs. and 21 minutes flying time. I notice that the Graduation Dance, held at the Lakeland Yacht and Country Club was on Saturday 6th December—the day before Pearl Harbour.

Many members of every pilot training class felt that they received an excellent grounding in flying at the Lakeland school.

Ian F.V. Hawkins of that same class was a pupil of Instructor Stanley Vossler, and with others completed pilot training and survived the war. More than forty years later, Hawkins reminisced about his early RAF training in America:

We arrived at Lakeland, Florida in our very ill-fitting gray Burton's suits in early October 1941. We received our flight training in PT-17 aircraft, and my instructor was Mr. Stanley Vossler, a very kind man. We were very impressed by the hospitality and kindness of many local people from whom we received a variety of invitations. I was particularly impressed by my early training in the warmth of Florida. I subsequently found, to my horror, that the most important instrument to a pilot (i.e., the ASI) was absent from the Stearmans we flew. Consequently, we enjoyed getting into clouds and coming out at all angles, and probably became better pilots because of it.

When the primary flying course ended for its members at Lakeland, Florida, on 9 December 1941, Class SE-42-D had the highest failure rate and the lowest graduation rate of the thirteen RAF classes trained at that school: 44 RAF students had been eliminated from pilot training (2 for non-flying reasons) and 56 graduated and were posted to basic flying school. Of the 380-man net intake for the first four classes at the Lakeland School of Aeronautics, 231 graduated as pilots, 148 were eliminated and 1 went missing.

CARLSTROM FIELD
ARCADIA, FLORIDA, 42-A-42-D

The Fifty-third U.S. Army Air Forces flying training detachment was established at Carlstrom Field, some seven miles south of Arcadia, Florida. As with Souther Field at Americus, Georgia, Carlstrom had been one of the twenty training airfields developed across the Southern tier of the United States in 1918–19. During 1918, the U.S. Army Air Service built large training stations and cleared landing grounds on the Florida prairie. Two Florida airfields each occupied 640 acres, a section of land and were subsequently named for fallen military aviators. Between 1918 and 1922, like Souther Field, Carlstrom and Dorr Fields trained a large number of pilots and, in the postwar years, served as depots for surplus aircraft and engines.

Eventually, both airfields were closed and their buildings were sold as war surplus and subsequently dismantled and removed, but the land on which they stood remained property of the United States government. During the next decade and a half, the cement foundations of barracks and hangars as well as the paved roadways and drainage ditches were hidden by grass, weeds and cabbage palms. Much of the remainder of the region became "citrus, sugar cane, and cattle country." On several occasions, responsible Florida leaders attempted without success to persuade the army air corps of the attractiveness of "Florida's Big Prairie" and these former airfield sites for the building of permanent military airfields.

In May 1940, as the war in Europe expanded rapidly, army air corps headquarters announced not only its seven-thousand-pilot training program but also new plans as well, which favored putting flying training schools in warmer, Southerly regions. Although disturbed by the European war, officials of DeSoto County, Florida, were nevertheless pleased to learn of air corps expansion plans. They immediately updated their brief describing the advantages of their county for airfields and resubmitted it to government agencies. Though civilian flying school proprietors were encouraged by army air corps expansion, those seeking government contracts to train military pilots were being steered away from large, already developed municipal airports with paved runways.

The army wanted civilian contractors to operate primary flying schools, but already developed flying facilities would be needed for the more advanced training of army and navy aircrews. As a result of that policy, army air corps site selection teams, as well as state government authorities and potential civilian primary school contractors, were scouting around the Southern tier of states seeking available, large, open, undeveloped spaces for flying school sites. Because Carlstrom and Dorr Fields had been used for flying training almost twenty years earlier and remained undeveloped and available in 1940, they attracted the immediate attention of state and federal government aviation agencies, which urged qualified civilian contractors to make use of them.

Undoubtedly, the Florida aviation entrepreneur best qualified to develop contract schools for the army air corps was John Paul Riddle, who operated a Civilian Pilot Training Program (CPTP) and other aviation enterprises in Miami. Riddle, who had been trained as a United States Army Air Service pilot at Carlstrom Field in 1922, had a varied career in the field of aviation. He had been a barnstormer, had flown air mail routes and had been active in American Airlines. In 1939, he was a fixed-base operator at Miami airport and had established a company to train pilots to fly both seaplanes and land planes. To meet the growing demand for aircaft maintenance staff, Riddle operated an aircraft and engine (A&E) mechanics school in Miami. He also had extensive interests in Brazilian aviation.

In 1939, when the newly created Civil Aeronautics Authority (CAA) launched its program to train thousands of pilots, Riddle was able to obtain a contract to use his flying school for training University of Miami students under the CPTP. During 1940, when the army air corps began its rapid expansion and launched plans for the establishment of a balanced number of flying training schools in each of three geographic zones in the United States, Riddle was at the right place at the right time.

With an excellent, well-established and deserved reputation in aviation, Riddle was in an ideal position to gain flight training contracts in south Florida or elsewhere, if he could get the necessary financial backing. He knew and had trained large numbers of pilots and aircraft and engine (A&E) mechanics and, as a result, had ready access to both well-qualified instructors and well-qualified maintenance staff. Moreover, he knew the organization and types of facilities that were necessary. His immediate task was to convince others that there was profit potential in the establishment and operation of contract flying schools aimed at providing primary flying for army air corps flying cadets.

Because of his reputation and the fact that contractors were needed in the Southeastern United States, especially in Florida, the army air corps was delighted to give him a contract to commence training cadets on 15 February, later changed to 22 March 1941. In order to undertake the contract, Riddle had to find an airport site away from the congested Miami area, gain approval of that site from air corps officers and then build and equip an airfield with hangars and all other airport facilities. In addition, he would have to locate and lease or purchase auxiliary landing grounds, and the schools he built would have to have utilities, barracks, dining hall, classrooms, infirmaries and recreation facilities.

In late 1940, when the site at Carlstrom Field was selected and approved by army air corps officers, the Embry-Riddle Company worked with DeSoto County officials, and they were able to purchase for $2,300 a 213-acre tract of land on the north side of the World War I flying school site. Located on the west side of a paved state road, this land appeared to be an ideal site for building a pilot training school and an aircraft overhaul depot.

The Embry-Riddle Company leased the contiguous 640-acre old Carlstrom Field site from the U.S. government and began to develop a flying field. The only work needed to prepare the airfield for use was to cut the tall grass, remove the bushes and cabbage palms, clean out the field's old drainage ditches and discourage a large population of snakes. In January 1941, once these basic tasks were completed, the company had use of a vast tract of land, and quickly developed two sod runways for training use.

The choice of architect Stefan Zachar of Miami as designer of the school proved to be an excellent one. Zachar's unique and distinctive plans for the school were a work of genius and made the Embry-Riddle School at Carlstrom Field one of the most attractive flying schools in the United States. The original design called for a capacity enrollment of 250 students, but the architect undoubtedly sensed that the school might be enlarged later, so he laid out the buildings on a circle one thousand feet in diameter five-eighths of a mile in circumference.

The six barracks, ground school building, infirmary, canteen, dining hall, dispatch office, gate house and administration building were to be equidistant, and two massive hangars were to be erected outside the circle on a curve, thus providing large parking spaces near the hangar line. The original two metal hangars with lean-tos around three sides measured 180 feet wide by 120 feet deep, housed thirty-two primary trainers each and would open on the south side to the huge, level airfield.

Carlstrom Field's administration building faced the entrance to the school on the north side of the circle. The original six barracks were arranged around an Olympic-sized swimming pool in the center of the circle, and the pool was flanked by basketball and tennis courts. The ground school building, with its six classrooms, two offices, toilet and large storage room, was located on the east side of the circle. The canteen was situated on the south side of the circle directly across the curved drive from the hangars and flight line. The school's dining hall was located on the west side of the circle. All of the other buildings of the school were designed to be aligned in such a way as to take advantage of prevailing winds and to provide maximum ventilation and cooling. Steel casement windows were installed wherever possible, and buildings were constructed of concrete blocks on reinforced concrete pads.

Each student room would be accessible through separate outside entrances under a covered, screened-in walkway, thus providing maximum comfort and at least some protection from insect pests. Though the military standard of the time called for communal toilets and showers, Zachar recognized the need for a greater measure of privacy for the elite flying students, and therefore incorporated in the school's design a separate bathroom for each four-student room. Many students who attended the school and lived and worked in the original Zachar-designed facilities were not aware until they left how lucky they had been in their housing accommodations at Carlstrom Field.

It is likely that Zachar suggested the swimming pool as a centerpiece, and that proposal was accepted. Though not absolutely required by the contract, Carlstrom Field was located in an isolated region far from a city, so a swimming pool and other recreational facilities were essential for good student morale. In a cost-conscious era, those schools that developed swimming pools also justified the expenditure by asserting correctly that, in the event of such emergencies, the pools would serve as reservoirs for use in extinguishing fires.

To make Zachar's plans a reality, the Embry-Riddle Company selected as general contractor the C.F. Wheeler Construction Company of Miami. E.W. Riley, job superintendent for the Wheeler Company, began construction on 24 December 1940 and used a daily average of one hundred men on the building site to complete the job in sixty-seven working days. One part of the original plan that was deleted by the Embry-Riddle Company was the construction of ten frame houses on the site for key school personnel. This omission proved to be a mistake.

As with other civil contractors, Riddle was able to use his army air corps contracts as collateral to secure loans guaranteed by the Reconstruction Finance Corporation. In January 1941, he gained such an RFC loan in the amount of $215,000 and borrowed through a second mortgage $75,000 from Standard Oil Company. In May 1941, when he was asked by the army air corps to expand Carlstrom Field, Riddle gained a further Reconstruction Finance Corporation guaranteed loan totaling $445,000.

At about the same time, he was encouraged by army air corps officers to develop a second contract primary school for the training of USAAC flying cadets. And what better place to do so than in the open land and air space of Florida's big prairie near Carlstrom Field. Dorr Field, another World War I army air service advanced flying training school, was located about fifteen miles east of Arcadia and twelve miles northeast of Carlstrom Field. Riddle agreed to build his second contract primary school on the Dorr Field site and made arrangements to begin construction there in July 1941. In addition, Riddle had signed another contract in May 1941 with British officers, and he planned to build and operate a British flying training school at Clewiston. The huge tract of land was almost identical to those used for Carlstrom and Dorr Fields.

As a result of these vast undertakings, Riddle had to look for other sources of capital. He already had the support of his wealthy partner, T. Higbee Embry, but he now gained the strong financial backing of Maurice Rothschild of Chicago and John McKay of Miami. With that support and the subsequent expansion to five major contract operations, the Embry-Riddle Company ultimately became a key army air forces training and maintenance contractor. Though financial backing helped him to obtain government contracts, success depended largely on Riddle and the experienced and competent staffs that he employed.

Riddle, as president and chief executive officer of the Embry-Riddle Company, selected Captain Leonard J. Povey to serve as vice-president and director of flying. Povey, who had also learned to fly in the United States Army Air Service, had spent several years in the Cuban Air Force and had built a strong reputation in aviation. In the field of aerobatics, he was credited with developing the maneuver called the Cuban 8. In 1940, Povey was employed by the Civil Aeronautics Authority (CAA) and had the responsibility of traveling around to assure the standardization of flight instruction being provided by dozens of civil contractors used in the Civilian Pilot Training Program (CPTP). With his reputation and vast experience in aviation, Povey was an excellent choice for the important managerial post with the Embry-Riddle Company.

As long as the operations remained relatively small, the staff functioned well, personnel problems were few and the company prospered. However, for a variety of reasons, that standard was difficult to maintain for very long. With few exceptions, those civilians at the helm of Carlstrom Field had served in either army air corps or naval aviation. Captain Leonard J. Povey was the civilian general manager at Carlstrom Field; James S. "Jack" Hunt served as director of flying; Thomas Gates was one of two stage commanders, and Wyman Ellis was the other; G. Willis Tyson, a native of Manchester, England, and an experienced aviator, was named flight commander and engineering officer. Of all Embry-Riddle personnel at Carlstrom Field, Tyson was the only company officer who lacked experience in military aviation.

Even before the school was completed, instructors and maintenance staff began to arrive in the area to prepare for 22 March 1941, the scheduled opening date of the school. In January, while construction was still going on, some of the flying instructors began to take a refresher instructional course at the Arcadia municipal airport in preparation for the arrival of students. With its population of about four thousand people and its economy based on cattle and citrus farming, the depression-ridden town of Arcadia, Florida, was attractive, but poor. There were few houses or even rooms available for rent. As a result, many school staff lived in trailers or commuted as much as twenty-five miles or more daily.

From the beginning, with its beautifully designed facilities and near-perfect flying weather, the Riddle Aeronautical Institute (RAI) was bound to become a very important station for the training of military pilots. In February 1941, Captain Stanley H. Donovan, graduate of the United States Military Academy, career officer and former USAAC flying instructor, arrived and took command of the detachment as the school's first air corps supervisor. Donovan's primary function was to ensure that the terms of the contract between the army air corps and the Embry-Riddle Company were fulfilled. The means of supervision included regular checks of the quality of flying and ground training provided to USAAC flying cadets. In addition, he was responsible for daily inspections to ensure the quality of aircraft maintenance and domestic facilities available for the care and discipline of cadets.

As the unit history of Carlstrom Field asserted, "It must always be kept in mind that the present contract primary flying schools are hybrid in nature, being part civilian and part army, with the division of authority and responsibility constantly shifting on some matters." Because of the nature of the organization, there was plenty of room for conflict. To avoid problems, it was important that personalities be taken into consideration and that efforts be made to promote cooperation. For these reasons, the choice of air corps supervisors and civilian management personnel was extremely important.

There was also no public transportation, so personnel involved in construction and later as school employees relied on private automobiles. The company provided a bus service, but it was never popular or profitable and was abandoned, only to be resumed a short time later when student numbers were significantly increased. When USAAC flying cadets of Class SE-41-H arrived in Arcadia to begin training in mid-March 1941, they were transported the seven miles from the Arcadia railway station to Carlstrom Field in the private automobiles of instructors and townspeople, and that practice continued for Class SE-41-I and for subsequent arriving and departing classes.

Although the twin problems of housing for "permanent" personnel and transportation for everyone at the school were aggravating nuisances and remained so, there were others. When the school was built, electrical service was readily available, but because of isolation of the school site, deep wells aimed at providing a potable water supply had to be drilled on the site. The company had nine wells drilled, and these provided an adequate flow of water until October 1941, when overcrowding and expansion of the school made it necessary to increase the water supply. To reach sufficient potable water to serve the increased population, more wells were drilled and in doing so, drillers struck a strata of sulfur, and from then on until late in the war, water at Carlstrom Field was less desirable in flavor and odor. Though the sulfur could be masked through liberal use of lemons and limes in drinking water, or a straightforward substitution of citrus juices or other cold beverages for water, hot beverages proved less palatable, and showers and shaves were less refreshing. The problem of water potability was not solved until about 1944, when a water purification system was installed to process the liquid pumped from the twenty-one shallow wells on the field.

Another problem of major proportions that developed later was that of groundwater. Elevation of the airfield was recorded as fifty-six feet; however, a small circular area in the center of the airfield that became a pond during wet weather had to be roped off and clearly marked with flags. Drainage of the airfield could be improved by the relatively simple expedient of ditching or installing pumps, but occasional very heavy rains left school management no choice but to suspend operations until the field drained.

The problem of sewage disposal in an area already waterlogged proved more difficult to solve. The only solution to the problem was to construct a sewage treatment plant some distance north of the domestic site, a project completed early in 1942. Such domestic problems, which were typical of many encountered in the rush of wartime defense construction, were naturally noticeable, but were a low priority of concern to those intent upon learning to fly. However, the addition of more people to the station forced these problems to the forefront. Because of his successful Miami organization for the training of A&E mechanics and the superior maintenance record at his flying schools, Riddle was encouraged in 1942 to build and operate an aircraft overhaul unit at Carlstrom Field. The addition of this unit and its personnel exacerbated already critical problems involving housing, transportation, potable water and sewage disposal.

In March 1941, when training commenced, there were five flying supervisors on station and twelve flying instructors. By the end of the year, that number had climbed to eighty-two flying instructors, with twenty-nine additional instructors being trained by the company in refresher courses at Carlstrom Field. Joseph H. Horton, formerly the CAA senior maintenance supervisor at LaGuardia Field, New York, became superintendent of maintenance. When Carlstrom Field opened, Horton had a staff of twenty-five qualified A&E mechanics and one parachute rigger. By 15 December 1941, production line maintenance had been introduced, so there were only eighteen CAA-rated mechanics, one hundred civil air mechanics (CAMs, who were mostly women) and mechanic's helpers and three parachute riggers.

Sidney Pfluger was director of the ground school and also taught navigation. In addition, Douglas Hocker, Larry Walden, Leroy P. Sterling and Joseph R. Woodward Jr. served on the ground instructional staff teaching theory of flight, aircraft and engines and meteorology. Though not required to do so by early War Department contracts, in March 1941 the Embry-Riddle School employed Robert F. Towson of Miami as director of physical education at the school. In July, Towson was replaced by Jesse Thomas.

On 16 March 1941, the forty-nine members of Class SE-41-H, the first group of USAAC flying cadets, arrived and commenced training six days later. At the 5 April 1941 dedication of the field, Brigadier General Walter R. Weaver, commanding general of the Southeast Air Corps Training Center (SEACTC), delivered the address. At the end of five weeks, the members of Class SE-41-I arrived at Carlstrom Field. These two small classes of USAAC cadets, most of whom were college and university graduates, arrived at the school in civilian clothing.

While undergoing primary flight training, the cadets were issued helmets, coveralls, goggles and other essential equipment; off-post they wore civilian clothing. Since the training of USAAC flying cadets in civilian-owned schools under contract with the War Department had existed in the air corps only since 1 July 1939, priorities were still shifting in 1941, and most schools were still open to visitors.

At most civil contract primary schools between 1939 and 1941, rigid discipline, inspections, hazing and the class system, which had been borrowed from West Point and Randolph Field practices, were modified or simply omitted. That aspect of cadet training was reduced because the schools were in a civilian setting and there was a shortage of military staff necessary to do the military training properly. Instead, the military part of officer cadet training was generally postponed until cadets reached the army-operated basic flying schools. Since 1938, regular air corps officers had complained that the training was getting too soft, and that it was not up to the standard that they themselves had endured.

Because these training officers pushed constantly for a greater emphasis on military discipline, their voices were finally heard and a general stiffening of military training spread to the emerging classification centers, pre-flight schools and the new civil contract primary schools. To complicate matters, British pilot training students entered into the American training program under the Arnold Scheme at precisely that transitional stage. Moreover, students at Carlstrom Field and other primary schools were also compelled to learn flying in the midst of considerable construction on the airfield.

Pressure had begun in spring 1941 to expand the school's facilities, and the work had commenced, so each class was increased in size at Carlstrom Field. During the summer and autumn of 1941, while Arnold Scheme Classes SE-42-A, SE-42-B, SE-42-C and SE-42-D were undergoing training, three more huge hangars were added to the two already erected. In addition, between 21 August and 25 September, four new two-story barracks were constructed. These new quarters did violence to Stefan Zachar's original design, but they were located within the circle between the existing six one-story barracks and the flight line. The dining hall was doubled in size, and both the canteen and administration buildings were enlarged. A separate infirmary building was also constructed. Despite problems created by construction and overcrowding, the attractiveness of Carlstrom Field facilities, the size of its airdrome and the record time in which it had been constructed had already attracted considerable attention in flying circles.

Besides General Weaver, other military officers who visited during the early months were Brigadier General Clarence L. Tinker, commanding general of the Third Air Force at Tampa's McDill Field; Brigadier General Charles H. Danforth, formerly commanding officer of the air corps training center at San Antonio, Texas, now retired and living in Punta Gorda, Florida; General Rush B. Lincoln, commanding general of the air corps technical training command; Major General George C. Brett, newly appointed chief of the army air corps; and Major General George Stratemeyer, commanding general of the SEACTC (who had recently replaced General Weaver). Among the noteworthy civilians who visited Carlstrom Field were actor Fred Stone, actress Sally Rand, novelist Rex Beach and Grover Loening, aviation pioneer, inventor and manufacturer of amphibian aircraft.

The arrival of Class SE-42-A on 9 June 1941 resulted in several more changes at Carlstrom Field. With the departure of Class SE-41-H, Class SE-41-I was elevated to upper-class status. With Class SE-42-A, British student pilots made up regularly enrolled classes at Carlstrom Field for the remainder of 1941. The arrival of ninety-nine British student pilots doubled the size of student pilot classes at Carlstrom Field and brought Flight Lieutenant Maurice A. O'Callaghan, an experienced ex-army officer, as the first RAF administrative officer. Whatever O'Callaghan's former experience, he must have found the climate of south Florida trying at best. He undoubtedly also found the occasional RAF student trying as well. Among the students, he was noted both for kindliness and for "tearing great strips" from the undisciplined or argumentive. Whether deserved or not, his reputation among at least some of the RAF students was that he was an officer whose bite, given reason, was at least equal to his bark.

Among the ninety-nine British students in that first RAF class at Carlstrom Field were cadets from a wide variety of occupations. There were ex-servicemen, as well as Reginald Trapp, professional golfer; George Butcher, engineer; Dennis Burgoyne, bank clerk; and Douglas May, tailor. Surnames of several other members of the class bespoke the district or region of the United Kingdom they represented, and included Vernon Lewis and Arthur L. Prandle from Wales; W.G. Fraser and William T.F. Hutcheson from Scotland; and Stan Forster, Alex Barrett, Roy Medland, Fred Chesney, John Hetherington, William F. Forrest and Robert K. Eggins from different parts of England. Eggins, who was to return to Carlstrom Field early in the spring of 1942 as a pilot officer check pilot, was very popular with his classmates. Regularly, at mealtimes, he played American-style tunes on the piano in the dining hall.

Following a few days' stay in the infirmary, nineteen-year-old "Woody" Forrest of Barkingside, Essex, returned to successfully complete his training. More than forty years later, Forrest still had vivid memories of the U.S. Army's aviation cadet regulations, which were based on the West Point and Randolph Field cadet systems and which defined the purposes of military, academic, flying and physical training in the making of a military aircraft commander. As part of that discipline, American and RAF cadets alike were marched everywhere on the station, even to meals. RAF student pilots were compelled to discard their own drill in order to learn and use American-style drill.

Especially shocking to Forrest and to other members of that first RAF class was the hazing, which meant that they believed they were constantly watched for minor infractions of what they perceived as ridiculous rules, and on occasion were required to recite nonsensical ditties. As a result, the British students at Carlstrom Field were less than happy when, as punishment for even minor infractions, they were compelled to walk fifty-minute "tours" in the hot sun for each demerit above five received in the course of any given week. To walk aimlessly at attention back and forth along a ramp or paved path for having been found with dust on a window ledge was perceived as a useless and wasteful punishment for a ridiculous infraction, but demerits and tours for flight line infractions and domestic sloppiness got their attention.

Since such "childish" hazing was associated with English public schools, it may well have been resented by non-public school men for precisely that reason. Whether or not that assessment is correct, the custom of hazing had not found its way into very many units of the British armed forces. Moreover, outside organized training sessions, the Royal Air Force concentrated on aircrew and technical training, presumed maturity among its trainees and used a more informal approach than did the American system of training. In the event of infractions of good RAF discipline, efforts were made to assign the miscreant to some useful and productive fatigue duty. Later, when USAAF airmen arrived in England, they were as shocked as RAF aircrew at what British authorities labeled LMF (lack of moral fiber) instead of combat fatigue.

The attitude of USAAF training and tactical officers as well as the cadet officer under their orders was that the RAF students were now undergoing *American* aviation cadet training, which was a set system not usually modified to suit any individual's tastes, regardless of nationality or customs. Those men who really wanted to become pilots were willing to tolerate almost anything for that opportunity. Those who were not willing to absorb the discipline were perceived as dangerous to themselves and to others, and were therefore deemed unsuitable for pilot training.

Despite such minor problems of adjustment, Woody Forrest and his classmates were thrilled with their flying. At first, as at every other station, the young men found their trainer aircraft superb, but there was the basic problem of communication. Because of engine noise in flight and the less-than-perfect Gosport tubes as a means of in-flight communication, instruction always took place before leaving the ground and reviews were done after landing. Depending on the instructor's personality and his assessment of each student, in-flight direction could be handled gently or not so gently. Flying required absolute concentration; daydreaming could get aircraft passengers maimed or killed. Forrest was taken aback to find that his civilian flying instructor was abrupt. Since there were several instructors around who were perceived by some classmates as blatantly anti-British, he felt that his instructor was as well.

After gaining more experience, however, Forrest understood the teaching methods better and concluded that his instructor was not only a superb, experienced pilot, but also an excellent psychologist. "I think he realised that I was (and still am) pretty lazy and readily discouraged," Forrest wrote many years later, "and the only way to get me through this difficult primary course was to make me determined to go solo and get rid of him." Even with problems and the fear of failure lurking constantly at the door, Forrest and his classmates had a "ball." Since their own country had more than thirty different dialects, they were especially taken with the soft Southern accents and pronunciations. Expressive terms and descriptions readily caught their attention. They were enthralled with "y'all" and with the pronunciations of their meteorology instructor, who regularly referred to "My-ammah."

Carlstrom Field was likened to a great country club. A large number of like-minded individuals were there and, together, they were doing exactly what they wanted to do. Even though it was necessary to adjust to a different training system and to the minor inconveniences caused by the construction of additional barracks and hangars and the enlargement of both the canteen and the mess hall, the food was magnificent and the quarters superb, but the water stank. The irritation that each RAF draft experienced while attempting to adjust to many new things at one time gradually gave way to mixed feelings about the differences between the two nations, their people, military customs and training systems.

Although that system may not have been used before 1942, many students at Carlstrom Field who were eliminated from pilot training were apparently removed from their regular billets and were sent to reside for several weeks in Barracks 11, "Sleepy Hollow," before being posted to Maxwell Field for reassignment or back to Canada. Although too many of that first RAF class remained "dodoes" (students who never soloed) before being washed out of training, many others did adjust to the pressures applied during the first few weeks of training. In fact, they thrived on the challenge and triumphed. For both groups, there were other distractions that also required adjustment. Although some areas of the Southeastern United States suffered from a drought during summer 1941, south Florida experienced periodic high winds, thunderstorms and heavy rains that interfered with flying when they flooded low-lying sections of the main airdrome and auxiliary fields.

The occasional six-foot-long rattlesnakes that undoubtedly crossed the huge airfield with some regularity sometimes attracted the attention of a flying instructor. Everyone except the RAF student in the aircraft was amused with Instructor Carl Dunn's battle with such a reptile in the middle of Carlstrom Field. It was reported that Dunn saw the snake and attempted first to crush it with the tires of his Stearman's landing gear. That effort failing, Dunn unbuckled his seat belt, got out of the aircraft with Stearman engine crank handle in hand and, after several wildly inaccurate throws of the heavy metal crank, returned to his airplane and student and continued the instruction session. Despite these little distractions, sunshine and airplanes were enough for most of the students to suffer virtually anything.

Moreover, the natives were decidedly friendly. The young RAF students were a novelty, and civilians of the region fell over themselves to do things for them. Dances were put on at Arcadia's Tourist Center. The Reverend Frank Robinson and his congregation of the Trinity Methodist Church made tremendous efforts to entertain as many of the young visitors as possible. However, all was not one-sided. Many of the cadets joined church choirs and described Britain's wartime experiences to civic clubs, to students in schools and other local groups.

LAC Arthur L. Prandle, a former newspaperman, became a one-man RAF public relations chief in that part of Florida. Regularly, he wrote interesting articles for the *Arcadian* telling of activities of the British cadets and their hosts. In "Serving in Three Air Forces," Prandle described how the members of Class SE-42-A were issued portions of uniforms by the RAF, RCAF and USAAC. In England, they had received blue uniforms, caps, shoes and socks, greatcoats, the heavy and complete flying kit, a set of heavy blue coveralls and a gray woolen civilian suit. However, all of this RAF-issue clothing was much too heavy to be worn on even the coldest days in Florida. The Canadian-issue khaki uniforms with sewn-in red insignias had not been measured when issued and had not yet been tailored. Since they had little clothing that could be worn, air corps officers issued them baggy, gray-green fatigue coveralls for general wear until provision could be made to tailor their khakis or to provide them the same proper-fitting summer uniforms that were issued to American aviation cadets.

Prandle's newspaper articles were not only entertaining but informative. His secret was that he found literally everything about Arcadia and Carlstrom Field fascinating, and he conveyed that enthusiasm to his readers. Diplomatically, he also expressed his own gratitude and that of his classmates for the hospitality being shown to all of them. If they did not walk tours for excessive demerits as, to his embarrassment, Prandle did on at least one Saturday afternoon, the cadets were permitted to leave Carlstrom Field on weekends. From shortly after noon on Saturdays until 4:00 p.m. (later 6:00 p.m.) Sunday afternoon, they often went on picnics or traveled to beaches, the Everglades, Lake Okeechobee and various towns and cities near and far.

Since it was seven miles into town from the airfield and there was no reliable public transportation, office secretaries, instructors, army officers, maintenance men and other staff regularly stopped their automobiles and picked up groups of cadets walking along the paved road toward Arcadia. Local citizens drove out and met the British boys at the main gate leading into the air station, drove them back to Arcadia or to nearby towns, farms or ranches, fed and entertained them and drove them about in large automobiles to see the glories of that part of Florida.

During the weekend of 28–29 June 1941, all of the members of Class SE-42-A were invited to Sarasota by three clubs. The sponsoring organizations were the Junior Chamber of Commerce (Jaycees), the Junior Woman's Club and the Bundles for Britain organization. The latter organization was chaired by Mrs. Karl Bickel, wife of the president of United Press, one of the major American wire services. As a result of that gracious welcome to the town and state, and many other similar sponsored weekends, Sarasota became the favorite town of RAF students from Arcadia as well as for many from the flying school at Lakeland. Within a short time, several of the SE-42-A students had modified a 1914–18 musical favorite, "Tipperary," and "It's a Long, Long Way to Sarasota" became a theme song. Evidently, it was passed on from one class to another at the Arcadia school and was sung as the occasion demanded.

On Sunday, 29 June, several couples and a large number of attractive girls were invited to have lunch with the cadets in the school's dining hall and to join them in the swimming pool during the afternoon. On Thursday evening, 3 July, the cadets were invited to a dance in Arcadia's Tourist Center, and the cadets were invited to it. Then, on Friday, 4 July 1941, local citizens invited the RAF students to their Independence Day celebration and their semiannual rodeo, which included not only entertainment but also barbecue and other foods. Citizens of other Florida towns such as Fort Myers, Sarasota and even Tampa also entertained the student pilots.

Around 15 July 1941, Class SE-41-I, the American cadet class, departed for basic flying school. Class SE-42-A, now halfway through its primary flying course, became the upper class, and LAC William Harrison was appointed cadet captain. A few days later, on 19 July 1941, 101 new RAF student pilots arrived at Carlstrom Field as members of Class SE-42-B. At around the same time, seasonal torrential rains came to south Florida. As a result, the already crowded training schedule was totally disrupted for everyone, and the flying schedule was extended to Saturdays.

On Saturday, 26 July, Major General George Brett, recently designated chief of the army air corps, and Major L.S. Stranathan accompanied several British officers to inspect Carlstrom Field. Among the visitors were Captain Harold Balfour, MC, MP, undersecretary of state for air; W.W. Wakefield, parliamentary private secretary to Captain Balfour; Air Commodore George C. Pirie, British air attaché; Group Captain D.V. Carnegie, director of UK training in the United States; and Wing Commander H.A.V. Hogan, DFC, RAFAO for the Southeast Army Air Corps

Training Center. Before departing for Washington, Captain Balfour was shown training records and addressed some two hundred RAF cadets.

Although under the circumstances it was probably unavoidable, problems developed in August and September 1941 in the management and operation of Riddle Aeronautical Institute at Carlstrom Field. If not caused by it, the Carlstrom problems were certainly aggravated by expansion that was attempted too quickly. During the summer of 1941, company administrators were developing four different sites simultaneously. The technical school in Miami was being enlarged, as was Carlstrom Field. Construction of another large USAAF primary school was underway on the site of Dorr Field. Progress was also being made in the construction of Riddle Field, the British flying training school near Clewiston.

Carlstrom Field was the parent pilot training school in the system. Originally designed to accommodate 250 students, it was also one of the first primary flying schools in the Southeastern United States to be enlarged so that it could accommodate 600 students at one time. Although the first small class commenced training on 22 March, construction at the airfield had been virtually continuous. Not only was Carlstrom Field a primary school, but it was also an overhaul station for Stearman trainers from a number of primary flying schools in the region. By early autumn, Carlstrom was still crowded, but its enlarged facilities were nearing completion.

Larger drafts were already being assigned to Carlstrom Field, and initial drafts were also scheduled to arrive at Riddle and Dorr Fields in August and September. However, each of these airfields and schools had suffered serious construction delays, and none was ready to commence training. Instead of delaying the drafts or having them reassigned elsewhere, army air forces training officers agreed with the contractor and his managers that there was sufficient space at Carlstrom Field to train its own drafts as well as the early intakes for the other schools. In June 1941 when Class SE-42-A arrived, intakes doubled, and in mid-July they doubled again when Class SE-42-B arrived.

In August, prior to the arrival of Class SE-42-C, an additional group of fifty RAF LACs and a consignment of aircraft arrived at Carlstrom Field. Their flying and ground school training would be conducted alongside that of Arnold Scheme Classes SE-42-A and SE-42-B. When construction of BFTS No. 5 was completed at Clewiston, some seventy-five miles east of Arcadia, the extra students and aircraft were to be moved there. Because of the additional men and planes and delays in training caused by high winds and rain, double training schedules were implemented and training time was expanded to a seven-day week. Because of its rapid expansion, Carlstrom Field was several months ahead of other training stations in expanding to a seven-day "wartime" training schedule.

On 25 June, slightly more than two weeks after their arrival, LAC Rae Smart became the first member of the class to solo and, as was the custom borrowed from American cadets, was duly dunked, fully dressed, into the school's swimming school. After five weeks of training, American cadet Class 41-I departed and a second RAF class, SE-42-B, arrived to take its place. Training continued, and men washed out of pilot training and regularly departed for Canada to be remustered for other training. A few days before Class SE-42-A graduated, LAC Bunyar became the fourth member of the Caterpillar Club at Carlstrom Field. He bailed out of his Stearman ten miles south of Carlstrom Field and walked back to the airfield. Fortunately, despite overcrowding, there were no fatalities at the school.

As the members of Class SE-42-A were completing their final flying hours, the finishing touches were being put on dining hall expansion. Though not yet absolutely finished, the dining hall had been doubled in size and was now air conditioned. Club rooms and a ladies' powder room had been added near the exits. Second only to air conditioning was the addition of a large and attractive patio built adjacent to the dining hall. It was surrounded by palm trees and, although not yet ready for use, was being equipped with a special dance floor and a band shell.

Finally, on 16 August 1941, when the fifty-three surviving members completed the course, Class SE-42-A became the first class to use the new addition to the Carlstrom Field dining hall for their graduation dance. Anticipating their departure, the *Tampa Morning Tribune* of Friday, 15 August 1941 contrasted the departing bronzed and lean British cadets with the young Britishers with "pink and white complexions" who had arrived on 9 June. The newspaper was also correct in reporting that among both graduated cadets and townspeople there was genuine regret at the cadets' leaving.

In an article in the *Arcadian*, Arthur Prandle expressed his and his classmates' appreciation for all of the care taken in their training. In thanking the school's flight commanders and flying instructors, Prandle left a description of a part of the ordeal of the first RAF class at Carlstrom Field:

> *It has not been an easy ten weeks. The bad weather in the middle of the course meant that pupils and instructors alike had to flog themselves, giving up all thought of week-ends for over a month, in order to make up for lost time, and our instructors stood by us like bricks, working hour after hour, their only concern to make us good, safe pilots.*

Although all of the British students obviously did not react to their early American experience in the same way, Prandle, in keeping with the lyrics of a popular song of the war period, diplomatically "accentuated the positive."

Since their arrival in two contingents between 17 and 25 July, Class SE-42-B had experienced difficulty in building flying time. At that time, Carlstrom Field was crowded. In the Embry-Riddle Company newspaper, Dale Delanty wrote, "Carlstrom is now at its highest peak to date in the number of cadets. Almost all available barrack space is in use." In describing other construction, he indicated that access to the recreation center was difficult owing to expansion of that building and the piles of building materials close by destined to be used in the new two-story barracks.

When a storm warning came on Tuesday, 22 July, Lieutenant George Ola discovered after a quick survey that an aircraft was missing with its solo student. Fearing repetition of the tragedy that had occurred three weeks earlier at Lakeland, Ola took an aircraft and searched for the missing student. Fortunately, the student was found at Parker Field, and his aircraft had been tied down to prevent damage from the heavy winds. On returning to Carlstrom, the wheels of the lieutenant's aircraft struck a huge mud puddle near the end of the airfield. No damage was reported but, much to his embarrassment, Ola and his aircraft were drenched with muddy water. Much of the entire summer continued wet and, as a result, flying training suffered.

Since the weather was less than kind, a Saturday schedule had been put into effect on 2 August, and a few days later the school was temporarily placed on a seven-day-per-week flying schedule. By 12 August about fifty members of Class SE-42-B had soloed. In six days, they were able to make up the lost time and to crowd into that brief period two weeks of flying training. In mid-August 1941, with the departure of Class SE-42-A for Gunter Field, Class SE-42-B became the upper class, and nineteen-year-old LAC Peter E. Tickner became cadet captain. Nicknamed "the Saint" by his classmates, Tickner was described as having a moustache and sandy red hair.

Other members of Class SE-42-B were noted in 1941 for prowess of a different kind. While in training, Bruce Smeaton regularly wrote a column in *Flypaper*. Eddie Kureen was described as the "sole support of the biggest mustache in Class 42-B," though some of his classmates expressed it slightly differently by asserting that "there's more mustache than there is Eddie." Unfortunately, for those who were able to keep them in primary school, they usually found moustaches forbidden in USAAF basic flying schools. Other students were noted for different achievements. Within a few days of Class SE-42-B's elevation to senior status, LAC Herbert Bunton became a Caterpillar Club member when he bailed out of a Stearman trainer.

For several days during August, two Canadian cinematographers used several thousands of feet of film in photographing activities of RAF student pilots in training at Carlstrom Field. As the end of the month approached, arrangements were made to have a large contingent of cadets travel to Sarasota, and there to be filmed being offered the hospitality of that town. Since Sarasota was already well aware of the British cadets, it was not difficult arranging entertainment over the long Labor Day weekend.

While some men remained on station, a busload of Class SE-42-B members traveled to Sarasota to be filmed for the *March of Time*. Since some of the men had to fly Saturday afternoon, 30 August, the school's bus did not leave the airfield until 4:15 p.m., but that did not seem to matter since they were not scheduled to return to the flying school until Monday afternoon, 1 September. When the bus arrived in Sarasota, it was given a police escort to Five Points and, as crowds stood aside and the cameras turned, the cadets piled out of the bus and were greeted by a number of attractive young ladies. During that enjoyable weekend, camera crews directed by Al Snyder and Bill Perry of the *March of Time* followed the young men to the Lido for dancing on Saturday night. Whether or not they recorded his performance for posterity is unknown, but Trevor Tate was described as one of the few British cadets capable of jitterbugging.

On Sunday, the young men were filmed while enjoying themselves swimming and sunbathing at Lido Beach. Among others, Sarasota hosts to cadets for that fabulous weekend included the Greens, the Reynolds and the Brooks. On Monday, before boarding the bus at 5:00 p.m. for the return to Carlstrom Field, the cadets visited the facilities of the Ringling Brothers Circus headquarters and a reptile farm, or did some lazy sightseeing in Sarasota. As the bus made its way back to Arcadia and Carlstrom Field, many tired but happy cadets exclaimed over the "fantastic" hospitality they had enjoyed, and they sang popular British and American songs and, no doubt, sang Class SE-42-A's composition, now adopted as their own nostalgic lullaby, "It's a Long, Long Way to Sarasota." Not all of the young British cadets traveled to Sarasota regularly, but many of them returned there as often as possible.

In the ensuing weeks, activities at the school continued as usual. Class SE-42-C had arrived in late August and had commenced training prior to the Labor Day weekend. In the ensuing weeks, as training continued at the school, quite a few members of Classes SE-42-B and SE-42-C were eliminated from pilot training and traveled back to Canada by way of Maxwell Field, Alabama. Others continued in training and began to enjoy aerobatics and precision flying. They were very busy and enjoyed the beautiful sunshine, clear skies and citrus groves of Florida's big prairie.

However, they were shocked to read and hear accounts of the disappearance of a fellow British cadet and his Stearman trainer from the flying school at Lakeland, Florida. Instructors warned them to be especially careful of rapidly approaching fronts or heavy weather during their solo trips and urged them to find a place to land quickly in the event of an emergency, rather than to allow themselves to get lost in the Everglades or over the Gulf of Mexico while attempting to remain aloft long enough to locate a particular auxiliary airfield. Despite the tragedy at Lakeland and fears on the part of instructors of an even worse disaster in the crowded airspace around Arcadia, Carlstrom's four RAF classes underwent training simultaneously on a double schedule, worked and flew and regularly logged additional hours.

LAC Stanley Slater, later Group Captain Stanley Slater, DSO, OBE, DFC, was another of Class SE-42-B's distinguished graduates. Some forty-two years after undergoing training in Florida, Slater fondly recalled his training days:

> *Carlstrom Field was an impressive camp and the standard of accommodation and general amenities were very good. The food, though somewhat unfamiliar to us, was excellent. I remember my first taste of peanut butter. I was assigned to Flight D at the Riddle Aero Institute whose general manager was Leonard J. Povey. My flight instructor was a civilian named [Ralph] Cuthbertson, and he had a group of 4 RAF students, the first he had taught. Mr. Cuthbertson was very enthusiastic and keen for us all to pass. He continually reminded us of the cost of the flying training per minute and emphasized the need to get the maximum value from every minute in the air.*
>
> *I recall that I had some difficulty understanding what he said in the air probably as a result of the limitations of the communications system, his Southern accent, and my inexperience and slight apprehension, but he was thorough and painstaking. Eventually, I went solo at 10 hours which may have been slightly longer than average. The course totalled 60 hours, and because of the high "wash out" rate, all of us were apprehensive about our chances of completing the course.*
>
> *I remember a few stories (rumours) which were circulated in order to keep up our morale. One concerned a famous Battle of Britain pilot who was sent incognito to report on Arnold Scheme training. He was reputed to have been suspended before going solo! Some of the suspensions occurred as a result of disciplinary offences, some of which, in our opinion, were very minor, but I think we did not appreciate always that we were then on a peacetime course where some of the regulations seemed petty and irksome to young men who were anxious to get back and start fighting. Furthermore, the upper/lower class system and the Honour Code were not fully accepted by the British cadets, and these and the "gig" system were irritants to some of us. Personally, I was eager to succeed as a pilot and was willing to put up with anything to achieve this ambition.*
>
> *I recall that the room inspections were very strict and we found it necessary to sleep outside the bedclothes so that we did not disturb the 45 degree angles. We also put toilet paper in taps before leaving the room in the morning if we were to avoid "gigs" for water in the wash basin. Punishments for these minor infringements of the regulations seemed severe; walking up and down a concrete path was a depressing way to spend a Saturday afternoon. Restrictions on our leisure time were criticized by some of the students who thought that we should be allowed out of camp more often than once a week from Saturday midday until Sunday 4 p.m., but I found the facilities on camp for sport adequate compensation. Apart from an occasional trip to Arcadia and a beach party with the instructor at Sarasota towards the end of the course, I had no other contact with the outside world, but quite a few of us were happy to remain on camp at the weekend.*
>
> *I enjoyed the heat and the sunshine, and since we flew in the morning before the clouds and turbulence built up, the temperature was no problem. However, I remember one*

student by the name of Rice who was suspended because his sunburn, after a weekend at the beach, was so bad that he could not bear to wear a parachute. My first flight at Carlstrom Field was on 27 July 1941 and my last flight was on 25 September, a period of approximately 10 weeks. During this time, we lost 7 days because of rain and a hurricane scare when the aircraft had to be flown elsewhere by the instructors to avoid possible destruction. Graduation Day was a big relief to all of us; we felt that the most difficult hurdle had been passed.

Evidently, the hurricane scare came to Miami on Friday, 20 September and simultaneously, another tropical storm in the Gulf of Mexico joined it to drench the entire Florida peninsula.

In mid-September, before Class SE-42-B completed its flying and left Carlstrom Field, a two-hour variety show called the "Carlstrom Field Follies" was presented in the dining hall. The class was filled with talented musicians, professional actors and other theater people. Producer-director of the show was Eric Hall of London, and the stars of the show were experienced actors: red-headed Derek Shelton, formerly of the Birmingham Repertory Theater, and Bill Sykes, prominent London actor. It proved to be a fitting way to celebrate the end of the ten-week primary flying training course.

Alan George Winchester, another member of the class, closed out his primary flying experience with a different kind of performance. While on a morning solo flight in late September, Winchester got lost and, instead of waiting until he ran out of gasoline, he followed orders and decided to make a forced landing in a field near Myacca City. Children were released from a school nearby to see him and his aircraft, and when he met some adults there, he was surprised to see that many of "the male population had additional digits on one hand or frequently on both. Shades of Anne Boleyn!!" Fortunately, Winchester's worry about the possibility of being washed out because of slight damage to the aircraft was needless. For getting lost, he received a reprimand, but he was praised for landing safely in a small field.

On Friday night, 28 September, Class SE-42-B held its graduation dance on the newly constructed patio adjacent to the dining hall. Although there was a shortage of girls, the dancing was fun and the food was delicious. Moreover, the comedy, which was produced and directed by Derek Shelton and starred Eric Hall and Bill Sykes and satirized the life of a cadet at Carlstrom Field, brought the house down. The show was food for the soul. However, a different kind of feeding could not go unnoticed for long. In the open air of the patio, the healthy Florida mosquitoes made a feast of both the cadets and their guests.

Of the total intake of 101 students, 27 had been eliminated and 74 members of Class SE-42-B graduated on 2 October and departed for a basic flying school. Since both Class SE-42-B and SE-42-C underwent primary training alongside two separate additional RAF contingents destined to make up Courses 1 and 2 at British Flying Training School No. 5, their experience was somewhat different from other Arnold Scheme pilot trainees. The addition of other RAF students undergoing a different, more relaxed, form of flight training under the RAF rather than the USAAF syllabus, however necessary, was apparently a mistake. Arnold Scheme RAF students on the station were jealous of the Clewiston contingent apparently because they followed the RAF training syllabus and did not have to undergo the strict USAAF aviation cadet discipline that was imposed on Arnold Scheme cadets.

Since Carlstrom Field was being rapidly expanded and construction continued during these hottest and wettest months of the year, the school's facilities and personnel were undoubtedly taxed to their limits. Although civilian flight commanders and instructors had to adjust their training schedules in order to accommodate the larger numbers, a primary concern was the exercise of extreme caution in order to prevent accidents. With so many aircraft in the air and so many airfields in use at one time, it was also necessary to keep the aircraft separated into flying zones and to maintain longer flying schedules.

The double schedule at Carlstrom Field, which was necessary to accommodate the Clewiston students, was unpopular with both instructors and students. Compared to the problems encountered by army air forces military training officers, those of civilian staff appeared almost inconsequential. The American commandant of cadets and his tactical officers were put in a position in which it was virtually impossible to do their jobs properly. If aviation cadet regulations were to be enforced for one group and the other was totally exempt, it was an impossible situation that could lead only to conflict at many levels.

Since strong resentments were expressed by both Arnold Scheme and Clewiston students, there were probably clashes as well between American training officers and the RAF officers in charge of the BFTS students. Since at least some of the RAF students of the Clewiston BFTS who were temporarily under training at Carlstrom had also been washed out at other Arnold Scheme primary schools and were getting a second chance at pilot training, which was denied American cadets and other RAF students, it is perhaps understandable that some of the army air forces officers and cadets were irritated. To some of the other British cadets in training, the double standard for the two groups of students was more than an irritant.

In glorious understatement, the USAAF unit history indicated that "unfortunately, this was a time of major expansion from a 250 school to 600." However, the overcrowding did not end in late September 1941 with the transfer to BFTS No. 5 at Clewiston of the contingent of 90 cadets of Courses 1 and 2, and their fifty-two aircraft.

Class SE-42-D, which consisted of 146 RAF students, began training at Carlstrom Field on 4 October 1941. With Classes SE-42-C and SE-42-D in training simultaneously, though five weeks apart in the syllabus, there were approximately 240 RAF students in residence and training at the school. Ninety-nine American aviation cadets, who were destined to be the first class of pilot trainees at nearby Dorr Field arrived, instead, at Carlstrom. In early October, they had been ordered to report to Arcadia for assignment to the Dorr Field segment of Class SE-42-D, but owing to weather problems and material shortages, Dorr Field was not yet ready, as had been projected.

Nevertheless, the Embry-Riddle Company had signed a contract to accept cadets on schedule, and the army air forces had enrolled and equipped aviation cadets and scheduled them for arrival at the school on 3 October. Precedents for doubling up training at established contractor flying schools had been established in June and July 1941 when contingents of RAF students scheduled to commence training in five of the six British flying training schools had been trained temporarily at other primary schools until their own schools were ready to receive them.

Thus, Riddle Aeronautical Institute at Carlstrom Field had already served as the parent institution of No. 5 BFTS at Clewiston. Not only had it spawned instructors, managers and maintenance personnel for the RAF school, but it had also provided all of the elementary flying training for Courses 1 and 2, and an introduction to basic trainers for Course 1. Ground staff, many of whom had received vital experience at Carlstom Field, were designated for transfer to Clewiston, and until that move provided aircraft maintenance at Carlstrom Field for Stearman PT-17s, PT-18s and Vultee BT-13 basic trainers.

Carlstrom Field also trained and furnished the initial ground and flying instructional staffs, maintenance and management personnel for Dorr Field. As with earlier parasite units, the detachment of army air forces supervisors, civilian instructors and maintenance staff worked at Carlstrom Field, but as a separate Dorr unit. The ninety-nine Dorr cadets were billeted at Carlstrom Field and trained there alongside the Carlstrom classes. According to the station's unit history, the initial Dorr Field contingent "never lived at Dorr, and at best used the field as an auxiliary."

Among the students trained in Class SE-42-D at Carlstrom Field were Francis W. Preston and Neville Hetherington of Yorkshire and L.G. Robson of Northumberland. As with others of that fourth Arnold Scheme student pilot draft, these men were processed through the RCAF No. 1 Manning Depot at the Canadian Exhibition Hall in Toronto and traveled directly to Arcadia via Detroit and Cincinnati, Atlanta and Jacksonville. At some point during their training in Britain, probably at RAF Wilmslow Embarkation Centre, RAF students were issued with small blue booklets entitled "Notes for your Guidance," which they were urged to read and keep. At various points along the journey, probably as early as ITW and certainly at RCAF No. 1 Manning Depot in Toronto, they also learned that large numbers of RAF student pilots had been eliminated from pilot training in Arnold Scheme primary flying schools.

At first there was much speculation as to the cause of such numerous failures and such an affront to British selection procedures and initial training. In casting around for answers, RAF staff arrived at some standard but inconclusive answers, and these were repeated *ad infinitum* until they became a part of the conventional wisdom of the time. Although these views were to be further modified in time, the accepted reasons for the terrible and unheard of wastage that were spread about in late summer 1941 to RAF students destined for training in the United States included the "peacetime" nature of American flying training, the rigid American disciplinary system and covert Italian and German sabotage activities imbedded in the American training system.

Since Germany and Italy were at war with Britain, it was perhaps understandable that RAF students in the United States should be somewhat wary of people with distinctly Italian and German surnames. Unfortunately, some students who experienced difficulty in learning to fly came to believe that enemy influences were to blame. That fear on the part of many RAF student pilots was fed by letters and news reports that occasionally appeared in regional newspapers.

One such letter ostensibly from a distraught German-born mother of Orlando, Florida, was picked up by and reprinted in many Florida papers during July and August 1941. In mid-July 1941, a writer using the name Mrs. Freida Ollenberg had written to the newspaper "enclosing an Iron Cross which she had received from the German government for the death of her husband in the other war." She said she was distraught because her "two sons, both born Americans and citizens of the United States are fighting in Hitler's army because they were lured there by German agents operating in this country." The writer asked that the *Orlando Sentinel* "warn the people of Florida of just what is happening here in Florida so that they will wake up."

Continuing, the writer insisted that "Germans in Florida and all over the United States of America are being approached by many Nazi agents who tell them that their duty is to the fatherland first." Although the writer may have thought her evidence true, a cursory critique of the letter indicates that it was probably spurious and may well have been planted. Although the *Orlando Sentinel* may have done a follow-up check to verify the existence of "Mrs. Ollenberg" and the truth of her statements, the newspaper that reprinted the letter apparently did not follow up the story, and evidence of verification was not available. At best, the conclusion is that the "Ollenberg letter" is suspect.

LAC L.G. "George" Robson of Class SE-42-D, who was popular among his classmates and a talented player of the Northumbrian bagpipes, became convinced in the closed society of Carlstrom Field that there might well be a German conspiracy to deny the RAF a large number of pilots. His instructor was George Eckhart, an assistant flight commander at Carlstrom Field and a very able flight instructor, and Robson kept meticulously detailed records with drawings illustrating every manuever, landing pattern and virtually every word of instruction, encouragement or correction administered by his instructor, as well as personal evaluations of his own efforts.

After ten hours of flying, George Robson recorded that he was still experiencing significant difficulties when he invariably stalled while attempting landings. On 30 October 1941, after a morning flight of thirty-eight minutes, which brought his total flying time to eleven hours, thirty-nine minutes, Robson noted in his diary, "I felt much more confident and landed the plane properly, which is a relief. I could have soloed. Mr. Eckhart told Spiers and Irwin [two other RAF students] he would have let me solo if there hadn't been so much traffic, however, he was handing me to the Flight Commander to solo."

On 31 October 1941, Robson wrote that he had a check flight of twenty-two minutes with Flight Commander Gordon Mougey, and still experienced difficulty with landings. After they landed, the civilian flight commander critiqued his performance, indicating he was not correcting for torque sufficiently on takeoffs and was leveling off too high during landings. Robson recorded that he had now logged twelve hours, one minute of flying time.

On 3 November 1941, an unnamed U.S. Army officer gave Robson a fifty-five-minute check flight, and during that check concentrated on his major deficiencies—takeoffs and landings— and once more Robson experienced difficulty, including what he described as several "hard landings." At the end of the check flight, the officer told Robson that "as much as he disliked doing it, he felt he could only eliminate me."

To his diary of events, George Robson confided his feelings of having been wronged: "I don't consider this was a 'check flight'—I wasn't asked to do stalls, spins, S-turns, rectangular courses, forced landings, series of turns, etc., and I don't consider the officer capable of coming to a correct 'conclusion' without, at least, some of these." He went on to describe how his instructor, Mr. Eckhart, was surprised at his elimination and told him to get into "another flying school as soon as possible, as he was confident I could 'do it'."

On 7 November 1941, Robson was called to the office of the Carlstrom Field RAF administrative officer, Flight Lieutenant Maurice A. O'Callaghan. O'Callaghan was a somewhat rigid, experienced soldier who was not noted for tea and sympathy. As Robson stood before O'Callaghan and Flight Lieutenant Pinnell and was offered alternate aircrew training, he related his feelings about not having had a "square deal" and his plans to "place the facts before headquarters in New Brunswick."

By way of explanation, Robson went on to state that he felt the RAF needed pilots, that he had waited a year to get a release from his job with a firm operating under the Ministry of Food and that valuable time and money had been expended bringing him to the United States for an unjust elimination from pilot training. This series of statements by LAC Robson induced in

Flight Lieutenant O'Callaghan something nearing a volcanic eruption. According to Robson, O'Callaghan "went into a raging temper and told me I was one of those stupid individuals, who thought, when they came into the Air Force, they could just do as they liked."

Robson was understandably surprised at the RAFAO's attitude, and resented the reprimand because his record in training was unblemished: "I have never been late for a parade of any kind," he wrote, "nor been punished for any offence, and I have had no 'demerit marks' here." Later during that interview, Robson was again asked to sign a paper indicating choice for further aircrew training or to apply for discharge from the RAF and be eligible for call-up by the army.

Robson applied for discharge, explaining in his diary: "My sole reason for doing this was that I have seen so many pilots eliminated because they haven't had a 'fair chance,' and I feel I should bring it to the notice of my C.O., as it is impeding our 'General War Effort.'" Flight Lieutenant O'Callaghan asked Robson to consider over the weekend altering the request for "discharge" to an application for observer training before the meeting of the elimination board on Monday.

At the elimination board meeting on Monday, 10 November 1941, four officers reviewed the medical, academic, disciplinary and flying records of each student appearing before it. Obviously, from the record, elimination was recommended for LAC Robson on the basis of flying deficiencies, so when board members asked Robson if he had any comments to make, he recorded his answer in his diary as: "No sir, from that report my flying seems to be terrible."

However, Robson further confided to his diary his true feelings at that time.

> I don't wonder, now that there are so many "so-called eliminations"—flying reports are made out in a manner so "black," regardless of the truth in many cases, that it is impossible to argue...Many cadets will have left Carlstrom Field under the same circumstances, and I only hope the R.A.F. can sort the "wheat from the chaff," otherwise our general war effort is being sabotaged at a time when we can least afford to sacrifice future pilots.

In another document that he had labeled "Progress Log," George Robson explained his experience more fully. In a dark, clearly written and neat script, Robson analyzed his experience under four categories. He felt that he had had two hours, seventeen minutes of good instruction on the seventeenth, twenty-seventh and thirtieth of October; and on ten other days he had completed six hours, fifty-one minutes of flying instruction under bad conditions, including three days when he was ill. His first flight, the familiarization ride of thirty-one minutes, he considered wasted time because he had no earphones (the PT-17s were equipped with a speaking tube), and the two check flights totaling one hour, seventeen minutes were also "wasted for instructional purposes."

The most telling argument that Robson made in this document is his assertion that civilian instructor George Eckhart gave him assurances of both his (Eckhart's) and the flight commander's (Mougey's) written recommendations with proviso (if the army would give them permission) that Robson be permitted to pursue further pilot training. But Robson would not leave it at that.

His "Progress Log" then deteriorated into a diatribe against the entire American system of flying training. The litany of complaints cited the sixteen-hour daily schedule; the requirement that cadets attain a 70 percent standard on every weekly ground school examination or suffer the penalty of required weekend study; the lack of facilities for extra instruction on weekends; insufficient leave time to escape daily camp routine; brief normal leave time only from Saturday noon to 7:00 p.m.

Sunday, provided no academic deficiencies or excess demerits necessitated walking tours or extra study on Saturday afternoon; the award of demerit marks for dust, buttons unfastened, damp floors, etc.; the elimination of a British LAC who had been confined to his room for two weeks by the RAFAO, and had not been allowed to fly or to attend class; an attack on the British students by the director of the ground school for violation of the honor system; and an RAF revolt at being put on "academic detention" for the weekend following failure of a pop quiz.

Even after delivering this massive overkill, Robson went further. He described how American tactical officers stood behind curtains trying to catch cadets late, out of step or talking in ranks, and the removal of the cadet captain from office, ostensibly because another student entered the cadet captain's room during evening study to borrow some item. Robson's closing remarks pointed to an unsympathetic medical officer and a large number of sick and "generally run-down" British cadets in training "at a camp eight [actually seven] miles from Arcadia on the Prairie, surrounded by swamps, and in a very unhealthy humid atmosphere."

LAC L.G. Robson was eliminated from pilot training. In Canada, he was persuaded to remuster for observer training, which he completed in Canada. During the course of the war, Robson distinguished himself on operations as an outstanding navigator and ended the war a squadron leader. Realizing that his perceptions would be controversial, but knowing that he was not alone in feeling as he did about his training experiences, Robson proved to be a historian's dream when he graciously permitted use of his documents to tell the full story of his autumn 1941 Carlstrom Field days.

Whether or not L.G. Robson was also the author of the parody on "Ten Little Indians" is unknown, but someone with the initials "L.R." produced it, and this clever rhyme circulated around Carlstrom and other American training fields in late 1941. Entitled "R.I.P.," it follows:

Ten Little LAC's sailed across the brine,
One fell overboard so then there were nine.
Nine little LAC's driving American rate,
Wandered on the left hand side so then there were eight.
Eight little LAC's spinning through the heaven,
Chewing gum choked one so then there were seven.
Seven little LAC's, solo, doing tricks,
One believed his altimeter so then there were six.
Six little LAC's, P.T. in a dive,
Didn't pull out soon enough so then there were five.
Five little LAC's, coordination poor,
Crossed controls at hundred feet so then there were four.
Four little LAC's thought they saw the tee,
Turned out to be the gas wagon so then there were three.
Three little LAC's hedgehopping they flew,
One didn't see the water-tower so then there were two.
Two little LAC's giving her the gun,
Too late he saw he'd undershot so then there was one.
One little LAC reached his graduation,
Took one look at Basic—and quit in desperation.

How accurately this parody expresses the way some RAF students felt about primary training is impossible to say. It does not reflect accurately the safety record of any known RAF contingent or American flying school. Although it is not possible to provide specific numbers, a few American as well as RAF student pilots simply gave up in 1941–42, but the numbers who did so in each air force increased signficantly during the final year of the war.

A different attitude toward American primary flying training was expressed by Francis William Preston of Yorkshire, some forty-two years after completing the primary flying course with Class SE-42-D at Carlstrom Field:

We arrived from Toronto at the U.S. Army Air Corps Training Detachment at Riddle Aeronautical Institute, Carlstrom Field, 7 miles southeast of Arcadia, Florida early in October 1941. The officer commanding was First Lieutenant William A. Hart. Flight Lieutenant Maurice A. O'Callaghan was the RAF administrative liaison officer…We were billetted in far superior accommodation (4 to a chalet) than we had come across in previous training—two tiered beds and a shower with wash basin, a table with 4 chairs and a wardrobe each. We were given the Aviation Cadet Orders, and an Absence Card to display in our room. An ex-policeman from Peterborough, LAC Wybourn, was appointed Cadet Captain.

There was a smell of sulphur about the water, but what a contrast to anything we had experienced before—sunshine, an open air swimming pool, blue skies—and at last we were to learn to fly. My first flight was on 8 October 1941, and my instructor was Mr. Tom T. Turner, Jr. All of the instructors at the base were civilians, but a military pilot also did checks on us after 40 hours and a final one after 60 hours flying. The PT-17 was a good aircraft, more sturdy than our Tiger Moth, and Tom Turner was a great instructor who gave me confidence.

It was, however, with some doubts that I went solo on 23 October 1941 for five minutes. The next flight was dual, going over spins, stalls, spiral turns, and everything we had done over the last three weeks. What a relief when on 29 October, I went up solo for 30 minutes without the instructor shouting in my ear. I was all alone in that big blue sky doing spins, loops, etc., and when I came out of my dream world, I realised that I had lost sight of the airfield. However, I set course westward and it came up in a few minutes, much to my relief.

November passed all too quickly; I passed the 40 hour check on the 22nd, and the 60 hour check on 2 December, thus completing my 60 flying hours and the course on 4 December 1941. I recall that we were allowed to do the British style of drill, and the Flt Lt. also got us some concession on haircuts at the post barber shop. (I forget the price, but I believe the normal price in the USA was at least a dollar whilst in England, it was no more than six pence or one shilling maximum.)

There were washouts, especially in the early stages, and it was sad to see cadets leave who had been washed out. Good habits were stressed, and we had to make our bed in a set pattern, have our clothes buttoned and in set order in the wardrobe and our toilet articles displayed in a set order on the stand. We were allowed to go to the Post Exchange (PX) for about an hour after dinner, then were confined to our rooms to study until "lights out" at 9 p.m. I recall the Juke box was almost constantly playing Gene Autry's "I don't want to set the World on Fire."

We were allowed on "Open Post" from noon on Saturdays till 6 p.m. on Sundays if we had not collected above the allowed number of demerits. These "gigs" were awarded for non compliance with regulations—having the wrong set of items in the wardrobe or other minor misdemeanors. I think the allowance was 10 or 12 a week and for every one over that number, one had to walk the ramp for one hour, usually on Saturday afternoon. The food was excellent. I enjoyed the cold iced tea with plenty of sugar. The quickness of nightfall was a wonder; looking out of the Dining Hall to the west, it was light, while to the east, it was pitch black.

Most weekends I spent in Arcadia; the local cinema always had a cowboy film. The local people were very hospitable, especially a Mrs. Smith whose husband was a major in the Army and, I believe, a son who was also in the Army. I had one weekend in Sarasota with a cadet named Steve Nunn. We were taken from the camp gate in a car (often there were cars waiting at noon on Saturdays offering cadets a lift or weekend hospitality). I have snapshots of Steve with some pets, alligators and snakes, when we visited a "farm"; alas, I heard Steve was killed on return to the UK. We had no trouble with accents, and the ground instruction was good. We were not too happy about the treatment of the coloured people; segregation was new and alien to us, but we had little time to worry too much on this question.

Thanks to the good weather, we finished the course a week early on 5 December 1941 and were to have a week's leave from the next Monday. Most of us planned to visit Miami and the Everglades, though one or two had contacts or relatives they were planning to visit. However, the whole course was invited to visit Lake Wales on Sunday 7 December 1941, and so we did, in buses and private cars. Lake Wales is the highest point in Florida (elevation: 324 feet above sea level) and the Bok Singing Tower with its adjacent sanctuary was dedicated and presented to the American people by President Calvin Coolidge.

The Program of recitals at the singing tower was changed to include all British tunes such as "Loch Lomond," "There'll always be an England," etc. We were also presented with a booklet entitled, "Sanctuary Thoughts." Of all places to be—a beautiful, peaceful place full of all the best things in life, of tranquillity and peace—to hear of the attack on Pearl Harbour—it was shattering not only to the good people with us, but to us as well. If we had been away from the reality of war for four months and in a dream world, this brought it back to us with a bang! Needless to say, our leave was cancelled on return to Carlstrom Field, and the next day, we had to dig the RAF uniforms from our kitbags and don them. After some three months in "civilian" clothes, it was strange to be in uniform again.

Between 17 July and 10 December 1941, while Frank Preston and L.G. Robson were undergoing pilot training at Carlstrom Field, the airfield remained congested and doubled in normal capacity. Despite such crowding, of the original Class SE-42-D intake of 146 RAF students, one student was held over to Class SE-42-E, 32 were eliminated and a record 113 men graduated.

When the Dorr Field American cadet detachment completed its primary training at Carlstrom Field in December and departed for basic flying schools, the overcrowding was eased somewhat. Because of a lack of evidence, the question of whether or not the presence at Carlstrom Field of extra courses of British students destined for BFTS No. 5 at Clewiston and American cadets scheduled to train at Dorr Field affected the training of those regularly assigned to Carlstrom Field cannot be answered firmly. Perhaps there was, is and always has been an optimum efficient size for educational institutions at all levels, as well as for training stations of all kinds, beyond which numbers a law of diminishing returns begins to take effect.

Although Carlstrom Field was too crowded during summer and autumn 1941, its pilot production rate remained high, and the school had one of the lowest elimination rates among the primary schools that trained RAF pilots. Of the 470-man net intake in Carlstrom Field's first four RAF classes, 327 men graduated and 143 men were eliminated. Since the Riddle Aeronautical Institute later received some criticism from basic and advanced flying schools about the quality of some of its graduates, perhaps some of its instructors compensated too much for crowded conditions. On the other hand, training at a crowded primary school might well have better prepared Carlstrom Field cadets for the training conditions to be encountered at basic and advanced flying schools and on crowded combat airdromes.

CHAPTER SIX

BACKGROUND TO EARLY ARNOLD SCHEME TRAINING AND RESPONSES FROM BRITAIN, CANADA AND THE UNITED STATES

Britain's leaders had long been aware of America's wealth of raw materials and world records in manufacturing. Although there had been friction between the two nations over 1914–18 war debts, strong cultural and financial ties remained. British army, air and naval attachés regularly observed and reported American innovations to London, as did the officers assigned to similar duties in other foreign legations in Washington. Experienced Royal Air Force officers were regularly sent to the United States to evaluate American air power, its organization, new aviation technology and aircraft. Since circa 1938, Group Captain George Pirie, air attaché in the British Embassy, had sought out American political and military leaders in efforts to ascertain new developments and to assess American attitudes toward Great Britain's chances of surviving the war, which had begun in November 1939.

In December 1939, Great Britain established the Empire Air Training Scheme and signed an agreement with Canada, Australia and New Zealand to provide joint aircrew training. At that time, the British Air Commission (BAC) was established in Ottawa, but since it was essentially an agency of the Ministry of Aircraft Production, its headquarters were moved to New York and, later, Washington, D.C. When Winston Churchill became prime minister in May 1940, he appointed the Canadian Lord Beaverbrook minister of aircraft production and Beaverbrook, despite his distrust of Americans, strengthened the BAC. At the head of the commission was Air Vice Marshal Arthur T. Harris.

In late June 1940, when Secretary of Treasury Henry Morgenthau Jr., without consulting the army air corps, allowed the British Air Commission to assume control over all French orders for aircraft and engines, U.S. Army Air Corps leaders were furious. The air corps had hoped to obtain the French materiel so as to build the expanding U.S. air strength. Later that summer, while the Battle of Britain air war raged, the Air Ministry sought every means possible to develop better relations with American political and military leaders. Group Captain Pirie and other attachés lobbied as much as possible in efforts to foster aid for Britain. The Ministry of Aircraft Production sought greater numbers of aircraft and the Air Ministry sought an absolute open and cooperative policy with the United States concerning secret experimentation and new technology.

Although there was a daring agreement in which the United States traded fifty destroyers and ten coast guard cutters to Britain in exchange for American defensive bases along the Atlantic shore and the Caribbean island chain, the 1940 national elections remained the greatest obstruction. When President Roosevelt won his unprecedented third term, and with one of the greatest air battles in history drawing to a close, Britain's Air Ministry dispatched Air Commodore John Slessor to North America.

Slessor's mission was to negotiate the best possible terms for Britain in the scheduled American, British and Canadian (A-B-C) Conversations. The RAF officer succeeded in meeting with Canadian officials, American civil aviation officers and later with Secretary of Treasury Morgenthau and President Roosevelt. While these planning sessions were underway, the Lend-Lease Bill (HR-1776) was pending in the Congress of the United States. A number of important and far-reaching agreements were confirmed, including a fifty-fifty sharing of American aircraft. By early 1941, the Refresher Scheme was yielding good results for both Canada and Great Britain. Then, on 11 March 1941, the Lend-Lease Bill passed and was signed into law.

In April 1941, after Major General Henry H. Arnold flew to England and proposed to train four thousand British pilots alongside army air corps pilots, his surprising offer was gratefully accepted by the Air Ministry. By June, four of the six planned British flying training schools were approved and equipped, and the Air Ministry recognized the need for a larger RAF administrative organization in the United States. When further friction developed between Britain's Air Ministry and the Ministry of Aircraft Production, the Air Ministry decided to form the Royal Air Force Delegation (RAFDEL), a surrogate Air Ministry in Washington, which more clearly responded to the needs of the Royal Air Force.

In July 1941, the Air Ministry established the RAFDEL as its own liaison agency in Washington, D.C. RAFDEL was charged with supervising all RAF aircrew training in the United States and overseeing the RAF side of aircraft and equipment acquisition. It was also expected to provide administrative support for the increasing numbers of RAF personnel being assigned to work in the United States.

After July 1941, RAFDEL staff worked with the British Air Commission in procuring materiel, and with United States Army Air Corps and U.S. Naval Air Service officers in the training of British aircrew in the United States. Since 1938, Britain had placed orders for numerous American aircraft and had received them in 1940, but none had fought in the Battle of Britain. After the Lend-Lease Bill became law, the British Air Commission (BAC) placed orders for greater numbers of American trainer aircraft for Canadian and British schools and for more American tactical aircraft.

The commission also entered into a contract with the Packard Motor Company to build a separate factory in which to mass-produce Rolls Royce Merlin aircraft engines. In addition, the BAC placed orders for numerous Link Trainer simulators, as well as Pratt and Whitney, Curtiss-Wright and other aircraft engines. For long-range anti-submarine reconnaissance patrols, the BAC ordered numerous Consolidated PBY-5 flying boats and B-24 Liberator bombers.

During July 1941, the United States Navy began to train aircrew for Great Britain. The broad-scale Towers Scheme proposed to train RAF and the Fleet Air Arm (FAA) aircrew, including flying boat and carrier fighter, torpedo and dive bomber pilots. In addition, the U.S. Navy agreed to train navigators and wireless operators (telegraphist)/air gunners. Following the creation of the RAFDEL in Washington, the Royal Navy established its own air liaison agency, the British Air Delegation (BAD), with offices in Washington. All RN personnel in the United States were assigned to HMS *Saker*, which maintained Royal Navy administrative offices in New York. Initially, Fleet Air Arm men traveled to Canada with RAF aircrew students, but drafts of RAF flying boat student pilots and FAA aircrew students were sent from RCAF No. 1 Manning Depot at Toronto to the U.S. Naval Air Training Station at Pensacola, Florida. RAF and RN officers supervised British students.

During June 1941, the United States War Department changed its designation, U.S. Army Air Corps (USAAC), to the United States Army Air Forces (USAAF), but both American and British officers and men found it difficult to abandon use of the "army air corps" label. The organization of the U.S. Army Air Forces was constantly expanding. Personnel had to be trained for administrative and myriad other duties. RAF and FAA administrative organizations also developed gradually and became larger and more complex as they adapted to the demands of combat operations and technical changes. As already described, Arnold Scheme training was administered by USAAF officers and a RAF administrative officer (RAFAO) at each flying school and a senior RAF administrative officer (SRAFAO) at Maxwell Field, Alabama.

Wing Commander Hogan regularly sent written reports to Group Captain Carnegie in Washington. "In primary schools," Hogan wrote, "the aim in training is to make the pilot completely at home with his aeroplane and to develop to a high degree his air sense and produce a well disciplined pilot." In describing instructional techniques, Hogan pointed out that much of the instruction is "given on the ground before and after flight." Practically no instruction was possible in the air because of poor speaking tubes, so Hogan reported personal experiments with different types of speaking tubes in an effort to bring about improvement. Of shock value to his superiors was Hogan's report that the total Class SE-42-A wastage in all three phases of Arnold Scheme flying training was likely to reach more than 50 percent. This information caused shock waves to reverberate amid Montgomery, Washington, Ottawa and London.

In further describing Arnold Scheme training, Hogan praised the American physical training program, but was disturbed by a new phenomenon among the RAF eliminees, three of whom had "requested to be eliminated from flying" and a couple of "suspected malingerers." In describing the elimination of students for flying deficiencies, Hogan described "several instances in every school of breaches of flying regulations." In comparing the primary schools, Hogan praised Tuscaloosa for its excellent instructors and good results, and in each school cited the addition of facilities, which would make it possible to increase class sizes in all of the schools except Darr Aero Tech at Albany, Georgia.

In the course of his normal duties, Hogan's prime daily concern was for the problems of several thousand students undergoing training in a foreign land. Only after he was absolutely inundated with work at Maxwell Field was he given significant assistance with which to carry out his varied duties. After the first RAF class became settled at the six Arnold Scheme primary flying schools, Hogan's labors increased. First, he sought to compare the USAF flying training syllabus with the subjects that British student pilots had already received in British initial training wing (ITW) courses. Within a few days of his arrival at Maxwell Field, Hogan was able to review the ground school syllabus used in all primary schools with Major Luke Smith, SEACTC director of training. Since RAF students had already studied a great deal of navigation and mathematics in their ITWs, Smith agreed to a number of changes in the ground school curriculum for British students.

Changes in the primary flying training syllabus for RAF students included the omission of mathematics and a reduction in navigation instruction to twenty-two hours and in meteorology to twenty-one hours. The thirty-four hours of ground instruction thus omitted would be replaced by ten hours of aircraft recognition, ten hours of current events, five hours of RAF organization, four hours on the Aldis signal lamp and five hours on RAF procedures and extra study. Owing to the level of academic training the British students had already received, if they had indeed completed an ITW course, the syllabus changes were undoubtedly good ones.

As soon as the changes were made for RAF students in the ground school syllabus of the primary schools, an Air Ministry signal arrived that indicated that RAF students arriving between July and September 1941 (Classes SE-42-B, SE-42-C and SE-42-D) would have covered only about 70 percent of the ITW syllabus. "In navigation," Carnegie wrote, "they may not have done any map reading, instruments, or meteorology." If the USAAF ground school syllabus had already been changed in the primary schools, these omissions in the ITW syllabus for the 1,650 students of these three courses may well have contributed to the increased number of washouts among them. At the time, there were other, more pressing, concerns.

During his survey of the schools, Hogan took great care to ascertain how the six RAF administrative officers were able to function in their new environments. He discovered that only Darr Aero Tech at Albany, Georgia, and Carlstrom Field at Arcadia, Florida, were providing on-post accommodation for the RAFAOs, and they were doing so only out of kindness. Hogan recognized that the RAFAOs would need automobiles in order to travel to and from where they lived in neighboring towns and their duty stations or vice versa, and he was determined that these officers should receive "board and lodging at government expense."

For the RAF administrative officers, there were many pressing problems much closer and more disturbing than concern about their own comfort. In the Arnold Scheme primary flying schools, they were in a most difficult position. They had their orders from Maxwell Field as well as official policy directives from Washington and London, and often they had within their jurisdiction a large number of rebellious students who condemned them for all of the problems the students themselves encountered and often helped to create.

The RAFAOs found that the requirements of army air corps discipline and drill was accepted by most students as part of the price to pay for learning to fly, but it was not appreciated by large numbers in every Arnold Scheme class. They were unaccustomed to and detested hazing, demerits or "gigs" for domestic sloppiness and restrictions on their freedom to come and go as they wished. Like firemen, the RAFAOs were engaged almost constantly in putting out small fires at many points, and the pyromaniacs were RAF student pilots. In addition to their normal duties, when changes were made in the air corps ground school syllabus, the RAFAOs found themselves teaching RAF procedures and leading public affairs discussions. Moreover, they were very popular speakers at meetings of local civic clubs.

On 28 June 1941, Wing Commander Hogan forwarded to Carnegie at the British Embassy "the lists you made out yesterday," which included the revised syllabus for navigation and meteorology training to be given RAF students in the Arnold Scheme primary schools. In doing so, Hogan was careful to point out that "Headquarters, Southeast Training area has instructions to forward to the War Department such matters before approval can be given for the alterations in the syllabus." Beyond that report on 28 June, Hogan was exceedingly busy with training matters.

On 2 July 1941, Hogan submitted his "Confidential Report No. 1" to Carnegie. Hogan provided a training progress report on the British students and the six primary schools in which they had commenced training three weeks earlier. The RAF officers and the British students were greatly impressed with the superior accommodation and dining facilities at the schools, but Hogan expressed the opinion that instead of commencing flying immediately, UK students needed at least a week to become acclimatized. In describing the khaki uniforms that members of Class SE-42-A had been issued, he indicated that "mis-fitting uniforms have had alterations carried out at public expense." He also recommended paying two-thirds of the seventy-five-cent weekly charge for the ten pounds of laundry that American and British student pilots usually had done each week.

In describing the training students were receiving, Hogan was evidently embarrassed to report that RAF students were posing "ridiculous questions as regards flying, indicating their complete lack of knowledge about aircraft and theory of flight." Hogan also proposed that ten hours of theory of flight be added to the ITW syllabus. He described as well the army air forces system of appointing cadet officers, and proposed that RAF "student leaders" be appointed to assist the RAF administrative officers in maintaining good student discipline. Hogan preferred too that all student pilots, including NCOs, be considered equal while under training.

In the American schools, Hogan also reported that RAF students were being treated "as if they were cadets, which suits the majority of them, although it is a little difficult for some of them to understand such treatment, owing to their different upbringing." In an attempt to prevent future problems, Hogan advised of the misinformation that RAF students had absorbed at some point before arrival in the United States. He asserted that RAF students were "grossly misinformed about the laxity of discipline in American primary schools." Having been given that wrong information, they objected to the discipline they encountered and this "caused some dissension between them and the school authorities." Hogan felt that if the RAF students "had known what they were coming to, these incidents and minor upheavals would not have occurred."

In describing student training, Hogan pointed out that students "rise at 5:20 a.m. and go to flights from 7:00 to 11:00 a.m., then after a large lunch they are given a lecture in a language which they have difficulty in understanding and it is no wonder that they get sleepy." The senior RAFAO was generally pleased with conditions in the schools and in the training, but embedded in much of what was reported was a concern that the RAF students behave themselves. Perhaps such concern was natural since the British officers and men were guests in the United States and were expected to conduct themselves properly at all times.

Within a very brief period, Hogan had developed excellent rapport with the entire Eastern Flying Training Command (EFTC) staff and was keen to be of as much assistance as possible. Hogan recognized that he was in a unique position, one for which rules and procedures manuals had not yet been written. In the course of his tenure, he would be stretched to the limit in dealing with his many tasks and with his superior officers. On the one hand, he had to deal with the recently promoted Major General Walter R. Weaver, the exuberant and energetic commander of the EFTC, who was, in Hogan's words, "flat out" in everything he did. On the other hand, the RAF officer also had to deal with more senior RAF officials in Washington whose work had different priorities centered on aircraft and equipment procurement and who were sometimes secretive and somewhat less than straightforward in both plans and pronouncements.

On 17 July 1941, Hogan wrote to Carnegie advising of his busy schedule in case the RAF group captain needed to contact him. It was essential for Hogan to visit the primary schools at Camden, Americus and Albany to speak to Class SE-42-B, the new RAF students who were scheduled to arrive on July 18. Hogan also described his other labors, indicating that there were now more than one hundred eliminated students at Maxwell Field whom he intended to recategorize for further RAF training. "The eliminations have now reached 24%," he wrote. "Most of the ones I saw today obviously had not the makings of pilots & one felt that the eliminations were well justified."

Ever conscientious and anxious about the increasing Arnold Scheme elimination rate, Hogan consulted with Major Luke Smith about the problem, and Smith urged army air forces primary school supervisors to carefully screen RAF pupils to salvage as many eliminated RAF students as possible by extending the training time, if necessary. Having identified problems, it was characteristic of him that Wing Commander Hogan sought both short- and long-term solutions. He had had discussions with responsible officers at Maxwell Field, and he had forwarded recommendations to improve RAF training in the EFTC, but these were rejected, so Hogan continued with his normal duties.

The RAF wing commander devoted all of his fifth fortnightly report to "Discipline and Social Conditions affecting British Pilots in American Basic Schools." Hogan described how Class SE-42-A arrived at Cochran Field, Georgia, five days before their course was to begin, and three of those days were used for "processing," whereby the RAF students were drilled continuously through the morning and afternoon and were required to change uniforms several times between drill sessions. Under the American system, USAAF aviation cadets were exempted from flying training for several days in order to haze the incoming lower class.

Hogan also reported on other problems affecting RAF student morale at the USAAF basic flying schools. The khaki uniforms, which had been issued to members of Class SE-42-A in Canada, were "in disgraceful condition, having been worn continuously for four months," and despite efforts to get replacements from Canada, many men still did not have caps. Food and accommodation at the basic schools was deemed excellent, and pay for the RAF students was described as adequate. "They collect at the pay table between $12.00 and $30.00 per fortnight." Differences in pay seemed to vary considerably from one pay period to the next, and it was worrisome to newly arrived RAFAOs that students had no opportunity of "inquiring into their personal accounts." Happily, Hogan was pleased to announce that as of 25 October, charges for haircuts, laundry and repairs to clothing and shoes had "become a charge on public funds." Around that same period, the USAAC began to issue summer dress and flying uniforms to all British students.

In describing the curriculum at the USAAF basic flying schools, Wing Commander Hogan was struck with their emphasis on "safety first" and precision flying. Although he felt that the procedures taught did indeed teach safety and judgment, he hoped that the curriculum would be modified to incorporate more operations-related exercises. Hogan also felt that RAF students would profit from the flying training received at the basic schools despite "teething troubles" at both schools. However, he was anxious to see the implementation of the proposed new basic flying school curriculum, which incorporated twenty-five hours of instrument flying and nine hours of night flying.

In the weeks ahead, as Group Captain Carnegie received reports from Wing Commander Hogan and other members of the RAF training staff, he compiled his own reports and submitted them to the Air Ministry. In such a report dated 8 July, the director of UK training described a few administrative problems in the United States and made some significant requests. To solve the problem of the loss of personal equipment such as RAF brass cap badges, he called for the establishment of an RAF central store at Maxwell Field and for smaller stores at the individual schools, so that these items of dress and equipment might be replaced more readily. To carry out the duties assigned to him, Carnegie also requested additional RAF staff.

Among new RAF officers assigned to the Washington office was Wing Commander Wilfred E. Oulton, who was in charge of navigation training at schools in the United States in which British personnel were being trained. Wing Commander A.A. de Gruyther was assigned to serve as deputy director of UK training in Washington. Wing Commander Priest, an expert in armaments, worked closely with instructors at the BFTSs as well as the USAAF schools. Group Captain Lord Nigel Douglas Hamilton was assigned to Washington to assist Carnegie in liaison work with a number of political offices and service headquarters.

In addition to officers already assigned to duty stations and those en route to Washington, Carnegie requested that the Air Ministry send three additional RAFAOs to the United States by

23 August 1941. These new staff officers were to be assigned to serve the needs of UK student pilots as they entered USAAF basic flying schools. Carnegie also anticipated the need for a further three RAFAOs by 8 November, at which time the first Arnold Scheme students were scheduled to enter three separate USAAF advanced flying schools.

Initially, Carnegie worked out of the office of the air attaché in the British Embassy, but as more RAF students and staff arrived, larger separate offices were obviously needed for the training organization. By mid-July, Carnegie was referring to the Royal Air Force Delegation (RAFDEL) in correspondence, and a short time later his offices were moved to office suites on K Street in Washington. The organization ultimately evolved into a miniature training group headquarters or, in many ways, a surrogate Air Ministry, which provided much-needed assistance to the director of UK training and the growing RAF staff scattered about the United States. In addition to staff officers assigned to RAFDEL offices, a number of combat-experienced RAF pilots traveled to the United States aboard the *Britannic*, visited, consulted with USAAF and RAF staff and, after a few months, returned to the United Kingdom.

Wing Commander Kenneth J. Rampling, DFC, arrived to serve as assistant to Wing Commander Hogan until construction of BFTS No. 5 in Florida was completed. Wing Commander R.S.S. Tuck and a number of other pilots flew with American pursuit groups during the United States Army's 1941 Carolina maneuvers. Group Captain Harry Broadhurst came to the United States to demonstrate fighter tactics to USAAF officers, and Wing Commander Edward M. "Teddy" Donaldson was assigned to duty as an expert in gunnery. Ultimately, Broadhurst, Tuck and Donaldson test-flew various models of American aircraft and visited many factories as well as USAAF and RAF training stations.

When the USAAF established its system of aerial gunnery schools in each geographic command, Donaldson was a major advisor and a strong influence on gunnery training at all USAAF and RAF schools in the United States. Before he moved to fame in the Western desert, Group Captain Broadhurst brought European fighter combat experience to the discussions held at various flying training command headquarters and in the USAAF School of Applied Tactics, which had been transferred from Maxwell Field to Orlando, Florida.

As Group Captain Carnegie traveled about the country visiting and inspecting various schools, he commiserated with staff officers about various training and personnel problems. As with Wing Commander Hogan and the RAFAOs in the Arnold Scheme primary schools, he too began to worry about the increasing number of washouts from pilot training courses. Regularly, Carnegie observed, read reports of subordinate officers and communicated his findings to the Air Ministry's director of flying training in London.

In July, efforts to serve the needs of large numbers of washouts had already become a problem at Maxwell Field. Since RCAF No. 1 Manning Depot in Toronto was too crowded to receive more Arnold Scheme washouts, an American bottleneck was created and many airmen were sent to Darr Aero Tech at Albany, Georgia, to await remustering. By late August 1941, the American bottleneck was nothing when compared with what had developed at RCAF No. 1 Manning Depot at Toronto. How that bottleneck developed in Canada can be discerned by observing the absence of sufficient transient stations in Canada, the continued arrival of large drafts from Britain and by examining the wastage figures from Arnold Scheme Classes SE-42-A, SE-42-B, SE-42-C and SE-42-D at the six USAAF primary flying schools.

As Arnold Scheme flying schools were being enlarged during the summer of 1941, the numbers of British pilot trainees in the United States were increasing, as were training problems. The first major problem involved the delivery of British trainees safely across the North Atlantic Ocean every five weeks. Although good reasons existed for at least two contingents to be late, portions of most remaining RAF drafts arrived at some American flying schools from one to three weeks later than scheduled, and their tardiness disrupted USAAF training schedules.

Primary flying school civilian and USAAF military staff were not unsympathetic with the RAF; they fully recognized the problems likely to be encountered in transporting men across the U-boat-infested North Atlantic Ocean. Both groups understood, but a new cadet intake was supposed to arrive at American primary flying schools every five weeks. The civilian contractors were to enroll and complete each class's training as scheduled. For BFTSs and the Pan American Airways navigation section, new classes were alternately scheduled to begin training every seven or eight weeks. The standard explanation in all references to late arrivals was that flying school contractors lost money, something few people had any sympathy for during wartime. However, for the sake of the record, it is important to detail some of their losses.

The system by which civilians contracted with the War Department to build and operate primary flying schools under USAAF supervision was completely new to the United States, and policies were not firmly established. Because of the late arrival of some cadets, civil contractors faced both personnel and financial problems. They had to pay the salaries of their civilian flight and ground school instructors, as well as service and maintenance personnel to wait for any late arrivals. And many of the same men had to be paid overtime in order to catch the late arrivals up to the level required for graduation on time.

Contracts stipulated that charges for billets ($1.00 per day per student) and for meals served in the dining hall ($1.25 per day per student) could be made only for the days men were actually present. For the USAAF training officers, such tardiness meant that instead of handling arrival details at one time, all procedures for orientation, supply, physical examinations and records preparation had to be repeated. Ultimately, the problem of late arrivals contributed to a number of changes in administrative procedures in Britain and Canada, as well as in the United States. Even so, the problem of late arrivals at Arnold Scheme schools continued.

The second crisis in the training of British aircrew in the United States involved the elimination of large numbers of British trainees from pilot training. Of approximately 2,200 RAF pilot trainees who made up the first four Arnold Scheme intakes, approximately 40 percent (about 950) were eliminated or washed out by 15 October. When wastage from the six BFTSs, the several Towers Scheme schools and the large number of flying schools in Canada are included, wastage undoubtedly approached 2,000. American flying instructors insisted that one of the main reasons for the elimination rate among British student pilots was that most of them lacked mechanical experience. Moreover, some of them were being eliminated for motion sickness and for a variety of other easily detected problems.

The Canadian Air Ministry was especially affected by the return flow of washouts from USAAF schools. RCAF No. 1 Manning Depot was already crowded with men: new drafts of trainees were arriving regularly from the United Kingdom and hundreds of washouts were arriving. Aircrew screening boards were established at RCAF Trenton, Ontario, but since that airfield also served as a training station, it had limited capacity. Many of the RAF washouts reported there to be interviewed, remustered and assigned to either RCAF, RAF or such American schools as the Pan American Airways Navigation School and the new Towers Scheme navigation and wireless operator/air gunner (WOp/AG) courses. However, these schools could absorb only a limited number of the eliminated pilot trainees.

Since Royal Canadian Air Force, British Commonwealth air training plan and joint air training plan schools in Canada already had long lists of men awaiting assignment to aircrew training, RCAF officers found it impossible to reassign all washouts immediately. Given time, they could have done so, but in the meantime something had to be done with the disgruntled men. In Toronto, many of the washed out RAF trainee pilots were cursing U.S. Army aviation cadet regulations, the Southern heat and in particular Arnold Scheme schools. In doing so, they were accidentally lowering the morale of new arrivals, and were helping to create overcrowding at Toronto and RCAF Trenton as well. Solutions to these complex problems rested in all three nations along the training pipeline.

The British Air Ministry's directorate of flying training in London was perfectly aware of these problems, but there was little it could do in the short term. Late arrivals in the United States were embarrassing and, although construction had begun in August on RAF No. 31 Personnel Depot at Moncton, New Brunswick, there had not yet been sufficient time to develop adequate transient facilities in Canada. In time, these problems would be addressed, but the reported shortage of British manpower demanded attention to the high wastage rate and made it one of the most critical problems associated with aircrew training in late summer 1941.

Air Ministry officers had gone on record as expecting about 20 percent wastage, not twice that much. Understandably, the loss of so many apparently qualified men posed a major threat to British aircrew production and aircraft procurement plans. The crisis caused shock waves to reverberate among Montgomery, Alabama; Washington; London; and Ottawa. In London, the concern over late arrivals, inadequate transient facilities in Canada and excessive wastage occurred at a most inopportune time. The summer of 1941 was a critical period when Britain suffered reverses in Greece, Crete and North Africa. That summer not only revealed significant weaknesses in the Mediterranean theatre of operations, but they also uncovered problems that threatened the development of British air strength.

However, there were positive developments as well. By 1 July 1941, the Nazi attack on Russia drew the *Luftwaffe* away from further severe bombing raids on Britain and brought Great Britain another much-needed ally. That event was welcome news, but it also brought problems. Russia requested military aid, and since the Russian front was absorbing Nazi ground and air forces, she had the prospect of relieving much pressure on British forces. It was essential that Britain not only supply tactical aircraft and other aid to Russia, but that she also urge the United States to do the same. In mid-August 1941, Prime Minister Churchill and President Roosevelt met at Placentia Bay, Newfoundland, and the Atlantic Alliance was formed. Both nations began to cooperate more closely in developing the means for stopping Nazi aggression.

British aircraft diversions to Russia caused a further drain on existing aircraft production and affected the air expansion plans of both Britain and the United States. However, both nations quickly reached agreement to supply Russia with as much air and ground weapons, food and equipment as possible. On 9 October 1941, the Air Ministry notified RAFDEL that delivery of heavy bombers from existing British contracts would be completed by December 1941. And since delivery from recent Defense Aid (Lend-Lease) orders would not begin before autumn 1942, there would be an eight-month gap "which can only be filled by diverting aircraft from the Air Corps."

From the British point of view, the United States was still enjoying peace and did not need a large air force. Britain hoped to be able to replace her own aircraft diversions to Russia from American production. However, the USAAF had recently announced its own thirty-thousand-pilot expansion program, and requests for more American aircraft were unwelcome. Although aircrew production figures appeared to belie it, the Russian drain on the British aircraft supply came at a particularly critical time. Despite heavy aircraft and crew losses in the Battle of France and the Battle of Britain, enemy attacks on airfields and cities and problems with aircrew recruitment and initial training, British aircrew strength had surprisingly increased.

Between 3 September 1940 and 2 September 1941, Britain gained 31,581 aircrew, more than half of whom were trained in the United Kingdom. These accessions in strength included 15,501 pilots (352 from the United States) and 4,279 observers (about 170 from the United States). Although by late summer 1941 more than 3,000 British aircrew were undergoing training in the United States, only a few navigators and several American Refresher Scheme pilots had completed their courses in the United States.

Owing to the transfer of RAF flying training schools overseas, and the British embargo on exporting trainers, Britain found herself with a temporary surplus of pilots and aircraft used in elementary and service flying training schools. If RAF pilot production continued as it had during the preceding twelve months, a larger surplus might build up. Owing to the diversion of British and American combat aircraft to Russia, it would be difficult to obtain sufficient tactical aircraft either to train pilots properly or to employ them in combat against the enemy.

Since British and Commonwealth aircraft production was not yet equal to enemy production and could not yet meet all demands placed upon it, the only way to acquire essential tactical aircraft would be to gain a larger share of the increasing American production. However, until surplus pilots and aircraft could be employed in the United Kingdom, care was essential lest USAAF officers learn of these temporary UK surpluses. If they did so, the United States might well suspend or further reduce RAF aircrew training in the United States and reduce aircraft deliveries to Britain and Commonwealth countries. If Air Ministry planners were beginning to panic, such a reaction was perfectly understandable.

During the summer of 1941, almost a year following his initial visit to New York and Washington, Captain Harold H. Balfour, MP, MC, undersecretary of state for air, returned to the United States. On this occasion, he joined Major General George C. Brett, the new chief of the air corps, and visited the Arnold Scheme schools. Balfour was impressed with the training, the student accommodation, food and Stearman (Boeing) biplane trainers. After his return to London, Balfour met with the Empire Air Training Scheme Committee on 1 August 1941 and declared, "In my view, this training will be more than an insurance to our main training plan. It can be, and should be, in itself, a great part of the main plan." However, Balfour was disturbed by the wastage in the primary schools, indicating that "these eliminees were mostly older married men, whom we shall cease to send…in future."

When in difficulty, the best strategy is sometimes to take the offensive, and although that may well not have been the original plan, it was the course ultimately pursued by Britain's Air Ministry training directorate. Initially, passage through the training pipeline was slowed, and further intakes were delayed. Since large numbers of aircrew volunteers had already been brought to the Aircrew Receiving Center (ACRC) No. 1 in London, an immense pool of aircrew candidates had built up, and training time was extended. Aircrew in-discipline plagued training officers in the United Kingdom and overseas, and it was addressed as well. The amount of foot drill or "square bashing" was increased throughout the preliminary stages of training as well as in transient depots.

Since it was believed that some otherwise qualified potential aircrew lacked sufficient formal education to complete their training successfully, efforts were also made to provide preparatory ITW training with the Air Training Corps, and special courses on RAF stations were conducted by education officers and other qualified personnel. Although efforts were being made to recruit as many eligible men as possible for aircrew training, the screening process was extended and tightened. ITW courses were expanded from the standard six to eight weeks to periods extending from three to nine months, and many of these longer ITW courses were established on active RAF stations or in universities.

Air Ministry planners also decided on several other courses of action in order to reduce the wastage of British pilot trainees in American flying schools and to eliminate the expense of shipping "unqualified" men great distances. In addressing the selection process and preliminary training, it was decided that aircrew candidates were no longer to be declared fit simply on the basis of documents, personality and a few questions by a board of senior officers. Entry was still relatively easy for men of average and above average intelligence and mechanical abilities, but they had to prove themselves in more demanding academic course work and a short period of flying.

In September 1941, as more volunteers from university auxiliary air force squadrons began to enter the RAF, the air services began to enroll larger numbers of aircrew students in excellent university facilities. Although some aircrew had been posted to a few scattered universities earlier, the number of universities enrolling aircrew students in ITW courses grew during the closing months of 1941 and continued to provide ITW training to the end of the war. Many qualified "deferred entry" aircrew trainees who might otherwise never have seen the inside of a university, were posted to scattered British universities for short courses or for year-long courses that encompassed all RAF ITW course requirements.

Although flight grading courses were introduced in order to make use of surplus elementary trainers and instructors, the innovation soon proved effective as a means for screening aircrew candidates and reducing training wastage overseas. Upon completing their ITW courses, between thirty and fifty men were detailed to each of sixteen elementary flying training schools (EFTSs) scattered about Britain. Instructors graded each student for further flight training under what came to be called the PNB system (pilot, navigator or air bomber).

At the flight grading schools, aircrew students were supposed to receive from eight to twelve hours of familiarization flying, but many of them were allowed to log between thirty and sixty hours of flying. At least one qualified pilot who had been trained in Egypt was enrolled in at least one Arnold Scheme course. Why? Was he checking on the quality of American training? Flight grading began in November 1941, and some instructors at assigned EFTSs conscientiously sought to screen airmen, but it was not until spring 1942 that more exacting standards were adopted in all flight grading schools. However, from the beginning, once RAF aircrew candidates finished their required ITW course and were further screened in flight grading courses, they formed a second pool of aircrew from which drafts could be drawn for assignment to overseas flying training schools. Flight grading courses continued to absorb surplus pilots and British trainer aircraft.

At the other end of the training spectrum, concern was being voiced about the quality of pilots trained under the hurried fourteen- to eighteen-week wartime system of training. Over a period of several months, accident rates increased at operational training units (OTUs) and on active air stations. These accidents cost Bomber Command and Fighter Command dozens of highly trained men and numerous aircraft, both of which were hard to replace. The inevitable conclusion of commanders and staff officers was that pilots had not received sufficient training.

In order to provide more flying experience before pilots reached OTUs, Air Commodore Cochrane, director of flying training in the Air Ministry, recommended changes. He proposed that the airdromes and facilities of four service flying training schools (SFTSs) that were slated to be transferred to Canada be converted instead into "Pre-O.T.U. Schools." Once that extension of training within the United Kingdom was approved by the Air Council, RAF advanced flying units (AFUs) emerged as a means of providing acclimatization flying for all aircrew trained outside the United Kingdom.

Many of the Arnold Scheme pilots who entered the early AFU intakes were less than pleased with the attitudes of some RAF flying officers. Evidently, some AFU instructors arrogantly expressed the view that the aircrew training undertaken overseas was somehow defective and of a lower order than that received exclusively on RAF training stations in Britain. In fact, during 1941 while most men trained to "wings standard" in RAF schools in the United Kingdom, Canada, South Africa and the American BFTSs were receiving about 150 flying hours, Arnold and Towers Scheme pilots were logging from 215 to 300 flying hours.

In addition to the introduction of "short" flying courses for screening aircrew candidates at the beginning, during autumn 1941, student pilots were posted to a new embarkation depot. The small, crowded, wire-enclosed embarkation depot at Wilmslow, Cheshire, was no longer sufficient to handle the larger drafts that were necessary to fill the increased number of overseas flight training schools. The fifth and sixth Arnold Scheme drafts, Classes SE-42-E and SE-42-F, as well as their equivalent BFTS and Towers Scheme intakes destined for schools elsewhere, constituted the final RAF drafts to transit through the Wilmslow Embarkation Depot.

Members of the sixth Arnold Scheme draft (SE-42-F) were among the first to enter the Aircrew Receiving Wing (ACRW) No. 1 in London's Regent's Park and Lord's Cricket Ground, labeled "Arsey-Tarsey" by some students. In October 1941, following the departure of Arnold Scheme Class SE-42-F, RAF Wilmslow was converted to other uses. Heaton Park, east of Manchester, replaced it and provided expandable space for larger numbers of tentatively qualified aircrew. During the remainder of the war, it continued to serve as a second aircrew pool and the major embarkation depot for RAF airmen. Obviously, the two new RAF aircrew pools (the one in London and the one in Manchester) would be interdependent, but officers at Heaton Park would coordinate their overseas drafts with initial training wings and Movements Groups.

Reorganization of the RAF preliminary training system had resulted in the creation of three aircrew pools in the United Kingdom, one at the induction stage, another after ITW and yet another after flight grading. In addressing the problems of embarrassing late arrivals for American flying courses and excessive wastage, RAF, USAAF and RCAF planners created three aircrew pools in North America as well. Perhaps a RAF and RCAF aircrew pool in Canada and one in the United States might solve some of the more serious problems such as late arrivals, crowding and the mixing of washouts with newly arrived aircrew volunteers. Certainly, they could serve as holding units in the event training had to be speeded up quickly.

ACCLIMATIZATION COURSES AT MAXWELL FIELD, ALABAMA, 42-E-42-G

By September 1941, 1,100 men of RAF Classes SE-42-C and SE-42-D were undergoing training at six American primary flying training schools, and about 600 surviving student pilots of RAF Classes SE-42-A and SE-42-B were undergoing basic flying training at Cochran Field, Georgia, and Gunter Field, Alabama. Between June and late August 1941, the number of British students who had been eliminated from pilot training in the United States had risen at an alarming rate, now numbering almost 1,000 men. These failed aircrew students boarded trains in small and larger groups and returned northward to Canada, disappointed and disgruntled, their dreams of flying RAF fighters or bombers shattered; but neither the British nor Canadian Air Ministries were ready for them. The RCAF No. 1 Manning Depot could not process large contingents of trainee pilots arriving from the United Kingdom in addition to huge numbers of failed aircrew returning to Toronto from Canadian and American flying schools.

The Canadian government was designing, building, equipping and staffing airfields for training RCAF aircrew as well as transferred RAF schools. The need for temporary facilities in which to house, feed and clothe thousands of aircrew awaiting posting to schools or awaiting transportation eastward to Britain had not been anticipated. A RCAF training and flying boat station at Trenton, northeast of Toronto, was developed as a facility for remustering hundreds of failed aircrew. A large and competent staff worked steadily to reassign failed pilots to other aircrew training, but the number of Canadian pilot, air observer and navigation schools (AONSs) and bombing and gunnery schools (B&GSs) ready to receive students was small, so the military rule of "hurry up and wait" endured.

Meanwhile Toronto's RCAF No. 1 Manning Depot continued to receive new student pilots from Britain as well as disgruntled failed pilots waiting impatiently for reassignment to another chance at pilot training or to other aircrew duties. The failed pilots were unwittingly destroying the morale of the newly arrived British students awaiting assignment to flying schools.

When a near mutiny occurred at the huge Toronto RCAF station, aircrew training officers in Ottawa, London, Washington and Maxwell Field, Alabama, were alarmed. An aircrew training conference was arranged, and British Air Chief Marshal A.G.R. Garrod, AMT (member of the Air Council for Training), came to Canada and the United States to meet with training officers. The purpose of the series of meetings was to implement means to solve the problem of the great number of failures among RAF student pilots. Except for a small number, the British student pilots had undergone almost five hundred hours of initial training and had traveled across the North Atlantic in troop transports to Halifax, Nova Scotia. There, they had boarded trains for a thirty-hour journey to Toronto, where they were processed for entry as aliens into the United States.

Since the U.S. Army Air Corps organized all air or ground crew training in order to produce as many pilots or other air or ground crew as possible, its training schedules were rigid. Pilot training began in civilian contract primary flying schools. Their training schedules were set to commence training each new draft of RAF and USAAC pilots class every five weeks. If classes from Britain failed to arrive as scheduled, the civilian contractors lost money because they had to pay flying and ground instructors and maintenance staff whether or not students were available. Moreover, classes arriving late disrupted U.S. Army Air Corps' training schedules and wasted training time.

What was needed was a large Canadian depot that would house and assign RAF students to USAAC flight schools as scheduled. Since the RCAF had receiving depots under construction, one problem was being solved, but the RAF No. 31 Personnel Depot at Moncton, New Brunswick, and the enlarged U.S. Army Air Corps Pre-Flight Center at Maxwell Field, Alabama, would not be ready to receive students until October 1941.

On 26 October 1941, Class SE-42-F arrived in Halifax aboard the *Pasteur*, a 29,000-ton French liner that was launched in 1939 and whose maiden voyage was from Brest to Halifax, Nova

Scotia, with France's gold reserves. As with many prior and later drafts, the passengers adhered to normal reception procedures, and following a brief medical examination aimed at guarding against the spread of communicable diseases, they boarded a train at dockside. This was the first westbound RAF draft to travel the relatively short distance of about 225 miles to RAF No. 31 RAF Personnel Depot on the northwestern outskirts of Moncton, New Brunswick.

Aboard the trains, care had been taken to provide a meal, relative comfort and as speedy a journey as possible. At a cost of about thirty-five cents per airman, the No. 2 (11) Movements Group arranged for sandwiches and pint cartons of milk to be distributed, regardless of the hour, to the airmen when their train stopped at Truro, Nova Scotia. In addition to the snack, which the RCAF provided, the local community also donated fruit and other items for free distribution to the young men. Such service and thoughtfulness boosted morale.

Harry E.V. Pinnell (Tuscaloosa, 42-F) was amazed that "when the train stopped at Truro in the middle of the night, the platform was crowded with people giving us tea and cake, etc.—a marvelous welcome." LAC Leonard Trevallion (Arcadia, 42-F), who had served for about six years as a member of the Metropolitan Police and had survived the London Blitz during service in Putney and Wandsworth, London, was one of the older members of Class SE-42-F.

Many years later, he recalled the arrival of his draft in North America:

> *After arriving at Halifax, we were taken by train to a camp at Moncton. The whole camp was knee deep in mud and we walked between barracks and mess rooms on duck boards, and the weather continued to be awful. However, our gloom was soon dispelled when we entered the mess room and were faced with more food than we had seen in years. There were dishes of freshly grilled crisp bacon, platters of fried eggs and mountains of feathery light white bread and masses of fresh butter, nowadays rather frowned upon, but then a delight to behold. I think many of us had guilty consciences when we remembered the folks back home.*

Regardless of conditions in the as-yet-incomplete camp, after proper documentation the transient airmen boarded trains in Moncton and traveled to aircrew training schools in the United States.

Of the first westbound RAF draft, the local newspaper duly reported:

> *The men were the first members of the R.A.F. to enter the United States in uniform. Training of British airmen has been carried out in the U.S. for many months, but prior to the entry of the men from Moncton, most trainees entered the country wearing civilian clothes.*

The newspaper also indicated that a number of Moncton citizens had invited RAF airmen for "Sunday dinner or a friendly evening in some private home," and urged other citizens to do likewise. To encourage people to take part in the hospitality scheme, the telephone numbers of welfare officers at the various nearby RAF and RCAF stations were provided. Members of the sixth Arnold Scheme draft, the first one to travel westbound through the Moncton depot, had found comfortable accommodation there.

Construction on the depot was not finished until April 1942, but ultimately the massive camp on the northwestern edge of Moncton would provide temporary housing and care for eight thousand aircrew at one time. The completed RAF depot contained a headquarters establishment and four separate squadron areas. Each of these divisions had lecture rooms, stores, a drill hall, huge two-story two-hundred-man barracks, a dining hall, recreation hall and canteen. The headquarters unit contained officers' quarters and mess, NCOs' quarters and mess, a motor pool, a guard house and a post engineering establishment for the maintenance of buildings and other facilities. The camp also had three parade grounds, three outdoor sports areas, a 150-bed station hospital and a huge YMCA facility.

Because of the convenience of the location and the economies that would be possible by the sharing of the hospital and other facilities, the RCAF constructed its own No. 2 Y Depot on a fifty-acre tract adjacent to the RAF facility. Bed and board accommodation would then be available for three thousand more men at one time. The RCAF facility was to be situated on a knoll between Wilbur Street, Mountain Road, Killam Drive and Edmonton Avenue. It contained three divisions with parade grounds and sports areas and was located on a tract surrounded in every direction by pine trees. When construction of both transient facilities was completed on 11 April 1942, there were sixty-eight buildings in RAF No. 31 Personnel Depot and twenty-four buildings in the RCAF No. 2 Y Depot.

The two-station project had taken the contractors—Carter, Halls, and Aldinger Limited—eight months to complete, and the company had employed 2,675 men on the construction projects. Costs for building the combined RAF/RCAF station were 3 lives, 1 serious injury, numerous minor ones and $3,250,000. During the construction, 2 contractors' employees were killed on the job in accidents involving heavy gravel trucks or other machinery. Another construction worker died under the wheels of a fellow worker's automobile. In addition, an RAF airman was seriously injured when he jumped from, and fell under the wheels of, a moving truck that had given him an unauthorized lift.

So pressing was the need for the camp that within two months of the beginning of construction, portions of it were being used. As each new section became available, the RAF/RCAF moved into it, so that well before completion of the combined stations, most of the buildings were already in use. Although the quality of the original construction was excellent, modifications and improvements continued into 1944. RAF personnel in transit to and from training stations in North America were provided with administrative support by RAF No. 31 Personnel Dispersal Center (PDC). The Moncton depot's supply organization issued khaki drill (later poplin shirts and gabardine tropical dress summer uniforms) and other essential clothing and equipment for use in such climatic extremes as sub-arctic Canada, tropical south Florida and the deserts of Arizona and California.

The seventh Arnold Scheme draft, Class SE-42-G, arrived in Halifax aboard the *Pasteur* on 2 December 1941 and was quickly transported to Moncton. LAC John Cunningham of SE-42-G, a native of Birmingham and former member of a territorial army battery of the Royal Artillery, had entered the RAF in June 1941. Years later, he recalled his first experience of North America and a famous classmate:

> *A train journey brought us to Moncton, New Brunswick where my first surprise was to see pure white bread on the Mess table at our first meal, after living with the gray look at home for so long. The crisp, dry snow was also noticeably different from the soft, wet variety we were used to at home. About the only other memory I have of Moncton is of going to the cinema in town and seeing Michael Rennie, the film actor, playing a part in a film of murder and suspense set in a lighthouse…to the jeers and catcalls of the mostly*

*RAF audience. Michael may not have caused such hilarity had he not been one of our
fellow cadets in transit at Moncton.*

Rennie completed his flight training in Valdosta, Georgia, before returning to the United
Kingdom for further assignment.

LAC George A. Stone from Crewkerne, Somerset, provided more specific details about
procedures at the as-yet-incomplete RAF No. 31 Personnel Depot. In a laconic, telegraphic
style, Stone described his stay at the Moncton PDC, and in doing so revealed some of the
depot's early procedures: "Camp in process of being built, no fence round camp, two barrack
blocks and one Mess Hall completed, one Drill Hall partially completed. Reported to drill hall
after breakfast each morning, if name not called out for posting, got lost till next morning.
Wonderful *food* after rationing."

Despite the abundance of food and the festive air of the approaching Christmas season,
Moncton, New Brunswick, was a small town far from home.

Spending a few weeks in what was perceived as almost a wilderness environment, many of
the British cadets were suffering from what later generations would refer to as "culture shock."
Everything was different! In letters home, the young men tried to describe what they saw in
Canada and the United States, and they automatically contrasted what they saw with what
they had left behind in Britain. A few of the obvious differences included vast amounts of open
land, the variety of trees and huge train engines and cars that one walked into "up steps" rather
than tiny cars that one boarded at station platform level. Since there were relatively few private
vehicles in Britain at that time, many of the young British cadets were intrigued by the fact that
most people in Canada, even the working classes, owned large automobiles or trucks and drove
them on the righthand side of the road.

As members of the westbound drafts were adjusting to culture shock, the new, incomplete
transient station and the vagaries of a Canadian winter, large and small groups of "displaced
airmen" were arriving at the Moncton depot from the interior of Canada. As will be recalled,
Air Commodore Critchley, AOC, 54 Group, had met with disgruntled RAF trainees at RCAF
No. 1 Manning Depot in Toronto and had promised them another opportunity to be assigned
to aircrew training. Some of the failed pilots had been or were being gradually absorbed into
observer, bomb aimer and wireless operator/air gunner courses in Canada. A few of them
filled out drafts to the Pan American Airways navigation section and to Towers Scheme USN
navigation and wireless operator/air gunner courses in Florida.

For one such failed pilot, the entire business proved to be too much. On Friday morning,
5 December 1941, a group of men entered one of the large drill halls at RAF No. 31
Personnel Depot and were shocked by what they saw. A Royal Air Force airman was
hanging by the neck from one of the rafters of the huge building. Whatever the cause of
the suicide, it was a terrible tragedy and must have had a devastating effect on those who
either saw or heard about it. The seventh westbound draft had arrived at the Moncton
depot a few days earlier, and Brian Davies (Arcadia, 42-G) recalled the incident when he
asserted that "even a report of the tragedy of a 'washed out' trainee pilot hanging himself
in a gymnasium could not dampen our spirits for long."

Existing documents record deaths and funerals of a number of RAF personnel in Toronto
and elsewhere, but rarely indicate cause of death. Evidently, most of them died from accidents or
illness. Despite modest efforts to do so, there was no way to substantiate these reports or rumors.

However, considering the numbers of RAF aircrew undergoing training in the various training schemes and the numbers who failed different courses in both the United States and Canada, it is indeed possible that others may have taken their own lives.

The Air Ministry evidently intended for the Moncton depot to serve as the administrative and financial records center for all RAF aircrew in both Canada and the United States. From its inception some, though not all, RAF offices in Moncton received reports of training casualties at scattered American airfields. Fatalities continued to be reported to Moncton for some time and names of such training casualties appeared in the "Daily Diary" of the depot, but more and more the expanded RAF Delegation (RAFDEL) offices in Washington, D.C., handled such administrative details. Administrative records and matters concerning RAF airmen in Canada were handled by staff members of the United Kingdom Air Liaison Mission in Ottawa.

Many of the young RAF airmen were unaware of the numerous military and air stations scattered over New Brunswick, and of the extraordinary labors of many civilians to provide entertainment and a hospitable reception to thousands of servicemen who the war brought into their midst. RCAF No. 8 Service Flying Training School, Lakeburn; RCAF No. 4 Equipment Depot, Scoudouc; and RCAF No. 5 Equipment Depot, Moncton, had been operating for several months when the Moncton city fathers learned that RAF No. 31 Personnel Depot would be built on the northwestern outskirts of their town.

In preparing for a large influx of servicemen, Moncton's aldermen were concerned about the potential problem created by the 1940–41 polio epidemic then raging. Even so, they made every effort to provide essential services and to encourage citizens, churches and other institutions to plan entertainment for the servicemen. Since Canada had no public houses (pubs) and very rigid laws governing the sale of alcoholic beverages, there was great concern whether the small Canadian town could entertain large numbers of young men. Despite the shortage of facilities, the entire town of Moncton made extraordinary efforts to accommodate staff and transients. Churches built additions or developed recreation facilities for servicemen, and YMCA board members arranged for the renovation and enlargement of Moncton's existing YMCA in order to serve the expected larger numbers of servicemen.

The YMCA in Moncton and the Salvation Army hostel were both popular places for the young airmen, and many of the transients found in these institutions warm smiles, a hot cup of tea, a place to write letters, read and play table tennis, cards or other games. If the airmen remained in Moncton very long, they soon discovered regular entertainment, such as Friday and Saturday night dances. Individual families from Moncton and nearby communities also did their part. As Christmas 1941 approached and Moncton's weather became bitterly cold, the RAF student population increased at a phenomenal rate.

The local newspaper called on citizens to make special efforts to invite servicemen into their homes instead of their having to "roam the streets with nowhere to go." The newspaper described the YMCA as overflowing, asserting that many young men had been invited into local homes for a meal, but greater numbers remained. "About 5 o'clock, they could be seen leaving in groups of two and four for the restaurants and then nothing to do but to stand in some doorway in the blizzard."

Other changes wrought by mutual agreement in the RAF/USAAF conferences resolved that British student pilots, like their American colleagues, would all be addressed as "cadets." The four-week-long acclimatization course for British cadets would include academic, physical and military training components. The course would be designed to help British cadets adjust to a different environment and a hot climate, thereby reducing the number of failures in pilot training and enhancing their chances of becoming successful military pilots.

At Maxwell Field, Alabama, headquarters of the Eastern Flying Training Command Pre-Flight Training Center, preparations were underway to receive 750 RAF cadets for the new four-week acclimatization course. The arrival of the RAF intake was delayed several days. First, an announcement was made that they would arrive on Tuesday, 7 October; then, the announced arrival date was switched to Monday, 13 October, and finally, 748 members of Class SE-42-E arrived at Montgomery's Union Station shortly after noon on Friday, 17 October.

LAC (later Squadron Leader) Andrew Maitland of Ayr, Scotland, and Class SE-42-E (Camden, South Carolina) provided a full account of his experience as a member of the first RAF draft to undergo an acclimatization course at the USAAF Cadet Replacement Center at Maxwell Field, Alabama.

> We left Toronto by rail for Maxwell Field, Montgomery, Alabama. Our route took us through Detroit, Cincinnati (at the station there at 4 a.m.), and on through Kentucky and Tennessee to Montgomery, Alabama. It was just after lunch time that we entered Maxwell Field at Montgomery where we were to become acclimatized and take another I.T.W., this one American style.
>
> The base here impressed me very much; it was so clean and tidy and had excellent facilities for everything. The discipline was of a very high standard, and the cadets seemed to be marching to attention at all times. The life at Maxwell Field was not easy, and coming on top of our I.T.W. in England, it was not surprising that there were a few moans and groans from the less enthusiastic British cadets, especially the older ones.
>
> I must say that I did not mind the routine, as the weather was good and I felt very fit. It was rather strange that we were taught American Rifle Drill, but I assumed that the course was the same as for American Cadets, so we were all treated in exactly the same way. There was quite a bit of rivalry between the American and British cadets, and this was good a thing. We took part in a drill parade each day when a pennant was presented to the best squadron on parade, and we managed to acquit ourselves quite well considering the (to us) new rifle drill.
>
> The big grievance which seemed to raise its ugly head with U.K. boys was the fact that they could not leave base in the evenings and were only allowed out on leave from two o'clock Saturday afternoon till two on Sundays. During I.T.W. in England, we had been allowed to leave base after work in the evenings and had to be back and in bed by 2200 hours (10 p.m.). Usually, outings in the evening were for a couple of pints of beer at a pub and back in time for lights out. This freedom probably didn't mean an awful lot, but it helped to break the monotony, and I think this was the privilege missed most by RAF cadets.
>
> Maxwell Field's routine did not bother many of us who felt that we needed to stay in, in the evenings, in order to use the time for private study. A typical daily schedule at Maxwell Field was as follows:
> 0500 Rise and parade [meet formation], be counted, then return, wash & shave, prepare for calisthenics.
> 0530 Calisthenics and games til 0730.

0730 Return to billet; wash & dress for breakfast.
0800 March to breakfast.
0900 Return from breakfast and collect rifle.
1030 Finish Rifle drill and proceed to classroom instruction.
1230 Wash and march to lunch.
1330 Proceed to classrooms for more instruction in maths, history, etc.
Rifle drill and daily retreat parade with all squadrons on parade—a very long stint on the parade square.
1800 Shower, shave, and prepare to march to dinner.
1830 Dinner.
1930 Private study period.
2100 Lights out.
This very full schedule was routine from Monday to Friday.

The demerit system was also in operation and was quite strict. On one occasion, a fly happened to mess up my mirror and that cost me a demerit. More than 10 demerits and one would be walking on the Parade Square for an hour on Saturday afternoon. Fortunately, I avoided the Saturday afternoon walking. Though I was anxious to get on to flying school, this course did not annoy me. The American cadets I met at Maxwell were in the main fairly tall, clean-cut, very healthy, athletic looking, and were polite and well disciplined. Obviously, they had gone through a very good selection procedure.

The good people of Montgomery were so kind to us when we escaped from base on Saturday afternoons and Sundays. They often invited us out for lunch after church on Sundays, and they crowded to the base on Sunday afternoons when the Drill Competition between Squadrons was on view to the Public. How they loved to watch the drill!

The weather at Montgomery was warm and sunny with clear blue skies all during our stay, and this always makes life a little easier. One or two little incidents have always stuck in my mind about my stay at Maxwell. The first was when I had a crew cut and couldn't believe it was me when I looked in the mirror. Then there was the day when I was playing football with the Volleyball and the voice of the Calisthenics Instructor filled my ear with, "Hey Mister, let's not kick the Volley Ball!" Then there was the occasion of seeing an American cadet eating a "Square Meal"—his punishment for some misdemeanor in the mess hall.

There was little doubt in my mind when we came to the end of our course at Maxwell that as an I.T.W. Course for American Aviation Cadets, this was very comparable with our own I.T.W. Course, but would say that the American course was a little more exacting when it came to matters of discipline. Finally, the great day arrived for us to climb aboard a Greyhound Bus to begin our journey to South Carolina.

The highlight of our trip from Montgomery to Camden was the few hours stop at Atlanta, Georgia where I managed to have a little look around the city. At that time, Atlanta struck me as one of the nicest cities in the USA. The countryside from Atlanta to Camden was beautiful and I sat there and enjoyed every minute of the ride.

For purposes of comparison, it is interesting to see some of the excerpts from a diary kept by Andrew Mathieson, a native of Essex and member of Class SE-42-E (Albany, Georgia).

Mathieson's diary briefly alludes to the 16–17 October 1941 train journey from RCAF No. 1 Manning Depot at Toronto to Maxwell Field and provides an excellent chronology of events during the acclimatization course:

> *October 17th. Aren't the rivers slow and muddy? Pass cotton and maize fields. At 2 p.m., we arrive at our destination, which is a British Receiving Centre for the first time. We take a dim view of the barbed wire and the sentries' six guns.*
>
> *October 18th. This morning, we have a dirty, grease-soaked rifle literally thrown at us, we spend hours cleaning it, and spend the rest of the day doing American rifle drill.*
>
> *October 19th, Sunday. We work all day, and no "double time." Great ceremony in the morning [afternoon], when the Governor of the State of Alabama presents us with a Union Jack. Understand we are here for three weeks. Discipline very strict. Confined to camp until further notice. Not allowed to visit the pictures or go to the P.X. (Post Exchange—NAAFI). "E" Squadron of British boys sends in a mass protest.*
>
> *October 23. '45 Automatic shooting on the range. 20 shots. I am graded as "snapshooter" [sharpshooter] having scored 60% and 64% in quick firing. I suppose the fact that as a farmer's boy I have been shooting for ten years has a lot to do with it. Daily "march past" as usual.*
>
> *October 24. Our protests bear fruit. Two free periods allowed today, and permission granted to visit Cinema and Post Exchange.*
>
> *October 25th. Parade in the afternoon, then free until 3.30 on Sunday. We tour Montgomery, visiting the Fair, snapping [photographing] buildings. Hitching a ride is easy here—and what cars!*
>
> *October 27th. After yesterday's dust, a downpour turns the whole "drome" into a mass of cloggy, sandy clay and mud.*
>
> *October 28th. Must draw attention to the Mess, which is beautifully run. Wonderful food. Strict discipline even here. March in, then stand braced behind chairs. We receive the command, "Cadets—sit!" We then sit, with arms folded, to attention. Next comes the command "Cadets—rest!" and we can get cracking on the food. Negro servants rush all over the place, fetching pineapples, iced tea, etc. Our status here is that of Junior Officers. We have batmen and other servants.*
>
> *October 30th. British and American squadrons parade for P.T., and huge cine cameras "take" us, apparently for film. Sweltering, prickly heat, and we shower three times a day. The snag is that if you lay your shirt down for a minute, "Sam" whisks it off to the laundry. How willing they are!*
>
> *October 31st. We are headlines here. We wanted coat hangers. Headlines! We'll get coat hangers! Chamber of Commerce approached. Girl Scouts canvass. Demerit system in full swing. Too many demerits means being confined to camp. We travel "abroad" in the civvies issued at Wilmslow, as America is not at war yet.*
>
> *We cannot walk two yards but what we are saluted in the streets with "Hyah, England! Can I drive you anywhere, England?" and so on. Truly a remarkable people, warm and friendly on their own, but appearing a little brash when in a crowd. Most also say, "How d'y'all like America?" Given free tickets for entry to the Fair. The cost will actually be 2 cents Federal Tax! At the Fair, we continually run up against reporters and photographers. We had to pose beside a kiddies railway and become headlines again.*

November 1st. Open Post (free) today, and we stroll about. Everyone wants to drive us somewhere, or to do something for us. Torrential rain falls. 1.11 inches, according to the papers. "Summer is over" they say, but to us it is still damned hot.

November 3rd. Definitely going on Wednesday [November 5]. Our American officers pose for photographs. Peter and I posted to Albany, Georgia, and the rest of No. 2 ITW to Tuscaloosa.

The two accounts of experience at Maxwell Field between 17 October and 5 November make up a fairly full description of the hurried schedule of activities and the necessary adjustments to a different system of training and discipline. Since Class SE-42-E was late in arriving at Maxwell Field, their acclimatization course lasted only three weeks instead of the scheduled four weeks before they were posted to a primary flying school.

ORIGIN OF ACCLIMATIZATION TRAINING

On 11 July 1941, plans were announced that a USAAF Aviation Cadet Replacement Center would be built at Maxwell Field and that Maxwell Field's USAAF advanced flying school would be transferred to Turner Field east of Albany, Georgia. By 13 August, sufficient buildings were complete to provide housing for the 866 USAAF aviation cadets who arrived and commenced the ten-week-long pre-flight course, and more than one hundred buildings were still under construction. One USAAF aviation cadet class completed pre-flight training before the British cadets of Class SE-42-E arrived.

Although acclimatization training was put into effect for Class SE-42-E at Maxwell Field in mid-October 1941, many of the subjects that were taught had been proposed several months earlier. In 1940, British training officers had expressed concern about posting aircrew overseas for flying training. During the essential long periods of delay consumed by preliminary training, waiting for ITW and for sea voyages, many RAF officers suspected that aircrew students might well forget much that they had learned in their various training courses. Although there was apparently little concrete evidence to support that view, there was probably some truth in it.

In order to prevent a loss of efficiency, Air Ministry planners were anxious to provide "refresher work" aboard ship for both westbound and returning eastbound aircrew. Refresher training was also provided in the various transient camps in the United Kingdom and Canada where students spent time between postings to the different stages of flying training. In June 1941, Group Captain Carnegie asked Wing Commander Hogan to procure materials about "Air Corps organization, geography of the United States, flying systems, aircraft recognition materials, etc. for use in preparing materials for student use at depots before departure to the USA for training." Interestingly, the materials requested by Carnegie cover virtually the same acclimatization course syllabus used for RAF drafts at Maxwell Field, Alabama, and later at Turner Field, Georgia.

Carnegie had originally proposed that if RAF students were to use U.S. Army Air Corps aviation cadet orders and other similar service manuals, these documents ought to be rewritten in the style of British training manuals. Then the manuals could be put to use at the depots and aboard ships well before the RAF drafts arrived in the United States. If these reasonable proposals could be implemented, much of the lost or wasted time at the Wilmslow, Cheshire, and Heaton Park, Manchester embarkation centers might ease student adjustment to the demands of flying training in the United States. Such manuals would also be useful aboard ship or in Canada. Unfortunately, as a result of delay and general British criticism of USAAF training, preparatory courses were not immediately implemented in UK depots and at other points along the westbound training pipeline.

THE AIRCREW REPLACEMENT CENTER
MAXWELL FIELD, ALABAMA

The purpose of the army air forces replacement center was to act as a receiving and screening depot for USAAF aircrew candidates from within the regional training center. The U.S. Army's investment of both money and time in training aircrew was high, so the replacement center was viewed as a means whereby candidates might be further screened and tested to determine their aptitude for aircrew training. Personnel screening would indicate whether cadets might best pursue training as pilots, navigators, bombardiers, flight engineers or aerial gunners. If successful, the pre-flight screening process would reduce the costly attrition rate in later training and would more quickly yield greater numbers of qualified aircrew.

Candidates entered the receiving branch of the center where they were "processed" and "classified." During that thirty-hour receiving, processing and classifying period, each candidate submitted to academic, psychological and physical examinations, the results were recorded on proper forms and these documents became a part of each student's permanent record. Other documents would record his having been classified according to examinations and having received proper issues of clothing and equipment. "Classification" meant that those with obvious deficiencies would be screened out and remustered to other duties or, on the basis of the screening process, if success was predicted, they would continue in the course.

In addition to clearing the hurdles of the initial thirty hours, aircrew candidates were further screened during a four-week academic, military and physical conditioning pre-flight training course. For example, academic and military preparation included sixty-five hours of lectures in citizenship, mathematics, current affairs, United States military organization and administration. This pre-flight course also included thirty-six hours of infantry drill, ceremonies, weapons and guard duty, plus thirty-two hours of physical training.

The aircrew reception center's pre-flight course suffered from a defective syllabus that was designed to do too much for too many in too little time. The system of aircrew training based on ten-week courses for primary (EFTS), basic and advanced (SFTS) flying courses dictated that students enter each phase of training every five weeks. It was a lock-step system that was designed to gain maximum performance from aircraft, instructors and cadets and allowed very little latitude for deviations in schedules.

USAAF aircrew trainees entered every phase of pilot training nationally at five-week intervals (later every four and a half weeks), so the amount of time spent in a reception center was dictated by that system. Such a course could run five, ten, fifteen or more weeks, and Air Ministry officers had initially suggested to USAAF officers that a ten-week-long course would be best. However, a number of other considerations persuaded planners to propose that the ten-week USAAF course should be cut in half for RAF cadets.

The decision was influenced by a number of factors, including the fact that most RAF students had already completed a rigorous ITW course and that Arnold Scheme primary pilot training intakes occurred every five weeks. If the ten-week course was approved, there was not a sufficient pool of trainees available in Canada to fill two drafts at once and ensure continuity of training. As a result, it was decided that a five-week acclimatization course was sufficient for RAF Arnold Scheme students who were all destined for pilot training. For apt and enthusiastic aircrew trainees, even a five-week course was too long; for those without adequate educational experience or motivation, it might prove to be far too short.

The rationale for such a course appeared to be perfectly sound—to screen USAAF aircrew candidates—and the thirty hours allotted to that single goal was sufficient and could be completed in four or five days. However, the total amount of time available before students were to be posted to primary flying schools was five weeks. As a result, the remaining portion of the pre-flight course had to be used profitably. An obvious answer to this question of what to do with the additional time was to provide refresher academic work that might better prepare weaker aircrew candidates for the demands of ground school.

If the twenty-four-hour academic portion of the course was designed to overcome deficiencies in mathematics and other academic training, it was of neither sufficient scope nor duration to provide more than a simple review. For example, the twenty-hour mathematics portion of the course encompassed the elements of arithmetic, algebra and a very basic introduction to principles of trigonometry and geometry. Had there been a serious attempt to provide sufficient academic refresher training to overcome the educational deficiencies of students with the aptitude for aircrew training but insufficient formal education, undoubtedly a long-term course of sufficient depth and intensity would have yielded better results. Since the weakest segment of the five-week replacement training center syllabus was the academic (twenty-four hours), however laudable its aim might have been, it was not to receive high priority.

Apparently the processing and classification of aircrew candidates (thirty hours) was first priority. All other parts of the course—academic (twenty-four hours), military (seventy-seven hours) and physical (thirty-two hours)—were simply included because training officers tended from experience to foster officer military training and rigorous physical training to the exclusion of much else.

For RAF Arnold Scheme students, the four-week-long classification and pre-flight course was viewed as an acclimatization course with an aim to assist British student pilots to adjust to USAAF cadet discipline and the climate of the region. Beginning in October 1941, all Royal Air Force student pilots completed the USAAF reception center course. Before undergoing their modified pre-flight or acclimatization course, Classes SE-42-E, SE-42-F and SE-42-G were received, processed and classified at the USAAF reception center at Maxwell Field, Alabama. From the perspective of Air Ministry officers, British cadets should attend the course primarily because of the attrition rate among RAF students in USAAF flying schools. That wastage was 25 to 40 percent higher than RAF rates, and the expense of training and shipping potential aircrew more than eight thousand miles via Canada to and from the United Kingdom for training, only to have large numbers of them fail, was both expensive and discouraging. Moreover, because such large numbers of failures occurred among men whom the Air Ministry considered to be carefully screened, apt and motivated aircrew candidates, RAF officials were anxious to persuade USAAF officers to modify their system of flying training and to adopt that of the RAF.

A part of the problem stemmed from the differences in physical and educational qualifications, as well as the population base and reward system of the air forces of the two countries. For the most part, the United States Army Air Forces competed with the United States Naval Air Service for aircrew trainees from a population totaling more than 100 million. Both American air forces retained similar qualifications and sought almost physically perfect men between the ages of twenty-one (later nineteen) and twenty-six who possessed a minimum educational qualification of two years of college.

The Royal Air Force, on the other hand, had to compete with the Royal Navy and the British army for recruits from a population of about 46 million. In the interest of qualifying as many men as possible, the RAF also had less restrictive qualifications. Britain sought aircrew candidates between ages eighteen and thirty-two, with correctable vision and other less strict physical qualifications.

The differences did not end there. There were also variations in training methods, priorities and rewards. The United States Army Air Forces pilot training system emphasized precision, smooth technique and safety from the beginning of pilot training to the end. And if the British system of flying training did not condone recklessness, it did very little to discourage the taking of chances. Until changes were made, men were rushed through RAF and RCAF elementary and advanced flying for basic qualification to "wings standard" with between 120 and 150 flying hours.

In June 1941, when British aircrew training in the United States began, RAF officers viewed the American flying training system as essentially "peacetime" and emphasized flying safety and officer cadet training. What they wanted and needed was barely qualified aircrew returned to the United Kingdom for further training. After gaining their wings, pilots would be given operational training and conversion training in British or other operational aircraft, and would be assigned to staff or combat flying. Whereas in 1941 the United States commissioned all of its pilots, Air Ministry regulations prohibited the commissioning of more than 33 percent of every graduating aircrew class, except those trained at the Royal Air Force College at Cranwell. Most RAF aircrew completed their training and received flying brevets (wings) and the tapes (stripes) of a sergeant.

Almost from the beginning, RAF training officers began to receive complaints from strident voices warning that the Arnold Scheme flying training system was not working. Too many British student pilots were being failed, the American disciplinary system was too rigid and housekeeping requirements too strict. In flying, some even said that there was too much emphasis on safety and precision. From the perspective of many Air Ministry officers, men who had completed the very tough, heavily academic British initial training wing course ought to have been able to complete aircrew training without significant problems.

In fairness to them, most Air Ministry officials and RAF liaison officers in the United States appeared to be pleased with the cooperative efforts between the United States and Britain. And even if many of the elements of USAAF discipline were at first unfamiliar to them, they fully recognized the merit of such personal discipline and leadership training. They also heartily approved the flying training. However, in order to avoid misunderstandings, problems needed to be addressed quickly and tactfully. Since so many British cadets were failing Arnold Scheme pilot training courses, their failure was on the verge of being recognized by some as a national insult.

Like the systems of other nations, Britain's pilot training had also been developed over a long period of time and was based on their incomparable elitist educational system. ITW training was effective, but many of the British students, according to American ground and flying instructors, lacked mechanical aptitude, and because so many of them had never operated anything more complicated than a bicycle, large numbers of them had great difficulty in developing smooth techniques in coordinating aircraft controls.

However much British and American training officers sought answers to their concern over the failure of British student pilots, the answers lay much deeper than anyone could say at the time without contributing to further misunderstanding. As a result, except in private conversations, both USAAF and RAF training officers failed to articulate their views about the reasons for failure. At the same time, inexperienced student pilots were critical of the American aircrew training system, giving voice to personal resentment against a system that was not their own.

Neither the American nor the British flying training system was wrong; they were just different. Both systems achieved superb results. The training of RAF aircrew in the United States occurred at the dawn of a new age when educational levels in both countries were relatively low. Demonstrative respect was very high and one-sided, and the basis for tolerance and understanding between the various elements of society was at a very low level.

Although leaving wartime Britain often involved hardship and danger, the experience of undergoing training in a different climate and environment resulted in a different kind of hardship: culture shock. In addition to the necessity for British students to adjust to the strong demands of flying training, they were also expected to undergo at least part of their training alongside USAAF cadets and, as a result, were expected to abide by the same regulations.

Although no one intended for the system to work the way it did, and few people recognized it at the time, the British airmen were systematically deprived of all but a few symbols of their national identity and service heritage. Initially, they either had no uniforms or poor ones, no flag and no service identity except each other. Rather than helping in a difficult situation, the wearing of gray suits off station undoubtedly added to British students' problems. Being compelled to abide by USAAF aviation cadet regulations and to perform drill and ceremonies the "American" way deprived them of a natural desire to compete and to gain special recognition for their own superb drill.

In comparing themselves with many of the American aviation cadets they met, some British cadets felt wanting in education and athletic prowess, but they were soon able to prove themselves in all kinds of competition. LAC Graham R. Hyslop of Lancashire described the intense heat that caused him and many of his classmates considerable discomfort. He and many of his classmates were also impressed with the fact that most of the American cadets he met were twenty-one years old and had two or more years of college. Many of the RAF students were pleased to get to meet and exchange views with their American classmates.

Beginning on Sunday, 19 October at 4:00 p.m. and most Sunday afternoons thereafter, a cadet parade was held at Maxwell Field, and the public was invited to attend. Since the newly arrived members of Class SE-42-E had just been issued rifles and had had only about two hours of American drill at the first parade, they naturally lapsed into British drill and proved themselves to the spectators that afternoon. During that initial review, Wing Commander Hogan presented a Union Jack to Major General Walter R. Weaver, and the American general presented it to the British cadets through Captain John R. Luper, commandant of cadets.

After the Union Jack was presented, it flew alongside the American flag and the RAF ensign. The first Sunday parade and flag presentation undoubtedly raised British morale considerably and helped smooth the way for adjustment to long daily schedules, restricted weekend freedom and guard duties. On weekdays during the following weeks, regular retreat ceremonies were held every weekday evening at the lowering of the flags, and this practice continued at the USAAF flying schools.

On Saturday afternoon, 25 October, after the first week at Maxwell Field, the RAF cadets were allowed to leave the post for the weekend, and large numbers of them walked about the downtown area of the city and visited the Alabama State Fair. Before the day was over many of them had met friendly citizens who invited them into their homes. On 1 November, before members of the RAF class left Montgomery for assignment to primary schools, they sponsored an English-style dance at the Dixie State Armory. Of the 749-man intake for Class SE-42-E, 3 men were held over for further training and 746 completed the acclimatization course and were dispersed to six primary flying schools on 5 November 1941.

Although they were not enamored of USAAF drill, hazing, inspections and rigid scheduling of activities, the members of Class SE-42-E had apparently adjusted to the demands of acclimatization training. "Although we had heard many worrying rumours of hazing, bracing, upper classes, square meals, etc.," wrote LAC Raymond Peter Grimwood of Class SE-42-E (Tuscaloosa), "we received every consideration and kindness throughout our stay." On a similar positive note, LAC Arthur R. Betts of Class SE-42-E (Americus) pointed out that acclimatization "proved invaluable help in the months that lay ahead." Therein lies an important point: learning the purpose of acclimatization training.

On Thursday, 6 November at about 11:45 a.m., Class SE-42-F arrived at Maxwell Field in their RAF blue uniforms, the first Arnold Scheme intake to enter the "neutral" United States in uniform rather than in the drab gray suits that earlier classes had been issued. As they proceeded southward from Canada by train, many of them had switched from the heavy woolen uniforms to khaki. Although the nights were cool, there was plenty of sunshine and warmth during daytime, so until adjustment to the climate was complete, most of the men wore RAF-issue khaki uniforms at Maxwell Field. Among members of that 750-man intake were 66 former policemen.

Even though they marched American-style with the rifles, to them, on the wrong shoulder, many members of that second RAF acclimatization course at Maxwell Field were glad that they were able to participate in a gigantic Armistice Day parade through downtown Montgomery during the chill morning of 11 November. Until training was dramatically changed after the 7 December Japanese attack on Pearl Harbor, each day was filled with activities. On Wednesday evening, 19 November, the new RAF class sponsored an English-style dance in the city auditorium, which was well attended and "great fun."

Off-post and on, a major redeeming feature for the British cadets was the food. LAC Philip Penfold never forgot those magnificent breakfasts following PT and the "appetite raising march to the mess hall," and few ever forgot celebrating Thanksgiving, the distinctive American holiday, when dinner included the traditional turkey (or baked ham) with all of the trimmings.

Another redeeming feature for the RAF cadets in strange surroundings was the well-developed British sense of humor. Shortly after 7 December, when a total "test black-out" was ordered for Maxwell Field, the members of Class SE-42-F were standing outside the barracks while an AT-6 from the advanced flying school flew over to check on the blackout conditions. Recognizing the ludicrousness of worrying about the Alabama airdrome's being attacked by Japanese bombers from five thousand and more miles away, the British cadets "became fractious and started making 'bomb' noises and giggling in the gloaming." Tactical officers called them down for their lack of discipline, but darkness was useful to cover the well-developed British rejection of authority.

LAC Chris Harrison of Derby recalled Class SE-42-F's experience at Maxwell Field:

> Doing the U.S. version of what we had done at I.T.W. was very fidget making, as was the (pre-Dec. 7th) monotonous reiteration of what was going to happen to those gentlemen from Japan if they were so foolish as to start anything. The "Upper Classmen" business, to all of us who had experienced war to some degree or other really upset us, and we became a little obnoxious.
>
> Hughie Edwards, with his V.C. (hero!!) visited Maxwell, and we all got together in a hangar and had a good old moan, as we didn't want the war to be over before we got back!

I well remember, and reminded Hughie [later Air Vice Marshal Hughie Edwards, VC, governor-general of western Australia] *some years ago in Sydney that one of the things he said was to the effect that when we got "into" the war, we might wish we hadn't been in such a hurry! (How true!) All agreed that as a special favour to Hughie we would behave.*

The three visiting RAF officers who had experienced active operations with Bomber Command included Wing Commander H.I. Edwards, VC; Wing Commander J.N.H. Whitworth; and Group Captain John N. Boothman. They arrived at Maxwell Field on 13 November and, accompanied by Wing Commander Hogan, they spoke to RAF cadets in the advanced flying school and in the replacement center.

In an effort to provide a means of welcoming the large numbers of RAF cadets in training at air stations around Montgomery, a number of ladies of the St. Johns Episcopal Church were joined in a meeting by Mrs. Venetia Hogan, and the British War Relief Society was established. In early November, the ladies developed policies for raising funds. According to the November 9 issue of the *Montgomery Advertiser*, the society sponsored for RAF cadets its first weekly Saturday afternoon tea at the church's parish house. Businessmen through the chamber of commerce and various civic organizations regularly supported this drive and other means of addressing the needs of both British and American servicemen.

Within the military, two major changes occurred while Class SE-42-F was undergoing its acclimatization course. The Southeast Air Corps Training Center (Eastern Flying Training Command) gained War Department approval of its specially designed insignia, which emphasized its training role. Moreover, at around the same time, Composer Robert Crawford's "Army Air Corps Song," encouraged by General Weaver, was being sung by marching units at Maxwell and other airfields. Another marching tune that also became popular during the time was the "Sixpence Song," which RAF cadets popularized.

On 10 December 1941, thirty-year-old LAC Stanley Holden of North Harrow, Middlesex, and a member of Class SE-42-F at the aviation cadet replacement depot, died in the station hospital at Maxwell Field. In mid-December when the acclimatization course ended for Class SE-42-F, 1 cadet had died, 2 others had been eliminated (apparently for health reasons) and 3 were held over for further training. The remaining 747 members of that class graduated and were dispersed to five Arnold Scheme primary flying schools. (The Camden, South Carolina primary flying school had ceased training RAF student pilots after the graduation of Class SE-42-E.)

In mid-December 1941, Class SE-42-G boarded train cars at Moncton and traveled for about thirty-six hours across eastern Canada, generally following a snow-covered route northward to the St. Lawrence River via Riviere du Loupe, and through Montreal and Toronto to Windsor, Ontario, where they crossed into the United States. As LAC Brian Davies of Cardiff, Wales (Arcadia, 42-G), recalled many years later, the Canadian rail cars were uncomfortable. But on changing trains at Detroit, his draft found "comfortably padded seats, which could be swung to face the window, dining car service, comfortable bunks and a standard of food and service of which we took full advantage."

On 18 December 1941, the 746-man Class SE-42-G intake arrived in Montgomery from Moncton, New Brunswick, and was joined by the 3 men held over from the preceding class. Apparently, strained relations quickly developed between the American cadets and staff officers and the British cadets of Class SE-42-G. Although precise reasons could not be readily ascertained, fault was shared by both.

Most of the RAF class members who responded recognized that many members of the Class SE-42-G were older and had served in the British armed services since 1939 or had served as policemen in British cities during the Blitz. A considerable number of them had served at Dunkirk or elsewhere in an active war zone, and they deeply resented the American system of discipline and leadership training, which appeared to be designed for "callow youth."

Canadian-born LAC Donald A. Williamson of Class SE-42-G (Lakeland) recalled an occurrence demonstrating the sense of humor of older RAF students under training:

> At Maxwell Field, we were paraded outside the hut of the U.S. Officer in Charge (O.I.C.). There may have been 50 to 100 or more of us, quite green to U.S. ways. We were "stood" to attention; the O.I.C. came out the door, saluted, cleared his throat and spat! On day number two, as soon as the O.I.C. appeared at his door, we at once greeted him by hocking as noisily as he had done the day before and then spat in unison. P.G. Wodehouse would have described the O.I.C. as "other than gruntled."

After some weeks of the acclimatization course at Maxwell Field, the large RAF contingent was split into smaller groups for transportation to primary schools. Williamson was posted with others to Lakeland, Florida, early in January 1942.

LAC Brian Davies, eighteen, of Cardiff, one of the younger members of Class SE-42-G, recalled that Maxwell Field facilities and food "were of a standard higher than we had experienced." Davies also recalled that the initial Alabama heat was intolerable, so the USAAF issued the British cadets lightweight gabardine summer uniforms to replace the heavier khaki drill that had been issued them in the United Kingdom. Davies felt that the retreat ceremony that was held each evening was impressive with its cannon salute and flag lowering, and it was especially good one evening for the reviewing officer to be Air Chief Marshal Sir Charles Portal, RAF chief of air staff.

But all was not roses. Davies also recalled RAF objections to American drill and unsuccessful efforts to persuade the training officers to permit them to use British drill. Evidently, this was the beginning of disagreements between RAF students and USAAF staff. When USAAF cadets attempted to enforce hazing and the cadet honor code, which required cadets to report each other's infractions, Davies asserted that "the British would have nothing to do with it—and said so to the individual cadets in terse soldier's language!"

Following a meeting with an American major, the British cadets were informed that they "should maintain their own system and would not become part of that aspect of the American training." Although it is now impossible to determine the sequence of events, it is possible that having won a single exemption from USAAF cadet regulations, the RAF cadets may have pushed a bit too hard for further concessions.

THE CHRISTMAS 1941 CONFRONTATION

Concerning subsequent events, there are probably as many versions as there were British students present. LAC Brian Davies believed that since the RAF cadets were accustomed to being allowed off-post every night, they were bitter about what they perceived as unnecessary restrictions on their freedom. Davies believed that RAF cadets had been promised open-post in Montgomery on Christmas Eve and had gotten dressed for the occasion. When the open-post was canceled for some unexplained reason, "the disappointment manifested itself in loud and bitter grumbling."

According to Davies, relations deteriorated after that.

> *Conditions were not helped when our American course [tactical] officers appeared with automatic pistols strapped to their belts. We were later ordered to attend a Carol Service being held on the base at which various civil dignitaries from Montgomery were attending. We joined in the singing with gusto, except we used all the bawdy RAF songs we knew. We had a party and ignored the rest!*
>
> *Next day, we were allowed to leave the base and visit Montgomery. Those of our colleagues who had remained behind on guard duties were clandestinely slipped miniature bottles of Scotch as we returned as ordered by 4 p.m. Christmas Dinner was served at 7 p.m., by which time the festive spirit had overtaken the ill will of the previous day.*

Davies went on to explain that a USAAF officer explained at the Christmas dinner that the cancellation of "open post" had resulted from the base's being put on alert because of reports that a Japanese carrier was in the Gulf of Mexico. Whether or not this was a simulated drill in which USAAF officers were supposed to assume that a carrier of the Imperial Japanese Navy was present in the Gulf of Mexico is unknown. If it was simply an "alert" designed to ascertain training station readiness, it apparently failed miserably.

LAC John Cunningham provided a different account of the chronology of Class SE-42-G's experiences. Although there are some slight differences in the interpretation of events, both Davies and Cunningham felt that the American and British perceptions of the honor system caused most of the problems:

> *The "Honour System" demanded that all cadets were bound to behave at all times in an honourable manner, to strictly observe all rules and regulations even when not being supervised, not to crib or cheat at examinations, to be subservient to their cadet leaders, and to report any observed breaking of rules by a fellow cadet to their superiors.*
>
> *At a meeting in the cinema, the British made it quite clear that they would have none of this nonsense. The Commanding Officer was aghast at such insubordination, but finally accepted that British codes of honour did not allow such ungentlemanly conduct. The American cadets were astounded at this British anarchy, and the cadet leaders lost their superiority.*
>
> *I well remember an incident, which occurred before the rejection of the "honour system" had been fully realised by the permanent staff, who set up an aircraft recognition examination in a room, the walls of which were adorned with photographs of aircraft with their names obscured with slips of paper.*
>
> *We examinees were directed in through the door in single file and moved around the room, noting on our examination papers as we passed our identification of each aircraft before leaving the room. Needless to say, we all scored full marks, and when a member of the staff went into the room to collect the photographs, he found the floor littered with bits of paper and paper clips.*

Since aircraft identification was new to the American instructors, the British cadets demonstrated the RAF WEFTL (W-wings, E-engines, F-fuselage, T-tail and L-landing gear) system of identification and assisted in the preparation of proper pictures of combat aircraft for use in the aircraft identification classes. The USAAF ground school instructors and tactical officers were undoubtedly appreciative of this cooperation, but they were no doubt disturbed by poor attitudes and obvious breaches of good discipline. The incidents described undoubtedly occurred, but perhaps the gravest clash over cadet disciplinary regulations occurred on Christmas 1941.

LAC George A. Stone of Class SE-42-G (Tuscaloosa) focused attention on the question of being permitted to leave the post during Christmas and provided yet another interpretation of the conflict. Stone was of the opinion that a full week of "open post" was granted over Christmas and was "cancelled 3 days before Christmas." According to Stone, the reasons given for the canceled leave included information "that there was believed to be a Japanese Aircraft Carrier in [the] Gulf of Mexico, and in case Maxwell Field was attacked by aircraft from same, it would be better to have all cadets in camp, instead of scattered around Montgomery."

Although to the British cadets this explanation sounded ludicrous in the extreme, the thing that apparently irritated Stone and other British cadets was that there was "no blackout anywhere and all pine trees along roadsides in camp [were] festooned with coloured lights." They believed that they were being lied to and held on post for other, unstated, reasons.

In Stone's further description of events, he asserted that "we were allowed to use the main PX over Christmas and actually buy some beer. As a result, of course, there were those who got drunk and made fools of themselves and caused a lot of ill feeling." Stone failed to mention any permission to leave the post. George A. Ebner of Glasgow and Class SE-42-G (Tuscaloosa) provided another variation and specifically referred to an "open post":

> We were given the same training as American cadets but kept separate. On Xmas Day, we were confined to camp (rumours said a Jap carrier in the Gulf) and entertained by a band in the hangar. We were not very well behaved and danced around (a ring of roses) and continued with carol singing after the band had stopped.
>
> The American officers and men were extremely patient with us, and humoured us with a Xmas Dinner & beer & released us on an unsuspecting public the following day. I believe this resulted in 5 cases of alcoholic poisoning among the class. The citizens of Montgomery couldn't have been nicer and many welcomed us to their homes. This was to be the main feature of our stay in Alabama.

Many other RAF members of Class SE-42-G ignored clashes over the honor system and other differences between the RAF and the USAAF but were highly critical of the way some of their classmates acted.

There is no clear evidence that points to a particular set of circumstances that caused the RAF Christmas "revolt." Although Class SE-42-G may have had a larger proportion of older pilot candidates, most of the RAF intakes contained some older ex-servicemen, and these were mostly sensible men. A number of the members of Class SE-42-G expressed the view that the real problem lay in the fact that a large number of their classmates were older, and that the many veterans among them rejected American training out of hand. It was believed that their actions and words might have encouraged other class members to reject USAAF cadet discipline,

American drill and upper-class hazing. Still others felt that many of the veterans counseled patience, as did RAF staff officers when they learned of the flap.

According to several other class members, the real culprit in the whole affair was excessively close supervision by student officers, the scheduling of every minute of the day and a failure to allow daily time off the air base to relax and get away from military service regulations. Although close restriction undoubtedly played a part in the "revolt," it was probably not the deciding element. Since the two previous courses had similar experience either in primary flying schools or in Maxwell Field's USAAF replacement center, the question as to why Class SE-42-G objected so strenuously still remains.

The prime difference between members of Class SE-42-G and members of earlier RAF classes is that most of the members of Class SE-42-G had undertaken at least part of a flight grading course in the United Kingdom. And although one may speculate that possibly that modicum of flying training might have produced overconfidence and led to ego problems, no documentary evidence was available that indicated that the new RAF policy of "flight grading" contributed to problems during acclimatization training at Maxwell Field.

However, evidence has been provided by a sufficient number of RAF cadets who underwent the different American discipline to conclude that when undertaken with the proper spirit and the proper attitude, the acclimatization course could be fun. The academic work of the acclimatization course (however unchallenging it may have been) did provide valuable information, and the rigid physical and military training did instill the self-discipline essential to succeed in the very tough pilot training courses.

Perhaps the rumors about American hazing and washouts that had been encountered in the United Kingdom and in Canada produced a mindset among some RAF cadets that did greater damage than anyone realized at the time. Whatever the reasons, apparently too many RAF cadets neither understood nor accepted the purpose of acclimatization training.

WHY THE CHRISTMAS REVOLT?

The many conflicting accounts that have arisen from the events of Christmas 1941 have clouded the story of Class SE-42-G's acclimatization so much that the exact details can probably never be determined. Each of the descriptions of Class SE-42-G's Christmas "revolt" at Maxwell Field has been told and retold for more than fifty years, and the narrators undoubtedly believe that their memories provide true accounts of what transpired.

The different versions possess immediacy because they all purport to be eyewitness accounts, but none of the witnesses could possibly have been privy to every detail. In the process of being remembered and repeated, the facts and rumors have sometimes become garbled, and narrators too often came to believe that the final version they delivered was the truest.

Although several course members registered disgust with the behavior of a few of their classmates, others repeated the tales over the years and nurtured strong resentments against "U.S. Army Air Corps discipline" for many years. As long as four decades after the war, many aging ex-aircrew, and perhaps a small group of ex-USAAF training officers as well, still bristle at mention of the RAF acclimatization course at Maxwell Field. Some readers may believe that the actions of some RAF cadets of Class SE-42-G at Christmas 1941 constituted an "ego trip" by men who assumed British superiority in all things, and who held Americans in contempt because Britain "had fought alone" since the fall of France in June 1940.

Unfortunately, Class SE-42-G's "revolt" did occur, and stories emanating from it may have influenced many people's views of American training and British-American relations. In raising questions about such interpretations, it is important to recognize that if a similar group of British cadets had refused to abide by regulations on a Royal Air Force training station in Britain, they would have quickly found themselves en route to infantry units. Similarly, if USAAF cadets had refused to abide by regulations on a USAAF or, alternatively, on a British station, it is highly likely that they would also have quickly found themselves in the walking army.

Why then were the USAAF training officers at Maxwell Field so patient and easy in their treatment of the men of Class SE-42-G? Did senior officers believe that their tactical officers had made errors in handling the difficult situation? Were they intent upon avoiding an embarrassing international incident? Did they agree to "turn the other cheek" out of respect for the Royal Air Force, Wing Commander Hogan and other RAF officers? Readers of World War II books cannot but be reminded of the insubordination of Britain's most famous and egotistical army commander two years later in 1944–45. Although the evidence available makes it impossible to reach even a tentative judgment as to the impact of Class SE-42-G's actions, one cannot but conclude that had there been a training agreement similar to that which existed at that time between Canada and the United Kingdom, the "revolt" at Maxwell Field might never have occurred.

When Class SE-42-G completed the acclimatization course in mid-January 1942, 8 men were held over, 3 were eliminated and 738 completed the course and were posted to five USAAF primary schools to commence flying training. Whether cause or result of Class SE-42-G's "revolt," the USAAF cadet reception center at Maxwell Field was enlarged and quickly converted wholly to American use. USAAF aircrew selection procedures were tightened, and a few months later an aircrew classification center was opened at Nashville, Tennessee. Following classification, the American pilot candidates would be posted to Maxwell Field to undergo ten weeks of pre-flight training. The four-week RAF acclimatization course was transferred to Turner Field, near Albany, Georgia, and many members of final six RAF intakes there were assigned to tent accommodations.

CHAPTER SEVEN

FINAL CLASSES OF THE TWO DISTANT PRIMARIES

CAMDEN, SOUTH CAROLINA, 42-E

In early November 1941, a few days following the tragic death of Cadet Pritchard, Class SE-42-E arrived at the Southern Aviation School. The actions of staff and students underscored the necessity for training to continue on schedule despite casualties. That November intake at the Camden flying school contained forty RAF cadets and forty American aviation cadets. Absorbing the five RAF students held over from Class SE-42-D, that brought the total RAF intake to forty-five for that final British class to be trained at the Southern Aviation School.

On 9 October 1941, the members of Class SE-42-E had arrived in Halifax, Nova Scotia, aboard the *Highland Princess*, and after spending a few days at RCAF No. 1 Manning Depot at Toronto, the entire 550-man Arnold Scheme draft had been sent by train on 16–17 October via Detroit, Cincinnati, Chattanooga and Birmingham to Maxwell Field, Alabama. Following a four-week-long acclimatization course there, the Class 42-E cadets were divided into separate contingents to be posted to primary flying schools. The forty RAF cadets assigned to Southern Aviation School traveled by Greyhound coach through Atlanta to Camden. During the final thirty miles of the journey, the RAF students witnessed one aspect of the United States Army's Carolina maneuvers as they saw thousands of troops from the bus windows. They also observed paratroopers being dropped from aircraft and U.S. Army engineers constructing a pontoon bridge across the Wateree River a few miles west of Camden.

Since Camden and nearby Fort Jackson served as headquarters for the military exercises, both of them drew a large number of visitors, including the Russian military attaché and two observers from the Russian air force. During their five-day stay at Camden, the Russians watched a polo match, inspected the Southern Aviation School and shocked some Americans by indicating a preference for lemonade instead of Coca-Cola.

One of the members of that RAF class, Raymond Dunn of Kendal, Cumbria (then Westmoreland, and still gateway town to the beautiful Lake District of northwestern England), graciously permitted use of a letter written to his mother and stepfather over a period of several days, and finally completed and mailed on 12 November. Extracts from that letter provide student impressions of the school, town and region in early November 1941:

> *9 to 12 November 1941. The field at Camden is small compared to most of them, and has about 40 training planes. There are about 60 RAF men here, and about 80 American cadets, and we sleep in double decker bunks, alternately American, British, American, etc. They are grand chaps and are training as officers. As at Maxwell Field, we are only allowed out on Saturday afternoons to Sunday evening.*

Several of us walked the 4 or 5 miles into the village on Saturday only to find the place crowded with soldiers undergoing manuevres here. After waiting two hours for a bus to Columbia, 32 miles away, we eventually got one, in which we had to stand all the way. We got to Columbia at about 8:30 p.m. only to find it also absolutely packed with troops. On the way, we ran into a real battle royal, with troops camping all along the road, and tanks and lorries in the hundreds.

The town of Columbia, usually about 50,000 population, also had 40,000 to 50,000 troops in as well. The streets were crowded with them, the cafés and the cinemas were full, and, after ringing up about 20 places to try and get a room, we packed it up as a bad job and got a bus back to camp.

The discipline at the camp is more strict than one might conceive possible. There is the same system of black marks [as in the acclimatization course at Maxwell Field] for the slightest error or accident, such as brushing a fly from your nose, or not folding the blanket with exactly square corners. If one gets more than five in a week, then he cannot go out on the Saturday until he has walked an hour for each one over five, on a rectangle of pebbles outside the barrack. It is known as the ramp, and several have had as many as 10 one-hour "tours" to do, so we are on our toes all the time against this.

We fly every morning in 2-seater biplane trainers, and usually about 30–35% and sometimes 40% do not pass out at this camp, as trying to fly unless one is air-minded is like trying to play the piano without a musical ear. We have to fly solo within 12 or 15 hours flying, or we are eliminated.

It is very cold here, equally as cold as it is in Kendal, and yesterday morning at about 6.30, we did a six-mile cross country run to keep us fit. There was a thick frost on the ground, but it didn't worry us when we ran into a field with a bull in it which wasn't tied as we soon found out.

We had yesterday off, as it was Armistice Day, and we were allowed to wear uniform on that account, instead of the thin common grey suits we were issued. In the morning, we went to the [memorial] service, as one of our lads crashed last week [actually a fortnight earlier, on 29 October] and was killed. It was the first accident of its kind here, as they have quite a good record.

Cadet Raymond Dunn's observations encapsulated a great number of observations within a relatively brief period. He was among the cadets who graduated from the USAAF advanced flying school at Selma, Alabama. Another member of Class SE-42-E was Andrew Maitland of Ayrshire, Scotland, who departed Camden early. Eliminated from pilot training at Camden, Maitland was remustered and trained as a bomb aimer (bombardier) and navigator in Canada.

More than four decades after leaving Camden, Squadron Leader Andrew Maitland, DFC with bar (RAF, retired), recalled how he felt when he washed out of pilot training:

There was no doubt about it, my world had fallen about me, and I remember sitting on my bed nearly in tears, and then coming downstairs at the Barrack block and sitting on the outside steps wondering where I would go from here. The scrub rate in the States was very high, but this did not appease me. I had a bit of advantage having been at Prestwick, and here I had failed to make the grade. When I got back to Canada, I would just have to plead with the Reselection Board to let me have another go, but I was not at all hopeful.

It is not surprising that we tended to overestimate our importance in the scheme of things, especially when removed from pilot training, but I do think this was quite a natural attitude to take considering all the excellent training we had received from the RAF and the U.S. Army Air Corps which was designed to build character and confidence, and to make us physically fit, mentally alert, personally disciplined, and leaders of men. This training did make us proud young men and, of course, when one was scrubbed, it tended to hurt one's ego; I think this was the most difficult thing to bear.

If the Arnold Scheme had contributed nothing more than the qualities I have mentioned, from my point of view, it would all have been worthwhile. I say this with conviction because I was to become a Regular Serving Officer of the Royal Air Force and was to remain in the service for 25 years. The scheme was to contribute more than this, much more than this.

A few weeks after Maitland's departure for Maxwell Field and Canada, the surviving members of Class SE-42-E graduated and departed by coach for basic flying school.

Twenty-two British cadets, or exactly half of Class SE-42-E's net RAF enrollment, graduated; the others were transferred elsewhere or were remustered in Canada for other service. Class SE-42-E had been the final RAF Arnold Scheme draft to transit through the Toronto depot for documentation, and it had been the first Arnold Scheme draft to report to the Maxwell Field Cadet Replacement Center for acclimatization training. In January 1942, the twenty-two RAF graduates of the Southern Aviation School were also the final British students to undergo pilot training at Camden, South Carolina.

As Class SE-42-E completed its training in winter cold, including snow, at Camden, the surviving members of the first Arnold Scheme class (SE-42-A), who had commenced training six months before in the heat and dust of June, completed their training at three USAAF advanced flying schools and were awarded their wings as qualified pilots. Except for a few former RAF students, such as Sergeant Arthur D. Moore (SE-42-A), who visited civilian friends in Camden in May 1942 when on leave from Moncton, New Brunswick, Canada, the RAF presence in Camden, South Carolina, ended for a while.

During the autumn of 1941, when the Hulse organization opened another primary flying school at Decatur, Alabama, problems began to develop at its Camden school. First, many members of the maintenance staff as well as experienced flying and ground instructors transferred to Hulse's new school or to other contractors' schools. Instructor Harry Howton and other reserve officers with extensive flying experience were posted to India to fly men and supplies over the mountains to and from China. As a result, instead of mellowing with experience, the instructional staff at Camden was almost totally new once again. Secondly, the school was still undergoing construction, and British officers felt that the main airdrome was inadequate for the numbers assigned to be trained there.

Consequently, British staff officers surmised that the number of RAF eliminees would continue at much too high a level. Although no specific written evidence could be found to confirm it, RAF staff were critical not only of the loss of experienced civilian staff at Camden, but also of the fact that Woodward Field was still "dusty, rough, and unlevel." The school was also said to be having difficulty getting an adequate number of replacement Stearman trainers. Given these conditions and the greater convenience in supervising primary schools located closer together, it is likely that these were the reasons the RAF Delegation decided to concentrate Arnold Scheme training farther southward to the states of Georgia, Florida and Alabama.

The Southern Aviation School had commenced operations in March 1941 and had trained American cadet classes SE-41-H and SE-41-I before the arrival of RAF cadets on 7 June 1941. Training for the five RAF classes (SE-42-A through SE-42-E), which had enrolled 298 British students, extended over seven months, from 9 June 1941 through 9 January 1942.

When the RAF students departed, the Southern Aviation School was only about ten months old. The school's physical facilities were only half completed, and its wartime training service had barely begun. In early 1942, shortly after the RAF departure from Camden, the U.S. War Department changed its policy. Instead of requiring the civilian contractor to continue paying for improvements, the Defense Plant Corporation purchased the facilities, equipment and auxiliary field leases of the Southern Aviation School. The USAAF continued to assign the military administrative staff, the maintenance inspection staff, the aircraft and the replacement parts, as well as periodic orders for engine overhauls. Later in 1942, the USAAF also began to provide all gasoline and oil used by the civil contract flight schools.

Following government purchase of the contractor-built facilities, school officials renegotiated their contracts and leased all facilities and equipment from the Defense Plant Corporation at a low fixed fee. Under this arrangement, the United States government now owned the contractors' buildings and equipment, and when improvements or additions were made to the school, they were done at government expense. Entry of the United States into the war brought about a greater demand for pilots, so training was intensified to seven days per week. At the urging of RAF officers, night flying was introduced into the primary flying syllabus. In 1939, the national production rate for USAAC pilots had been set at 2,250 per year, and from that point it climbed to 7,000; then 12,000; 30,000; 50,000; 75,000; and finally 104,000 pilots per year. Class sizes at the Camden flying school expanded to meet each new USAAF expansion goal.

The Southern Aviation School, as a miniscule but no less important part of that vast training establishment, had originally enrolled around fifty cadets in each of its first two classes, and gradually increased enrollments as facilities and staff became available. During 1942, school officials were asked to double capacity and output and, as a result, changes came rapidly. As enrollments climbed to more than two hundred men per class (more than four hundred cadets in training at one time), the school's domestic, ground school, physical training and flying training facilities were enlarged. In October 1942, an air-conditioned Link Trainer facility was added. More aircraft and equipment arrived, the number of maintenance staff was increased and more Link Trainer instructors, tactical officers, administrative and medical staff were assigned. Captain Edwin P. Hoyt, who later became famous as author of numerous World War II histories, was among the new officers assigned to the Camden flying school.

A long-awaited addition, a very large swimming pool, was completed, and playing fields were developed to the rear of the hangars. A first-rate obstacle course was installed in the pine grove behind Barracks B, C and D. Owing to sandy conditions that prevented its continued use, the lease of Pritchard Field (formerly Funderburk Field) was not renewed, and Stevens Field was leased. In order to accommodate the larger numbers of student pilots and to reduce the pressure on maintenance facilities at Woodward Field, the school's staff found it necessary to add satellite airfields. Two of the existing three auxiliary fields were converted into satellite fields when small hangars and stage houses were erected on them, thus making it possible to carry out routine maintenance without returning aircraft to the main airdrome.

During 1943, a national shortage of qualified flying instructors and A&E mechanics, most of whom had entered the armed forces in increasing numbers, led to large-scale on-the-job training.

Older, qualified, as well as younger civilian pilots and A&E mechanics who were ineligible for active service because of age or physical defects, such as diabetes, were recruited and trained in CAA-sponsored instructors' schools or technical schools. Many civilian contract and USAAF schools also implemented a nighttime production line maintenance (PLM) system. Finally, women were employed and trained on the job as civilian aviation mechanics (CAMs). They learned to repair, inspect and maintain correct records of aircraft maintenance. When women replaced qualified male technicians who were being drafted in increasing numbers, the number of aircraft available and ready on the flight line remained at a very high level, but the ladies never received credit for their outstanding achievements.

By mid-1943, newly assigned military staff, many of whom had combat experience, were available to increase the supervision of every aspect of training and to begin the process of making further changes dictated by wartime experience. Strenuous efforts were made to standardize and to improve every phase of flying training. When War Department planners discovered that the casualty rates among aircrew had been much lower than expected, the number of aircrew already trained or currently undergoing training exceeded the numbers required to end the war. As a result, pilot and other aircrew training was made much more difficult than before, and in April 1944 the USAAF deliberately eliminated some nine thousand student pilots and reassigned them to the ground forces.

Beginning in April 1944, many civilian contract primary flying schools were closed. In late spring, Southern Aviation School staff were notified that the school would close when Class SE-44-K completed its primary flying training in July 1944. More than six thousand student pilots had been enrolled in the Southern Aviation School, and the Defense Plant Corporation reported that it had disbursed $694,512.71 in the original purchase, the assumption of leases, the construction of additional buildings, the purchase of equipment and the paving of two runways at Woodward Airport. After 1 August 1944, all of the Stearman trainers were flown away, the school buildings and hangars were closed and leases on auxiliary and satellite airfields were canceled. The Southern Aviation School and its civilian and military staffs had completed their assigned mission.

When all of the airplanes, cadets, military and civilian staff were gone, the chamber of commerce and the Camden and Kershaw County Airport Commission began to seek other potential users of the flying school and its excellent facilities. However, since there were dozens of similar closed flying schools and military camps scattered over the region and the nation, local officials had little luck. Finally, the United States Army leased the domestic facilities of the former flying school and brought nearly five hundred German prisoners of war there. The barracks that had housed American and British student pilots now housed German POWs who were sent out on agricultural work details during the remaining months of the war.

By late summer 1945, the POWs were being repatriated and the United States Navy gained control of the airfield and its hangars. Although the recently paved runways were kept open, practically all of the remainder of the airfield served as a park for every known type of carrier-borne aircraft, many of which bore the marks of combat damage from the war in the Pacific. It was a sad ending for a once proud primary flying school, as well as for a number of carrier-borne aircraft from several of the U.S. Navy's veteran fighter, torpedo and dive bomber squadrons.

However, it was not only the airfield that the cadets remembered; it was also the tiny town and its hospitable citizens. Close by Camden's old Quaker Cemetery, even today, are a number of graves of British soldiers dating from 1780–81 when a garrison was located nearby. Within the Quaker Cemetery under massive headstones lies the dust of generations of Carolinians, including veterans of every war in which the nation has fought. Many veterans of the American Civil War were buried there, including at least two of the six generals that the district produced. In the shadows of a giant cedar tree is a plot called "Little Arlington," which at the time contained memorials to Civil War hero Richard Kirkland, "the Angel of Marye's Heights," and to heroes of World Wars I and II, including the remains of two World War I recipients of the Congressional Medal of Honor.

Most reminders of the RAF presence in Camden are in the hearts and minds of many of its citizens. However, the grave of RAF Cadet George James Pritchard, RAFVR (SE-42-D), is located in one corner of Little Arlington, and its simple memorial stone placed there by the Commonwealth War Graves Commission serves as a sad but permanent reminder of the RAF presence in Camden, South Carolina. Another memorial that serves as a link with the RAF is a silver paten that is still used in communion services at Camden's Grace Episcopal Church. The silver was presented to the church in 1942 by the Pritchard family as a thanksgiving memorial of their son's birthday.

In 1944, the Hulse organization published an honor roll in the company magazine, *Southernaire*, detailing in a straightforward way a few of the achievements of 442 of its USAAF graduates who flew and fought in every wartime theatre of operations. Although one issue of *Southernaire* asserted incorrectly that Captain Robert K. Morgan (who died in 2004), pilot of the Boeing B-17 bomber *Memphis Belle*, received his primary training in the company's school at Decatur, Alabama, in truth the Camden school could claim Morgan as one of its own. Southern Aviation School staff could also take pride in having trained many men who flew as instructors in the United States, and many others who flew combat missions in New Guinea, the Aleutian Islands, in the air war over North Africa, Sicily, Italy, Western Europe, India, Burma, China, the Pacific Islands and the final B-29 assault on Japan.

During the war years, a few British cadets returned from basic or advanced flying schools to visit friends in Camden before leaving North America. In the years since 1945, a number of former British cadets returned from time to time to visit wartime friends. Many of them simply drove through en route to or from Florida and drove around the Woodward Airport while they reminisced. In the 1980s, John Dudley "Mac" McCarthy of Essex, Laurence Buckley of South Africa, Peter Nelson of Australia and Richard Locatelli of Tasmania came back for a visit.

In September 1991, Paul White, a retired Hawaiian Airlines pilot who in 1943 was a Link Trainer instructor at Southern Aviation School, managed to gather a large number of former staff to celebrate the school's fiftieth anniversary. Brigadier General Hulse (USAAF, retired), former Lieutenant Colonel Leonard Hauprich and numerous former instructors and former USAAF cadets also came to celebrate the anniversary.

In October 1991, during the fiftieth anniversary of Arnold Scheme training, four former RAF pilots—John R. "Joe" Petrie-Andrews, DFC, DFM; William S. "Peter" Ellenshaw; Arthur Leighton-Porter (all of Class SE-42-A); and Charles B. Ross (SE-42-E)—made a nostalgic return visit to Camden. Later in 1991, H.J.P. "Pat" Cattrall (SE-42-B) of western Australia remarried and moved to Camden for two years. Although the school staff may have attempted to determine the fate of the 298 RAF men who were enrolled in the small flying school, they were never able to record as part of the school's honor roll the experiences of British fliers who trained at Camden.

All British aircrew were volunteers. Many of them had obtained releases from critical jobs and, if they did not successfully complete their aircrew training, they had the option of being remustered for another assignment in the RAF, or of applying for release in order to return to their war jobs.

As the statistical record shows, 298 British student pilots were enrolled in primary flying training at Southern Aviation School, Camden, South Carolina. Of that number, 164 graduated, 133 were eliminated, 1 was killed in training, 1 was transferred to Darr Aero Tech at Albany, Georgia, and another to BFTS No. 3 at Miami, Oklahoma, to complete his training.

It is known that a small number of Arnold Scheme primary flying school washouts were assigned to other schools to continue their pilot training. Although there is no record to indicate how many or which RAF eliminees at Camden were reassigned to continue pilot training, from the experience of Camden cadets Fred Fish, Harry Hepplewhite, Hugh Leighton Mowbray, John Morden and Michael S.J. Mycroft, it can be assumed that at least some Camden eliminees continued pilot training in another flying school either in Canada, Britain or South Africa. Even so, most British student pilots who were eliminated from pilot training were remustered to duty as observers (navigators), bomb aimers, (radio) wireless operators/air gunners or, later, as flight engineers. Some of them rejected further flying and were assigned to ground duties or were discharged in order to return to critical jobs.

It is impossible to account for all of the 298 RAF student pilots who were enrolled in the Southern Aviation School at Camden, but a description of what happened to a few of them will provide insight.

WHERE HAVE ALL THE RAF CADETS GONE?

42-A. CLIVE L. BROOKS, twenty, of Fakenham, Norfolk (Camden, Macon, Selma), entered the RAF at 17 at the RAF School of Technical Training, Halton, Buckinghamshire. He served with 456 Royal Australian Air Force Squadron flying deHavilland Mosquitoes, June 1943 to December 1944. Brooks flew eighty operational sorties and was credited with destroying one Messerschmidt 410 and two flying bombs. He served as test pilot at the Royal Aircraft Establishment (RAE), Farnborough, from 1944 to 1949, where he flew British and captured German aircraft, including jets. His RAF service ended in 1961 when Wing Commander Brooks retired, having logged approximately 2,500 hours. At that time, he was commanding a Venom jet Night Fighter Squadron. He subsequently joined the BBC in administration.

42-A. WILLIAM S. "PETER" ELLENSHAW, twenty-eight, of Uxbridge, Middlesex (Camden, Macon and Class 42-H Valdosta), worked in films as a special effects artist. He was the first member of Class SE-42-A to solo, but he became ill while undergoing training at Cochran Field, Georgia. For several months he was confined to Lawson General Hospital, Fort Oglethorpe, Atlanta, Georgia, and at the Turner Field Hospital. Ellenshaw reentered and completed advanced flying training at Moody Field, Valdosta, with Class SE-42-H. In the United Kingdom, he was assigned as a flight instructor; later, he was sent to Canada as an instructor. He completed service as flying officer with almost two thousand hours. Following active RAF service, Ellenshaw joined the Disney Studios in Hollywood and continued with them to retirement in 1983. He won an Academy Award for technical work. He was a successful California artist.

42-A. JOHN PETER "ACORN" MOSS, twenty, of Wimbledon, Surrey (Camden, Macon, Albany), was selected to take Wing Commander H.A.V. Hogan on a flight in a Stearman biplane while at Camden. (Ironically, both Hogan and Moss rose to the rank of air vice-marshal/major general.) On returning to England, Moss was assigned for several months as a flying instructor for Royal Navy pilots. In 1944, he completed fighter OTU, and after the Normandy invasion he flew

Spitfire XIVs with No. 2 Squadron of the Tactical Air Force. In 1948, he and his wife immigrated to southern Rhodesia. There, he joined the Royal Rhodesian Air Force and served until he retired as an air vice-marshal, second in command of the Rhodesian Air Force. Although several others achieved air rank during their RAF careers, Moss attained the highest rank of all RAF student pilots trained at the Southern Aviation School. He died on 2 January 2002, while a resident of Hermanus, Cape Province, Republic of South Africa.

42-B. RICHARD "STUKA" GUTHRIE, nineteen, of Bedford (Camden, Macon, Selma) was labeled "Stuka" by his Camden classmates because of his habit of dive-bombing Camden's Hermitage Lake, or people he saw in or on it. Flight Lieutenant Guthrie won a Distinguished Flying Cross before he was killed in Normandy on 18 August 1944. At the time, he was assigned to the British Second Tactical Air Force flying a heavily armed Hawker Typhoon of 247 Squadron in close support of the Allied armies at Caen, Mortain and the Falaise Gap in Normandy. According to one account that could not be confirmed, his aircraft was struck by enemy AA fire and he dove it into an enemy formation near Vimoutiers, Normandy. His remains were interred in one of the British cemeteries nearby.

42-E. GRAHAM ALAN "TAILSPIN TAFFY" RICH (Camden, Macon, Dothan). Graduated May 1942 and returned to United Kingdom via Canada as a sergeant pilot. Further training at 7 AFU and Nos. 8 and 9 OTU on Spitfires. His demonstrated expertise as a pilot led to a photo reconnaissance unit (PRU) assignment. In April 1943, he flew his first sortie with 541 Photo Reconnaissance Squadron from RAF Benson. His Spitfire XIs were stripped down and unarmed, and he flew a further twenty-four sorties over targets that had been hit by Bomber Command. His sorties included PRU trips to the Mohne Dam after 617 Squadron's successful raid; to Dusseldorf; and three visits to Cologne following the "1000" aircraft raids. Subsequently, Rich served with 543 PRU Squadron at Malta and Gibraltar.

Back in the United Kingdom, Rich was assigned to No. 1402 Meteorological Flight flying Spitfire XVIs on three hundred high-altitude flights, many to forty thousand feet or more. He then served as an instructor in Canada and at No. 5 Advanced Flying Unit (AFU), Tern Hill. During the postwar period, he remained active in the RAF, RAAF and civilian flying clubs. He flew aircraft in motion pictures such as *633 Squadron*, *Blue Max* and *Dam Busters*. Rich evidently owned his own Spitfire and worked closely with Cliff Robertson, the American actor. He retired as squadron leader, AFC, and died circa 1992.

HARGROVE VAN DE GRAAF FIELD
TUSCALOOSA, ALABAMA, 42-E-42-G

Following their reception at Regents Park, an extensive ITW course and a brief wait before entraining for Liverpool, the huge draft of British aircrew students boarded a transport bound for Canada. Mess officer aboard the *Highland Princess*, later RAFAO at Tuscaloosa, was Flight Lieutenant A.T. Grime. Accompanied by the *Pasteur* and an escort of several destroyers and a small aircraft carrier, the transports arrived in Halifax, Nova Scotia, on 21 September 1941. The men entrained for Toronto at dockside and for about thirty hours passed through the most colorful and beautiful autumn scenery they had ever seen. Theirs was to be the final RAF draft to enter the United States from the very crowded RCAF station in Toronto.

At the RCAF No.1 Manning Depot, the Arnold Scheme Class SE-42-E draft was posted to Maxwell Field, Alabama, for an acclimatization course. This short pre-flight course was one of the several changes agreed to at an RAF/USAAF training conference aimed at reducing the wastage in Arnold Scheme primary flying schools. The first short pre-flight course, lasting from 15 October to 11 November, provided a brief introduction to American history, the army air corps, American drill and ceremonies and extensive physical training. For the students, the best part of the course was well-prepared and plentiful food, and the fact that their acclimatization course lasted only three weeks.

Having been divided into drafts assigned to the six Arnold Scheme primary flying schools, the 120 student pilots of Class SE-42-E boarded coaches or train cars and left Montgomery. The men assigned to the Tuscaloosa draft traveled by coach and arrived at the Alabama Institute of Aeronautics around 12 November 1941. There, they were joined by the 3 student pilots held over from Class SE-42-D, and their numbers rose to 123. They were well received by the USAAC officers and local citizens, but many of the RAF cadets began to experience difficulties with the civilian flying instructors. Many of the Alabama Institute's highly experienced ground and flight instructors had been transferred by the Parks Company to its new primary school in Missouri, and were replaced by recently "qualified" but inexperienced instructors. Clashes occurred between RAF cadets and the instructors, and the RAFAO was evidently of little or no help in the difficult situation.

LAC Harold Charles "Harry" Leng of Dawlish, Devon, and Class SE-42-E had a slightly different, but confirming, experience:

> *My own experience of the civilian instructors was unfortunate. From the first, there was a thinly veiled antagonism from him (my own instructor). He "forgot" to teach me cross-wind landings & when I refused to carry on doing them after nearly killing myself & others, I was put up for a "washout" check with the U.S. Army captain. He discovered immediately that I had not been instructed in X wind landings & taught me himself. I had no further problems. I was probably unlucky in my civilian instructor: some mornings he was too drunk to move away from the hangar wall in case he fell over!*

In his evaluation of primary training, Leng unintentionally may have indicated why Class 42-E lost ten RAF cadets as washouts (the greatest number from any Tuscaloosa class) for unspecified reasons listed as "other than flying deficiencies"(usually disciplinary or medical):

> *Evaluation of Primary—wasteful of good material; made even worse by the instructors not understanding the British temperament. The administration were still applying the "West Point Cadet System" & this did not go down at all well with people like air gunners who had done a tour of operations & then re-mustered as pilots—or Sergeants from the Army who had fought at Dunkirk.*
>
> *…I hope this helps to give credit to the U.S.A. for their invaluable efforts to provide aircrew in bulk when Britain was so desperately short. It is tragic that so many of them must have "got the chop" in the Bomber Command "meat grinding" period from 1943 to March 1944, when only one out of three survived.*

Coincidentally, before flying six combat operations as pilot of an Avro Lancaster bomber, Leng served as a flying instructor from November 1942 to October 1944, and was promoted to flight lieutenant.

LAC Raymond Peter Grimwood of Cheshunt, Surrey, also a member of Class SE-42-E, had different experiences. Grimwood could have had no idea that he was embarking on a career leading to his becoming a flight lieutenant bomber pilot in 57 Squadron, where he was awarded a DFC. Following that wartime experience, he became an airline pilot with British European Airways. During his career, Captain Grimwood became a member of the Royal Aeronautical Society and the Guild of Air Pilots and Air Navigators, which designated him master air pilot. Having logged almost twenty thousand flying hours, he retired in 1977.

Shortly after arriving in Tuscaloosa, Grimwood and four other RAF student pilots were invited to celebrate Christmas with Dr. and Mrs. Thetford of Boliger, Alabama. However, when the Japanese attacked Pearl Harbor, all leaves were canceled. The United States became an ally, and aircrew training was speeded up to seven days per week. On Christmas Day, the Thetfords drove sixty miles to visit their RAF friends at Tuscaloosa and to present them with gifts. Later, Peter Grimwood and several of his fellow RAF student pilots were able to visit the Thetfords in Boliger. As he recalled many years later, "We spent a couple of weekends with them, and for many years after, I am told, our names were still called for attendance at the Boliger Episcopal Church."

John Boaden, twenty, of Helston, Cornwall, also a member of Class SE-42-E, washed out of pilot training at Gunter Field. During his primary flying training, he recalled going to Saturday socials at Tuscaloosa's First Methodist Church and visiting Cornish people in Birmingham, Alabama. Before returning to Canada for navigator training, he spent a weekend in New Orleans and managed a short trip on a Mississippi River boat. After graduating as a sergeant navigator in Canada, he returned to Britain, joined 106 Squadron and earned a DFM during his thirty operational trips.

LAC Michael Gardner, former journalist of Maidenhead, Berkshire, and Class SE-42-E, wrote an article in *Fins and Flippers* entitled "Thanks For the Memories." Acknowledging that he was making mock use of actor-comedian Bob Hope's theme song, he launched his witty remarks, which might well apply to every British cadet who entered training in the United States, except for the evident steady diet of beans:

> *Those who graduate from the Alabama Institute of Aeronautics will take with them a firm grounding in elementary flying, a certain, perhaps hazier, knowledge of C sub L and strato-cumulus clouds. But everyone will take with him—those who graduate and those who fail—memories…which we'll hold and which will cling to us with fond tenacity. And when I leave I'll be able to say to Tuscaloosa and the Air Corps…Thanks for the Memory.*
>
> *And I have a lot of them…maybe some of mine are shared by you. Here are just a few that neither distance nor time will fade or tarnish…The irate cadet who took off his gosport and tried to shout down the earpieces back at his instructor—an eliminee who humorously cracked, "why all these Keep 'Em Flying notices? Why not Stop 'Em Flying instead?"…beans for breakfast…The Air Corps officer who looks like Henry Fonda, and confounded us all by talking like Jimmy Stewart…Another who grew a mustache that should have made him look like Gable, but instead made him look like the same officer with a mustache that should have made him look like Gable…*
>
> *The suggestion that marriage licenses should be sold at the canteen* [this probably referred to Cadet J.S. "Scottie" McLennan of Edinburgh, whose potted biography stated that he "took greater risks with local girls than with flying,

and married one of the Alabama University girls, after being here four weeks"]…*beans for tea…The sharp-shooting sheriff whom rumor suggests can split a cadet at fifty yards…The morale officer who, since coming to Tuscaloosa, has more than 1000 hours dual (on the ping pong table)…The sudden outburst of mustache-growing among the cadets (know the blonde cadet lieutenant who sports seven hairs on the left, six on the right of his upper lip?)…*

The Ground School Instructor—that key chain—is he fixed to it or it to him? And does he swing it, or is he swung?…The admonition to a cadet, who jumped headlong into the stormy seas of matrimony, by an officer, "This is disgraceful. Don't let it happen again."…The blonde who asked the cadet if V.R. stood for very romantic…Oh yes! I almost forgot—beans.

In that same issue of the cadet magazine, the potted biography of LAC W.A. "Bren" Brenard reconfirmed Gardner's dietary concerns, indicating that Brenard's pet aversions were "beans, early morning flying, athletics, and beans."

The talented LAC Michael Gardner also wrote another article entitled "The Lights Dim Twice," which dealt with the execution of a prisoner who envisioned killing the warden and escaping prison in the minutes before being executed in the electric chair. The clever tale was reminiscent of Ambrose Bierce's famous American short story, *An Occurrence at Owl Creek Bridge.*

Fortunately for the British cadets, recreation was available from the friendly people of the University of Alabama and Tuscaloosa. During the time that RAF students were in training at AIA, the civil contractor made very few improvements to the school. Despite efforts of several USAAF commanding officers to pressure the contractor to provide cadet recreational facilities and other amenities, very little was done. In September 1942, one month before RAF training ended at the primary school, a recreation building was finally completed. But even that effort proved inadequate, as the building was crowded with a canteen and soda fountain, a game room, a cadet library, a miniscule motion picture theatre and a short-wave radio.

In 1943, after the RAF students were gone, the contractor finally made significant efforts to improve the appearance of the school. By May 1943, a six-hundred-foot-long fence and an entrance gate were completed along U.S. Highway 82, and trees were planted along the circular drive, which ran past the infirmary, barracks, recreation building and metal hangar. In 1944, the unit history finally stated the case clearly: "The entire contract performance at this Detachment—[has been] to meet the barest minimum requirements with the least expense and least number of personnel possible." Positive change by the USAAF included the addition of five RAF pilot officers to the instructional staff at AIA. The British officers included Denys D. Ding and C.J.C. Manning, who had graduated from AIA as members of Class SE-42-D, and F.R.C. Pusey, J.J. Woods and H.W. Moore, who had completed primary flying at other Arnold Scheme schools.

After Class SE-42-E had completed almost five weeks of primary flight training, Class SE-42-F arrived from Maxwell Field, and its enrollment rose to 128 with the addition of the 4 men held over from Class SE-42-E. Among the new UK students was Cadet Christopher E. "Tiger" Harrison, twenty-seven, of Derby, a highly skilled expert on Rolls Royce Merlin aircraft engines. Harrison's potted biography described him as having "known the 'Merlin' since it was a two-stroke." En route to North America aboard the *Pasteur*, he recalled that distinguished passengers included Hughie Edwards, VC; and "Sailor" Malan, DSO, DFC, fighter ace. In describing some of his experiences at Tuscaloosa, he was specific:

Barrack type accomodation; one night the "sheriff" (probably the Officer of the Day [OD]) on his rounds was put into a shower, but not wetted, and threatened to shoot someone. I was not active in this but admit I said little contra, but thought it all very foolish. And our 6-shooter friend had my sympathy. Quite an "inquest" on this.

Chris Harrison graduated from primary training and was posted to Gunter Field, where he soloed after a few hours flying solo in a Vultee BT-13. Then he was pulled out of pilot training and embarked on a unique non-military assignment in Detroit, Michigan.

The 42-F student officers included LAC Leonard W. Thorne of London as group commander. A former Metropolitan Policeman, Thorne had been awarded the George Medal (second only to the Victoria Cross) for rescuing a large number of citizens from fire during the London Blitz. Cadet Ronald Slade-Betts of Bromley, Kent, served as adjutant. Cadet Brian M. Jubb, graduate of Rugby with a year at Oxford before joining the RAF, gained fame as one of the masters of ceremonies when Class SE-42-F instituted a weekly RAF radio broadcast on a local radio station.

Cadet Michael Gardner's memory of beans for breakfast and beans for tea had indicated some serious problems with food service at the Alabama Institute of Aeronautics, a problem that was addressed head-on by Class SE-42-F. Class officers joined the student squadron officers to form the Gripe Committee. On 22 January 1942, the committee met with Mr. R.M. Davies, the AIA dietician, and gained significant changes in the RAF cadets' diet. Servings of beans were undoubtedly reduced.

On Wednesday afternoon, 14 January 1942, RAF Cadet Derek M. Sharp of Yorkshire and his civilian flight instructor, Mr. J.A. McCausland, took off from an AIA runway in a Stearman PT-17. After hitting some turbulence, the aircraft began to climb, and when the instructor looked back to the rear cockpit, his student was missing; a further look revealed that Sharp was sitting astride the fuselage in front of the stabilizer. Obviously Cadet Sharp had failed to fasten his seat belt, and the turbulence had thrown him out. McCausland quickly grabbed the controls and climbed to about two thousand feet before attempting to persuade Sharp to take to his parachute. Sharp refused, and then McCausland saw that, since Cadet Sharp had also failed to secure his parachute properly, the instructor had no choice but to attempt a safe landing of the tail-heavy aircraft as soon as possible. Fortunately, he was able to do so, and they both survived. As could be expected, there are numerous versions of the events.

Six days later, while Sharp was taxiing into position for a solo flight, another trainer flown by Cadet Sidney A. Sims landed on top of Sharp's aircraft, shearing off part of a wing and narrowly missing Sharp's twice very lucky head. Shortly after his most famous experience at AIA, "Bare Back Sharp" was elected president of the board of the Killers and Wreckers Club of Class 42-F. Another board member, LAC Les B. Cameron of Scotland, was credited with "badly damaged wings and landing gear" from attempting to land his trainer "from a height of one hundred feet without any preliminary glide." LAC William "Bill" Mason, also of Scotland, became lost and landed his PT-17 on a dairy farm near Birmingham; LAC Fred Hollingberry also lost his way and experienced a forced landing, but he was best known for "using his propeller as a reaper in a cornfield." Unfortunately, Derek Sharp's luck ran out. He went "missing" on a bombing raid, and since his body was never found, he is commemorated on one of the panels of the beautiful RAF Memorial high on a hill above Runnymede.

Members of the club included LAC Jack Powell, who made a forced landing near Gordo, Alabama; Reginald A.J. Shotbolt, who chased two civilian boys off Moody Auxiliary Field with his PT-17 propeller; David C. Smith of Chesterfield, Derbyshire, whose first solo landing was a three-point one—his trainer's two wheels and propeller; and LAC Sidney A. Sims of London, who was noted for "attempting the assassination of the K and W president." It is unknown if the K&W club existed beyond Class SE-42-F, but the unit history described how in the summer of 1942 "British cadets wrecked 18 planes in four days, and 15 LAC's were eliminated." Even so, the maintenance department had the planes back in service at the end of three days.

A few days after Class SE-42-E departed for Gunter Field basic flying school, Class SE-42-F became the senior class, and Class SE-42-G arrived at Maxwell Field, Alabama, around 19 December 1941.

The Tuscaloosa draft was transported across Alabama in trucks on 11 January 1942 and trained there until 28 March 1942.

LAC George Ebner's assessment of his experiences at AIA were also revealing:

> *Instructors were civilian with a sprinkling of military, who gave progress checks. My only check lasted 20 minutes and was conducted by Lt. Simonds, USAAC. Instruction in the air was good. Ground instruction was good, but heat made it difficult to stay awake. Exam questions were of the multi-answer type, and the previous course passed on the answers, so we did tend to cheat at exams. When they changed the answers, the failure rate was high!!*
>
> *The Southern drawl was conspicuous among instructors, and pronunciation & spelling could be a little confusing. There was no lack of hospitality shown to cadets by local inhabitants. If you went to church, the minister invoked the audience to entertain the British, and every one of us was taken into someone's home & dined & wined.*

Among other members of Class SE-42-G at Tuscaloosa was Cadet Kenneth A. Curzon Wright of Warlingham, Surrey, who survived a flying miracle on a par with that Derek Sharp had experienced in Tuscaloosa. In June 1945, Flying Officer Wright bailed out of a tailless North American P-51 of 126 Squadron. At about six hundred miles per hour, he landed in an oak tree, then a hedge, skidded into a grain field and survived with minor injuries.

Wright with his several classmates, including David Howell of Glasgow, Scotland, were regularly entertained with food and conversation at the Hotel McLester by Dr. George Lang, who held a chair in philosophy at the University of Alabama. Dr. Lang was noted for paying the hotel to serve free coffee to all British cadets who visited there. After the war, Dr. Lang sent food parcels to Wright's parents and to him and his wife. Professor Lang visited Wright and his wife in England every year until he died. Such were the bonds of friendship that were firmly established by many British cadets and American citizens.

Other RAF cadets were Arthur W. Fearn of Chilwell, Nottingham, who had been an inspector of armored cars and tanks at the Chilwell Arsenal before entering the RAF. Fearn ultimately flew two tours of operations on Lancaster bombers with 57 and 617 Squadrons, and won a Distinguished Flying Cross. Geoffrey F. Snow of Wallington, Surrey; George A. Stone of Hythe, Southampton, Hampshire; and Henry Bull of Ayrshire, Scotland, all had distinguished war records, and after the war became airline pilots. Cadet David Howell of Glasgow, Scotland, enjoyed all of his experiences in the United States and made many friends; he spoke often of gardening on Tuscaloosa's RAF radio program, and he also came to know Professor Lang of the University of Alabama. Howell washed out of pilot training at Tuscaloosa, returned to Canada and was posted to Coral Gables, Florida, for training as a navigator. Subsequently, Howell flew on Stirling aircraft of 218 Squadron, won a DFC and became a prisoner of war.

In late February 1942, Robert Reginald Farrow and 123 other RAF students arrived in Tuscaloosa and joined 5 men from previous classes who had been held over to continue training. The 129 RAF students were designated Class SE-42-H. Farrow's instructor had a reputation for being tough. Out of six pupils for flying instruction—three in the morning, three in the afternoon—he failed five and was known as "Washout Wade." During Farrow's brief stay at Tuscaloosa, he made many friends at the University of Alabama and, although he went solo, he was eliminated from pilot training and was sent back to Moncton in Canada to be remustered to other aircrew training. Bob Farrow was assigned to training as a wireless operator/air gunner and joined an RAF draft that traveled southward by rail to the U.S. Naval Air Station at Jacksonville, Florida.

Thomas C. Overend of Ayrshire, Scotland, also had the misfortune of being eliminated from Class SE-42-H at Tuscaloosa. He too was sent back to Canada, where he was remustered to other aircrew duties. Forty-two years afterward, with understandable mixed feelings, he described his experiences as a trainee pilot in America. He thoroughly enjoyed the heat and, with others of his classmates, recalled shocking local people by lying in the Alabama sun in the "cool" of March and April 1942.

Although he and his classmates also enjoyed the cafeteria-style self-service dining hall, they could soon easily predict meals because of the lack of very much variation in the menus. Barracks at the school were very comfortable with four men to a room, "each person with a bed and chest of drawers, all highly polished," but it soon became obvious how and by whom the dusting and polishing was done. Overend thought the alternating morning and afternoon training schedules was an orderly, workable system.

Although he recognized and accepted the fact that he and his classmates were enrolled in an American rather than a British school, Overend believed, with others of his contemporaries, that order and discipline were carried too far. In retrospect, the West Point–type discipline "where leadership was secondary to blind obedience," Overend felt, "was a form of hyper-discipline, not at all suited to wartime training." Although he did not personally object to the orderliness essential for lockers and other kits, many RAF students who were less prone to neatness found it a constant trial, especially if they walked tours regularly as a penalty for sloppiness.

Why many of the RAF classes at the Tuscaloosa primary flying school experienced anti-British views is unknown. With the university there and a strong military tradition dating back more than a century, one would expect it to be different. However, precisely because the University of Alabama had a more sophisticated population than surrounding counties may well account for what Overend and others called "mixed feelings." As he recalled, while most people in Tuscaloosa and other Alabama towns were kind and friendly, there were two vocal elements who appeared to be anti-British in sentiment. One group believed that Britain had "once again dragged America into a war," and another expressed the view that the United States once more had to "help pull Europe out of the mire."

However these sentiments were articulated, they were manifestations of resentment. They were the same sentiments that were cloaked with other words and accents that American servicemen encountered in Britain during the war. Just as many British citizens resented the fact that some

British girls found the Americans attractive and different ("overpaid, oversexed, and over here"), many people in the United States resented the fact that American girls found the young RAF types attractive. The words hardly masked the true feelings, especially in a university town.

For the RAF cadets, the University of Alabama sometimes provided the means for a social life. Officers of the educational institution issued "regular invitations to students' activities, concerts, barbecues, sporting occasions" and, as Thomas Overend remembered, "some of us always took part." Churches in and around Tuscaloosa also attempted to welcome the British students as often as possible. Understandably, there was a considerable amount of what sociologists refer to as culture shock. The young visitors were shocked at the practice of racial segregation. Overend recalled the "two-part buses in which whites sat in front, and the occasional outraged argument erupted when one or two of us Brits had the temerity to sit in the Jim Crow department rather than wait for the next bus."

Of many experiences gathered and savored from being thrust into a different world, different culture and much heat, none was perhaps more disturbing than seeing "appalling conditions, but where, despite the apparent poverty, new chevvies and Oldsmobiles would be parked outside." But one experience that obviously delighted Overend and his friends was described as follows:

> Whilst wandering about a somewhat seedy part of Tuscaloosa one Sunday morning, we chanced upon a small red-painted Negro church, where from within came the most soulful singing I had ever heard. We sat there fascinated by this, and as time passed, it developed into a frenzy of sound and a performance that would be accepted today in Carnegie Hall.

When Overend and his classmates of Class SE-42-H completed primary training on 28 April 1942, eight men were held over for further training, forty-three students were eliminated from pilot training and eighty-three graduated and were posted to Gunter Field Basic Flying School.

Class SE-42-I arrived at the Tuscaloosa flying school on 31 March 1942, within a few days after Class SE-42-G graduated. Since 7 December 1941, all RAF and USAAF pilot training had been intensified. Instead of the standard ten-week course and five and a half days per week, most flying training now continued seven days per week and was completed in eight weeks, after which students received a few days' leave before reporting to the next phase of training. Even with the inclusion of leave time within the training schedule, the entire pilot course had now been reduced to twenty-six or twenty-seven weeks, instead of thirty.

When the Defense Plant Corporation purchased most primary schools, thereby relieving contractors of their investment in war projects, the Parks organization refused to sell its Tuscaloosa school, and also refused to make essential improvements. On 10 March 1942, Lieutenant Andrew J. Kinney, commanding officer at the Tuscaloosa school, requested a reduction in the number of students being posted to the Alabama Institute of Aeronautics. Kinney asserted that no more than seventy cadets should be sent until "all improvements are made." Although he evidently did not intend to sell the Alabama school, the contractor's response to the request for recreational facilities was that he hesitated because the DPC might purchase the school.

Indications of political influence emerged when the unit history asserted that the school ws being improved "despite the limitations imposed by the War Production Board." Another fiction evidently intended to please the contractor was a further assertion that the "smooth operation" of the detachment was attributed to "the complete and willing cooperation between Air Corps and civilian supervisors." The AIA contractor was noted for always doing the absolute minimum, but the excellent reputation of the ground and flying instructional staffs prevented cancellation of their contract.

Although there were undoubtedly many others, there was at least one RAF student who completed primary pilot training at the Tuscaloosa school in about seven instead of eight or nine weeks. Just as his draft was formed into groups at the Turner Field Replacement Center in order to be posted with Class SE-42-I, Gordon John Cadman became ill and was hospitalized. Instead of reporting on 31 March, Cadman did not arrive at Tuscaloosa until the end of the first week in April 1942.

Forty-two years later, from his home in Sussex, Cadman described that early training experience:

> With the help of a kind and considerate hospital staff and an understanding RAF liaison officer, I made my way by Greyhound coach to Tuscaloosa, Alabama, a week late. My instructor was Mr. Kulzer, and after several hours instruction, I was sent solo on 16 April 1942 and ground-looped on landing! Mr. Kulzer said I had the basic ability, but lacked confidence, so he assigned me to another instructor, Mr. Kalb, and I never looked back. I soloed successfully on 22 April and graduated from primary on 27 May 1942.
>
> I found the people of Tuscaloosa most friendly and hospitable—I spent many pleasant days or parts of days as guest of a local family. I was amazed at the number of people of British stock in the region—surnames such as Green, Brown, Johnson, Stevens, Robinson, Black, Jones, etc. abounded—rather like thumbing through the London Telephone Directory. Our reception by school personnel was more mixed—generally it was good, but there were occasions when remarks such as "goddammed colonialists…defeat at Dunkirk" and other similar jibes were uttered, but, even so, our reception was generally good, warm and friendly.
>
> After graduating from Primary, on the very next day, I flew from Birmingham to New York in a DC-3 to visit my Uncle Bill Sterritt who worked for Bell Telephones and lived in a quite palatial flat in New York. After several memorable days of seeing the sights and travelling to Buffalo and Niagara Falls, I returned to Tuscaloosa in time to gather my kit bag and move to the basic flying school at Montgomery, Alabama.

Including 8 men who were transferred from the preceding class, there were 120 RAF students in Class SE-42-I at Tuscaloosa. Of that number, 5 were held over to continue training, 49 were eliminated and 66 graduated.

Near the midpoint in Class SE-42-I's primary flying course, Class SE-42-H graduated and left for basic flying school, and ninety-nine new RAF students arrived from the RAF acclimatization course at Turner Field, Georgia. The new draft was designated Class SE-42-J. In an effort to reduce the number of eliminees at the Alabama Institute of Aeronautics, two RAF pilot officers were assigned to that primary school. Pilot officers were Denys Ding and C.J.C. Manning, both of whom had completed the primary flying course at the Tuscaloosa school as members of Class SE-42-D. They had recently completed their advanced pilot training, received commissions and, according to an experiment begun at several primary schools in February 1942 with several Class SE-42-A graduates, were assigned to their alma mater. Three other pilot officers would join them later.

In an even rarer instance, Pilot Officer C.J.C. Manning was able to have his wife join him. C.J.C. "Johnnie" Manning had been born in Barbados, British West Indies, in 1913. Audrie

Manning, his wife, who was three years younger, had also been born there. In April 1942, following his graduation at Maxwell Field, Manning and several of his classmates were permitted a brief leave before returning for the wings ceremony. At that time, they were also commissioned and were told that they would be assigned as instructors in an American flying school for at least six months. Immediately, Manning informed Audrie, who had remained in Barbados with their two small daughters, and the young couple made plans for her to join him during his six-month instructor's tour in Alabama.

Fortunately for the Mannings, Audrie Manning's mother, who had been bombed out of her London flat, had come to Barbados to live with them. As a result, once Manning received permission for his wife to join him, Audrie quickly prepared to travel to the United States while her mother kept the children in Barbados. She managed to get to Trinidad, where she caught the regular Pan American Clipper from there to Baltimore. Audrie recalled that the flying boat was "roomy and luxurious and had Pullman bunks and excellent service." The other passengers were "Diplomats and King's Messengers," and the journey to New York took about twenty hours.

After landing and sending her husband a telegram before catching a train, Audrie traveled south to Montgomery, Alabama. On the train, an elderly Southern gentleman was so concerned that she might not be met at the station that he told Audrie that he would ask his wife to come there and offer her the hospitality of their home. In the meantime, he would contact the commanding officer of Maxwell Field, who was a personal friend. Audrie Manning was to write many years later, "It was the first of many kindnesses which were shown to me in particular and the R.A.F. personnel in general."

Johnnie Manning did meet his wife at the station, but at first he thought the telegram was a hoax. He did not understand how his wife could possibly reach Montgomery that quickly from Barbados. He had just returned from an "end of course" leave in New York where he and several other newly commissioned RAF pilot officers had been royally entertained by one of many patriotic organizations in that city. They were shown the town, but the most outstanding event was being given tickets to see Gertrude Lawrence in *Blithe Spirit* and going to meet her in her dressing room afterward.

Shortly after his wife arrived in Montgomery, Johnnie Manning attended the wings ceremony at Maxwell Field, and Audrie watched as Lieutenant General Henry H. Arnold awarded class members their wings. When Johnnie and other newly promoted RAF pilot officers left for Toronto, Canada, to receive regulation RAF officers' uniforms, Audrie traveled by Greyhound coach to Miami, Florida, to stay with friends there. While in Miami, despite the war, she was able to go tarpon fishing off the coast of Florida and, with the luck of the neophyte, she caught one!

Years later, she recalled that during her stay in Miami, it was impossible to completely escape the war, because one could "hear explosions out at sea and see the oil slick, which meant yet another ship blown-up." After Audrie returned from Miami and met Johnnie, they traveled to his duty station at the Alabama Institute of Aeronautics at Tuscaloosa, the same primary school where Johnnie had completed his primary flying training. Now the Mannings discovered a small Southern town, and the town discovered them.

As in much of small-town America during that era, virtually the entire population was very careful to be identified with a particular church and to maintain the reputation of being good citizens and Christians. Life went on much the same as anywhere else, except that there were a number of social taboos that newcomers were compelled to learn quickly and were careful not to violate, because violation of these taboos meant almost certain social ostracism.

Most of the American military and civil personnel at the flying school had their families with them, but the only other British couple in the town besides the Mannings were Flight Lieutenant Arthur T. Grime, the RAFAO, and his wife. The two British women were quite conspicuous when they went about the town together shopping or just walking. All of the townspeople were kindly, but Audrie Manning recalled that a family named Little were exceptionally so. Mr. and Mrs. Little lived with their two daughters and a niece in an antebellum house where the "Welcome" that was printed on the doormat was sincerely applied in relations with the British visitors. The Mannings and many RAF cadets from the nearby primary flying school enjoyed the informality, good food and happy family atmosphere of the Little home. "I don't know what I would have done without the Littles," Audrie Manning wrote many years later. "Through them we found our apartment, they lent us linen and pots and pans, introduced us to their friends, instructed me in the ways of the Deep South, encouraged me to go to classes at the University of Alabama, and generally befriended us."

Occasionally, they went with a larger group to a roadhouse out of town to "watch and join in with some fantastic jiving." Then there were picnics on the Black Warrior River and visits to Moundsville, the site of an ancient tribe of American Indian mound builders who, a thousand years earlier, had developed a town site among an unusual group of hills along the river a few miles south of Tuscaloosa. And then came the day when John Manning got permission to take Audrie on a flight in the open cockpit Stearman, with strict instructions "on no account to be sick and let the Brits down." She didn't.

Because of Johnnie's check pilot flying and assistant engineer ground duties, Audrie Manning was understandably alone much of the time, but she found many activities to occupy her. She spoke to two ladies' clubs in the town. Considering the relationship between the United States and Britain in 1941–42, it was perhaps natural that a British subject should be asked to address the local chapter of the Daughters of the American Revolution (DAR). Audrie Manning also joined an American Red Cross group, which made bandages and swabs for sterilization and shipment overseas.

Since she and her husband came from a racially mixed community in Barbados, they were not surprised by the strict segregation of blacks and whites in Alabama in 1942, but they observed how shocked others from north of the Mason-Dixon line were. Johnnie Manning was compelled to buy an automobile with which to travel to and from work, a round trip of about ten miles daily, but that requirement strained the financial resources of the young couple. An RAF pilot officer simply was not paid very much money monthly, even with flying and overseas pay allowances, so they were often unable to buy gasoline for their car, even at less than twenty cents a gallon, as it was then. Perhaps even more difficult was the problem of window shopping and seeing so many items in shops, yet being unable to buy them.

The Manning apartment became a rendezvous on weekends for British officers who were serving at various naval and air stations in the region. It proved to be a nice setting for the entertainment of new friends such as Dr. Sandy Levine of New York, the medical officer (MO) at the Alabama Institute of Aeronautics. The young British couple managed occasional weekend jaunts to New Orleans or Mobile, or a simple evening out to dine in the McLester Hotel in Tuscaloosa.

In September 1942, on completion of his duty assignment at Tuscaloosa and before reporting to RAF No. 31 Personnel Depot at Moncton, New Brunswick, for shipment to Britain, Manning and his wife flew to Barbados for a two-week family leave. Audrie remained in Barbados with her two daughters until 1943, when she was fortunate enough to get passage aboard a ship traveling to Britain. The ship stopped off in New York for a brief time before continuing the journey in convoy, and she "met with great kindness, particularly from one taxi driver, who drove me around to see the sights for free, because, as usual, I was short of dollars."

Audrie Manning proceeded on to Britain, where she joined her husband, an instructor at RAF Burnaston, an elementary flying training school (EFTS) near Derby in the English Midlands. In 1944, Flying Officer Manning finally got an operational assignment with 77 Squadron and flew Halifax bombers on thirty-eight missions over enemy territory. Shortly after Germany surrendered in May 1945, Manning, then a flight lieutenant and thirty-two years old, was discharged and returned with his wife to Barbados. Some years later, they moved back to England.

Anthony E. Vidler and his Class SE-42-J RAF draft departed from Turner Field, Georgia, in a "fleet of coaches" on the morning of 30 April 1942 and arrived in Tuscaloosa that evening at 9:30. On 1 May, Vidler recorded in his diary that he "went out for an hour in Tuscaloosa with Bonnie Boardman, Bob Woodall, and Ron Burnett. 'Smashing friendly girls.' I remember some of the local young U.S. males weren't too keen on us!" On Sunday, 3 May, Tony Vidler reported sick with a rash; it was diagnosed as German measles, and he was removed to the huge Veterans Administration Hospital in Tuscaloosa. After he was discharged from the hospital on 19 May, he commenced flying on 21 May with his instructor, W.E. Spotts.

Vidler enjoyed the food and accommodation on-post and the hospitality off-post, but on 5 June, after slightly more than nine hours of flying instruction, he had an elimination check flight with Mr. Garl and Pilot Officer Manning and was eliminated. Whether they were his true feelings at the time or later rationalizations, he adopted a realistic view toward what happened to him: "I don't think I would've made a good pilot anyway. The upper/lower class system was probably appropriate for U.S. cadets—straight from civilian life to flying school and needing discipline as officer cadets. But we were not officer cadets and had already had up to 1 year having rough edges knocked off by disciplinary NCOs." On 16 June 1942, Tony Vidler departed by train for Canada to be remustered to another aircrew category.

By July 1942, according to the unit history of the USAAF flying training detachment at Hargrove van de Graaf Field, Link Trainer simulators were introduced into primary schools. Since the first intake at the Alabama Institute of Aeronautics early in July 1939, the number of Stearman PT-17 biplane trainer aircraft had gradually increased from seventeen to sixty and the number of civilian employees from 35 to 183. In addition, the USAAF staff and student enrollment had more than doubled. However, the number of RAF students sent to Tuscaloosa had been reduced for Classes SE-42-I and SE-42-J, and would be reduced even further for the final three RAF drafts sent from the Turner Field RAF replacement depot in Georgia.

The seventy-eight members of Class SE-42-K arrived in Tuscaloosa from Turner Field during the last week in May and, with five men held over from the preceding class, commenced flying training on 3 June 1942. Among members of that class were LACs George W. Childs, Stan Chadwick and Eddie Colton. These three RAF cadets, better known as "The Unholy Three," were accomplished evaders of regulations and, except for USAAF discipline, apparently enjoyed their stay in the United States. Sadly, Chadwick and Colton were killed during the war.

Childs survived to continue flying as an airline captain with British Airways until his retirement in 1975. Reminiscing about his wartime American training, Childs, with twenty hours of flying logged, recalled a unique experience while shooting stages at Rice Field, a satellite of the main airdrome:

On the last landing, a cumulo nimbus was over the field and I had a strong cross wind. Billy Miller [American civilian instructor] was sitting on the fence. I lost control. The aircraft spun round with the wing hitting the ground & dust all over the place. Centrifugal force threw me outwards and as I put my arm out for protection, my sleeve caught the throttle & it all got worse. I told myself to close the throttle, for then it must all stop. It did.

Billy Miller came over with a wry smile on his face, inspected the plane & said that we could fly back to Hargrove van de Graaf (Tuscaloosa). Then, he looked at me and said, "you did the right thing…full throttle and opposite rudder." Back at Hargrove, I was taken in to the chief instructor who wanted to see this only 20 hour real natural pilot who, when caught in a strong crosswind, instinctively applied full throttle & opposite rudder. Perhaps they were right, since I didn't have another accident in the next thirty-four years of flying! How life's courses hang on a thread.

Of the eighty-one net RAF enrollment for Class SE-42-K, two students were held over, thirty-three were eliminated and forty-eight successfully completed primary training.

During the months in which RAF cadets underwent training at Tuscaloosa, the town had changed very little. Its population remained at about twenty thousand, and the university student body remained at around five thousand. Gasoline rationing reduced travel, so there was very little entertainment available. The bowling alley and the four motion picture theatres were popular and always busy. The Bama Theater still showed the best films; the Druid showed "B" pictures; the Ritz showed cowboy films; and the Diamond was reserved for blacks. Often, the British cadets walked about Tuscaloosa with new friends and just talked. Sometimes three or four cadets would join five or six male and female university students, and they would go to someone's house to play charades or word games and to sing RAF songs. Occasionally, such groups met at one of the drugstores for Cokes.

Around 1 July 1942, the seventy-three-member draft designated Class SE-43-A arrived at Tuscaloosa from Turner Field and commenced flying on 7 July. Of the total enrollment of seventy-five RAF students in that class, four were held over, thirty-five were washed out and thirty-six graduated in early September 1942.

The final draft of RAF students to be trained at the Alabama Institute of Aeronautics were sixty-five new arrivals from Turner Field who joined the four men held over from SE-43-A. Among the members of Class SE-43-B was John Clark, one of "Trenchard's brats," a former RAF fitter who had been trained at Halton, the famous RAF technical school. Among other pupils were Albert E. Moulder of Gloucestershire, Frederick John Evans of Havorfordwest, Harry "Jack" Richardson of Surrey and John McKenzie-Hall of Australia.

On completion of pilot training in the United States, McKenzie-Hall was commissioned and assigned as a pilot officer flying instructor first at an American advanced flying school at Eagle Pass, Texas, then at British Flying Training School No. 1 at Terrell, Texas. Subsequently, McKenzie-Hall had a distinguished career in the RAF and Fleet Air Arm, and was finally assigned to the Queen's Flight on helicopters.

Some forty-two years later, McKenzie-Hall provided an excellent description of his primary flying school experiences with Class SE-43-B:

In early August 1942, groups were formed, and I joined 65 RAF cadets and 51 Americans to make up the contingent of Class 43-B at the Tuscaloosa, Alabama primary school. There were no tents this time but dormitories with polished wooden floors and furnished with tubular metal double-stacked beds, metal cabinets, and wooden tables and chairs with study lamps between each set of beds.

In addition to the regular American cadets, we also had a number of Americans who had transferred from the RCAF to the USAAF. We were introduced to Major Kinney, C.O., and Mr. Gammon, Director of Ground School. Our Chief Flying Instructor was Mr. G. Reavis Nelson. There were some 11 USAAF officers and one RAF flying officer, P/O C.J.C. Manning.

My first flying instructor on the PT-17 biplane was E.L. Raynor, but after three hours, 45 minutes of unadulterated hell for both of us, he threw in the towel. Fortunately, I was transferred to Mr. Henry, and unlike Mr. Raynor, he not only believed in ground briefing before a flight, but also in the simple method of building up confidence through gentle in-flight demonstrations of the aircraft's attitudes and controls, and clear-cut in-flight explanation of maneuvers required.

Tuscaloosa was a small dusty, sleepy town with mainly wooden buildings where, in the hot mid-afternoon sun, we sought refuge in a drugstore to cool down with chocolate malted milk and ice cream. I met an extremely nice farming family called Strobel, and spent very relaxing hours at their small wood-built home. I visited Bessemer and saw the steel works, and went into Birmingham to see the night life which, at this time, we could not afford.

On post, activities never ceased, and once again, the upperclassmen descended upon us underclassmen. The British contingent stood the indignities for a week or so and then rebelled against the system by confining themselves to the dormitory and refusing as a whole to undertake further training until "hazing" stopped. Two days later, successful RAF Liaison took place, and from then onwards, I cannot remember further clashes between senior and junior classes.

Link trainer practice was encouraged, and Sergeant Gibson was very effective in imparting to me a very sound basic knowledge. Much of my success firstly as a night-fighter pilot, then an instrument examiner, and finally a transport pilot stemmed from this early interest in the psychological approach to instrument flying.

As with many others, McKenzie-Hall's American flying training led to a career in aviation.

The members of Class SE-43-B completed their flying and were preparing to go on a short leave prior to departing for the USAAF basic flying school at Gunter Field near Montgomery. In order to salute Tuscaloosa's final RAF class, the University of Alabama prepared their marching bands to entertain the fans attending football games during a halftime intermission. The RAF guests were seated in a special section of the Denny Stadium for the football game between the University of Alabama and Mississippi State University.

On that bright, sunny Saturday afternoon, 3 October 1942, the British guests gained some new experiences. In the midst of a storm of noise and cheering, they observed pretty cheerleaders, tough-looking well-padded players and waving banners, and became as confused as Americans usually did at British cricket matches. Halftime activities at that particular American football game included the loud and stirring music of two university bands, and on that memorable occasion, the University of Alabama formally introduced their new pep song entitled "Hail Alabama," and the band played it with gusto.

It was appropriate that "Hail Alabama" should be played; those were the sentiments of quite a number of the graduating RAF and American cadets who had trained together for ten weeks. The University of Alabama band, which was directed by Colonel Carleton K. Butler, also played a tribute to both British and American aviation cadets who were in training at the Alabama Institute of Aeronautics at Tuscaloosa. Of that final sixty-nine-man RAF contingent, a part of Class SE-43-B, one student died following surgery, twenty were eliminated from pilot training and forty-nine went on leave for a few days before returning to graduate on 7 October 1942.

Although civilian instructor Carl Knauer had been killed and several RAF cadets had been injured in aircraft accidents during the sixteen months in which British cadets were trained at the Alabama Institute of Aeronautics, only one fatality occurred among the British student pilots. On 4 October 1942, Kenneth McGregor Moore, a twenty-six-year-old cadet from Willowfield, Londonderry, Northern Ireland, died following surgery in a Birmingham, Alabama hospital. As former classmates were arriving at the USAAF basic flying school at Gunter Field a few days later, Moore's body was interred in the RAF plot of the Oakwood Cemetery Annex high on a hill overlooking the Alabama River in the heart of Montgomery.

Between 8 June 1941 and 7 October 1942, thirteen classes containing 1,254 RAF pilot trainees were enrolled in the Alabama Institute of Aeronautics. Of that number, 758 men (60.45 percent) successfully completed the course.

Of the 497 RAF pilot trainees (39.55 percent) who failed to complete pilot training at Tuscaloosa, 450, or 35.89 percent (an average of 35 for each of the thirteen classes), were washed out for flying deficiencies and 46 cadets (3.57 percent) were eliminated for "other than flying deficiencies."

The lowest number of eliminated cadets occurred in the first and last RAF classes, SE-42-A and SE-43-B, with nineteen and ten, respectively. The highest number of RAF cadets eliminated at the Alabama Institute of Aeronautics occurred in classes SE-42-E and SE-42-F, with sixty-four and fifty-seven, respectively.

In an effort to reduce wastage, it is worthwhile to note that seven of the thirteen Arnold Scheme classes (Classes SE-42-G through SE-43-B) underwent flight grading courses in Britain. There they flew Tiger Moth biplanes for from ten to thirty-six hours before sailing to North America. They also underwent four weeks of acclimatization training before being assigned to a USAAF primary flying school. Similarly, the American Civilian Pilot Training Program (CPTP) and some College Training Detachments (CTDs) allowed USAAF aircrew students to complete twenty-five or more flying hours in light aircraft before entering army or navy primary training schools.

Another indication of problems that beset Classes SE-42-E and SE-42-F is that they recorded the greatest number of eliminated cadets (ten and nine, respectively) for "other than flying deficiencies," a phrase usually reserved for either medical or disciplinary problems. Perhaps some significance attaches to the fact that both of these classes were undergoing primary training when the Japanese attacked Pearl Harbor. At that time, flying training was immediately intensified, and leisure time for students undergoing training all but disappeared for several weeks.

After 7 October 1942, the Alabama Institute of Aeronautics continued training USAAF aviation cadets, student officers and aviation students (enlisted student pilots). However, in July 1943, French student pilots were also assigned to the Tuscaloosa flying school. Flying and ground school instructors were assigned to French classes at night. Americans continued in training alongside French students through Class SE-44-D. More than 1,200 French pilots were trained at Tuscaloosa over a period of thirteen months. French student casualties were interred in a section close by RAF casualties in Montgomery, Alabama's Oakwood Cemetery Annex.

According to the USAAF unit history, conditions at the Tuscaloosa flying school worsened during the last twelve months of its existence. Maintenance of aircraft declined because the company refused to hire sufficient staff. USAAF commanders and technical inspectors attempted without success to gain the cooperation of the contractor's representative. Sadly, months before the school closed in September 1944, contractor cooperation with military staff returned to the miserable status of its early years. On 28 July 1944, USAAF Flying Training Command notified officials of the Alabama Institute of Aeronautics that the school would close in August 1944, and that French pilot training would be shifted to Orangeburg, South Carolina.

WHERE HAVE ALL THE RAF CADETS GONE?

42-A. HARRY REED, nineteen (Tuscaloosa, Gunter, Selma). Following additional training in Britain, he was assigned to 533 Squadron flying turbinlite night fighters. Later, Reed flew Mosquito aircraft with 264 and 169 Squadrons. During the war, Flight Lieutenant Reed was credited with the destruction of two enemy aircraft and was awarded the DFC. He logged 1,340 hours flying time.

42-B. SIR ARTHUR GORDON NORMAN, twenty-four, of Shanghai, China (Tuscaloosa, Gunter, Maxwell). Following additional training in Britain, he joined 295 Squadron in North Africa and flew numerous sorties in North Africa, Sicily and Italy. Subsequently, Norman flew SOE sorties with 298 Squadron and 644 Squadron in Europe. Wing Commander Norman was knighted, was twice awarded the Distinguished Flying Cross (DFC with bar) and logged almost two thousand hours of flying time.

42-D. GORDON KENNETH FRANK WADE, twenty-one, of Birmingham (Tuscaloosa, Gunter, Maxwell). Following additional training in Britain for Bomber Command assignment, he joined 10 Squadron and flew four-engine Halifax bombers on thirty sorties. Following his combat flying, Wade served as an instructor in a conversion unit. Toward the end of the war, he was assigned to 242 Squadron in the Air Transport Command. Flight Lieutenant G.K.F. Wade was awarded the DFC and logged more than two thousand hours' flying time. In the postwar era, he became an airline pilot, and from 1946 to 1972 he flew for Aer Lingus. From 1972 to 1982, Captain Wade flew for Britannia Airways. In all, he logged about twenty thousand hours of flying time.

42-F. DAVID JOHN PRICE MATTHEWS (Tuscaloosa, Gunter, Selma). After receiving additional training in Britain, Matthews joined 154 Squadron in North Africa and flew Spitfires in North Africa, Malta, Sicily, Italy, Cyprus, Sardinia and Elba. During World War II, he was credited with destroying five enemy aircraft in 180 operational sorties. Flight Lieutenant Matthews was awarded the DFC, continued service in the Royal Air Force and served as an exchange pilot with the U.S. Marines at El Toro, California.

42-F. SIDNEY JAMES PERKINS, eighteen, of Buckden, Huntingdonshire (Tuscaloosa, Gunter, Maxwell). Following additional training in Britain, he flew fighter aircraft with 268, 2 and 16 Squadrons. Postwar, Group Captain S.J. Perkins, OBE, AFC, MiD, served as a test pilot at Boscombe Down and went on to command 85 Squadron.

42-H. GORDON MACDONALD BRAIDWOOD, twenty, of Leeds, Yorkshire (Tuscaloosa, Gunter, Selma). Following additional training in Britain, Braidwood was commissioned pilot officer and joined 126 Squadron flying Spitfires and Mustangs. Flight Lieutenant G.M. Braidwood, DFC, also flew with 74 Squadron from Malta, Sicily and Italy, and was credited with destroying six enemy aircraft during 209 sorties. Postwar, he studied at Leeds University and served in HM Diplomatic Service from 1948 to 1979.

CHAPTER EIGHT

RESPONSES TO THE WASHOUT RATE IN THE UNITED STATES

THE FOUR GEORGIA AND FLORIDA PRIMARY FLIGHT SCHOOLS

SOUTHER FIELD
AMERICUS, GEORGIA, 42-E-42-G

During the afternoon of Wednesday, 5 November 1941, the three Central of Georgia rail cars bearing the one-hundred-man Class SE-42-E and their baggage arrived from Maxwell Field, where its members had undergone the initial acclimatization course. As the new class arrived, the west runway was being paved with asphalt and other construction was underway. Although a few members of the new class hailed from other parts of the British Isles, most of them came from England. Prior employment among class members ranged from student and ex-serviceman to schoolmaster, draughtsman, architect and engineer. Several of the young men had worked in the post office or in other civil service posts, and a few of them had been employed in industry.

During early November 1941, Souther Field had almost two hundred cadets in training and, since flying instructors were apparently reluctant to take their charges to the auxiliary field for practice, flying conditions deteriorated at the main airdrome, and congestion became a serious problem. The Graham Company failed in its attempt to purchase a piece of land adjacent to Souther Field. However, the company did purchase a large tract of land south of Plains, Georgia, which was intended for use as a satellite airfield. However, since Americus lacked sufficient housing for additional staff, USAAF flying training command was reluctant to approve the purchase.

When the members of Class SE-42-E arrived at Souther Field, they discovered that the cadet billets in the long barracks were divided into bays with a dozen wooden bunks in each bay. With its coin-operated Coca-Cola machines, piano, radio, short-wave wireless receiver, easy chairs and variety of magazines, the student lounge within the barracks was very comfortable. Regularly, the British cadets listened to BBC and local radio broadcasts. They became fascinated with the tone and delivery of the radio advertisements as well as the maddening repetition of hillbilly songs on local commercial radio stations.

Although fields, courts and pitches for playing softball, football, basketball and volleyball required only a small investment and a minimum of equipment, Souther Field was not yet well-endowed with outdoor recreational facilities. Except on Wednesdays, when the cadets swam in the heated swimming pool at Georgia Southwestern College, the physical training ritual almost every morning included calisthenics, or warm-up exercises, followed by a variety of games. For leisure time, the cadet recreation room, which was located near the dining hall, was equipped with a number of games, including table tennis, cards, chess and darts.

It was good that at least some games and limited sports facilities existed on the airfield, as there was little recreation to be found off-post. However friendly the citizens of Americus and other small Southern towns close by flying training airfields, all of the towns were notorious for their lack of recreation facilities. During the summer months, there were adequate opportunities for swimming in a nearby lake and picnics, but in wintertime, with only one cinema and a small bowling alley available, indoor recreation was severely limited. In a letter home, one RAF cadet described the town as follows: "Americus once was a one-horse town, but the horse died. There are only three things to do; go to the one and only picture house, go to the bowling alley, or the drug store."

With the enlarged RAF classes, which were almost double the size of the first three classes, it became more and more difficult for the relatively small population to entertain all of the young men in their homes. The United Services Organization (USO) operated canteens and organized recreation and travel assistance near major wartime bases, but efforts to establish a USO in the small town of Americus failed. The community took another approach. James McKinley, field representative of the Farm Security Agency (FSA), announced plans to meet any interested groups at the Windsor Hotel to assist in planning a downtown recreation center for the cadets.

Transportation was as critical a problem in Americus and Souther Field as it was at numerous other wartime training airfields. If the cadets decided to take advantage of the "open post" available to them on Friday nights, or the period extending from Saturday noon until early Sunday evening, they could either hitchhike or pay fifteen cents for a truck ride into Americus. The return fare was the same rate. The truck normally returned to the airfield before meals were served at the station dining hall and made its final Saturday run at midnight. On Sundays, a truck left Souther Field early enough to deliver the men to church and returned after church hours. Those men who remained in town during Sunday afternoon were usually able to reach the airfield quickly by hitchhiking.

On 17 December 1941, the 103-man Class SE-42-F arrived from Maxwell Field wearing their RAF blue uniforms. They were the first class to enter the United States who had not been issued the gray woolen suits for wear when off-post. Although members of Class SE-42-E had been wearing their RAF uniforms since 7 December, RAF blue became a much more common sight around Americus, Georgia, by Christmas 1941. The new arrivals commenced flying training immediately and, with their arrival, USAAF training policy changed dramatically. Until further notice, flying training would be carried out seven days per week, and the training time was reduced from ten to eight weeks.

Despite plans by the citizens of Americus to entertain the RAF cadets during Christmas, the entire class was restricted to Souther Field. Although Christmas gifts from townspeople were delivered to the primary school, it was not the same. Risking being caught and washed out of training, LACs Geoffrey Perks and Ron Sullivan climbed a fence and started walking toward town. They must have had quite a scare when an automobile identical to that of the commanding officer of Souther Field rolled to a stop on the road alongside them. However, when the complete stranger offered them a ride into Americus, they breathed a sigh of relief and quickly accepted.

When the class was nearing the end of training, an editorial staff was selected to compile and publish the class magazine. This group included Bryan S. McCann, editor; Edward Slinger, assistant editor; Philip C. Williams, art editor; and Roy Parker, office boy. The magazine staff was able to persuade a number of men to submit materials, and LAC Charles R. Parker produced an amusing page. Although his article had special application for men trained at Souther Field, it could well have been adapted to each of the six primary flying schools:

The Cadet's Ten Commandments

1. Thou shalt not make errors in Form #1, lest a fair damsel request conversation with thee.

2. Thou shalt not fail to return thy parachute to the appointed place, lest it be damaged by the elements and thou receive due retribution.

3. Thou shalt not sleep on thy master's time, neither shalt thou ask foolish questions lest no answer be forthcoming.

4. Thou shalt not bow down to adjust thy boot-lace after the klaxon hath sounded, neither shalt thou communicate by word of mouth with thy fellow man.

5. Honour thy Instructor that thy days may be long at Souther Field, and Moncton remain a reverie.

6. Thou shalt not covet thy neighbour's cap, nor his English cigarettes, nor anything that is his.

7. Thou shalt not fly to Fort Benning that they may kill the fatted calf for thee, lest thy fellow men become jealous.

8. Heed not the plea of thy classmate to indulge in follow the leader in the air, lest the camp become thy prison for many moons, and the soles of thy boots become thin.

9. Thou shalt not get thee to bed before the appointed hour, neither shalt thou lay abed, when thou shouldst be labouring for the cause.

10. Thou shalt not answer the Quiz either "Yea" or "Nay" of thy own accord, and refrain from wheedling the answer from the teacher lest thou be led astray.

Sadly, one page that the Class SE-42-E staff inserted announced that theirs was the final issue of the cadet magazine. For security reasons, there would be no future issues of the *Souther Cadet* or indeed of similar publications by most other flying schools.

In that final issue, LAC Gordon K. Thorne of Taunton, Somerset, produced a set of word-pictures that undoubtedly expressed some of the homesickness that descended on each of the RAF cadets in quiet moments as the Christmas season came to the Georgia airfield:

Oh! To Be In England
Just before I turn to sleep,
Oft my thoughts will roam
Away across the oceans deep,
Wondering what it's like at home.

Maybe rolling Yorkshire dales,
Are covered deep in snow,
Perhaps the siren's lonely wail,
Echoes through the streets of Bow.

Factories of Lancashire
Beneath a greyish heaven;
The moon that shines so frosty clear,
High over glorious Devon.

The waves dashing with a roar,

On Cornwall's rocky coast,
Skylarks that over Surrey soar,
Good beer—still England's boast.

The low hills of Somerset,
Misty blue at eventide,
The English sky at sunset,
The gentle countryside.

Then the lovely Sussex Downs,
That gave towards the sea,
All the countless Midland towns
Still guardians of our Liberty.

Is Fair England's garden,
Sleeping down in Kent;
Remember Shakespeare's Arden,
The Wye—The Thames—The Trent.

Vast endless Wiltshire plains,
Oh! Derby moors of blue,
Soon I'll be back again
To stay at home with you.

On 5 November 1941, when Class SE-42-E arrived at Souther Field, it had a net intake of ninety-nine RAF students. By the time the class departed for basic flying school on 14 January 1942, twenty of the students had been eliminated and seventy-nine graduated. That record represented one of the highest percentages of graduates among the RAF classes trained at Americus.

As the off-post recreation problem increased, Mrs. Herschel A. Smith agreed to chair a committee that would establish and operate a servicemen's club. Through church and social organizations, Mrs. Smith and other committee members were able to gain wide community support for their project. On the fourth floor of their building on Forsyth Street, the Bank of Commerce provided space (rent free) for the Servicemen's Center. Committee members solicited donations and collected furniture, a piano, magazines and other essential items, and the Servicemen's Center opened on 14 January 1942, the day that Class SE-42-E departed for basic flying training.

The surviving members of Class SE-42-F completed their primary flying training near the end of February 1942. To the 103 arrivals were added 3 men held over from the preceding class. During the afternoon and evening of 16 February, the Servicemen's Center sponsored a dance for the men of Class SE-42-F, and during the evening of 20 February, a farewell banquet was held for members of that class. Of that class's 106-man total, 3 men were held over to the next class, 37 were eliminated from pilot training and 66 graduated.

In January 1942, when the 101 men of Class SE-42-G arrived from their acclimatization course at Maxwell Field, the 3 men held over from the preceding class joined them, and the total enrollment for Class SE-42-G rose to 104. Primary flying training for that class took place during the winter months, and for most of the time they spent in Americus, the weather was cool and enjoyable. In March 1942, when the course ended, 26 of the 104 RAF cadets had been eliminated, 5 were held over to the next class and 73 graduated.

One week before the surviving members of Class SE-42-G graduated, several citizens of Americus suffered another tragedy involving an RAF student pilot. On Thursday evening, 5 March 1942, the day before his graduation from the USAAF advanced flying school at Napier Field, Alabama, twenty-five-year-old LAC Clarence Melville Johnson was injured in an automobile accident. It was thought that his injuries were not serious and that he would soon recover, but Johnson died on Saturday morning, 7 March. Members of the Frank P. Harrold family of Americus were devastated by the tragedy. Since the Harrolds had "adopted" Johnson while he was a member of Class SE-42-C at Souther Field, Mr. Harrold arranged through Flight Lieutenant Sir Anthony Lindsay-Hogg, the RAFAO at Napier Field, to have Johnson's body interred in Americus. The funeral was conducted in the Calvary Episcopal Church, and Johnson's body was interred in the Harrold family plot in Americus's Oak Grove Cemetery on 9 March 1942.

DARR AERO TECH
ALBANY, GEORGIA, 42-E-42-G

On 5 November, the 172 members of Class SE-42-E arrived at Darr Aero Tech, and their numbers were increased when they were joined by 2 of the 3 men held over from Class SE-42-D. When that large class arrived at the Albany train station, they were dressed in RAF blue winter uniforms and were met by a smiling khaki-clad Flight Lieutenant A.G. Hill. As a news photographer snapped a picture of the group and recorded it for posterity, the young men were crowded along the train station facing the tracks, some smiling, some unsmiling.

Thus far, their experiences had been different. The first four RAF drafts (Classes SE-42-A through SE-42-D) had traveled directly from the RCAF No. 1 Manning Depot in Canada to their primary schools. However, since so many men had been late in arriving at the primary schools, army air forces officers in Washington consulted RAFDEL and the Air Ministry seeking a solution to the problem. By October 1941, it had been decided that a pool of British trainees would be formed at the Aviation Cadet Replacement Depot at Maxwell Field, Alabama. On that station, the British trainee pilots, after completing a four-week-long acclimatization course, were to be distributed to primary schools to which they were scheduled to report.

The syllabus for that USAAF course allowed little free time and included a rigid physical training program, plenty of wholesome food, drill, ceremonies and inspections, something of American history, customs of the American services and aviation cadet regulations. The food was excellent, and the physical training program, however unpleasant at first, did indeed prepare the young men for the hard months ahead. Many of the young Britons thoroughly enjoyed the course and the rigid schedules; others accepted it as simply a small hurdle to overcome in order to enter flying training; and still others were contemptuous of the course and rebellious at having to "suffer" it.

Andrew Mathieson of Class SE-42-E kept a diary during his RAF career and permitted use of a transcript copy of the portions of it that dealt with part of his training in the United States. Selected excerpts from the diary provide insight into the experience of RAF student pilots:

November 11th. Armistice Day. Parade in town, but this is quite disappointing. We tried to march to three bands—our own, the Americans, and a majorette band—while over all there is the hooting of trains, shriek of sirens and the banging of firecrackers. It seems festive even here.

November 12th. *Airborne again; on steep turns, etc. I feel sick but otherwise enjoy it. Rather "rigid" at controls, but I can't hear half of what my instructor says. Shows me once only how to do a particular manoeuvre, then "packs up" in a bad temper when I can't do it. Someone said he felt he had too many pupils, and he tries to "eliminate" one. On our "Open Post" day, Pete and I ask a taxi driver to take us through "Ragsdale," the red light district. Just like the films, with ladies at the doors dressed in revealing dressing gowns. We are scared stiff.*

While Mathieson and his classmates were finding their way around Albany and the vicinity, many of the students who had left the town and its hospitable people a fortnight earlier were visiting Albany as often as they could.

Most RAF cadets training in America found a friendly reception and extraordinary hospitality in every town where primary flying schools were located. However, the U.S. Army Air Forces basic flying training schools at Cochran Field near Macon, Georgia, and Gunter Field near Montgomery, Alabama, to which Arnold Scheme students were sent were located near cities that had very large military populations. Moreover, by the time the RAF cadets moved to basic flying schools, they were no longer the novelties they had been in the small towns where the primary schools were located.

For all of the RAF men, but especially those of the first four classes, the towns where they learned to fly drew them like magnets, and they sometimes did some foolhardy things. They pooled their resources, rented automobiles from noncommissioned officers at their basic flying schools and drove long distances regularly on weekends to visit friends in Albany and other primary school towns.

Typical of the hospitality afforded some RAF men by Albany citizens was a drive to Florida during November 1941. John A. Davis, business manager and travel columnist for the *Albany Herald*, wrote of taking LACs Eddie Barron, Joe Trull and Ken Taylor on a Sunday trip to the Florida Gulf Coast and returning them to the flying school by 7:30 that same evening. From his article, it is obvious that Davis and his wife enjoyed showing the visitors some of the features of that rich farming and resort area.

At Baconton, the RAF cadets observed a turpentine still; at Thomasville, they were surprised at the hundreds of roses blooming in November and the giant and shapely oak tree, a town institution. Once they crossed into Florida, they drove via Tallahassee to Wakulla Springs and the Gulf Coast, then returned by a different route to Albany. The kindness of Mr. and Mrs. Davis provided rich and colorful memories for the young RAF cadets and was typical of citizens of Albany and surrounding towns.

Toward the end of November 1941 and the celebration of Thanksgiving, LAC Andrew Mathieson and his fellow members of Class SE-42-E continued their training. Life was becoming more complicated for them. They had been at Darr Aero Tech for only three weeks and were steadily building up hours and experience for their solo flights. Their fear of failure caused anxiety levels to increase almost daily, as excerpts from Mathieson's diary demonstrate:

November 21st. *First letters arrive from home, which cheers me up. Flying. We are* *called "Dodos" at the moment, but now the first cadet has soloed. He is no longer a Dodo. In accordance with tradition, he gets flung into the swimming pool with all his clothes on.*

November 26th. Have flown 6 hours, 27 mts. Winter is here officially, and we wear blues instead of khaki and civvies.

November 27th. Good God! Instructor asks me if I think I can solo in time. (We must solo in 10 hours or—OUT) I say, "Yes," but he puts me in for a Flight Commander's check. This is usually the short cut to elimination. I cry.

December 3rd–6th. Rain and thunderstorms. Drome unfit. United States airship cruises around afterwards.

The most exciting event of December 1941 was the Japanese bombing of Pearl Harbor and America's subsequent entry into the war. In Albany during the two weeks prior to that eventful day, a great deal of excitement had been generated about a pending sports contest.

With the consent of Darr officials and the cadets themselves, civic clubs of Albany decided to sponsor a benefit rugby football game in the Albany stadium at 2:30 p.m., Sunday afternoon, 7 December 1941. Halftime entertainment would include music by the Albany High School band and the Turner Field Drum and Bugle Corps. There would also be a demonstration of RAF drill. The RAF men deferred to their new American allies and refused to allow any contributions to be made to British war relief. Proceeds from tickets sold throughout the city and in some neighboring towns were to go to charities determined by the sponsoring civic clubs.

As a local newspaper described the events of the afternoon of 7 December, the Spitfires and Hurricanes, two rugby football teams from Classes SE-42-E and SE-42-F at Darr Aero Tech, were playing before a crowd of about five thousand people. Among those present were Reginald Levy and many of his Class SE-42-A classmates, who at the time were undergoing twin-engine advanced flying training at nearby Turner Field. The game was a mystery to the Americans, and the announcement of the Pearl Harbor attack was undoubtedly both exciting and sobering. The Spitfires won. Following that Sunday respite, training continued, only now the rules had changed.

USAAF officers were more security conscious now that the United States was at war. The pace of training also quickened. Andrew Mathieson flew a record three check flights with the flying school's civilian flight commander, and after the third check he was allowed to go solo. Immediately following that flight, he was assigned to Ted Dantis, his new instructor, and from that point on his progress continued. By the second week of December, the newspapers were more filled than ever with war news, there was more rain and the air became crisper, but there were still sunny days that made it possible to enjoy outdoor sports.

On 21 December, Flight Lieutenant Hill began his seventh month in Albany with very good luck. According to the local newspaper, he scored a hole in one on the eleventh hole of the Radium Springs Golf Course. Although it was too warm for the British students to even think about the Christmas season, and even though there was concern about the necessity for wartime blackouts, local leaders decided that the city should use its traditional Christmas streetlights and decorations.

LAC John Clark (SE-42-E) recalled the experience of learning a new term at Christmas 1941. Clark and several classmates caught a ride into town with an insurance agent. After they were seated in the automobile, the driver indicated that he had two or three stops to make en route to town, but would get them there. The young men were shocked when they found themselves in the Ragsdale community, a place that the insurance agent referred to as a "red light district." Although there had been whispers about it on the station, it was a place and a label entirely alien to them. As Clark recalled the experience more than forty years later,

> *We were in Ragsdale picking up insurance premiums, and every one of us trying to act as though it was the most natural thing in the world to be doing, until our driver let us out downtown. We were all just about to explode with laughter and couldn't wait to get back to the base to tell our friends.*
>
> *Our fascination with the term, "red light district," was further enhanced since it was about Christmas 1941, when we found most of the homes in Albany had little single red, lighted candles in the windows, and several of us concluded this then was a pretty wide spread problem. With Christmas approaching, we soon learned differently.*

Although some members of Class SE-42-E and perhaps all of the men of Class SE-42-F, the new class that arrived around 15 December, may have remained on the station on Christmas Day, other RAF men were entertained royally in Albany and neighboring towns.

Further excerpts from Andrew Mathieson's diary trace events of the last weeks of Class SE-42-E's primary flying training and record the advent of colder, nastier weather:

> ***December 26th***. *More solo, doing lazy eights and other manoevres. Three more fellows get checks (and elimination) by Army check pilots. Hell! There's hardly anyone left! Who's next?*
>
> ***January 1st, 1942***. *Rain. Who cares? We'll be home this year! I didn't mention that during the Christmas period, when we were confined to camp, several lads nipped out. The local sheriff catches one, "sticks 'em up!" and marches him to the Officers' Mess. Another makes a getaway in an ordered taxi, but escapes, with the car holed by a bullet. Many cadets, we are told, get "eliminated" at Tuscaloosa after being caught out of camp after hours.*
>
> ***January 9th***. *Pay day. Draw 17 dollars, as I send 7 dollars home. Foggy. We should move out soon.*
>
> ***January 14th***. *Only about 3 hours to do. Go up solo for two hours and 10 minutes, then up again for a front seat ride, with the instructor in the back, instead of the pupil, for 42 minutes. All acrobatics. Every book and leaflet in the aircraft is lost, and we find torn pages on the struts and tail when we land. I appear to have been missed for the 60 hour check.*

Of the 175-member Class SE-42-E, 4 were held over, 60 were eliminated and 111 successfully completed the course. At 6:30 a.m. on Saturday, 17 January 1942, Mathieson and his surviving classmates boarded buses and arrived at the Gunter Field, Alabama USAAF basic flying school four hours later. On that same day, the popular and efficient Flight Lieutenant A.G. Hill, who had served as RAF administrative officer at the field since June 1941, departed for assignment to the USAAF advanced flying school at Napier Field, Dothan, Alabama.

A few days before Christmas 1941, Class SE-42-F, a 173-man RAF intake, had arrived from Maxwell Field and joined the 4 men held over from the preceding class. By mid-January, SE-42-F moved to upper-class status, and a new junior class arrived to commence training. Of Class

SE-42-F's total enrollment, 5 men were held over for further training, 90 were eliminated and 82 RAF students graduated. Unfortunately, their class was to have one of the highest failure rates of any Arnold Scheme class.

Class SE-42-G, another 173-man intake, arrived in Albany at the end of the first week in January 1942. It absorbed 5 holdovers from the preceding class for a net enrollment of 178 men. This was the last class to complete the acclimatization course at Maxwell Field, and the first class to have partially completed a flight grading course before leaving Britain. The eight- to twelve-hour course of dual flight instruction in Britain, which was eventually perfected, was intended to screen out students who became airsick or could not otherwise adjust to flying, thereby reducing the number of men eliminated from pilot training in American flying schools.

While Classes SE-42-F and SE-42-G were undergoing training, the city of Albany experienced two disasters. On Tuesday afternoon, 27 January 1942, an unexpected and violent storm struck Albany and the vicinity. Thunder rolled and lightning flashed over a wide region. A bolt of lightning struck a downtown building, doing some minor damage. Winds reported at sixty-seven miles per hour were accompanied by hail and heavy, blinding rain. A train shed roof was blown off, some equipment at the railway station was damaged, a number of streetlights were broken and several plate-glass store windows were either cracked or shattered. At Darr Aero Tech, the winter storm ripped a number of aircraft "loose from their moorings and smashed them into others nearby in the most serious quirk of the storm."

The other "disaster" that perturbed some citizens of Albany, Georgia, was an article that appeared in the February 2, 1942 edition of *Time* magazine. Evidently, the "damnyankee reporter" was less than kind in his inferences and inuendoes about the impact of military stations in Albany. On 30 January, shortly after the magazine was distributed, the editorial columns of the *Albany Herald* struck back at the author and expressed concern that the magazine should "print the slime that drips from his pen." Whether or not the magazine article changed visitors' attitudes toward the community is unknown. It was still the same town and, with one notable exception, it would be difficult to discover any measurable changes that the *Time* article might have inspired.

However, the change was not long in coming. On 9 March 1942, at the opening of the Dougherty County Superior Court, Judge Carl Crow charged the grand jury with responsibility for "a thorough investigation of the alleged gambling conditions in the county." On 30 March, the *Albany Herald* reported that the grand jury "failed to come to a conclusion," and Judge Crow was not pleased. The judge's displeasure was felt in official quarters.

Within a brief time, both the Albany Police Department and the Dougherty County Sheriff's Department banned the sale of alcoholic beverages between Saturday midnight and 12:01 a.m. Monday morning, and ordered removal of all gambling devices. Whether this city and county cleanup also affected private clubs such as the casino at Radium Springs was not specifically mentioned, but it is probably safe to assume that the clampdown applied only to Ragsdale and to "juke joints and night spots" that had proliferated in the city and county following the establishment of the military installations.

But there was other news as well. On 31 January 1942, a Roosevelt Birthday Ball was held at Radium Springs, and hundreds danced to the music of Sammy Graham and his orchestra. Albany had become an air force town now, so a huge cake was decorated with an airplane. The evening also included what the British cadets called a "singsong" or "singalong," and the Americans a "community sing." Money raised from auctioning the cake, from the dance and other events would go to the Infantile Paralysis Foundation, President Roosevelt's favorite charity.

Evidently, because of the normal wintertime disruption of training by the weather and the new post–Pearl Harbor seven-days-per-week training schedules, it became more and more difficult for the cadets to meet people at a set time at the gates of the school and to accept invitations, which continued to pour in from people in Albany and other nearby communities. In order to relieve the anxiety that many cadets had that they might offend gracious hosts, and also to reassure local citizens, Flight Lieutenant Judge, who had replaced Flight Lieutenant Hill as RAFAO at Darr Aero Tech, wrote to the *Albany Herald* about the problem:

> *Owing to service and other reasons—particularly weather conditions—open post periods are never certain and inconvenience is unavoidably caused to so many generous residents. I know from what the cadets have told me and from personal experience how great is the care taken to entertain them, and if I can be of any assistance to would-be hosts and hostesses in this matter, it will be a pleasure to do so.*

From 15 to 17 February, gentle rain fell slowly but fairly steadily, and the weather bureau recorded 2.68 inches in three days.

As a result, some members of Class SE-42-F had difficulty completing the required flying time. However, they squeezed in enough time and departed for a basic flying school around 20 February. Class SE-42-G moved into upper-class status, and a new class replaced SE-42-F. Of the 178 RAF students of Class SE-42-G, 6 were held over, 71 were eliminated and 101 successfully completed the primary flying course in late March 1942.

LAKELAND SCHOOL OF AERONAUTICS
LAKELAND, FLORIDA, 42-E–42-G

On 6 November 1941, the 115 RAF members of Class SE-42-E arrived at Lakeland from the USAAF Aviation Cadet Replacement Center at Maxwell Field, Alabama. The two high points of their training at Lakeland included the Japanese attack on Pearl Harbor on 7 December 1941 and the visit to the school one month later by Air Chief Marshal Sir Charles Portal, chief of air staff of the Royal Air Force, and Lieutenant General Henry H. Arnold, deputy chief of staff of the United States Army and commanding general of the army air forces. Now that war had come to the United States, security regulations were in force, so no publicity was released to news media in advance of their brief visit to the Lakeland school.

Among the members of Class SE-42-E were eighteen-year-old Norman Plum of London and Sydney James Williams, a twenty-one-year-old former London "Bobby" (policeman). Since in the view of numerous RAF cadets the Lakeland primary school was a "plum posting," Norman Plum was undoubtedly the victim of many puns and much good-natured ribbing from classmates. Plum successfully completed pilot training and returned to the United Kingdom for further training and combat operations. During the course of 1943–45, Plum won a commission, a Distinguished Flying Cross with bar and flew a record eighty combat sorties (nineteen on twin-engine Wellingtons, eleven on Lancasters and fifty on DH Mosquitoes of 692 PFF Squadron).

Jim Williams also completed pilot training successfully and gained a commission as pilot officer. He too returned to Britain to fly combat operations. Later, he returned to his duties as a police constable in London. Forty-three years later, Williams described his Florida days from his retirement home in Sussex. He and his classmates had boarded a train at the USAAF replacement center at Maxwell Field and traveled eastward and southward to Lakeland. From the Lakeland Railway station, they were transported by truck to the huge barracks at the flying school. There, they were assigned three men to a room. Williams had been appointed cadet sergeant at Maxwell Field and his responsibility was essentially disciplinary. Since it would normally have been cold and wet at home in Britain, it took some time for the men to become accustomed to mild weather and daily sunshine.

Their training commenced immediately, and Williams found himself attending ground school in the morning and flying in the afternoons, alternating about weekly. Of course, there was special flying kit, and issue leather jackets were worn with blue uniform trousers for ground school classes. However, since the United States entered the war in December, and U.S. Army regulations had required a changeover to winter uniforms by 1 November, members of Class SE-42-E wore RAF uniforms both on and off station after that date. The classes at Lakeland were also permitted to march to British-style drill. On 11 November, the entire RAF student body at the Lakeland school formed up into two groups for an Armistice Day Parade through downtown Lakeland. The first group of fifty-four men was led by Duncan MacKinnon of SE-42-D, a Scottish cadet playing the bagpipes, and a second echelon of thirty-five men followed. Behind them were American ex-servicemen of 1917–18.

As his dual flying training continued, Williams recalled the "great shock" when, after landing at the auxiliary field near Plant City, his civilian instructor, C.D. Oakley, stepped out of the front cockpit onto the wing of the Stearman, reached back to connect the front seat belts and then climbed down from Stearman No. 28 and sent him solo. To that time, Williams had received only four and a half hours of dual flying instruction, but he soloed successfully. Now his flying instruction really began. During weekends, if there were no demerits to walk off on the ramp during Saturday afternoon, Williams and others usually walked downtown, had a snack or glass of beer and surveyed the town and its environs.

On Sundays, most of them attended church in town. At the Methodist church, Williams and several friends found that they enjoyed the friendly atmosphere and the people. Usually, they were invited to Sunday lunch and/or dinner and were driven about the town and countryside. From his perspective, "Southern hospitality was beyond our comprehension." During these travels, the British cadets found a genuine friendly welcome everywhere they went, and were impressed with the citrus groves and the ability to buy "a sack full of beautiful grapefruit" for ten cents.

Of his experiences early in 1942 as he and his classmates were winding up their flying training at Lakeland, Williams recalled hearing about LAC Derek Sharpe's falling out of a trainer at Tuscaloosa, Alabama. He also remembered that

> another cadet went "missing" and that was the last we saw of him. His nickname was "Steve," possibly short for Stevenson. We heard later that he was picked up in Canada as a deserter but could get no real confirmation of this. Flying Officer Wooley was the RAF Liaison Officer at Lakeland, but we had very little contact with him. We took our flying tests…some failed for not looking around before turning or starting aerobatics…and we passed our written examinations. The successful cadets were posted for further training. On 9th January 1942, we left Lakeland Railroad Depot amid very emotional scenes. Half the town had turned out to see us depart. The elderly and the young had tears in their eyes.

When Class SE-42-E had been in training for five weeks, Class SE-42-D graduated and moved on to a basic flying school. Within a few days, Class SE-42-F arrived to commence training.

As Class SE-42-E completed its ten weeks of training at Lakeland, the editor of the *Lakeland Ledger* took that occasion to respond to remarks reputed to have been made in the British House of Commons by Richard R. Stokes, a Labor Party MP. The editorial asserted that Stokes had been correct in his observation that the United States was already beginning to displace Britain as the most powerful western democracy and, in the light of the realities of early 1942, his deploring Britain's loss of power was perfectly understandable. However, journalists rightly or wrongly interpreted Stokes's remarks as an irresponsible attack on the United States at a time when solidarity was needed and desired by all thinking people.

In summary, the Lakeland editor deplored divisiveness and called upon the British students in training in the United States to set the record straight once they arrived back home:

> *Americans and Englishmen simply have to keep in mind that they're temperamentally different. The successive groups of English students with whom Lakelanders have come in daily contact have made an extremely favorable impression. We've been quick to accept them as regular fellows, decent chaps. They're above the average and they've made many friends here.*
>
> *And so we feel confident they've gained a pretty good insight into American temperament and will tell their folks back home that we aren't such a bad sort, after all. Englishmen and Americans have too much in common to let awkward speakers and trivial differences impinge upon the treasured bond of democratic friendship which now exists between their countries.*

Of the 115 intake for Class SE-42-E, 41 were eliminated (1 for other than flying reasons) and 74 graduated around 12 January 1942 and were posted to basic flying school.

Class SE-42-F had arrived at Maxwell Field, Alabama, around 20 November 1941. They had been among the first westbound RAF students to be processed through the new RAF No. 31 Personnel Depot at Moncton, New Brunswick, Canada, rather than through the RCAF No. 1 Manning Depot at Toronto. Their documentation had been completed quickly, and they had boarded trains in their RAF blues for the journey via Toronto on southward to Montgomery, Alabama. They arrived in the United States as the first Arnold Scheme students to enter the country in uniforms rather than in gray civilian-issue suits.

After the four-week acclimatization course at the Aviation Cadet Replacement Center at Maxwell Field, they were transported by train to Lakeland. The class arrived at Lakeland, Florida, 119 strong on 18 December 1941 and commenced flying training a few days later. Among its members was twenty-eight-year-old Phillip G. Penfold, who graduated as a pilot officer and served as a flying instructor at the USAAF basic flying school, Cochran Field, Macon, Georgia, from August 1942 until 30 April 1943.

More than forty years afterward, Penfold remembered those early training days in Florida:

> *On 17 December 1941, we entrained* [at Montgomery, Alabama] *for Lakeland, Florida and arrived there next morning. My instructor was R.H. Harvey, and I trained on Stearman PT-17s. I was average and soloed after 10 hours. Many fellows started being washed out left and right, sometimes for ridiculous reasons. I learned after the war that most of the chaps who were washed out were shipped up to Canada and were put right*

back into training there. We finished 6 days early and were given leave. Six of us went to Clearwater, Florida, and it was here that I met my future wife. She came from New York State, and when I graduated from Advanced, we got married in Macon, Georgia.

During my stay in training, the friendship and generosity of the American public was absolutely beyond description. On Christmas Day, everyone in camp was taken out to Christmas Dinner by different families. When we wanted to go somewhere, we didn't have to thumb rides, we just stood by the road, and the first car would stop and take us virtually anywhere we wanted to go. The hospitality became overwhelming.

For instance, when we were staying in Clearwater, we ate all our meals in the cafeteria. The public soon found out, and every time we were there, we would get phone calls, all with invitations to dinner or to stay with people. Our pay was $11 every two weeks, but we had reached the stage when we preferred to be poor and independent. There were too many strings attached to many of the invitations. We were not ungrateful, just overwhelmed. I always hoped that the British people would be as hospitable to the "Yanks" when they were in England.

One weekend, fourteen of us hired two cars and drove to Miami. We hadn't realised it was so far, so we didn't arrive until 10 p.m. When we arrived there, we wanted to clean up, so we asked a taxi driver where we could get "a wash and brushup," as it was called in England. He said he knew just the place, so we piled into two taxis, and off we went.

In about 5 minutes, he off-loaded us and led us up some stairs, with me in the lead. He knocked on the door, a trap opened, he spoke, and in we went. There was a room on the left with a juke box and several good looking girls. We all sat down and then one of the girls got up and walked across the room, and I realised that I could see right through her dress. A pregnant silence fell on the room, as we all realised at about the same time exactly where we were.

Finally, we explained to the Madam whose name was "Jackie," that we had just arrived, were going out on the town, and would be back later. The girl that Ted Clayton was talking to finally said, "Wouldn't you like to go to bed?" To which the great Ted replied, "No, I'm not tired." We left in good order and went out on the town; at one bistro, we sang for our drinks. A little later that Sunday morning, we all collected together and started back for Lakeland where we had to be in by 7 p.m.

As with many classes at different schools, Class SE-42-F at Lakeland had an abundance of talent among its members. One evening several days before their departure, a group of RAF students, each with extraordinary talents and a keen sense of humor, presented a variety show called "It's in the Air." Among the singing groups in the variety show were Tom Dingwall, the "Scots Baritone"; LACs Adams, Boal, D.P. Jones, MacLeod and Baker as "The Quintet"; "Harmony at Its Best" with Riley and Wilkins; and "The Welsh Choir" led by Dai Davies. Interspersed between the singing talent were performances by Bob Drinnan, "Our Syncopating Pianist"; "The Band"; Hugh Tattersall, "Pianist"; and a variety of satirical skits.

Such amusing individual and group performances included "Military Memories" with Alan Wade and John Thomson and company; Charles Duncan as "The Carefree Cadet"; "I Want To Be An Actor" by Alan Wade; "Antiques" by Wade and Duncan; "The Manual of Arms" by Eric Armitage and company; "Impersonations" by Nick Berryman; and "Oh Doctor" by Ron Pate and Bill Behrens. The master of ceremonies for the show was Bill Ottewille; the stage manager was George S. Holme; and the property manager was Corporal Rance. As was customary, the show closed with a "Music Hall Finale" that included the entire cast.

Of the 119 RAF intake for Class SE-42-F, 49 were eliminated for flying deficiencies and 70 completed the primary flying course at the Lakeland School of Aeronautics around 23 February 1942. The number of eliminees for this class was greater than that of any of the thirteen RAF classes trained at that Florida school. The 118 members of Class SE-42-G arrived at Lakeland from the RAF Replacement Depot at Maxwell Field in the early hours of 11 January 1942. Both classes were in training at the time the USAAF more than doubled its objectives for the training of pilots from thirty to sixty thousand per year. In order to reach that level of production, it was necessary to increase the numbers of cadets and airplanes at each school and to compress the training schedule. Instead of five days per week, directors of training at all flying training schools were ordered to extend their training schedules to seven days per week.

The speed-up of training was not just in intensity, but in length as well. Each phase of training was then reduced from ten to nine (later eight) weeks. Since there was already a constant fear of failure and a need to escape from regimentation, even if only for brief periods, many British and American cadets objected to the rush of training. However, in early 1942, with the Nazi sweep into Russia, Greece, Crete and North Africa and the Japanese assaults on the Philippines, Hong Kong, Malaya, Singapore and the Netherlands East Indies, the future looked bleak, and no one could be certain as to the number of pilots that might be needed.

Among the members of Class SE-42-G in training at Lakeland was Donald Alexander Williamson, who was born 13 March 1919 in Canada but was living in Scotland before the war. Williamson served in the British army and transferred to the RAF in early 1941. As with other members of his course, he underwent a somewhat brief flight grading course at an elementary flying school before embarking for Canada and the United States. As he recalled many years later from his home in Vancouver, British Columbia:

> *Flying began for me at Lakeland on a PT-17 (Stearman) on 13 January 1942. My instructor was G.D. Dewey who, if memory serves correctly, was from Texas and a long-term believer in flying "by the seat of his pants." It goes without saying that housing and food were, after war-time Britain, outstanding. Instruction was of the highest quality, and the Stearman was a much more robust plane than the Tiger Moth, and it even had brakes!*
>
> *Then and later, heat became a problem, but they simply fed us salt tablets, and large quantities of Coca Colas were consumed. There were the usual number and types of incidents: We were carefully warned of the different meanings, some offensive, that would be given to certain phrases that were in common use in Britain; and, of course, because of the warnings, those phrases were used whenever it was possible to use them. The last line of the Air Corps Song was "Nothing can stop the Army Air Corps." It was essential for us to add yet a new concluding line: "Except the weather!" This was an oblique reference to the practice of stopping flying when it was suggested that there was a cumulo nimbus somewhere in the Gulf of Mexico.*

The sarcastic but good-natured ribbing that went on constantly between American and British cadets was simply an expression of the British sense of humor and was not to be taken seriously. Such remarks were made constantly and were meant to elicit similar responses.

However, Williamson's comments about the weather are of interest because the USAAF emphasis on flying safety was much stronger than that insisted on by many RAF flying officers. Whereas the RAF syllabus called for teaching night and instrument flying early in training, the United States Army Air Force syllabus emphasized training safe and skillful pilots in an orderly progression from the simple to the complex. From the perspective of USAAF officers, it was essential that pilots first learn to handle an airplane well in every conceiveable attitude. Only then would it be possible to teach them to fly safely at night and in all kinds of weather.

Since the Lakeland school had lost a British student pilot on 2 September 1941, when an unexpected storm approached rapidly, perhaps its staff was more aware of what weather fronts could do to inexperienced pilots. Owing to a rapid deterioration of weather conditions in May 1942, about a dozen members of Class SE-42-G while in basic flying training at Gunter Field were to suffer one of the worst training disasters to befall Arnold Scheme student pilots.

Another member of Class SE-42-G at Lakeland, Florida, was Edgar Lancelot Spridgeon, a native of Peterborough, Northamptonshire. Subsequently, Spridgeon served as a pilot officer/flying instructor at the USAAF advanced flying school at Napier Field, Dothan, Alabama, and on return to the United Kingdom in 1943 found it impossible to escape assignment to further flying instructional duties.

After retiring from a machine tool company, Spridgeon recalled the end of his Lakeland days:

> After the 60 hours, 7 minutes of Primary School, I was proficient in the handling of the PT-17 Boeing-Stearman and flying it was certainly a joy, including the spinning and aerobatics. We were given seven days leave at the end of the Primary course, as the basic school was not ready for us and a party of eight of us went to Miami for five days. We stayed at the Colony Hotel on Miami Beach which was run by Sid Burrows from Manchester, England, who never turned away an RAF cadet. He charged 75 cents a night in his sea-front hotel, which included bed, bath, shower and toilet, which was very generous as the normal terms were $2 a night. Sid's father-in-law ran a nearby cafe and we had breakfast of ham, 2 eggs, cereal, and toast for 55 cents.

Sid Burrows of the Colony Hotel became a legend among RAF men trained in Florida. Of the 118-man intake for Class SE-42-G, 2 were held over for further training, 40 were eliminated and 76 graduated from the primary flying school at Lakeland in early February 1942.

CARLSTROM FIELD
ARCADIA, FLORIDA, 42-E-42-G

The original Arnold Scheme intake was 550 student pilots due to arrive every five weeks. During the autumn of 1941, as the total Arnold Scheme intake rose to 750, the five RAF primary flying school contingents had continued to climb in numbers. By early November, the pace quickened at Carlstrom Field. Additional flying instructors were being put through their paces by senior pilots in preparation for an increased enrollment. On Thursday, 6 November 1941 at 9:30 a.m., 198 RAF students of Class SE-42-E arrived in Arcadia by Atlantic Coast Line train. RAF Administrative Officer Flight Lieutenant Maurice A. O'Callaghan had escorted members of Class SE-42-C to Gunter Field and proceeded on to Maxwell Field to escort the new draft to Carlstrom. Although many of the RAF cadets felt that ITW courses in Britain were superior in content to the new Maxwell Field four-week-long course, they had spent the preceding month undergoing an acclimatization course.

When members of the new 198-man RAF contingent arrived at Carlstrom Field, they joined the approximately 120 members of Class SE-42-D, now the upper class. Still on the same airfield, and undergoing training in separate units, were the survivors of the first 100-man contingent of American aviation cadets who were supposed to receive their primary flying training at Dorr Field, which was still under construction. The second 100-man Dorr Field American aviation cadet draft (Class SE-42-E) dribbled into Carlstrom Field between 6 and 9 November, an estimated 50 to 60 of them driving their own private automobiles.

Training had reached the "stages" level for members of Class SE-42-D, and initial flying commenced immediately for the newcomers of the Carlstrom and Dorr contingents. As the month wore on, the sun continued in the bright blue skies and the evening and early morning air became cooler and everyone, including the British cadets, was issued a leather flight jacket and switched to winter uniforms and winter flying togs as required by army air forces regulations. Among the British cadets were LACs Edward "Ted" Slinger, Edwin B. Dean and Gerald A. Percival.

With the crowding at Carlstrom Field, Arthur Lee Harrell, correspondent for *Fly Paper*, indicated that "the quadrupled staff of flight instructors will certainly have to do some 'heads up' flying and teaching to maintain the unparalleled safety record that has been established." Harrell went on to describe how one instructor's reaction to the increased traffic was to sing a ditty to the tune of the nursery rhyme "Old MacDonald Had a Farm," which ran, "Here a plane, there a plane, Everywhere a plane, plane…John Paul Riddle had a field."

Carlstrom Field was not the only place that was crowded. The town of Arcadia had about four cafés or restaurants, three drugstores and a terrible housing shortage. The influx of civilian and military personnel at Carlstrom and Dorr Fields was only beginning to be felt. The Embry-Riddle Company owned only one bus, which was used to transport people to both fields and cadets to and from Arcadia and other towns. For much of the time, the system seemed to work because people resorted to carpooling and hikers were usually offered rides by those with space in their vehicles. However, with the increasing numbers, transportation was becoming a severe problem.

Near the end of November, the British students were introduced to what was for most of them their first Thanksgiving Day. The sumptuous feast of turkey with all of the trimmings ably prepared by the dining hall staff was a marvel to students already impressed with the quality and quantity of so many foods that were still rationed in Britain. Unfortunately, the idyllic scene was marred by the fact that a number of the newly arrived American and British student pilots had already washed out and were having their turkey dinner at Maxwell Field while awaiting transportation to Canada. For those remaining in training at Carlstrom Field, the excitement of a special holiday was only the beginning.

On that fateful Sunday, 7 December 1941, total strength at Carlstrom Field was recorded as 8 USAAF officers, 15 enlisted men and 440 RAF and American aviation cadets. Around 17 December, all of the American aviation cadets of the Dorr Field contingents in training at Carlstrom Field departed for Dorr Field with their aircraft and civilian and military staffs. The initial Dorr intake had done its entire primary flying course at Carlstrom Field and had used the Dorr landing ground only as an auxiliary field. Its graduates were assigned to basic flying schools.

Since the second Dorr class (SE-42-E) had completed only five weeks of the primary flying course, it moved to its home station as the upper class to a newly arrived junior-class intake. As the American contingents left Carlstrom Field, RAF members of Class 42-D also departed for basic flying schools. Within a few days, the 233-member Class SE-42-F arrived from Maxwell Field and took their places at the Riddle Aeronautical Institute, which continued to train about

600 student pilots per class. Each course now enrolled mixed American and UK cadets instead of assigning them to separate classes.

Not too long after American entry into the war, the army air forces asked journalists and company public relations men to be careful about what they printed. As a result, there was a virtual blackout of information for a time, and even after *Fly Paper* resumed publication the quality and quantity of information had become a casualty of war. Most of the British flying training schools in the United States continued to publish class sketches, as did at least one Arnold Scheme basic flying school, but the other Arnold Scheme basic flying school and most of the advanced schools stopped doing so for eight months. The primary schools resumed the practice of publishing class books only sporadically during the autumn of 1942.

Training officers responsible for American flight training syllabi bent to RAF pressure and American entry into the war. Orders were issued that reduced each phase of training from ten to nine weeks and expanded the training schedule to seven days per week instead of five. The former regular weekend pass also became a casualty of war, and with its demise, eliminations climbed alarmingly at all primary schools. By the time Class SE-42-E completed its primary course around 9 January 1942, 59 students had been eliminated, 4 were held over to the next class and 135 graduated and boarded a train for the journey to the basic flying school at Gunter Field, Alabama.

Heretofore, with Classes SE-42-D and SE-42-E, the presence of USAAF aviation cadets destined for Dorr Field had provided an international flavor. Beginning with the arrival of Class SE-42-F in December 1941, the classes at Carlstrom were officially mixed. British cadets, no longer required to "hide" their nationality off-post with drab gray suits, wore RAF blue uniforms. Class SE-42-F with its record enrollment of 233 RAF students was reduced by almost one-third during its first five weeks of training. As the graduates of Class SE-42-E departed, Class SE-42-F moved to senior-class status in time to receive its juniors, Class SE-42-G.

At about that same time, cold weather came to south Florida and John Paul Riddle returned from a three-week visit to the United Kingdom, where he and several other Americans were guests of the Royal Air Force. Riddle and his American companions had traveled to Dorval Airdrome near Montreal, where they boarded a Ferry Command aircraft for the eight-and-a-half-hour flight to Britain. During their stay in the United Kingdom, they visited a variety of British training stations and returned to the United States on the regular Pan American Clipper run to New York.

Among the students of Class SE-42-F at Carlstrom Field were Norman Bate, Ronald Bloor, Robert L. Brook, Frank Newman, Edgar "Tommy" Evans, Raymond R. Lassiter and Edward Jacobs. Ray Lassiter was twenty-one years old when he was eliminated from pilot training and returned to Canada to remuster to other aircrew training. As he recalled from his home in Surrey forty-three years later:

> *I was suspended at Carlstrom Field for dangerous flying and used the day of suspension to look around Florida in company with one or two others. I recall a small van stopping outside Arcadia, the driver asking whether we would "like a lift." We accepted and some hours later found ourselves at Miami Beach! There was no way of getting back the same day, and we were very fortunate in finding excellent accommodation at the Colony Hotel, Miami Beach. It was owned by an Englishman who made us wonderfully welcome—as did the other guests. Needless to say, we were not at all popular with the C.O. at Arcadia*

when we returned and were "deported" to retrain in Canada!

Among the members of the class who graduated were Ronald Bloor and Norman Bate, both of whom won their pilot's wings and served as flying instructors with the USAAF before returning to the United Kingdom.

More than forty years later, Bate recalled from his home in Leicester his days at Carlstrom Field:

> *At Carlstrom, our billets were first class and were built around a swimming pool. Flying instruction was given by civil pilots, monitored by Air Corps officers who performed check flights. Wash-out or pass decisions were partially based on grade slips. Ground lectures were given by civilian lecturers. The skies were cloudless and it was hot to very hot there, so most of our meagre pay was spent on cold drinks and toiletry articles and toward share costs of car hire. My instructors on the Stearman PT-17 biplane were Mr. Gould and Otto von Schaick, both outstanding civil instructors with a great deal of flying experience. I soloed after 7 hours, 40 minutes and completed primary training on 15 February 1942. Learning to fly by the "seat of my pants" from experienced instructors helped to ensure that I flew accident free during the war years.*

Bate also recalled activities away from Carlstrom Field, indicating that he and several friends often walked to and from Arcadia, "with its tiny cinema, saloons [cafés], and roller skating rinks at 50 cents an hour." In January, they visited deserted beaches, but found Sarasota too expensive.

W. Ronald Bloor was twenty-three years old and a former police constable in Lichfield, Staffordshire, when he underwent pilot training in the United States. With Vernon G. Bull, Norman Bate, Eddie Barron and other members of the class, Bloor arrived at Carlstrom Field from the acclimatization course at Maxwell Field, Alabama. Forty-two years later, from his home in Macon, Georgia, Bloor recalled his primary flying training:

> *Housing was of the chalet type, spartan, but quite adequate. Food was excellent, of type and quantity not experienced for a long time. This did require some adjustment, as did the Florida climate, but neither was a problem. The quality of instruction was very good. I remember the very friendly relationship with my instructor and his insistence on nothing but my best efforts. After the initial shock, accents presented no problem. Recreation on post consisted of team games, a building where we could gather to drink cokes and shoot the bull, but there was little time for this since there was quite a load of "homework," and we were eager.*

But all had not been absolutely smooth for Class SE-42-F. The Christmas season came and went, and early in the new year, tragedy struck.

On Sunday night, 4 January 1942, nineteen-year-old Alfred Thomas Lloyd of New Radnor, Wales, was thrown into the school's swimming pool and tragically drowned. As news of the tragedy spread, the detective in many people rose to the surface, and the rumor mill began to churn out many versions of what had happened. Was Lloyd dead already? Had he been thrown into the pool in an effort to revive him? Or had he been thrown in the pool to cover up his being accidentally killed in a scuffle? Did Lloyd drown or did his head strike the edge of the pool when several playful classmates threw him in at night in the usual horseplay following a successful first solo flight?

Evidently, all of these questions occurred to investigating USAAF officers as well as to a Florida grand jury. Investigations were conducted by military and civil authorities, and the ruling was that LAC Lloyd's death was "accidental." The most likely explanation is that Lloyd drowned when he was thrown into the chilly pool in mid-winter as the traditional "reward" for a successful first solo trip. The tragedy probably resulted from boredom and horseplay among a group of "overgrown schoolboys," as many of the British cadets labeled themselves and their classmates.

Attention was at least partially diverted from the tragedy by receipt of a letter from Sergeant Pilot Arthur L. Prandle, formerly of Class SE-42-A, and RAF correspondent to the *Arcadian*. Of the fifty-three men of that first RAF class that had graduated at Carlstrom, one had been washed out at Gunter Field, another had been killed during advanced training and the remaining fifty-one members graduated on 3 January 1942 and received their wings. To those still in primary training and worried about failing, Prandle's comments were like a light at the end of a tunnel.

In Class SE-42-G, which arrived at Carlstrom Field in mid-January 1942, there were 227 UK cadets and 56 American cadets assigned for a total enrollment at Carlstrom Field nearing 600 student pilots. Among the RAF cadets were G.G.K. Gray, Derek V.A. Curley, Eric Polak and Brian Davies. Forty-two years later from his home in Bristol, Davies used his logbooks and an excellent memory to reconstruct his 1942 adventures in south Florida:

> Our indoctrination and acclimatisation completed, we travelled by rail to Carlstrom Field, Arcadia, Florida, arriving there 12 January 1942. The atmosphere at this civilian contract school was very much more relaxed than at Maxwell Field, but we were still kept up to scratch with formal parades and room inspections. Our arrival at Carlstrom demonstrated the difference between American and British attitudes. The American cadets were immediately hazed by their senior course while the British were welcomed by their senior course as old friends.
>
> We now began our primary flying training on Stearman PT-17 airplanes. Most pilots would probably say that this was the most enjoyable time of their flying career. They learn how to handle a simple aircraft, enjoy the thrill of flying solo for the first time, revel in the excitement of aerobatics, and are quietly exultant at performing new "tricks" with precision. Three instructors were involved with my training: Messrs. O'Brien, T.N. Taylor, and Quesenberry. Of these, only "TNT" is fixed in my memory as he carried out most of the instruction.
>
> Small in stature and avuncular in manner, he had been flying for many years along the American west coast as far north as Alaska. He claimed to have ceased logging his flying hours, but thought he had done about 9,000. He entertained several of us at his home one night and allowed us to participate in his hobby of model trains. He kept a King snake indoors as a deterrent to other reptiles and rodents. Every 20 hours flying time became time for a progress check, the final being at 60 hours. A Mr. Lampmann checked me out and warned that he was letting me go forward for further training with some doubt in his mind. He urged me not to let him down.
>
> At Maxwell, there had been little or no social contact with American cadets. All this altered at Carlstrom. We were billeted in our rooms in alphabetical order, but the nationalities were kept separate. This apart, we were fully integrated and found there was much we had in common. Early in 1942, a team of reporters and photographers visited

us and they produced a piece, which was published in Time *magazine, on how Britons had settled into the American way of life.*

Each week, from 4 p.m. Friday to 10 p.m. Saturday, we were given Open Post. A Greyhound bus had been chartered to convey us to Sarasota which became our playground. On $25 pay each two weeks, the first weekend was done in style, the next on a shoestring; often the second visit was done by hitchhiking to save on bus fare. One time, during the return to Arcadia, I caught a ride in an auto in which were three middled aged ladies, and all through the journey, after it was determined that my uniform was not that of a private military academy, I was subjected to intense questioning on the political implications of American participation in the war. This was the first contact made with anyone who espoused the isolationist viewpoint.

Eventually, they dropped me off about halfway to Arcadia, and I began to walk along an arrow-straight road devoid of anything living. Some large birds were soon observed pecking at something in the middle of the road. They scattered on my approach, and the object of their concern turned out to be a dead rattlesnake. My latent snake phobia came to the fore, and with great trepidation, the walking continued. Part fact, part imagination, I heard the ominous rattle from the ditches along each side of the road, and when enough courage had been mustered to look at a ditch the first thing seen was the head of a water moccasin snake swimming along at my pace. The relief at getting another ride after about an hour was beyond description. Never again was hitchhiking attempted unless a through ride was guaranteed.

In those days, Sarasota was not as large or popular as it is now. Many of the vacationers came in family groups and, it must be confessed, we lived our "poor" weekend on their generosity. It was a two-way exchange, insofar as they were curious about us and anxious to learn firsthand about war experiences. This fact we unashamedly exploited to the full without pangs of conscience. If we had to "sing for our supper" then we sang!

We must have appeared quite eccentric to local people as each Saturday morning, we rushed into the sea, and were the only ones doing so. Mostly it was done to clear our heads from the excesses of the previous night, but partly to enjoy sea temperatures of around 72 degrees. We played on the beaches like the overgrown schoolboys that many of us were. We did the usual tourist's round of Ringling Brothers Circus Winter Quarters, the snake farm, and other attractions, and took photographs of each other in Red Indian headdress, etc. In a small way, we contributed to the vacation orientated economy of the area.

One weekend, five of us pooled our resources, hired a car and drove to Miami. None of us had a valid U.S. Driver's License, but an American cadet, whose physical description fit one of our party, was persuaded to part with his on loan. We reached Miami without mishap, arriving well after dark. On attempting to cross the causeway to Miami Beach, we were stopped by police who ordered us to proceed seawards without headlights. This measure had been introduced to counter U-boat activity offshore by reducing shore light against which shipping would be silhouetted. We found that once the headlights were off, there were no other demands from the police, so we slunk away.

In one night, we were spent out, so set off on the return journey early the next afternoon. Most of the driving was being done by Bob Simmonds, a burly, dark haired ex-soldier. On the open road, with no oncoming traffic, and just for the hell of it, he reverted to the British practice of driving on the left. The wail of a Florida Highway Patrol car siren was soon heard, and we were stopped and questioned by two officers. Apart from the traffic violation, the driver had no licence, and the borrowed licence description fitted one of the passengers.

Visions of our instant deportation from the U.S.A. by the RAF, with the attendant disbarment from further flying training were paramount in our minds. We made a clean confession, pointed out the consequences to us if action were taken, and ended up exchanging cigarettes with the officers as we related exaggerated war stories to them. One of the officers was Patrolman Lewis whose grandfather had come from Wales, and I was pushed forward by my colleagues to talk about Wales! They played ball and sent us on our way with a verbal caution that, should we get into trouble during the remainder of the journey, they would have to take action as well.

Finally, in the spring of 1942, the USAAF training program was switched to nine weeks training on a six-day-per-week schedule, but even so, the number of pupils at Carlstrom Field continued to climb, as did the number of eliminees. Of the enrollment for Class SE-42-G, 80 RAF men were eliminated, 3 were held over and 150 graduated in late March 1942 and moved on to basic flying schools.

CANADIAN INTERLUDE FOR THE FINAL SIX ARNOLD SCHEME CLASSES

In January 1942, a large draft arrived in Halifax aboard the *Ausonia*, a small 14,000-ton Cunard Liner, now an armed merchant cruiser, capable of a speed of fifteen knots. The class's numbers were increased by several men who had been held over from preceding classes. LAC Thomas C. Overend of Ayrshire, Scotland (Tuscaloosa, 42-H), recalled that experience more than forty years later:

Moncton and the surrounding area was buried under heavy snows, but the town had many lighted shops, an abundance of goods available, and drug stores and small restaurants where one could eat well for the very little money that most of us had. I remember as well the Royal Canadian Mounted Police in their scarlet and black uniforms, of whom the more irrepressive of our numbers came to know even better. After about four weeks at Moncton, I was delighted to find myself on a posting to the United States as part of the Arnold Scheme. Arnold Allay was stenciled on our luggage, and we embarked on the Canadian National Railway for a journey to Windsor. I believe the cars were very old, and the quality of the food on board little better than we had been accustomed to in Britain.

From Moncton, New Brunswick, Class SE-42-H was posted to Turner Field near Albany, Georgia, for a month-long acclimatization course before assignment to flight training, but all Arnold Scheme student pilots did not disembark from transports in Halifax, Nova Scotia.

Early in February 1942, Arnold Scheme Class SE-42-I disembarked in New York from the small six- to eight-thousand-ton American troop ship, *Chateau Thierry*, and entrained for Moncton. Arthur E. Drinkwater of London (Americus, 42-I) recalled that other trainee pilots had been eliminated from training in the United States since the *Letitia* had sailed with a large number of washouts in December:

The train journey from Halifax to Moncton through a snow-covered Canada was a pleasure and marching through the snow from the station to the depot was a unique experience. Our documentation was carried out by aircrew cadets, acting as clerks, who had been "washed out" in the USA, and it was then that we first learned of the huge numbers of cadets who were eliminated in the USA and viewed the future with mixed feelings—excitement at going to the USA and trepidation of being failed as a pilot. When we marched out of Moncton to board the train for Turner Field, it did nothing for our morale to hear calls of "see you back here in a few weeks."

Still, with each westbound train, RAF aircrew continued to arrive in Moncton. Students destined to be members of Class SE-42-J arrived in North America aboard the USS *Neville*, another small six- to eight-thousand-ton American troopship. Those men assigned to Arnold Scheme Class SE-42-K arrived aboard the *Banfora*.

As the population fluctuated at the RAF No. 31 Personnel Depot and changed month in and month out, RAF and FAA airmen presented variety shows regularly in the town and on the station, and the young men won the hearts of young and old. On 18 March 1942, men of the RAF and Fleet Air Arm presented a three-hour variety show in the Moncton High School auditorium. Even with a seating capacity of between 1,200 and 1,300, there was not enough room. The extravaganza was described as "a combined English Music Hall Show, a vaudeville performance, and a minstrel show." The RAF portion of the show included a Beach Resort skit and "The Mikado with Wings." The Fleet Air Arm performance included a baritone solo and "Blackout Sketches." The show ended with a combination of performers presenting "A Toast to England," which included "There'll always be an England," "Land of Hope and Glory" and "Rule Britannia."

It was inevitable that many local young ladies found the dashing young Britons attractive in their blue uniforms and exciting to meet and flirt with. And though these reactions were normal and even to be expected, some local young men became jealous and developed a strong and particular dislike for the RAF men. In March 1942, a young Moncton civilian was found unconscious in a lavatory of the sergeant's mess at RAF No. 31 Personnel Depot. He had been shot with a .25-caliber Colt automatic pistol, and the bullet had entered his throat and exited through his upper jaw near the temple. The judgment was that the wound was self-inflicted, but no motive was speculated on in the columns of the local newspaper.

After 11 April 1942, once construction of RAF No. 31 Personnel Depot was completed and its permanent staff was augmented, more recreational activities were provided for servicemen on the RAF station. Sports activities such as boxing shows and a five-team basketball league occupied large numbers of men, while two showings nightly of motion pictures in No. 1 and No. 4 Recreational Halls proved very popular. Movies, quizzes and musicals became standard and regular on-post recreational fare, and there were the inevitable table tennis and card games.

To supplement the military diet, YMCA canteens on the station served more than eighty thousand airmen a month and a Y library, which was located in No. 4 Squadron Lounge, issued about 2,500 books per month. Hospitality was still available in abundance within the town and its service clubs. The faithful YMCA continued to operate its hostel and to provide large numbers of service personnel with stamps, air-graphs, stationery, games and food, either free or at very low cost. In addition, the sewing corner in the Y and the Salvation Army Hostel continued in operation, and volunteer women workers mended clothing and sewed on stripes and brevets for eastbound sergeant pilots.

Walter Leon Frank Randall (Americus, SE 43-A) was barely nineteen years old when he arrived in Canada on 9 May 1942. Excerpts from Randall's diary capture the feeling of adventure that he and others felt on arrival and during their stay in Canada:

> **Saturday, 9 May [1942].** *It is now near tea time, and at the moment I am sitting in a none too comfortable leather seat in one of the Canadian National Railway's coaches literally flying across country on our way from Halifax to the camp at Moncton, where we expect to stay for some time before we are sent to U.S.A. We landed at about 2:30 and I was truly amazed at the remarkable efficiency displayed by the personnel at the port in their efforts to get us away as quickly as possible.*
>
> *The countryside is very beautiful with its towering hills and deep green valleys, divided by the winding courses of the rock and boulder strewn streams. Trees are everywhere and the slopes are a patchwork of green, brown, and purple while close at hand along the side of the railway track the white bark of the silver birches lends a contrast to the dark rocky earth that is visible between the trees. We have passed several small villages nestling in a hollow and they are very pretty and colourful in comparison to English hamlets, but I think this is due to the fact that the houses are made of wood and are painted in vivid whites, greens, reds and blues.*
>
> *We stopped at Truro some half an hour ago and enjoyed for the first time the nourishment of good Canadian food. True, it was only a sandwich and a glass of milk, but when you receive ham and eggs in sandwiches you realize the difference between the present English food and that which we are due to receive in a very short time from now.*
>
> **Sunday, 10 May.** *The Canadian air force is even more sensible than I imagined, for not only did they give us a hot meal when we arrived, but also allowed us to remain in bed till 2.30 this afternoon. Our train drew into Moncton at 10.30 p.m., and after marching round a number of lighted streets, we came to the large camp. It was rather funny to see all the lights blazing forth, especially in the huge hangar [drill hall] where we were mustered for the usual form filling and detailing for billets. We were put in huts of 18 per room with double bunks and a locker apiece. We turned in at about 2.0 a.m., after having a very tasty meal of bacon and eggs. I managed to rise at 10.0 this morning and after a good clean up had a marvelous meal followed by a welcome pay parade, when each man received 11 dollars to tide him over a few days.*
>
> **Wednesday, 13 May.** *It has rained during the night and the red clayey mud has formed a bad habit of sticking to our boots. We spent most of the day dodging PT and signals, but we had to succumb to some work although we finished at a fairly early hour. I had decided to remain in camp all evening and write letters, but there was a film show at the camp cinema and I visited that place instead. It was a very good film, "She Knew all the Answers" with Joan Bennett, and I was very amused the whole time. I am rather alarmed at the rate my cash is disappearing, for I seem to buy pounds of chocolate and apples every day, not to mention the numerous ice-creams and milk shakes in town.*
>
> **Monday, 1 June.** *We have been on a Canadian Pacific train all today since 7.30 this morning and have spent the day rattling through the endless pine and birch forests interspersed with small fields on our way through New Brunswick into Quebec where we now are. The weather has been warm and sunny today and although it was rather cold at*

first, we are now fairly sweltering in the stuffy sleeping car. The accommodation aboard the train is quite good and although we have to fetch our food, it is very tasty.

It quickly becomes obvious from Randall's descriptions how much change had occurred in the feeding and rail transport of aircrew trainees in the months since the first RAF drafts arrived in Halifax in June 1941. In May 1942, LAC Randall and the Class 43-A draft arrived in Halifax aboard the *Letitia*, an Anchor Donaldson Liner of some 14,000 tons, now a troop transport. That same transport quickly returned to the United Kingdom, and in June 1942 she transported the final Arnold Scheme Class, SE-43-B, to North America.

Early in the morning of 22 January 1942, as the temperatures hovered around zero degrees Fahrenheit, the 750-man Class SE-43-A Arnold Scheme draft marched through crisp dry snow blanketing RAF No. 31 Personnel Depot to the Moncton, New Brunswick train station. With the noise of clanging bells and huge train engines in their ears, they boarded a train with their RCAF escort officers and the train pulled out of the station. On the train they had their passports checked, and in the dining car black waiters served what one RAF cadet described as "the best lunch he had ever tasted." As the train sped southward down Canada's east coast, it crossed over the border into the United States at Vanceboro, Maine, in mid-afternoon and the men were instructed to put their watches back one hour. They were now six hours behind the time in England. At Portland, Maine, they changed trains before continuing the journey southward during the night.

Between about 5:30 and 6:00 a.m. on Friday, 23 January, the train rolled through the outskirts of New York City and stopped for a few minutes at Pennsylvania Station. The young RAF men were much impressed by the new engines and cars in New York. They had become accustomed to snow in Canada, but now it was all gone, and they saw only light frost on the trees and browned grass. From New York, they continued southward via Philadelphia to the busy Union Station in Washington, D.C. In the national capital, the RAF cadets enjoyed a two-hour layover and were able to see a small part of the city before continuing their train journey southward for another twenty hours.

TURNER FIELD, GEORGIA
RAF ACCLIMATIZATION, 42-H–43-B

On Saturday, 24 January 1942 at around 7:30 a.m., the train rolled into the station at Albany, Georgia, and the RAF cadets were transported in U.S. Army buses to Turner Field, about three miles east of the town. Eight additional RAF cadets who had been held over at Maxwell Field joined the 750 newcomers, raising the intake to 758. Before the RAF draft arrived, First Lieutenant P.J. Von Weller, commandant of cadets, had made a fortuitous arrangement. Instead of being assigned to a separate dining hall, the men of the replacement center would be fed in the cadet mess hall on the new station.

The new arrivals were assigned billets in new barracks. Cadet Geoffrey A. Barnett (Arcadia, 42-H) recalled that "the weather on arrival at Albany, Georgia was fine and warm. The airfield must have been recently constructed as it was more or less free of vegetation and the wooden barracks released a very pleasant aromatic resinous scent. They couldn't have been up all that long." Shortly after arriving, the RAF intake marched to the cadet mess hall for breakfast, and there they were astounded when black waiters delivered to their tables milk, cereal and fruit as well as huge mounds of eggs, bacon and sausages and apparently unlimited quantities of orange juice and pancakes.

Following breakfast and time out for unpacking their kit bags, the new arrivals were welcomed by Captain A.H. Davisson, commanding officer of the cadet replacement center, and by the senior RAF administrative officer and his staff of three officers and seven enlisted men. While many of the new intake were assigned to tent accommodations at Turner Field, Cadet Thomas C. Overend (Tuscaloosa, 42-H) recalled that his contingent of that first intake was assigned to "two-story wooden accommodation blocks in individual beds with, to us at that time, the unbelievable comfort of sheets and soft blankets."

Other elements of accommodation were deemed not so pleasant. Although some of the British cadets felt that central heating was "an unnecessary luxury," the warm days and cold winter nights of the region brought home to them the need for a modicum of heat. However, none of the UK contingent appreciated the American design of community toilets and showers. Since the British place extra value on privacy, there was initial concern and embarrassment upon seeing and being compelled to make use of "the long row of loos back to back with no cubicles or doors."

Later on the day of their arrival, the RAF cadets underwent physical examinations, and since individual medical records were unavailable, the senior RAF administrative officer certified that the men had received the required vaccinations and other innoculations. During the ensuing medical examination, it was apparent that none of the RAF cadets suffered from communicable diseases, but about 10 percent of their number required dental work, and five of them were admitted to the station hospital. Robert Reginald Farrow (Tuscaloosa, 42-H) was one of the RAF contingent who suffered from tonsillitis and spent a week in the Turner Field Station Hospital.

On Sunday morning, 25 January 1942, the British cadets gained a shocking introduction to American aviation cadet life. At about 5:50 a.m., a drum and bugle corps marched and counter marched before cadet billets playing "a medley of tunes including 'You're in the Army Now,'" a specific piece that would haunt many of the RAF men for years to come. The RAF draft soon learned that the band marched past their barracks and tents as a warning that they had ten minutes to dress and parade (meet in formation) in front of their billets. LAC Thomas C. Overend recalled that "our privacy was invaded by a large gentleman dressed in T-shirt and slacks, who informed us in no uncertain terms, that we were expected on the games field immediately for one hour of 'calisthenics,' whatever that was."

At least one RAF cadet, Peck, was so impressed with the new word "calisthenics" that he felt compelled to write a ditty about this strange activity. Although the verse was produced at a primary flying school, it applied equally well to the exercises whatever the station:

Throughout the U.S. armies wide
Stand formations side by side
Their contempt they'll never hide
For Calisthenics.

When the British Air Force bold
Came to this land that's never cold,
No exact science, they were told,
It's Calisthenics.

Requires complicated explanation,
From that we hope for preservation,
We're daily driven to desperation,
By Calisthenics.

Then comes "Corporals, Report!"
Along the lines there runs a snort,
For absentees must now be sought
For Calisthenics.

The notices have all been read,
These o'er half an hour spread,
Turn and twist and screw the head
In Calisthenics.

The formation then proceeds to waddle
Astride an invisible Texan saddle,
A queer position, this "hop straddle,"
It's Calisthenics.

The U.S. draftees go rolling past
In camouflaged army lorries "fast"
And many an envious glance they cast
At Calisthenics.

Then midst grumpy groans and grumbling,
Order given, "Commence Tumbling!"
Throughout the ranks there grows a rumbling
"This Calisthenics."

The tired cadets, a melodious lot,
Underneath the showers "hot"
Remove the perspiration got
From Calisthenics.

And now to end this tale of wit,
I'm compelled sadly to admit
There is no means of stopping it
This Calisthenics!

However, LAC Geoffrey W. Smith of Norfolk (Arcadia, 42-H) indicated that the American form of physical exercises made a lifelong impression upon at least two members of his acclimatization course:

At Turner Field, we were also introduced to what Americans called "calisthenics."

The NCO who supervised our 0530 exercises every weekday morning was a huge, barrel chested, heavily muscled, close cropped, bullet-headed, deep voiced he-man (I had won a silver trophy at school for physical training, and I thought I was good, but he frightened me!). On the large field where we took calisthenics, demonstrations were given and orders were shouted by the NCO instructor from a large square platform some 12 feet high, thus: "the next hexercise is a body-bending hexercise done to four counts in the following manner—hut—hoo—hree—hoor—hut—hoo—hree—hoor! Kaydets! in cadence count—hut—hoo—hree—hoor."

Many years later, I was sitting in the Eastgate Hotel, Lincoln, having supper and a glass of wine when a voice from about 4 tables away started, "and the next hexercise will be a body-bending hexercise!" It's a good thing there weren't many people in the restaurant at that time, because my automatic response was "hut, hoo, hree, hoor." I was then joined by my old friend, Les Meehan, whom I had not seen for about 30 years.

Since the British cadets had had little opportunity for exercise during the preceding month, USAAF training officers assessed their physical condition on arrival as "little better than fair," but that would change.

On that first Sunday, the cadets gained an introduction to calisthenics, ate a massive breakfast and, except for other mealtimes, spent the rest of the day looking about the station, having haircuts and going to the post exchange with American cadets. That evening, many of the British cadets made their first trip into Albany to do some shopping and visit a cinema. Some of them went to Radium Springs, and Cadet Victor F. Moore (Albany, 42-H) described "queer cobwebby moss on trees" (Spanish moss) and a "bubbling deep hole [artesian well] where [the] spring came up." A brief introduction to the area surrounding Albany, Georgia, was not the only adjustment necessary for the UK student pilots.

A very basic problem that all of the British students faced was the adjustment to the change in climate. They had left Britain in the cold and damp of early winter, and in Canada they had experienced below zero temperatures. Now, in southwest Georgia, they found warm, sunny days and cold nights. Such changes of climate were not easy to adjust to. As Jim Double (Arcadia, 42-H) observed in his diary, there were other variations: "The sun is just about cooking me, and this afternoon we got a dust storm followed by terrific thunder and rain." Since the RAF draft had arrived dressed in heavy blue woolen uniforms and were also wearing woolen underwear, USAAF officers decided that they should be issued summer-weight underwear and khaki uniforms so as to survive the climate of southwest Georgia in greater comfort.

The syllabus for the acclimatization course at Turner Field contained four parts: reception, processing, military and academic. The curriculum was only slightly different from the course introduced at Maxwell Field in October 1941. Given the experience gained with the first three classes at Maxwell Field, 9 hours were scheduled for indoctrination in the customs and courtesies of both the RAF and the USAAF. "Reception and Processing," which included documentation, medical examination, pay parades and the issue of clothing and equipment, took 19 hours. "Basic Military Indoctrination" consumed 101 hours and included 44 hours of physical training, 20 hours each of infantry drill and ceremonies, 10 hours of inspections and 5 hours of interior guard duty.

Two additional hours were set aside for addresses by Wing Commander Hogan, senior RAFAO, Maxwell Field, and Lieutenant Colonel Harbold, commanding officer of navigation training at Turner Field. Although some effort was made to provide RAF students with a basic introduction to American history, government and geography, most of the fifty hours scheduled for academic preparation were devoted to military indoctrination, including six hours of training films.

Following reveille, calisthenics and breakfast, the RAF cadets quickly learned how to prepare their quarters for inspection. In doing so, there were special problems encountered in learning to make a bed so that all four corners of the covering blankets were folded at forty-five-degree angles. Blankets were to be so taut that either a nickel or dime had to bounce a certain percentage of the height when dropped on it. Following completion of these domestic chores, the official day began.

The normal schedule for a day of activities at the Turner Field replacement depot ran as follows: lectures were scheduled from 7:30 a.m. to 11:30 a.m. After lunch, sports (games) of choice were scheduled until 4:30 p.m. Following showers and dressing in proper uniforms, the men marched to the mess hall for the evening meal. Then, at around 7:00 p.m., a full retreat parade was held, and all cadets not engaged in other duties marched to the flagpole in front of headquarters and observed the lowering of the colors, the traditional end of day on a military post. Unless they were authorized to leave the station, the remainder of each evening until lights out was normally spent in the post exchange canteen, reviewing studies and writing letters.

The American emphasis on training for leadership in the acclimatization course was "strange and bewildering" to the British students. Proud of their own drill forms, very few of them cared for American-style close-order or ceremonial drill. Whereas American cadets rarely hesitated to gain practice in moving large bodies of men through the skillful use of proper military commands, RAF students were usually taken aback when they were placed in command of a large group of men. Since such a practice did not exist in the RAF, many of the UK cadets failed to accept the view that such practices were designed to provide them with valuable experience. Cadet James Double's diary entry spoke for dozens of British cadets: "After supper had another parade and what a laugh! LACs chosen to be Corporals, Sergeants, even C.O. What a joke! Saluting each other like a lot of boy scouts." Apparently, many other RAF cadets agreed with Double, but others gave it a try and benefited accordingly.

Some men interpreted such practices as efforts to make of them "little Americans," but other, more sensible cadets rejected such a notion and with LAC Geoffrey W. Smith accepted the idea that "when in Rome, do as the Romans do." Smith approached acclimatization with a well-developed sense of humor and undoubtedly profited from it.

> We also had a certain amount of drill—American Army style—hilarious to us as we had to take a squad in turn and bawl out all the different words of command. One of our bunch, Cadet Hunt (nicknamed Pee Wee after the jazz musician), had a complete blank when he had to advance his squad with two other squads which had already been given the order by their respective commanders. Pee Wee was stuck for the word—we stood smartly to attention, hanging on his every word, until finally, in desperation, he gave a most unusual command—"For—ward Chaaaarge!"
>
> We nearly had hysterics, as we stumbled forward in a shambles, some trying to break into a run, some trying to march, and the rest doing their best to stand up. Pee Wee got us back into order—I don't know how, but probably by the good old British standby—"As you were!"

Smith was also impressed by other less formal but nonetheless entertaining activities, such as

Susan Myrick's talks on Southern dialects. Mrs. Myrick, a columnist with the *Macon Telegraph*, had coached Vivien Leigh for her role as Scarlett O'Hara in *Gone with the Wind*.

During their stay at Turner Field, each of the RAF drafts gained open-post privileges early on and regularly after that. On one occasion, Geoffrey Smith and several classmates were invited to visit Dublin, Georgia, to be entertained by families there. Two elderly ladies, the Misses Baum, entertained and fed several of the British cadets. The ladies employed an old black cook whose accent was so difficult to understand that the UK cadets had to ask for translations. Smith recalled that "the food was indeed marvelous!" Helen Baum said, "I guess if us white folk put our minds to it, we could cook as good as our Nigras!" Other British cadets experienced similar hospitality.

Friday, 6 February was payday, and many of the RAF cadets went into Albany that evening and during other free time. They soon discovered that the citizens of Albany already had some eight months of experience with British cadets from Darr Aero Tech primary flying school and were well aware that the "British Boys" had little money. As a result, they were exceedingly generous with hospitality, and those UK cadets who wished to meet Americans in their homes had no difficulty in doing so. Some of them quickly learned an effective *modus operandi*. LAC Leslie Meehan (Arcadia, 42-H) recalled being "made very welcome. Derek Joss and I were adopted by a family, after standing around outside a church on Sunday, purposely looking lost. The food was incredible after wartime England."

On Wednesday, 11 February, near the end of the course, a dance was held in town, and fourteen army trucks conveyed the cadets to and from the dance. A week later, the entire course was divided into groups destined for five separate primary flying schools. They handed in their books and rifles, and a few days later, on Sunday, 22 February 1942, they left Turner Field by coach, train or army truck. Of the 758-man intake for Class SE-42-H, 10 men were held over for further training and 748 were dispersed to assigned primary flying schools.

Regularly scheduled sessions of vigorous calisthenics, classwork and games, plus excellent food and adequate rest, quickly produced the desired results. The four-week-long acclimatization course at Turner Field did help the RAF cadets adjust to the different climate and prepare for the demands of flying training. Julian Burkness, director of physical training at the replacement depot, was careful to maintain "before and after" records on every cadet who passed through the station. When the first RAF class completed its acclimatization course at Turner Field, Burkness reported that the average weight gain for the RAF cadets was $4\frac{1}{2}$ pounds, a total weight gain of 3,384 pounds for Class SE-42-H. LAC Thomas C. Overend of Ayrshire, Scotland, recalled that "I have never eaten so well at any time as in those days at Turner Field in 1942."

The USAAF civil contract primary schools continued to train American aviation cadets, but RAF authorities decided to consolidate pilot training in Georgia, Florida and Alabama. As a result, the Southern Aviation School at Camden, South Carolina, ceased training RAF cadets after Class SE-42-E completed its training. Perhaps since sulfur water invaded the wells and water mains of Carlstrom Field, Arcadia, Florida, by the end of 1941, that flying school trained no more RAF cadets after Class SE-42-H completed the primary flying course.

On 25 February 1942, the 509 members of Class SE-42-I arrived at Turner Field from RAF No. 31 Personnel Depot in Canada and absorbed the 10 men held over from the preceding class. The standard reception and processing procedures were adhered to, medical examinations were conducted and summer-weight clothing was issued as a replacement for their heavy woolen apparel. As with the preceding class, the physical condition of the RAF intake was recorded and showed such marked improvement during the four-week-long acclimatization course that the average weight gain was four and two-thirds pounds per man.

Except for minor modifications, the training and indoctrination syllabus remained essentially the same. Reception and processing was increased from 19 to 23 hours; basic military indoctrination increased from 101 to 106 hours; and academic preparation was increased from 50 to 51 hours. Academic work was impaired because the aviation cadet recreation building was the only place available in which to conduct classes, and it was not large enough for the entire intake.

Captain Arthur H. Davisson was pleased to report that many cadets "accepted invitations from families in nearby communities, which often included invitations to dinner or supper." Cadet George F. Pyle of North Yorkshire (Americus, 42-I) recalled his own experiences at Turner Field:

> Here we also had our first taste (an appropriate word) of American hospitality, which was to be a continuing feature of our sojourn. A party of sixteen (first on parade) was trucked some miles to a small farming community where our hosts awaited us outside their church. We were welcomed, and after morning service, taken in twos & fours to different households for "Sunday Dinner." The warmth, friendship, & generosity shown to us is beyond description, as was the novelty & richness of the meal which ranged from Southern Fried Chicken, creamed corn, sweet potatoes, & so on (all strange to us), to the Angel Food Cake & ice cream.
>
> It was at that moment, I think, that a feeling of guilt overcame me at the thought of my family enduring the shortages of rationed Britain. Needless to say that, such pleasures apart, we were all impatient to be away from the classroom & parade area and on to flying school, such impatience being goaded by the constant sound and sight of AT-9s in the circuit and on the ground.

Other members of Class SE-42-I had similar experiences. LAC Oliver Villiers Brooks (Albany, 42-I) recalled many years later,

> Our introduction to the U.S. Army Air Corps: "Get your hair cut, Mister!" "Take a brace, Mister!" "Take a demerit, Mister!" Turner Field was our introduction to the disciplinary and punishment system of the Air Corps as well as to American drill to which we had to adapt ourselves in pretty quick time. Some of the older and more responsible looking cadets were selected to act as section, squad, and squadron commanders, and most of these positions were filled by the fair proportion of ex-policemen we had within our ranks. It was about the time that police were permitted [actually since March 1941], if they wished, to volunteer for aircrew duties. Theirs was a reserved occupation, so those who fell down often simply went back to their civvie street jobs in the police. Other section leaders came from the fair number of cadets who were already serving members of the Air Force. I recall that the senior cadet on 42-I was an ex-policeman, R.L.W. Cheek, a massive citizen, who was to win a D.S.O. on one of his first operational flights and got chopped very soon afterward.
>
> The toilets in the barrack blocks were a little more civilized, all in a line without partitions. We paraded for everything: meals, ground school, calisthenics, etc. We did some guard duties. I remember guarding the base sewage works at night and listening to the "rattlesnakes" in the nearby undergrowth. Food, of course, was wonderful compared

with what we were used to—all of the steaks, eggs, ice cream, etc., that one could eat. This standard was maintained throughout our training. On completion of our 4-week acclimatization course at Turner Field, a large contingent of us was sent across town to Darr Aero Tech to begin flying training.

The same system of open-post hospitality offered by families in Albany and neighboring towns continued to be a huge success. Of a total intake of 519 members of Class SE-42-I, 12 were held over to the next class and 507 graduated and were posted to primary flying schools.

For unknown reasons, the 495 members of Class SE-42-J, the third and smallest RAF intake at the new RAF replacement center, arrived at Turner Field in five separate contingents over a period of seventeen days. On 30 March, 268 men arrived from Moncton via Halifax, and 169 others arrived that same day by way of the Port of New York. And on three dates in April, other smaller groups arrived at Turner Field from Canada. These drafts included 18 men on 3 April, 16 more on 5 April and a final contingent of 24 men on 16 April. Twelve men who were held over from the preceding class were added to the 495-man intake, so the total enrollment for Class SE-42-J was 507 RAF cadets.

Anthony E. Vidler (Tuscaloosa, 42-J) arrived in New York aboard the USS *Neville* and departed almost immediately by train for Albany, Georgia. At Turner Field, Vidler and his classmates were astounded at the quantity and variety of food. They found the south Georgia climate in early April 1942 very hot by day and cold by night. Many of Vidler's draft were assigned to live in tents, which they found very comfortable despite a constant problem with sand. Vidler and many of his classmates enjoyed socials at Albany's First Baptist Church, dances in the high school gymnasium and "walks in Tift Park admiring the azaleas."

Garnet G.A. Whitehead (Lakeland, SE-42-J), whose draft had attended the same ITW, recalled being "warned of sensitive areas where lack of tact might offend." Taboo subjects in the indoctrination program included an effort to describe the relationship between whites and Negroes in the Southern states and a prohibition against "discussions of the War Between the States, which we felt was still very much a live issue. (Certainly to avoid singing 'Marching through Georgia.')" Because of the delayed arrival of Class SE-42-J, some of the men received less than the four-week acclimatization course and for that reason undoubtedly considered themselves among the blessed. Of the 507-man total intake, 12 men were again held over and 2 were eliminated, so the number of graduates posted to the four primary flying schools at the end of April 1942 was 493.

The arrival at Turner Field of the full Class SE-42-K intake was also delayed for more than two weeks. On 1 May 1942, 433 RAF cadets arrived from Moncton, New Brunswick; on 7 May, an additional 30 cadets arrived from Moncton; on 9 May, 21 more cadets arrived; and on 16 May, the final contingent of 24 cadets arrived from Canada. The 12 men held over from the preceding class were added to the 506 new arrivals, bringing the total enrollment to 518 RAF cadets.

John Lilley (Albany, 42-K) recalled leaving Moncton by train near the end of April and arriving there on 1 May. As Lilley remembered,

Turner was some sort of holding unit where we became orientated to our surroundings in a new country. Not least was getting used to the climate, which was hot and humid as well as to the Army Air Forces' way of doing things. Here we played lots of games, had plenty of calisthenics, and classes on history and customs. Tropical kit was issued here to replace the heavy RAF uniforms which we wore. From the rationed diets in England, the food at Turner Field seemed out of this world, and the combination of good food and exercise was the essence of getting students fit for the demanding courses to come.

Other members of the class had similar reactions to their new experience. Colin Armstrong (Albany, 42-K) was fascinated with everything during his journey from Moncton, New Brunswick, to Albany, Georgia, during the spring of 1942. As he recalled his experiences many years later,

We spent about a month at Turner Field, 3 miles east of Albany, Georgia and were told that the purpose was to become acclimatized to the heat and to prepare us physically for the courses ahead. We lived in tents and spent our days doing drill and "calisthenics." I also recall the AT-9 aircraft, which were used for twin-engine pilot training and navigator training at Turner. I also remember being introduced to Coca Cola machines and the scrumptious bars of chocolate on sale there. It was here that we began to be introduced to the strange rituals of aviation cadetship.

Donald G. Saunders (Americus, 42-K) summed up with a memorable experience: "At Turner Field, we lived in tents and every aspect of our lives was excellent, but we did not get a lot of open post. I spent my 19th birthday at Turner, and a few of us went to the beer tent to celebrate later, and a few American soldiers joined in, and it became a friendly, comradely night to remember."

Robert J. Parish (Americus, 42-K) later trained with Class 43-A at Gunter Field, Alabama, and then came back to Turner Field for advanced twin-engine (TE) flight training. Parish celebrated his twenty-first birthday while he was undergoing basic flying training at Gunter Field, Alabama. From the time he left Heaton Park, Manchester, until he returned, Parish maintained a diary that described in contemporary RAF slang the events of each day.

At midnight on 3 June 1942, the 507-member Class SE-43-A arrived at Turner Field from Moncton, New Brunswick. The next day, after being allowed to sleep late, 11 men held over from the preceding class joined them, bringing the total to 518 RAF cadets. Training for Class SE-43-A went on much as usual with few, if any, variations in daily regimen. At the end of four weeks, 4 men of the 518-man net enrollment were held over, and 514 graduated and were posted to four USAAF primary flying schools.

Since the preceding class arrived at Turner Field on schedule, it is assumed that the final contingent of 514 RAF men arrived at the Albany, Georgia station on 8 July and were joined by the 4 men held over from Class SE-43-A. John E. McKenzie-Hall (Tuscaloosa, 43-B), a member of that final RAF acclimatization course, ultimately completed flying training, served as an instructor and returned to the United Kingdom for further RAF and Fleet Air Arm service.

Many years later, McKenzie-Hall recalled his days at Turner Field:

At Albany, Georgia, we detrained into buses and were carried to Turner Field, a hot, dry, and sandy reception centre. We had gradually become acclimatised to the increasing heat on the way, but beginning our stay at Turner Field with a sun blistering parade of some two hours duration burnt up a little of our enthusiastic feelings. We were lectured and praised, harangued and insulted, and finally allocated to four-man tents that were too hot to enter. It was hard for us to realize that whatever our nationality, education or training, we were now to be treated as raw recruits on a "pre-flight" course. We proceeded to be tested by 4 weeks of dawn calisthenics, drill, and lectures, which appeared to have little to do with aviation.

I believe the outstanding memory for me of this stage was the impact made in the mess hall by the long wooden tables almost collapsing under the weight of fresh fruit, jugs of milk, fresh bread, butter, and mouth-watering food of all descriptions. Although our time for eating was short, the amount put away was adequate and memories of rationed England with many foods in short supply soon faded or were conveniently brushed aside, as were the initial feelings of guilt at the availability of such a glut of food.

This was the first opportunity we had had to meet our American allies and fellow cadets, and a period of adjustment took place on both sides. Despite our very differing backgrounds, many incidents drew us together as comrades and broke the ice. For instance, we were certainly of one mind during an invasion of rats in our tents, and I was forgiven for hitting one sleeping American over the head with a wooden tent peg in an effort to kill a rat about to crawl over his face. Another common interest was, of course, girls, but contact with them was infrequent on base and, at this period of our training, we were not allowed outside the gates.

Cadet George Lee of that same class recalled similar experiences at Turner Field, ending on a positive note by calling the training "a good experience—drill, calisthenics, sports, guard duty, sunshine and good food." Of that 518 total enrollment for Class SE-43-B, 1 man was eliminated, 14 were held over and posted to Canada to complete aircrew training or to be remustered to other service and 503 graduated and were posted to the four USAAF civil contract primary flying schools.

Original gravestone of Cadet G.J. Pritchard, Quaker Cemetery, Camden, South Carolina. *Courtesy of J.D. McCarthy.*

Aircraft on display before Union Jacks at 1941 Canadian Exhibition, Toronto. *Courtesy of W.C. Warner.*

British equivalent of "jock straps and helmet liners." *Courtesy of R. Gregory*

Major cause of chronic constipation among newly arrived RAF cadets. *Courtesy of J. Moss.*

North Atlantic westbound convoy from an armed merchant cruiser, summer 1941. *Courtesy of D. Coxhead.*

October 1941 visit of RAF Air Marshal A.G.R. Garrod, AMT, Maxwell Field, Alabama. *Courtesy of the SEACTC.*

RAF aircrew walking around train at Moncton, New Brunswick, winter 1942. *Courtesy of J. Moss.*

Man and Jeep. *Courtesy of R. Gregory.*

Moncton High Street scene. *Courtesy of D. Shellock.*

Georgia marble, gift to RAF from English-Speaking Union, Atlanta, Georgia. *Courtesy of R. Skolfield.*

RCAF cadets marching, Toronto. *Courtesy of F. Jones.*

Main Street, Albany, Georgia. *Courtesy of F. Jones.*

St. Clement Danes, the RAF church, London. *Courtesy of D. Howell.*

RAF u/t pilot George Adamson sprawled aboard ship bound for Halifax, 1941. *Courtesy of F. Miller.*

Canadian memorial to those war casualties who have no known grave, Ottawa. *Courtesy of Dr. S.H. Guinn.*

Three RAF aircrew in heavy RAF flight garb. *Courtesy of F. Jones.*

No. 8 intake, St. John's Wood. *Courtesy of T. Adams.*

Four RAF cadets in gray woolen clothes. *Courtesy of R.F.H. Martin.*

Instructor with pupils. *Courtesy of J. Lett.*

Six-man aircrew in flying togs. *Courtesy of F. Jones.*

Kitchen staff girls in front of Darr Aero Tech dining hall. *Courtesy of J. Lett.*

RAF cadets seated on a French 75-millimeter cannon, Macon, Georgia. *Courtesy of R.F.H. Martin.*

RAF cadets wearing great coats at Dothan rail station. Band in back. *Courtesy of R.F.H. Martin.*

DeHavilland Tempest. *Courtesy of D. Coxhead.*

RAF Cadet D. Coxhead in flying clothes. *Courtesy of D. Coxhead.*

Instructor and three cadets in engines classroom. *Courtesy of G. Wheeler.*

RAF cadet Class 42-B, Darr Aero Tech. *Courtesy of D. Coxhead.*

Instructors before PT-17 at Darr Aero Tech. *Courtesy of D. Coxhead.*

RAF ITW Class, Aberystwyth, Wales, March 1941. *Courtesy of the RAF.*

Aerial view of Darr Aero Tech–Albany in the distance. *Courtesy of E. Roberge.*

Stearman PT-17 in the clouds. *Courtesy of G. Wheeler.*

Three wireless operators/air gunners relaxing. *Courtesy of J.R. Johnson.*

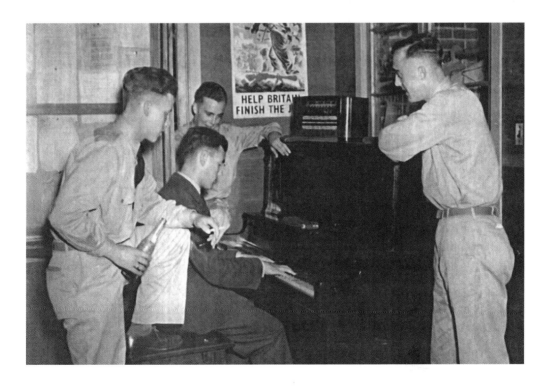

Four RAF cadets in recreation room with piano. *Courtesy of P. Penfold.*

Barracks at Lakeland. *Courtesy of P. Penfold.*

Stearman PT-17 biplanes aligned on the flight line. *Courtesy of R.F.H. Martin.*

Group of RAF cadets in civilian clothing, Americus. *Courtesy of R.F.H. Martin.*

Graduation dinner. *Courtesy of R.F.H. Martin.*

RAF cadets aboard a train headed for Canada and home. *Courtesy of R.F.H. Martin.*

RAF graduates Watson and McKenzie await a train for Canada and home. *Courtesy of R.F.H. Martin.*

Loading charter bus for transfer to basic flying school. *Courtesy of G.R. Hyslop.*

Lieutenant Webber, instructor, and four cadets at Cochran Field. *Courtesy of R.F.H. Martin.*

British cadets and instructor in front of a Harvard at Napier Field, Dothan.

Reginald McCadden with others from Americus at Butler, Pennsylvania CPT school. *Courtesy of M. Gracey*.

Instructors on the flight line, Americus, Georgia. *Courtesy of R.F.H. Martin*.

THE FINAL SIX RAF CLASSES IN GEORGIA

SOUTHER FIELD
AMERICUS 42-H-43-B

After some four weeks of acclimatization training at the newly established RAF reception center at Turner Field, Class 42-H was split into smaller groups to be transferred to primary flying training schools. A group of ninety-eight students was sent by Greyhound coach about forty-five miles northward to Souther Field, and they arrived there on 25 February 1942. One of its students was John A.L. Currie of Harrow, Middlesex. Currie later became famous as Squadron Leader Jack Currie, DFC, who wrote several outstanding aviation books, including *Lancaster Target*, which was made into a BBC-TV production. He also wrote a short volume entitled *Wings Over Georgia* describing his training and other real and imagined experiences while in the United States.

A classmate, Kenneth C. Evans of Bedford, also kept good records of the class's activities in the intensified and shortened USAAF pilot training program. More than forty years later, Evans recalled his American experience:

On meeting us, he [Flying Instructor Holloway] told us to look hard at one another, because there would shortly be only two of us left, and this proved to be the case. Later, two further students were assigned to him, and the speech was repeated, but I believe three of us finally graduated.

Housing and food were good, and by this time, we were already adjusted to the climate. The quality of instruction was excellent. As I remember it, there was little or no time for recreation on or off the post. Open post was only one day in eight, but we were most impressed that we were able to hitch-hike as far away as Atlanta and return on that day off. At that time, I recall little opportunity to meet residents of the area socially.

The outstanding incident for me at Americus occurred on 17 April 1942 when Mr. Holloway, my instructor, fell from the plane when I was rolling it at 3,000 feet. He opened his parachute, and I followed him down and attempted to land, but did not appreciate that the field was some 300 feet lower than the base aerodrome for which the altimeter was set. In any event, Mr. Holloway landed OK and indicated that I must return to base; I did. On my return, the despatchers allege that, in a marked British accent, I said "I say, old boy, to whom do I report that I have dropped my instructor out?" [This incident was reported in the local press, and there was some controversy as to whether he would be allowed to become a member of the Caterpiller Club.]

I personally experienced no difficulty with instructors' accents, although we were all impressed and intrigued by the Southern accent. Some difficulties were experienced in

reconciling the American Honour System with our own esprit de corps. I had collected
rather a large number of demerits while at primary flying school, but these were cancelled
on my transfer to basic. Both my ground school and my flying results were very satisfactory,
and I felt that the school standards had been very high.

When Class SE-42-H completed its primary flying training at the end of April 1942, thirty-six students had been eliminated and posted back to Canada, and the surviving sixty-two were sent to basic flying schools.

Class SE-42-I, 103 strong, had arrived early in March, and one of its members was LAC George F. Pyle of South Shields, County Durham, who later had a distinguished wartime flying career as a fighter pilot. More than forty years after undergoing pilot training in the United States, Pyle recaptured how it felt to be in flying training far from home during wartime:

My instructor was Mr. Featherstone, a civilian from Kansas City; the aircraft were Stearman PT-17s, and flying commenced on 31 March. The housing was roomy, with bunk beds in open plan...fairly spartan but adequate. The food was excellent...eight cadets to a table with table service. Breakfasts were usually of juice, cereals, milk, unlimited bacon, eggs, & hot cakes with maple syrup, hot apple rolls, coffee & fresh fruit. Main meals occasionally raised eyebrows (fruit salad with brown stew) and new items to our diet were not always received enthusiastically. Nevertheless, after the rations at home, we ate like fighting cocks & I suspect that many cadets had never eaten so well before!

Flying training was excellent from a quiet, courteous Mr. Featherstone, who had four pupils and whose one ambition appeared to be to get his hands on the stick of an AT-6 (better still a P-40). Solo came after 9 hours, & the thing I recall most was the sight of an airspeed indicator on the instrument panel of the empty front cockpit. We were being made to fly by aircraft attitude & the sound of the struts and wires!

One cadet claimed to have done a snap roll shortly after going solo (he had been taught in the barracks by a senior classman) & before having reached the aerobatics aspect of the course. As a result, most cadets proceeded to frighten themselves stupid & enjoy the glow of achievement by carrying out the manoeuvre at some distant and (hopefully) unobserved corner of the sky.

The constant topic of conversation and personal fear of every cadet was the prospect of "washing out," and for those who had soloed successfully (many did not reach solo) both increased as the 20-hour and 40-hour check rides approached. Some cadets were washed out, not for flying deficiencies but for disciplinary reasons, having acquired too many demerits or "gigs." Even so, in this small school hazing was minimal, since all cadets were British & senior classmen were reluctant to impose a form of discipline which they disliked and felt unnecessary. Lectures and study hall were regarded as necessary evils not to be ignored, but which must not interfere with the serious business of flying.

Perhaps the instructors had as much difficulty with the variety of British accents as the cadets did with the instructors. The gentle, lazy speech of Mr. Featherstone presented no difficulty, and he did not need to shout. We listened! He was that sort of nice man, and I always remember his parting words at the end of the course—"Don't forget, guys—never lose flying speed!" (He didn't mention take off in course pitch; we hadn't got that far!)

Off-base leisure was pursued in Americus with church on Sunday mornings and lunch with a local family (invitations to lunch were posted on the camp notice board). There were visits to the cinema, bowling alleys and a service club, and one memorable visit to the cemetery at Andersonville helped me to understand the bitterness & tragedy of that piece of American history.

Overall impressions of primary training were of a life totally undreamed of just six months earlier. I was flying (my boyhood ambition) in a delightful aeroplane, in ideal conditions & superb climate—save for one terrible storm which almost caught me out—with an instructor I admired, and friends and comrades in the same determined state of mind as myself. Save for the news from home, the war was a long way off and the only shadow was the ever present fear (diminishing) of washing out.

As George Pyle recorded above, during the time that Classes SE-42-H, SE-42-I and SE-42-J were undergoing training, an expansion program was underway at Souther Field.

Early in 1942, the United States government bought most of the facilities that had been constructed by civilian contractors at primary schools scattered across the United States. Although a small number of contractors would not sell, the Graham Company at Souther Field agreed to sell. With the Defense Plant Corporation (DPC) acting as its agent, the United States government assumed the lease of Souther Field from the town of Americus and Sumter County. It also purchased the buildings and much of the equipment from the Graham Aviation Company and assumed existing leases on auxiliary fields. The Graham Company then leased Souther Field from the DPC at a very small cost and continued to operate the school under contract with the army air forces. However, since the government now owned the former civil contract flying school, USAAF officers would decide what additional facilities were needed. The DPC would make the equivalent of an impact study and, if there was sufficient local housing to supply the needs of additional military and civilian staff, would build essential new facilities.

Although officers would later balk at further additions to Souther Field, there was apparently no difficulty in approving construction that doubled the school's enrollment by July 1942. By the time the new construction was complete, Souther Field's two very long two-story barracks building were being used exclusively for billets. Other separate buildings completed during that time included an administration building, a classroom building, a Link Trainer building, a small hospital and a two-story dispatcher's booth. In addition, the dining hall was enlarged and three massive steel hangars were added close by the original wooden shop hangar. The concrete apron stretching along the flight line was widened to seventy feet, and new paved parking ramps were added around hangars.

Since the 148-acre Bill Graham Auxiliary Field No. 1 was located only three miles northwest of the main airdrome, USAAF officers had always considered it too close to the main airdrome for proper and safe training. Because of the Graham Company's failure to lease another auxiliary field, enrollments at the primary flying school had been kept small. However, when the Graham holdings were purchased, the lease on the small auxiliary field was given up and arrangements were made to develop a more appropriate auxiliary airfield. Auxiliary Field No. 2, which was located some thirteen and a half air miles due west of Souther Field near Plains, Georgia, was purchased by the DPC. Although only 203 acres were used for flying training, the tract at Plains contained 757 acres of land.

Only with the arrival of Class SE-42-K in June 1942 did real expansion of student enrollment begin. With that 175-member class in early June 1942 came Robert J. Parish of Essex. A few excerpts from Parish's manuscript diary, interlaced with the youthful and refreshing RAF jargon, provide an excellent account of his experiences and observations from the time of his arrival at Americus:

> *2:6:42* [2 June 1942] *Shift off for Americus by coach. Arrive 10:00. First impression nice place. Good food. Personal waiters. Shoe shine & haircutting at own leisure. Receive goggles, helmet & flying overalls. Woe is me.*
> *5:6:42 Elected Flt. Ldr. bags of bull. Choose Charlie Dalziel as my Sergeant, and 3 Corps. bags of saluting. Decent flight of lads under me. Start ground school.*
> *6:6:42 Visited Americus. Bags of coloured folks. Not bad place—not good either.*
> *12:6:42 Had crash. Sand storm caused my port wing to drop while landing* [ground loop]. *Don said I did well & averted a nasty spill. Boy did I shake for awhile.*
> *14:6:42 Went to Decoto* [DeSoto] *with Ric & Eddie. Had a swell time with Mr. & Mrs. Wilkinson & Jane & nieces. Went to morning church with them & had a bloody fine lark. Got their own cow, 3 dark servants, took us swimming. Swell dinner. About our best day so far. Wizo do.*
> *23:6:42 Leave circuit & just my luck, fly straight into a storm. Didn't mind until a bit of lightning crops up, so lost no time, with a crafty 180* [degree turn] *& full gun, back to 'drome, & to my surprise, safe touch down—more by luck than judgement.*

Despite such occasional summer storms, the pace of training continued. The Link training instructional and maintenance staffs arrived at Souther Field and ten Link Trainers were installed in the new building built for that purpose. Each cadet was required to complete six hours on the Link Trainer during the primary phase of training. Of comfort to some students was the fact that getting adjusted to the instrument flying in a simulator had none of the dangers of flying real aircraft.

On 29 June, a fatal aircraft accident undoubtedly had a sobering effect on the two classes in training at the time. LAC Robert Parish described the incident in his diary as follows:

> *LAC Hislop with Instructor, Mr. McLoughlin* [L.E. McGlaun], *were killed today near Ellaville. As far as could be established, they were doing aerobatics, & it's believed that the pupil froze on the controls. The plane spun in, & an eye witness said the instructor was seen hanging on the side, trying to pull pupil out, he later jumped at 150 ft. but had his throat cut by tail plane. The wreckage came in at night, & the pieces didn't much resemble an airplane. I flew over in afternoon, & circled the spot, but could only distinguish a nasty crater.*
> *We figure there'll be a full military funeral—the flag flies half-mast. Later in the day, a second crash occurred; a kite touching down collided with another taxying—a most disturbing Monday to try & not remember.*

LAC Hislop's remains were transported to Montgomery, Alabama, for interment in the RAF plot of the Oakwood Cemetery Annex.

In the ensuing week, Parish and his classmates were deeply concerned about the large number of eliminees departing for remustering in Canada. Then, on 7 June, the crash of an advanced trainer near Americus took the lives of four American cadets and further upset the RAF trainees at Souther Field. But the primary flying course was rapidly drawing to a close for Class SE-42-K. On completion of their navigation exam on 1 August, several class members hitchhiked to Atlanta for the weekend.

During the following week, on completion of Link Trainer time and the final flying hours and checks, the course was finished and the graduates busily packed for transfer to a basic flying school. By the time Class SE-42-K completed primary flying training at the end of July 1942, 1 cadet of the 175 enrolled had been killed in a flying accident, 5 were held over for further training and 37 students were eliminated and posted back to Canada for remustering. A record 138 of the RAF cadets completed primary flying successfully and were posted to a basic flying school, an indication that flight grading in the United Kingdom was finally producing good results.

As the class completed its training, a large physical training area was finally completed west of the new No. 2 Barracks. The Graham Company should have built these facilities at least a year earlier. The physical training facilities were concentrated in an area encompassing slightly more than three acres and included four basketball courts, four volleyball courts, four badminton or tennis courts, two combination football-soccer fields and a huge obstacle course.

In early July 1942, Class SE-43-A, two hundred strong, the largest of all the RAF classes enrolled at Souther Field, arrived and absorbed the five students held over from preceding classes. Among its members were Joe Hitchman of North Derbyshire and Lee Randall of Sussex. Walter Leon Frank Randall was barely nineteen when he arrived at Souther Field to commence pilot training. Both Hitchman and Randall completed their training successfully and returned to the United Kingdom for further training. Randall flew Spitfires and Tempests on operations and was shot down in September 1944 during the Market-Garden Campaign, but managed to evade capture.

Excerpts from Randall's diary, which he graciously lent the author, provide an excellent picture of cadet visits to the small town of Americus and primary training, including night flying, at Souther Field in one of the final classes of the Arnold Scheme:

> **Monday, July 6 [1942].** *Souther Field, Americus, is a pretty nice place as far as I can tell up to the present. We arrived here at 10.30 this morning after a short journey in streamlined buses, and were immediately put into barrack blocks similar to those at Moncton except that there are large lockers for each man, lovely spring mattresses, and several arm chairs in which we can recline.*
>
> *The school is quite a large affair with roughly 80 planes, but as there are some 350 of us here, I am afraid there is likely to be a shortage when we start flying. We have had to store a large percentage of our kit and have all we need in the lockers which unfortunately have to be laid out in one way and one way only. I find the upper class, of which there are some in each room, are very helpful although they naturally tend to "shoot the line." However, I am itching to get cracking and am looking forward to Wednesday when we are scheduled to start flying. We have been issued with more flying kit, this time very light stuff, especially the helmets and overalls.*
>
> **Wednesday, July 8.** *The Stearman PT-17 is quite a decent plane with controls which are much heavier than the Tiger. There are also many adjustments which can be made to suit the pilot, including adjustment of the seat, rudder bar, etc. The plane flies very steadily and stalls very smoothly, although it is rather hard work recovering from manoeuvres such as turns where very hard opposite stick and rudder seem to have to be applied. As far as other lessons are concerned, we have had none except PT which was cut short by a terrific dust storm which suddenly arose at 5.30 this afternoon.*

Saturday, July 11. *As we had open post tonight, most of us visited the town, or city, I am not sure which, of Americus which turned out to be somewhat larger than I had expected. The amusements being on the same lines as at Albany, we visited the cinema which unfortunately seems to specialise in "rootin-tootin-shootin" western films that don't appeal to me very much. However, as the price of admission was only 20 cents and the programme was as long as an English one, if not slightly longer, I think the visit was worthwhile. We paid a visit to the New York Cafe, the most sophisticated joint in town where the food is reasonably cheap, and consumed ham and eggs and tea as was our usual wont at Albany* [Turner Field acclimatization course].

Sunday, July 12. *While walking, we visited a peach orchard and calmly took half a dozen peaches apiece in order to help us on the road. I am afraid my day in Americus has been more or less wasted, for there is nothing whatever to do, and I spent most of the time wandering round the town and its outskirts, or sitting in the Service Centre, or eating and drinking, the last of which I did a great deal. Finally I, with three other fellows, took a taxi back to camp, and after shaving I am about to retire until the rush of early breakfast and flying starts me off again tomorrow.*

Monday, July 13. *We have had a classic thunderstorm today which dispensed ably with our 2 hours PT period. The rest of the day has been very hot, so that I was even sweating while flying this morning. We are on early flying this week and fly theoretically from 7.0 till 10.0, but, owing to the fact that the instructor did not arrive on the field till 8.20, we did very little and that consisted wholly of "circuits and bumps" on the right hand circuit.*

Tuesday, July 14. *There has been another worse thunderstorm today which reduced a great part of the "drome" to slimy red mud and also the athletic square. Luckily, it came in the late afternoon when flying was nearly over so that few planes were caught up and all those landed safely. During the PT period, a visit was paid to the local swimming baths where I swam 100 yards in order to qualify as a potential swimmer and also to gain the permission to do as I like in any future swimming periods. During the evening, we have had another study hall in the classrooms…*

Thursday, July 23. *I am beginning to realise that we have been very lucky in coming to Americus for the ground school seems to be negligible and we have hardly any drill, while the PT is worth doing especially when we enjoy an hour in the Americus swimming baths twice a week. A great deal of time also seems to be spent in the barracks dozing in chairs or writing letters when it is possible to summon up the strength.*

Friday, July 24. *It has rained very hard again today and the whole parade ground is about 2 inches deep in water, as well as the paths and roads of the camp. The aerodrome is like a bog and it is now practically impossible to land on it without grave risk of a nose-over. All this happened just before I was due to fly, so it rather seems as though I have had my share of flying for the day.*

Saturday, July 25. *Another step has come in the advancement of my flying career, for I have had a solo-ship for the first time today. I rather shook myself, however, by nearly running into the tee on a takeoff and just missing another plane by doing a climbing turn at 10 feet. Did I feel weak at the knees when I got safely up into the air? My landings were pretty lousey owing to the fact that I did not discover the throttle did not shut properly and I was trying to land at about 500 revs. which caused the plane to float for miles over* the aerodrome before dropping to the ground. We had open post tonight which was spent wandering round Americus, eating, and visiting the late film show at 11.0 where we saw the musical film "Swing it Soldier" which was good in comparison with the everlasting western films which are usually shown.

Sunday, July 26. Another of those unfortunate Sundays when nothing can be accomplished. As it has been hot, we decided to go to Americus with the vague idea of bathing somewhere in spite of the fact that the only swimming pool we know of has just been banned because of ear trouble among the lads. Anyway, we arrived in town and after sitting in the services club for some half-hour, we ventured to the Episcopal Church and heard a very dry sermon, and also watched the queer customs that go on in American churches.

After a light dinner at the New York Cafe, we attempted to hitch-hike to a local bathing place, some four miles out of town. However, when the fortieth car had passed, we changed our minds and went to the cinema which cooled me off and also used up a couple of hours. After a walk round the suburbs during which I became more and more browned off and tired, I returned to camp after waiting in the service centre for a bus to turn up.

Tuesday, July 28. The sight of several eliminees on their way out, bound for Trenton served to remind me of the fate awaiting the unwary and has resolved me to get on with the job in hand even though things may look on the black side during some of the "off" days.

Sunday, August 2. One of the laziest days I have had for some time, for apart from getting up for breakfast, I remained more or less in bed until dinner time. I spent the whole of the afternoon with George Palmer in the Americus swimming pool, only coming on to dry land once for a drink and a chocolate bar. The water was very warm and I felt no cooler when I dressed at 4.15 than I did before entering the baths. However, the cinema proved very refreshing and we spent a couple of hours watching a film "Sweater Girl" which was quite exciting and rather different to the usual "high school" tales. Ham and eggs tasted good in the New York Cafe afterwards, and we returned to camp early with our appetites thoroughly satisfied.

Thursday, August 6. We are now in the upper class for the old upper class left today for its basic school and we are expecting the new lower class tomorrow. Owing to the fact that there are so many in this new class, another bed has been installed in our bay which tends to make it rather crowded. We have had a meteorology final exam today which was fairly simple and I am fairly sure I have passed it or "made the grade" as they say out here.

Friday, August 7. The new class has arrived today and things have been in rather a mess especially in the bays where kit bags have been strewn all over the place and men have been frantically unpacking, filling lockers, and signing forms. Flying today has been pretty good for I have shot my 90 degree stages again and have passed. The wind tee was going round in circles all the afternoon which caused landings to be rather fast and awkward in some cases, but I didn't ground loop which is no doubt one feather in my cap.

Monday, August 10. I have had rather a sudden shock today for I found to my surprise that I was on night flying. This has been in addition to an hour's flying this morning when I was taught lazy eights and chandelles officially and made a few attempts at these manoeuvres. My steep turns today were literally terrible for I not only lost a terrific amount of height on one, but went into a spin off another which is unpardonable.

As regards the night flying, I found it a very interesting experience, although I wouldn't relish the idea of being up in the black void alone. Once we left the ground, all that could be seen was a huge blue flame round the exhaust and the string of lights dotted round the drome. All the rest was a solid black engulfing darkness with maybe one or two small pin points of light on the ground. I could just make out the horizon, but it was of very little use and I had to use the unfamiliar instruments in the cockpit. Owing to fear of stalling out on the approach, I always came in much too fast and failed to make a decent landing. However, next week I should improve. We had a lecture tonight in how to fill up our log books and I now have the additional worry of seeing that there are no mistakes in this all important record.

***Thursday, August 13.** I have spent some time listening to the radio which we now have in our bay. It is quite a powerful set and besides hiding a camera for one of the lower class, is capable of picking up England and other places where one doesn't hear the continual "Eat Crispy flakes" or other "snappy" advertisements. I filled up my RAF log book today and much to my surprise discovered that my times agreed with the office which I believe is a miracle of accuracy on their part.*

***Saturday, August 15.** What a day I have had—not that I have done a great deal of flying, for I haven't had any, but I was "Officer of the Day" all morning and the rush has nearly driven me dotty. Firstly, I had to rise at 5.30 in order to blow the hooter for reveille at 6.00, put the flag up, and run everybody's errands all the time. The C.O. would phone up and say "find so and so" and as soon as that was done, "find somebody else."*

Also there were papers to be delivered to each bay, a new innovation, and mail to be sorted and re-addressed if necessary. I had to go to every parade to see whether any one was absent and "gig" them accordingly. The worst job of the lot, however, was answering the telephone with a "Souther Field, Aviation Cadet Randall, Senior Officer of the Day, speaking," a speech which is confusing to remember and difficult to say correctly, one phrase usually getting lost on each occasion that I had to use it.

On Monday, 17 August, a civilian flying instructor and nineteen-year-old LAC Douglas W. Flatau of Flax Bourton, Somerset, and Class SE-43-A were killed when their Stearman trainer plunged into the ground. According to Randall, this accident "tended to put a number of us off our stroke for a short time."

On 23 August and succeeding days, members of Class SE-43-A did the 160-mile-long cross-country exercise to McRae, Georgia, and return. For most of them, skimming across the Georgia countryside was an interesting daylight experience, but at least one man missed Souther Field and landed 40 miles northward at Butler, Georgia. Two days later, freak weather conditions set in, and for several days and nights the RAF cadets and local citizens had the unusual experience of shivering in the cold during the last week of August 1942.

During the first week of September, as class members rushed to finish the scheduled six hours of instrument flying exercises on the Link Trainer, they were mindful of the necessity to complete their final flying hours and the dreaded sixty-hour check. Sandwiched into these activities was a lecture on "the terrors of basic flying school" and an extensive explanation of the Vultee BT-13A trainer, about which so many rumors had circulated. Although most of the LACs undoubtedly thought that the official verdict that all were likely to graduate was optimistic at best, they were pleased that they had almost made it.

On Sunday, 6 September, members of Class SE-43-A packed their bags and attended a lecture that described the travel to be undertaken the next morning. On Monday, 7 September 1942, Class SE-43-A had completed its primary flying course at Souther Field, and LAC Lee Randall summed up the class's experience at Souther Field as follows:

> *On the whole, I think I have enjoyed myself quite a bit since I have been here, and if only Americus had been more of a town with a little more to do, I should have enjoyed myself a great deal more. However, the work has been light, although the hours have been rather long, the flying has been fun, apart from the fact that waiting for planes is not a pleasant occupation. I have been pleased with the food and also the living conditions. The public services are, however, appalling and I am highly disgusted with what we have had to put up with in connection with buses and taxis. The huge quantity of cowboy films that we have seen lately has completely removed the desire to see another for a long, long time and I sincerely hope that neither the Post Theatre at Cochran nor the Cinemas in Macon specialise in this particular type of film.*

Class SE-43-A had begun training in July with a net intake of 203 RAF students. One student died in an airplane crash, 2 were held over for further training, 42 were eliminated from training and 160 graduated and were posted to basic flying schools.

In the middle of SE-43-A's course, the 197 members of Class SE-43-B, the final RAF Arnold Scheme intake, arrived at Souther Field and absorbed the 2 men held over from SE-43-A, thus having a net enrollment of 199 students. Of that number, 33 members of Class SE-43-B were eliminated from primary training and were posted to Canada to be remustered. On 7 October 1942, the 166 graduates of that final RAF class completed the primary flying course at Souther Field and embarked on a short leave before reporting to a basic flying school.

In classes 42-A through 43-B, the Graham Aviation Company at Souther Field enrolled 1,419 British students, an average intake of 109 pupils for each of the thirteen classes. Of these RAF student pilots, 1,037 (73.08 percent) successfully completed primary training and 382 (26.92 percent) were eliminated.

Of the 382 eliminees, 339 (23.89 percent, an average of 26 RAF cadets for each of the thirteen classes) were washed out for flying deficiencies. A total of 39 (2.75 percent) were eliminated for reasons "other than flying," and 4 (.28 percent) died while under training, two from drowning after graduation but before entering basic flying school, and two during training from accidents involving aircraft.

At the request of the Harrold family, twenty-five-year-old LAC Clarence Melville Johnson of Wakefield, Yorkshire, who was trained with Class SE-42-C at Americus and was killed in an Alabama automobile accident in March 1942, was buried in the Harrold family plot in the Oak Grove Cemetery in Americus. The other training casualties were buried in the RAF plot in Montgomery, Alabama.

WHERE HAVE ALL THE RAF CADETS GONE?

42-A. VICTOR DAVID JOHN SHAPLEY, twenty (Americus, Macon, Turner), twin brother of Ernest, with whom he trained as a pilot. Back in the United Kingdom, the two brothers were split up. Victor was assigned to Bomber Command and ultimately flew Lancaster bombers on thirty missions. He was subsequently commissioned and promoted, and was demobilized as flight lieutenant. After World War II, Victor Shapley flew for British South American Airways, and in January 1949, his aircraft disappeared in the Bermuda Triangle with the loss of all aboard.

42-B. DOUGLAS CHARLES LOWE, twenty (Americus, Macon, Dothan). Back in Britain, he underwent further training for service in Bomber Command. He completed training at a twin-engine advanced flying unit (AFU-TE), an operational training unit on Wellington medium bombers (OTU) and a heavy conversion unit (HCU) on Stirling bombers. On active service, he flew twenty-six sorties with 214 Stirling Squadron and 75 Stirling Squadron, and was awarded the DFC. Later, as a flight lieutenant, Lowe served as an instructor at an OTU and at the Bomber Command instructors' school. He continued service in the Royal Air Force and retired as Air Chief Marshal D.C. Lowe, GCB, DFC, AFC, ADC to HM the Queen, 1978–83. After retirement, he served as chairman of Mercury Communications, Ltd.

42-C. ROBERT WILLIAM GEORGE GRIMSWADE, twenty-two, (Americus, Macon, Dothan). On returning to Britain and further training at an advanced flying unit and a flying instructors' school, he served as an instructor for several months. After completing an OTU, he was assigned to 31 Dakota (C-47) Squadron of the Air Transport Command flying to and around India and Burma. During the postwar period, he joined British European Airways (BEA) and that airline's successors, and retired in 1975 as senior captain.

42-I. GEORGE DUFFEE, eighteen, of London (Americus, Macon, Dothan). On return to the United Kingdom and further training for service in Bomber Command, he was assigned to 78 Squadron, flying as co-pilot (second "dickie") on Halifax bombers. On 22 June 1943, the aircraft was shot down by a night fighter while returning from a raid on Mulheim. With help from the Underground, Duffee evaded capture for four months, during which time he traveled from Holland to Gibraltar. Back in Britain, he was allowed to rejoin 78 Squadron and continue flying combat missions. During the war, Flight Lieutenant G. Duffee, DFC, flew forty sorties and logged 750 hours' flying time. He rejoined the RAF in 1948–49 and flew four hundred flights into Berlin during the Berlin Airlift. Afterward, he flew for British European Airways (BEA) and its successors. Captain Duffee retired in 1979, having logged about twenty thousand hours of flying time.

43-B. HARRY KENYON-ORMROD, twenty-five, of Reading, Berkshire (Americus, Macon, Dothan), had served in the British army from 1939 to 1941. On returning to Britain and further training for assignment to Bomber Command, he was assigned on 17 February 1944 to 578 Squadron at Burn, Yorkshire. On 23 August 1944, his aircraft was shot down over Belgium, but he managed to evade capture for three weeks. Ultimately captured, he was imprisoned in Brussels. As a POW, he was transported to Bankau Prison in Germany, where, in June 1945, he and other Allied prisoners were marched across Germany to Luckenwalde. They were liberated by the United States Army and were fed white bread and peanut butter. Back in Britain, Kenyon-Ormrod completed his education and retired in 1978 as headmaster.

DARR AERO TECH
ALBANY, GEORGIA, 42-H-43B

Around 22 February 1942, Class SE-42-H arrived at the primary flying training school from the RAF replacement depot at Turner Field on the opposite side of Albany. At Darr, the 175-man intake joined 6 men held over from the preceding class, bringing the total enrollment to 181. This was the second class of British cadets whose members had undergone a flight grading course in the United Kingdom. However, as with the preceding class, flight grading was not done well primarily because harsh winter weather interfered. As a result, although some of them had done better, many of the students of Class SE-42-H had spent eight or more weeks getting about six hours of dual flying instruction in the United Kingdom, and that training was hardly enough to affect the primary flying training that they commenced several weeks later in the United States.

During March, spring slowly evolved over all of the Southern states. After the drought of the preceding summer and the heavy autumn and winter rains, the spring of 1942 in southwest Georgia was particularly beautiful. Chartreuse leaves covered the hardwoods and provided a beautiful backdrop for the gray Spanish moss that clung to their branches. Conifers glistened with new needles and cabbage palms (palmetto trees) were pushing out new shoots that would become huge green fronds.

Trees of the massive pecan groves were covered with blooms, and the inevitable yellow pollen filled the air and covered everything it reached. Daffodils, tulips and other bulbs were a delight and, before the end of the month, soft rain-washed buildings, walks and streets and other flowering plants and trees brought color to residential streets, parks and public places. Along streets and throughout the forests and woodlands of the whole area, wild white dogwoods were in full bloom. It was a time of renewal, and a time for people to enjoy the outdoors.

LAC Anthony V. Rippengal from Kent was nineteen years old when he commenced flying training at Albany, Georgia. As a student pilot, LAC Rippengal had a facility for entertaining his classmates by mimicking people. Some forty years after qualifying as a pilot, he recalled happy experiences in the Southeastern United States:

> On one or two weekends, some friends and I made our way to Tallahassee where we succeeded in disturbing the studied calm of the State College for Women. Six of us were on a visit to Tallahassee, and a gentleman we met suggested that we visit the college and call at one of the "sorority houses"—a new word and concept to us. He led us to a tree-lined avenue and pointed to one of the houses and turned to go. "Aren't you going to introduce us?" we asked. "No, that's O.K.," he said, "Just tell them who you are"; then he left. After we had recovered from the shock, we held a council of war and arranged for our social secretary to press the door bell. The door opened a crack, and a worried young female face appeared and gazed at us in some alarm and astonishment.
>
> The social secretary said his piece, and we waited expectantly. The young face looked nervously round behind her, and then spoke the dread words, "I am afraid there is no one here at the moment." Her discomfiture increased rapidly as a whisper started in the upper reaches of the house and floated down the staircase in an increasing crescendo of sound which said, "Oh yes, there is!!!"
>
> Fortunately, the impasse was resolved as a door opened inside, and the House Mother appeared and duly invited us in. As we entered the hall, we saw a winding staircase, and as our eyes followed it up, they encountered a host of smiling faces peering over the hand rail. In no time at all, we were being royally entertained. I believe we went on a picnic the next day, and we were invited back the next weekend for the house dance. A very pleasant interlude indeed.

Of the 181-man enrollment of Class SE-42-H, 7 were held over for further training, 63 were eliminated and 105 successfully completed primary flying training around 28 April 1942.

Just one week before the next large RAF draft was divided at Turner Field's replacement center and was posted to primary flying schools, Albany and vicinity experienced a flood. On 20 March, owing to heavy rains throughout the state, the level of the Flint River rose by almost two feet. By Monday, 23 March, the turbulent and muddy, mustard-colored waters had risen more than five feet and swept along all sorts of debris. For several days before the waters receded, flooding occurred in lowlands along the river and in Albany itself from the Flint River Bridge southward along Front Street, but damage was reported as "minimal."

South of Albany close by the river, damage was more extensive. Since the casino and clubhouse received heavy water damage, and for several days the springs as well as the swimming pool and most of the entire golf course were inundated by the reddish-brown flood waters, Radium Springs received the greatest damage from the flood. Farther down the river, lowlands did not escape flooding, but houses and other facilities on higher ground were spared. Although muddy water apparently surrounded much of River Bend Park, there was little serious damage. On 31 March 1942, the 168-man Class SE-42-I intake arrived at Darr Aero Tech and was joined by the 7 students held over from the preceding class, bringing the total enrollment to 175 men.

From his home in Harrogate, North Yorkshire, Squadron Leader Douglas A. Boards, DFM, described how, though training schedules were tight, he and several classmates were able to meet people and enjoy themselves:

> At Thomasville, we met some people who on several occasions arranged barbecues, horseback riding, and swimming. At the end of the primary course, we had a graduation dance to which we invited two of our girl friends from Thomasville. We also had a 4-day leave, and spent some of it with our friends in Thomasville, and also hitched along the Gulf Coast to Appalachicola and Panama City.
>
> On another occasion, while two of us were visiting Thomasville, we were hailed from a passing car. The man driving it stopped, and turned out to be a wealthy New Yorker enroute through Thomasville. He said he had been looking for some RAF cadets, and he took us to have tea at a very plush hotel, "The Three Toms Inn." We had a very pleasant time.
>
> I thoroughly enjoyed the constant warmth in Albany, quite different from an English summer, but no problem. On post, training took up most of our time. My instructor, Mr. Freye, had 5 students and graduated all five of us. There were no accidents that I recall, though, on occasion, there were training stoppages due to thunderstorms, rain, or haze, but much less than in the U.K.
>
> The quality of instruction was very good. The quiz system of exams was new to me. I thought it a good quick way of putting down quickly what would otherwise take a long time; it was easy to mark. The flying instruction was also excellent. One thing I particularly thought good was that all through the course, we never used an Airspeed Indicator, and the other instruments were basic—tachometer, cylinder head temperature gauge, oil pressure gauge, and magnetic compass. This stood me in good stead in my subsequent flying career. Even now, I cannot think of any changes I would like to have seen. We were taught to fly "by the seat of our pants."

Of course, the primary flying students did not know much about flying at the time, but in the light of later experience, not all RAF students agreed with Douglas Board's assessment of his initial flying experience.

LAC Oliver Villiers Brooks was twenty years old when he underwent pilot training at Darr Aero Tech. His flying instructor was Leslie H. Freye, an experienced, patient and competent pilot from Chicago who always tried to graduate all five of the students assigned to him. "We did not have much open post," Brooks recalled, "but when we did we were taken about and entertained well." Another member of Class SE-42-I, George Beattie Smith, a native of Belfast, Northern Ireland, recalled that on one occasion, he and several other RAF cadets caught a ride with a man who, "because he was not going our full distance, lent us his car until the following morning, in order that we could be back on time."

One weekend, LAC George Allan Findlay and a classmate were sent to nearby Camilla, Georgia, as guests of a church. During that visit, he met Florence Whiting, a young lady who in 1943 became Mrs. Findlay. Their courtship was sometimes carried on by air. "On several solo flights from Darr," Findlay recalled, "I would make a point of flying over the Whiting farm and would occasionally drop messages in a 'coke' bottle."

The 167-man Class SE-42-J draft that traveled from the Turner Field replacement depot to Darr Aero Tech in late April 1942 joined the 7 men held over from the preceding class, bringing the total intake to 174 men. The class remained at the Albany school until late June. When students of the class began to fly, spring was in full bloom and it was good to be alive. For instructors and cadets alike, maneuvering a Stearman PT-17 with its open cockpit over miles of fields and woods and swamps in the bright southwest Georgia skies was an exhilarating experience.

Below, life went on as usual in the rich agricultural country. Grains and grasses planted in winter converted huge fields into multiple shades of velvet green. Spring plowing and planting had begun. Along the edge of wooded areas, many farmers had begun to remove covers from tobacco plant beds and these strips of ground stood out in contrast to the surrounding green and the reddish-brown plowed fields. When covered with the long white cloth strips, these spots guarded tobacco plants from either cold or sun until they could toughen enough to be planted. Dogwood blossoms and other wild flowers and trees still dotted the forests and swamps.

John A. Davis and his wife must have been one of the kindest couples in Albany. Mr. Davis, the business manager and columnist for the *Albany Herald*, regularly "adopted" a couple of UK cadets, enjoyed their company, provided hospitality and drove the young men about showing off the country, its flora and fauna, narrating a large measure of its local history and either explaining or showing them local customs. Earlier, they were described as having taken two British cadets on a Sunday trip to the Florida Gulf Coast.

One Sunday afternoon in April 1942, the Davises were driving northward into Lee County when they saw beside the road "two British cadets walking in the direction we were headed." Vic Moore and Ron Pickler rode with the elderly couple in their "Flying Ford" through the winding, back roads of Lee County, Georgia, savoring the violets, wild azaleas, wisteria, honeysuckle, old houses and springtime greenery. Soon the party came upon Mount Pleasant Church, an African American institution. They entered the church and witnessed what Mr. Davis later described as "one of the most earnest, and in some respects, inspiring services I had ever attended." In a powerful delivery, accompanied by chants and songs, the black minister's sermon "swayed his congregation to constant exclamations of approval of his declarations." When the white guests withdrew, they were deeply moved.

Soon their course would be finished and the two young RAF cadets would move on from Albany to a basic flying school. They would take with them formidable memories. Unfortunately, as with earlier classes, too many young RAF cadets were spending only three or four weeks at the flying school before they washed out of pilot training and joined other sad and disappointed young men on the long rail journey back to Canada for remustering. Many of them got other opportunities for aircrew training in Canada, and from there went on to service against enemies over Europe, the Middle East, North Africa and Southeast Asia.

Of those RAF students in Class SE-42-J who continued their labors and qualified as pilots were many men of uncommon valor. One of those quiet and deeply religious young men of the class whom destiny was to single out for the ultimate sacrifice was Cyril Joe Barton. Though he may have originally entered the school as a member of either Class SE-42-H or SE-42-I, Barton was apparently delayed in his training, but successfully completed primary training at Darr Aero Tech on 4 July 1942 with Class SE-42-J. Subsequently, he finished basic flying at Cochran Field, Macon, Georgia, and graduated on 10 November 1942 as a sergeant pilot from the USAAF advanced flying school at Napier Field, Dothan, Alabama.

Less than a year later, on 26 September 1943, by then captain of a seven-man Halifax Bomber crew, Barton was commissioned pilot officer. On the night of 30–31 March 1944, Barton and his crew flew Halifax LK797 on his nineteenth and final mission. That was the now famous Nuremberg Raid, which cost RAF Bomber Command more aircraft and crews in a single night than any other raid of the war. En route to the target, Barton's aircraft was severely damaged by night fighters, but he pushed on to bomb a target and bring his giant aircraft and the remnants of his crew back home to fight another day.

Flying through the night fog and mist, with his fuel supply diminishing rapidly and without proper navigation, Barton finally crash-landed the Halifax around 6:00 a.m., 31 March 1944 at Ryhope, County Durham. The fuselage broke in half on contact with the ground, and much of the remainder of the aircraft disentegrated. The three crewmen in the rear section of the fuselage survived, but Barton was unfortunately dead on arrival at a nearby hospital. On 6 April 1944, Barton was buried in a cemetery near his home in Kingston-on-Thames, Surrey. Several weeks later, on 27 June 1944, exactly two years after he had completed his sixty hours on Stearman PT-17s at Darr Aero Tech and was awaiting his final sixty-hour check ride, Cyril Joe Barton was posthumously awarded the Victoria Cross, Great Britain's highest award for valor.

To Class SE-42-J and the more than 4,000 men who successfully completed Arnold Scheme pilot training courses, Flying Officer Barton's sacrifice brought a signal honor; he was the only Arnold Scheme graduate to receive the Victoria Cross. Of the 174-man gross intake for Class SE-42-J, 6 students were transferred or held over to Class SE-42-K for additional training, 63 were eliminated and 105 graduated near the end of June 1942. Following a few days' leave, they left for a basic flying school.

On 2 June 1942, following the four-week acclimatization course that the *Albany Herald* erroneously reported as a "four months pre-flight course," but which anxious British cadets believed to be an accurate accounting of time, Class SE-42-K traveled the few miles across town from Turner Field to Darr Aero Tech and commenced primary flying training.

Including the 6 holdovers, Class SE-42-K had a total enrollment of 179 students, and when they arrived Class SE-42-J, which had become the upper class with the departure of the men of SE-42-I, announced its cadet officer and noncommissioned officer appointments.

Unlike earlier classes, many members of Class SE-42-K had completed in excess of thirty hours flying in flight grading courses at scattered elementary flying training schools (EFTSs) in the United Kingdom. As a result, their progress in primary flying training was much more rapid than earlier classes', and their failure rate much lower. Within two weeks, as many of them were soloing for the second time, some distinguished British visitors arrived on an inspection tour of selected Arnold Scheme schools.

From his headquarters at Fort Worth, Texas, came Major General Barton K. Yount, commanding general of the army air forces Flying Training Command, and he was accompanied by several visitors including Captain Harold Balfour, MC, member of Parliament and undersecretary of state for air; Air Marshal A.G.R. Garrod, air (council) member for training; and Air Vice Marshal Robert Leckie, Royal Canadian Air Force air member for training (AMT).

Among the graduates of Class SE-42-K were Colin Armstrong of North Yorkshire and John Lilley of Nottinghamshire. Although he enjoyed himself when he did get off the station, Armstrong "did not get a lot of open post" because he received a large number of demerits and spent most weekends walking tours in the hot sun. John Lilley also successfully completed pilot training and served as an instructor in the USAAF advanced flying school at Douglas, Arizona. Back in Britain, he saw combat, survived the war and returned to his native Nottinghamshire.

More than forty years later, John Lilley wrote from his home in the Midlands about his training days in the United States:

> *The hospitality of the locals was superb. They went out of their way to entertain us and brought into being a new meaning to "Southern hospitality." However, one had to have the right modus operandi to make contacts. Many RAF men following the English tradition that the pub is a community centre, thought that by going to bars, they would meet the locals. I quickly found out that this was not the way to "get one's feet under the table" or meet a family. The best way, or at least I thought it was because it worked, was to go to church and sit there looking lost. This was in the Bible Belt after all, and after the service, one could rely on people coming up to you and introducing themselves and inviting you to their homes!*
>
> *The course ended at the beginning of August 1942 and we were given a few days leave before going on to basic flying training. I went to Valdosta, Georgia, Jacksonville and Tallahassee, Florida. Travel was by coach and brought me to the then existing attitudes to Negroes of the South. Unwittingly, I boarded a bus and walked to the back to sit down. I didn't realise that whites got on in the front half of the bus and blacks at the back. I was regarded with suspicion and hostility by both blacks and whites on the bus, and was told roughly by a black to get the hell out of their part of the bus. My confusion must have been evident, because there was nothing on the bus to show any division, but someone explained to me the convention of the locals, which I, of course, acceded to.*

As Lilley and his classmates savored each of their experiences during the summer of 1942, changes were occurring everywhere.

The heat and humidity were oppressive. The swimming pools at Darr Aero Tech, Radium Springs and Riverbend Park were in almost constant use. There was plenty of recreation, but so little time to enjoy it. However, being able to fly was enough, except that the intensified nine-week course seemed to pass so rapidly that there was hardly time for anything. There was understandable shock and concern, however, when word came on 16 July that four twin-engine advanced trainers from Moody Field near Valdosta had collided in the air near Madison, Florida, killing seven RAF cadets and one American officer-instructor. On 17 July, RAF contingents from Darr and Turner Fields demonstrated their superb drill when they marched in the American Heroes Day Parade, which was sponsored by Albany merchants for the purpose of promoting the sale of war bonds.

Three weeks later on Tuesday evening, 4 August, Class SE-42-K held its graduation dinner-dance in the dining hall at Darr Aero Tech. Mr. H.D. Goodman ("See Sub Ell"), director of ground school, acted as master of ceremonies. During the course of the evening, Goodman presented an award to LAC James Meadows for the highest academic average for the class. The next day, the class graduated and an announcement appeared in the newspaper that RAF training in the United States would likely end soon. Of its 179-man gross enrollment, 8 men of Class SE-42-K were held over to the next class, 35 were eliminated and 136 graduated and were posted to a basic flying school.

In early July 1942, the 168 RAF members of Class SE-43-A arrived at Darr Aero Tech and joined the 8 students held over from Class SE-42-K, bringing the total enrollment to 176. When Class SE-42-K departed on 4 August, SE-43-A was elevated to upper-class status and made preparations to receive Class SE-43-B, the final RAF class to be trained at Darr Aero Tech. As the senior class began to practice aerobatics and precision flying, the new class commenced initial flying.

On Wednesday evening, 2 September 1942, a dance was held in honor of the graduating class at the school's dining hall, and the RAF cadets helped to provide much of the entertainment. After Mr. Goodman, master of ceremonies, presented the academic award to LAC Douglas J. Traini, LAC Allen Mottershead, known professionally in the United Kingdom as "Max Madison," presented comedy and music specialties, and several other British cadets, including Bryan Walker, John Trinder, George Lee and Jerry Tibbetts, presented an amusing skit entitled "Bungled Badley." The next day, 3 September 1942, Class SE-43-A departed for a basic flying school. Of the 176 students, 11 were held over, 32 were eliminated and 133, or a whopping 80.6 percent, graduated and were posted to a basic flying school. This success record was the best of any RAF class trained at Darr Aero Tech.

Since the 172 members of Class SE-43-B had arrived at the primary flying school in early August, they were halfway through their primary flying course when SE-42-K departed. During the course of their training, they were joined by the 11 men held over from the preceding class. All of them had already gained a degree of familiarity with Albany during their four-week acclimatization course at nearby Turner Field. And most of them had already flown more than twelve hours on British flight grading courses before arriving in the United States. As a result, they were quite anxious to continue flying training.

Among the members of Class 43-B were Christopher Horn of Ashington, Northumberland; George Lee of Bromley, Kent; John Marcus Greenhow of Huthwaite, Nottinghamshire; and William "Jock" Riddell of Ayrshire, Scotland. Except for Greenhow, they all completed the course successfully. John Marcus Greenhow was one of Instructor Carl Siemer's two students of the class who washed out. On 24 September 1942, Greenhow was eliminated from primary training. However, as with five RAF student pilots from Class SE-42-A the year before, Greenhow received some further flying training in a war training program (formerly CPTP) with Graham Aviation School at Butler, Pennsylvania. Afterward, Greenhow was posted to Canada, where he successfully completed pilot training.

On Friday afternoon, 11 September, two Stearman trainers with a British cadet at the controls of each collided in the air ten miles northwest of Albany. Although the aircraft were virtually destroyed, both students fortunately parachuted to safety. Then, on Sunday, 13 September, Class SE-43-B was joined by USAAF aviation cadets of Class SE-43-C.

On 7 October 1942, exactly sixteen months after Class SE-42-A, the first Arnold Scheme intake, arrived to commence training at Darr Aero Tech, Class SE-43-B, the final RAF Arnold

Scheme course, completed its primary flying training. On 9 October 1942, the eleven RAF cadets remaining at Darr Aero Tech who had been delayed in training or held over from one class to another for illness or other reasons departed Albany by train destined for Canada, where they would continue aircrew training.

RAF pilot training was concluded at Darr Aero Tech. Squadron Leader A.G. Hill, who had served from June 1941 as RAF administrative officer at the primary school, had been sent on other detached service assignments in January and returned to Darr in May 1942. It was fitting that Hill should be present when the last class completed its training. The Darr Aero Tech graduates who had returned to the school to serve as check pilots also departed. Pilot Officer Guy E.C. Pease had been reassigned as an instructor at an advanced flying school earlier, and on 26 October 1942, Pilot Officers Edwin Hibbert and Jack E. Gilder departed for Canada and return to the United Kingdom, while Pilot Officer Robert H. Weighill followed via Montgomery, Alabama, a few days later.

That was not the last that would be heard of the British cadets. There were other British students in training at Turner Field's USAAF advanced flying school who would not complete their flying courses until February 1943. There were also some RAF administrative officers and instructors on duty there. Even if there had not been others still present, Albany would never hear the last of the more than 3,500 RAF personnel who were wartime visitors between June 1941 and March 1943. Of all the Southern towns where RAF Arnold Scheme schools were located, Albany, with primary and advanced flying schools as well as an RAF replacement depot, served the greatest numbers of British student pilots of any town.

Between 1941 and 1943, a great mutual admiration society was established. The British student pilots had impressed the people of Albany and other nearby towns, and had themselves been greatly affected by the Americans. When the calendar rolled around to Christmas once more, the *Albany Herald* published a long article by Ernestine Sherman that captured memories of the British presence and defined its impact. She wrote of much teasing about American and British pronunciations, and of lively discussions about literature, history, philosophy and religion. There had also been pleasant winter evenings "before the fire" listening to phonograph recordings. The UK officers and pilot trainees had brought friendliness and goodwill and had promoted understanding. One RAF student who was washed out of pilot training was quoted as saying, "I shall never forget you two, for you and my instructor will always personify America to me."

As Ms. Sherman asserted and dozens of others confirmed, the British cadets gave Americans a new perspective on both the United States and Great Britain. "The map of Britain is now dotted with familiar places," she wrote, "for I know boys, and their families who live in them, many whom I have been invited to visit when peace has come again." Being able to have places described by young men who lived there brought British geography alive and helped many readers "to know" the specific places when they read the literature of the islands.

In classes SE-42-A through SE-43-B, Darr Aero Tech at Albany, Georgia, enrolled 2,208 RAF students, an average intake of 170 students for thirteen classes, each of which commenced training approximately every four and a half to five weeks during the period extending from 8 June 1941 to 7 October 1942, when Class SE-43-B completed primary training and departed.

Of these 2,208 RAF students under training at Darr Aero Tech, 1,392, or 63.04 percent, graduated, and 816, or 36.96 percent, were eliminated. A further statistical breakdown of the eliminees indicates that 766, or 34.69 percent, an average of 59 for each of the thirteen classes, were washed out for flying deficiencies; 48, or 2.17 percent, for "other than flying deficiencies"; and two, or .09 percent, were killed in accidents involving aircraft.

Including all eliminees, five of the RAF classes, SE-42-C, SE-42-E, SE-42-K, SE-43-A and SE-43-B, had fewer than the average of fifty-nine eliminees, and the latter three classes, the lowest numbers of which were thirty-five, thirty-two and thirty-seven, respectively, demonstrate the effectiveness of flight grading in the United Kingdom. The greatest number of eliminees occurred in Classes SE-42-F, SE-42-A and SE-42-B.

WHERE HAVE ALL THE RAF CADETS GONE?

42-A. REGINALD LEVY, nineteen (Albany, Macon, Turner). On return to Britain and additional training for assignment to Bomber Command, he joined 51 Squadron flying Halifax bombers. In the course of the war, he participated in major raids on Hamburg, Peenemunde and Berlin. Later, he converted to DH Mosquito aircraft and flew with 105 Squadron on low-level daylight bombing raids. In 1943, he was awarded the DFC, and by the end of the war he had flown seventy-five sorties. In 1948–49, Levy flew numerous missions in the Berlin Airlift. Subsequently, he joined Belgium's Sabena Airways. On his fiftieth birthday, 8 May 1972, Levy was hijacked to Tel Aviv by "Black September." In the shoot-out that followed, two passengers were killed. Captain Levy was awarded the Knight's Order of the Crown, and continued as an airline pilot until retirement in September 1981.

42-B. JOHN C. BLISS, twenty-eight (Albany, Macon, Dothan), was a veteran of service with the London Metropolitan Police. After graduation as a pilot officer, he served as a flying instructor at the USAAF advanced flying school at Dothan, Alabama, until 17 October 1942. Back in Britain and further training, he was assigned in June 1943 to 227 Squadron, flying Beaufighters in the Middle East Command. Bliss flew forty sorties over the western desert, Greece and the Dodecanese Islands. During this time, he developed tuberculosis and spent two years in hospital. On returning to Britain and the Metropolitan Police, he served in various capacities until retirement in 1971. During the war, Detective Inspector J.C. Bliss was promoted to flight lieutenant and logged 1,194 hours of flying time.

42-B. EDWIN ALDRIDGE HADDOCK, twenty, of Grimsby (Albany, Macon, Selma). Back in Britain for further training, he was ultimately assigned to 181 Squadron flying Hawker Typhoons with the Second Tactical Air Force. On 15 July 1944, his aircraft was shot down near Abbeville, France. With the aid of five different resistance groups, Haddock was able to evade capture for seven months. While receiving arms by parachute, he was charged as a spy and arrested by the Gestapo. He then spent five months in solitary confinement in Tours, Anger and Fresnes in Paris. Finally recognized as a POW, he was transferred to Stalag Luft IIIA. As the war was drawing to a close in early 1945, the Germans forced Allied POWs to march westward to Luckenwalde. E.A. Haddock completed his wartime service as squadron leader, completed his medical training and obtained his MD degree. As a hobby, he is a surrealist artist.

42-F. STANLEY McCREITH (Albany, Macon, Selma). At graduation, he was commissioned pilot officer and was assigned as a flying instructor at the USAAF advanced flying school, Dothan, Alabama. Upon returning to Britain in May 1943 and receiving further training, he was assigned to 680 Photo Reconnaissance Unit flying Mosquito aircraft. Assigned to the Middle East Command, his aircraft was shot down by flak over Hungary on 13 October 1944. Captured by German forces, he was imprisoned in Stalag Luft III until May 1945. McCreith was assigned to PRU unit at RAF Benson, and subsequently, in 1947, he was assigned to the Empire Test Pilot's

School, then to Boscombe Down for three years. Wing Commander Stanley McCreith, AFC, retired from the RAF in 1966.

42-G. JOHN CUNNINGHAM (Albany, Macon, Dothan). Commissioned on graduation, he served as a flying instructor at the USAAF basic flying school, Gunter Field, Alabama, from 28 September 1942 to 26 May 1943. Back in the United Kingdom, he underwent further training in preparation for assignment to Bomber Command. Between 26 July 1944 and 8 November 1944, Flight Lieutenant Cunningham flew Lancaster bombers of 115 Squadron on thirty-five sorties and was awarded the DFC. Subsequently, Cunningham was posted to Air Transport Command in Southeast Asia and the Pacific.

42-I. GEORGE ALLAN "MAC" FINDLAY (Albany, Macon, Dothan). Commissioned on graduation, he attended central instructors' school at Maxwell Field, Alabama, and was then assigned as a flying instructor at the USAAF basic flying school at Bainbridge, Georgia. In February 1943, he returned to the United Kingdom for further training. He then volunteered for service in the Far East. Ultimately, he was posted to 54 Squadron at Darwin, Australia, flying Spitfires. In mid-1944, he reported to RAF authorities in Sydney and was assigned transport to San Francisco. While in the United States, Findlay was determined to see his wife in Camilla, Georgia, so he caught a plane to Atlanta and rode a bus to Camilla. Upon returning to Britain, he was assigned to a P-51 Squadron and was credited with shooting down two flying bombs and assisting with four more. Until Flight Lieutenant G.A. Findlay was demobilized in September 1946, he was assigned to other flying duties. Upon release by the RAF, he returned to his wife in Georgia and began developing his own business.

CHAPTER TEN

THE FINAL SIX RAF CLASSES IN FLORIDA

LAKELAND, 42-H–43-B,
AND CARLSTROM FIELD, 42-H

Near the end of February 1942, within a few days of the graduation of Class SE-42-F, the 122 RAF members of Class 42-H arrived at the Lakeland school by rail from the new RAF replacement center at Turner Field, Albany, Georgia. The 2 men held over from Class SE-42-G joined them and increased the intake to 124. Among the members of Class SE-42-H at Lakeland were John B. Lyke, a former local government officer in Hereford, England; Cyril D. Pearce of London's Metropolitan Police; and Leslie J. Clay of Coventry. Lyke and Pearce completed pilot training, but Clay was eliminated at Lakeland and trained in Canada as an air bomber. Of the 124 RAF cadets of Class SE-42-H, 1 was held over for further training, 27 were eliminated and 96 graduated from the intensified training course early in April 1942.

The 122-man intake for Class SE-42-I arrived in Lakeland on 31 March 1942, and 1 student who had been held over from the preceding class was added to the intake. Since RAF pilot training ended at Carlstrom Field at Arcadia, Florida, with Class SE-42-H, 6 RAF students who had been held over for further training were transferred to Lakeland. One of these Carlstrom trainees, LAC A.J. Daniel, had contracted measles, and since he was unable to finish primary training with his class he joined the 5 LACs who were transferred to Lakeland. As a result, enrollment for Lakeland's Class SE-42-I climbed to 129 men.

Besides LAC Daniel, other members of that class were two twenty-one-year-olds, Victor H. Johnson of Birmingham and Basil S. Wood of West Bromwich. Other class members included twenty-year-olds James L. Beveridge of Falkirk, Scotland, and Stephen A. Heard of Sussex; twenty-three-year-old Frank W. "Bing" Bingham and twenty-six-year-old Harold F. "Harry" Warwick, both former police constables in London's Metropolitan Police; and Herbert Nevil Mottershead, a Shropshire farm lad. Mottershead completed his pilot training at Cochran and Moody Fields in Georgia, returned to the United Kingdom, built a distinguished record as a bomber pilot, won a commission and a Distinguished Flying Cross and managed to survive the war.

More than forty years later, from his home in a Derbyshire village near the center of Britain, Mottershead recalled the exciting days he spent at Lakeland:

> *Instruction was thorough, irrespective of the instructor, and each one had plenty of patience. I cannot recall serious accidents…Oranges and grapefruit grew everywhere, and fresh orange juice was to be had in every store and cafe. With the town of Lakeland so near, there was plenty to do off post. Many cadets took a keen interest in the local college; others made use of the school's sports facilities, and some would head for Tampa-St. Petersburg or even*

the Everglades. One of our cadets was a very fine pianist, his talents being put to good use as accompanist to the cadet choir which sang British songs on the local radio each week.

"Harry" Warwick and "Bing" Bingham completed their pilot training at Cochran and Turner Fields, were awarded commissions as pilot officers and served as flying instructors at USAAF flying schools before returning home to Britain.

Of the primary flying school at Lakeland, these two LACs recalled the abundance of good food and fresh fruit. "We used to pass by orange groves which bore the notice, 'these fields are posted,'" recalled Frank Bingham. "This didn't mean much to us until wandering into them we were confronted by a guard with a shotgun." Except for this part of their education, they found both their civilian instructors and local citizens practitioners of "traditional Southern hospitality." Having served as a police constable in London's devastated East End, Warwick was much impressed with the "sun, warmth, and beauty of Florida," recalling especially the "scent of orange blossoms whilst flying low in open cockpit Stearmans."

At Lakeland, LAC Daniel recalled "a splendid lady who ran a taxi in the town of Lakeland, and who used to ensure we got back to the base on time, and I am sure, undercharged us in the process." On 1 June 1942, as the orange and lemon blossoms in the surrounding groves opened and were maturing to an aromatic peak, 85 of the 129 RAF students in Class SE-42-I graduated and were posted to the USAAF basic flying school at Cochran Field near Macon, Georgia. Of the remaining members of the class, 2 were held over for further training and 42 were eliminated.

On 1 May 1942, the 122-member intake of Class SE-42-J traveled by train from the RAF replacement center at Turner Field, Albany, Georgia, and joined the 2 RAF men held over from the preceding class at Lakeland. Among the members of that course were Ronald W. Cumbers of London and Garnet G.A. Whitehead of Cambridgeshire. Before joining the RAF, Cumbers worked on the London Stock Exchange, and Whitehead was a "solicitor's articled clerk." Cumbers was later eliminated from pilot training, became a bomb aimer and flew on sixty-two operational sorties. Whitehead completed pilot training and won a DFC with Bomber Command. When the war ended in 1945, Whitehead was second pilot aboard a Douglas C-47 Dakota transport, the first British aircraft to land in Japan.

More than forty years later, Circuit Judge Garnet G.A. Whitehead recalled his Florida experiences:

We travelled by coach from Albany to Lakeland, Florida. I started flight instruction there on 3 May 1942 on Stearman PT-17 aircraft. My instructor was Jack V. Maguire who had a reputation of being "fierce." We had been warned about him before we even got to Lakeland, and received sympathy when we were assigned to him. He was an extremely good flier and instructor. He certainly balled us out if our flying fell below his expectations, but he never failed to compliment us for good work when justified.

I always felt he had a poor opinion of my flying ability initially, but his attitude towards me changed dramatically after I did a forced landing. On that occasion, I was flying solo and practicing aerobatics when the engine cut out at 3000 feet. I was near one of the auxiliary landing fields and made a textbook 180 degree overhead approach and landing—a technique he had taught and demonstrated to us. The landing was witnessed by another instructor, who reported it to Maguire, and from then on I could do no wrong!

Our reception by the citizens of Lakeland was marvellous. I was one of four who had a standing invitation to stay with a Tampa accountant and his family at Lake Carroll every weekend. I understand they entertained four of us from each class during the whole of the time the British were training at Lakeland. Their name was Mr. and Mrs. T. van Rhyn Carty and were better known as "Uncle Van" and "Aunt Maizie." They were wonderful people, and I continued to correspond with them until the early 1960s when they died.

On base, the food and accommodation was of the highest order. We had come from England where food was severely rationed, to a land of plenty, and there were never complaints about food, or about accommodation. Some of us had minor physical problems resulting from the climate and the transition from rationing to plenty. "Prickly heat" was a problem with some—I suffered a series of boils which was very painful, especially as our seat-type parachutes were not designed to accommodate such protrusions!

Discipline was strict despite the civilian nature of Lakeland. The 0545 reveille was not popular; it meant we had 15 minutes to dress, shower and shave before gathering at the flag at 0600. The Cadet Officer of the Day, in addition, had to collect the flag (stars and stripes) from the Guardroom locker. On the occasion when I was O.D., I conceived the bright idea of collecting the flag before going to bed. It was a particularly cold night, and during the night I spread it over my bed as an additional blanket. At about 0300, the US Army O.D. decided to carry out a bed check, and observed the recumbent figure lying under the flag! Thus, I (and everyone else in the dormitory) learned one of our earlier lessons about the respect to be shown the flag.

Ground school was unpopular; we had covered most of the material at ITW. Ground school alternated with flying—i.e., one day flying in the morning, and ground school in the afternoon, next day vice versa. We found it extremely difficult to keep awake in the afternoon ground school sessions. We felt too much academic stuff was included in the subject, "Theory of Flight." The instructor had a very boring voice, and was obviously a mathematical genius, which meant that most of us were not on the same wave length most of the time. He was given the nickname, "See-Sub-Ell" which had reference to his favourite theme, i.e., (C/L) Coefficient of Lift.

Although Lakeland graduates of the early classes had continued training at Gunter Field, many of those in the fall of 1941 and winter of 1941–42 through Class SE-42-I had been posted to Cochran Field at Macon, Georgia.

Of the 124 men of Class SE-42-J, 2 were held over for further training, 41 were eliminated and 81 graduated in early July 1942. With RAF training closed with the graduation of Class SE-42-E at the Southern Aviation School, Camden, South Carolina, and at the Riddle Aeronautical Institute, Carlstrom Field, Florida, with the graduation of Class SE-42-H, only four Arnold Scheme primary flying schools continued to train RAF student pilots. With that reduction in training schools, Lakeland primary graduates were once more assigned to the USAAF basic flying school at Gunter Field, Alabama.

The final three Royal Air Force classes at the Lakeland School of Aeronautics were different from the preceding ten classes. They were combined British-American classes, and all of the members of the RAF contingents had completed a flight grading course plus additional hours of dual and solo instruction. On 3 June 1942, when Class SE-42-J was halfway through the primary flying course at Lakeland, they were joined by Class SE-42-K, which consisted of a seventy-nine-man RAF draft from the Turner Field replacement depot. The new class's numbers were increased to eighty-two by the addition of three men held over from preceding classes, and the remainder of the two-hundred-man class was filled out by USAAF aviation cadets.

Among the members of Class SE-42-K were LACs Eustace C. Youngblood of London; Robert T. Bowring of Derby, a former Halton boy; Michael Beetham of Leicester; John H. Appleton of Worcestershire; and Douglas H. "Peter" Pratt of Surrey. Pratt was eliminated from primary training at Lakeland and subsequently trained as an air bomber in Canada. Eustace C. Youngblood completed flying training at Craig Field and subsequently served on 136 Squadron in Southeast Asia. Robert Bowring, John Appleton and Michael Beetham successfully completed flying training at Turner Field and arrived back in the United Kingdom in time for the 1943–44 RAF bomber offensive. During the next forty years, Beetham rose to the rank of marshal of the Royal Air Force and chief of air staff, the highest-ranking American-trained British airman.

During the postwar years, Robert Bowring of Derby also remained in the Royal Air Force as a career officer. In the process of flying in the Berlin Airlift, attending a number of schools and exercising responsibilities in staff, command and administrative posts, Bowring rose to the rank of squadron leader. During his aviation career, Bowring achieved recognition as an exceptional aviation writer and was selected for membership in the Guild of Air Pilots and Air Navigators. Subsequently, the guild awarded him its Pike Memorial Trophy and Medal for his international contributions to the development of pilot training plans.

When Class SE-42-K was halfway through its primary flying course, they were joined by Class SE-43-A, which included USAAF and RAF cadets. The seventy-four-man RAF contingent arrived at the Lakeland train depot at 5:00 a.m. on 6 July 1942 and received one holdover from the preceding class, which brought the total enrollment to seventy-five. After eating breakfast, being assigned quarters, receiving a medical examination as well as an issue of personal supplies and training manuals, their first day was complete. Among that RAF intake at Lakeland were LACs Eric S.V. Ryland, Frederick W. O'Brien, John D. Silvester, William E. Greenwell and Eric N. Bailey.

As with the members of preceding classes, their daily schedules were filled with flying, ground school lectures and physical training. When they were able to leave the flying school, they usually traveled into Lakeland by bus or taxi, had lunch, played carpet golf and strolled about the town taking snapshots. During their sessions of open-post, most of the RAF cadets visited the local USO. While some of the cadets read or wrote letters, others were involved in playing table tennis or cards, and occasionally all of them joined in an organized singsong. The remnants of Class SE-42-K completed primary flying training on 4 August 1942, and of that strength, one RAF student was held over for further training, thirty were eliminated and fifty-one successfully completed primary and were posted to a basic flying school.

Priorities for off-post activities during the summer of 1942 were food, swimming and sightseeing. When time permitted, RAF cadets, usually traveling in pairs, hitchhiked to nearby towns and resorts. On Sunday, 19 July, LACs Eric Bailey and Stan Baker hitched a ride to Winter Haven with Mr. and Mrs. E.L. Hoskins, and the American couple drove them about the town showing them the sights before dropping them off at nearby Cypress Gardens. During subsequent weekends, they hitched rides to and from Sarasota, Plant City and Tampa.

On Friday, 4 September, final flying hours, sixty-hour checks and ground school examinations were completed. Then, at 1:30 p.m. on Sunday, 6 September, the surviving members of Class

SE-43-A departed by train for Montgomery, Alabama, and the Gunter Field USAAF basic flying school. In his diary, Eric Bailey described the scene at the Lakeland railroad depot when a large number of friends crowded in and around the railroad station to say goodbye to the RAF cadets: "One chap really said it was just like leaving home a second time."

On 24 July, Albert I. Lodwick, owner-operator of the primary flying school, announced that only one additional RAF class would be trained at the Lakeland school. A fortnight later, that final RAF intake, Class SE-43-B, containing sixty-eight RAF cadets, arrived at the Florida primary school. Among the RAF members of the course were Ronald A.E. Allen of London and Reginald C. Schofield of Boston, Lincolnshire. As they followed the established training regimen and the usual open-post activities of the cadets who had preceded them, life on the air station went on according to usual schedules for day and night flying, ground school, six hours of Link Trainer exercises and physical training.

In September, when Class SE-43-A left the Lakeland (Lodwick) School of Aeronautics, Class SE-43-C, an all-USAAF cadet class, arrived as the junior class. Of the seventy-five-man Class 43-A RAF intake, twenty-four men were eliminated and fifty-one graduated from the primary flying school on 8 September 1942 and were posted to Gunter Field, Alabama, for the basic phase of their training.

Then, in early October 1942, it was all over. Eight RAF cadets had been eliminated from primary training, and the remaining sixty members of Class SE-43-B departed for a basic flying school. Almost exactly sixteen months had passed since the arrival of the first RAF class in June 1941. Wing Commander Ronald A.E. Allen, AFC (RAF, retired), was a lowly LAC member of Class SE-43-B, and forty-five years after commencing training at Lakeland, he wrote of his American training, "I would not have missed the experience of training in the USA for all the tea in China!"

In Classes SE-42-A through SE-43-B, the Lakeland (Lodwick) School of Aeronautics enrolled 1,326 RAF students, an average intake of 102 British pupils for each of the thirteen classes. Of these RAF pilot candidates under training at Lakeland, 875 (65.99 percent) graduated. Although Classes SE-42-E to SE-42-H numbered from 115 to 124 students, the largest number of RAF students enrolled in a particular class was 129 in Class SE-42-H.

Of the 1,326 students enrolled, 451 (34.01 percent) were eliminated. Of those students who were rejected for further pilot training, 440 (33.18 percent) were eliminated for flying deficiencies and 10 (0.75 percent) washed out for "other than flying deficiencies."

As at other primary schools, difficulty is encountered when trying to correlate eliminees with class size. At Lakeland, the greatest number of eliminees came from classes SE-42-F and SE-42-D and numbered 49 and 44, respectively, but SE-42-F enrolled a total of 119 students while SE-42-D had only 100. The smallest number of eliminated RAF students was 8 and came from Class SE-43-B, the last (and smallest) UK class trained at Lakeland.

CARLSTROM 42-H

The practice of mixed RAF/USAAF classes continued with Class SE-42-H at Carlstrom Field when 233 UK students were joined by 43 American cadets. In February 1942, 2 RAF check pilots, Pilot Officers Jack H. Gilder and Robert K. Eggins, advanced flying school graduates of Class SE-42-A, returned to Carlstrom to serve there as check pilots until about April 1942, when Class SE-42-H departed for Gunter Field. Among members of that last RAF class at Carlstrom were Vic Hewes, Samuel Liggett, Geoffrey Smith, Les Meehan, Jim Double, L.G. Lunn and Geoffrey A. Barnett.

James Charles Double of Essex, England, kept a diary during his pilot training. A few excerpts from that diary provide insights into what it was like when Class SE-42-H arrived at Carlstrom Field:

> **Monday, 23 February 1942.** *Arrived early in the morning at Carlstrom Field. Very pretty place—so far cleaned up billet, then shower and to bed after talks by officers. Raining hard, not quite the Florida I expected. Saw oranges growing while being taken to camp. Palm trees growing outside billet, tennis courts and swimming pool just outside too.*
>
> **Tuesday, 24 February 1942.** *Shown some usual routine things. Introduced to new flying instructor. Started up my first Stearman plane, but did not fly. No flying today owing to bad weather. Spent evening cleaning up billets, boots, etc.*

Because of rain, getting in flying time proved to be very difficult for everyone on the course, but the winter rainy season was nearly over.

Finally, on Saturday, 28 February, even though it was very cold, Class SE-42-H commenced flying. They also flew again on Sunday, but there was no flying again until Tuesday. However, Double and his classmates continued to attend ground school regularly and to build up flying time gradually. On days when they were not flying and could get off-post, they traveled to Sarasota, met the McLaren and Binze families, spent some time at Ledo Beach and occasionally the families that had "adopted" Double and three other RAF cadets visited them at Carlstrom Field.

On 17 March, Jim Double flew the Stearman PT-17 solo, the first time with an American aircraft. On 27 March, he passed his twenty-hour check, and on 13 and 14 April he took course examinations. His final check in the front cockpit of the Stearman came on Monday, 20 April 1942, and he passed. On Wednesday, 22 April, Jim Double and three other RAF pupils of Mr. Holmes met the instructor in Arcadia, and they drove northward for dinner and nightclub hopping in Sarasota and Bradenton, and finally got to bed around 6:00 a.m. Primary flying training was over.

On 9 April 1941, eighteen-year-old LAC Leslie G. Lunn enlisted in the Royal Air Force directly after leaving school. Lunn, who successfully completed pilot training and later flew Spitfires and Mustangs, had "some success" against the V-1 flying bombs and continued on in Bomber Command during the postwar jet age. More than forty years afterward, Squadron Leader L.G. Lunn, AFC (RAF, retired), recalled his training days after leaving Turner Field:

> *We were all sent our various ways and I landed up at Carlstrom Field, Florida. The Riddle Aeronautical Institute were responsible for our training, with civilian, Army Air Corps and some RAF instructors. I still have my Cadet Handbook, issued to me on arrival to start the serious business of training to become a fighter pilot. My instructor was Mr. Ryan, a civilian, and my first flight with him was on 28th February 1942.*
>
> *The weather was glorious and you could smell the orange blossoms at 5,000 feet in the open cockpit Stearman biplane. It was all very basic with no airspeed indicator or attitude reference. Our check rides were with Army Air Corps officers, and I went solo on 17th March 1942. I felt very proud of myself. The washout rates were high; I was the sole "survivor" of four students who had begun with Mr. Ryan. We had check rides at 20-40-60 hours and I was successful, finishing primary training with exactly 60 hours.*

We were given four days leave—where to go and what to do—with no money—was the major problem. We were given an address in Sarasota, a Servicemen's Club. With five dollars to my name, four of us set course. We registered at the club and, with some embarrassment I might add, but we need not have worried, as a Mr. Whitney collected us and took us to his home and private beach on Long Island. They could not have been kinder to us—they gave us a well stocked bungalow on the beach and entertained us royally. I have always been most grateful to them and all their friends. We lost track of them during the war.

Others who completed primary training at Carlstrom Field in late April 1942 included Geoffrey A. Barnett. His description of Carlstrom Field is of interest because he describes the new compressed training schedule, which pushed cadets through each phase of training in nine weeks or less.

As Barnett recalled,

The instructors were mainly civilian. My instructors were a Mr. Galloway followed by a Mr. Holmes and the Flight Commander who was a Mr. Worley. The 60-hour check was by Lt. Richardson. I'm sure we were very impressed with the superb flying ability of the U.S. Army men. I know the latter were always on the watch that the civilian instructors in general fulfilled the U.S. Army requirement, i.e., went through the full range of exercises. I think we worked 12 days and then had two off. We would hire the odd car and drive to Sarasota or run down to Miami, calling at Palm Beach on the way back.

Once on a trip down the West coast road to Fort Myers, we were followed by "cops" for quite a long way. They finally brought us to a halt with sirens and all the usual ritual, e.g., taking their time and standing with a boot on the running board of the car, plus blowing cigar smoke into the driver's face. However, on perusing my Florida driver's licence, they saw that I was British. The atmosphere changed immediately. They were very friendly and said they had followed because the car's steering looked slack—as it probably was.

While at Carlstrom, we did as much swimming as we could. Local Americans on the Gulf Coast warned us against entering such cold water. We would surely get pneumonia as it was only just March! I don't know what the water temperature was, but it seemed better than a good English summer. It became apparent that Northern instructors and those from the South had not forgotten the Civil War. Odd remarks about each other would be made from time to time. The PT-17 aircraft didn't have airspeed indicators in the rear cockpit, as we had to "fly by the seat of your pants, Mister!" This was probably a good thing. Carlstrom Field at that time prided itself on no fatalities and aimed to keep it that way.

In many ways, the Florida prairie country was ideal for flying training. However, there were occasional rains that still overloaded the drainage system and left the airfields of the region flooded.

In February 1942, LAC Samuel Liggett, another member of Class SE-42-H, recalled one such storm that virtually drowned Carlstrom Field. Forty-three years afterward, from his home in Ayr, Scotland, Liggett described his Florida experience:

The evening prior to one of our days off, a recreation bus took us into Sarasota, and we returned late afternoon the following day, and another bus load took off to enjoy themselves, but when the field was flooded, almost the entire school was stood down for two days, so when the bus arrived, they were going in emergency doors and windows. After a lot of to-ing and fro-ing, we set off, but the bus broke down, and when they counted us off the vehicle, if my memory serves me right, I think there were 92 bodies counted out.

We were really very well treated by the citizens of Sarasota—with accommodation, wining and dining, etc. Our biggest problem was trying to show our appreciation, as they would not let us buy anything. The almost 40% washout rate at Carlstrom upset the British lads as we had all done a flight grading course in the U.K., and we seemed to have the same number of washouts as our American buddies who had their first taste of flying.

Liggett's observation about the American cadets may not have been absolutely accurate. Many American aviation cadets had been enrolled in the College Pilot Training Program (CPTP) and had flown enough hours to solo. While awaiting a call to flying training, other American cadets were assigned to College Training Detachments (CTDs), where they received ground training as well as twelve to fifteen hours of flying similar to flight grading courses offered in the United Kingdom.

Leslie Meehan had memories similar to those of his classmates. Some forty-three years afterward, Meehan recalled his Carlstrom experiences:

We did find the "demerit" (gig) system extremely petty and did not accept "hazing." The training was first class, extemely meticulous. I was nearly washed out at Carlstrom Field and had three checks with Second Lieutenant Klopfenstein, two of which I talked my way through! In one, I actually did a stage downwind! I changed my instructor after my third Army check to the assistant flight commander, and from then on, I had no difficulty. It seems that although I got on well with my original instructor, we were not compatible in the air.

The instruction in America was much more precise than in England where precision for single-engined pilots was only practised on the Link Trainer. To try to land a plane, without the help of the engine, on a spot was unheard of. People still won't believe me when I say that we had no air speed indicator on our primary trainers, and we gauged our speed by revs., altitude, wind noise, and the seat of our pants.

Whilst we had our Tiger Moth and Miles Master for training in England, the Stearman and Harvard were certainly superior machines. The Stearman had no vices, whilst ground looping was the only Harvard problem. There was too little free time available. We were only allowed out one day in eight, with only about three days between courses. At the British BFTSs, they had queues of cars waiting to take them home for the weekend. Still, we managed to enjoy ourselves at Sarasota, St. Petersburg, Tampa, Atlanta, and Birmingham, in addition to local towns.

Another member of that class was Geoffrey W. Smith. Before returning to the United Kingdom, Smith completed his pilot training and served several months as a pilot officer flying instructor at a USAAF basic flying school at Bainbridge, Georgia. From his home in the United

Kingdom forty-two years afterward, Smith recalled the departure of Class SE-42-H by train from Turner Field on 22 February 1942 and its arrival later that same day at Carlstrom Field. As he recalled,

> Our reception by the military was quite tough—"we had to toe the line!" "'The Demon King" was Second Lieutenant A.B. Klopfenstein, who gave us the impression that he was there to cause us the maximum irritation. When he was there, there was no rest—and he appeared from the shadows in his dark glasses at all hours, jumping on any poor mortal who crossed his path. Off post, the people we met were generous to a fault. We were entertained by families and service organisations; in Sarasota and Punta Gorda, barmen and waitresses would invariably tell us that "the gentleman at the table in the corner had picked up your tab—he's just left."
>
> Our course began on 25 February 1942, and my first flight in a Stearman PT-17 was on 28 February. My first solo flight came on 21 March, and it was sheer magic! After 41 years, I can almost smell the orange blossoms and feel the exhileration and euphoria that I felt then. My first instructor was Mr. J.T. Gramentine, a rather stern gentleman. On 12 March, I reported to the wrong aircraft (the instructor had changed planes and had not informed the despatcher), and I thought he would kill me.
>
> Perhaps I would've been better off if he had done so, because the humiliation of having to record in the log book, "did not fly today—late" was worse than hanging. I had 7 trips with Mr. Gramentine, and as his student load was reduced from 7 to 5, two of us including myself, were allocated to a new man from Wichita, Kansas named Delmar D. Jones (I did have a couple of rides of about 40 minutes each with A.R. Jaynes before D.D. took charge of me).
>
> We completed the course on 22 April, by which time I had logged 60 hours, 38 minutes flying time. At the end of the course, D.D. Jones and his lovely wife took all of his "stoodents" to Sarasota for a steak dinner and drinks. I remember stopping at the roadside for a pee on the way back. I disturbed a rattlesnake, and ever since that time, I've had trouble passing water at the roadside!
>
> We had a few days leave after primary training. I remember hiring a car after taking a driving test. I set off to visit Fort Myers with various mates—David Sara, James Wallace, Jack Roberts, Bill Saddler, and B.N.E. Ford-Coates. The car had a blow-out while travelling at about 60 MPH, and it rolled over a couple of times. If James Wallace hadn't been cooling his feet out of the window, he wouldn't have broken his ankle and ended up, eventually, in the military hospital in Atlanta, Georgia (and I wouldn't have got to see Atlanta when I visited him, if he hadn't been hurt).
>
> An instructor at Carlstrom Field, who must have been in his fifties, had the loudest voice in Florida. When he was briefing his students on the flight line, he could be heard at least 50 yards away—and he was speaking "normally." On one occasion, David Sara, a timid and polite young man, experienced a somewhat unnerving encounter with his Stearman soon after his first solo. He entered traffic in the normal way, but on the downwind leg, it was obvious to those on the ground that all was not well. The engine noise was horrendous, and the aircraft was batting on like a demon—his throttle was stuck open!
>
> I am not sure if an instructor in another aircraft flew alongside to signal to David what to do or not do, but I do know that his excellent and vociferous instructor was out on

the field in his familiar pigskin flying jacket signalling and giving voice with instructions to David Sara. David got the message, switched off the engine, and glided to a perfect landing in the middle of the field, having been talked down by his instructor of the loud voice from some point on the downwind leg. The instructor greeted David like a hero; until then, he was thought to be a hard man by most of us. David Sara apparently spent the evening playing Brahms on the Canteen piano.

The quality of instruction both in the air and on the ground was high. It did not appear to me that the system was unduly harsh. We all wanted to succeed—those who failed simply didn't make the GRADE. *I was sorry to see some lads wash out, but it was the name of the game. There was no truth in such rubbish as "Teacher's Pet," being the "Fair-haired boy," or the "Blue-eyed Boy," or "not who you are, as who you know."*

Certain cadets were given particular duties that appeared to favour them, but in my mind they earned the distinction through natural abilities. Some had a commanding presence—being 6 ft+ tall with a deep voice—I'm sure if they lacked military bearing and got drunk they would not have made it. Very few instructors were difficult to understand; we got used to the deep Southern drawl, but instructors seemed to come from all over the States. They seemed more amused at our English accents (I had the greatest difficulty in understanding my Scottish room-mate; Bill Sadler's accent—even after two years).

In late April 1942, when Smith and his classmates completed primary training, theirs was the eighth and final course of RAF student pilots to be trained at Carlstrom Field. Of the 233-man RAF intake, which included 3 men held over from the preceding class, 6 men were held over for further training and transferred to Lakeland (Lodwick) School of Aeronautics. Of the 227-man net intake for Class SE-42-H at Carlstrom Field, 72 were eliminated and 155 graduated and were posted to a basic flying school.

In the eight intakes of British students that trained at the school, Classes SE-42-A through SE-42-H, Carlstrom Field enrolled 1,345 RAF pupils, an average intake of 168 students for each of the eight classes. Of these 1,345 British student pilots who entered training, 923 (68.62 percent) graduated. Of the 422 eliminees, 399 (29.67 percent) of the Carlstrom Field RAF intake were washed out of pilot training for flying deficiencies and 22 (1.64 percent) were washed out for "other than flying deficiencies." Based on the increased enrollments, Classes SE-42-B, SE-42-D and SE-42-C had the lowest number of eliminees with 27, 32 and 40, respectively. Classes SE-42-F, SE-42-H and SE-42-G had the highest number of students eliminated from pilot training at Carlstrom Field with 79, 72 and 68, respectively.

Despite continued construction and severe crowding for several months in 1941, the 1,300-acre Riddle Aeronautical Institute at Carlstrom Field maintained an outstanding record of pilot production, a relatively small percentage of eliminations and one of the lowest fatality rates of any civil contract flying school in the United States. During its four years and three months of operation, Riddle Aeronautical Institute trained 7,500 cadets with only one fatality.

WHERE HAVE ALL THE RAF CADETS GONE?

42-B. THOMAS HENRY BLACKHAM, nineteen, of South Glamorgan, Wales (Carlstrom, Gunter, Selma), was a student in Scotland before entry into the RAF. He was trained at and served as an instructor at Cochran Field. On returning to Britain in late 1942, he underwent further training and was assigned to Bomber Command. He few Halifax and Lancaster bombers on twenty-six sorties and was awarded a DFC. On 3 May 1944, his aircraft was shot down over France. Blackham evaded capture and joined the *maquis*. In July 1944, he was captured, charged as a spy and sent to Fresnes political prison in Paris, later to Buchenwald. In 1945, he was designated a POW and was sent to Stalag Luft III. Liberated at the end of the war, Blackham resumed flying, gained a permanent commission and was posted to RAF Cranwell and numerous staff positions until retirement in July 1977. T.H. Blackham retired as air commodore, OBE, DFC, and served as deputy lieutenant for mid-Glamorgan.

42-B. STANLEY SLATER, twenty (Carlstrom, Gunter, Maxwell). He graduated as a sergeant pilot, and after further training he was assigned to Bomber Command. He flew Halifax and Lancaster bombers, and in 1943 he was promoted to pilot officer and awarded a DFC. Subsequently, following service during raids on Berlin and Nuremburg, Slater was awarded the DSO and a bar to his DFC. His aircraft was shot down over Denmark, but he evaded, escaped to Sweden and three weeks later returned to Britain. Slater was awarded a permanent commission in the RAF and served as an exchange pilot in the USAF (Washington state). Stanley Slater retired as group captain, DSO, DFC with bar.

42-B. ROBERT C. STOCKBURN, nineteen (Carlstrom, Gunter, Selma), graduated with Class 42-E. On returning to Britain and undergoing further training, he was assigned to Fighter Command. On 11 July 1943, his 501 Squadron Spitfire was shot down near Dunkerque in northern France by flak. Stockburn evaded, escaped through Gibraltar and returned to the United Kingdom. He rejoined 501 Squadron and covered the D-Day landings, after which 501 was re-formed as night fighter squadron flying Tempest Vs. In February 1945, he joined 33 Squadron in Holland, then in September 1945 transferred to 74 Squadron, flying Tempest Vs. During World War II, Stockburn was credited with destroying nine enemy aircraft (plus one shared) and three V-1 flying bombs. In April 1946, Flight Lieutenant (captain) R.C. Stockburn, DFC, was demobilized.

42-F. DONALD M. BLACKEBY, twenty, of Broxbourne, Hertfordshire (Carlstrom, Macon, Selma). Between June 1943 and June 1944, he flew Boston medium bombers (Douglas A-20s) with 88 Squadron. He survived the war and was demobilized as a flight lieutenant (captain), having logged 1,027 flying hours "It was my opinion based on many others that we received the best training available anywhere in the world."

42-G. GEORGE GORDON KENNETH GRAY, nineteen, of Manchester (Carlstrom, Gunter, Turner). On return to Britain and further training, he flew Boston IIIs (Douglas A-20s) with 88 Squadron. On 6 June 1944, his aircraft was shot down by flak and he crashed in the English Channel. He was picked up by a Walrus ASR flying boat and was then assigned to the communications flight of the RAF Second Tactical Air Force. In 1946, he was seconded to BOAC and flew C-47s with them. Subsequently, until 1977, Gray flew as an airline pilot with British Airways, logging more than 21,000 flying hours. Captain Gray became a member of the Guild of Air Pilots and Navigators.

42-G. WILLIAM FRANCIS POLLEY, twenty, of Hillsborough, County Down, Northern Ireland (Carlstrom, Gunter, Selma). On return to Britain and further training, he was assigned to 501 Squadron flying Spitfire Vs. Later, the squadron was converted to Tempests and assigned to flying as night fighters. In that capacity, Polley was credited with shooting down six V-1 rockets and sharing another. In July 1944, his aircraft was shot down by enemy flak, but he evaded capture and made it safely to American lines. Postwar, W.F. Polley, DFC, received an MA degree from Trinity University, and from 1948 to 1984 served as principal of schools.

CHAPTER ELEVEN

USAAF Basic Flying School

Gunter Field

In 1940, the municipal airport site that was located four miles northeast of Montgomery in Montgomery County, Alabama, on the south side of Alabama State Highway 14, became Gunter Field, the first United States Army Air Corps basic flying school in the Southeastern United States. In June 1940, Colonel Walter R. Weaver, commanding officer of the army air corps tactical school, and Lieutenant Colonel Ira C. Eaker, commanding officer of the newly organized Southeast Air Corps Training Center (SEACTC), received a directive from army air corps headquarters in Washington to establish a basic flying school near Maxwell Field, Alabama. As senior officer, Weaver also commanded the Maxwell Field station. Before the summer was over, Colonel Eaker was posted to the Carolina maneuvers and subsequently to the Eighth Air Force in England. Colonel Weaver relinquished command of Maxwell Field and assumed command of the SEACTC.

In late May 1940, when the decision was made to expand air corps training and locate training airfields in the warmer regions of the country, the information was quickly circulated nationwide by aviation organizations and others, and every state was anxious to obtain air bases or other military installations. Since local officials were expected to purchase or lease such facilities from private owners at minimal cost, improvements made to such property by the War Department might be put to civilian use later. Colonel Weaver's promotion to command the SEACTC gave him prime responsibility for the selection of sites and the construction of all new training stations within the Southeastern states.

The history of Gunter Field reaches back to 1940 and the army air corps' seven-thousand- and twelve-thousand-pilot production plans. Air corps planners felt that schools might be established quickest by leasing and using municipal airports. Montgomery's municipal airport comprised 187 acres of a 600-acre tract between the Seaboard Airline Railroad and Alabama State Highway 14. The airdrome was 221 feet above sea level and was situated directly across that paved highway from Kilby Prison in the midst of rolling hills and very rich farmlands abounding in cotton, corn, sugar cane, fruit, pecan trees and scattered dairy farms. Because of the relatively small size of the tract and both private and public ownership of the airfield and contiguous land, arrangements were finally made with officials of Montgomery County, the City of Montgomery and the State of Alabama to lease the site and enlarge it.

Within several miles in any direction of the airfield tract, the region contained many scattered swamps with pines, cypresses and several varieties of hardwood trees. There were also numerous creeks and other small streams and a number of deeply eroded gullies. On the south side of the tract was a dammed up stream forming a small lagoon, and two miles away to the southeast was the Veterans Administration Hospital. A few miles north-northwestward from the site, the mighty Alabama River and its tributaries descended from the north and northeast and snaked their way across the middle of the state westward along the northern edge of Montgomery, around Maxwell Field and on westward through Alabama's Black Belt to Selma, there curving southward and emptying into Mobile Bay.

Information about the climate of the immediate region was reassuring to air corps training officers. Past experience at nearby Maxwell Field indicated that, on average, there were 102 clear days per year, 102 days during which there was .01 inches of rainfall or more and 4 days in which trace amounts of snow fell. Although the highest recorded temperature was ninety-nine degrees Fahrenheit and the lowest sixteen degrees, the average daily maximum temperature was around seventy-five degrees Fahrenheit. Annual rainfall stood at about fifty inches and was usually spread throughout the year, and the humidity level ranged between 86 and 54 percent. In addition, the area averaged 117 partly cloudy days and 117 cloudy days, and the sun shone 66 percent of the time. Records also showed that thunderstorms occurred every month, or an average of 60 days per year, mostly in summer, and that high winds occurred during both winter and spring.

Official wind rose data indicated that, if buildings were properly located, the municipal airport tract could be an excellent site for a military airfield. Prevailing winds during spring and summer were from the south, and during late summer northeasterly winds dominated, shifting in late autumn and early winter to a more easterly direction. Such data made it possible to properly site the runways, decide the safest potential landing approaches to the airfield and select the proper locations for quarters, instructional and domestic buildings in relation to maintenance areas, the flight line and runways. Obviously, the field would have to be enlarged and other runways would have to be added before the airdrome could accomodate the large volume of air traffic required by an army air corps basic flying school.

The first stage of construction at the new basic flying school was completed during the summer of 1940, at the same time as the Battle of Britain. In September, the base was officially opened and the domestic site was declared ready to receive army air corps flying cadets. Although U.S. Army Air Corps officials would have preferred that the new station be named for a deceased airman from Alabama, an official policy for naming such installations had not yet been publicized by the chief of the army air corps, so for the first seven months of its existence, it was simply labeled "Army Air Corps Basic Flying School, Municipal Airport, Montgomery, Alabama." On 4 December 1940, when William Adams Gunter, longtime mayor of Montgomery, died, city officials petitioned air corps officials to name the airfield in his honor, and they reluctantly agreed.

If army air corps officers had not rigidly adhered to their plan to use semi-developed municipal airports for basic and advanced flying schools and operational stations, they would have been wise to avoid Montgomery's municipal airport altogether. Although domestic and instructional buildings were easily developed around the municipal airfield site, the landing field, with its single runway, was never quite satisfactory as a basic flying school site because it was too small. Instead of expending a phenomenal amount of money developing an air corps station with a limited landing field, Taylor Field, the old World War I training base that was located several miles southeast of Montgomery, might well have been redeveloped at lower cost.

Since early Gunter Field construction was done in 1940 before the United States Army Corps of Engineers was charged with the responsibility of building air bases, the task was assigned to Colonel George S. Deadrick, quartermaster construction and contracting officer at Maxwell Field. On surveying the municipal airport site, Colonel Deadrick and his staff found already located there one large permanent hangar, a 3,500-foot paved runway running northwest-northeast, an operations building with weather station, a rotating beacon, boundary lights and floodlights, several large gasoline storage tanks and a large two-story brick veneer structure, which had originally been used as a hotel and restaurant. Located nearby was a municipal swimming pool, and east of the airport was an eighteen-hole municipal golf course.

On approval of the site, the station was to be built to accommodate 316 cadets, 1,073 enlisted men and 63 officers. A railroad spur line would be extended into the station from the south and would allow regular deliveries of bulk fuel and other supplies. The school buildings and domestic site would be situated on the northern and northwestern sides of the huge tract leased for that purpose, and the landing field would be located on the east and southeast, adjacent to the domestic facilities. Since the airdrome was the only basic flying school in the Southeastern United States, it was expected to absorb all of the graduates of primary schools east of the Mississippi River.

Before the municipal airport and surrounding acreage was leased from the city, county and the State of Alabama for the development of a flying school, a site selection board had also surveyed the county and neighboring lands in order to locate potential auxiliary or satellite airfields. It was standard practice to obtain several such landing grounds within a fifteen- to twenty-five-mile radius in order to divide students into different groups according to their flying experience, then to assign them to flying zones centered on auxiliary airfields. Such well-established safety precautions made sense in order to avoid excessive congestion around a single airdrome.

In casting around for auxiliary airfields, Taylor Airport, which had been used in 1918, and another airfield near Shorter, Alabama, were selected for development. With proper authorization, Colonel Aubrey Hornsby, station project officer, negotiated leases for Shorter and Taylor Fields. However, the topography, soil quality and drainage of these auxiliary fields was such that neither could be enlarged nor prepared in time for the intensive use required for winter flying operations. With luck and a great deal of labor removing obstructions, grubbing out stumps and leveling the landing grounds, the auxiliary airfields might be ready for significant air traffic by May 1941.

After negotiating cancellation of two of the city's airport contracts, one with Gulf Oil Corporation and another with Eastern Air Lines, the army air corps leased the six-hundred-acre municipal airport tract from the city and county and the golf course tract from the city. An additional tract of about ninety acres was leased from the State of Alabama, including the new, but never used, Kilby Prison Tuberculosis Hospital. The rooms of that building, unsuitably equipped with steel bars, would never be quite satisfactory. However, at different times, the building was used for post headquarters, administrative offices, ground school and a variety of other purposes. New buildings added to the airfield site by the army air corps followed standard mobilization patterns already developed by the U.S. Army Corps of Engineers.

Owing to the availability of inexpensive building materials and a large WPA workforce, Brigadier General Walter R. Weaver, the recently promoted commanding officer at Maxwell Field, proposed that permanent hollow-tile and stucco facilities could be built more cheaply by the WPA than could standard wooden mobilization buildings. Construction began, and no sooner was one phase completed than another began. "Weaver-type construction" was ultimately used for building much of three Alabama air bases: Maxwell, Gunter and Craig Fields, as well as other stations within the SEACTC. However, in several instances when these USAAF stations were later expanded, some two-story wooden barracks were built.

In addition to General Weaver, three other men were instrumental in planning the basic flying school. Colonel Deadrick's staff supervised construction and contracting, Mr. R.G. Brasswell was construction superintendent for the WPA and Lieutenant Colonel Aubrey Hornsby was air corps project officer for the airfield. Had the standard camp layout been followed, it was believed that 65 percent of the large grove of pecan trees would have been cut and removed, but Colonel Hornsby recommended a different layout, which led to the removal of only six trees. In preparing the site, some drainage problems were encountered, but the stages of construction proceeded rapidly. Contracts were handled through the WPA, and 1,500 men (65 percent black and 35 percent white) worked on the site.

The construction of Gunter Field represented a link between the Great Depression of the 1930s and World War II. It was built by a New Deal agency at phenomenally low cost, and not only was the project to be used for national defense, but it also brought an identifiable economic boost to the immediate area. Perhaps no one was more suprised than the project directors and supervisors, but they discovered that the workforce, instead of fitting into the stereotyped "shiftless and lazy" mold, proved willing to work and were not tied to rigid ways of doing things. In short, they were superb, and the project was an excellent demonstration of why the Works Progress Administration was so effective as a New Deal work relief measure.

The project used an apprenticeship on-the-job training system, which paid the men a regular wage while also serving as a means for quickly training unskilled workers in a number of building trades, including plumbing, carpentry, masonry and plastering. Such training made it possible for many black and white unskilled former agricultural workers and tenant farmers to escape the poverty of low-paying seasonal employment and to learn trades that enabled them to abandon agriculture, pursue a different career and better provide for their families than ever before. In organizing and supervising the workforce, the managers developed some new building techniques that made Gunter Field a model project and influenced the course of other defense construction that would soon begin in every part of the United States.

Instead of taking three or four weeks to construct each building, the new techniques produced finished buildings in one week. Some building materials were brought in from elsewhere and delivered to the site by truck from the Kilby rail siding almost a mile away. Some of the lumber came from a dismantled, transient National Youth Administration camp that had been located near the lagoon, but most building materials were obtained locally. Roof rafters, ceiling joists and wall sections were prefabricated on the site, then workers used an assembly line system of construction. In the meantime, drainage and water supply lines were run, plumbing was "roughed in" and concrete pads were poured. By the time the floor pads were dry, prefabricated frames were erected quickly, then in rapid order came brick (hollow tile) masons and plasterers.

No sooner were the plasterers finished with a building than heater-blowers were installed, if necessary, for both day and night "curing" or drying of the pads and masonry walls. Next came the plumbers, electricians, "finish" carpenters, painters and inspectors. Even with these methods of construction, preparing the site and building the entire basic flying school would absorb more than two years because of later expansion. Obstructions to flying were removed around the airfield, and an attractive military camp began to emerge in the shade of the large pecan grove.

Work had begun on the domestic and school buildings and on the airfield itself but, despite the efforts of construction personnel to meet the established deadlines, problems of drainage and delayed arrival of construction materials prevented the airfield from being completely ready for training until late November 1940. Because of these delays, staff personnel reporting to the new station lived and worked in tents amid dust and mud, and the June and July cadet intakes, Classes SE-41-A and SE-41-B, completed their basic flying instruction at nearby Maxwell Field.

In late August 1940, an operations office for the new basic flying school was established on the second floor of the Maxwell Field operations building. Thirty-four North American BT-14 trainer aircraft were assigned on loan from Randolph Field, Texas, and new Vultee BT-13 trainers began to arrive in small groups from the factory in Downey, California. Within a relatively brief period, young air corps officers had delivered a total of 160 basic trainer aircraft to Maxwell Field for use at the new basic flying school. On 25 November 1940, the operations building and several other flight line buildings opened at Gunter Field, and regular flying operations were begun at the new airfield.

The first class to undergo training at Gunter Field was Class SE-41-C, which arrived there on 26 November 1940 and moved into buildings that had neither windows nor heat. The class consisted of a total of two hundred army air corps student pilots (mostly flying cadets, but including a few student officers). The class, consisting mostly of graduates of Harvard, Yale, Princeton and Columbia Universities, commenced training immediately, and its companion junior class of another two hundred students was due to arrive on station in early January 1941, thus bringing Gunter Field's total enrollment to four hundred. In order to accommodate and train the initial two hundred student pilots, one-half of the class flew in the morning, the other half in the afternoon.

When it was put into service in November 1940, the 187-acre main airdrome at Gunter Field with the single macadam-paved runway proved adequate to serve only during daylight hours. The single hangar was used for maintenance and to serve commercial airline traffic still using the airfield. Until adequate hangars and other flight line buildings were available, and when not flying or being serviced, the canopied monoplane basic trainers were parked on the airfield apron in all kinds of weather. The airfield was too small for east-west night landings, and it lacked the maintenance buildings, lighting, radio control system and other equipment necessary to handle regularly scheduled night flying and the requirements of the large numbers of students and aircraft.

In January 1941, with the arrival at Gunter Field of Class SE-41-D, problems began to develop. With two hundred students scheduled for training in the morning and another two hundred in the afternoon, it was necessary to stagger takeoffs and landings for each of the three squadrons in order to reduce congestion and allow necessary servicing of aircraft. One squadron operated from 7:40 to 11:40 a.m. and from 12:40 to 4:40 p.m. Another squadron used the schedule of 7:50 to 11:50 a.m., and from 12:50 to 4:50 p.m. The third school squadron used 8:00 a.m. to 12:00 p.m. and 1:00 to 5:00 p.m. However, it was discovered that only about eighty aircraft could be safely operated from Gunter Field, and once large numbers of students were doing solo flights, safety dictated a reduction at the main airdrome.

Auxiliary fields were needed well before they were available. In addition to the absence of auxiliary airfields, a maintenance problem developed at Gunter Field. The established North American BT-14 basic trainer, labeled the "Yale" by Canadians, was reliable and easy to maintain, but problems developed with the new Vultee BT-13s. Oil and gas tank leaks were bothersome, but there were other problems of a more serious nature. During September 1940, while Class SE-41-A, the first course, was in training at Maxwell Field, three air crashes occurred within one week, killing three officers and two aviation cadets. Some aircraft appeared to be working well and having few problems while others were constantly undergoing repairs.

Fearing sabotage, air corps officers notified the manufacturer and requested that the Federal Bureau of Investigation (FBI) evaluate the evidence and look further into the matter. However, intensive air corps and FBI investigations revealed that these fatal crashes had most likely resulted from structural weaknesses in the BT-13, not from sabotage. The aircraft were temporarily grounded, a team of technical representatives swarmed over Maxwell and Gunter Fields and modifications were undertaken. Because of such teething problems with the new trainer, the aircraft availability dropped from between 80 and 90 percent for the North American trainer to about 60 percent for the Vultee.

Until the Vultee trainers became serviceable in greater numbers and problems with the main airdrome and auxiliary fields were solved, Colonel Aubrey Hornsby, now commanding officer at Gunter Field, was faced with many dilemmas. As a temporary solution, he proposed significant modification of the existing training curriculum. In the past, air corps training officers had worked with a two to one student/airplane ratio at basic schools. Since so much solo flying time was essential, they had deemed 171 North American BT-14 trainers adequate for the training of 342 students. Now, because of the problems with the Vultee, Hornsby believed that the ratio of aircraft to students should be increased to 250 trainers for every 400 students.

Since it would be impossible to handle such a tremendous volume of traffic at the small main airdrome, and neither Taylor nor Shorter Fields would be available for full use until May 1941, Gunter Field could not possibly reach its projected goal of training four hundred students at the same time for at least five months more instead of the projected two months. If the only basic flying school in the Southeastern United States could not meet its output goal, the entire air corps flying training program might be compromised. Primary, basic and advanced flying training schedules were so interlocked that one such delay placed all of them in jeopardy.

If the number of flying instructors and serviceable airplanes remained the same, Hornsby felt that Class SE-41-D and subsequent classes would have to be significantly reduced in size. Furthermore, he presented a good case for reducing the basic flying course from seventy to fifty hours and intensifying training. By shifting some flying training to the advanced stage, moving to a seven-day-per-week schedule and permitting students to fly every other day, Hornsby believed that two hundred students could be trained at Gunter Field, but not four hundred.

The Gunter Field commander's communication of 17 December 1940 is important because it reveals how the availability of aircraft and instructors, as well as construction and maintenance problems, threatened the training program. Evidently, Colonel Hornsby's proposal to reduce the basic flying training hours fell on deaf ears. About six months later, RAF officers would attempt to persuade USAAF training officers to reduce the hours in the training syllabus for RAF students. However, since USAAF officers had already considered and rejected such a change, they would seek temporary and long-term solutions to specific problems and would alter the syllabus as experience dictated, but they steadfastly refused to reduce basic school flying training hours below seventy hours.

Beginning in 1941 with the twelve-thousand-pilot production program, it appeared that construction projects at Gunter Field were to be interminable. In February, construction began on fourteen additional buildings, and in late April contracts were let for building a chapel and a large officers' club. Then, within a few months, priorities changed once more. The thirty-thousand-pilot production plan was implemented, the staff and student populations were further increased and more buildings were necessary. Included among these new structures were a separate Link Trainer building; a sub-depot of the Air Materiel Command, which handled supply and maintenance for aircraft and equipment; a medical and dental detachment; a finance office; a weather office; control towers; signals offices; a skeet range; two swimming pools; two theatres; and other recreational buildings.

Additional construction included some buildings for administrative purposes, numerous barracks for student pilots and permanent maintenance and other staff personnel, bachelor officers' quarters, dining halls, supply and storage buildings, warehouses, hospital buildings and other buildings for miscellaneous uses. In addition, construction proceeded on such essential installations as water storage tanks, underground fuel storage tanks, a water supply system, a sewage system (including a treatment plant) and miles of paved service roads and aprons for parking and servicing aircraft.

Effective 20 June 1941, the United States Army Air Forces, a new, enlarged organization, was formed from a nucleus of personnel in the old army air corps. As USAAF plans and training officers proposed and approved further expansion plans, all training stations were enlarged. By 10 December 1941, there were 109 buildings either completed or under construction at Gunter Field. Then, with the announcement of an increased pilot production goal, plans were laid to build another twenty-one buildings on the station. Beginning with fewer than two hundred students in September 1940, the municipal airport at Montgomery evolved into a complex of buildings called Gunter Field. Initially, Gunter Field was the only basic flying school in the region, so its personnel trained administrative, instructional and maintenance staffs for other basic schools that were planned for the Southeast Air Corps Training Center.

Since the main airdrome was so small, the only solution available to permit an enlarged training program was for Gunter Field flying instructors to put into use as soon as possible a number of auxiliary landing grounds. Until some stages of training could be shifted away from the busy main airdrome to flying training areas centered on scattered auxiliary fields, aircraft used both the single Gunter Field runway and, when possible, the three-hundred-acre Maxwell Field for practicing takeoffs and landings and for soloing students.

Although USAAF policy aimed to lease land for auxiliary fields that required little grading or other expense, there were no such open fields available within the proper distance (fifteen to twenty-five miles) from the main airdrome. As a result, considerable work had to be done on each of the four sites. Clearing flying obstructions from the approaches to these fields required the purchase and removal of several hundred acres of pine trees. Preparation of landing surfaces required grading, installation of drainage lines, seeding and compacting. All of these tasks were not only expensive but took more time than was either intended or desired, and therefore interfered with flying training.

The Corps of Engineers experienced other delays in getting the fields inspected and leased from private owners, but ultimately the auxiliary fields were leased and contracts were let to prepare them for use. Shorter Field, located fifteen miles east of Gunter Field and one mile north of Shorter, Alabama, contained 240.5 acres and was rented at a cost of $1,202.50 annually. Taylor Field, the World War I airfield that was located twelve miles southeast of Gunter Field on Pike Road just north of the Central of Georgia Railroad, required only $5,644.62 to prepare it for use, and annual rental charges for the airdrome were set at $2,419. McLemore Field, which was located one mile northwest of Mount Meigs, Alabama, contained 225 acres and cost $21,946.65 to prepare it for use as an auxiliary field. The Mount Meigs auxiliary field was leased at a cost of $2,250 annually.

In 1942–43 three additional auxiliary airfields were added. The fourth auxiliary field was located two miles east of Waugh, Alabama, on the south side of U.S. Highway 80. Preparation of the 299.37 acres of what was confusingly called Mount Meigs Auxiliary Field cost $30,792.50 and was leased for an annual fee of $2,993.70. The 295-acre Elmore Field was located one and a half miles southwest of Elmore, Alabama, and the site cost $111,859.06 to prepare for use as an auxiliary airfield. Deatsville Auxiliary Field was added in 1943, but no details of its size or cost for preparation could be located. Gunter Field had begun training in November 1940 with

200 students, a large ground support staff and a small contingent of army officer-instructors. In December 1942, shortly after Class SE-43-B, the final RAF course, left Gunter Field for advanced flying schools, the USAAF basic flying school had an enrollment in excess of 700 student pilots and employed more than 130 flying instructors and supervisors.

When Gunter Field officers encountered problems in getting the new basic flying school under operation, they set about to resolve them quickly and, in the process, discovered ways to improve efficiency. While construction continued on the airfield and the domestic site, normal aircraft maintenance was carried out in the open air or in the single hangar on one side of the airfield. In September 1941, after about ten months of operation, a production line maintenance (PLM) system was implemented at Gunter Field for all fifty- and one-hundred-hour checks. Under the system, two lines of aircraft were routed through a hangar, and teams of engine, airframe, instrument and radio mechanics swarmed over each aircraft at four separate stations to provide thorough maintenance and inspections.

This efficient system permitted maximum use of highly skilled and experienced maintenance specialists and replaced the more wasteful, labor-intensive system that preceded it. Though the system had been proposed and implemented in 1940–41 by the chief of maintenance at the civil contract primary flying school at Glendale, California, it was first used on the more powerful and complex basic trainer aircraft at Gunter Field. From there and from Glendale, it was adopted for use on other primary, basic and advanced training stations. PLM was also used on operational stations and at maintenance depots in the United States and overseas.

Gunter Field's organization and administration was patterned after long-established procedures developed and used at Randolph Field, Texas. Gunter was commanded by Lieutenant Colonel Aubrey Hornsby, originally the station project officer, and his staff included Major Donald Fitzgerald, executive officer; Major Leonard W. Rodieck, director of training; Major J.E. Mallory, director of ground school; Captain Robert E.L. Choate, operations officer; Captain Richard H. Wise, post adjutant; First Lieutenant Arthur E. Brown, personnel officer; Lieutenant J.R. Luper, commandant of cadets; and Lieutenant Colonel Richard T. Edwards, post quartermaster. It was this latter officer who had responsibility for the smooth running of the domestic side of this sprawling military town. The post quartermaster administered a billeting office and all warehouses and supply depots on the station. In administering to the needs of a military population five thousand strong, these service units issued and accounted for clothing, food, equipment, transport, utilities, recreation and fire protection. By 1 December 1941, such routine base activities were centralized under the new office of post engineers.

Staffing the offices, service units, hospital and school squadrons followed common practice of the time. Usually, some experienced personnel were transferred from already established basic schools or other installations. To these men were added newly trained staff from scattered air corps technical and administrative schools or directly from short military indoctrination courses. In line with pre-war command and staff studies, any expandable military force would be compelled to devote a great deal of effort to training personnel needed to operate other organizations.

Like other older air corps bases, Gunter Field established its own school system and continued formal instruction and on-the-job training (OJT) programs to qualify men and improve the efficiency of new staff as duty assignments were enlarged. Into Gunter Field schools went raw recruits or men remustered from other branches of service, and out of the schools came qualified men, many of whom continued to serve on the station while others were posted to new training stations.

Since Gunter Field was the initial basic flying school in the Southeastern United States, it performed an especially vital function in SEACTC expansion plans. Every staff office, unit and detachment at Gunter Field brought in new staff, trained them in their duties, provided active duty organizational, administrative and instructional experience and, after a few months, these men were posted to newly activated air corps stations. Many of the original staff officers rose to the rank of general or colonel in the USAAF Training Command before the end of the war. Of those who managed to escape the Training Command to combat assignments, many distinguished themselves in various parts of the world during 1941–45. Captain Louis W. Schneider (medical corps reserve, the original Gunter Field post surgeon) and Captain Frederick V. Whitman (dental corps, the first dentist assigned to Gunter Field) went to the Philippine Islands, where Dr. Schneider was killed in action and Dr. Whitman was made a prisoner of war.

Among the staff schools that were operated successfully at Gunter Field and trained a large number of air corps personnel included the following: an aircraft mechanics' school, a weather school, a military police school, an administrative school, a post quartermasters' school, a noncommissioned officers' course, a radio code school, an air traffic control school and a Link Training instructors' school. When plans were being developed to open a new training station, extra squadrons at Gunter Field trained maintenance and administrative personnel for those stations as well. Just as most of the original staff at Gunter had come with squadrons from Randolph and Maxwell Fields, Gunter Field trained squadrons that were later transferred to new basic schools at Macon, Georgia; Greenwood, Mississippi; Malden, Missouri; and others when those stations were ready to commence training.

In addition to training student pilots and ground staff, Gunter Field also trained many flying instructors. Since there was no air corps or USAAF central instructors' school before 1942, each station conducted its own instructor training courses. From the beginning, experienced senior flying officers provided refresher and instructors' courses for newly assigned pilots and continued to provide regular flight checks for instructors even after students arrived on station. Younger, less-experienced instructors were junior officers who had demonstrated exceptional abilities as pilots during training and who, despite protestations, had been assigned as instructors.

An important part of the flying training curriculum at every stage of training was ground school. At Gunter Field, Major J.E. Mallory, air corps, was the original director of the ground school. When training commenced in November 1940, the ground school used rooms in the post headquarters building, formerly the unused Kilby Prison Tuberculosis Hospital. The rooms of that building, unsuitably equipped with steel bars, would never be satisfactory, but it was August 1942 before a new, larger building was completed, and it was October 1942 before sufficient expandable ground school classrooms and instructional aids were adequate for the task of training the large student population.

The ground school syllabus was more flexible than that in the flying department. Instructors were told what courses were to be taught and how many hours were to be used for each, but there was no common syllabus. For example, navigation was taught for fifteen hours, meteorology for thirty hours, airplanes and engines for twenty hours, radio code for thirty hours and radio communications for three hours. From the beginning, ground school instructors developed their courses according to their own views as to the emphasis required. When the British cadet classes arrived, the ground school staff modified the curriculum so as to better serve the needs of the UK students. Greater coordination between ground and flying training followed later.

Since Gunter Field's mission was basic flying training, its training organization was of central importance. At first, Lieutenant Colonel Leonard H. Rodieck served as both director of training and director of flying. As the school grew, the two offices were separated. Reporting to the director of training were a director of flying, director of ground school, director of military training, commandant of cadets and school secretary.

In the initial flying training directorate system, organization was fairly standard at all flying schools. Reporting to the director of flying were two group commanders and six squadron commanders. Each squadron commander had an assistant and from eight to twenty flying instructors. Group I included Squadrons 1, 3, 5 and 7, and Group II included Squadrons 2, 4, 6 and 8. The lower class (new arrivals) flew from 8:30 a.m. to 12:30 p.m., while the upper class attended ground school. Then the two classes exchanged places and the upper class flew from 1:30 to 5:30 p.m., while the lower class attended ground school. In order to assure flying experience at all times of the day and night, schedules were shifted about for the various squadrons. In addition to these refinements, a two-hour night navigation flight was added to the syllabus.

As each new expansion plan and curriculum change was implemented, more buildings, aircraft, instructors and students were added to the station. By December 1941, there were 108 flying instructors and 108 trainer aircraft at Gunter Field. For the early instructors, adjustment to teaching flying was very difficult owing to inadequate facilities and shortages in equipment, personnel and instruments. Although most of these shortages were remedied in time, the first Vultee BT-13 trainers had no instruments in the rear cockpits, so on night flights, with the student in the front cockpit, early instructors were put to the "supreme test."

During 1942, new sources of flying instructors were found. By February 1942, several RAF pilot officer graduates of Class SE-42-A were given an instructors' course in the new central instructors' school at Maxwell Field, Alabama, and a number of them were assigned as instructors at Gunter Field. In the ensuing months, additional RAF instructors were posted to Cochran Field from Arnold Scheme and BFTS courses until there were fifty-five RAF pilot officers and flying officers serving on the Gunter Field instructional staff. Another potential source of flying instructors was the huge pool of older American civilian pilots who were not qualified for active military service. In 1942, a number of these civilian "service pilots" were sent through the instructors' school and were hired at Gunter Field as civil servants, but most of them were later commissioned.

By September 1942, Gunter Field had changed dramatically. The total number of instructors climbed to 170, then dropped back to 128, and the number of aircraft rose to almost 200, and flying training was once more reorganized and further expanded. The earlier group organization was disbanded and four school squadrons were established. The eight former squadrons were redesignated flights A through H and two flights were assigned to each of four school squadrons. Each flight commander had an assistant and 13 or 14 instructors. As a result, the new training organization was stabilized with approximately 128 flying instructors and another dozen or more supervisory staff officers. As part of that change, orders came in from USAAF headquarters ending hazing as a part of the cadet training syllabus. Criticisms of overly harsh military cadet training had finally brought results.

United States Army Air Corps training officers deemed military discipline as important for producing officer pilots as other parts of the aviation cadet training syllabus. When the training sequence was reduced from one year to thirty-six weeks, then thirty weeks, and primary flying training was dispersed to civilian contract schools with very tiny air corps staffs, primary school syllabi were modified to omit most of the military training formerly required at that stage of training. As a result, the basic flying schools were directed to increase the amount of military training in their curricula.

In September 1940, Gunter Field complied with that order and established a flying cadet basic training group. Military and physical training and cadet discipline came under the group's plans and training office (S-3), and Second Lieutenant James R. Luper assumed command of the group. He was assisted in the performance of his duties by six other second lieutenants, most of whom were graduates of the United States Military Academy at West Point, New York. In May 1941, Luper, then captain, was transferred to Maxwell Field as commandant of cadets at the Aviation Cadet Replacement Center. Other officers of the original staff, including Lieutenants Frank W. Iseman and John H. Knight, were later transferred to Cochran Field, Georgia, the second basic flying school in the SEACTC.

Together, the military training staff used the Aviation Cadet Handbook, which had been developed through long experience and practice by the Air Corps Training Center at Randolph Field, Texas. The cadet code dictated that officer-cadets be exposed to a prolonged period of hazing at meals, in quarters and everywhere on station during their first five weeks of training at every school. The idea was that enforcement of that rigorous code would produce an outstanding officer who could withstand pressure and retain his composure despite efforts to bring about a perfectly normal reaction of anger or defiance.

The disciplinary system, which was peculiar to the American ground and air forces, aimed at stripping individuals to the barest essentials and remolding them according to a tested code of behavior. It proved an excellent means of training American military leaders. Those who accepted the system as an important and necessary part of their training exerted self-control, laughed at it (quietly), survived it and discovered that they indeed possessed greater self-discipline, which improved their abilities to master details and lead others.

However, it was not a system designed to salvage either sore-heads or the hopelessly undisciplined. The cadet code was not a mystery; it was published in a manual that was issued to all cadets. It was enforced by the senior class in varying degrees during primary, basic and advanced flying schools, and all juniors, students newly assigned to the training station, would comply with the code until released from it. For those who lost their control and were defiant, the screws were tightened in an effort to eliminate them from the cadet corps as undesirable officer material. Until changes were wrought in 1942, all American aviation cadets were trained as officers, and the cadet code was widely known by civilian and military applicants to be a part of the course to be suffered by those who entered flying training.

Perhaps it was essential that all students undergoing the system of cadet training be treated the same and that favoritism not be shown to anyone. However, what was forgotten in fostering this egalitarian view was that the British students undergoing pilot training were unaware of the system until they arrived, and parts of their culture rejected it out of hand. To many RAF students of working-class origins, the code smacked of the rigid class structure and the hated system of "fagging" that then prevailed in British public schools. Because of these similarities and the working-class ethos that labeled such practices as "poofy" and "bullying," it was natural that they should resist it. Some of them failed to recognize the benefits to be derived from such experience and resented being placed under the authority of cadet officers who had only slightly more experience than themselves.

Realities that promoted defiance included the fact that many of the British student pilots had left school at age fourteen to take jobs. On graduating as pilots or other aircrew, most of them became sergeant pilots, and only one-third of each graduating course was commissioned. Many of these men expected to remain NCOs, and being awarded a king's commission was considered beyond either their interest or their abilities. Other RAF student pilots had already served as "other ranks" in one or the other of the uniformed services, including the British Army, Navy, Maritime service and RAF, and these experienced old hands knew all the tricks for evading the rules and counseling defiance. Despite the fact that some men and the occasional officer promoted an "us" and "them" interpretation of relationships between the RAF cadets and their American counterparts, many of the young British students enjoyed the USAAF training system while others were embittered by it.

Looking back to early training, many junior and senior USAAF officers were critical of using even a modified West Point disciplinary system with either American or foreign cadets. They felt that pilot training had enough built-in pressures without adding an extra burden of trying in a limited period to indoctrinate students in the complex honor code and its uses. These USAAF officers expressed the view that the discipline and tactical training of foreign students should be handled by officers of the same nationality. However, until higher headquarters accepted their arguments and permitted modification of the training system, they had no choice but to carry out established policies with as little pain as possible. Just as Class SE-42-J entered basic flying school in September 1942, the "class" hazing system was finally abolished in the USAAF aircrew training programs.

FLYING TRAINING AT GUNTER FIELD

Officially, flying training began at Gunter Field on 20 November 1940. Between that date and 17 August 1941, seven courses totaling 1,328 American flying cadets had arrived at Gunter Field. Beginning with 200 members of Class SE-41-C and continuing through five classes, a total of 970 flying cadets and 51 student officers, or an average of 194 student pilots per class, had entered the school. When the massive Cochran Field opened some nine miles south of Macon, Georgia, in June 1941, it received a larger number of students than Gunter and began to remove some of the pressure from the older basic flying school.

Enrollment at Gunter Field for Classes SE-41-H dropped to 137 aviation cadets, and that for Class SE-41-I was reduced to 170 cadets. Beginning with Class SE-41-H on 22 March 1941, the new title "aviation cadet" replaced the older label, "flying cadet." Of the first five classes (SE-41-C through SE-41-G), 82 American flying cadets were eliminated, 3 were killed and 936 graduated. Of the final two Gunter Field basic flying classes made up exclusively of 307 American aviation cadets, 15 were eliminated and 292 graduated.

When Class SE-41-H graduated in August 1941 and moved to advanced flying schools, Class SE-41-I became the senior class, and its place as the lower class at Gunter Field was taken by Class SE-42-A, which included 158 British cadets and 30 American aviation cadets. Some of the classes arriving at the basic flying school would later be all British, but most British cadets would complete training alongside American cadets. During the seventeen months extending from 17 August 1941 to mid-January 1943, a total of 2,394 British pilot trainees entered the basic flying school at Gunter Field, Alabama. Of that number, 22 were killed in accidents, 262 were eliminated (248 for flying deficiencies, 14 for "other than flying" reasons) and 2,110 completed training successfully and were posted to advanced flying schools.

Early in the course, the American and RAF members of Class SE-42-A learned the value that USAAF officers placed on the basic flying training course. In 1938, debates had begun as to the importance of each of the three phases of flying training, and those officers who perceived basic flying as most important were generally adamant in their opinion. Most of the instructors and staff officers took their jobs very seriously and were also careful to inform their students exactly what was expected of them. In measuring individual student abilities, the instructors submitted for the official records an army air corps tabular assessment form, which listed the instructor's evaluation of each student's natural aptitude, airmanship, skill in landing, cockpit drill, aerobatics, instrument, night and formation flying. Flying instructors also assessed each student's judgment, map reading and navigational abilities.

In making assessments of their students, the instructors were also required to evaluate persistence, sense of responsibility, endurance, leadership, method, deliberation, enterprise, dash, distribution of attention and self-control. After judging both flying abilities and personal qualities, basic flying school instructors recommended each student for bomber (TE) or fighter aircraft (SE), for instructor duty and for noncommissioned or commissioned rank. Although all of their recommendations were not accepted, the instructor evaluations helped to determine the school to which each student pilot would be sent for advanced flying training.

The standard 1941 USAAF basic flying school syllabus was covered in seventy hours and included an introductory and a diversified stage. The first to the eighteenth hours included learning instruments and technique. After soloing in the BT-13, the student pilot was introduced to further experience, including night and instrument flying, but much of that experience was gained with an instructor aboard. At Gunter Field, it included six hours of instrument flying, one and a half hours of aerobatics, three hours of local night flying and five cross-country flights. The cross-country was a dual-instrument flight (student under the hood) of approximately one hour's duration and usually ran from Gunter Field to Alexander City, Alabama, and back, a distance of approximately 100 miles. Four navigation flights during daytime included a straight-line flight from Gunter to Columbiana, Alabama, and return to Gunter (120 miles), and several triangular flights, including Gunter to Opelika, Alabama, to Troy, Alabama, and return to Gunter (175 miles); Gunter to Ozark, Alabama, to Greenville, Mississippi, return to Gunter (200 miles); and Gunter to LaGrange, Georgia, to Eufala, Alabama, and return to Gunter (230 miles).

In addition to these day flights, the syllabus included one night navigation flight of approximately two hours and ran from Gunter via Green Airway 5 to Newnan, Georgia, and returned to Gunter along the same airway. The latter group navigation flights were usually carried out in loose formations of four-plane elements with one instructor in each element. The route for the Gunter-Newnan cross-country flight was modified in the spring of 1942, and the new plan was to follow a triangular route that ran southeastward from Gunter Field to Crestview, Florida, where the aircraft landed, then they flew westward, turned northward at Mobile, Alabama, and, without landing, flew back to Gunter Field. Shortly after this new route was implemented, a sudden weather change in May 1942 produced one of the worst disasters of the entire period of British aircrew training in the United States.

Class SE-42-A, the first of thirteen courses in which British student pilots were trained at Gunter Field, arrived in several separate contingents from primary flying schools located at Arcadia and Lakeland, Florida, and Tuscaloosa, Alabama. Former journalist Arthur L. Prandle (Carlstrom) continued to write articles for the *Arcadian* newspaper relating the activities of the students on his course. In describing their send-off from the Arcadia railway station by a huge crowd on Saturday, 16 August 1941, Prandle and his classmates were "touched by this outward and visible sign of the bond of affection which exists between us." He and his classmates were also pleased that their journey to the basic flying school was aboard an air-conditioned train, rather than a steam-heated train like the one on which they had arrived in Arcadia, Florida.

As they traveled northeastward across Florida via Lakeland to Jacksonville, and then northwestward via Thomasville, Georgia, to Montgomery, they tried to get some rest in the reclining seats and to see as much of the country as possible. Sunday evening, 17 August at around 6:00 p.m., they arrived at Union Station in Montgomery and boarded army trucks for the four-mile drive to Gunter Field. Following assignment to quarters and an excellent meal, they were exhausted enough to sleep.

On Monday, 18 August, nine British members of the class were ordered to shave off their moustaches. Despite pleas to reverse the order, it stood, and their facial hair was shaved off in accordance with cadet regulations. Within ten days, Brigadier General Walter R. Weaver, commanding general of the SEACTC, reversed that particular standing order, but for members of the first RAF class, it was too late at basic and primary flying schools. Other than the removal of "those mustachios of which we were so proud," Prandle felt that the British cadets had adjusted to Gunter Field. Several of them soloed after only three or four hours of dual flying.

Just following lunch on Friday, 26 August 1941, in celebration of Gunter Field's first birthday and the departure of Class SE-41-I, the final "all-American" class, ice cream was served for dessert along with slices from a red-white-and-blue cake weighing thirty pounds. During the few days following the departure of Class SE-41-I and the arrival of Class SE-42-B on 30 August, members of Class SE-42-A drilled regularly in preparation for a station parade scheduled for Saturday morning, 4 September.

Following the arrival of Class SE-42-B, it was decided to hold an all-British military review on the lawn of the Kilby Prison dairy, so that course began to sharpen their drill as well. Then, on 4 September, using RAF drill, the all-RAF formation, except for an American color bearer and color guard, marched past the reviewing stand. Especially confusing to the RAF students was that the guest of honor at the parade was Jack Dempsey, who at that time was traveling with Cole Brothers Circus. Sports figures were praised in the United Kingdom, but not yet to the extent that they felt Americans appeared to regard them at the time.

As the British students at Gunter Field settled into the routine, many of them discovered that people in Montgomery and the vicinity were just as friendly as the Americans they had met while undergoing primary flying. When they were able to go into Montgomery, they met people at the USO, at churches, at the Cadet Club and elsewhere, and were welcomed into homes. During the last weekend of September, thirty RAF cadets from Gunter Field were guests of the small town of Andalusia, Alabama. On Friday afternoon, Lions Club members drove to Gunter Field and transported the cadets to the south Alabama town, where they were entertained royally until the club members delivered them back to Gunter Field on Sunday afternoon. Not to be outdone, some people in Montgomery sponsored a dance the following Friday evening and paired fifty RAF cadets from Gunter Field with fifty young ladies from Montgomery.

During October, the British cadets probably expected to gain a reprieve from the heat that they had suffered from since arriving in the United States in June and July, but that was not to be the case. Although cool nights were making it easier to sleep in the otherwise hot barracks, daytime temperatures ranged higher than normal, and brilliant sunshine was a regular occurrence. On 10 October, the high temperature was a record ninety-four degrees, but within a week, a cold front moved in, bringing rain with it, and temperatures moderated from cool to chill.

Around 30 August 1941, 155 British student pilots of Class SE-42-B had arrived at Gunter Field. As with the members of Class SE-42-A, those from south Florida schools traveled by rail via Jacksonville and Thomasville, Georgia, to Montgomery. Alan George Winchester (Arcadia, 42-B) recalled that at the time of their arrival at Gunter Field their uniforms "had been vandalised for keepsakes to give local girls." When Class SE-42-A departed, 2 of its members were transferred to Class SE-42-B, bringing the intake of the latter class to a total of 157. Of the student pilots who made up that first RAF contingent at Gunter Field, plus the 30 Americans in the class, 10 members of the class did not complete the course. On 20 November 1941, 149 British and 29 American student pilots graduated and were posted to advanced flying schools. Two British students were held over to continue training with a subsequent class, 7 UK students were eliminated and 1 American was killed in an aircraft accident.

James Cook of Yorkshire (Lakeland, 42-B) was a veteran of Dunkirk. Owing to excellent weather, Cook's class finished the basic course at Gunter Field about a week earlier than scheduled, so they were allowed a seven-day leave. As with so many members of the RAF classes, Cook and a classmate decided to hitchhike to Lakeland, Florida, to visit friends from their primary training days. On Sunday afternoon, 7 December 1941, he and his friends were visiting the Bok Tower in the heart of Florida's citrus district when they heard the news of the Japanese attack on Pearl Harbor, Hawaii.

LAC Stanley Slater (Arcadia, 42-B) recalled that the Vultee BT-13 was a noisy but effective trainer. Slater also recalled that after attending a circus performance, he and two RAF classmates were given a lift by the Williamson family, who befriended them and remained close friends of the airmen for the remainder of their stay in the United States. Of the 157 net enrollment for Class SE-42-B, 1 student was held over to the next class, 6 were eliminated and 1 British cadet was killed while on leave. On 9 December 1941, while on leave visiting friends in Arcadia, Florida, before reporting to an advanced flying school, nineteen-year-old LAC Louis Wells of Bootham, Yorkshire, England, was killed in an automobile accident. Funeral services were held in Florida, and Wells was interred in Arcadia's Oak Ridge Cemetery. As a result of this loss, 149 instead of 150 RAF cadets graduated at Gunter Field in December 1941 and were posted to advanced flying schools.

On 4 November 1941, the 204 UK student pilots of Class SE-42-C arrived at Gunter Field. Members of this class came from primary schools at Lakeland, Florida; Tuscaloosa, Alabama; and Albany, Georgia. The addition of 1 student held over from the preceding class brought the total enrollment to 205. Of that number, 19 were eliminated (18 for flying deficiencies, 1 for other reasons) and 186 graduated in January 1942.

Many years later, Kenneth I. Pearson (Tuscaloosa, 42-C) recalled his training:

> *The basic flying course at Gunter Field was carried out on Vultee BT-13As. The instructors were U.S. Army Air Corps officers, and my logbook shows that those who suffered me were Lieutenants Tucker, Henderson, and Stearn. There is no doubt in my mind that the experience of induction into the U.S. Army Air Corps, the training, the contacts at an impressionable age with our hosts and the travel involved was intensely pleasurable and could have been nothing but a benefit to me.*
>
> *In later years, when my job took me many times to the States, I never went as a stranger. My work brought me into contact with many Americans, both civil and military, and I am sure that I possessed a greater understanding of them as a result of the Arnold Scheme.*

It is strange how great events seem only to attain their correct dimension in one's consciousness with the passing of time. This is particularly true of Pearl Harbour. I was at Gunter at the time, and we heard the news over the radio in the flight hut, and our only thought was that if America came into the war, ceasing to be neutral, we would have to go back into RAF uniform which was not attractive in that the material was heavier, rougher, and perhaps less smart than that which we were accustomed to as cadets.

Following the Japanese attack on Pearl Harbor, rumors spread rapidly. Many RAF cadets wrote home that, instead of returning home, they might be assigned to join American air force units in the Far East.

By mid-December 1941, the members of Class SE-42-B departed for advanced flying schools, and Class SE-42-C moved to upper-class status. Then, on 16 December 1941, 197 RAF students of Class SE-42-D arrived at Gunter Field to commence training. Changes had been made: blackout conditions were being observed, military staff were on guard against potential sabotage and the pace of training had quickened to seven days per week. Moreover, students from Camden, South Carolina; Tuscaloosa, Alabama; and Arcadia, Florida, were posted to Gunter, while those from the other three primary flying schools were posted to Cochran Field, Georgia. Why men who had been trained at Camden were shifted from Cochran Field to Gunter is unknown, but it is likely that RAF cadets trained at Camden had held senior rank at the Macon, Georgia basic flying school for each of the first three RAF classes, and USAAF training officers possibly wanted to evaluate primary training by comparing cadet performance in a different basic flying school.

Among the members of Class SE-42-D at Gunter Field were a large number of men from the empire and from British companies located in South America and the Far East. C.J.C. "Johnnie" Manning of the Barbados and Denys R. Ding of China and the British-American Tobacco Company were among the men who had trained at Tuscaloosa, Alabama. More than forty years later, Joe Crossman (Camden, 42-D) of Coventry, England, recalled his experiences:

Of the 50 who had started training at Camden in October, 27 survived primary and moved on to basic flying training at Gunter Field, Alabama on 15 December 1941. We flew Vultee BT-13s. Discipline was very strict, we used to do rifle drill and marching early in the morning before breakfast. The meal times at Gunter stand out in my memory. You had a set time, and if you hadn't finished when the officer called, that was it.

At breakfast, they brought plates of flapjacks and maple syrup. Some meals they put out great platters of steaks, fried onions, and eggs on the table and you just stuck your fork in and took as many steaks as you wanted. I used to watch all that meat being picked up and think of the meagre ration of meat people were having to live on in Britain at that time.

The weather was much colder now, and one day it actually snowed, which caused a sensation. The first snow seen for many years. My instructor was Lt. Renz, a young Army lieutenant. We were now introduced to blind or cloud flying, where you pulled a hood over your cockpit and flew entirely on instruments. With a pilot in the back seat of course to keep a look-out. Night flying and cross country trips were now part of the course. The townspeople were very hospitable here too, and there were always invitations out to meals and so forth. I was invited to Xmas dinner with one family.

Other members of Class SE-42-D had different experiences. During his stay at Gunter Field, Frank William Preston (Arcadia, 42-D) recalled that American news photographers called out to the staid and dignified visiting RAF chief of air staff, Air Marshal Sir Charles Portal, "Hey Marshy, look this way!" Unfortunately, after fifteen hours of instruction with several different instructors, Preston was washed out at Gunter Field and returned to Canada for remustering to other aircrew training. Of the 197 students in Class SE-42-D, 36 were eliminated, 5 were held over to subsequent classes and 156 graduated.

On 9 January 1942, 240 British students of Class SE-42-E arrived at Gunter Field. John Clark (Albany, 42-E) and his classmates traveled by coach from Albany, Georgia, to Montgomery, Alabama. When John completed his pilot training at nearby Maxwell Field, he was commissioned pilot officer and was assigned as a flying instructor at Gunter Field. Earlier, while undergoing pilot training, Clark met Jean Harmon of nearby Wetumpka, Alabama, and the young couple were married in 1942 while John served as an instructor at Gunter Field. After four and a half weeks, 5 students from Class SE-42-D were held over for further training and brought Class SE-42-E's enrollment to 245.

Unfortunately, on Monday, 9 February, shortly after taking off on a routine training flight, a BT-13 trainer aircraft bearing Instructor Lieutenant Vincent DeGolyer—a Cornell University graduate of Castile, New York—and RAF Corporal Reginald A. Price (Albany, 42-E) crashed some six miles east of Gunter Field, and both men were killed. The twenty-two-year-old Price, a former London police constable and student at Oxford University, hailed from Slough, Buckinghamshire. He had been cadet captain during his primary training at Darr Aero Tech, Georgia.

Raymond Peter Grimwood (Tuscaloosa, 42-E) remembered instrument flying at Gunter and recalled that for the first time they used Link Trainers for instrument training and followed that a few days later with instrument flying under the hood. Many of the RAF cadets were concerned about the "gig" system and "walking tours," but Grimwood was not bothered; in fact, he apparently enjoyed the discipline. In recalling the cadet code after more than forty years, Grimwood, who had become an airline captain, indicated that he still had a card with the code printed on it, indicating that it "has always meant something to me in life."

In early March 1942, as the course was drawing to a close for Class SE-42-E at Gunter Field, the *Montgomery Advertiser* published an in-depth article describing night flying at Gunter Field. The first night flight was described as exciting, "exceeding even the thrills of the first solo flight in primary school." The article emphasized the potential danger, the sense of isolation in the darkness and the necessity of relying on instruments to maintain the proper attitude of the aircraft in flight. In tracing the feelings of a young RAF student pilot during his first night takeoff, zone flying and landing, the newspaper article described how night flying experience was so vital to later cross-country flying training and to future bomber combat operations.

Within a few days after the article appeared, two BT-13s collided some fifty miles from Gunter Field while on a night flight. The wing tip of the aircraft flown by RAF LAC J.B. Blackett was so severely damaged in the collision that the ailerons were made "virtually immovable." Following the directions given by his instructor in a nearby aircraft, Blackett approached Gunter Field at a low level and brought the aircraft safely straight onto the runway, thereby attesting to "the quality of training received at Gunter Field."

When Class SE-42-E departed Gunter Field for advanced flying schools in mid-March 1942, its record was as follows: of a total enrollment of 245 student pilots, 4 were held over for further training, so the net enrollment dropped to 241. Of that number, 41 were eliminated, 2 were killed in flying accidents and 198 graduated and were posted to advanced flying schools.

By February 1942, with the extended training schedule in effect, cold weather had come to Montgomery and on occasion there were some light snow flurries. At Gunter Field, the domestic site was in excellent condition. Most of the barracks, recreation facilities, classroom and utility buildings were now complete. On the airdrome, the flight line was the heart of the school's activities, and it was still located on the east side of the field. There the USAAF sub-depot repaired and overhauled BT-13 aircraft in a huge hangar, and the individual school squadrons conducted operations from the extensive flight line. Cadets and instructors were still being transported from their living quarters to the flight line on the east side of the airfield.

In late February 1942, the 175-member Class SE-42-F arrived at Gunter Field. With the addition of the 4 students held over from the preceding class, the net enrollment climbed to 179, but the total cadet population of the basic flying school was around 400, and the personnel strength of the station exceeded 5,000. Training was proceeding as usual, although the weather was now more to the liking of many of the RAF cadets. Since the pace of training had quickened in December, some of the British students continued to experience difficulties; the elimination rate had climbed and still remained inordinately high. Those who entered training were constantly under pressure, and fear of failure was their prime concern, but as they gained more experience and the new became the routine, they settled down to their training. Another addition to Gunter Field that helped was the assignment of a number of RAF pilot officers to the station as instructors.

One student of Class SE-42-F who apparently adjusted quickly to Gunter Field and his flying training was Lionel C. Ewens (Tuscaloosa, 42-F). The gregarious Ewens recalled his training at Gunter Field and the many friends he and his classmates made among American citizens. During his stay in the United States, Ewens may have set a record for travel among Arnold Scheme students. During Easter leave, he and several classmates visited New Orleans. Then, during his seven-day leave between basic and advanced flight training, Ewens and Don Jordan, a classmate, hitchhiked to Gloversville, New York, the town to which Charles Booth, the British social reformer, traveled regularly in pursuit of his glove manufacturing interests. Ewens was successful in locating and visiting some distant cousins who had immigrated to the New York town from the glove-making region of Somerset. Since Ewens and Jordan had to return to Alabama, their visit was necessarily a short one.

They traveled by bus to New York City, where they visited the Stage Door Canteen, and Ewens was thrilled at being able to dance with actress Paulette Goddard. Then after hitchhiking to Baltimore and Washington, seeing the sights in the nation's capital and meeting a number of hospitable people, the two RAF cadets hitched south to Atlanta, where they caught another Greyhound bus from Atlanta into Montgomery. Ewens arrived back at Gunter Field "with 50 cents in my pocket." Sadly, Don Jordan, Ewens's companion on that odyssey, was killed in a flying accident shortly after they returned to Britain. Of Class SE-42-F's intake of 179 UK students, 10 were held over to the next class, thus dropping the net enrollment to 169. Of that number, 21 were eliminated, 3 were killed in flying accidents and 115 graduated and were posted to advanced flying schools.

Of the students killed in training at Gunter Field, it is difficult to be precise because following entry of the United States into the war, information was more restricted than in the past. Although newspapers reported flying accidents when they were able to ferret out the information, any details concerning military personnel were now considered restricted, and newspaper accounts of such fatalities were sketchy at best, often following an official news release pattern such as "while on a routine training flight," etc. However, a careful examination of extant newspapers revealed some information, and official records continued to confirm numbers, if not names.

The three members of Class SE-42-F who were killed while in training at Gunter Field were LACs Shotbolt, Nash and Atkin. Twenty-year-old LAC Reginald Arthur John Shotbolt (Tuscaloosa, 42-F) of Luton, Bedfordshire, was killed on 7 April 1942. On 10 April 1942, USAAF Flying Instructor Lieutenant William S. Mudd Jr. and twenty-four-year-old RAF LAC Frederick Nash of Dover, Kent, England, were killed when their BT-13 went into a spin and crashed on an auxiliary field east of Gunter Field. That same night, twenty-three-year-old LAC Thomas Walpole Atkin of Acklam, Middlesbrough, Yorkshire, was killed when his plane crashed some five miles southeast of Perote, Bullock County, Alabama. Class SE-42-F completed training during the third week of March and its members were permitted the usual seven-day leave before graduating and being posted to advanced flying schools.

On Monday, 30 March 1942, Class SE-42-G, totaling 205 UK cadets, arrived at Gunter Field and commenced training at the now crowded USAAF basic flying training school. After four and a half weeks, the 10 students held over from Class SE-42-F were added, bringing the total class enrollment to 215. Before being posted to five primary flying schools (Camden, South Carolina, ceased training RAF students with Class SE-42-E), members of Class SE-42-G had spent about half of December 1941 and January 1942 undergoing acclimatization training at Maxwell Field. As a result, those who came to Gunter were familiar with the city, and many of them were able to renew friendships from their earlier assignment in Montgomery.

Although construction at the station was now almost finished, Gunter Field was a USAAF military station, and its training routine was therefore quite different from the more casual form prevailing in the civilian contract primary schools. Instead of two men per room, there were now six; instead of black waiters serving food to individual tables, there were now compartmentalized steel mess hall trays and cafeteria-style lines. Although there was unlikely to be very much agreement concerning that critical area, hazing was gone, and cadet discipline was more orderly and reasonable, as one would expect on a crowded military station. On the flying side, rumors of disasters made adjustment to the powerful and noisy BT-13s more difficult. But once the cadets soloed and overcame their nervous anticipation of the first night flight, they quickly adjusted to night flying, formation flying, instrument flying, Link Training time and aerobatics.

However, Class SE-42-G proved to be the hard luck class of both Maxwell and Gunter Fields, as well as of the Arnold Scheme. Tragedy struck members of the class at Gunter Field and later in an advanced flying school as well. The routine at Gunter Field was steady; cadets were awakened in the wee hours of the morning, and following physical training or close order drill, or both, they ate breakfast, dressed appropriately for assigned duties, straightened their kits, made beds and reported for classes or for transportation to the flight line.

The trail of tragedies began early in the month of May 1942, when flowers were in bloom and the warm Alabama sunshine accented the different shades of green that blanketed the entire region. During the evening of Thursday, 7 May, nineteen-year-old flying instructor Pilot Officer Geoffrey H.A. Butler of West Hartlepool, County Durham, was killed when his BT-13 trainer slammed into the earth some five miles southeast of Gunter Field. On that same night, twenty-year-old LAC Oswald Hendrie McDonald crashed about one mile east of Gunter Field and was killed. It could not be established whether or not the two aircraft had collided before they crashed individually, but the two deaths resulting from these accidents were only the beginning for the month.

On the afternoon of Wednesday, 20 May 1942, Captain Joseph O. Garrett's Training Squadron 6 flew for two hours, making up for flying hours lost owing to weather problems. For three days running, Garrett had scheduled a navigation training flight for the squadron, but each time, owing to a front in the vicinity of Evergreen and Atmore in south Alabama, Lieutenant O.S. Graf, the station meteorologist, had advised against flying. However, Lieutenant Garrett and his group commander, Captain Macready, were anxious for the squadron to complete that stage of its training, so they watched weather developments closely.

After the squadron had flown for two hours during that Wednesday afternoon, Garrett made his decision and ordered that preparations be made to depart on the routine triangular navigation training flight. The route ran southeastward 110 miles to Crestview, Florida, then westward to Mobile, Alabama, and then, without landing, the squadron aircraft were to turn northeastward and fly 160 miles back to Gunter Field; total flying time for the entire trip was about five and a half hours.

By 3:45 p.m., the squadron was winging its way toward Crestview, Florida. It had been dispatched from Gunter Field in flights of four aircraft each, one flying instructor in the lead aircraft of each flight. If the flight had gone according to plan, the thirty-five aircraft should have returned to Gunter Field before midnight. However, after arriving in Crestview at 6:13 p.m., departure on the remaining two legs of the flight was delayed owing to the passage of a small storm. There were no dining facilities at Crestview, so the already tired instructors and cadets evidently did not have access to either coffee or food.

Instead of leaving Crestview at 8:00 p.m. as scheduled, the small storm did not lift until around 11:00 p.m., so it was at 11:20, almost five and a half hours after landing, that the thirty-five aircraft took off in darkness from Crestview and flew directly west across the pine barrens of the Florida panhandle toward their turning point near Mobile, Alabama. All of the thirty-four cadets and nine flying instructors had already been on duty for almost eighteen hours, and they were understandably tired and anxious to get home and into bed.

The instructors and cadets encountered light rain and saw some lightning flashes, but decided to push on. According to later reports, all of the aircraft reached Mobile, Alabama, around midnight and turned onto a heading for Montgomery. Then, at around 1:20 a.m., 21 May 1942, in the vicinity of Evergreen, Alabama, the weather deteriorated rapidly. The pilots encountered heavy haze, light rain and what appeared to be a rain squall. Having been criticized a great deal by colleagues for allowing "a little weather" to interfere with training, the instructors decided to push on. As the aircraft entered this storm, it became much worse than anticipated, and the small, loose four-aircraft formations separated in order to avoid mid-air collisions.

According to the unit history, during the ensuing storm, twelve aircraft crashed, seven men died and several others were injured. Of the wrecked aircraft, two solo students parachuted to safety near Atmore, Alabama, and their two aircraft crashed and were destroyed. Two aircraft crash-landed near Evergreen, Alabama, and seven others crashed within a twenty-mile radius of Atmore, Alabama. The remaining twenty-three aircraft were scattered over the region: five aircraft reached Gunter Field; two BT-13s returned to Crestview, Florida; two airplanes landed at the U.S. Naval Air Station, Pensacola; three airplanes landed at Mobile; one aircraft landed at Napier Field, Dothan, Alabama; one aircraft at Atmore, Alabama; five at Evergreen, Alabama; and four at Greenville, Mississippi.

The account of the "British accident" in the station history was fairly detailed, but strangely accounted for only thirty-four of the thirty-five aircraft. Apparently, the station historian failed to list the crashed aircraft with a dead RAF student aboard that was finally found in a remote area of Butler County, Alabama, on the seventh day following the disaster. Why this important detail was omitted is a mystery.

Regional newspapers reported the accident after they received information from USAAF authorities on Friday afternoon, 22 May. In its initial report, the *Macon Telegraph* listed four young men who lost their lives in that series of air crashes in south Alabama in the early hours of Thursday, 21 May 1942. The list included nineteen-year-old LAC Victor William Lear of Radstock, near Bath, Somerset, England; twenty-one-year-old LAC James Edward Maddick of Dundee, Angus, Scotland; twenty-two-year-old LAC Patrick Geoffrey Marshall Overton of Porthcawl, Wales; and twenty-six-year-old LAC Ronald Edward Randall of Moseley, Birmingham, England.

On Friday night, 22 May, after their bodies were located and transported to the White Chapel Funeral Home in Montgomery, the *Montgomery Advertiser* was informed and, in its Saturday issue, added to the list of four reported dead the names of twenty-two-year-old LAC Michael Ernest Peachell of Broadway, Dorset, England, and nineteen-year-old LAC David Stanley Peattie of Knock, Belfast, Northern Ireland. At 3:00 p.m. on Saturday, 23 May 1942, graveside services were held for these six British cadets, and their bodies were interred alongside others in the RAF plot of the Oakwood Cemetery Annex.

Until all of the men and aircraft were accounted for, Gunter Field officials were understandably reluctant to release information. However, on Saturday afternoon, 23 May, as search planes continued to fly in and out of Gunter Field, the *Montgomery Advertiser* gained a more full account of events. They learned that thirty-four of the thirty-five aircraft were accounted for, and that a seventh missing cadet had not yet been found. Finally, on Wednesday, 27 May, the seventh day following the accident, Gunter Field Instructor Lieutenant G.M. Elmore, while flying yet another search mission, reported sighting a wrecked aircraft in a remote, heavily forested area near Garland, Butler County, Alabama. It took several hours for a crew of men to reach the crash site, but when they did, they recovered from the wreckage the body of twenty-two-year-old LAC Arthur Vernon Lowe of Millhouses, Sheffield, South Yorkshire, England.

The loss of seven young men was a disaster of such proportions that it sent shock waves from south Alabama to Eastern Flying Training Headquarters at Maxwell Field, to Air Training Command Headquarters in Fort Worth, to USAAF and RAFDEL Headquarters in Washington and to the Air Ministry in London. The USAAF was justly proud of its training system and its magnificent safety record. A disaster of such proportions was very rare and unusual. As required by army regulations, an investigation was launched, a report with recommendations was presented and the axe fell.

The official report indicated that the accident was caused by pilot fatigue and unexpected and unusual weather conditions. Responsibility for the accident was placed on the instructors. Inexperience on the part of the nine instructors present on the exercise was blamed for the breakup of the flying formations, which led to the dispersal of students. The conclusion was that the scattering of the students, who were too inexperienced to cope with the emergency, had led to the disaster.

The accident was a horrible tragedy that cut off seven young men in their prime and cost the Royal Air Force seven potential combat pilots, nine if one counts the two fatalities of 7 May. Since these deadly accidents cast a long-term pall of gloom over Gunter Field, it obviously harmed both that station and the USAAF and UK training systems in general. Members of succeeding classes indicated that Gunter Field was not "a happy station." More important, however, and unknown to the UK cadets, were the short- and long-term effects of the "British accident" on USAAF training.

The Accident Board delved into navigation training at Gunter Field and the details of the accident of 20–21 May 1942. The board then made a series of recommendations to the commanding officer. In light of what had happened, they felt that clearance for continuing night exercises involving students must come from an airfield with a complete weather station and a forecaster on duty. The board also recommended restriction of student navigation flights to within a radius of one hundred miles of Gunter Field. Flight routes and airfields along the route of navigation flights were to be thoroughly checked beforehand, and both takeoffs and landings were to be made on "strange" fields before they were to be used in an emergency.

In order to prevent the recurrence of such tragedies, the board also urged the inclusion in the curriculum of a "problem-solving course in practical navigation." And finally, control aircraft, with which the students might check, were to be stationed along cross-country flight routes, and these aircraft would await the passage of all student aircraft and would then follow them back to Gunter Field.

The board's recommendations were quickly put into effect, and greater emphasis was placed on flying safety. Training Bulletins 19, 20 and 21 were revised, and the board's recommendations were incorporated as follows: the importance of air discipline was stressed; methods for selecting strange fields were clarified; the provision of food for men flying at night was required; knowledge of the use of blind flying instruments and of aircraft radio were stressed, as was the necessity for checking the weather by radio before takeoff on any night flight; installation of a complete set of instruments was required for the front cockpits of all aircraft being used in navigation flights; and the exercise of greater care in soloing students at night.

Wing Commander Wilfred E. Oulton from RAFDEL and Wing Commander H.A.V. Hogan, RAF administrative officer for the SEACTC, had been trying for almost a year with moderate success to persuade USAAF officers to modify their navigation training. British students were flying in the United States and obviously needed to know American navigation in order to survive while in training in North America. However, the USAAF and the Royal Air Force used different maps, charts, weather symbols and terminology. The dilemma for the RAF cadets was that they were compelled to learn two kinds of navigation: USAAF methods and terminology in order to survive, to complete training or to instruct in the United States and then, on return to the United Kingdom, in order to survive in British units or in combat, they would discard the USAAF navigation and have to learn that of the RAF.

The British officers had requested a change in the curriculum at the basic flying school, favoring a greater number of individual hours rather than group hours of navigation training. Gunter Field officers had concurred in the RAF suggestion in January 1942, and had evidently sent their recommendation on through channels to Washington via Maxwell Field and Air Training Command headquarters in Fort Worth, Texas. Evidently, the request was either ignored or went astray and, as a result, group navigation training continued at Gunter Field.

As early as 4 April 1942, fully six weeks before the "British accident," another warning of problems with navigation training had arrived at Gunter Field and had evidently been ignored. In an effort to better coordinate basic and advanced flying, the director of training at the USAAF advanced flying school at Craig Field, fifty miles west of Gunter Field, had notified the basic flying schools of problems that Craig Field instructors were encountering with students. According to the Craig Field officer, cadets arriving at that station did not know how to use their aircraft radios in flight; they had little knowledge of cockpit lights or how to trim their aircraft in the air; some students were not aware of "the proper use of brakes, rudder and throttle in landing"; and their cross-wind and accuracy landings were poor.

One of the most telling criticisms by Craig Field staff was that students arrived there lacking air discipline and were not aware that "a constant speed, and constant altitude are necessary for holding in single lane traffic patterns—day and night." Anxious to address student problems and resolve them during that final phase of training, Craig Field training officers urged that basic flying schools send student grade slips to advanced schools so that weaker students might be placed with the better instructors for specific attention to problem areas.

On 27 May 1942, orders were issued prohibiting further group navigation flights and night formations, and substituting during both day and night individual navigation training. A subsequent unconfirmed report indicated that as a result of the accident on 20–21 May 1942, the Gunter Field director of training was relieved and transferred, the group commander was relieved and transferred and the weather forecaster was relieved. Although the "British accident" was probably not the only reason for it, a number of official visitors arrived at Gunter Field within three weeks of the tragedy.

Undersecretary of State for Air Captain Harold Balfour, air member for training; Air Chief Marshal A.G.R. Garrod, air member for training; and Director of Training Progress M.S. Laing flew to the United States and were joined by Air Vice Marshal Robert Leckie, the Canadian air member for training and visitor to the United States in 1937. The visitors were met by Major General Barton K. Yount, commanding general of the Air Training Command, and together they visited and inspected Gunter Field and a number of other training stations in the Southeastern United States. Unfortunately, a record of the discussions of this formidable group of men could not be located, but a part of the discussions no doubt concerned the Gunter Field "British accident" and USAAF plans for coordinating and standardizing flying training.

Whether self-examination followed the accidents of May 1942 and whether criticisms of training methods contributed to reform is unknown, but it is likely that they did. Within six months of the Gunter accident, the Air Training Command announced the creation of four new training wings within each regional flying training command. Appointed to command one of these wings was Colonel Aubrey Hornsby, who had supervised construction of Gunter Field and served as its commanding officer for two and a half years. The reason for creating the wings was to better coordinate, supervise and standardize all USAAF flying training.

The system that emerged from the first two years of army air corps expansion extended from 1 July 1939 to 20 June 1941, then the United States Army Air Forces came into being and expanded training to such an extent that it was producing pilots at the rate of thirty thousand per year before December 1942. During 1943–44, the quantity production of USAAF training was double that of 1942, but increasingly there was greater concern for maintaining quality. Better coordination of flying training had been needed for many months, but it took a May 1942 tragedy during a stormy night in south Alabama to serve as one of the catalysts that brought it about.

On 30 April 1942, 209 British cadets of Class SE-42-H arrived at Gunter Field. Added to their numbers were the 7 students held over from the ill-fated Class SE-42-G. Among the new class members was Alfred Sidney Dove (Tuscaloosa, 42-H), who recalled his experiences at Gunter Field some forty years afterward:

Basic flying training was conducted at Gunter Field, a regular Army Air Corps base with good brick-built living accommodation and army instructors. The training aircraft was the Vultee BT-13A which looked something like a Harvard but had a fixed undercarriage and manually controlled flaps. Memories of this period center around the strict discipline, sticky heat, and the much frequented coke machines, which were liberally spread throughout the living quarters, and which for a modest 5 cents would dispense an ice cold bottle of welcome refreshment.

The quality of instruction was again of a high calibre, as was the content of the course itself—virtually at a peacetime level. The eventual wash-out rate was quite high, but was lower than primary. Free time was minimal; I can remember visiting the city of Montgomery only once or twice during the 2 month's stay.

Members of Class SE-42-H had begun their basic flying training during the fateful month of May 1942 amid reports of accidents and deaths.

On Thursday, 28 May, the day after LAC Lowe's body had been found in his wrecked aircraft, Class SE-42-H experienced its own first fatal accident. Twenty-three-year-old LAC Frank Rogers of Pontardulais, Wales, and his flying instructor were killed in an aircraft accident near Taylor Field, several miles southeast of the main airdrome. Two weeks later, on Saturday night, 13 June 1942, Class SE-42-H suffered its second and third fatalities when two trainer aircraft collided near Mount Meigs Auxiliary airfield, some fifteen miles east of Montgomery, killing twenty-one-year-old LAC James Arthur Barnes of Preston, Lancashire, and twenty-year-old LAC Walter Samuel Bowden of Exeter, Devonshire, England. So many accidents heavily affected training and morale.

In recalling his own experiences and attitudes, Samuel Liggett (Arcadia, 42-H) of Ayrshire, Scotland, gave evidence of low morale and dissatisfaction with conditions:

After Carlstrom Field, my next stop was Gunter Field, Alabama, and training on the Vultee BT-13A—probably the least enjoyable part of my training. Although the flying side was first class, the tin trays in the Mess Hall and general attitude towards all cadets, both British and American, did leave a great deal to be desired. The food was adequate but was served on wet tin trays; the contrast with other stations was unbelievable. It used to be said that the convicts in the State Penetentiary adjacent to the airfield were warned if they did not behave, they would be moved to Gunter.

Our senior course, 42-G, had lost quite a number of cadets returning from their day/ night cross country flight…Class 42-H had also lost one or two cadets in other flying accidents, so morale was somewhat low. That we had not had a day off for about three weeks made it even lower.

One day, we were due to parade after lunch for a rehearsal for a parade to be held in Montgomery to mark six months after Pearl Harbour; with no previous arrangement, no one went on parade. You can guess there was soon a bit of shouting, and eventually about six cadets—a case of 6 volunteers (you, you, and you) were marched to the RAF Liaison Officer's office, and the base commander was there, where, much to everyone's surprise, everything was quickly sorted out. None of the senior officers had known that we had been in camp for three weeks, and how low morale was at that time. On Sunday, we went on parade and marched through the town with heads high and colours flying.

> *The citizens of Montgomery were very good, but there was a strange feeling about the base. It was at Gunter that I had my first taste of night flying and thoroughly enjoyed it, except one night when 12 of us were kept circling the auxiliary field for almost 3 hours waiting for a fire tender to arrive from Gunter.*

Liggett recorded some misinformation about the "British accident" of 20–21 May, a communications problem that plagued all aircrew students undergoing flight training.

Nineteen-year-old Leslie G. Lunn (Arcadia, 42-H) gave yet another variation in understanding what had happened to members of Class SE-42-G in the early morning hours of 21 May 1942:

> *I found that transition was very difficult. My first flight at Gunter was on 3rd May, Lt. Marshall my instructor. Once I settled down, all went well, but it was hard work and very long hours—up at 5.30 a.m. at the flight line at 6.30 a.m…Flights all morning, ground school all p.m., with night flying thrown in. It was while I was at Gunter that disaster hit the senior course on a night flight…It was a setback, to say the least.*
>
> *All still went according to plan for me, but I did nearly fail my 40-hour check ride by making a mess of a practice forced landing. I was given another chance! I completed basic training on 3rd July and, without any time off, left the following day for Craig Field, Alabama.*

Anxiety about possibly failing was the greatest problem facing aircrew under training everywhere, and the experience of Lunn simply reconfirms the haste with which men moved through the training pipeline in 1942.

James Double (Arcadia, 42-H) kept a diary that recorded his experiences and observations during the course of training.

> *We left Carlstrom Field on 29 April 1942 at 1730, and arrived at Gunter Field the following morning at 0830. We met the remains of other courses and got news of other failures. On arrival, we also heard stories of engine failures and people getting killed here on these BT-13As, but I should soon be able to find out for myself. My instructor is 1st Lt. Crockett, and he is very relaxing and helpful. I'm sure I'll be O.K. The programme continues alternative ground school and flying except when weather stops flying, then we catch up on school work.*

Rumors were rife, and one of the most difficult problems facing training stations at every level was how to handle the problem of eliminees. If they remained on station very long, it was easy for them to frighten newcomers into believing virtually anything.

Double's diary entries for the final ten days in May confirm the rumors mixed with facts that ebbed and flowed around the "British accident." On 21 May, he entered into his diary, "Bad night last night. Senior course were night flying home from Mobile, Alabama and ran into a tropical storm. So Far, 5 dead and five more missing; only 3 out of 30 got back to Gunter Field." On 22 May, he reported, "Sixth body found from night of the 20th." And on 23 May, "Search parties are still out looking for wreckage." Finally, on 27 May 1942, "Last aircraft found—pilot dead." Double and his classmates were undoubtedly disturbed by the terrible tragedy to their senior class, but when tragedy struck Class SE-42-H, he made laconic entries: On 28 May, "Cadet

Rogers and his instructor killed today near Taylor Field." And on 13 June, "Cadets Bowden and Barnes killed in collision while night flying at Mt. Meigs."

A month later, on 22 June, Double became ill while walking to his assigned aircraft and was rushed to the station hospital at Maxwell Field with a severe case of food poisoning. After having his stomach pumped, doctors decided to keep him under observation for several days and ordered complete bed rest. Despite such orders, a few of the nurses got him dressed and took him to the base theatre to attend the visiting Kay Kyser Show. Finally, on 29 June, he was restored to duty at Gunter Field and was immediately told that he was transferred to Class SE-42-I.

Since he was already far ahead of Class SE-42-I in his training, he was granted four days' sick leave on 3 July, and used that time to explore some of the region. Double hitchhiked to Pensacola, in the process catching a series of four rides. The last couple transported him into Pensacola and invited him to spend the night. He did so and was able to conserve some of his limited funds. From Pensacola, he hitched to Mobile, but had a difficult time getting a room in that "dirty shipbuilding town," so he returned to Montgomery by train, showered and changed clothes at Gunter, then returned to Montgomery and spent the night at the Exchange Hotel. On Monday, 6 July, Double caught a train to Birmingham, spent the night, saw the town and returned to Gunter Field at 1:30 p.m. on Tuesday, 7 July. All in all, the four-day leave had been exhausting, but Jim Double had covered a considerable amount of travel.

Finally, Double returned to flying with Class 42-I and, despite summer storms from mid- to late July, managed to complete the required flying time. On 4 August, he visited the UK cadet graves at the cemetery in Montgomery, and on 5 August, the graduation parade was held. Of the 209 British cadets who had commenced training, plus the 7 added from the preceding class, 3 members of Class SE-42-H were held over to continue training, so the net enrollment for the class dropped to 213. Of that number, 25 were eliminated, 3 were killed in flying accidents and 185 graduated and were posted to advanced flying schools at Craig and Napier SE Fields in Alabama and at Turner and Moody TE Fields in south Georgia.

The 148 British students of Class SE-42-I arrived at Gunter Field on 2 June 1942 and received 3 students held over from the preceding class, thus boosting enrollment to 151. George F. Pyle (Americus, 42-I) described in detail some of his experiences and observations while in training at Gunter Field:

> *Travel to Gunter Field, Montgomery, Alabama, was by bus & reception was by the Course Commander who read the rules, followed by a tour led by a senior classman. Basic was a totally different set up to Americus and came as a rude shock after the friendly family atmosphere of primary. It was, by comparison, a large training base with runways, scores of aircraft, and thousands of personnel. Gone were the civilian instructors—this was Army—and American cadets outnumbered the Brits. Hazing was apparent even in the cockpit; mess hall was cafeteria style with long lines of enlisted men also waiting to be served. The food was poorer and sloppy (no teeth required) & served on metal trays (shades of the Chateau Thierry).*
>
> *Compared with Mr. Featherstone [at Americus], my instructor was an impatient bully who shouted constantly, jagged the throttle & punched the control column on me, and quickly filled me with despair. He would not let me solo; to me his training methods were wrong, and after one particularly unhappy trip, and sensing my early return to Canada, I was discourteous but desperate enough to tell him so.*

The stoney silence on the next trip was unnerving, to say the least, but wonder of wonders, I was allowed to solo the BT-13 at a satellite field. On the following day, my three pals and I were handed over to an RAF instructor because Lt. Wilkins had to take over a "bunch of difficult American cadets and lick them into shape!" The fun had gone out of training. This was impersonal mass production & friendships became more important and valuable. Seeing friends washed out was depressing.

The tour of the base at the outset had not helped with a visit to the aircraft graveyard and the information that twelve [really only nine] *British cadets had been killed on a previous course (42-G), seven on one night cross country flight. The BT-13 "Vultee Vibrator" seemed to be an unforgiving beast with a tendency to drop a wing on the unwary. It had radio, flaps and a variable pitch prop.*

We learned to fly formation, fly on instruments, make blind approaches by beam, fly cross country, and fly at night, all in addition to the stalls, spins, loops, lazy 8s, chandelles, and practised forced landings which had been part of primary training. I do not recall trying a snap roll in a BT-13 (or an AT-6 for that matter).

My RAF instructor was little older than myself, and an earlier product of the system, who had stayed behind like many others with a commission and done an instructor's course. We were only his second class. He was quiet & lacked the authority of experience, but we reacted favourably and worked hard for him (& ourselves), perhaps realising subconsciously that the Army would have the last say.

And who should be my end of course check pilot but the dreaded Lt. Wilkins—now Captain. But I knew what he liked and disliked, and apart from a slight altercation on my runway positioning on landing, he finally announced, "A good ride, Pyle! But all that hazing at the beginning didn't do any harm, did it?" The last word, as I said, was with the Army.

Accommodation on the post was good, with three to a room and shared ablutions with the three next door. Recreation followed the earlier pattern, though with diminished contact with the public. On 7 June 1942, the British participated in a large march past of troops through the streets of Montgomery to mark the first six months of war for America. We smiled wryly about this, because Britain had been taking the brunt of things for 2 and ¾ years, but we marched, heads up, as smartly as we could, and felt a little proud.

LAC Pyle learned well and subsequently flew Spitfires and Mustangs. But everyone did not take the same view of the June parade.

Jack Tate (Americus, 42-I) recalled his days at Gunter:

On 2 June 1942, we arrived at the U.S. Army Air Forces Base, Gunter Field, Montgomery, Alabama for Basic Flying Training. Our greeting by a very senior officer on arrival was somewhat less than friendly. At least, it was frank in that it spelled out to us in simple language that we were not wanted. The U.S. resources would have been better employed training American cadets, and the sooner we were gone the better. If anyone so much as stepped out of line for any reason, however trivial, our chances of graduating were nil.

The training schedule was hard but acceptable. Reveille at 0420 hours, parade at 0500, breakfast at 0600, drill at 0700, and either ground school or flying from 0800 to 1300 hours. After lunch, the programme was reversed with respect to flying and ground school. During the evenings, a student was liable for a one-hour link trainer session two or three times per week, with little or no time off base. Many of Course 42-I were remusters from the Army with several years service in Europe behind them, including Dunkirk.

It was particularly inept and rather foolish for the U.S. Army to try to change not only our deeply ingrained drill procedures but to try to impose the cadet honour system on people to whom it was unnecessary and indeed anathema. It was ludicrous to tell an ex-Grenadier guardsman, whose arms drill is among the best in the world, that he must change to a system that looked to our eyes as decidedly sloppy, at least as performed on this base.

Few of 42-H or 42-I were happy on this base, but worked hard in spite of a great many provocations, the happiest times being when in the air. The many infringements of a multiplicity of impractical rules led to the imposition of many gigs and indeed an award of 42 tours "walking" for the whole of 42-I in one punishment. In effect, the limited Open Post time vanished overnight.

On 6 June 1942, flight training commenced on BT-13 and BT-13A aircraft. My instructors were RAF Pilot Officers Cain and Sharpe, Lieutenant Cellotto, and Captain Garrett. In all I flew 70 hours, 20 minutes at Gunter, including 33 hours dual, 37 hours solo, 1 hour night dual and 7.20 hours night solo.

John Spooner, a friend, was killed flying from Gunter shortly after we had dined with his relatives in Birmingham, Alabama. Another friend, Alec Musto, an ex-Grenadier Guardsman, washed out, and was being retrained as a pilot, but was killed on active service...

In retrospect, I was not impressed by some aspects of this basic course. The unnecessarily high washout rate, the small minded petty disciplinary quirks by senior officers, the minimal experience of instructors, and the total lack of combat experience either in the air or even on the same continent.

Perhaps Tate's attitude toward American training was influenced by British army veterans classmates. Like many British student pilots, Tate presumed greater expertise than was his at the time, forgetting or not realizing that his classmate, Gordon John Cadman (Tuscaloosa, 42-I), recorded somewhat different observations:

My next stop was Gunter Field, Montgomery, Alabama for basic flying in Vultee BT-13A aircraft. My instructor was Pilot Officer May, who, of course, was from an earlier RAF contingent and who stayed in America as a flight instructor. I was 20 years of age at the time, and he wasn't much older, but he was very painstaking in his instruction.

The BT-13A was a low-wing monoplane with fixed undercarriage, two-pitch propeller, radio and manual flaps, a few new things to contend with. We lost one cadet because he tried to take off with his prop in course pitch. He failed to get off the ground and was killed as his aircraft hit some trees on the airfield boundary.

I found the BT-13A very easy to fly and went solo on it after 5 hours, 5 minutes dual on 14 June 1942. My first check ride was with Lieutenant Worton and came on 18 June, after which I progressed to the more detailed aspects of basic flying. On 10 July 1942, I started night flying, and after 1 hour, 20 minutes dual with P/O May, went solo. I was given upper zone four in which to circle until I was called in for my turn to land.

Just before P/O May left the aircraft, he gave me final instructions, and wished me good luck over the intercom…at which point I should have flicked the radio control from "intercom" to "transmit," but in my anxiety at finding myself in charge of this throbbing monster, alone for the first time at night, I failed to do so.

I took off with no trouble at all and climbed to my appointed upper zone four, where I settled into a steady left-hand circle awaiting my radio call to come in for a landing. I circled and circled and circled, but no call…in fact, I hear nothing on the radio at all. After awhile all the other circling lights had slipped away—by then I had been circling for well over an hour, and I saw what I took to be a green flashing light directed, I was certain, at me.

I said to myself that of course, the ground radio must have failed and they are calling me in by lamp! (which indeed they were doing). I joined the circuit and on my approach felt not a qualm that I was landing in the dark, alone for the first time, and I made what I thought was a very good landing. I taxied back to the flight line, to be met by a nearly demented P/O May, who said (in essence, if one removed the expletives) "Cadman, have you gone mad? We've been calling you in for nearly an hour—did you freeze up there?—why in hell didn't you answer our calls?" Then, he checked the radio, discovered my error in not switching over to "transmit" and added, "if you hadn't made such a bloody good landing, the best we've seen tonight, you would be for the 'washing machine!'"

Further excitement at Basic concerns a night cross-country solo! It was a very sultry, steamy, and heavy night (1 August 1942), we were to fly solo from Gunter to Newnan and back to Gunter, a trip which was timed to take about three hours. On take-off, I had the cockpit canopy open because of the heat (a practice which was frowned upon) and had my maps and flight plan tucked into my safety harness.

As I gained height, the rush of air from the open canopy sucked the maps, etc. from under my harness, so there I was map-less and without a flight plan, faced with a 3-hour night cross-country flight! First thoughts were to turn back and admit my stupidity, but as this was the last flight of my basic training, I had no wish to do it all the next night amidst a gale of laughter from my fellow cadets—and so I pressed on, having remembered some of the headings I had worked out on my flight plan, along with turning points, the odd beacon or two, and one or two night-recognisable landmarks.

I found my way to Newnan, flew low to make sure I was right (giving my radio call sign as I passed over), swung over onto a reciprocal heading which was not right I knew, but was more or less the only hope I had of arriving back at Gunter. There was, by the way, no wind to speak of on this sticky, airless night which meant I had no drift to contend with!

I realised that if I flew straight back, I would arrive far too early, and long before the others, which would appear odd, as I was not flying a noted speedster. I therefore decided on a few dog-legs, always keeping in sight a main highway, which appeared to run in the right direction (which I could easily distinguish by vehicle head lights).

Having crossed and re-crossed the highway what seemed like hundreds of times, I decided to proceed directly down its length to bring me to Montgomery and so on to Gunter Field. Alas, my guess that the road led to Montgomery was misguided. It led to a place I was unable to identify, but as I circled the small town below, I saw a light beacon on the horizon, whose code I recalled from my long-gone flight plan.

I headed towards the beacon and found my way to Gunter without further trouble. Everyone else had landed, I found—I was roughly half an hour late, and, of course, had quite a lot of explaining to do, both to my instructor, P/O May, and to the C.F.I. (Chief Flying Instructor).

With this escapade and the trauma of my first night solo, it may seem strange that I was able to graduate from basic, but graduate I did, with most of my friends. A few, perhaps 5% or less, fell by the wayside and were sent to Trenton, Ontario, Canada for remustering as Navigators. I quite well recall the glum faces and forced smiles with which they left the remainder of us and took the "wash out train" to Canada. I was lucky to still be amongst those continuing in pilot training.

Of the 143 British students enrolled in Class SE-42-I, 10 were eliminated, 2 were killed in flying accidents and 131 graduated in early August and were dispersed to the four available advanced flying schools.

The 143 RAF members of Class SE-42-J arrived at Gunter Field around 4 July 1942 and became the junior class to SE-42-I. On 10 August, twenty-six-year-old Cyril Evan Gray of Sanderstead, Surrey, was killed with Lieutenant Torbert Slack Jr., his instructor, when their BT-13 crashed about one mile southeast of Gunter Field. That evening, nineteen-year-old Albert Edgar Ayling of Cowplain, Hampshire, died in a separate accident. Both UK student pilots were interred in the Oakwood Cemetery Annex.

Garnet A. Whitehead (Lakeland, 42-J) recalled his experiences at Gunter Field:

I did my Basic flying training at Gunter Field, Montgomery, Alabama on BT-13s. I do not recollect having any one particular instructor, but several Army pilot instructors, whose role appeared to be to give a short period of instruction, and then leave it to the student to practice. This appeared to work pretty well, and we acquired confidence (too much in some cases).

Emphasis was on cross country, instrument, and night flying. Here we suffered some casualties caused, I suspect, by a combination of overconfidence and inexperience. It was my sad duty to act as coffin bearer at the funerals of casualties, perhaps because I was six feet in height, as were the other bearers.

At Gunter, discipline was strict, but conditions, i.e., food, accommodation, etc. were good, and there was generally a very good spirit in the place, with friendly rivalry with the U.S. cadets. We always felt we outsmarted them in marching, with our 140 paces per minute, and arms swung up to shoulder level!

We did not have a great deal of contact with the civil population in Montgomery, although I did have a couple of week-ends with one family. With two other cadets I used to visit the coast (Panama City) or Birmingham at weekends, in both of which places we found the natives very friendly! At Gunter, there was some fraternising with the U.S. cadets, with whom we spent a lot of our spare time in Montgomery. We were not allowed off the station in the evening, only at weekends.

After almost five weeks at Gunter Field, the senior class departed, Class SE-42-K arrived and SE-42-J became the senior class. On 5 September 1942, Class SE-42-J graduated. Of the 143-man 42-J enrollment, 2 were killed in flying accidents, 10 were eliminated and 131 graduated.

GUNTER FIELD, 42-K-43-C

With the arrival of Class SE-42-K, British enrollment once more climbed upward. Donald G. Saunders (Americus, 42-K) recalled his experiences:

> *On 6 August 1942, we boarded buses and went by road to Basic Flying Training School at Gunter Field, Montgomery, Alabama. Here we were back in the Army again, and this was our first mix with American boys who were striving for the same aims as ourselves. Our billets were in long, low barrack blocks with stoops, four persons to a room.*
>
> *Until now, food had been prepared by civilians, but now good food was ruined by bad cooks (U.S. Army). We flew Vultee BT-13 aircraft and had excellent instruction by a mixture of American and RAF pilots. Although Gunter did not have the creature comforts of Americus, Montgomery was a much better place for Open Post. Moreover, Gunter had a good Post Exchange, whereas Souther Field had only a small shop.*
>
> *We were back in the Army with a vengeance, but West Point and the RAF combined together well to buck the system and do as little work as possible and have more time for fun. One bad spot at Gunter: one night while taxying for a night take off, I heard my dear friend Norman Downs on the radio ask permission to take off. He did so, his engine cut out, and we buried his remains in a cemetary at Montgomery. I still think of that incident all these years later.*

For Saunders and many others, flying could be fun and, at the same time, dangerous.

Robert J. Parish (Americus, 42-K) continued with his manuscript diary to basic flying school. In doing so, he provides an excellent day-to-day account of life at Gunter Field. The longer he stayed in the United States, the more intense his RAF jargon became, but increasingly, American jargon crept into his narrative.

> *6:8:42* **[6 August 1942]**. *We left Americus, with many regrets at 0800 & arrived at Gunter Field 13:30. Had a good journey down, with bags of breaks en route. Spend half the day filling in forms. Alphabetical billeting. Separated from Ric, but allotted to a decent room for 5. Two Americans—George Conder & Eddie Coleman—and 3 Raf. Malcolm Parkinson & George Palmer with self. Have some eye trouble. Poor Joe.*
>
> *7:8:42*. *Lectures & more lectures, meet instructors (sprog P/O) & have a look at these mechanical monsters.*
>
> *8:8:42*. *Hang about flight line all morning, but don't fly. About as much ambition to fly these damn things, as to climb Mt. Everest. Guess its my chosen career.*
>
> *9:8:42*. *Take a flip. P/O Stewart a decent old cock. Rather a vicious machine. Go to Montgomery again (went yesterday)—It makes a break anyhow!*
>
> *10:8:42*. *Flew. Phew! What a kite. Lectures throughout afternoon. Then calisthenics.*
>
> *11:8:42*. *No fly. No regrets!*
>
> *12:8:42*. *Bull parade only outstanding thing during the day—super war effort.*
>
> *13:8:42*. *Receive new instructor. Decent sort of wallah. P/O Conus from Ilford. Did 13 different types of stalls with him & spinning.*
>
> *14:8:42*. *As per b——usual.*
>
> *15:8:42*. *Bull parade—then open post. Saw Mrs. Luinius,—gave us a warm welcome! Returning in cab, the driver knocked down a guy—but he still lived,—no excitement.*

Another week over. Thank God. Monday morning, a cadet with instructor went for a burton, & late evening a solo student got killed. Nice outlook.

16:8:42. *At last, instead of usual 05:00 rise, have a little lay in, made a nice break. Shot some landings p.m. Am still far from enthusiastic about this lousey place. "Oh To Be In England..."*

17:8:42. *No flying—bad weather. Hear I'm due for solo check with P/O Smeaton, hell of a binder, am afraid we won't get on too well together.*

18:8:42. *No flips—bad weather & P/O Smeaton is due to leave tomorrow. Good Show—Joe. Managed another lay in, owing to late night link* [Link Trainer].

19:8:42. *Was OKed for solo by P/O Fields but storm came up, & had to fly back to Gunter on instruments. 12 Cadets were allotted as funeral party to bury Dougie Flateau, who was killed with his instructor at Americus, after being kept back for further training. Bull parade at night (war effort).*

20:8:42. *Bags of St. Peter. No flying. Leave line about 11:00.*

21:8:42. *Still, I don't fly. Mac is sent to Maxwell with water on the knee. MPs keep us up half the night, conducting a search for a stolen $200 (L50).*

22:8:42. *Fly at last, also solo, after 5½ hrs total dual, on Vultee. Bull parade & then free. Cadet Lincoln crashes, & chews tail plane off another kite, nobody seriously hurt; two ships busted up bad.*

23:8:42. *Lay in bed. Then out 'till 18:30. Write a few letters home. Am completely & thoroughly browned off!*

24:8:42. *Making pretty good progress with P/O Fields, so for no reason at all, they kindly condescend to change me to P/O Linton—he seems OK, but I don't like his face. The bull & bad system at this place, is about the most tantalizing, & disgusting show of cock I've ever experienced. Poor Poor Show!*

25:8:42. *Meteorology Quiz. Had a row with the messing officer about the piss poor food,—& came out top,—even got him to agree that half the stuff wasn't fit to eat. Went solo over Taylor again, but fly at all times with my canopy open. I don't like this kite, & my view is, that if it as much as coughs, I'm out of the bloody thing quick. Usual tendency to get bags of speed & height, & carry a good parachute.*

Bull here is getting increasingly ridiculous. Have to keep our sleeves rolled up on the flying line, turned down at other times. Mustn't read books, while waiting to fly. Except for personal pride, I'd throw this course in, but my obstinacy makes me all the more determined not to let these goddam Yankees put one over on me. Receive 7 letters from G.B. which helps a lot to make me feel better. Bad ear again, full of minor ailments since I've been in this part of the world. Hear news that Duke of Kent has been killed in flying accident.

26:8:42. *Bull parade in morning. Meteorology results through. I've managed 96%. Must have been a lucky nickel I was spinning for True or False. Do some instrument in the B.T. for first time. About 2 hrs. open post at night so went to camp cinema. Freedom in the camp appeared most unnatural.*

27:8:42. *Game of English football in the morning. Flag not at half mast* [for the death of the Duke of Kent], *most disrespectful in comparison to the way we're always compelled to salute it, & do their bull parades. After all, the majority of cadets here are RAF.*

28:8:42. *Shot 90 degree stages at Mt. Meigs. Cadet Pack eliminated & Gordon fails a check.*

29:8:42. *Bull parade, & then free.—Thank God! Went to see Malcolm at Maxwell Hosp. He's pretty comfortable, but unlikely to get out for a few days. Later went to a dance for ½ hr at USO. Then about 8 of us went skating. Had about the best time, so far, at Montgomery. Later went to see "Reap the Wild Wind." Returned to camp about 0220 Sunday morning, cheesed off because we couldn't have made it even later,—that's how much we like Gunter, still had a decent time, considering.*

30:8:42. *Lay in. Then 3:10 hrs of flying. Gordon has another check ride & fails. After being in our section all through Primary, he's now slung off the course, after nearly 100 flying hours. Damned hard. It is very hard to see him go, because he is one of my better friends. Poor show, but the very best to you Gordon Yeo of Cornwall.*

31:8:42. *Nothing erratic happening.*

1:9:42 **[1 September 1942]**. *A senior class lad didn't return from X country last night, & a Squadron was mobilised to search from the air. They found the plane & his body, but little pukha gen exists. Had supper in PX (as usual) because cook house food is so disgraceful, & was talking to another cadet. Learned he came from Palmers Green & originally lived in Hamilton Park. Home Sweet Home. Good job I'm saving to take some stuff home, otherwise, I think I'd get hellishly tight!*

2:9:42. *Goddard (who used to go to Highbury County School) was eliminated today. Food here is worse than ever. Living mainly on Ham & eggs bought from the P.X. each night.*

4:9:42. *Pay day. Consequently can afford a little more to eat. Few more lads eliminated, totalling some 3 dozen in all.*

5:9:42. *After 3 yrs. of war, still another bull parade, then dinner in Montgomery. Saw a film, then went skating.*

6:9:42. *Awaited on flying line, but bad weather kept us down. Had another decent dinner at Montgomery, then saw "Eagle Squadron." Back to prison at night.*

7:9:42. *Poor devils of Junior Class arrive. "Poor Devils." Food still reasonable—for the pigs.*

8:9:42. *Had a X Country this afternoon, & two lads got lost. However, they had enough gumption & sense to return to base, but their punishment is to walk around the flying line, with a darn great poster on them reading, "I got lost easily." Apparently the Yankee flight officer doesn't realise the war has been on 3 yrs. & that we are trying to win, also that we're all over 6 yrs. old.*

9:9:42. *Had a check with Lt. Barrett. When we came down, he said my flying was OK, but he guessed I should have another check, because of the fact that I was behind in instrument and night flying time. He asked me if that would be OK, & I probably told him NO, because I'd gone up for a flying check & passed one. Consequently, after arguing for about ½ hr. he passed me. Most typical, of the unfairness of this bloody rotten course. At night, Maurice Mann crashed after a stabilizer stall. Fortunately not hurt.*

11:9:42. *Two crashes last night. Reggie Lumsdaine went through a hedge, & plane caught fire. He got out, & is only suffering from shock. 2nd was a minor accident. I'm night flying.*

12:9:42. *George Palmer's kite was about 30 ft. above the T when engine cut, fortunately he has presence of mind, to get all flaps down, ended up over the boundary, but no accident. On investigation, a spark plug was found to be missing from engine. Mechanics,—I s—— 'em Met Gus Youngblood, old school waller.*

13:9:42. Day off, so decent dinner for a change.

14:9:42. X Country. I took off, & about 10 ft. above the ground, engine went for a burton. I stalled in from that height, & was glad to get out of that kite. The mechs. found out after I'd tried to fly it that the kite was u/s [unserviceable]. Shook me pretty badly. Took off soon after in another ship, & maps went flying out the side. What a day. John Moriarty was practising a forced landing, & went to clear his engine, but it was dead. Finished up a pukha forced landing, fortunate for him, he wasn't coming out of a stall or spin. Nice place, this!

15:9:42. Dougie Gell spun in last night & was killed. Apparently confused rudder stabalizer with elevators. Damn nice chap. I fly tonight.

16–17:9:42. Everything as per usual.

18:9:42. Dinner consisted as usual of roll, & a cup of water. Felt like crying, at this insulting disgusting treatment.

19:9:42. Further progress check with Barrett. Managed to squeeze through, a pass. Had a drink with Don & Cyril in the evening.

20:9:42. Scheduled for night flying, but a cold front cancelled it. Sunday, so bit of a rest.

21:9:42. Landed at Shorter Field in formation, tail wheel busted, & couldn't steer with it, so remainder of formation returned to Gunter, & Linton & I were stranded there, until another fetched over here with a spare wheel. Formated on him going back.

23–24:9:42. Nothing particular to log.

25:9:42. Norman Downs was killed last night. His engine failed on take off. Our flight commander complimented him on being the 1 in 100 people to make a successful night forced landing. He did everything OK, & made a good touchdown, but in the dark, rolled on & plunged down a 20 ft. ditch. Plane caught fire, & he was burned to death. A 15-month fine friendship ended.

26:9:42. We asked special permission that Norman should be buried solely by Waddington lads. At first, it was doubtful, because they said flying took preference (second to bull parade). Most of us decided to buzz up the cemetery in salute, but at the last minute, we buried Norman—All Harry's Air Force. He was given full military honours…7 officers, 8 bearers…Escort of 12 & firing Squad of 8.

2:10:42 **[2 October 1942]**. Pay Day—Speaks for itself. Slap up feed for a change.

3:10:42. Flying. Bull Bull Bull. Decent eats in town. Pictures; Behind in flying time, so tomorrow we stay in all day (Sunday). OK to lose 1 hr. flying for bull parade today though. Flight Commander must be a Physiologist!

5:10:42. Bad weather stops flying, but few of the lads gain about 1 hr. (last period).

6:10:42. Instr. Check with P/O Frost. Passed OK. Finish up formation time…Have now finished all basic flying, thank God!

7:10:42. Say cheerio to Instructors. Start a bit of packing. Settle all queries at Flight Office. RAF Navi Ex.

8:10:42. A chap (42-I) from Selma was buried by our lads today. He was due to graduate this morning. Packing most of the day, then a wash & brush up for the party. Wow what a time. Get really bruised for a change, but think I deserve it after putting up with this dump. Had damn good time with the boys & P/Os Frost & Field. Halfway

through the evening, became total blackout, & didn't remember another thing 'till I was back at camp. How I arrived there I fail to realise. Really good time, though.
9:10:42. *What a hangover. Sick as a dog. Horrible liquor they sell over here. Apparently have to re-take engines exams. Don't feel like it. Lot of bilge.*

Of the 189 students in Class SE-42-K, 8 were held over, leaving a net enrollment of 181, of whom 3 were killed in flying accidents, 15 were eliminated and 163 graduated.

Parish was not among the graduates. He was also notified that he would not be able to retake the engines exam. Instead, he was assigned to continue that phase of training with Class SE-43-A. Further excerpts from Parish's diary reveal his feelings about his setback and his final days in training at Gunter Field:

10:10:42 **[10 October 1942].** *Said goodbye to the Fighter Boys leaving for Selma. Eric, Eddie, Trev., Johnnie. Damn good lads. All packed & ready to leave, & 3 hrs before pushing off time, am told I'm not going for 6 RAF lads failed engines. The lowest was 66%; I was 68% instead of 70. Felt like crying when saying goodby to Bomber Boys. Cec. Mutch. Geo. Palmer, Jim Pezaro, Trev Dawson, Bryan, Bill Smith, damn fine chaps. Hope they crib like hell.*

Visited Miss Osbourne, who helped us have a pleasant week-end. Nice English style dinner with her. Visit next door neighbours, from Birmingham, England. Mrs. Osbourne is from Ilford, Essex. One of the chaps next door, commits suicide. Don't blame [him] if he looked at us poor wretches. Apparently, was perturbed that his calling up papers were due to arrive. Visit bags of people. Arrive home late.
11:10:42. *Visit Minnie again. Have quite a good time. In late once again.*
12:10:42. *After waiting 3 hrs., get interview with Major Brett who says we'll comply with 43A schedule. Oh Yeah!*
13:10:42. *Join new Squadron & am "told" to do sweeping up. Have hell of a row with Flt. Com. Anticipate improvement in conditions.*
14:10:42. *So far haven't taken any Studies. Engines unheard of on this course. Having easy time. Out at night. In bed till 8:30 every morning (unofficially). Flying mostly Observer rides—& what rides. Guys new to instrument flying. Nose in all positions.*
15:10:42. *Just lazing about & skiving.*
16:10:42. *Send cable to Mom. Pay day.*
17:10:42. *Minnie's birthday. Skip Bull parade. Bob & Ken return after being out all night. XC to La Grange. Dual with CSP Weaver. Complimented me on my Navigation & landing. Minnie had fixed a date with 3 girls for us. Took them to the pictures. Most boring time. Later visited Minnie which brightens things up a bit.* [Popular Minnie Osbourne of Ilford, Essex, and Montgomery, Alabama, was always entertaining RAF cadets.]
18:10:42. *Went to dinner at Minnie's. Real English cooking "Oh Boy." Later visited her Grandma. 82 yrs. Owns real Georgian style house. Very interesting. Finished week-end off by sitting outside shop in a car, eating hamburgers. Return 10 p.m.*
19:10:42. *Special schedule made out for us. May learn a little about Engines now.— May?*
20:10:42. *Bad weather. Rest from flying. Saw "Gunga Din" for about the 4th time.*

21:10:42. Engines last period every day now. Quite interesting. Went out at night in Cleaners' car.

22:10:42. Had a formation flip with McLane & Wiley, ended up in a rat race. Very nice.

23:10:42. As per usual.

24:10:42. Went up with Ken & found Minnie's place from the air. Later, went round there, had chili for tea, very nice indeed. Had knock about in the evening. Phillips' daughter was there; smashing kiddie about 7. Wouldn't let anybody but me put her to bed that night. Pleasant change.

25:10:42. Had dinner in town. Went to Minnie's. Pam still there. Mrs. Phillips arrived in afternoon to take Pam home. Introduced to her; very nice person. Elizabeth & Sarah came round for a few hours in the afternoon. Had wizard tea, at Minnie's, real English type. Got soaked at night going round to Janet's with Ken, then bugger. Anyway had nice week-end. Took eats home. P/O Frost joined us en route & expressed his thoughts of what a filthy trick had been played on us.

26:10:42. McLane took off on my wing in formation, & flicked my aileron, cadet in back of us nearly had a baby. Change from khakis to Blue.

27:10:42. Engines Quiz. Me 66 probably pass, but not so good. No flying. Good job we've been kept behind. We're learning a lot.

28:10:42. Ted Render had his engine give out on a XC just after Eufala. Landed in a field cut & bruised, & a wrecked plane. Later, a student officer & cadet got lost on a team ride. Nothing heard of them. At night, one plane landed upon another, on the flarepath. Bad show, but no one hurt.

29:10:42. Student officer & cadet reported down safely & OK at Selma. Not much doing. No flying again.

30:10:42. 21 today. Recd. cable from Mom, Joy & Kay & Will. Very dreary sort of day for a 21st [birthday]. No flying again.

31:10:42. Skiv Bull parade go out instead of flying—cheesed off. Can't go to Minnie's this week-end because her Grandmother has died. Makes our week-end pretty hopeless, but went in Montgomery Fair, found ourselves in children's dept. & started playing with the toys 'till we got thrown out. At a cafe, Ken was putting salt on his dinner & Bob kidded him it was sugar. Ken said, "I don't mind, I like sugar on my dinner," so Bob put some actual sugar on. Later, we bought some marbles to throw about in the dark. Bags of fun, especially in pictures.

1:11:42 [1 November 1942]. Went for decent walk with Bob. Had chicken dinner at Cloverdale. Walked to town & saw a show then back to camp. Nevertheless, this joint & bloody country is getting me down.

2:11:42. Went up in back seat with McLane. 3-ship formation. Broke into a dog fight & he just about blacked me out. Nice time, also had 1 hr. transition. First since being held back.

3:11:42. Had an Army Check ride with P/O Thompson. Good egg only up 25 min. passed with ease—a cinch. Visited Minnie's place at night.

4:11:42. Had commission interview with Flt. Lt. Phillips & recommended, don't particularly want one though. Figure it'll keep me in this lousey Air Corps.

5:11:42. Had final engines exam. Bob & Wiley 94%. Sam & Bennett. 100%. Me 96%.

Parish had finally finished his engines exam satisfactorily; he had also gained a significant amount of flying experience.

His diary describes in some detail his leave between flying courses, which was standard for the time:

> *6:11:42* **[6 November 1942]**. *Applied for a spot of leave & got it. Had dinner round Minnie's place, tried to hitch about 8 o'clock. Didn't get picked up 'till 10. & then only for 6 miles. In finish, got a lift to Tuskegee (where we stayed the night at a Hotel. $1 per head) by 3 Negro officers. Well educated chaps, & very decent indeed. Bob got a single room. Ken & I shared.*
>
> *7:11:42. Lift by a cadet & his fiancée, took us very nearly to Atlanta. Booked up at a Hotel, & found after that "the Cunninghams" would have been very pleased to have us. Went to U.S.O. dance, & apparently interested 2 gals who wanted us to visit their people.*
>
> *8:11:42. Went to church. Met some very nice people. Went back to dinner with Dr. Stauffer. Wizo feed. Took us in his car to Francis & Lois. Went for a stroll with them, & returned to their house for tea. Really good apple pie. Went to pictures later. Had a good time, but these girls bore me. Went home to a bed at the U.S.O.*
>
> *9:11:42. Woke up pretty late. Had breakfast at U.S.O. Saw a RN (Canadian) sailor. Lift from Atlanta to Columbus. Then got a lift the wrong way, & went back to La Grange nearly. However, after about an hour, got a lift all the way to Montgomery. Visited Janett & Elois to say goodbye, Bob got me playing the violin. So & so.*
>
> *10:11:42. Pay parade & packed. Bought Min. a cocktail set between us. Had dinner at Minnie's. She was really taken aback by the present. Had a nice time out with Anne, Doris, and Minnie & said goodbye to everybody.*

Class SE-43-B had the same intake of 184 British students, to which the 1 holdover from 43-A was added. After losing 3 men as holdovers to the next class, the net intake dropped to 182. Of that number, 13 men were eliminated and 169 graduated.

LAC John E. McKenzie-Hall (Tuscaloosa, 43-B) was posted to Gunter Field for basic at a time in which USAAF flying training was being tightened up and standardized. Since he was later to serve as a flying instructor en route to a distinguished career in aviation, his comments about training at Gunter Field are significant:

> *By the time my class began basic flying training at Gunter Field, Montgomery, Alabama on 12 October 1942, I had become acclimatised both to the country and to the methods of teaching, and experienced no difficulties in adapting to the Vultee "Valiant," BT-13A. For the first time since leaving the U.K., I had a British flying instructor, Pilot Officer D.W. Fields. He was very thorough and led me progressively into the more advanced techniques of instrument flying, night flying, formation and cross country navigation. We also carried out a number of exercises called "chandelles" and "lazy eights."*
>
> *This course also introduced for the first time student pair flying, and I appear to have carried out a number of hours instrument flying with an American student called Theiler. Captain J. Garrett gave me a 40-hour flight check and an above average rating which gave me a strong sense of confidence. I have no recollection whatsoever of any social life*

during these two months at Gunter Field and don't think I left the airfield. Quite a few bodies disappeared off the course for one reason or another, and I seem to recall that a greater percentage of American cadets were eliminated than British at this stage. This was probably quite logical because the American intake was so much greater than the British at all stages of training.

In my opinion, the USAAF system of flight training was highly wasteful of potential pilots. If a student for any number of minor reasons was not up to scratch in his exercises or fell behind in the accumulated hours required, he was given a check ride. This was enough to unsettle any student who knew that if he made a mistake or fell out with the instructor it was a "washout" for him…

The "upper" and "lower" class system was still in full swing and by this time the "upper" class had learned by experience to be more sadistic and bullying than in Primary. Staff bureaucracy in discipline and punishment was also at its height, and we were rigorously introduced to the system of receiving punishment "gigs" and the result of collecting too many of these produced a number of hours "walking tours" wearing white gloves and backpacks. Gigs or demerits would be awarded for almost anything that displeased an inspecting officer.

However necessary for disciplinary or character-building reasons, this type of imposition was bitterly resented by the British contingent. However, most of us had come to realise by this time that no good to our future progress would come by fighting the system, and we therefore became resigned to the childish indignities, and persevered with an intense period of ground school and pre-flight study.

I carried out a further 15 hours of link training and progressed on to beam systems, bracketing and let down, as well as continuing the usual sequence of climbing and descending turns and timed exercises. At the same time, I was carrying out these exercises in the air as well and found that instrument flying, although as physically demanding as aerobatics and mentally far more exhausting, was becoming easier and more enjoyable.

What I wouldn't have done in those days for a modern instrument panel and servo controls. With the artificial horizon always liable to topple, the needle and ball the only secondary instrument, and the gyro compass frequently spinning, one had a tiring task in maintaining accurate flying attitudes over long exercise periods.

The USAAF system, which emphasized learning to fly by the seat of the pants, was a time-tested system that taught students to fly without any but the most basic instruments. Since most of the Arnold Scheme students of the final three classes had soloed in the United Kingdom on Tiger Moths (with instruments), the USAAF system appeared strange and did not meet their expectations.

CHAPTER TWELVE

USAAF BASIC FLYING SCHOOL

COCHRAN FIELD

In June 1732, more than two hundred years before British student pilots began training in the United States, King George II granted a charter to a group of twenty men for a portion of what came to be the British colony of Georgia. James Oglethorpe, MP, and his associates received the charter and were granted executive and legislative powers for a period of twenty-one years. Unlike most other grants for lands in North America, Oglethorpe and his group aimed to give acreage to the poor of London and to European religious dissidents. King George II, for whom the colony was named, granted the charter primarily as a buffer against coastal encroachments by the Spanish in Florida. The new southernmost colony would provide protection for the prosperous and very rich coastal areas of Carolina.

In 1733, Oglethorpe brought a group of about 125 colonists to Georgia, and the colony grew rapidly. Among the settlers in 1736 were John and Charles Wesley, who came to Georgia as Anglican clergymen, but returned to England to found the Methodist Church. Oglethorpe recruited Scottish Highlanders to serve as defense forces. He also made peace treaties with Indian tribes living in the vicinity of the main settlement at Savannah. Later, Oglethorpe led military operations against Spanish invaders and finally, on 7 July 1742, defeated a formidable Spanish force in the Battle of Bloody Marsh.

In 1763, near the end of the colonial period, the Treaty of Paris set the boundaries of Georgia southward to the St. Mary's River and westward to the Mississippi. In 1775, when the Second Continental Congress met, Georgia had only one parish represented, and was soundly condemned by the other colonies. Within the year, Georgia gained representation, but in the ensuing War for Independence, Georgia's struggle, like that of South Carolina, was largely a civil war that led to the seizure of Loyalist (Tory) lands when the war ended. For example, after the war, the huge Cumberland Island was presented to General Nathanael Greene, successful commander of the Southern Department of the Continental or Patriot forces.

In 1793, Eli Whitney, a visitor from Connecticut to coastal Georgia, succeeded in his efforts to invent a workable cotton gin, which promoted cotton production and revived slavery. As the state grew and prospered, its leaders pressured and forced "treaties" with all Indian tribes within its boundaries, thereby increasing land available for expansion and white settlement. Around 1800, during the struggle with France, the United States government established Fort Benjamin Hawkins near the site of Macon, Georgia. The fort was named after the famous Indian agent of the 1783–89 Confederation period. As treaties with Indian tribes pushed the natives out, whites rushed in from states to the north and towns and counties were quickly established, often named for the former homes of the immigrants.

Large numbers of North Carolinians settled in middle Georgia, and their major town was called Macon, in honor of early North Carolina statesman Nathaniel Macon. The area south of Macon, in Bibb County, where Cochran Field was built, was originally the plantation of the MacArthur family, formerly of North Carolina. The plantation house burned after the Civil War, leaving only the MacArthur family graveyard. Many people moved into the region during the 1870s and 1880s and planted peach orchards and cotton. In time, peaches were produced for local markets, but soon cotton, pecans and peanuts rivaled peach production. However, during World War II, many army, navy and air stations displaced agriculture within the state.

COCHRAN FIELD, MACON, GEORGIA

In 1941, the airfield site on the Hawkinsville Road, nine miles south of Macon in Bibb County, Georgia, became Cochran Field, a United States Army Air Forces basic flying school. Since it was common practice for municipal and county governments to purchase the land and convey it without charge to the federal government, the army air corps would likely have accepted virtually any name proposed by local authorities. However, proposals that the airfield be named Vinson Field in honor of Representative Carl Vinson, MC, then the powerful chairman of the House Naval Affairs Committee, were rejected. Agreement was finally reached that it should be called Cochran Field in honor of First Lieutenant Robert J. Cochran, a native Georgian and member of the Eighth Aero Squadron of the United States Army Air Service who had been killed in action on 10 October 1918.

Built and put into operation in 1941, Cochran Field was further expanded until, by the time the war ended in 1945, the airfield had cost approximately $5 million and its basic flying school had trained almost 2,500 British pilots and in excess of 8,000 American pilots. The history of the school reaches back to 1940, when plans were being developed for the army air corps' 12,000-pilot production plan. In late May 1940, when the decision was made to expand air corps training to a rate of 7,000 pilots per year and to locate training airfields in the warmer regions of the country, the information was quickly circulated to the leaders of Southern and Southwestern states.

Members of Congress, who were ever watchful of programs that might bring economic activity to their districts, notified state, municipal and county officials of the specific requirements of the United States Army Air Corps. The congressmen also advised of how, when and to whom to submit proposals to attract military installations. Having been advised of requirements and procedures, officials of Bibb County and the city of Macon proposed several sites within the county as ideal locations for an army airfield. Accompanied by two business leaders, the mayor of Macon made an appointment with Brigadier General Walter R. Weaver and traveled to Maxwell Field, Alabama, in order to plead the case for locating an army airfield near Macon.

The Macon delegation must have impressed army air corps planners, for on several occasions during the summer of 1940, General Weaver, commanding general of the Southeast Air Corps Training Center (SEACTC), visited Macon with Major Luke S. Smith, his director of training. Evidently, Weaver and his staff examined all of the sites proposed by the Georgians and agreed that a tract of land adjacent to the Georgia Southern and Florida Railroad, and twenty miles south of the exact center of the state, was ideal for an airfield. The fairly level 1,009.78 acres of land were about 350 feet above sea level and contained many farm houses, a church, a peach packing shed and pecan groves.

When city officials had difficulty in purchasing the site, they resorted to condemnation proceedings through the U.S. District Court of the Middle District of Georgia. As a result of the civil action, a portion of that valuable land was condemned, and a total of 1,009.78 acres was purchased for public use by the city of Macon for a total cost of $103,247.15. Following actual purchase, the City of Macon and Bibb County split the cost of the property equally and conveyed it to the United States government for use by the army air corps as a basic flying school. As part of the agreement, a clause in the document stated that if the government ceased to use the airfield, it would revert to local government ownership.

After the war, the flying school closed, the reversion clause went into effect and Cochran Field became the property of the City of Macon and Bibb County. Most of the structures were sold and removed, and what had been a large military town was swept away. The airfield was improved, runways were paved and for more than fifty years after the war, it was the municipal airport for the city of Macon.

As with other military installations of 1940–41, the United States Army Corps of Engineers had been charged with responsibility for concluding and supervising contracts for designing and building army installations. Project engineers were Lieutenant Colonel H.L. Robb and Major Clinton J. Muncie. The army air corps project officer was Lieutenant Colonel Donald P. Fitzgerald, formerly executive officer at Gunter Field, Alabama. The contract for topographical surveys of the land area was awarded to the William M. Brown Company of Macon, and the engineering and architectural contract went to J.B. McCrary Engineering Corporation of Atlanta. On 19 February 1941, the McDougald-Nunnemaker-Griffin Company of Atlanta became general contractors for the huge construction project. Apparently the army engineers awarded all contracts under the standard cost plus fixed fee arrangement then in use by government agencies.

The original plans called for building the basic flying school alongside the railroad and the paved Hawkinsville Highway running southeastward from Macon. The school buildings and domestic site would be clustered near the highway and the railroad spur line on the northern end of the huge tract. The large landing field would be located adjacent to and south of the domestic facilities. The spur line connecting the main railroad line with the airfield made possible regular deliveries of bulk fuel and other supplies. The station would include eleven administrative buildings, thirteen barracks for student pilots, thirty-five barracks for permanent maintenance and staff personnel, four bachelor officers' quarters (BOQs) and six dining halls. Service facilities would include thirteen supply and storage buildings, ten warehouses, fifteen hospital buildings, forty other buildings for miscellaneous uses, two water tanks, six underground fuel storage tanks, a water supply system, a sewage system—including a treatment plant—and several miles of paved service roads.

Although parts of the airfield were under construction during the summer of 1941, the original main airdrome served its purposes well until February 1942. In that month, two tracts of land totaling 41.2 acres were condemned through court action and added to the west of the airdrome. Adjacent to that combined tract, another 97.8-acre tract was likewise condemned and absorbed by the growing USAAF station. This most recent additional land was obtained for the purpose of building much-needed housing for military personnel already suffering from the critical housing shortage in and around Macon. With these 1942 land acquisitions, the size of the USAAF basic flying school at Cochran Field increased from 1,009.78 acres to about 1,150 acres.

The airfield at Macon occupied seven hundred acres, and the area adjacent to the domestic site consisted of a paved parking apron 450 feet wide by 2,400 feet long. Two taxi-ways 100 feet wide by 900 feet long connected the paved apron to the runways. Two paved runways measured 300 feet wide by 4,500 feet long. In order to use most of the airfield and keep down dust, it was deemed necessary to grade the field and plant three million yards of Bermuda grass. That ground cover was hauled in on trucks, and the task of keeping it damp and sprigging the vast area began. The sodded areas of the airfield were finished shortly thereafter. While construction continued on the airfield and the domestic site, normal aircraft maintenance and service was carried out under tents or in the dust and heat of the open air.

Since the original plans for Cochran Field authorized construction of a building to house bombsights, the army air corps undoubtedly planned to train both pilots and bombardiers at the station. After all, Turner Field, the advanced flying school then being built almost fifty miles southward at Albany, Georgia, trained pilots and navigators jointly for a time. In April 1941 and again in May, plans for the basic flying school were further modified; bombardier training was deleted, and a post chapel, an officers' recreation building and an officers' mess were added to the plans. In May, thirty-six additional buildings were authorized.

Separate offices that eventually operated at Cochran Field included a sub-depot of the USAAF Materiel Command, which handled supply and maintenance for aircraft and equipment. Other facilities included medical and dental detachments, a finance office, a weather office and a signals office. A communications squadron would staff the control towers, weather and signals offices. Later additions included a skeet range, two swimming pools, a Link Trainer building and housing. Several miles away to the southeast, the USAAF was also building a huge materiel depot, which would serve the needs of training and other stations in the Southeast.

Evidently, because of a shortage of steel and the necessity to provide hangars for the open-cockpit Stearman trainers at the increasing number of primary flying schools, the construction of hangars at some of the basic flying schools was delayed. Ultimately the materials for building four huge steel hangars were delivered to the Cochran Field, and the hangars were finally erected between September 1941 and April 1942. Until such facilities were available, and when not flying or being serviced, the Vultee BT-13 monoplane basic trainers, equipped with fixed landing gear and plexiglass canopies, were parked on the airfield apron in all kinds of weather. While there, the aircraft sometimes attracted snakes and other nocturnal creatures seeking shelter.

Effective 20 June 1941, the old U.S. Army Air Corps gave way to the United States Army Air Forces, a new, enlarged organization. By the end of June 1941, the operations building, which included offices for the dispatchers as well as weather, communications and control tower staff, was completed. Cadet squadron buildings were also completed at about the same time. As construction continued, Class SE-41-I arrived and joined Class SE-41-H at the basic flying school. Then, in August, when Class SE-41-H graduated, Class SE-42-A, a new, larger British course commenced training. In 1941–42, as USAAF plans and training officers proposed and approved further training expansion plans, Cochran Field and all other training stations were enlarged. Beginning with fewer than 100 students in June 1941, Cochran Field grew as the USAAF goal for the production of pilots rose steadily from 30,000 to 50,000, to 60,000, to 75,000 and finally to 104,000 pilots per year.

In order to prevent collisions or excessive crowding in the airspace of the main field, safe operations required the use of several auxiliary airfields within a fifteen- to twenty-five-mile radius. Until some stages of training could be shifted away from the busy main airdrome to air space centered on auxiliary fields, Cochran Field fliers were permitted to use the Civil Aeronautics Authority's airfields at Butler and Cochran, Georgia, for practicing takeoffs and landings and for soloing students. Meanwhile, negotiations were continuing in an effort to procure three auxiliary landing grounds. The City of Macon leased the 269-acre No. 1 Auxiliary (Gunn Field) for $1,345 per year. The city also leased the 127.75-acre No. 2 Auxiliary (Perry Field, originally called Nunn Field) for $894.25 annually. The 253-acre No. 3 Auxiliary (Fort Valley Field, formerly called Harris Field) was leased from a group of owners for an unreported sum.

Before the end of 1941, student enrollment doubled, so additional auxiliary airfields were required. Auxiliary Field No. 4 (Byron Field), containing 157.91 acres, was leased from local owners, but difficulty was encountered in attempting to lease or purchase an additional site, so property was once more condemned by the court, a fair value was established and the site was conveyed to the USAAF. This tract of land, Auxiliary Field No. 5 (Myrtle Field), totaling 245.95 acres, cost $14,115 and made it possible for the USAAF basic flying school to increase its enrollment significantly.

Subsequently, improvements were made at several of these auxiliary fields. Stage houses were constructed at Byron and Perry Auxiliary Fields, and a small wooden hangar was added at one of the airfields. Cochran Field had begun training American aviation cadets in June 1941 with fewer than 100 flying cadets and a small contingent of army officer flying instructors. Following two initial classes of American flying cadets, Cochran Field began in August 1941 to receive British cadets, and for the next sixteen months RAF student pilots continued in training at the Macon Airfield. In December 1942, Class SE-43-B, the final RAF course, departed for advanced flying schools, and a few days later, when Class SE-43-D arrived at Cochran Field, the military population included 750 student pilots and 130 flying instructors.

Organization and administration at the basic school was patterned after long-established procedures developed and used at Randolph Field, Texas. The airfield was commanded by Lieutenant Colonel Donald D. Fitzgerald, originally the station project officer, and his staff included Major Claire Stroh, executive officer; Captain Richard H. Wise, post adjutant; First Lieutenant James W. Clark, personnel officer; and Major Moses D. Johnson, post quartermaster. It was the latter officer who had responsibility for the smooth operation of the domestic side of this sprawling military town. The quartermaster administered a billeting office and all warehouses and supply depots on the station. In administering to the needs of a military population nearly five thousand strong, these service facilities issued and accounted for building repair and maintenance, food, clothing and equipment for ground and flying personnel, as well as transport, utilities, recreation and fire protection.

Staffing the offices, service units, hospital and school squadrons followed common practice of the time. Usually, some experienced personnel were transferred from already established basic schools or other installations. To these men were added newly trained staff from scattered air corps technical and administrative schools or directly from short military indoctrination courses. In line with pre-war command and staff studies, any expandable military force would be compelled to devote a great deal of effort to training personnel needed to operate larger organizations. Because of the rapidity of USAAF expansion, each established station accepted as a normal part of its mission the necessity to train their own staffs, as well as those for new schools. Like other older stations, Cochran Field established its own school system and continued formal instruction as well as on-the-job training programs to train qualified men, and to improve the qualifications of new staff as their duty assignments were enlarged.

Into the various schools at Cochran Field went raw recruits or men remustered from other branches of army service, and qualified men came out of the schools, many of whom continued to serve on the station. Others, after gaining some job experience, were posted to new training stations. Some of the staff schools that were operated successfully at Cochran Field and trained a large number of army air corps personnel included an aircraft mechanics' course, a weather school, an administrative school, a noncommissioned officers' course, a radio code school and an administrative officers' school.

Moreover, when plans were being developed to open a new training airfield, established older stations such as Cochran Field and Gunter Field formed extra squadrons and trained maintenance and administrative personnel for those stations as well. Just as most of the original staff at Cochran Field had come from Gunter and Maxwell Fields in Alabama, Cochran Field trained squadrons that were transferred to new basic flying schools when they were ready to commence training. Many staff members who received training and experience in school squadrons at Cochran Field were posted to such stations as Shaw Field, a new USAAF basic flying school near Sumter, South Carolina.

Cochran Field's flying training organization was of central importance. At first, Major James T. Patterson served as both director of training and director of flying. Reporting to the director of training was a director of ground school, a director of military training, a commandant of cadets and a school secretary. Later, as the school expanded, Major Patterson relinquished his assignment as director of flying. Captain Casper P. West replaced Patterson as director of flying, and he had two group commanders and eight squadron commanders reporting to him.

Each training group consisted of four squadrons, and squadron organization followed a standard pattern derived from experience. Each squadron commander had an assistant and from eight to twenty flying instructors. The original flying instructors were recently graduated student pilots who had demonstrated exceptional flying abilities. In addition to their duties as commanders, older, experienced military pilots, all of whom had earlier been qualified as instructors, set up schools on station and trained new flying instructors. Original staff and instructional personnel at Cochran Field were U.S. Army Air Corps officers, but later included a RAF flight lieutenant administrative officer and approximately forty RAF pilot officer flying instructors.

Ground school was also an important part of flying training at every stage. At Cochran Field, Captain Edgar C. Lakey, U.S. Army Infantry, was the original director of the ground school, but in December 1941, First Lieutenant Arthur L. Huff replaced him. In June 1941, when training commenced, the ground school used four classrooms in Buildings 20, 21 and 22, but by the end of August 1941, Building 34 and a room in Building 8 were added. The ground school syllabus was more flexible than that in the flying department. Instructors were told what courses were to be taught and how many hours were to be used for each, but there was no common syllabus. From the beginning, ground school instructors developed their courses according to their own views as to the emphasis required.

When the larger British cadet classes arrived, the ground school modified its syllabus and expanded its staff and facilities. United States Army Air Forces training officers deemed military discipline as important for producing officer pilots. When the training sequence was reduced from one year to thirty-six weeks, then to thirty weeks, then to twenty-seven weeks, the syllabus for primary flying schools was modified to reduce the amount of military training. In order to compensate for the reduced emphasis, the basic flying school syllabus of 1941 tried to remedy the deficiencies of the civil contract primary flying schools. Military training was emphasized, and in 1943 ground and flying training were better coordinated.

During the summer of 1941, Cochran Field and other basic flying schools established aviation cadet basic training groups. Military and physical training and cadet discipline came under the authority of the group's plans and training office (S-3), headed by Second Lieutenant John H. Knight. First Lieutenant Frank W. Iseman served as commandant of cadets, and several tactical officers assisted him. Until a qualified army officer replaced him, Earl D. James, a civilian, was employed as director of athletic programs.

The ground school, military and flying departments were intended to complement each other and, together, their mission was to produce excellent pilots and officers. From the perspective of American student pilots, this was the standard, expected course of training, and they rapidly adjusted to its requirements. The military training staff used the USAAF Aviation Cadet Handbook, which had been developed by the Air Corps Training Center at Randolph Field, Texas, through long experience and practice. The cadet code provided for the appointment of cadet officers who had the responsibility of enforcing cadet regulations. On station during their first five weeks (half of the ten-week course) of training at each primary, basic and advanced flying school, officer-cadets were to be hazed. The enforcement of that rigorous code would produce outstanding officer pilots who could withstand pressure and retain their composure despite efforts to bring about a normal reaction of anger or defiance.

An unsigned Macon, Georgia letter of 9 March 1942, from WBK [his sister] to "Dear Walter," which was found in Box 501 of Records Group 18 in the National Archives, complained of low morale of British cadets due to excessive drill, weapons handling and little recreation. Her closing remarks were:

> As a whole, they [the British boys] come from the lower stratas of society, and they do not quite know what to make of this strange America. Maybe their confidence in the superiority of all that is British is shaken, and they take it out in resenting the officers on the ground that they are not gentlemen, and so have no right to command his majesty's subjects.

A view perhaps excessive, but that revealed that British cadets were encountering significant problems in USAAF flying schools.

As indicated, some of the British pilot trainees did not like the USAAF system. Later, looking back to that early American training experience, many senior officers at Cochran Field were critical of using even a modified West Point disciplinary system with either American or foreign cadets. Pilot training had enough built-in pressures without adding an extra burden of attempting, in a limited period, to indoctrinate students into the complex honor code and its uses. These USAAF officers, including Colonel Fitzgerald, CO of Cochran Field, expressed the view that, in the future, officers of the same nationality should handle discipline and tactical training of foreign students. However, until higher headquarters permitted modification of the training system, there was no choice but to continue established policies. Coincidentally, just as Class SE-42-J entered basic flying school in September 1942, the "class" system was officially abolished in USAAF aircrew training programs.

During the first six months the school was in operation, the flying training organization at Cochran Field evolved gradually. Initially, Squadrons I and III accommodated the ninety-seven American flying cadets of Class SE-41-H when they arrived in June 1941. When the ninety-five members of Class SE-41-I arrived five weeks later, Squadrons II and IV were activated. It is assumed that each of the four squadrons then had approximately forty-six students, and because of the initial staff shortages, instructors were often assigned eight or nine students each until more instructors could be added. The ratio of students to instructors was reduced to five or six, and later to four students per instructor.

As each new expansion plan was implemented, more buildings, aircraft, instructors and students were added to the station. By December 1941, there were 108 flying instructors and 108 trainer aircraft at Cochran Field. For the early instructors, adjustment to teaching flying was very difficult, owing to shortages in facilities, equipment, personnel and instruments.

Although most of these shortages were remedied in time, the first Vultee BT-13 trainers had no instruments in the rear cockpits, so on night flights, with the student in the front cockpit, early Cochran Field flying instructors were put to the "supreme test." During 1942, new sources of flying instructors were found. A number of RAF pilot officer graduates from Class SE-42-A, the initial Arnold Scheme course, were given an instructors' course at the basic or advanced flying school to which they had previously been assigned.

Later, newly appointed USAAF and RAF instructors were posted to one of the USAAF central instructors' schools (CISs) within each of the geographic training commands. The CIS for the Eastern Flying Training Command (EFTC) was located at Maxwell Field, Alabama; for the Central Flying Training Command (CFTC), the CIS was established at Kelly Field, Texas; and in the Western Flying Training Command (WFTC), the CIS was located at Mather Field, near Sacramento, California.

In the ensuing months, as each new class graduated from advanced flying schools, additional RAF instructors were posted to Cochran Field. By mid-1942, there were forty RAF pilot officers and flying officers serving on the instructional staff. Another potential source of flying instructors was the huge pool of older American civilian pilots who did not possess qualifications suited for active military service. In 1942, twenty-two civil service pilots were trained at Cochran Field to become service pilot-instructors at other schools. During 1943, several Cochran Field–trained instructors were posted to a course at the central instructors' school, and when they returned they offered the same course to other instructors serving at Cochran, thereby spreading the benefits of standardization of instructional techniques.

Following the arrival of two courses of British students during the summer of 1941, total enrollment at Cochran Field rose from 200 to more than 320 student pilots, and the training organization at Cochran Field was expanded. More instructors and aircraft had to be added quickly, and the training and maintenance staffs had to be significantly increased. The director of training, Major James H. Patterson, and his staff evaluated that early experience and expressed the belief that the first four classes (two American and two British) had spent too much time performing maneuvers. On 8 November 1941, after the arrival of Class SE-42-C, the third RAF course, the department of training was further changed.

From the original four-squadron configuration, as at Gunter Field, the school's organization changed quickly to two groups and eight squadrons: Group I included Squadrons 1, 3, 5 and 7; and Group II included Squadrons 2, 4, 6 and 8. The lower class (new arrivals) flew from 8:30 a.m. to 12:30 p.m. while the upper class attended ground school. Then the two classes exchanged places, and the upper class flew from 1:30 to 5:30 p.m. while the lower class attended ground school. To assure flying experience at different times of the day and night, schedules were shifted about for each squadron. In addition to these refinements, a two-hour night navigation flight was added to the syllabus.

By September 1942, when a further expansion plan was implemented and the total number of instructors at Cochran Field had climbed to 170 and then dropped back to 128, and the number of aircraft had reached almost 200, flying training was once more reorganized and further expanded. The earlier group organization was disbanded, the eight squadrons were relabeled flights A through H and the personnel of the original eight squadrons were combined into four school squadrons. Each flight commander was assigned an assistant and 13 or 14 instructors. As a result, the new training organization was stabilized with approximately 128 flying instructors and another dozen or more staff officers. Long before these changes were wrought, before construction on the main airdrome was complete and before all of the necessary auxiliary fields had been developed, flying training had flourished at Cochran Field, Georgia, for two years.

The *Macon Telegraph* was one of the most powerful newspapers in Georgia and served the vast region of middle Georgia well. While the "Letters to the Editor" column of that newspaper served as an equivalent of London's Hyde Park "Speaker's Corner" and allowed every shade of opinion to be expressed on the issues of the day, the paper generally tended to support conservative Democrats in state and national politics. The separate page devoted to news items of the "colored community" smacked of paternalistic racism to the British cadets and to a later age of Americans more attuned to greater equality. However, the *Macon Telegraph* was truly a voice for moderation, and one of its editors became not only one of the South's leading journalists, but also was appointed by President Roosevelt to the wartime Civil Rights Commission.

In a 20 August 1941 editorial, editors of the *Macon Telegraph* interpreted public reaction to the arrival of RAF student pilots at Cochran Field by asserting that "everything possible will be done to make them feel at home." That declaration, from the perspective of many young Britons, proved to be typical American understatement. For the next sixteen months Macon and other communities of middle Georgia virtually adopted the RAF and the USAAF. As the leaves of wartime calendars were torn away, Macon citizens followed RAF action worldwide, while at the same time following the service of their own adopted "sons" from other states in different theaters of operations.

Letters written by distraught parents, wives or girlfriends informed many RAF pilots' "American families" of the dead, missing, wounded and heroic, and members of many Georgia households often joined them in prayers and mourning. When the war ended, Atlanta's English-Speaking Union sponsored the installation of a special memorial corner in St. Clement Danes, the RAF church, close by St. Paul's Cathedral in London's Strand. The massive circular tribute, made of Georgia marble, is still there symbolizing a historical and emotional link between the 1940s and the ages.

Not willing to defer completely to Macon and other nearby communities, the tiny towns of Fort Valley and Montezuma, which were located a few miles south of Cochran Field, sought to entertain as many of the British cadets as possible. During the Labor Day weekend from Saturday, 30 August through Monday, 1 September 1941, approximately one hundred British cadets enjoyed their visits to these two small towns during their first leave from Cochran Field. Many of them developed associations with a number of citizens of these towns that led to permanent friendships. In writing to friends in Montezuma, RAF Cadet John Burney inspired an editorial praising middle Georgians for their hospitality to servicemen. Burney, who washed out of pilot training at Cochran Field and returned to the United Kingdom in September 1941, asserted that "the hospitality of your people will remain with us forever."

A natural desire to demonstrate their particular brand of Southern hospitality, and the notice that the towns of Montezuma and Fort Valley received, must have inspired the citizens of Dublin, Perry, Milledgeville, Grays, Greensboro, Vidalia, Hawkinsville and numerous other small towns around the region to host the British student pilots. Dublin invited fifty of them to visit the town on Sunday, 5 October. The town and the Methodist church of Fort Valley entertained a considerable number as well. The people of Perry were somewhat embarrassed when they invited ninety-six RAF cadets to enjoy a steak dinner with them. The steaks were huge and delicious, but most of the young men, knowing that such portions were equal to at least an entire week's ration for a family in wartime Britain, felt guilty eating so much meat. People in the small towns of middle Georgia almost monopolized the free time of many of the RAF cadets.

Since Camp Wheeler, an army training station, had been built a few miles east of Macon in 1940, the town was becoming accustomed to being a garrison town. However, owing to natural inclination, many citizens of Macon were air-minded and anxious to provide hospitality for the increasing numbers of airmen stationed at Cochran Field. In cooperation with the ladies of Macon's Junior Defense League, the Servicemen's Recreation Center and the Shrine Mosque, a tea dance was sponsored for the British cadets on Saturday afternoon, 6 September 1941. The dance began at 4:00 p.m. and lasted until 7:00, and it gave the young RAF men a chance to meet many of the young ladies of Macon.

At around the same time, a Cadet Club was established in the basement of the Dempsey Hotel, but those British cadets who attended churches in the city are the ones who met Macon families. On Friday night, 26 September, a large number of RAF cadets joined the graduating American cadet class at a dance held at the Idle Hour Country Club. During the so-called cooler month of October, when temperatures rose to more than eighty-five degrees in daytime and dropped to the sixties at night, 106 RAF cadets at Cochran Field got an opportunity to watch the play of the football teams of Mercer University and the University of Georgia. Apparently, the British visitors were confused by the game, enjoyed the crowds and loathed the weather.

On 30 October 1941, the RAF students served hot dogs and soft drinks to their guests at a Royal Air Force–sponsored dance at the Idle Hour Country Club. Anxious to express their appreciation to their civilian guests who had entertained them often during their stay at Cochran Field, they had pooled resources for the party. During the evening, one cadet led a singalong, and everyone joined in singing the popular tunes of the day. During their seven-day leave before reporting to advanced flying schools, many citizens of Macon and vicinity drove "the RAF boys" to towns and communities in the region, and several groups visited Atlanta.

The second RAF class arrived at Cochran Field around 2 October 1941, and the first class departed for advanced flying schools around 1 November. On 2 November, Class SE-42-C arrived to replace them. On 23 November, two teams chosen from each of the two classes played an exhibition rugby football game at Mercer University's Porter Stadium. The Optimist Club sponsored the game, and proceeds were divided between Bundles for Britain and the Community Chest. As writer Bob Fackelman described it, "As the Lanier band wove the melodies of 'God Save The King' and the 'Star Spangled Banner' into one thought-provoking sequence, there was a knot tied that years cannot unloosen." Following the game, ten young ladies of the Macon branch of Bundles for Britain honored the British cadets with a tea. RAF Cadet John H. Barnes and Miss Kathleen Black of the Wesleyan Conservatory played the piano, and the guests sang a number of American and British songs until mid-evening.

On 30 November, a large number of RAF cadets were entertained by members of the Cherokee Heights Methodist Church, after which they joined members of the congregation in their homes for dinner. In late December, another RAF cadet was an accidental guest at Douglas, Georgia. Lost during a night flight, LAC Robert Granger of Scotland saw hangars and lights and landed at the primary school at Douglas. He was told to remain there and return to Cochran Field the next morning, so townspeople fed him, took him to a dance at nearby Union College and put him up for the night. Even with all of the hospitality offered by people in Macon and neighboring towns, many of the RAF cadets felt the pull of the towns where they had received their primary training. Unfortunately, the distances were great, and the cadets attempted to make long journeys between Saturday at 1:00 p.m. and Sunday afternoon at 6:00 p.m.

During the weekend of 15–16 November, two accidents occurred that injured eleven RAF cadets from Cochran Field and alarmed the USAAF and RAF administrative officers. The first accident occurred on Saturday afternoon, 15 November, near Andersonville, Georgia, when an automobile conveying six RAF cadets to Albany, Georgia, for the weekend wrecked and sent the young men to a hospital in Americus. On Sunday evening, another automobile returning five RAF cadets from a weekend in Camden, South Carolina, wrecked at Haddock on a hill near the junction of Highway 80 and the Cochran short route and sent two RAF cadets to the Cochran Field hospital.

In accordance with regulations, the accidents were reported through channels to higher headquarters, and the responses reverberated through communication channels for several days. Flight Lieutenant J. Leonard Keith, the RAF administrative officer, was compelled to issue orders restricting RAF cadet driving and forbidding weekend travel over distances greater than 150 miles.

As the Christmas season came and the weather worsened, many of the RAF cadets of Classes SE-42-B and SE-42-C were entertained by families they had met. Others attended the Wesleyan College Christmas Dance. On Tuesday, 6 January 1942, a farewell dance was held once more at the Idle Hour Country Club. Class SE-42-C had completed its basic flying course and was preparing to depart. The club was beautifully decorated for the occasion. In the days that followed, life in middle Georgia continued much as in the past, except now that the United States was at war, there was a greater urgency about everything. Class SE-42-E replaced the departed Class SE-42-C and joined the members of Class SE-42-D at Cochran Field. Schedules were lengthened, and the pace of training increased.

Macon and the nearby small communities continued their efforts to provide hospitality to the RAF students. In late January 1942, the town of Forsyth entertained its third group of fifty British cadets. On 24 May, Dublin repeated its entertainment of another large group of RAF cadets. The little town of Montezuma became a favorite of RAF cadets who trained at the primary flying schools at Americus and Macon. Many Montezuma families, including that of Dr. and Mrs. C.P. Savage, regularly offered hospitality to two or more RAF cadets from each Americus class, and many of these students returned from their basic and advanced flying schools to visit the small town. It did not take long for the airmen from Cochran Field to discover the friendly town. The girls of Montezuma enjoyed teaching many of these young men "jitterbugging," and one of their most apt pupils proved to be LAC David Anderson of Scotland. The girls of Montezuma undoubtedly enjoyed the dancing and socializing and the months of new friendships.

To commemorate the visits of RAF students from Americus and Cochran Field, the high school girls of Montezuma started a fad that spread to other schools in the region. Two artistic RAF cadets, when requested to sign their autographs on some shirts, not only signed but also drew numerous designs on the white shirts. To preserve the memories, the young ladies then embroidered the signatures and designs in vari-colored thread. Wearing the distinctive shirts became a "rage" among high school girls in Montezuma and several towns after that.

The kindness of many people from Macon and the other towns brought a large numbers of letters from appreciative British parents. Many Cochran Field flight instructors received letters from parents of former RAF cadets expressing appreciation for the excellent training their sons had received. Mr. and Mrs. Clay Murphey, who had regularly entertained many British cadets, including LAC Peter Norris, entered into a considerable correspondence with Arthur O. Norris, Peter's father. Mr. Norris wrote praising the treatment accorded British student pilots by American civilians. Mr. Murphey's reply that the RAF cadets were in every way "gentlemen" and were "a credit to their nation" was evidently transmitted to the Air Ministry and brought a reply from an air commodore thanking Mr. Murphey for his compliment to the RAF cadets.

Beginning with Class SE-42-F, which arrived at the end of February 1942, the pace of change quickened, and each month brought a new RAF class to Cochran Field. On Monday, 25 May, RAF cadets of Class SE-42-G threw a party at the Green Lawn, and on Wednesday night, 27 May, it was time for the traditional graduation dance and party at the Idle Hour Country Club honoring the departing Class SE-42-G. The final six RAF classes—SE-42-H, SE-42-I, SE-42-J, SE-42-K, SE-43-A and SE-43-B—arrived at the basic flying school during either the first or second week of the months extending from May 1942 until the final RAF class arrived on 11 October 1942.

When Class SE-43-B departed around 12 December 1942, RAF pilot training ended at Cochran Field and the station returned to the training of aviation cadets, student officers and aviation students of the USAAF. In the course of learning to fly heavier basic trainers at Cochran Field, many young British student pilots had also learned to drive automobiles (some none too well). Some RAF cadets felt that they had been treated like convicts during part of their stay at Cochran Field, but in Macon and neighboring towns they were treated like royalty. For those who would relax and enjoy it, Southern hospitality had meant friendships made at church and picnics and introductions made over fried chicken, potato salad, barbecues, corn on the cob and many other strange dishes.

The town of Fort Valley, Peach County, Georgia, is located approximately thirty miles south-southwest of Macon and fifteen miles southwest of Cochran Field. During 1941–45, Harris Field, one of the major auxiliary fields developed by the basic flying school, was located east of the town. Another auxiliary field lay close by Byron, a tiny community located between Fort Valley and Macon. When many RAF instructors were assigned to Cochran Field during the months following March 1942, and since the city of Macon was crowded with military families from Camp Wheeler and Cochran Field, accommodation was difficult to find. As a result, many of these young RAF instructors gravitated to Fort Valley.

FLYING TRAINING AT COCHRAN FIELD

Officially, flying training began at Cochran Field on 4 June 1941. Between that date and 14 August 1941, two courses totaling 192 American aviation cadets arrived at Cochran Field: 97 members of Class SE-41-H arrived on 3 June from Arcadia, Florida, and Albany and Americus, Georgia; the 95 members of Class SE-41-I arrived on 14 July 1941 from Arcadia, Florida, Camden, South Carolina, and Americus, Georgia. During their training, several students were eliminated and flying accidents occurred that took the lives of 3 air corps officers and 1 American aviation cadet.

On Sunday, 14 August, the 88 graduates of Class SE-41-H departed for advanced flying schools. The 144 members of Class SE-42-A, the first of thirteen courses of British student pilots, arrived at Cochran Field in several separate contingents between 14 and 17 August. During the next sixteen months extending from 14 August 1941 to 14 December 1942, 2,759 British pilot trainees entered the USAAF basic flying school at Cochran Field, Georgia. Of that number, 11 were killed in accidents, 267 were eliminated (238 for flying deficiencies, 29 for non-flying reasons) and 2,476 completed training successfully and were posted to advanced flying schools.

The standard 1941 USAAF basic flying school syllabus encompassed seventy flying hours, with a minimum of twenty-five hours dual flying, but within that framework there was great latitude. At Cochran Field, it included six hours of instrument flying, one and a half hours of aerobatics, three hours of local night flying and three cross-country flights. The first such flight followed a triangular route southeastward from Cochran Field to Siloam, Georgia, northward to Cochran, Georgia, and westward back to Cochran Field. A second flight ran from Cochran Field northwestward to Greenwood, South Carolina, southwestward to Anderson, South Carolina, and back southeastward to Cochran Field. The third cross-country followed the route southward to Jasper, Florida, and return.

Before graduation day, pilot trainees underwent a strenuous ten-week course, including military, physical, academic and flying training. The standard cadet day began with reveille at 5:20 a.m.; at 5:50 a.m., they marched to the dining hall, and with steel compartmentalized trays in hand moved through the cafeteria line. At 6:25 a.m., the students reported for drill or calisthenics. At 7:05 a.m., half of the student body reported to the flight line while the other half marched off to ground school and physical training classes. Between 12:15 and 1:00 p.m., the cadets ate lunch in the dining hall and then reversed the training.

In the afternoon, students who had been undergoing academic and physical training in the morning hours flew, while the other half of the students marched to classrooms and physical training fields. At 5:40 p.m., the evening meal was served, after which students had free time until 7:30 p.m. when the "call to quarters" was sounded. From that hour, study time continued until "lights out" at 9:15 p.m. When night flying began and the student population at the basic school doubled then quadrupled, schedules were modified somewhat, but from the beginning, training days were always inordinately long and busy.

Unless the student pilots had applied for and were eligible for overnight weekend passes, the only free time they had at first was on weekends between 1:00 p.m. on Saturdays and 1:00 a.m. Sunday morning. Unless a special schedule was in effect, Cochran students were also free most Sundays until 9:15 p.m.

Bernard Victor Anthony Thompson of Derby, England, and Class SE-42-A, who had completed his primary flying training at Camden, South Carolina, remembered his introduction to a "full-fledged military base" and standard army barracks. Forty-two years later, Thompson recalled the bugle call at the lowering of the colors at the regular evening retreat formation and ceremony. In physical training, he and his classmates discovered a new word, "calisthenics," and thoroughly enjoyed sports and physical fitness. For those who had not been exposed to preparation for a "commando course," tumbling and an obstacle course were also introduced. While at Cochran Field, Physical Instructor Earl James introduced the British students to American football, softball and volleyball, and the students, in turn, taught American cadets the principles of rugby football.

Thompson no doubt spoke for many of his classmates when he compared the Stearman PT-17 and the Vultee BT-13A. "My first love," he declared, "was and still is the old Stearman, but comparing it with the Vultee was rather like comparing a motor bike with a car. Here was a real airplane!" Flying was their reason for being stationed at Cochran Field, and it now became fascinating. Sitting in the front cockpit of a canopied aircraft, using radio for communication, formation flying, cross-country flying and instrument flights under the hood were all so much more sophisticated than flying in the open-cockpit Stearman biplane. Thompson's reaction to this was, "I really began to feel as though things were beginning to move."

When there was time to go off-post, the men of Class SE-42-A found the people of Macon and surrounding towns very friendly and hospitable. Since money was in shorter supply for the British cadets, they had no way of returning the extraordinary hospitality that they encountered everywhere. In return, many of them sang in church choirs or entertained groups with programs of English ballads. Others joined the RAF glee club that had been formed on-post and regularly broadcast over local radio stations.

It was possible to be detached about some things, even very serious matters such as the occasional training fatality one heard about, but matters of a more personal nature were often upsetting, to say the least. In accordance with Aviation Cadet Regulations that stated that "no cadet shall have a horse, dog, cat, wife, or mustache," many members of the class were ordered to shave and have their hair close-cropped. The "GI haircuts" and enforced shaving of well-cultivated moustaches produced a great deal of anxiety among men who were accustomed to a different training system.

On Thursday, 25 September 1941, following delays caused by two separate showers of rain, the eighty-three members of Class SE-41-I graduated and received their diplomas, after which they were honored by a march past of the RAF cadets of Class SE-42-A. Immediately following the ceremonies, the RAF cadets were elevated to the exalted status of upperclassmen, and student officers were appointed. RAF Cadet Frederick W. Bradford (Camden, SE-42-A) was named cadet captain and group commander, and Bradford's staff included Cadet Captains Frederick W. Harrison, Rycherde H.H. Hogarth, Guy E.C. Pease, Reginald Levy and Arthur Smith. Appointed cadet lieutenants were Melville H. Ball, John J. Mulrooney, Norman Platt, Arthur Bradshaw, Michael F. Goodchap, Clement R. Sar, Ronald E. Nutley, Ernest A. Ellerby, William C. Phillips, Peter H. Campbell, Wallace F. Freshwater, Anthony Notley and Stanley S. Morrow. Within a few days, members of Class SE-42-B arrived and became the lower class at the basic flying school; Cochran Field was now all RAF.

When Class SE-42-A was nearing completion of its basic flying training, Wing Commander Harry A.V. Hogan, DFC, senior RAF administrative officer, visited Cochran Field again. Hogan's fourth report to senior officers of the Royal Air Force Delegation (RAFDEL) in Washington included his first description and assessment of the basic flying schools. Excerpts from Hogan's report provide insight into adjustment problems experienced by that first RAF course of trainee pilots:

> *Cochran Field is situated nine miles south of the town of Macon. The aerodrome itself is of tremendous size, with runways about 100 yards wide, which are broad enough to permit aeroplanes to taxi on both sides of the runway while other aircraft land and take off. Owing to the newness of the surface of the aerodrome, the earth has not yet settled firmly, and runways have to be used continuously except in very dry weather. There are no hangars as yet, but two are to be constructed shortly, and will be used for maintenance only. At present, the maintenance of approximately 160 aeroplanes is carried on out in the open.*
>
> *The camp itself is of temporary wooden construction, the barracks being two stories high, and each barrack containing small rooms to accomodate two students with adequate*

ablutions at one end of the building. The school opened in June and this course of R.A.F. students is the third course to undergo training at this school. The authorities are intensely keen to make the school a good one and possibly the routine has been unduly strict.

The British students arrived at Macon five days before the course was due to commence and their first three days were assigned to "processing," as it is called. The first day they were given drill continuously through the morning and mid-afternoon. It was an extremely hot day and the students perspired excessively. Between drills they fell out and changed their uniforms but were not permitted to take showers until 9 p.m.

The upper class "hazes" the newcomers who have to be initiated in a number of cadet rules, such as sitting on only three inches of the form at meals, no talking, looking nowhere except at their plates, etc., and being confined to their rooms when not on organised duty. The officers give encouragement to the upper class to carry out the hazing as effectively as possible.

In the past, the upper class has been exempted from flying training for periods up to one week in order that they may haze the lower class to the greatest extent. This method of dealing with the British students drove them to the point of exasperation. The situation was made worse by the fact that they did not fly for the first three days.

It is felt that had there been an R.A.F.A.O. present at the school at the time, the hazing, processing, and severe discipline might have been lessened by a tactful word from him, and the attitude of the British students might have been less antagonistic toward their initiation into Basic School. The hazing however, at this school has now been abolished, and the students are not so severely treated.

The students have now reached the 8th week of their training and undoubtedly have created a very favorable impression at both schools. The instructors at Basic School had heard certain distasteful rumors about the behavior and general attitude of the British students in Primary, however, the majority of the trouble makers having been eliminated, there has been no cause for further comment.

The students have now reached an average of between 55 and 60 hours, and should complete their course a week ahead of schedule. They have completed between 3½ and 4½ hours night flying, some cross country flying and without doubt have done very well. The standard of handling aircraft reached by the British students is undoubtedly high and the students are safe and reliable.

In closing that portion of his report, Wing Commander Hogan described the flying instructors as "very young and instructing for their first time." But he pointed out, "They have been most patient and have made every effort to get our students through, some students being given up to 20 hours dual before elimination."

As Wing Commander Hogan indicated, there was no RAF administrative officer at Cochran Field when the RAF cadets first arrived. However, that omission was remedied on 9 September 1941, when Wing Commander Kenneth J. Rampling arrived to serve temporarily as coordinator of basic flying training. The nature of Rampling's assignment is unclear. From official accounts, it appears that owing to Wing Commander Hogan's heavy burden of work as senior RAF administrative officer for the Southeast Air Corps Training Center, Rampling was intended to be his assistant. In order for the new wing commander to learn the region, its schools and schools' staffs, Hogan evidently assigned Rampling to Carlstrom Field, Florida, for a time before sending him to Cochran Field with instructions to coordinate RAF training at Cochran and Gunter Fields.

Neither Group Captain Carnegie nor Wing Commander Hogan indicated Rampling's assignment, but the *Macon Telegraph*, in reporting Rampling's departure from Cochran Field on 15 October 1941, indicated that he was being assigned to Clewiston, Florida, for "an indefinite period before being transferred to Maxwell Field as assistant liaison officer." In Rampling's place at Cochran Field came Flight Lieutenant C.C. Hirst, who could have passed as an identical twin of Robert Benchley, the American author, actor and humorist. Formerly of Burnmouth on the North Sea coast in the Lowlands of Scotland, Hirst had served as an officer in the British army until he transferred to the Royal Flying Corps in 1916. During the 1920s, he immigrated to Canada and lived in Toronto and Montreal, where he was secretary of the Aviation League of Canada. As required by RAF regulations, when he was promoted to squadron leader (major) on 10 November 1941, Hirst was transferred and his replacement was Flight Lieutenant J. Leonard Keith, MBE, formerly RAFAO at the Camden, South Carolina primary flying school.

Before they themselves left Cochran Field, the members of Class SE-42-A recalled their basic flying school experiences. In Class SE-42-A's edition of the cadet magazine, *Cochran Control*, one of their members modified comedian Bob Hope's farewell theme song and dedicated his tongue-in-cheek version of "Thanks for the Memories" to American aviation cadet Class SE-41-I:

Thanks for the memories of walking on the ramp
Weekends spent in camp;
And gigs and stars and walking tours, that left you hot and damp
How lovely that was.

Gee, thanks for the memories of three inches on your seat
Mosquitoes and the heat;
And processing and bags of bull and weary arms and feet
How lovely that was.

Many's the time we've grumbled
And never thought we'd last it
But now that we know that we've passed it
We did have fun and no harm done.

So thanks for the memories of haircuts "a la mode"
Inspections on the road
And staggering up the barracks steps with lockers—what a load!
How lovely that was.

We said good-bye with reluctance
And all got as high as a steeple
We met such intelligent people
That line should bring
Three cheers for the King
So thanks for the memories and all jokes put aside

We rather think we "tried"
So let's shake hands and leave it
As we would want you to
Awfully glad we met you
Cheerio and Toodle-oo

And thank you so much.

One memory that they might not have retained for very long was that, owing to good flying weather, Class SE-42-A set a record and completed its basic flying training course nine days early. Following leaves, graduation ceremonies for the class were held at 4:00 p.m. on Thursday, 30 October 1941.

Of the 144 RAF students who arrived at Cochran Field in mid-August 1941 to commence basic flying training, 2 pupils were held over to subsequent classes, so the net intake was 142 students, of whom 4 were eliminated and 138 graduated. Separate contingents from Class SE-42-A departed Cochran Field on 1 November 1941 for the three advanced flying schools located at Turner Field, Georgia, and Maxwell and Craig Fields in Alabama.

The contingent of Class SE-42-B men who traveled to Cochran Field in a Greyhound coach "fully laden with bodies and luggage" from Camden, South Carolina, joined others from Arcadia, Florida, and Albany and Americus, Georgia, at the basic flying school at 6:00 p.m. on 30 September 1941. As the coach from Camden entered the gates of the basic flying school, the huge plywood RAF insignia was still intact, stretching across the front bumper of the chartered Greyhound coach, and many of the men were singing and cheering. After eating and being distributed to different squadrons, members of this second RAF class on the new station were disconcerted to discover that their welcome appeared less friendly than at primary school. Thirty minutes of close-order drill on a dusty drill field in the muggy twilight was only the beginning of hazing and military training at the basic school. It and other similar adventures during the next few weeks left a bitter taste and affected many RAF student attitudes toward the basic flying school that would endure for a lifetime.

During the morning of 1 October 1941, the cadet squadrons were issued supplies, uniforms and equipment and were introduced to the post exchange (PX). In addition, before lunch, the new arrivals had their hair close-cropped "convict style" and those students with moustaches had them removed. Then, during the entire afternoon, from 12:30 p.m. to 5:40 p.m., they drilled and were rushed back into the barracks at intervals and ordered to dress in different uniforms—khaki coveralls, khaki uniforms, then blue flying coveralls, then back onto the drill field.

Close-order drill, the inevitable calisthenics, games and inspections during the next few days were steady reminders that they were now attending a military rather than a civil contract flying school. At some point during their first few days on the station, they were divided into groups of six and assigned to a flying instructor. The first thrill at the new station came when they reported to their instructor on the flight line to receive an introduction to the mysteries of the sleek Vultee BT-13 monoplane trainers and a familiarization flight.

On Saturday afternoon, 4 October 1941, they went on open-post and investigated the city of Macon, going to the cinema, eating snacks in cafés and restaurants, drinking Cokes and hot tea and listening to popular, romantic tunes. Popular songs included "You Are My Sunshine," "Yours," "Green Eyes," "I'll Come Back to You" and others being played on the fascinating

Wurlitzer jukeboxes that seemed to abound everywhere. At the beginning of the new week, depending on the squadron to which they were assigned, the RAF student pilots settled down to a routine of ground school in the mornings followed by lunch, then flying and physical training, or the reverse order of that same schedule.

During the following days, which seemed to rush by so rapidly, the routine of ground school and other activities continued, and almost every student was adding flying hours at a steady rate. On Sunday morning, 12 October 1941, at the request of the many people in Perry, Georgia, army trucks transported one hundred RAF students to the nearby town. There, they attended church services, after which they were invited in twos and threes to Sunday dinner (lunch) with church members. After several hours of visiting, they re-boarded the vehicles and departed for Cochran Field at 3:30 p.m. During the next week, after two weeks on the station, many of the students began to solo after having completed from four to six hours of dual flying. Later in the month came the shock of receiving grease-encrusted rifles, which led to unwelcome arms drills for the remaining weeks of basic flying training.

Inevitably, the RAF students discovered everything there was to find in and around Macon, Georgia, including the reminders of the American Indians who had lived along the Ocmulgee River and its tributaries, and many later additions. If they were not busy walking off tours for demerits, many of them caught rides into town on Saturday or Sunday afternoons, or boarded one of the red buses of the Suburban Transit Lines in front of the post exchange.

In Macon, they might visit families in the city or ride to the vicinity of Dixon's Drug Store or Dempsey's Hotel, attend one of several downtown cinemas or make use of the cadet lounge in the hotel. When they visited Macon, they were often taken to churches and Mercer University and Wesleyan College. At the latter college, they invariably met several of its attractive female students. Sometimes, they hitchhiked or traveled by train or coach exploring neighboring towns and meeting people. During several autumn Sunday afternoons, the RAF cadets were persuaded to put on exhibition rugby games for established charities. On one such occasion, they played before nearly six thousand infantrymen from nearby Camp Wheeler.

During at least one late October evening, many of the RAF cadets found themselves in the midst of crowds moving slowly among large tents and a few permanent buildings of the local fairgrounds. Carousel music was wafted through the chill evening air, and glaring lights caused tents and people to cast deep shadows. The county fair was great entertainment and its sights and sounds ranged from the commonplace to the bizarre. Sideshow barkers maintained a steady chant trying to entice customers to come into different shows or demonstrate their skill with rifles, baseballs or a sixteen-pound sledgehammer. There were rides for children of all ages on merry-go-round horses, creaking Ferris wheels and whirring specialty rides intended to test the nerves. Smells of popcorn, hot dogs and hamburgers, onions, mustard and other delights mixed with the pine odor of fresh sawdust or wood chips covering the fair's walkways. In addition, there were barns full of prize livestock and displays of farm produce. But such evenings were merely brief interludes during which the young men escaped military discipline and sampled some of the flavor of the region or shared some of their own interests.

In early November, Flight Lieutenant J. Leonard Keith, MBE, arrived at Cochran Field to replace Flight Lieutenant C.C. Hirst and assume the duties of RAF administrative officer. As a mariner, Keith had made many trips from Britain to Dunkirk and had helped to organize the small boats and yachts into an effective force for helping to remove the thousands of British and French troops who were saved to fight another day. For this service, Keith had received recognition from the hands of King George VI, but few people knew of this honor that had been bestowed upon this pleasant, mild-mannered Scotsman.

Keith had entered the RAF and served at a flying school in western Canada before being posted first to the primary school at Camden, South Carolina, as RAFAO, then five months later to the basic flying school at Cochran Field. Keith would remain there until his tour of duty in the United States ended and he was returned to the United Kingdom for further assignment. After D-Day, 6 June 1944, as a RAF squadron leader (supply), he would serve as a RAF beach master in Normandy directing the flow of equipment and other materiel to RAF units on the continent.

After slightly more than a month of training and accumulation of the requisite flying hours, RAF students of Class SE-42-B were introduced to night flying. Within the following week, they also did the first of three cross-country flights. Just at the end of October, cold weather had set in, and the men had dug out their RAF flying boots and gloves. Underneath their USAAF-issue blue flying coveralls, many of them also wore their RAF blue woolen shirts and trousers to ward off the cold. They had become upperclassmen and had completed approximately half of their required seventy hours of flying at the basic school.

As a result of this newly won status, several members of the class were to assume greater responsibilities than they had before. Cadet officers were appointed, and R. Payne became cadet captain and group commander. His staff included J.C. Adey, John C. Bliss, D.J. Rowe and Stanley W. Holmes. Cadet lieutenants included F.W. Pawsey, R. Anthony Bethell, Dennis A. Forknall, L.S. Bell, R.W. Findlay, D.S. Green, M. Penman, S.M. Kent, F.A. Harper, N.J. Dixon, William Hughes, R.G. Higgins, A.A. Brannigan, J.H. Barned, K.V. Panter, T.S. Perry, J.B. Thornton and P.S. Compton.

After they adjusted to the basic flying school, members of Class SE-42-B began to venture farther afield than Macon and neighboring towns. Primary flying schools in Florida were too far away to be visited during weekends, but many of the RAF cadets returned on several weekends to the small towns of Camden, South Carolina, and Americus and Albany, Georgia, to visit primary schools, instructors and civilian friends. That most of the RAF students had never had a driver's license and had never driven anything more mechanical than a bicycle was hardly a deterrent; after all, they could fly airplanes.

Because of the obvious dangers inherent in hurried weekend travel over long distances, RAF administrative officers cautioned their charges against them. Despite such warnings, groups of six or seven men could and often did pool their resources for the common welfare. Willingly, they paid one of the Cochran Field maintenance or administrative NCOs for the rental of his automobile. These "wild" RAF types, who had neither driver's licenses nor insurance and to whom the proper handling of an automobile clutch was still one of life's mysteries, often lurched out of Macon in a dozen or more short jumps before exceeding stalling speed and getting underway in the blue or maroon convertible or other similar new automobile. No doubt, many shuddering USAAF enlisted men car owners were left in clouds of dust with closed eyes and prayers on their lips.

In mid-November, six RAF men were driving the two hundred miles back from Camden, South Carolina, and were near Milledgeville, within about thirty-five miles of Cochran Field, when they had a collision with another auto. Two men from the Camden accident were lodged in the post hospital, and the other four suffered from bruises and contusions; the miracle was that no one was killed. The left front wheel of the auto was ripped from the axle and mangled; the convertible's engine was driven almost into the front seat, and the auto was deemed a total loss.

Ultimately, the insurance company paid most of the cost of replacing the car, but the RAF cadets pooled resources to make up the $100 deductible from the sergeant-owner's insurance.

In another auto smash-up near Andersonville, Georgia, several other RAF cadets were injured. Fortunately, no one was killed in that accident either, but they suffered more extensive injuries and several of them were admitted to the Sumter County hospital in Americus. As a result of these accidents, orders were issued through Flight Lieutenant Keith's office that all British cadets at Cochran Field were forbidden to drive. For fear of being washed out of training, most of the men complied with that order. Many of them continued to travel great distances on weekends, but now they simply hired, whenever possible, a USAAF-enlisted man with an auto to drive them wherever they wanted to go, including the towns where their primary flying schools were located.

Even with these restrictions, yet another RAF cadet was injured following the class party for instructors when an instructor collided with a bridge abutment near Cochran Field. Both men were hospitalized with minor injuries. It was probably just as well that the driving restriction was imposed; with their low pay, the RAF cadets could hardly afford very many forays away from the vicinity of Macon. Anyway, qualifying as pilots was by far the most important of their activities, so most of them concentrated on attaining that goal.

On occasion, sobering and disconcerting news intruded and temporarily dampened their spirits. From Turner Field, the advanced flying school near Albany, Georgia, came the shocking news that two RAF members of Class SE-42-A, which had left Cochran Field a short time before, had been killed in an air crash. Members of Class SE-42-B also received sad, disheartening letters from friends who had been eliminated from pilot training in American schools and had joined hundreds of others at the new RAF depot at Moncton, New Brunswick, Canada. On 23 November 1941, after considerable practice, two teams of RAF cadets from Cochran Field played an exhibition rugby game at Porter Field, Mercer University's stadium in Macon. The rugby game was very popular and was attended by an estimated four thousand people, the proceeds going to the Community Chest and the Bundles for Britain Fund.

In reminiscing about basic flying school at Cochran Field more than forty years later, Peter A. Morgan (Camden, 42-C) recalled that "American Air training was still at peacetime standard, was unhurried, careful, and selective. The people who got through and graduated to a RAF operational training course had the best of two worlds. By the time we reached Macon, we had grown up a bit and become less bristly—our contrariness waned—and we saw the funny side of it." John Dudley "Mac" McCarthy (Camden, 42-B) also remembered on arrival at Cochran Field that "it was pretty certain at that stage, that most of us would go on for our wings. It was put rather more succinctly by my own personal civilian instructor who said—'unless youse guys kill your goddammed selves en-roooote!!!'"

Whereas most of the RAF cadets were quite critical of USAAF military discipline, McCarthy took a healthier attitude. Discipline at the basic flying school was stricter than at the primary schools. The upper- and lower-class basic training group organization with cadet ranks and the West Point honor system with hazing was worrisome at best, but McCarthy felt that it was "not vicious, and if you entered into it in the right spirit, it could be somewhat enjoyable and amusing." In describing an incident when his course was leaving Cochran Field, McCarthy recalled that "we chipped in money and bought Lieutenant Knight, an extreme martinet at the airfield, a farewell box of toy soldiers!! In retrospect, it was a silly gesture which was heartless and school boyish!"

RAF cadet John C. Bliss, who had undergone primary training at Albany, Georgia, was on one occasion serving as a cadet officer and drilling a group of RAF cadets, American style. As they became worse at the American drill, he recalled energizing them through the simple expedient of reverting to RAF drill. No doubt, many USAAF officers witnessed similar reactions, and some of them, including Colonel Fitzgerald, later questioned the wisdom of insisting on the imposition of American drill and discipline on foreign cadets in pilot training. Most of the RAF students who recalled their days at Cochran Field were critical of hazing on the ground, and only rarely was hazing mentioned in connection with flying.

Although most RAF students were either critical or passive concerning training experiences, some had more extended experiences of hazing directly connected with their flying training. So different from the usual was the experience described by Stanley N. Freestone that it deserves quoting in full:

> It was at basic flying school after some 2 and ½ hours dual that for some reason, my instructor was changed. Then occurred the only crisis in my whole time in the Arnold Scheme. The new instructor was particularly aggressive towards me and did nothing but ride me with constant and severe criticism and ridicule. Perhaps this was part of the hazing system again, but I did begin to react, not being completely without spirit. I was put up for a progress "check" ride with the Flight Commander. I know now that it was meant to be "in" or "out."
>
> For three days, I was made to report to the flight line at 0600. I then sat waiting in a stuffy, hot wooden building until about 11 a.m., when I was told to go to a certain aircraft and prepare for a check ride. Each day I flew, I was made to have the aircraft heater full on, even though it was still very hot in Georgia. All through the flights, several times in the middle of a manuevre, the instructor would cut the engine and shout "Forced Landing!"
>
> These constant interruptions in the rhythm of flight were, of course, intended to pressurize me into some form of stress failure. I wanted to get those wings, and I held both my tongue and my temper. The final result was that I acquitted myself and the Flight Commander said, "you coped O.K.; I'm going to put you back with your original instructor." That was that!

Eddie T. Castle (Camden, 42-B) did not undergo the same experience as Stanley Freestone, but he undoubtedly spoke for many RAF cadets when he remembered more positive attitudes and recalled the normal anxiety over students' nervous reaction to night flying at Cochran Field. "The exhaust stubs of the Vultee BT-13A belched flame and frightened us a lot before we got used to it. The level of instruction was high and I recall few, if any, washouts at this stage of our training."

Like Eddie Castle, Albert Victor Dorman, who also trained at Camden, South Carolina, developed a pet aversion at Cochran Field in the form of "a seven foot high bean pole with a cavalry hat" named Lieutenant Knight. Knight appeared to enjoy hazing the cadets by asking for details about Betty Grable, his favorite film star. However, in recalling his experience at Cochran Field, Gerald Fraser Collis (Albany, 42-B) was very positive.

> The climate was pleasant, the food good, and accommodation in regular timber barracks was comfortable. My instructors were all Air Corps second Lieutenants and pilots and

included C.P. Patton, G.R. Root, and a Mackinnon and Baker; these instructors were friendly and informal and the quality of instruction was superb!

However, there was little time for recreation, especially after the Japanese attack on Pearl Harbour, when during the last few days of training, we were on a 7-day per week schedule. After heavy elimination of students in primary, there were very few in basic, but after Pearl Harbour, there was some easing of discipline and probably some losses resulted from the intensification of training.

As news of historic events and the thousands of rumors they generated ebbed and flowed around Cochran Field, men began to wonder if the American-trained RAF pilots might not be sent to the Pacific rather than back to the United Kingdom for combat assignments.

Forty years later, Vic Dorman remembered the aftermath of the Japanese attack on Pearl Harbor. "For the first time since we arrived here," he wrote, "we felt at one with the American people. It was now their war too, and we could feel the change in attitude towards us." He also recalled that the RAF cadets switched from the well-worn light gray flannel suits to their blue woolen RAF uniforms for off-post wear.

Probably because of being hospitalized, 3 members of the class were held over at the end of training, and the net intake for the class totaled 171. Of that number, 5 were eliminated from training and 166 graduated on 13 December 1941. Two days later, on 15 December, a large contingent of the members of Class SE-42-B were awakened at 2:30 a.m., packed their last kit bags, ate breakfast in the cadet mess hall and departed by bus at 6:00 a.m. for Napier Field at Dothan, Alabama. Others were undoubtedly posted that same day to the advanced flying schools at Maxwell Field and Craig Field, Alabama.

On about 4 November 1941, the 201-member Class SE-42-C traveled from the primary schools at Americus and Albany, Georgia, and Camden, South Carolina, and joined the students of Class SE-42-B at Cochran Field. The loss of two members of the class to drowning at the Jacksonville beach depressed members of the contingent from Souther Field at Americus, Georgia, but training had to go on. Most of the heat was now gone, heavy rains and cooler weather had arrived in middle Georgia and the men at Cochran Field began to experience delightful cool nights and a mixture of cloudy and sunny days.

Cadet discipline with its inspections and system of student officers continued, but the all-British Class SE-42-B was not unduly harsh in its relations with members of Class SE-42-C. What was harsh from the perspective of some of the British students was the daily schedule, which was routine for wartime flying training. An essential difference was that many of the men had been spoiled while in the primary flying schools because there was often a janitorial staff assigned for routine cleaning. Now in the environment of a USAAF basic flying school, each man had to clean his own area and equipment, and details were rotated among classes to clean and prepare the showers and toilets for daily inspection.

While the student pilots were away from their quarters, they were required to leave everything properly clean and aligned in inspection order. Regular inspections of quarters brought the assignment of demerits or gigs, and students receiving more than five in a single week were required to walk off the demerits at the rate of one hour for one demerit in a special area designated for that purpose. Some of the men found that they were able to evade tours while others accumulated so many demerits that there was no time to complete their walking before departing for advanced training. Most of the men accepted this form of disciplinary training, while others groused almost constantly. Such was life!

Although hazing disappeared from the scene, the daily schedule at the flying school was perceived by some as a form of harassment. In looking back, many men who experienced the training were glad that the discipline and schedules were so much a part of the training because so much of flying involved attention to detail. During autumn 1941, the daily schedule at Cochran Field was:

0515	*Reveille*
0520	*Parade*
0550	*Breakfast*
0610	*Clean up room, make bed, etc.*
0700–1000	*Ground School*
1010–1100	*PT*
1145	*Lunch*
1245–1700	*Flying*
1745	*Retreat parade, lowering flag, then march to mess*
1930	*Confined to barracks for study*
2115	*Lights out*

That standard schedule remained for some time, but after reaching solo and night flying stages, and especially after training was intensified following American entry into the war, the schedules were modified.

As with so many members of his own and other classes, Frank Jones had made a great number of friends and had enjoyed himself while in primary training at Albany. He was still enthralled with everything he saw, but one of his experiences was unique. On his twenty-first birthday, he was flying solo and became lost while out of radio range with Cochran Field. On seeing a town and circling to attract attention, he dropped a message attached to his flying goggles requesting that the finder point in the direction of Macon. Since his fuel was low and he could get no response to the message he had dropped, Jones decided to land. He crash-landed the aircraft on the town's golf course without doing injury to himself, but he managed to damage both the airplane and the golf course.

He soon discovered that he was in Thomaston, a town considerably north of Macon. He managed to telephone Cochran Field, and both he and his aircraft were returned to the flying school. The remains of his broken flying goggles were found and posted to him. Jones managed to survive the usual "check rides" following such an incident and ultimately graduated as a pilot. Apparently the forced landing convinced the town fathers of Thomaston that they should pay some attention to improving the local airport if it was so impossible to see that fliers landed on their golf course instead.

Richard F.H. Martin (Americus, 42-C) had no such similar experience while undergoing training at Cochran Field. In describing the training routine in letters to his parents, Martin was distressed about the terrible wastage of food at Cochran Field when there were so many shortages in the United Kingdom. As with many of his classmates, he was not amused with having to clean heavy grease from issued rifles and drill with them, and the very short haircuts required by training officers were ludicrous. "My comb is useless," wrote Martin, "except for scratching my head with it, as they have cut nearly all our hair off." However, all of the experience was not painful.

Martin, Reginald McCadden and several others of his classmates had made many good friends during their stay at Americus, which became their hometown during their stay in America. They returned there regularly to visit several of their former flying instructors and other friends in Americus and nearby communities. During these weekend visits, they attended local high school football games and a class dance at Souther Field. Toward the end of November, they celebrated their first American Thanksgiving Day with the Holston family. Occasionally, they reached Americus by hitchhiking the eighty miles by way of Montezuma; at other times, they caught either the bus or train from Macon and arrived in the wee hours of the morning.

Occasionally, there was entertainment in Macon as well. On one occasion, Class SE-42-C was provided with transportation and free tickets to a three-ring circus in a huge tent at the fairgrounds in Macon. The show was long and enjoyable, but they did not return to Cochran Field until almost midnight and, after rising at 5:15 the following morning, were much too tired. However, they survived and continued training.

But the entertainment was not exclusively for the British students. On Sunday, 23 November, the RAF cadets from Cochran Field played an exhibition rugby match at the Mercer University stadium. Large numbers of people from Macon and from nearby Camp Wheeler attended, and everyone enjoyed both pre-game and halftime performances. Included activities were a U.S. Marine color guard, a U.S. Army equipment display, RAF demonstrations of British drill and music and marching by the Lanier High School band with its attractive majorettes.

During the following week, an unusual incident occurred at Cochran Field. Several months earlier, more than one thousand observers were treated to a similar display of airmanship by an American aviation cadet, but this was the first such incident at the Georgia basic flying school and the first one involving an RAF cadet. While doing some solo exercises from an auxiliary field, twenty-one-year-old LAC George Viner of Bristol (Albany, SE-42-C) struck a boundary marker with his landing gear and knocked it askew. As he was preparing to land, the damage was noticed and he was quickly warned off by radio.

An instructor then flew alongside to check the damage. Believing that a normal landing would cause the wheel and landing gear to buckle and might result in a fire, Viner was ordered to fly back to Cochran and await further instructions. It was 2:30 p.m., and the trainer's fuel tanks were at least half-full, so on arrival over the main airdrome the British cadet was told to climb to five thousand feet and continue circling in order to burn some fuel before making what would likely be a crash-landing. At about 5:00 p.m., Viner had burned most of his fuel, so he radioed for permission to land. In doing so, he followed instructions closely, landed safely on one wheel and the craft settled down and stopped undamaged. It was a good example to others of coolness under duress and putting flying instruction to use in an emergency.

Before Richard Martin had left Britain, his mother had given him the name of a Miss Ellis of Atlanta, Georgia, a university classmate in Britain. Richard wrote to Miss Ellis on Peachtree Street in Atlanta, his letter reached her and she wrote back and invited him for Sunday lunch. On Saturday, 29 November, he traveled by bus to Atlanta and arrived amidst a huge crowd of people attending Georgia's most competitive sports event, the football game between arch rivals the University of Georgia and Georgia Institute of Technology. Luckily, Martin found accommodation at the YMCA for the night in the downtown area of Atlanta. He joined a crowd to have a good look at a displayed ME-109 that had been shot down during the Battle of Britain.

Following Sunday lunch at the home of Mrs. Newman (formerly Miss Ellis), Martin was shown the sights of the *Gone with the Wind* city before catching a late afternoon bus back to Macon and Cochran Field. During his journey, Martin was both amused and shocked at the casual belligerent attitudes he encountered among many American recruits he saw. Just a few days before Pearl Harbor, they gave the impression that the United States would be in the war soon and would "win it for Britain."

Within a few days of his return to Cochran Field, Martin was excited about being involved in night, instrument and formation flying. Then, on 6 December, he and a classmate who had been invited to attend the graduation dance at Souther Field returned to that small town for a visit. Luckily, they were able to catch a ride with Flight Lieutenants J.L. Keith and Easton-Smith. On Sunday afternoon, 7 December, Martin and several friends attended a cinema in Americus, and in the middle of the picture, the manager stopped the film and came onstage to announce that the Japanese had attacked American forces in Hawaii.

Following his return to Cochran Field, security regulations were tightened and a blackout began. While he and his squadron mates were waiting in the flight line ready room a few days later, they listened to President Roosevelt's war speech on the radio. In writing to his parents about the week's activities, Martin described how strange it seemed "to be in a position to watch America going to war."

During the rush of the next several weeks at Cochran Field, there were the sounds of sirens, air raid drills and stronger station security checks. There was also pleasure to be extracted from a minor accident. Martin fell and sprained his ankle while running from the barracks to an early morning formation, so he was compelled to spend several days in the station hospital for x-rays and other tests. Although his ankle proved not to be broken, he was the envy of his barracks for being excused from physical training for a week.

During the evening of 22 December at around 7:00 p.m., the skies opened up and a deluge fell on much of the state of Georgia. During the thirty-hour period following, 2.39 inches of rain fell, flooding streets, causing automobiles to stall and washing out roads and small bridges. The Ocmulgee River rose and flooded lowlands. On the main airdrome at Cochran Field and on the auxiliary fields, ponds were created where there had been none before. Not only did the heavy rain cancel last-minute Christmas shopping, but it disrupted training schedules as well, since the condition of the landing fields contributed to the loss of at least two days of training.

As a result of this loss, the training schedule was increased immediately to seven days per week, and the student pilots were restricted to the post so as to be available for schedule changes. In describing the ensuing problem, Martin indicated that the RAF students were in a state of "near mutiny." They had been flying every day, including Saturdays and Sundays, and were now scheduled for flying on Christmas Eve and with time off on Christmas Day only until 9:00 p.m. According to Richard Martin, a number of members of Class SE-42-D who had arrived at Cochran Field on 18 December "asked to be washed out unless we got some time off and were allowed out of camp." Undoubtedly, the training officers at Cochran Field were distressed at losing training hours because now that there was a war on, it was imperative that pilots be produced in large numbers as soon as possible.

Flight Lieutenant Keith may not have been successful in gaining more leave time for the British cadets than a few more hours on Christmas Day, but even so, the RAF students scattered to many communities for the holiday. All of the RAF cadets, according to LAC John Greening, were invited out for Christmas. Martin had intended to go to Fort Benning to visit some family friends there, but because of the changed schedule decided instead to accept the invitation of the Holston family to eat Christmas dinner with them in Americus.

As Class SE-42-D continued its heavy training schedule, ground school classes and examinations for the upper class were completed, and they were now flying their final stages. One morning in January, Lieutenant Knight attended the 5:15 a.m. formation to check on attendance and found that about a dozen men from each squadron were still in bed, having dodged reveille by getting others to answer to their names. Though Martin himself was not caught, he indicated that it was a near thing, as many members of his squadron were hiding under beds and in the shower when the lieutenant came in. "Anyway," Martin reported to his parents, "after the usual row, all is back to normal and all on 0515 parade."

On Sunday night, 4 January, members of the RAF Chorus (formerly Glee Club), composed of men from Classes SE-42-C and SE-42-D, performed for a national radio program. The program was heard on the Mutual Radio Network series entitled *I Hear America Singing*. Lieutenant A.L. Huff directed the chorus and LAC William Gordon served as master of ceremonies. A special feature of the program was a bagpipe solo by LAC Duncan MacKinnon, former regimental pipe major of the King's Own Scottish Borderers. According to the newspaper, the chorus presented a program of tunes, including "Drink to Me Only With Thine Eyes," "Sweet and Low" and "All Through the Night." In addition to that special Sunday night program, the chorus presented its usual program on a local radio station that Thursday evening.

On 9 January 1942, Class SE-42-C completed their basic flying training course at Cochran Field, and most of them had now logged between 130 and 135 flying hours. In the course of their training, they had been evaluated by their instructors and were now allocated to single-engine (SE) training at Craig Field, Selma, Alabama, or twin-engine (TE) flying training schools at Maxwell Field, Montgomery, or at Napier Field, Dothan, Alabama. On Saturday morning, 10 January 1942, Class SE-42-C graduated and entered the historical record as Cochran Field's fifth graduating class and its first of 1942. Following graduation ceremonies and a dance on Saturday, 10 January, the students joined their instructors for a "bash" at the Idle Hour Country Club close by the Ocmulgee River.

Before departing the next day, several members of the class traveled to Americus to see friends and advise them of where they were being posted. On returning to the post, they packed their bags, separated to different buses according to destination and left Cochran Field. Much of the detail that Richard Martin wrote about flying training at Cochran Field would have brought many anxious nods of agreement. When Class SE-42-C departed, 3 men had been held over from Class 42-B and 9 members of 42-C were transferred to the next class for training, so the net intake was 193 students. For Class SE-42-C, 7 were eliminated and 186 graduated and moved on to one of the three advanced flying schools to which RAF student pilots were posted at that time.

As a check on the proficiency of the basic flying schools, the cadets of Class SE-42-D from the primary schools at Camden, South Carolina, and Lakeland, Florida, were switched when they were assigned to basic flying. Those from Camden went to Gunter Field, Alabama, and those from Lakeland, Florida, came to Cochran Field. The remaining 202 members of Class SE-42-D were sent from the primary schools at Albany and Americus, Georgia, and all of them arrived at Cochran Field on 19 December 1941. When Class SE-42-C departed for advanced flying school on 11 January, 9 of its former students transferred to SE-42-D, bringing its total intake to 211. As SE-42-D assumed upper-class status, Class SE-42-E arrived to commence training.

Instead of a ten-week schedule for basic training, it was now officially a nine-week one, and it was conducted on a seven-day schedule. Reginald W. Everson, who had received his primary training at Albany, Georgia, recalled many years later that "at the end of basic training on 12 February 1942, we had a thorough knowledge of aerobatics, instrument flying, night flying, formation flying and cross-country at the basic level. Without question, we had had first class instruction in military flying."

For a time, William E. "Bill" Pearce, who had graduated from the Lakeland School of Aeronautics, was a cadet lieutenant at Cochran Field and wore "a Sam Browne belt as a badge of office." However, after attending a film about VD during which his classmates howled with derision, Pierce was punished for not controlling them better. The next day, he was restricted to his room. However, since that was his twenty-first birthday, the punishment, though memorable, was not exactly the pleasant milestone in life that it might otherwise have been. Raymond George Spear, who had attended primary at Albany, Georgia, also recalled a few instances of indiscipline at Cochran Field, but more sobering events occurred when "Assistant Flight Commander Loehrke and Cadet Briers were killed; also Lt. Hardy and Cadet Thomson."

On 26 December 1941, Boxing Day, Flying Instructor Lieutenant Loehrke and twenty-one-year-old LAC John K. Briers of Alvaston, Derby, England, were killed in the crash of a Vultee BT-13 near Skipperton, Georgia, some twelve miles southeast of Macon. Witnesses to the accident indicate that the aircraft engine faltered, then stopped, and the aircraft dived into the ground from about one thousand feet. Loehrke, football letterman and mechanical engineering graduate of the University of Wisconsin, had served at Cochran Field since training began there in June 1941. Memorial services for Loehrke and Briers, a member of Class SE-42-D who had arrived at Cochran Field 18 December, were held at Cochran Field, and Briers's remains were shipped to Montgomery, Alabama, where funeral services were conducted at graveside in the Oakwood Cemetery Annex.

Exactly two weeks later, on Friday, 9 January 1942 at 4:00 p.m., Flying Instructor Lieutenant Dalton Hardy of Syracuse, New York, and twenty-seven-year-old LAC Kenneth N. Thomson of Edinburgh, Scotland, were killed when their BT-13 stalled on a landing approach and crashed in the southeastern corner of Cochran Field. These were the first two training fatalities among British cadets at Cochran Field, but unfortunately they were not the final ones.

George R. Billany recalled that Cochran Field was a military flying school and they encountered the system of inspections, demerits, extensive drill and rushing about, as well as hazing at meals. However, Billany admitted that it may have been beneficial, for "when I got my commission later in my RAF career, I feel that what we had been through gave us a certain confidence in being able to cope with harsh conditions."

Nineteen-year-old William David Parker did not complete his training at Cochran Field; he was eliminated from pilot training on 24 January 1942. "My real problem was with the course," wrote Parker. "I could fly an aeroplane O.K., but I didn't understand the mechanics of it all, nor did I relish the instrument flying or aerobatics." Parker had completed primary flying successfully and had almost finished basic flying training (he had 51 hours, 45 minutes flying at Cochran Field) for a total flying time of 111 hours, 45 minutes. From Macon, as with so many others before and after him, he was posted to Canada in order to remuster for other aircrew training.

Many British cadets kept in touch with the men who taught them to fly. Tony Mason of Weston-Super-Mare, Somerset, wrote to Stan Vossler at Lakeland, Florida, and described training at Cochran Field. After describing what it was like flying the BT-13, Mason mentioned having flown on three long cross-country trips. "When we arrive back from these long trips," he wrote, "we are in flights of six and we come over the field in trail and peel off in turn and have a 'rat dance' all over the sky that's great fun."

During the coldest weather of the year for middle Georgia, basic flying training for Class SE-42-D was drawing to a close. As they were completing their pilot training, Eastern Flying Training Command Headquarters at Maxwell Field established at Cochran Field a basic flying instructors' school. Lieutenants S.S. Riddle and C.C. Pratt were detached from school squadrons and appointed supervisors of the school. Immediately, they began to put the new officers in the rear cockpits of BT-13 trainers and emphasize the maneuvers required for instructing students.

As the new instructors' school commenced training, Class SE-42-D graduated. Since 6 members of the class were held over to Class SE-42-E for completion of their training, the net intake for Class SE-42-D totaled 205 students, of whom 2 were killed in accidents, 11 were eliminated and 192 graduated on 20 February 1942 and were posted to advanced flying schools.

The 236-member Class SE-42-E arrived at Cochran Field on 12 January 1942. The 6 students held over from SE-42-D brought their total number in training to 242. In recalling their arrival at the basic flying school, Frank W. Savage remembered that his contingent of the class traveled by army truck from Americus to Macon and "were almost red from the dust of Georgia clay roads by the time we got to Macon." Savage, who was later to marry a Georgia girl, discovered that his social life improved in Macon. He and other RAF cadets found a warm welcome among families in Macon and Fort Valley and in other small towns scattered about the region. The cadets traveled the few miles to nearby Rivoli to attend dances and other socials as guests of students at Wesleyan College. There was a mutual fascination with accents; the British cadets were drawn to the pretty girls with the warm, soft Southern accents, and the girls often remarked in their direct manner to the British cadets, "We just loooove to hear y'all tawk!"

Although Savage and many other RAF cadets expressed the view that many of their classmates were washed out because of "tough disciplinary measures taken against minor violations of the Air Cadets' honor code," no evidence was found to support the claim that there were many such failures. There were always a few students in each primary flying school class who failed for "other than flying reasons," but there is no evidence of wholesale washouts in basic flying schools. The lament that RAF cadets could not understand why flying students were punished "for not 'squaring corners' when walking or not saluting a cadet officer who a week prior was 'just another chap in our class'" is just a simple objection to the system of cadet discipline.

It is true that eighteen students were eliminated for flying deficiencies in Class SE-42-E, nine in Class SE-42-D and nineteen in Class SE-42-F. The number of RAF cadets washed out in several later classes at Cochran Field was almost equal to the combined totals for all three of these courses. For the three classes that were in training for at least part of the time in which Class SE-42-E was stationed at Cochran Field, only six students are recorded as having been washed out of training for "reasons other than flying." Although there is no way to prove that some of those students listed as eliminated for "flying deficiencies" were not washed out for other reasons, it is necessary to accept the written official records contained within the unit history, since there is no other documented source of information.

Comments from the Cochran Field unit history concerning the elimination of British cadets from pilot training deserve quoting in full:

> *Eliminations increased at a constant rate while British cadets were at this field. It is not believed due to any failure on the part of this school. It is attributed to immaturity on the*

part of many of the British students, to "over age" on the part of some, and to mechanical ineptness. This condition seemed to increase with each succeeding class of U.K. cadets.

The Cochran Field unit history also remarked that the British students "appeared always ready with excuses" and "often they would say that a particular directive or policy was 'not British.'" Such encounters were not the kinds to win friends and influence them, and they understandably irritated not only American tactical officers but American aviation cadets as well. If the latter could abide by existing regulations, it was patently unfair to give others, even guests in the country, preferential treatment by allowing them to disregard those features of training that were required of everyone else but that they deemed unpleasant or inconvenient.

Perhaps the most telling argument that British cadets had in their objections to the disciplinary elements of American aircrew training was this: "To us, there was a war on and we wanted to get our wings and get back and get on with it." American aviation cadets were likewise anxious to get their wings and get on with it, but the training system was a strenuous one designed to instill discipline and regard for safety, while at the same time training effective military pilots.

In most instances, American civilian and military flying instructors did everything in their power to give British and American cadets the benefit of the doubt and an opportunity to prove themselves. Many did just that and either completed the course or gave it up. A case in point is that of LAC W.D. Parker of Class 42-D, who was eliminated from pilot training at Cochran Field with more than 51 hours of flying the Vultee trainer and a total flying time of almost 112 hours. One has to accept Parker's verdict as to his reaction to the training. His "I wouldn't have made a good military pilot" is an acceptable argument. When Class SE-42-E completed its training on 10 March 1942, the net intake was 233. Of that number, 19 were eliminated and, after a brief leave, 214 graduated on 12 March 1942; 9 SE-42-E cadets were transferred to Class SE-42-F.

The 260-member intake of Class SE-42-F arrived at Cochran Field in late February 1942 and joined members of Class SE-42-E, who were at that time halfway through their basic flying training. When Class SE-42-E departed in mid-March 1942 for advanced training, they were replaced by Class SE-42-G, so Classes SE-42-F and SE-42-G were in training at Cochran Field during the spring of 1942 when cool nights and warm, sunny days produced a profusion of color. As the young men of these classes were trying to concentrate their efforts on flying, the chartreuse fields and hardwoods, darker green pine forests and the brown and orange ploughed fields presented colorful contrasts. Gradually, huge squares, rectangles and scattered odd-shaped peach orchards burst into giant patchworks of pink blossoms. Shortly after the peach blossoms began to fade, thousands of pecan groves began to pollinate, and the yellow dust covered everything.

LAC Phillip G. Penfold of Class 42-F traveled by train with his contingent from Lakeland to Cochran Field. Penfold later served there as a flying instructor, so he was able to view Cochran Field and its personnel from two perspectives. As a student, he remembered Major John Knight, "who ran us around a lot," but as a pilot officer/instructor, he discovered that Knight was "quite a good sort." Penfold also recalled "the usual number of cadets who died in accidents, mostly their own fault, with unauthorized flying."

Since Class SE-42-F lost five men in flying accidents, it proved to be Cochran Field's hard luck class of RAF students. On Wednesday night, 18 March 1942, twenty-five-year-old LAC John F. Latta, formerly a student at the University of Glasgow, was killed when his BT-13 crashed on Cochran Field while he was attempting a night landing. Latta's parents lived in Bombay, India, and his wife in Stevenston, Ayrshire, Scotland. A week later, on Tuesday, 24 March at around

5:00 p.m., two aircraft collided in midair some twelve miles east of Sparta, Georgia. Evidently engaged in a "rat race" chase, indications were that one aircraft chewed the tail off the other and they both crashed, killing twenty-year-old Thomas H. Hedger of Sunderland, County Durham, England, and twenty-three-year-old Richard E. "Red" Davies of Kenilworth, Warwickshire.

Two weeks after these two tragic deaths, two separate night flying accidents within about an hour claimed the lives of two additional members of Class SE-42-F. Shortly after 2:00 a.m., 11 April 1942, the BT-13 trainer being flown by twenty-year-old LAC Philip W. Winter of Gowerton, Swansea, Glamorgan, South Wales, crashed seventeen miles southeast of Macon. A little more than an hour later, thirty-year-old Wilfred J. Hawes of Hatfield Peverel, Essex, England, crashed to his death near Jeffersonville, Georgia, in another BT-13 aircraft.

While at Cochran Field, Frank Norman Bate of Class SE-42-F met a family from nearby Fort Valley and therefore had an extra morale boost from this close family relationship while undergoing the harsh discipline of basic flying school. Between June 1941 and December 1942, the Bassett family, which included Papa, Mama and daughters Marguerite, Simone, Maris and Patsy, regularly "adopted" members of every RAF class and entertained them in their large rambling home at Pineola Farm, a few miles northwest of Fort Valley.

Ralph Bassett, a Georgia native and graduate of the University of Georgia, served in France as a United States Army officer. While in the army of occupation just after the war, he met and married his wife, Henriette, in Paris, and since about 1920, they had made their home in Georgia. Mrs. Bassett, who as a girl had studied in Leicester, England, was anxious to welcome and provide true Southern hospitality to the young British students who were so far from home. When she and her husband contacted the morale officer at Cochran Field, Mrs. Bassett asked him to be sure to send any cadets from Leicestershire, where she had attended school, and that was the beginning of a long and warm relationship between an American family and dozens of British cadets.

As Norman Bate, a native of Leicester, described his experience at Pineola Farm and Cochran Field, his words give evidence of increasing maturity and obvious adjustment to his new environment:

> *How much it meant to experience a fairly well-off family in such restful surroundings, well away from the harshness of Cochran Field and the coldness of Macon city itself… Evenings on the porch were spent drinking cocktails, mint juleps, whilst from inside one heard the piano and the singing of Marise. Here I was to have my first real experience of household chores, and for this I have also been grateful, for, if need be, I am fully independent of others in the running of a home, cooking representing no problem.*
>
> *Papa Bassett wished his girls to take up professional careers as doctors or teachers. I think I have known as many as sixteen Britishers present at Pineola Farm on a single occasion or one group leaving as one arrived. Papa, whose health seemed ailing, listened intently in his room to every single news bulletin from around the world; he was a shrewd man, and a good judge of character.*
>
> *My instructors at Cochran Field were Lts. Hall and Thomas. Lt. Hall was very strict at first, but he began to soften and smoothe away his antagonisms; rumour had it that he had himself a woman to whom we were eternally grateful, for they married and went off on a honeymoon.*
>
> *In his place came Lt. Thomas, a man who, somehow, one warmed towards. He was a man who had been grounded for three weeks for low flying along a main highway, causing*

two cars to go off the road, as his wheels were touching the road heading straight towards them. I felt immediately at home with him and rapidly made up for any lost ground. He was helpful in every way, and communicated well.

My flying improved, he was not too aloof to express appreciation for a manoeuvre well done. We carried out far more exercises than within the syllabus or within the allotted time. Night flying was a headache at first, yet I was later to both enjoy it and seek it while many never came to enjoy night flying.

It was Lt. Thomas, who taught us the dividing line between ostentation and sense by flying us down railway tracks flanked by embankments and trees. With a margin of error down to a few feet when our own height was barely 10 feet above the lines, the first branches of trees being above our heads.

RAF officers played no effective role within the training, the U.S. military methods thereby were preserved, as, I believe, was the correct process. Those who objected to the system, scorned or abused it, filled me with shame at the time. In my view, they did not deserve to be present, and did not deserve to ultimately have wings pinned to their breast pockets.

Having said that, I must acknowledge that I was not without resentment myself, often feeling that I'd received demerits unjustifiably. Perhaps I'd spent hours ensuring [that] my rifle was spotless, my bed immaculately made, yet both were found to have a speck of dust or a cloth fold not "knife edge." Retrospectively, I believe the principle of nothing short of perfection had much to commend it.

The approach to perfection was also applied, but much more humanely, within the flying training itself, and it was here at Cochran Field that my instructor demonstrated the consequences contingent with any deviation from air discipline. Again, retrospectively, the combination of ground and air disciplines probably brought, at least within me, a strong consideration of Airmanship.

Flying officers of the USAAC were friendly, good humoured, helpful, and essentially human. "Penguins" (Ground officers) were remote, inflexible, stern, and unapproachable, conveying thereby the impression that we were their prisoners, though doubtless they were both human and friendly within a non-service environment. We were never to know.

Growing self-confidence released the tensions of disciplines encountered away from the aircraft environment, and, I believe, it engendered an easing of tension and authoritarian attitudes of Ground Officers. From Cochran Field, was an admixture of great sadness on leaving a disciplined, busy, well run outfit, the realization of the great love developed for our off-base friends who had made us one of the family, and the tense excitement of wondering what now lay ahead at Advanced training.

When Class SE-42-F completed basic flying training in late April 1942, 9 members had been added from the preceding class, bringing the total intake to 269. However, 14 members of Class SE-42-F were transferred to Class SE-42-G, so the net intake was 255. Of that number, 5 were killed in flying accidents, 22 were eliminated from training and 228 graduated on 30 April 1942.

RAF FORT VALLEY

On 30 March 1942, just as the pink peach blossoms were in full bloom throughout middle and south Georgia, the 286-member intake of Class SE-42-G arrived at Cochran Field and joined

Class SE-42-F, which had completed half of its basic flying training. At about the same time as the arrival of Class SE-42-G, kudzu also arrived at Cochran Field and many other airfields in Georgia. Following heavy autumn and winter rainfall, post engineers had used cement in an effort to control erosion of clay hills on the periphery of the airfield, but these efforts failed.

As a result of erosion around the cement, a decision was made to plant 186,000 crowns of kudzu to halt the erosion. That vigorous Japanese import was probably suspect at the time, but even so it was widely recognized as providing an excellent ground cover and good animal feed. The fact that kudzu put down roots some twenty feet into the earth made it an ideal erosion fighter. However, forty years later, kudzu had become a regional pest. It proved itself almost indestructable by growing strong vines twenty or more feet and climbing anything in its path, including trees, power and telephone poles and almost anything else that remained stationary long enough for its vines to take hold.

A pest of a different kind was also developing near Cochran Field. The massive permanent USAAF air depot at Warner Robins Field was being built near Wellston, Georgia, just a few miles southeast of Cochran Field. As the authorities were planning a housing project for military and civilian employees of that important post, a nuisance was developing directly across the highway. The commander of Warner Robins Field described the "honky tonk" community as large enough to "put Coney Island to shame." "People out there," he continued, "have gone hog wild, and something has to be done to bring the situation under control."

Similar establishments were developing near Macon and most other towns that had military stations, but local authorities generally tightened law enforcement only after complaints came from military authorities and responsible citizens. Even so, honky tonks or beer joints continued to flourish, but few of the RAF cadets ever visited one, most likely because they never had time. At Cochran Field, concern was with completing the nine-week flying training course on schedule, so it was rush! rush! rush! and little time for anything else.

Within a week after the arrival of the new RAF class at Cochran Field, Flying Instructor John B. Hoffman and twenty-year-old LAC Geoffrey Holmes were killed in a flying accident. At about 2:30 p.m. Wednesday, 6 May 1942, their BT-13 crashed about one mile northeast of Byron, Georgia. Hoffman was a native of Columbus, Ohio; Holmes hailed from Wakefield, Yorkshire, and had attended Durham University. Memorial services were conducted for the two fliers at Cochran Field, and Holmes's body was shipped to Montgomery for burial there in the Oakwood Cemetery Annex. Fortunately, this was the only Class SE-42-G fatality at Cochran Field. Sadly, that was not the case with those assigned to Gunter Field, Alabama, and news of a tragic series of night crashes that killed seven RAF cadets at that station disturbed Cochran students some two weeks later.

By May, there were at least twenty RAF instructors assigned to Cochran Field and they rendered excellent service, especially in dealing with the RAF cadets, but two of them had some difficulty with an out of place reptile. Pilot officer/instructors Peter A. Morgan and Alfred A. Cross, both former Class SE-42-B students at Camden and Cochran Field, had taken off in a Vultee BT-13 when Cross called the Cochran Control Tower and announced that they were "coming in for an emergency landing. Snake in plane. That is all."

The aircraft did land safely. It quickly taxied to the paved ramp, and the two pilots hurriedly got out of the aircraft. A thorough search was made of the front and rear cockpits, and ground crew finally found and removed a bull snake that was coiled around wires behind the instrument panel. Since Cochran aircraft had covered canopies and were parked outside much of the time, it is likely that the snake had simply climbed up a wheel and an oleo strut and found a way into the aircraft. Fortunately, such incidents were rare; the nerves would not take too many.

Another member of Class SE-42-G was LAC Michael Rennie, the British actor, and he took considerable ribbing when a movie was shown at the Cochran Field post theatre. The movie was entitled *Ships with Wings*, and Rennie starred in the film as one of the ace pilots. At Cochran Field, he had not yet gotten quite that far with his flying. Ultimately, Rennie completed training at Cochran Field, did his twin-engine advanced training at Moody Field, Valdosta, and returned to the United Kingdom. Although it could not be confirmed, it was reported that owing to a surplus of pilots he was released from flying in 1943 and assigned to make war films. While he was in Macon, he was naturally very popular and was constantly invited to dances and other socials. Quite naturally, the people associated with Macon's Little Theater anxiously sought his opinions of their productions.

Another member of the class was Edgar Lancelot Spridgeon, who had completed his primary flying training at Lakeland, Florida. Spridgeon recalled leaving Lakeland by train and arriving the next morning at Cochran Field. In describing the intensive training schedule, he wrote, "A typical day was to get up at 6 a.m., breakfast, drill, P.T., ground school, lunch, flight line 1.0 to 6.0 p.m., parade for lowering the flag, dinner, study period in our barracks and in bed by 9.45 p.m." In describing the clothing issue for the spring of 1942, Spridgeon indicated that each RAF cadet received "3 pairs khaki trousers, 3 khaki shirts, 8 prs. socks, 6 vests, 6 prs. underpants, 2 belts, 2 prs. brown shoes…It was much better suited to the climate than RAF blue," he continued, "and much smarter than the khaki we had been given at Heaton Park. We wore RAF blue forage caps and black ties, which identified us as RAF. The U.S. cadets wore khaki ties and caps."

As with most of the British cadets, Spridgeon did some sightseeing during his end-of-course leave in late May. The English-Speaking Union in Atlanta had indicated a willingness to entertain 150 British cadets during the weekend of 29 May through 1 June 1942. As a result, Spridgeon and others traveled to Atlanta by coach, spent Friday night in the YMCA and were taken to Grant Park to see the large circular painting (cyclorama) of the Battle of Atlanta and other sights.

At the end of the day, they were delivered over to Atlanta families. As Edgar Spridgeon described it,

> At about 5.30 p.m., we were driven to meet our hosts and found ourselves with a family living in a house which was quite palatial. We spent two nights with them living in a luxurious style and really enjoyed our stay. The hospitality was most generous and we were told that when we wanted to come to stay again, just to send a postcard. We were made to compile a list of items, which would be appreciated by our fiancées and several parcels of "goodies" (cosmetics, silk stockings, etc.) were sent. We certainly learned the meaning of "Southern Hospitality."

No doubt, other members of the RAF contingent visiting Atlanta received an equally hospitable welcome during that late spring weekend leave before departure from Cochran Field for advanced flying schools.

Since Class SE-42-G received 14 students held over from 42-F and also had 14 students held over, the two canceled each other, and the net intake for the course remained 286. Since most of the members of this RAF class had undergone a "flight grading" course in Britain, its high record of eliminees might appear surprising. However, the number of eliminees is understandable when it is recalled that flight grading courses were conducted in winter at scattered airfields in the United Kingdom, and the RAF students often spent several weeks acquiring the requisite number of flying hours. Grading courses would improve in time, but the first two courses were severely hampered by weather conditions, especially on more northerly airfields. Of the 286 student pilots, 41 were eliminated, 1 was killed in training and 244 graduated on 2 June 1942 and were posted to advanced flying schools.

Class SE-42-H, the 288-member largest and final all-RAF Arnold Scheme course, arrived at Cochran Field on 1 May 1942. The several classes following it would be about two-thirds British cadets and one-third American aviation cadets. LAC Anthony V. Rippengal and many of his classmates found Macon less friendly than Albany and, when there was time, naturally gravitated back to the site of their primary training and early friendships. As with the preceding contingent from Darr Aero Tech, Rippengal and his SE-42-H classmates traveled the dusty roads from Albany to Cochran Field by army truck, and on arrival found discipline much looser than it had been in the past.

Whether the credit was merited or not, Rippengal felt that their immediate predecessors, Class SE-42-G, had been a moderating influence on the training staff at Cochran Field. "As we spent the first month in company with 42-G," Rippengal wrote, "we too benefited from their new status and thus were able to watch with much more equanimity as our American counterparts were put through the hoop!" Rippengal's assertion about easier discipline being permitted for Class SE-42-G and its companion course could not be substantiated. However, there is no reason to doubt him either. Indeed, it may well be that this "experiment" helped to convince USAAF authorities to do away with the hazing system and modify its disciplinary code officially some three months later.

William H. Gordon, who was also trained at Albany, Georgia, later became a career RAF officer. In looking back on what he judged to be the excellent training he received while in the United States, he pointed out that since total blackout conditions in the United States were impossible, criticism of the system of navigation and night flying training was "unfair due to the conditions obtaining." Applicable as well was the philosophy underlying particular training systems. The three-phase system of flying training in the United States aimed to produce qualified pilots with a very strong emphasis on safety. In two hundred flying hours in progressively more complicated aircraft, student pilots were expected to master the technique of flying increasingly more powerful airplanes in every conceivable attitude.

In the interest of safety, many things were done by the wartime training commands of all nations that were not deemed possible under combat conditions. As Gordon insisted, it may well have been "a mistake to use high-powered floodlights to illuminate runways for night landings." However, as he rightly concluded, the aim of the United States Air Training Command was not to duplicate combat conditions during the first two hundred hours of flying but to teach the safe handling and use of military aircraft under a variety of conditions. When students were assigned to operational aircraft, they quickly applied techniques they had already learned, but they would of course be expected to adapt to different types of aircraft as well as to changed flying conditions in the part of the world in which they were serving. As every aircrew learned early on in his career, training was continuous.

United States Army Air Forces officers learned a great deal from the Royal Air Force, but by mid-1942 they had begun to learn much from their own combat experience. Before that time, USAAF training officers bent to RAF pressure and modified their flying training syllabus in an effort to produce sufficient pilots for the prosecution of global war. In accordance with the RAF pilot training syllabus, American flying training was reduced from thirty to twenty-seven weeks (from three ten-week phases to three nine-week ones, sometimes even less), night flying was introduced in primary flying schools and a number of maneuvers were cut from each phase. Although experienced training officers argued in favor of teaching student pilots every maneuver and recovery technique for virtually every type of stall or spin, they had no choice but to yield to the strong pressures for modifying wartime syllabi and leaving many things for tactical squadrons to teach the young pilots.

As would be later discovered in analyzing the use of aircraft in operations against the Axis powers, the ability to apply air power according to the body of theory that had developed over the preceding thirty years did not exist until 1944–45. That same conclusion applied to flying training as well. Most experienced flying training officers were well aware in 1941 of what was needed for the "ideal flying training program," but neither the aircraft, training simulators nor instructors were available in sufficient numbers to make the ideal a reality. As a result, it was necessary to improvise constantly until it was possible to achieve something akin to the ideal. For example, it had been widely recognized since about 1938 that the Link Trainer simulator was ideal for teaching instrument flying, but until 1943 there were not enough such simulators available.

Until the supply could be increased, available Link Trainers were divided between flying schools in Canada, the United Kingdom, the British flying training schools in the United States and the USAAF basic and advanced schools. During 1941–42, while RAF Arnold Scheme students were in training in the SEACTC, there was such a shortage of simulators at Cochran Field and other schools that shifts were maintained, and students often completed scheduled Link Trainer hours late at night. The supply remained so limited that primary schools were unable to obtain the simulators until the summer of 1942.

By late 1943 and early 1944 simulators were installed in auxiliary field stage houses at many schools and in transit camps such as those at Moncton and Halifax, or wherever qualified pilots and navigators spent any time awaiting further training or combat assignments. New simulators designed to teach the GEE and H2S navigation techniques and to simulate actual combat conditions were developed by Britain, but were available only in limited quantities until much later in the war.

During the 1939–45 war, the arts of navigation and meteorology, which were interwoven and inseparably dependent upon each other, remained in a state of flux. Since neither was yet an exact science, they could not be better than the knowledge and theory underpinning them. One of the great failures in these two important areas was the lack of standard terminology for use on maps and aerial charts and in teaching use of the same terms to American and British airmen alike. Since no such standardization of terminology occurred, British pilots discovered, sometimes to their detriment, that having learned a particular system in training and in practice, they had not learned enough about variations that existed in different parts of the world.

Many young airmen discovered on operations in more "exotic" parts of the world that reliable charts were not always available, nor was there an easy means of learning essential details and dangers. Beginning aircrew did not yet have sufficient experience to realize that most such knowledge usually was purchased at the cost of human lives and aircraft. Cautionary notes that were blandly disseminated in briefings or through notations on charts often emanated from accidents involving the loss of life and aircraft, knowledge of which was uncovered through the thorough and painstaking labors of dozens of accident investigating teams. Even though improved aerial charts for many areas of the world that had never before been properly charted were finally devised during 1939–45, there were still things to be learned.

Even though rendered more than forty years afterward, Bill Gordon's linkage of training and service flying in a war zone are of particular value:

> In Georgia, magnetic variation was zero, whilst in the U.K., it was around 14 degrees, if I recall correctly. Thus, having measured the true track required to get from A to B in Georgia, I applied a wind correction factor and flew the subsequent calculated course. On my return to the U.K., however, I was to get temporarily lost a number of times before it dawned on me that I had to take magnetic variation into account when calculating my required course. In Georgia, meteorological data was fairly reliable, so applying the wind factor to one's course calculations was no problem.
>
> However, in Britain, forecasting was notoriously inaccurate and winds were constantly shifting, so pinpoints were vital to check one's track. Also, map reading in Georgia was very easy with mostly clear weather and easily identified landmarks, while in the U.K., the surfeit of detail, the large number of built up areas, railroads, rivers, etc., and the usually inclement weather created problems.
>
> Theory of Flight was not taught at all as far as I can recall, and this, I believe, caused my subsequent downfall. In 1945, when I was flying a four-engine York Transport aircraft on 3 engines, I may have failed to appreciate the dangers involved due to lack of directional control at a low airspeed, and ended up by crashing at night into the New Forest. The details of this accident were, as far as I know, never fully established, but from subsequent training I received on asymmetric flying I have to conclude that my airspeed was too low to maintain directional control of the aircraft.
>
> I now firmly believe that had I had adequate training in the principles of flight and asymmetric flying, this accident would not have happened. In all fairness though, maybe the RAF should also have given me this training when I converted onto four-engine aircraft; in fact, they subsequently did at the Central Flying School when I did another instructor's course, but it was a bit too late then.

Apparently, theory of flight was a normal and regular part of aircrew training curricula before and during the war in both USAAF and RAF schools. However, it is likely that during the period of 1942–43, when training was intensified at every stage, the subject was not emphasized to the same degree at training stations and in operational squadrons.

Class SE-42-H was undergoing basic flying training during the late spring, one of the most beautiful periods of the year in the Southeastern United States. However, the same warming conditions that produced a profusion of trees, flowers and shrubs also produced cold and warm air masses that clashed high above the entire region, spawning thundershowers and electrical storms with a fair degree of regularity. Cochran Field cadets who read local newspapers learned that seven RAF student pilots from Gunter Field died in aircraft accidents during a south Alabama storm. At the same time, they learned that a farmer near Dublin, Georgia, was killed by lightning, and the next afternoon another farmer in the same county was caught in the fields during a storm and was also struck by lightning and killed. All of these weather changes affected flying training, but as soon as the storms passed flying was resumed.

At about 10:00 p.m., Tuesday evening, 2 June 1942, a Vultee BT-13 with Instructor RAF Pilot Officer John J. Mulrooney and LAC B. Dix was evidently taking off from Harris Field near Fort Valley, Georgia, when the plane slammed into an automobile parked on the periphery of the airfield. The auto contained five people, two adults and three children. Mulrooney and Dix received slight abrasions in the accident, and the three children who were passengers in the automobile were also slightly injured. However, Mrs. Avis McDonald, manager of Fort Valley's telegraph office and driver of the car, was killed outright, and Maurice Jones, a passenger in the automobile, was seriously injured and died in a Macon hospital four days later.

Within twenty-four hours of the first accident, another occurred near Harris Field that took the life of LAC Arthur W. Wakley. Investigating officers were unsure of the cause of the accident, but it probably resulted from failure to properly adjust the propeller pitch. The twenty-year-old Wakley of Bournemouth, Hampshire, was on a routine solo flight when his aircraft crashed about a half-mile south of Harris Auxiliary Field. As with other Cochran Field fatalities, following memorial services at Cochran Field, Wakley's body was shipped to Montgomery, Alabama, for interment in the RAF plot in Oakwood Cemetery Annex.

Since Class SE-42-H received 14 students who were transferred from Class SE-42-G and itself had 14 students held over, the numbers canceled each other, and the net intake remained 288. Of that number, 45 were eliminated from pilot training, 1 was killed and 242 graduated on 4 July 1942. Since there had been a steady increase in the number of eliminees among the British cadets, there was great concern among Cochran Field training officers and instructors over the high elimination rate.

With the arrival at Cochran Field of Class SE-42-I on 3 June 1942, British and American cadets were mixed again at Cochran Field for the first time since Class SE-42-A followed as the junior class five weeks behind Class SE-41-I. Slightly more than 100 American cadets joined 190 British cadets at Cochran Field. More than forty years later, Oliver Villiers Brooks recalled his memorable arrival at Cochran Field from Darr Aero Tech. He instinctively liked the American aviation cadets and felt that USAAF discipline was harder on them than on the RAF cadets. He found the schedule of seven days' duty and one day off difficult to adjust to, but since there was plenty of flying, few people objected. That is what they were there for.

While doing some night flying, Brooks made a mistake that could easily have cost his life, but he managed to catch it in time. He "failed to do a proper cockpit check and did not go into fine pitch (propeller adjustment)" until his BT-13 had used about two-thirds of the runway. A quick adjustment was made, but he barely "scraped over the trees at the end (Luckily, I was not seen)." Brooks found discipline at Cochran Field "pretty ruthless." However, it was worth it to suffer virtually anything for the chance to fly. After Class SE-42-I had been training at Cochran Field for four and a half weeks, Class SE-42-H departed for advanced flying school postings and Class SE-42-J arrived to commence training. New Class SE-42-I officers who were appointed included Cadet Major R.L.W. Cheek, group commander, and Squadron Captains W.A. Molyneux, A.G.J. Taylor, R.M. Goodwin and W.N. Roberts.

Another class member, Douglas A. Boards, who later won a much deserved DFM with RAF Bomber Command, recalled his basic flying training. He found the barracks with their arrangement of three cadets to a well-furnished room comfortable but hot, and he found the local population anxious to entertain RAF cadets. "On open post," he wrote, "a line of people in cars would be outside the camp gates to 'snare' U.K. cadets as they came out!" Boards did not particularly care for the demerit system and during his stay at Cochran Field, he walked

"6–7 tours during off duty time." Regardless of the heat and the discipline, Boards enjoyed both ground school and flying.

H. Nevil Mottershead had a similar experience at Cochran Field. He and his contingent arrived from Lakeland, Florida, by train on 2 June 1942. His instructors were RAF Pilot Officer T.J. Parry and American Lieutenants Golinsky and Black, and Captain James T. Patterson gave him his army check ride. Mottershead completed fifteen hours on the Link Trainer, which he "put to good use when we began 'beam flying.'" All in all, he enjoyed the intensive training. Since the summer of 1942 in Georgia was unusually hot, Mottershead learned of a nearby lake where he went during his first day off.

After swimming a while, he began to walk back toward Macon when he was "overtaken by an automobile, which stopped, and the driver, a young lady, asked in a gorgeous Georgia accent, 'You want a ride into town?'" Mottershead gratefully accepted the offer, the driver and a girlfriend introduced themselves and the Briton accepted an invitation to go home with the driver. They drove past Cochran Field, the car pulled up at a white house among the trees and Mottershead was introduced to the girl's mother. In his words, it was the "beginning of a wonderful friendship." The Georgia family "adopted" Nevil.

For the remaining weeks Mottershead remained at Cochran Field, he spent as much time as possible visiting his new friends. On occasion, when he could not leave the post, his friend delivered "either a bag of peaches or a watermelon" to the Cochran Field gate for Mottershead and his classmates. During his final evening at Cochran Field, the RAF cadet had dinner with the family and spent the night in their home. The next day, he joined his classmates for the trip to the USAAF advanced flying school at Moody Field near Valdosta, Georgia.

A week after his departure from Cochran Field, "a telegram arrived telling me that my friend was dead and that the funeral was the next day." Owing to his training schedule, Mottershead could not obtain permission to get back in time for the funeral, but he did get a short leave two days later and returned to the home of his adoptive family. He persuaded the driver to let him off the bus at the driveway entrance on the highway, and walked the remaining yards for "a sad return to some people who had given me much happiness." The one of the gorgeous Georgia accent was no more.

There were other tragedies. On 7 July, two USAAF officers were killed in a crash at Fort Valley's Harris Auxiliary Field. Then, in the early hours of 8 July 1942, Pilot Officer Eric J. Holman and twenty-one-year-old LAC Eric W.F. Charrosin of Upper Norwood, Surrey, crashed at the same auxiliary field. Holman received only slight lacerations, but LAC Charrosin was critically injured and sent to the Camp Wheeler military hospital. Ten days later, Charrosin died at the army hospital from the effects of his injuries, and his remains were shipped to Montgomery, Alabama, for funeral services and burial in the RAF plot in the Oakwood Cemetery Annex.

The 190-man RAF intake received 14 RAF transfers from Class SE-42-H, so the total RAF enrollment for Class SE-42-I climbed to 204. However, since 10 members of the class were held over to subsequent courses for the completion of training, the net intake was 194 RAF students. Of this number, 1 was killed, 13 were eliminated and 180 graduated with their American classmates on 6 August 1942.

On Friday, 3 July 1942, at almost the same time that some of the surviving members of Class SE-42-F graduated, Class SE-42-J completed their primary flying course at four USAAF civil contract primary schools and traveled to either Gunter or Cochran Fields. The large class that arrived at Cochran Field contained 186 British cadets and 117 USAAF aviation cadets, a total of 303 students.

At the time of their arrival on the station, summer heat was at its peak and construction on the most recent expansion of the school was being completed. A swimming pool was being constructed in a grove of pines to the rear of the officers' club and was to be opened in mid-July. Until other pools could be built, arrangements were being made to divide the daily schedule in such a way that officers, cadets and enlisted men could use the pool at different times. On the field were 198 Vultee BT-13 trainers and 157 instructors, including about 40 RAF pilot officers.

As the men of SE-42-J commenced training and adjusted to the new station, changes were taking place all around them. Lieutenant Colonel Caspar P. West, who had served as director of training since Cochran Field opened, was posted to Bainbridge, Georgia, to assume command of that new USAAF basic flying school in southwest Georgia, and Captain James T. Patterson replaced him at Cochran Field. By 18 July, the Cochran Field swimming pool was being used, and the two huge mess halls on station had been redecorated. In Mess No. 1 the cadets were permitted to view the blue ceiling with twenty-two silhouettes of the latest enemy aircraft. They now had an excellent opportunity to practice aircraft identification.

On 22 July 1942, Major General Barton K. Yount and a large party arrived in a C-47 Dakota transport and made an inspection tour of Cochran Field. It is unknown if there was any significance attached to the visit, but General Yount, commanding general of the Air Training Command with headquarters in Fort Worth, Texas, made his inspection at the very time that an announcement was made bringing to an end RAF training in the United States. Public relations officers at Cochran Field announced prematurely that the "present class of RAF youths would be the last to train here." The classes in training when the announcement was made included SE-42-J and SE-42-K.

According to an Associated Press announcement of Thursday evening, 23 July 1942, the Air Ministry in London and the War Department in Washington simultaneously announced that RAF cadet training was being shifted to the dominions in order to "make way for the rapidly increasing numbers of American aviation cadets." Evidently in answer to questions concerning whether all RAF training was ending in the United States, a USAAF press release of 5 August indicated that except for two British flying training schools to be taken over by the USAAF, the others would continue to operate.

When Class SE-42-I graduated during the first week of August, Class SE-42-J moved to upper-class status and within a few days Class SE-42-K arrived on station. Then in the latter part of August, as Class SE-42-J was completing its flying training, two accidents in rapid succession marred the class's record. On Saturday afternoon, 29 August 1942, LAC George E. Parsons of Norwich, Norfolk, England, was seriously injured in a plane crash near Cochran Field and was hospitalized. Not too long afterward, LAC Eric J. Reid of London parachuted to safety from another aircraft. Fortunately, no one was killed in either accident.

Of the 186-man class RAF intake, an additional 10 were added from those held over from the preceding class. Since Class SE-42-J also had 10 students held over, the net intake was 186, of whom 11 were eliminated and 165 RAF men graduated during the first week of September and departed Cochran Field for advanced flying schools on Sunday, 6 September 1942. Of their 117 American classmates, 4 were held over, 8 were eliminated and 105 graduated.

On 6 August 1942, the 184-man British pilot trainee intake with 122 American aviation cadets of Class SE-42-K joined the 10 students held over from the preceding class. Since the class had 13 RAF students held over to subsequent classes for training, the net intake was 181 RAF cadets and 122 American cadets. Several changes were implemented during the nine weeks Class SE-42-K was undergoing training at Cochran Field. Competition increased for aircrew training in the United States, and owing to reports from war fronts of the need for greater stamina and discipline among aircrew, renewed emphasis was once more placed on military and physical training. As a result, training standards were restored to what they had been with the earlier classes.

Official orders were issued requiring extensive physical training for all personnel on every USAAF station. Instead of relying on profits from post exchange sales as a means for financing swimming pools and purchasing athletic equipment, as had been done in the past, military appropriations paid for improvements. At Cochran Field and other military stations, this order made significant amounts of money available for building swimming pools and obstacle courses and purchasing equipment for archery, tennis, fencing, basketball, volleyball, baseball and rugby football.

The teaching of self-discipline and unit discipline came from military drill and ceremonies through the subordination of selfish desires to the common good. The underlying principle behind this time-honored tradition was that before it was possible for an officer or noncommissioned officer to give orders and command respect, he had first to learn to take orders and respond to them properly. Although they generally never liked it, most men who served in the armed forces of any nation learned early that close order drill and military ceremonies helped to develop unit and individual self-discipline, and aided in building *esprit de corps* and individual morale. Perhaps the most important point was that responses to drill were automatic and not subject to debate.

Colin Armstrong of Class SE-42-K completed his primary training at Albany, Georgia, and later became a career RAF officer. Armstrong recalled that on arrival at Cochran Field, he and his classmates were informed that they were now in a military environment and that discipline was the rule rather than the exception. "We were told," he wrote more than forty years later, "that we thought we were hot stuff because we had gone solo, so for the first few days this cockiness was going to be knocked out of us." And so it was. It was double time, change clothes, drill, double time some more and run, run, run! "Our haircuts," Armstrong insisted, "received whether we needed them or not, would have made the Beatles cry."

Whereas a few differences had been made with some classes in the past, absolutely no differences were now permitted in treatment of British or American cadets. Most of the three-bunk barracks cadet rooms were allocated to an American aviation cadet, a British aviation cadet and an American aviation student. Since about 1940, the United States had been training navigators, bombardiers and gunners who were awarded the rank of staff sergeant on graduation. In 1941, pilot training was opened to enlisted men who had the health and aptitude, but not the cadet's minimum educational requirement of two years' college. Aviation students who were trained as pilots usually graduated as staff sergeants, later flight officers, but much later most of them won commissions. "At first, we resented being split from the friends we had made," Armstrong wrote, "but we soon realized the benefits." Since they were allies in this global war, it was good that they were learning more about "each other's countries and customs."

In describing the reactions of British cadets to American military regulations and the Aviation Cadet Honor Code, Armstrong was specific about RAF cadets' objections. "All we wanted to do," Armstrong asserted, "was learn to fly and get back home; what fools we were!" Everything was indeed pushed harder during the first month of basic training, then for the remaining weeks, there was a general easing of discipline but not of standards. "It was all hard work but great fun," Armstrong concluded.

At the end of the basic flying course Armstrong and his classmates received several days' leave. Many of the young men traveled back to the site of their primary training to visit old friends there. According to their means, others either hitchhiked or rode coaches to Miami, New Orleans or Atlanta, and some of them were entertained by people they had met during the course of their training. For example, the Kiwanis Club representing membership from the small towns of Gray and Haddock had sponsored a steak supper and party on Saturday night, 12 September at Lake Jonesco, some miles north of Macon. Many students who had gained friends from that evening social, as well as from other evenings and weekends in Macon and neighboring towns, were drawn back to those friends before departing for advanced schools.

Armstrong and several other class members hitched rides to Atlanta and enjoyed the hospitality of Mr. and Mrs. E.R. Smith of Superior Avenue, Decatur. Sadly, in 1943, Armstrong was to learn that the Smiths' son was killed in a flying training accident while undergoing USAAF pilot training and Armstrong's brother, a navigator on a Lancaster bomber, was killed on operations over Germany. It was such continuing sacrifices in both countries that welded permanent bonds of friendship and respect.

John Lilley, another member of Class SE-42-K who received his primary flying training at Albany, Georgia, also remembered that "it was a shock to find ourselves doing 6 hours of drill in the first two days at Cochran." He also remembered that many RAF students were "generally rather rebellious" about the discipline.

> Our American colleagues counseled caution as they seemed to have been expecting it and understood it. So far as the RAF men were concerned, it was the sort of thing Guards Regiments went in for rather than air forces, and our hearts were never in it…However, students learned to adapt to the situation and stagger from one crisis to another, but eventually they developed a number of strategies to keep crisis at bay.

Crises outside the realm of training understandably captured their attention and made them long to complete training as soon as possible so as to be able to join the war effort. Of special importance in August 1942 were the disastrous Canadian commando raid at Dieppe on the coast of France and continued depressing reports coming from the India-Burma frontier and from the western border of Egypt at a small railway station called El Alamein. Of importance as well in August 1942 was the news of fighting on the Eastern Front around Leningrad and close by Stalingrad, far to the southeast of Moscow. The American cadets were excited about news of the naval and air battle at Midway, the marine invasion of the Solomon Islands and the continued Allied buildup in Australia and New Guinea.

A darker tragedy worked itself out within about four days in late August 1942. Although it did not directly affect flying training at Cochran Field, it captured the attention of everyone living in the region. In an attempt to arrest an AWOL black soldier at the Macon bus station on Friday, 21 August 1942, a white policeman was killed and a black military policeman and another black soldier were injured. The AWOL soldier fled, and there was great excitement during the ensuing manhunt. City officials were anxious to avert a worse disaster, so efforts were rushed to capture the fugitive. Emotions were evidently at fever pitch as whites excitedly condemned the killing of a "white man," and African Americans, necessarily, were on the defensive against possible violent acts against them as individuals or as groups. Carloads of officers raced about streets and country roads, and bloodhounds coursed fields and woods searching for the soldier. "With the exception of a small quickly improvised fiery cross burning atop Reservoir hill, overlooking the city, at 1:45 a.m., Friday," reported the *Macon Telegraph*, "there was no outward demonstration." The fugitive was captured within three days, jailed and later tried and sentenced.

During September 1942, there was a USO program and a war bond drive in Macon, which deflected attention away from the recent tragedy. Near the middle of the month, plans were laid for a huge USO show to be presented at Camp Wheeler for military personnel stationed in the region. In the course of that show, theatrical history was made when Arthur "Harpo" Marx was reported to have spoken for the first time ever in a theatrical performance. Other performances were presented at Cochran Field on Sunday evening, 19 September.

Ten days later, near the end of September, two events disturbed the relative tranquility of the city. In the early morning hours of 29 September 1942, one of the most dramatic fires in Macon's history destroyed the Biltmore Apartments in the heart of the business district of the city. A few hours later, an attractive young actress arrived in Macon and focused the attention of the citizens on war bonds. Veronica Lake, the tiny blonde actress who in 1941 had starred in the aviation movie *I Wanted Wings*, was engaged in an exhausting schedule of personal appearances, and appeared at most cities where extensive air training was going on. At Macon, Miss Lake stayed at the Dempsey Hotel and was escorted about the city and the military posts during her work promoting the sale of war bonds.

As the members of Class SE-42-K finished their flying training and departed on leave before returning to pack and depart for advanced flying schools, Macon held a different kind of celebration. A street dance was held on Friday night, 2 October, in honor of middle Georgia heroines and heroes, including native son Colonel Robert L. Scott, who was building an enviable combat record as a fighter pilot in the skies over Burma and China. Of Class SE-42-K's 181-man net RAF enrollment at Cochran Field, 25 were eliminated and 156 graduated on 10 October 1942. Of the 122 American cadets, 4 were held over, 17 were eliminated and 100 graduated with their British classmates.

The 196 British members and the 158 American members of Class SE-43-A arrived at Cochran Field from primary schools at Americus, Georgia, and Tuscaloosa, Alabama, on 7–8 September 1942. They were joined by 17 students (13 UK and 4 U.S.) held over from the preceding class and these additions brought the total enrollment to 209 UK and 162 U.S. cadets.

LAC Joe Hitchman of Class SE-43-A, who completed his primary training at Americus, Georgia, recalled that Mr. H.T. Connor of Macon befriended him and his friend Len Dorman. Mr. Connor regularly met them on their days off, treated them to a movie and hospitality and delivered them back to the camp with a bag of fruit. Although many British cadets objected to olives, peanut butter and sweet potatoes as part of their diet, Hitchman recalled that "food on all of the stations could only be described as excellent."

Just after Class SE-43-A arrived at Cochran Field, Colonel William W. Welsh, commanding the Southeast Air Corps Training Center, made an important announcement. Welsh indicated that the United States Army Air Forces were not working to any quota system for cadet promotions to second lieutenant or flight officer or for the different aircrew categories such as pilot, navigator, bombardier, etc. Aviation cadets would be eliminated only for demonstrating a lack of ability in ground school and flying training, not for disciplinary reasons.

Whether this announcement was made in response to criticisms or was simply intended to reassure and boost the morale of aviation cadets and aviation students is unknown. Although records indicate that most of the young men expelled from pilot training were eliminated for flying deficiences, Colonel Welsh's announcement implied that at least until September 1942, some such flying deficiency eliminations may well have been made for disciplinary reasons.

Near the end of their course at Cochran Field, RAF and American cadets were entertained at a tea held at the Christ Church Episcopal Church Parish House. The Macon Bundles for Britain organization helped sponsor the tea; they also persuaded girls from Wesleyan College to attend, and again many cadets traveled to Atlanta and elsewhere during their short leaves before traveling to the advanced flying schools.

When Class SE-43-A departed on 11 November 1942, Class SE-43-C replaced them at Cochran Field and Class SE-43-B, the final RAF class at Cochran Field, moved to upper-class status. Since 16 (8 UK and 8 U.S.) cadets were held over to subsequent classes for training, the net RAF intake for Class SE-43-A was 201, and the net U.S. intake for the class was 154. Of the British net enrollment, 23 were eliminated and 178 men graduated around 11 November 1942, while 9 Americans were eliminated, 1 American cadet was killed in a flying accident and 144 graduated.

The intake for the final Arnold Scheme course of RAF student pilots totaled 226, to which was added the 8 students held over from 43-A, raising the total to 234. Since 5 of these students were held over and subsequently posted to Gunter Field to complete their basic flying training, the net RAF intake for Class SE-43-B was 229 RAF cadets and 124 American cadets. During the early autumn of 1942 while the final two RAF classes were in training at Cochran Field, the basic flying school was reorganized. The eight squadrons at the school were designated Flights A through H, and two flights were attached to each Cochran Field school squadron. Each flight commander had an assistant flight commander and 13 or 14 instructors, and each instructor was generally assigned 8 students.

Each of the flying schools was once more being expanded. By November 1942, more than 750 students were in training at Cochran Field, and there were 205 aircraft and 127 flight instructors stationed at the field. In addition to the three auxiliary fields that had been in use for some time, two additional auxiliaries were added during the summer of 1942. Moreover, the addition of stage houses, lights and radio communication at Byron and Myrtle Fields improved safety considerably. Now the main airdrome and these two well-equipped satellite airfields could be used for night flying exercises to prevent excessive congestion in the air space surrounding the main airdrome.

On Wednesday, 2 December 1942, following storms over different parts of Georgia, tornadoes were spawned and came to earth in north Georgia directly along the path used by Cochran Field students on their long-distance cross-country flights to Greenwood and Anderson, South Carolina. Considerable damage was done in Washington, Georgia, and five people were killed in Lincolnton. High winds ranging upward of two hundred miles an hour ripped up huge trees, damaged roofs and chimneys of houses and industrial plants and injured numerous people at Millen as well as near Dublin and Wrightsville.

A few days before Class SE-43-B graduated, many cadets from Cochran Field attended the Grand Theater in Macon to see a motion picture about the training of RAF pilots. The script for *Thunderbirds*, a film about pilot training that starred Edward G. Robinson and Richard Attenborough, was written and produced by Lamar Trotti, formerly a resident of Macon. A part of the motion picture was filmed at Falcon Field, Mesa, Arizona, and in return for the use of that British flying training school and a number of its RAF cadets in the film, a swimming pool was presented to the school by the film company. Among the young RAF men who saw the film in Macon were two RAF cadets who had "starred" in it. Evidently, Charles Lyon of Yorkshire and Nikolai Schwartz of London had been in training at Falcon Field when the film was made, were subsequently eliminated from pilot training there and were transferred to Class SE-43-B to complete their flying training with Arnold Scheme Class SE-43-B.

On Thursday evening, 10 December 1942, before the final RAF class departed, Macon's Bundles for Britain organization entertained the British cadets with a dance at the Idle Hour Country Club. Within a week following the departure of that final RAF class, officers at Cochran Field held a farewell dinner for Flight Lieutenant J. Leonard Keith, MBE. Except for a brief period during which Keith conducted a group of pilots and other aircrew back to the United Kingdom, he had been a RAF administrative officer since June 1941 at the primary school at Camden, South Carolina, and at Cochran Field. Subsequently, Group Captain C.E. Maude of the RAF Delegation in Washington wrote to the chairman and members of the organization expressing appreciation for their "providing entertainment and recreation for the RAF cadets during their stay in Macon."

Of the net intake of 229 for the final British class at Cochran Field, 41 were eliminated, 5 were transferred to Gunter Field to continue flying training and 188 graduated. Of the 132-man American intake, 8 were held over, 6 were eliminated and 118 graduated on 14 December 1942 and were posted to advanced flying schools.

CHAPTER THIRTEEN

SINGLE-ENGINE ADVANCED FLYING SCHOOLS

CRAIG AND NAPIER

In early November 1941, the members of Class SE-42-A completed their basic flying training at Gunter and Cochran Fields and were assigned to complete their pilot qualifications in USAAF advanced flying schools. Initially, British cadets were divided between Craig and Maxwell Fields in Alabama and Turner Field, Georgia; later, two other schools were opened, and some schools were shifted to other locations. RAF cadets who were destined to fly bombers underwent twin-engine (TE) advanced flight training at Maxwell Field, Alabama (Classes SE-42-A through SE-42-F), Turner Field, Georgia (Class SE-42-A only, then SE-42-G through SE-43-B), and Moody Field at Valdosta, Georgia (Classes SE-42-G through SE-43-B). Although the airfield was equipped with AT-6As only, from December 1941 to June 1942, Napier Field at Dothan, Alabama, also served as a TE advanced flight school for bomber pilots, but after June 1942, it became a second Arnold Scheme single-engine (SE) fighter training school.

While Class SE-42-A was undergoing advanced flight training, the Japanese struck Pearl Harbor, Hawaii, and American flight training changed radically. During the next six months, the pace of training was hurried, and several schools were shifted. Until June 1942, Arnold Scheme advanced flight training was conducted at only three Alabama air stations: Maxwell, Craig and Napier Fields. After that date, Maxwell Field became the Eastern Flying Training Command's central instructors' school; Napier Field at Dothan was converted into a single-engine flight training school; Turner Field resumed Arnold Scheme advanced training as a twin-engine school; and Moody Field, near Valdosta, was opened as a twin-engine school. The Cessna AT-17 and the Curtiss AT-9 had been improved and were being produced in larger numbers, and sufficient twin-engine trainers were now rapidly flowing from factories to the advanced TE flight schools. Until March 1943, two SE flight training schools—Craig and Napier—and two TE schools—Moody and Turner—continued to train RAF pilots.

USAAF SINGLE-ENGINE ADVANCED FLYING SCHOOL
CRAIG FIELD, SELMA

Even before 1810, when the United States government purchased West Florida, the rich soil of the Alabama Black Belt and the navigable Alabama River drew American traders and settlers like a magnet. Around 1809, those who settled on the lands of a high bluff on the west side of the Alabama River began to refer to their settlement as "High Soapstone Bluff." When the Creek were defeated at Horse Shoe Bend in 1814 and were removed from their traditional lands, large numbers of Carolinians, Virginians and Georgians flooded into central Alabama and lands to the south. In the wake of the Napoleonic Wars, other settlers migrated to the region from France and Britain. Within a short time, crude maps of the region referred to the river promontory as "Moore's Bluff."

In 1817, two years before Alabama was admitted into the federal union, speculators bought large sections of land. Many families residing on the worn-out lands of Tidewater Virginia and of the pine barrens of North and South Carolina, as well as on the sand and red clay hills of Georgia, purchased land and began the great trek overland with their household goods, slaves, farm implements and livestock. William Rufus King of Georgia organized a land company, gained control of much of the area around Moore's Bluff and is said to have renamed the settlement "Selma" from Ossian's *The Song of Selma*. Given the romantic mood of the period, selection of the name from one of the several frauds perpetuated by the eighteenth-century Scots writer James "Ossian" McPherson may have been the natural thing to do.

Except in late autumn and winter, perhaps the only way to survive the back-breaking labor of clearing land in this wilderness was to adopt a romantic notion of identity not at one with reality. The heat and humidity of the region, its clouds of mosquitoes and its regular visitations of chills and death induced by malaria and yellow fever were not mental aberrations. As the populations of many cemeteries and family burial grounds attest, they were real. Yet the melodic name Selma glides from the tongue easily and has implied a place far removed from the fields and swamps and eternal troubles of the south central Alabama frontier. The idea of this place undoubtedly produced great nostalgia in the dispossessed Creek, but not in the slaves that the domestic slave trade brought into the region in large numbers. They learned quickly what was meant by the expression "sold down the river."

As most of the forests were rapidly removed and the land was opened up to the cultivation of cotton, Selma became a market town. Steamboats that delivered supplies to upstream landings for anxious planters and merchants just as regularly returned downstream to Mobile with huge cargoes of cotton, lumber and other products. The cotton culture and lumber business enriched planters, ordinary farmers and the owners of storage warehouses and steamboats. Many of these successful men gravitated to Selma and other river towns to build their business structures and their versions of huge and attractive houses and public buildings.

As the town grew, its size was largely dictated by geography. Eastward, extensive swamps prevented early expansion; southward, high bluffs and the streams that cut through them stopped movement in that direction. As a result, the town grew westward in the direction of Marion and Centerville. According to standard nineteenth-century practice, roads radiating from Selma and leading to other communities were labeled simply by the town at its terminus and included, among others, the Camden Road, the Marion Road, the Centerville Road and the Montgomery Road. Within the town, early leaders established a pattern of designating as "avenues" those thoroughfares that ran in an east-west direction, while those running in a north-south direction away from the river were labeled "streets."

During its first century, numerous changes occurred to the town, the people and the surrounding land. A railroad was extended to Selma from Montgomery. German settlers established a foundry, which served the mechanical needs of the railroad, the town, farms and steamboats. The Civil War of 1861–65 led to the formation of numerous regiments of tough Alabama infantry and carried many of them to the bloody battlefields of that war, too many of them never to return. That same war, which significantly reduced the white population, also led to the relocation of the Confederate Naval Arsenal from Virginia and North Carolina to Selma.

Until Union naval vessels cut their way through heavy defenses at Mobile and Federal cavalry swept through the countryside, Alabama had not been a major field of action. Selma's war ended when Federal raiders destroyed the Confederate Arsenal, foundry and railroad shops. During the postwar era, another railroad was pushed through the Alabama countryside southwestward from Dalton and Rome, Georgia, to its terminus in Selma. During these years, much of the land of Alabama's rich Black Belt changed hands, most forests along the rail route were cut and the region increased its production of cotton.

Largely because of its relative isolation and rural insularity, the people of Selma and Alabama, and those of other towns and states of the region, found it difficult to come to terms with the massive changes being wrought during the late nineteenth century. As textile mills spread over the South, two such mills were built in Selma. Railroad consolidations brought the Southern and the Louisville and Nashville lines through the town, and railroad shops in Selma undoubtedly contributed to an increase in the local population.

During the early years of the twentieth century, although a few of the town's streets and avenues were given the names of former citizens or benefactors, many new streets were simply given numbers, as if their existence was too disturbing to established residents of the older sections of town. The relatively brief American participation in World War I produced an awareness of another world, but the standard of education for all except the very wealthy was exceedingly low. The changes wrought by that conflict and by other forces at work in the world hardly rippled the placid surface of the region or its conservative people.

The agricultural depression of 1925 to 1939, which worsened between 1929 and 1933, produced great human suffering, especially among tenant farmers. Unemployment and underemployment became the rule, rather than the exception, and the effects of this economic disaster further diminished the quality of life of the rural population as well as others dependent on agriculture for a livelihood. Two textile mills in Selma failed and were closed. New Deal agencies that came to Selma, Dallas County and other neighboring counties of central and south Alabama helped to relieve the burden of poverty for the very poor, but the more affluent element of society disliked the government's intrusion into their private domain and were critical of its effectiveness. The outbreak of global conflict in 1939–41 shook the world and, for most people, pointed the way to other things, even different careers.

As the year 1940 and the Great Depression were simultaneously drawing to a close, change was in the air, and cautious optimism spread. Warring Europe would have need of food and fiber, and the United States would have to begin to get its house in order before it too was drawn into that tornado-like conflict. Agricultural prices began to climb, and other businesses were experiencing slight improvement. When Congress passed bills enlarging the armed forces and implementing the Selective Service System, these changes were to have a dramatic effect on the lives of most people of Alabama and neighboring states.

During early summer 1940, Colonel Walter R. Weaver assumed command of the Southeast Air Corps Training Center at Maxwell Field, some forty-five miles east of Selma. The War Department directed Weaver to establish a basic and an advanced flying school in close proximity to his headquarters. Montgomery's municipal airport was selected for development as an army air corps basic flying school. With Gunter Field located on the northeast side of Montgomery and Maxwell Field on the northwest side, safe flying training in less congested air space dictated that the new advanced flying school should be built either to the south or west of Montgomery.

Following considerable study and examination of potential sites, Colonel Weaver and his staff selected a site six miles east of Selma in Dallas County, Alabama, for building an advanced flying training school. In July 1940, the City of Selma purchased 1,986 acres of land east of the Alabama River. The huge tract that was located between U.S. Highway 80 and the Camden

Road consisted of a huge cotton field, a juke joint, rolling hills, a lake and vast wooded areas. Huge stretches of swampy low land that lay between the Alabama River and the proposed airfield served as a breeding ground for mosquitoes. The advanced flying school tract was leased to the U.S. government for the sum of one dollar per year, and Colonel George F. Deadrick, construction quartermaster at Maxwell Field, assumed the tasks of designing, laying out and building the new station. Air corps Colonel Vincent B. Dixon was designated project officer.

On Thursday, 8 August 1940, Selma officials, army air corps officers and representatives of the Works Progress Administration attended a groundbreaking ceremony. Then, while WPA workers cut brush and small trees and grubbed out roots on the tract, machinery was moved in to commence grading and leveling land specified for the airfield and its domestic sites. For the remainder of the summer and autumn of 1940, while the Battle of Britain raged three thousand miles to the northeast, the Alabama construction site alternated between dustbowl and quagmire.

Until some new buildings could be completed, headquarters for the military contingent at the site was established in "Jack's Place," a two-story brick building that had formerly been a juke joint. Until the building was demolished in December 1940, officers lived upstairs and men assigned to the new station were compelled to live in tents located in a huge cotton field close by. As work began, men engaged in grading and construction began to contract malaria, and shortly thereafter, each worker was issued fifteen grams of quinine daily. The plague continued into the winter of 1940, when influenza replaced the malaria. Lieutenant Alfred O. Colquitt, medical officer, treated military and civilian staff as well as tenant farmers within a range of twelve miles.

On 27 August 1940, the new army air corps advanced flying school was activated. As at Gunter Field, WPA labor built the first forty-three buildings at the Selma base, using hollow tiles or "Weaver construction." The barracks were low, one-story, yellow stucco buildings containing sixteen four-man rooms with connecting baths between rooms, and a wide screened porch along their entire length. By December, the first stage of construction was completed and staff members moved from tents into more comfortable quarters and work areas.

Until more permanent tarmac runways were completed, gravel was hauled in, dumped, leveled and covered with clay and a topping of calcium chloride to provide temporary landing strips. Further grading and preparation of drainage for remaining areas of the huge airfield continued for several months. In September 1941, when all of the paving contracts were finally completed, Craig Field contained 175 acres of streets, runways, taxiways and parking areas, but a marshy area on the periphery of the station remained a concern of future medical officers.

Since more than two thousand military support staff were assigned to the school and service squadrons, the air station was a miniature town with airfield, administration and classroom buildings. The airfield also had hangars, a post chapel, repair shops, post exchanges, a post cinema, radio and weather offices, the dispatcher's tower/water tower, a separate cadet area and a sewage treatment plant. The addition of a twenty-five-acre lake and spillway between the flight line and the domestic site made the air station very attractive.

In rushing to complete the airdrome, special temporary expedients were tried. Three wells had been drilled, and a 100,000-gallon water tank located on the flight line also held the control tower. As the school expanded, pumps had to be run almost constantly to maintain a proper amount of water for the growing military population. In November 1941, another larger steel water tank with a storage capacity of 300,000 gallons was erected near the entrance to the flying school.

When construction costs were calculated for the original forty-three buildings, it was discovered that by using WPA workers and "Weaver" hollow tile construction, costs—which included all electrical, plumbing and other work done in preparing the buildings—had been held astonishingly low at $1.73 per square foot. By the time flying training began, there would also be a heavy demand for housing USAAF-enlisted personnel and their families, so approval was gained for the construction of Nathan Bedford Forrest Homes, a 100-unit duplex apartment complex.

Late in April 1941, Major Earle E. Partridge, the school's first director of training, arrived from Barksdale Field, Louisiana, with a number of instructors, school squadrons and North American AT-6 Harvard trainers. On Saturday, 3 May 1941, forty U.S. Army Air Corps flying cadets arrived from their gunnery course at Eglin Field, Florida. Major Yantis H. Taylor replaced Partridge as director of training, and during the next six weeks, the American cadets completed their required flying hours.

Within that period, army air corps Class SE-41-E arrived to commence advanced flight training. On 29 May 1941, the first graduating class of flying cadets paraded through the streets of downtown Selma and marched to the Wilby Theatre for graduation ceremonies, presentation of wings and promotion to second lieutenant. Shortly thereafter, Major Taylor was transferred and assumed command of Spence Field, a new USAAF advanced flying school at Moultrie, Georgia. Major Charles H. Anderson became the Selma air station's director of training.

From the beginning, there was concern as to the name to be given to the new flying school. Local citizens advocated naming the field after Edward Hobbs, a Selma native who had distinguished himself while serving with the U.S. Army Air Service during 1917–18. That was not to be. In late July 1941, it was announced that the field would be named for Bruce Craig, an Alabama native who was killed in a June 1941 flying accident while testing a B-24 Liberator bomber for assignment to Great Britain.

As was required for such flight schools, arrangements were made to lease auxiliary airfields at strategic points in several directions from the main airdrome. Trees were cut to clear approaches to selected sites, and machinery was brought in to level and pack the runways and to plant durable grass in unpaved areas. An auxiliary field in nearby Perry County was used for two months and was found to be unsatisfactory. One of the replacement auxiliary fields was Furniss Field in Dallas County, seven miles from Craig Field; another was Henderson Field in Wilcox County, twenty-eight miles from the main airdrome. Before 7 December 1941, three additional auxiliary landing fields were added.

In August 1941, Colonel Vincent B. Dixon, project officer and first commanding officer of Craig Field, departed for assignment as commanding officer of Brookley Field Air Depot near Mobile. During Colonel Dixon's tenure, construction of school buildings and barracks for cadets and support staff were completed; school squadrons were organized and training commenced. As at other advanced flying schools, the alignment of the school squadrons along Craig Field's extensive paved ramp was standard procedure and made it easier to coordinate schedules and control the movement of aircraft on the field. The station's Link Trainer building was also opened and equipped.

During autumn 1941, when the USAAF thirty-thousand-pilot program was put into effect, additional training schools were being established more quickly than ever before. As with each established basic flying school, new advanced flying bases were also directed to establish schools on base to train personnel to man other new stations. In addition to providing indoctrination training to new USAAF recruits, Craig Field trained a number of these and other men to perform special duties. On-station schools were established to train ground staff to maintain aircraft, engines and Link Trainers, as well as to provide a variety of administrative and technical skills.

As at most USAAF basic and advanced schools, the training directorate was divided into flying and ground training. The director of flying supervised flying training, which was organized into two training groups, each of which was commanded by the most senior and experienced flying instructors. The supervision of squadrons was assigned to other experienced instructors who had served as squadron or flight commanders. Generally, Group No. I included Squadrons 1, 3, 5 and 7, while Group II included Squadrons 2, 4, 6 and 8. As new students arrived, they were divided into small groups and distributed among the training squadrons that had most recently graduated a class. Each squadron handled much of its own standard maintenance and adhered to the station's master training schedule.

During the summer and autumn of 1941, enrollment in advanced flying schools doubled, then tripled. In early November, when the student intake doubled, it was necessary to add more instructors and aircraft to each squadron. Craig Field also established an instructors' school to train instructors for service in other advanced schools. In this way, the Selma school became the "mother station" of other USAAF single-engine training schools in the SEACTC or Eastern Flying Training Command. Older flying schools in the Central and Western Flying Training Commands served in the same capacity within their regions.

From the beginning, experienced members of its staff had been regularly drained off to assume supervisory posts at newly established schools or to fill priority overseas drafts to the Philippine Islands and the American Volunteer Group (AVG) in Burma and China. Among early instructors who joined the AVG and fought for China were aces Major "Ajax" Baumler, who taught fighter tactics at Craig, and Lieutenant Robert J. Sandler, early director of ground school. Sadly, Lieutenant Sandler was killed in a crash in Burma.

Before a central instructors' school was established in each USAAF geographic training command, the graduates of each pilot training class were screened and large numbers of young second lieutenants were assigned to the instructors' schools at basic and advanced flying schools to be trained and employed there as flying instructors. Around October 1941, Squadron 9 was established and designated Craig Field's instructors' school. Some thirty-one graduates in Class SE-41-G and about forty-one members of Class SE-41-H were retained and assigned to Squadron 9.

Owing to teething problems with some early models of North American AT-6 trainers, aerobatics had not been taught to the first few army air corps classes. The original model of the North American AT-6 was determined to have structural weaknesses in the aircraft's tail assembly that were deemed design flaws. Models in use were strengthened, and the improvements were incorporated into later models of the advanced trainers. When the AT-6A trainer was distributed to schools, it was necessary to teach the newer instructors aerobatics in the craft before they could teach that portion of the syllabus to cadets.

In August 1941, two months before RAF cadets arrived at Craig Field, Lieutenant Colonel Julian B. Haddon replaced Colonel Vincent Dixon as commanding officer. During the thirteen months in which Haddon served at Craig Field, student enrollment more than doubled. The number of buildings climbed from 43 to 111, and cadets who occupied the new buildings often mentioned the fresh aroma of yellow pine wood. Some of the new barracks were two-story mobilization-type structures divided into four- to five-man cadet rooms, while others were open-bay types. The eight-acre athletic field that was developed on the west side of the station near the original entrance gate proved adequate for physical training and sport.

On Saturday, 2 November 1941, a large contingent of British student pilots arrived by bus from Gunter Field, and on Sunday, 3 November 1941, they were joined by a contingent from Cochran Field. After each draft was fed, its members were assigned to quarters and given time to hang their clothing and straighten equipment. On Monday morning, following breakfast, the 122-member Class SE-42-A was welcomed by Lieutenant Colonel Julian Haddon, commanding officer, and by Major Charles H. Anderson, director of training. Anderson introduced First Lieutenant W.O. Davis, director of the ground school.

Later that same day, photographs were taken for identification cards, and then the entire class reported to the station hospital to receive the thorough Form 66 flight physical examinations. At 4:30 p.m., the cadets joined their American classmates in front of base headquarters for the lowering of the flag in the evening retreat ceremony. After eating dinner in the dining hall, they met there at 7:00 p.m. with Flight Lieutenant H.S. Hurrell, the RAF administrative officer at the station.

Since they were supposed to commence flying training on Tuesday afternoon, 4 November, the new student pilots reported to the cadet supply room that day following reveille, physical training and breakfast. They were issued flying equipment but, owing to inclement weather, flying was delayed until next day. On Wednesday, following familiarization flights in the AT-6A trainers, the student pilots began to master cockpit procedures and learn more about aircraft and engines. Before a full week of training passed, most of the students had soloed the sleek monoplanes and were enjoying flying immensely.

As they concentrated on learning to fly the sophisticated advanced trainers, the terrain the student pilots saw began to become commonplace. Although the sun shone most days, the nights were relatively cool and the mornings were always chill, with occasional white frost covering the brown grass. As they flew over the patchwork of open fields, farmsteads and forests through which the great Alabama River snaked its way toward the Gulf Coast, columns of smoke trailed upward from the chimneys of houses in towns and dispersed over the countryside. That far south, the leaves had changed colors on the hardwood trees, but they had not yet fallen to the ground. However fascinating the pastoral scenes, the main object of the young men was to complete the flying course as rapidly as possible and get back home to join combat forces.

On Wednesday, 5 November, the attention of some RAF cadets was undoubtedly diverted when they read the local newspaper. Edward B. Field, editor of the local newspaper, condemned the group of Detroit women who had insulted Great Britain and the United States by throwing eggs and tomatoes at Lord Halifax, British ambassador to the United States. In a separate article in the newspaper, Columnist C.C. Seay agreed with the *Christian Science Monitor* in its condemnation of American commercialization of the "V" for Victory symbol of British defiance, and suggested that Americans use "U" or "W," either or both symbolizing unity.

There were slight rumblings of resentment against the training of British pilots being heard in the streets of Selma. In response, Seay observed that such remarks were in no way intended as personal attacks on the young student pilots, but were normal growing public expressions of concern about the need for the United States to rearm and increase its own air strength. Within a few days, as if in response to insensitive remarks by some of its citizens, other more thoughtful people demonstrated support for the new arrivals.

On the domestic side at Craig Field, a room 37 feet wide by 150 feet long was allocated as a cadet recreation room and lounge. Since there were no funds available with which to furnish the room and equip it with necessities, Mrs. Julian Haddon, wife of the commanding officer, joined Post Chaplain J.E. Stockman in seeking public support for furnishing the room. Within a few days, a piano, numerous chairs, tables, lamps, pictures and other items were provided by thoughtful citizens of Selma. In the absence of proper wintertime physical education facilities on the air station, arrangements were also quickly made for the 122 British cadets to use the swimming pool of the Selma YMCA on Tuesday and Thursday evenings between 7:00 and 10:00 p.m.

Among the 122 RAF students was Cadet Frederick H. Bradford, who had served as cadet captain at Camden and Macon. Another cadet at Craig Field was one who had visited Selma before. During summer 1939, Cadet Roger W. Hall, who had graduated from Rugby and Cambridge, had traveled to the United States with James Hall, a South African classmate, and had visited a cousin, Mrs. Ronald Forrest, in Selma. Following that visit, Hall returned to the United Kingdom, where he served as an administrator with the Cambridgeshire War Agricultural Executive Committee until October 1940, when he volunteered for RAF pilot training.

Having arrived in Canada on 29 May 1941, Hall and his classmates traveled to Toronto, and within a few days were assigned to Arnold Scheme Class SE-42-A. Following primary at Lakeland and basic flying at Gunter Field, Hall was posted to Craig Field for advanced flying training. On Thursday, 13 November, Hall performed a vital public relations function when he addressed members of Selma's Exchange Club and expressed appreciation for American assistance to Great Britain.

John R. Petrie-Andrews (Camden and Macon) was among the large draft that had boarded coaches at Cochran Field bound for Selma. An experience at Craig Field almost ended his flying career and resulted in his not being recommended for further training as a fighter pilot. On 19 November, Cadets Pease, Petrie-Andrews and Phillips were detailed for a cross-country flight at 11:00 a.m. As Petrie-Andrews recalled the events more than forty years later,

> As there was time to spare beforehand, I think we started flying at 0700 hours, we were sent up to carry out instrument beam orientation. Well, it was a lovely morning as usual, and after riding the beam for awhile, the three of us met up, perhaps by arrangement, and had an invigorating half-hour of "follow the leader." Anything you can do…loops, rolls, etc., and we may have beaten up the odd lake or two. It was great fun, but at odd times there seemed to be more than just three aeroplanes.
>
> Later in the day, while stooging around the very boring cross country, so easy with all the roads and railways going E to W and N to S, my map slipped off my knee into the bottom of the aircraft. It was soon to be my turn to lead this open formation, so the only thing to do was to turn the aircraft (AT-6A, Harvard) upside down and shake it out. Well, all the filth and rubbish fell out but no map.
>
> The next thing I see, when I look out, is the other two aircraft doing the same thing—it got a bit silly there for awhile, and in the end, it was my turn to lead home. Not being quite sure of my position, I flew over to the nearest railway station and gave it a gentle buzz in order to be able to read the sign. But then next to the station I noticed a football game in progress, so we had to see who was playing.
>
> On arrival back at Craig Field, the three of us had to report to the Chief Flying Instructor, and he was furious! He was yelling about unauthorized this, that, and the

*other, and I was trying to say that it all happened because I had lost my map, and, after
all, we weren't dangerously low. Well, it turned out that the other odd "bod" who had
enjoyed our earlier "Chase me Charlie" was an instructor, and he had reported us. The
result was that we were summarily "washed out."*

*However, that was not quite the end, because Wing Commander H.A.V. Hogan and
Wing Commander K.J. Rampling (later killed on "Pathfinders") were able to get us
reinstated. They reasoned that it was a lack of discipline rather than flying skill, and as
the RAF was short of pilots, they should punish us as much as they liked, but should let
us finish the course, if we were good enough.*

*From that time on, we didn't leave the camp. Every weekend we walked the "ramp"
in full kit. We didn't mind that so much, but on graduation, we all got "E" category
grades whereas all the rest had B, C, or D. When we got back home to Britain, instead
of going into Fighter Command for which we had been trained, the "E" grade sent us to
Bomber Command.*

Petrie-Andrews may well have borne the brunt of the penalty for the group of three; he
was assigned to Bomber Command and, before he reached twenty years of age, had built an
extraordinary record as a bomber captain.

Pease, an Etonian, was commissioned pilot officer and later flew fighters, but Phillips's later
assignment is unknown. Whether or not the penalties for "rat racing" were justified is a moot
question. Air discipline was important, but it was deemed equally important to promote initiative,
daring and aggressiveness for those who would be fighter pilots. Ironically, "rat racing" later
became standard practice in American single-engine advanced flying schools.

As American Class SE-41-I was attempting to complete the required number of flying hours,
winter rains deluged the region. On 3 December 1941, the rains began, and by twenty-four
hours later, almost three inches had fallen. Four-mile branch (creek), which cut across the military
reservation, flooded out of its banks, and the lake separating the domestic site from the flight
line overflowed its spillway by about four feet. Despite the heavy downpour, flying resumed and
the final USAAF cadet class was able to complete its flying hours within a few days after the
Japanese attack on Pearl Harbor. On 12 December when Class SE-41-I graduated, Craig Field
had graduated 510 USAAF flying cadets since its establishment.

During that second week of December 1941, as the members of Class SE-42-A reached the
halfway point in their advanced training course, the 120 surviving members were posted to
Florida for their fixed gunnery training course. During their two weeks at the Florida gunnery
station, the RAF student pilots established an outstanding gunnery record and impressed the
USAAF instructors with their aggressiveness and accuracy. While they were enjoying the gunnery
exercises, the 155 men of Class SE-42-B arrived at Craig Field from the two basic flying schools.
With the exception of USAAF Aviation Cadet John Charles Green of Halifax, Virginia, who had
been held over from Class SE-41-I, Craig field was now totally British, and the United States
was at war.

Within a week of their arrival at Craig Field, LAC John Allam of Class SE-42-B wrote a
Christmas letter to Stan Vossler, his primary flying instructor at Lakeland, Florida, and described
his adjustment to the demands of the advanced flying course. In describing the speed-up of
training, which USAAF headquarters ordered following the Japanese attack on Pearl Harbor,
Allam described how the days were full from 5:10 a.m. to 5:30 p.m., and further open-post was

canceled. Schedules were extended to seven days on duty and the eighth day off, and although others disagreed, Allam felt that, with the issue of rifles and the implementation of regular drill sessions and inspections, discipline at Craig Field became as strict as it had been at Gunter Field. Since the students were on an intensive training schedule, they had little time to worry about Christmas. However, most of the young men who were free from training for that day were invited to have Christmas dinner with Selma families.

As the members of Class SE-42-A, the first RAF class at the advanced single-engine school, scrambled to complete the required flying hours, tragedy struck. During the early hours of Saturday, 27 December 1941, an AT-6A trainer crashed on the approaches to Craig Field. Twenty-year-old LAC Douglas Fairer Leman of Cartmel, Lancashire, became the first training fatality since Craig Field commenced operations, and his flying instructor, Lieutenant Walter W. Wilson Jr. of Rutland, Vermont, was seriously injured. While Wilson remained confined to the station hospital, Leman's funeral was held at Maxwell Field on Monday, 29 January 1941, and interment followed in the RAF plot of Montgomery's Oakwood Cemetery Annex.

On 3 January 1942, the 119 men of Class SE-42-A marched to the post theatre enjoying the chill, sunny air. Lieutenant Colonel Julian Haddon was ill, so Major Charles H. Anderson, director of training, presided over the graduation ceremony. Squadron Leader P.F. Heppel of the RAF administrative staff at Maxwell Field delivered the graduation address. Of its 123 members, 1 student was killed, 1 was eliminated for flying deficiencies, 2 were held over to the next class in order to complete the course and 119 (1 USAAF and 118 RAF) cadets graduated.

On 15 December, the 155 members of Class SE-42-B had arrived at Craig Field and were joined by the 2 men transferred (held over) from the senior class, which was then undergoing gunnery training at Eglin Field. Class members included Cadet Douglas Green, a former journalist on the staff of the *Northeastern Gazette*; Cadet E.J. Lischke, a Czechoslovakian member of the RAF; and Cadet Jack E. Gilder, former sergeant in the British Territorial Army. Gilder had served in the Battle of France, and later became cadet battalion commander at Craig Field. The new class went through the normal indoctrination and familiarization period learning the new, faster aircraft and getting adjusted to the advanced flying school schedule.

The advanced flying school syllabus also called for an intensive physical training program of one hour in the morning and one hour in the afternoon. Orders from USAAF headquarters also required officers and enlisted staff members to undergo the intensive physical training program. J.M. Elder, director of cadet physical training at Craig Field, introduced the British students to American games such as basketball and volleyball. In a newspaper interview, Elder also indicated that Craig Field did not have either the equipment or facilities for rugby football and soccer, but that plans called for the introduction of soccer in the spring.

The intensified training program reduced the amount of training time from 9 weeks to about 7.5 or 8 weeks, but since the students were tired most of the time, the new schedule may have contributed to the increased number of accidents. Late Tuesday night, 13 January 1942, nineteen-year-old LAC John F. Rimer of Southgate, London, was killed when his AT-6A trainer evidently stalled and crashed in a cornfield southeast of Craig Field. Less than twenty-four hours later, during the early evening of 14 January, twenty-one-year-old LAC George B. Whigham of Falkirk, Stirlingshire, Scotland, who was noted for his skill in playing the bagpipes, was killed in a similar accident near Craig Field. A double funeral for Rimer and Whigham was conducted in one of the Maxwell Field chapels at 10:00 a.m., Friday, 16 January, and interment of the two young pilots of Class SE-42-B followed in the RAF plot of Montgomery's Oakwood Cemetery Annex.

On Tuesday morning, 20 January at 8:30 a.m., tragedy struck once again, but this time the victim was a member of Class SE-42-C, the recently arrived junior class at Craig Field. While on a routine early morning solo flight, twenty-year-old Cadet Alfred Bolton Kinnear of Caerleon, Monmouthshire, crashed six miles from Selma, adjacent to U.S. Highway 80 and Craig Field.

At around that same time, Cadet Albert Victor "Shorty" Dorman, Class SE-42-B (Camden and Macon), of Port Talbot, Glamorgan, was involved in an accident almost identical to the one in which LAC Leman had been killed on 27 December. As Dorman recalled more than forty years later,

> Perhaps I was too eager, for it was January 1942 when I crashed while landing at night. I had been up for an hour practicing flying the beam around Birmingham with an Air Corps Lieutenant in the back seat of the North American "Harvard" AT-6A. I had wheels and flaps down for the final approach, and everything was lined up for a perfect landing. Suddenly, my left wing hit a clump of very tall pine trees some distance from the beginning of the runway. The plane swung around, and the right wing and tail struck the trees. Both wings and tail section broke off leaving only the two cockpits and the engine, which plunged into some very soft ground upside down engine first. I was knocked out for awhile, and when I came to, I was trapped with my head and shoulders pushed into some very soft mossy earth.
>
> The Lieutenant had succeeded in getting out via the broken off rear end of the cockpit. He told me later that it was dark, and he was confused. He had searched in his pocket for a match to light, but thank God, he didn't find one because the whole area was drenched with aviation fuel. He then heard me yelling from the front cockpit, and was able to dig away some of the dirt with his hands and then to tear off a side panel. I can remember releasing my harness and parachute and again, thank God for being "too small to be a pilot." I was able to squirm through the fuselage struts and away from the plane. An Army ambulance crew arrived, and off we went to hospital at Craig Field.
>
> I spent a couple of weeks there, whilst my main injury to my right eye and the right side of my face were patched up. The Lieutenant had only some small cuts. That's what I call a good landing! I never did find out what actually happened except that we were too bloody low. Later, I went to see the remains of the plane, which were collected together in a hangar, and I nearly gave up flying on the spot. This incident resulted in my missing the passing out of Class 42-B, and I had to start over again on Advanced flying with class 42-C.

Dorman was much luckier than six of his classmates; three men each from Classes SE-42-B and SE-42-C were killed in flying accidents at Craig Field.

About two weeks later, on Tuesday afternoon, 3 February, an AT-6A trainer failed to return from instrument flying exercises. On Wednesday, a massive air search was launched, and that afternoon, almost exactly twenty-four hours since the aircraft took off from Craig Field, its wreckage was sighted in a wooded area north of Miller's Ferry, Alabama, some seventy miles south of Craig Field. Found dead in the wreckage were nineteen-year-old Cadet David William Turner of Caterham Valley, Surrey, and twenty-year-old Cadet Paul Derek Underwood of West Ewell, Surrey. Turner had attended Haileybury College and was a medical student at London's St. Mary's Hospital when he volunteered for RAF pilot training. Underwood, who was praised by his classmates for his talent as a pianist and singer, had also been an active member of glee clubs at primary and basic flying schools.

Hardly had the bodies of Turner and Underwood been retrieved from the wreckage of their aircraft and transported by ambulance to Selma than yet another accident near Craig Field claimed the life of Cadet George William Rowley of Class SE-42-B. That third fatality among members of Class SE-42-B occurred Thursday afternoon, 5 February, as a few members of Class SE-42-B were rushing to complete their final flying hours in order to graduate the next day. Unfortunately, two aircraft being flown solo by Cadets Rowley and John T. Rhys collided at a point above the River Road about three miles east of Craig Field in the Houston Grove area. Following the collision, Rowley bailed out at very low level and was killed, but LAC Rhys was able to land his damaged aircraft safely at Craig Field.

On Friday morning, 6 February 1942, at 10:30 a.m., a graduation ceremony was held in the post theatre for the graduates of Class SE-42-B. Wing Commander H.A.V. Hogan, senior RAF administrative officer for the SEACTC, gave the address, and Lieutenant Colonel Julian Haddon presented diplomas to the men. Lieutenant Colonel Charles H. Anderson, Craig Field's recently promoted director of training, awarded the graduates both RAF and USAAF wings.

Of a total enrollment of 157 students in Class SE-42-B (including 2 holdovers), 4 RAF cadets, including LAC A.V. Dorman, were held over to Class SE-42-C to complete the advanced flying course. Three cadets were killed, 5 were eliminated (1 for non-flying reasons and 4 for flying problems) and 145 graduated. Sadly, that very afternoon at 3:00 p.m., services were held at the White Chapel Funeral Home in Montgomery for the three most recent victims of training accidents. Burial followed in the RAF plot of Montgomery's Oakwood Cemetery Annex for Cadet Rowley of Class SE-42-B and Cadets Turner and Underwood of Class SE-42-C.

From RAF No. 31 Personnel Depot at Moncton, New Brunswick, Sergeant Pilot John Allam wrote once more to his primary flying instructor, Stan Vossler, this time thanking Vossler for getting him and several classmates started off on the right foot at Lakeland. Allam was apologetically critical of the intensified training program at Craig Field:

> Somehow, I think they are speeding it up just a little too much. I don't see why I should know better than the authorities, but I do know that we flew a seven-day-week at Craig with an average of three hours a day, and we all got to the stage that they had to give us a rest—the instructors were even feeling it more than we did, as they were naturally doing more.
>
> One cannot but wonder whether USAAF authorities, in bending to RAF criticisms that American training was "peacetime," might have over-reacted by increasing the pace of training too much.

Before spring 1942 was over, USAAF authorities were in agreement: the tensions induced by long hours of concentration and intensified day and night flying were not eased by increased physical training. Rest and relaxation and greater coordination between the advanced and basic flying schools were needed to prevent accidents and fatalities. Addressing such problems required that training syllabi be modified.

Some two months later, Neville Hull of Birmingham, England, father of Michael Hull, who had trained with Class SE-42-B at Tuscaloosa, Gunter and Craig Fields, wrote to the recently promoted Colonel Julian B. Haddon to thank him for "giving my son his ambition, 'wings.'" In expressing his appreciation, Mr. Hull, a former non-flying member of the Royal Flying Corps, echoed the sentiments of many of the former RAF students when remarking on the effectiveness of the American instructors. Mr. Hull asserted that "it must be a heart-breaking job for them, licking the youngsters into shape, and pig-headed Britishers at that! They are doing a magnificent job and doing it well."

The 154-man Class SE-42-C arrived at Craig Field around 10 January and commenced advanced flying training immediately. On 28 January, Flight Lieutenant James L. Laurillard, a native of Edinburgh and former London resident, replaced Flight Lieutenant H.S. Hurrell as RAF administrative officer at Craig Field. After having been in training at the Selma airfield for about one month, Class SE-42-C was posted to Eglin Field, Florida, for their fixed gunnery course. It was cold, and it rained for several days while they were in Florida, but they were finally able to complete their required ground and air firing and return to Craig Field.

As the end of the course was drawing near, a RAF Commissioning Board convened at Craig Field and interviewed a large number of students for commissions. Frank Jones of Blackpool, Lancashire (Albany and Macon), had aspired to commissioned status. Although skill, experience and recommendations accounted for some promotions, commissions in the RAF, in general, were still being awarded according to the British pre-war standard of education, class and status.

Jones recalled that members of the board that convened at Craig Field asked such questions as, "Are you a university man? Did you captain your school football team? Did you gain any certificates at school? How many years were you at school?" It was standard RAF practice at that time for about one-third of each class to be commissioned pilot officers, and the remainder to graduate as sergeant pilots. Jones was disappointed at not receiving a commission, but he and many others who were passed over at the time of graduation were later encouraged to apply for commissions after surviving some eighteen months as a pilot.

Frank Jones also recalled that at Craig Field "stars were given for small mistakes in flying, i.e., leaving the flaps down, and the penalty for each star was 25 cents." Although many student pilots considered this practice petty, others found it a very positive way to focus attention on potentially dangerous omissions in procedures and flying discipline. In assessing the training he had received in primary, basic and advanced flying schools, Jones ended on a positive note:

> The Honour System, hazing, demerits, and tours were all part of the American way of life, and I personally felt it was up to us to accept, at least in part, the system. We were the visitors and, in my opinion, it was not reasonable to expect the American Air Force to change or amend their training system to accommodate comparatively few foreigners. We also had the advantage over many pilots trained by the RAF in England—large numbers of them were operational with far less flying hours than we had.

As could be expected, many of the young men who trained in the United States would probably be classified as "Little Englanders" who could accept no other system as comparable to anything British, while others were much more tolerant and positive about experiences in the United States.

As RAF men graduated from advanced flying training, many of those who were commissioned were asked to volunteer for six months' service in the United States as flying instructors. Although a small number of RAF pilot officers were assigned to primary and advanced flying schools, the most critical area of need was in the basic flying schools, so Gunter and Cochran Fields apparently had first priority on assignment of early RAF graduates. Pilot Officer D.M. Johnstone, formerly of Glasgow, Scotland, and Class SE-42-A graduate, who had been serving as a flying instructor at Napier Field, Dothan, Alabama, for several weeks, was reassigned to Craig Field on 16 March. Johnstone, who was on assignment as an assistant RAF administrative officer and flight instructor, was soon joined by Pilot Officer Ian D. MacMillan and Pilot Officer Philip Jones, who had graduated with Class SE-42-B. These three RAF instructors were the first of many to serve at Craig Field.

As with the two preceding classes, a great deal of flying was squeezed into the final three weeks of training. On Friday, 6 March 1942, the RAF cadets who had successfully completed the course formed up in front of their barracks in freshly pressed RAF blue uniforms and marched smartly to the post theatre. At the graduation ceremony, Major General George E. Stratemeyer, commanding general of the Eastern Flying Training Command (formerly SEACTC) at Maxwell Field, was the speaker. Evidently, since the class completed its training ahead of schedule, their wings, sergeant's stripes and pay were not ready in time for graduation, and were not presented until several days later at pay parade.

Of the 154-man total enrollment, 7 men were held over to Class SE-42-D to complete their training, 3 were killed in flying accidents, 3 were eliminated (2 for flying deficiences, 1 for other than flying) and 141 men graduated. Within three weeks of graduation, 13 members of Class SE-42-C returned to Craig Field as flying instructors. They included Pilot Officers C.E. Bearman, John B. Cunningham, A.E. Dowling, A.C. Flood, R. Kirker, Ray T. Raby, G.C. Robinson, Eric Woolley, R.F. Bass, C.C. Kane, G.D. Stephenson, E.J. Lischke and F.L. McLeod.

On 19 February, the 120-man Class SE-42-D arrived at Craig Field from the basic flying schools and commenced flying immediately. With the addition of the 7 men held over from Class SE-42-C, total enrollment climbed to 127. The intensified schedule continued in effect, and a training experiment went awry and proved to be embarrassing. There was always great concern among the flying instructors about the tendency of the British cadets to ground loop the advanced trainers. On a particularly foggy day when flying was delayed for some time, it was decided to experiment by teaching the handling of the advanced trainers under power on the ground.

A dozen pairs of instructors and students boarded AT-6As (students in front, instructors in the rear) and began to move about the airfield practicing braking. After about five minutes, seven tires went flat. On other trainers, heat had melted inner tubes and crystalized the wheels and brake drums, causing them to fracture even with a light tap. As a result of this experiment, Craig Field maintenance staff had to replace the tires, wheels and brake assemblies of most of the dozen aircraft used in the experiment.

During the remaining cold and often wet days of February, the class pushed on with its training. When they were free from concentrating on flying and technique, they were able to see vast distances from their aircraft. Winter grain began to show green in patches. During some relatively dry and still days, farmers in the region began their time-honored means of preparing for planting by burning the stubble and debris of the previous year's crops from their fields. LAC Graham Hyslop recalled that during his final cross-country flight from Cochran Field to Waycross, Georgia, and return, the large number of fires along the way "looked as though someone had been before us with a load of incendiaries; it reminded me of the blitz a year ago."

Despite warnings from agricultural agents and others knowledgeable in such matters, many farmers, in seeking to destroy the hated boll weevil, continued to burn large tracts of timber and underbrush adjacent to fields where cotton was to be planted. Sometimes the wind would rise while the burning was going on and forest fires would spread over several miles, destroying everything. This waste was a terrible sight to see either from the air or the ground. However, the time of annual renewal was near; in March, color portended spring.

Yellow forsythia blooms, referred to locally as "the first breath of spring," made their appearance in clumps and hedges close by homes and farmsteads. And in swampy lowlands, the purple and red buds of maple trees and other hardwoods appeared first before new leaves made their appearance. As March waned and April arrived, flying training continued at Craig Field, and the region's woodlands, parks and residential sections took on more color. Dogwoods burst into bloom, and their white blossoms dotted the forests and the edges of fields and along the streets of Selma and other towns. Daffodils and other bulbs began to bloom, as did azaleas and other shrubs. The pecan trees shed bright yellow pollen that covered everything. Springtime was special at Craig Field, Alabama, especially if the advanced flying course was drawing to a successful close and the award of pilot's wings was no longer a distant and doubtful prospect.

On 17 March 1942, within a week following departure of Class SE-42-C, the 170-man Class SE-42-E, the largest RAF class yet assigned there, arrived at the advanced flying school. The training schedule that new classes normally followed was as follows: squadrons assigned to flying in the mornings flew from 7:00 a.m. to 1:00 p.m., had lunch at 1:30, attended ground school and physical training from about 2:00 p.m. to 5:00 p.m. and had dinner at 6:00 p.m. Squadrons flying in the afternoon reversed the schedule, and had ground school and physical training in the mornings, lunch at 12:00, flying from 1:00 to 7:00 p.m. and dinner at 7:30 p.m. Lights out in cadet barracks was scheduled at 10:00 p.m.

Within a week of their arrival, most members of the new class had soloed, and after about three weeks, when they had accumulated around thirty hours in the AT-6As, their training schedule was modified to accommodate night flying. Since there were so many men in training, experience dictated that it was easier to abandon stringent schedules and concentrate all of the night flying exercises for a particular class. Some squadrons were scheduled for night flying on the first shift, which lasted from 6:00 p.m. to midnight. These men had breakfast at 7:30 and could sleep or otherwise relax until they had lunch at 1:30 p.m. Before reporting for flying at 6:00 p.m., their afternoons were taken up with ground school and physical training. The remaining squadrons, which were assigned to the second shift, began at 1:00 a.m. and worked until 7:00 a.m. They had breakfast at 7:30 a.m., then ground school and physical training in the mornings. During the afternoon and early evening before reporting to the flight line, they could sleep.

Between 9:30 a.m. and 6:30 p.m. on Army Day, 6 April 1942, Craig Field held an open house. Although routine flying and ground school training continued during the day, more than 2,600 visitors in groups numbering from 20 to 50 people were escorted about the air station, viewing representative quarters and other facilities and seeing aircraft. A large and varied number of military aircraft, some of which had been brought in for the day, were aligned along a part of the ramp near the main hangar.

Alongside a Stearman PT-17, a Vultee BT-13 and several North American AT-6As were a Curtiss P-40 fighter and a huge Consolidated B-24 Liberator bomber. Civilian visitors arrived and departed the airfield throughout the day, but for those remaining on post at the end of the day, the final attraction was the retreat parade. That evening, just as darkness came, several trainer planes dropped flares over the Alabama River near Selma, winding up the day's festivities and signaling the beginning of a radio address by Colonel Julian Haddon, Craig Field's commanding officer.

On Thursday afternoon, 23 April 1942, four aircraft that were flown by RAF Cadets Walter R. Eason, R.S. Ellis, W.B. Felder and Flight Commander Lieutenant B.H. Aszman made forced landings at Lumberton, Mississippi, while on a routine training flight. The three British cadets, who were rushing to complete their final required flying hours, were scheduled to graduate the next day with Class SE-42-D, but were compelled to stay overnight in Mississippi before returning to Craig Field.

On Friday, 24 April 1942, 2 American officers who had trained in grade and almost 300 British and American cadets marched to the post chapel for graduation ceremonies. Chaplain James E. Stockman delivered the invocation for this first ceremony conducted in the chapel; Colonel Julian B. Haddon delivered the address and presented the graduation certificates; and Captain Edward Herbes, director of flying, presented wings to the graduates. Of the total Class SE-42-D enrollment of 127 RAF student pilots, 1 was held over, 4 were eliminated (1 for non-flying reasons and 3 for flying deficiencies) and 122 graduated.

Between the February 1942 arrival at Craig Field of Class SE-42-D and the May 1942 departure of Class SE-42-E, major changes occurred that would affect the course of British flying training in the United States. British officials greeted American entry into the war with mixed views; they sought quick solutions to multiple problems. Glad to have a powerful ally now fully committed to the war, the Air Ministry remained anxious to preserve the January 1941 agreements reached in the A-B-C Conversations. These talks led the neutral United States to agree to share American aircraft production with Britain and Canada on a fifty-fifty basis.

There had already been many conferences and much talk about joint training systems for aircrew, ground and naval forces, and such talks would continue but would not be fully implemented. There was, however, general agreement to defeat Germany first and to provide minimal assistance to forces fighting the war against Japan in the Far East. When anxieties about American production of pilots for Britain increased, the British government, through its Air Ministry, made an awkward error. Instead of voluntarily reducing its training in the United States, the Air Ministry's Directorate of Training sought to expand British aircrew production in the United States.

In December 1941, after the United States entered the war, American air forces joined British air forces in the United Kingdom. Britain provided airfields and other services in what was called "reverse lend-lease." However, the British Air Ministry hoped that the United States would compensate Britain for its loss of airfields in the United Kingdom by building, equipping and providing aircraft and maintenance staffs for eleven British operational training units (OTUs) in the American west and one in the Bahamas. In March 1942, Canada graciously offered the United States Army Air Forces a large number of places in the pilot training schools of Canada's vast British Commonwealth Air Training Plan.

Although Canada's offer was a generous one, it indicated to American air training officers that neither Britain's nor Canada's aircrew training facilities were being used to maximum capacity. USAAF officers had long been critical of small aircrew training courses and large allotments of training aircraft and equipment assigned to the British flying training schools. As a result, the Canadian offer was declined, and USAAF officers became determined to reduce British aircrew training in the United States as quickly as possible. In June 1942, when the United States sought to obtain control of BFTS No. 2 on the edge of the Mojave Desert at Lancaster, California, USAAF and RAF commanders clashed. In that same month when, without consultation, the British persuaded Messrs. Plosser and Prince to build and operate BFTS No. 7 at Sweetwater, Texas, the USAAF hastened to assume control of it.

Indirect support for the American decision to reduce British aircrew training came from an unexpected quarter. Air Vice Marshal Arthur T. Harris, who had been serving on the British Air Commission in the United States since early 1941, was posted back to Britain early in 1942. In February 1942, Harris assumed the post of officer commanding in chief (OCIC) of Bomber Command. Within a brief period of his return to the United Kingdom, Harris argued successfully for a major change in aircrew policy. Instead of assigning a pilot and a copilot for each heavy bomber, as was the practice in many air forces, British bombers would, henceforth, have only one pilot. That significant change immediately and dramatically reduced the number of pilots required to man existing aircraft.

Given Britain's manpower shortage, Harris's decision may have been a correct one for the United Kingdom, but the new policy probably encouraged area bombing and excessive aircrew combat losses. On the other hand, American insistence on a daylight bombing policy led to great American combat losses. The USAAF refused to follow suit in the British one-pilot system. Instead, United States Army and Navy officers believed that the greater the number of aircrew qualified, the greater the weight of air power that could eventually be brought to bear against specific targets that would disable enemy forces. Regular officers of the United States Army Air Forces respected their British colleagues and were anxious to imitate Britain's separate air force organization by developing a United States Air Force equal to the army and navy as a third branch of the American armed services.

In the course of the preceding eight months, USAAF training officers had experienced difficulties in efforts to train British aircrew alongside American cadets. As a result of these daunting experiences, which the USAAF air training officers believed disrupted American pilot training and the USAAF goal for an autonomous air force, they were anxious to train as many USAAF pilots and other American aircrew as possible.

As a result of pressures brought about by the war, conflicting national goals and differences in temperament, criticism mounted in different quarters of the United States Army Air Forces to bring British aircrew training to a close in the United States in order to expand American air power more rapidly. The Canadian offer of excessive training capacity, coupled with appeals from hundreds of American personnel serving in the Royal Air Force and the Royal Canadian Air Force for transfer to the U.S. Army Air Forces, convinced USAAF headquarters to take action.

By late April 1942, the Canadian and United States governments reached an agreement that permitted some fifteen thousand Americans serving in Canadian forces to transfer to the military forces of the United States, if they wished. Many men chose to remain in the Canadian ground and air forces and did not exercise the transfer option, but when some of them were found eligible for transfer to the USAAF in equivalent Canadian rank, a larger number of Americans in the RCAF decided to do so.

Colonel Julian Haddon, commanding officer of Craig Field, was assigned to temporary duty in Canada and joined "a trainload of interviewing officers plus physicians, examiners, clerks and stenographers." During a period of about six weeks, these USAAF officers and men traveled the breadth of Canada to meet, examine and document the Americans who were qualified to transfer to USAAF service. A specially equipped train made about fifteen stops between Halifax, Nova Scotia, and Vancouver, British Columbia, and screened American citizens who had applied to transfer to the armed forces of the United States. The train had several cars including a reception car, a State Department car, a medical car, an examining board car and an adjutant general's car.

The mobile production line processing system for these direct entry airmen took about three hours to complete, and receptionists maintained a steady flow of men through each stage of processing. The staff of the State Department car confirmed and documented citizenship. Staff of the medical car provided standard Form 64 U.S. Army Air Forces physical examinations for each RCAF transfer candidate. Officers of the examining board interviewed prospects before they were sworn in, and adjutant general staff personnel prepared the proper documents, records and files on each man and issued proper travel orders and vouchers.

As a result of their work, large numbers of experienced pilots and other aircrew, many of whom had served as flying and ground instructors, arranged to transfer in equivalent commissioned grades they had held in the RCAF. Some men deemed too old to obtain USAAF commissions were employed by the Civil Service Commission as flying instructors in USAAF basic and advanced flying schools, or as ferry pilots. Other American citizens who had received their RCAF wings after some 130 hours of flying training were entered into USAAF advanced flying schools in order to complete the required 215 hours deemed essential for service as a military pilot in the USAAF. Near the end of May 1942, five former RCAF officers were assigned to Craig Field as flying instructors.

On 17 March 1942, while some of these decisions were in their early stages, Class SE-42-E arrived at Craig Field. With the addition of 1 cadet held over from the previous class, total enrollment rose above 300 student pilots, including 171 RAF cadets. Following the standard USAAF advanced training syllabus, the men proceeded through the training course at the new, rapid wartime pace. Ground school at Craig Field was different from earlier courses of study.

Cadet Graham R. Hyslop of Lancashire evidently appreciated the practical system of ground school that prevailed at Craig Field:

> *We spent 3 hours a day for a week down at the hangars inspecting the various workshops, visiting about 3 in the morning. We visited the electrical shop, propeller shop, cable and tube shop, parachute dept (where we saw a 'chute packed), instrument shop, etc., etc., and the last day we wandered around the hangar inspecting planes that were being overhauled. We have had lectures on anti-aircraft employment, air fighting and technique, armaments, practical navigation (or how not to get lost), and several other subjects.*

RAF and USAAF officers who had experienced combat also presented occasional lectures to the student pilots.

Hyslop became more enthusiastic about his flying training and, in another letter home, he provided an excellent description of his trip to Eglin Field, Florida, for gunnery exercises:

> *We set off for Eglin Field at 6 a.m. in army trucks. We arrived about 7 hours later and were about melted away with the Florida heat. We started flying the next morning at 6 a.m. (we got up at 4:30). When we were flying in the mornings, we went down to the beach at Fort Walton, about 10 miles away, from 2 p.m. to 5 p.m. Most of the time was spent in the Gulf of Mexico which was warmer than the indoor baths at home, and we were all very much sun burnt after about 2 days.*
>
> *We flew with nothing on but a pair of gym pants and overalls with neck wide open and sleeves rolled up, with the results that my neck and forearms became crimson and*

finally skinned. My right arm, after it had peeled, started to blister just like a burn. When we flew in the afternoons, we went down to the Beach in the mornings.

At ground gunnery and ground strafing, my scores were about average, but in aerial gunnery, I had the second highest score in the squadron. I really enjoyed aerial gunnery. The only snag about flying down there was that we were flying from an auxiliary field about 8 miles from the barracks, and had to be transported to and fro. The auxiliary field resembled Libya slightly; we had a kind of tent to lie in when we weren't flying, but planes were always coming along and blowing clouds of sand over us. It was very hot and dusty, and I never want to go out to any desert place after that.

Following fixed gunnery training at Eglin Field, Florida and hurried completion of flying hours, the class graduated on 8 May 1942. Once more, the graduation ceremonies were conducted in the post chapel and the main speaker for the occasion was again Major General George E. Stratemeyer. Members of the class were presented with USAAF pilot's wings and certificates of graduation signed by Lieutenant Colonel Charles S. Anderson, director of training.

Of the total RAF enrollment of 171, 4 cadets were held over to the next class for completion of the course, 7 were eliminated and 160 men graduated. One of the 4 men held over to Class SE-42-F was LAC Graham Hyslop. A fortnight prior to graduation, Hyslop became ill with appendicitis and was compelled to undergo surgery at the Craig Field Post Hospital. After recuperating for two weeks in the hospital, Hyslop was granted two weeks' leave before resuming training with Class SE-42-F. Fortunately, he was invited to spend that time with the Harper family at their farm some five miles from Selma.

On 1 May 1942, while the senior class was undergoing gunnery training at Eglin Field, Florida, the 153 RAF members of Class SE-42-F arrived at Craig Field. At an assembly in the post theatre that afternoon, USAAF and RAF officers welcomed the new class. Within a short time, 4 men who had been held over from the preceding class joined them to raise the RAF total enrollment to 157. In addition to the RAF and USAAF cadet contingents, several hundred newly inducted USAAF aviation cadets arrived at a newly organized aviation cadet reception center, which occupied a portion of Craig Field's domestic facilities.

On Monday, 4 May, Class SE-42-F commenced flying, and within a short time tragedy struck once more. At 7:45 a.m. on Saturday, 9 May, while taking off from the main airdrome on a solo flight, twenty-year-old Cadet Ernest George Gulliver of Knaphill, Woking, Surrey, was severely injured. Shortly after being removed to the post hospital, he died, and his body was sent to Montgomery for services and interment in the Oakwood Cemetery Annex.

During the following week, a few days before the 160 RAF pilots of Class SE-42-E graduated, the RAF staff was boosted in strength by the addition of twenty-two-year-old Squadron Leader John C. Freeborn, DFC with bar. Formerly a member of RAF 74 Tiger Squadron during and after the Battle of Britain, Freeborn had flown Spitfires and was credited with having shot down twelve enemy aircraft. Freeborn was sent to Craig Field to teach the latest fighter tactics to instructors and students at the advanced flying school. On Monday, 25 May, the young squadron leader thrilled members of Selma's Kiwanis Club with an address about 1940 air fighting over northern France, Dunkirk, the English Channel and the south of England.

As Freeborn, other RAF staff and the members of Class SE-42-F were continuing their flying and becoming acquainted with Selma and Craig Field, important changes were taking place on the station. For some time, there had been general flooding of the small creek that ran through the airdrome close by U.S. Highway 80, and this flooding often resulted in severe drainage problems in sections of the military reservation as well. In order to solve the drainage problem while at the same time providing recreational facilities, the U.S. Army Corps of Engineers designed and constructed a spillway and graded the banks of the twenty-five-acre lake, which was formed by damming the creek.

According to the contemporary news report, "the sides of the lake will be terraced and sodded, with kudzu crowns planted in eroded areas along the banks." (Ultimately, the lake was stocked with fish and sandy beaches were created, but there is no record as to how long the beach areas lasted before succumbing to the creeping, heavy vines of kudzu, the erosion fighter that three decades later was being referred to as "Japan's revenge.")

On 25 May, a modification of training policy was announced. Since established RAF training policy called for the production of two or more bomber pilots for every fighter pilot, and since Class SE-42-G was scheduled to arrive at advanced schools early in June, it was decided to implement changes so as to provide both twin-engine and single-engine flying training. Craig Field had already been expanded so as to be able to absorb the RAF men designated for fighter training, but as the number of RAF cadets increased, it was necessary to establish additional schools for the training of bomber pilots.

Since Maxwell Field was needed for other purposes, female auxiliary service pilots (WASPs) were ferrying twin-engine trainers from factories to Turner Field and to the newly completed Moody Field near Valdosta, Georgia. RAF cadets would be assigned with USAAF cadets to TE training at these schools. Since these two advanced twin-engine schools in Georgia could probably handle future drafts of RAF cadets and Napier Field at Dothan was already equipped with AT-6A trainers, it was decided to keep Napier Field an advanced single-engine flying school.

In anticipation of these changes, some of the most experienced RAF instructors in the command were reassigned to Turner and Moody Fields in time for them to qualify on the TE trainers before the arrival of the next class. Since some, though not all, of the members of the next RAF intake (Class SE-42-G) had undergone at least part of a new and (owing to winter weather) largely ineffective flight grading course in the United Kingdom, they were now almost ready to enter advanced flying schools.

June 1942 was believed to be an opportune time to make changes. At Craig Field, these changes meant that some instructors would be transferred and other new instructors would be assigned to the single-engine advanced school at Dothan. Until these changes were effective, the ten pilot officers assigned from Class SE-42-E would enter an instructors' course and Class SE-42-F would continue its normal flying training.

Among the members of Class SE-42-F was Cadet Frank Norman Bate (Arcadia and Macon) who, some forty years later, recalled the course of events that brought him to Craig Field for several months of stimulating duty.

> *We were driven by Greyhound Bus several hours by road to our new camp, Craig Field, near Selma, Alabama. Here the American training system reached its perfection point— there was the water tower, the immaculate Main Gates and smart guards, the hugeness of the Base and the distinctive noise of AT-6 aircraft, the sense of precision, organization, everything large scale. In contrast to this newness and efficiency, we had passed on the bus so many seemingly tumbled-down wooden homes, not unlike our home country's garden allotment buildings or summer bungalows; the region seemed poverty stricken.*

Electricity and telephone posts and cables appeared as eyesores, many a black or coloured person trudged the roadside, and, we were to find, could only use the rear few seats of buses. If a white person entered the bus, and no seat was available, a coloured person automatically got off the bus, even though it may have been the last bus, and he or she might be faced with a long walk home. This greatly distressed me, for, as with most Britishers, I had been brought up to respect all colours, creeds and cultures through schooling influences. Here in the USA, I respected the terms "the other side of the track," the culture of the South, and learned to accept it without much question and without criticism.

Craig Field training was, to my mind, faultless. Everything there was organized to bring the American and British Cadets closer together, whereas at other stations we had been largely isolated from each other. In those changed conditions, one found food for thought, recognizing that the Americans applied themselves to everything with purpose and vigour. The system itself was perhaps far better tailored to their pre-conditioning procedures but, if a British cadet did not benefit from Craig Field in particular, I would believe that he failed himself, that the system was good in its entirety.

Following graduation on 3 July 1942, Bate and several other RAF students who had received commissions were sent on a five-day leave. Of the 157 RAF gross enrollment in Class SE-42-E, 2 were held over to Class SE-42-G to complete their training, 3 were eliminated, 1 was killed and 151 graduated and received their wings.

On Tuesday, 2 June 1942, the largest class of student pilots ever to enroll at Craig Field arrived there from USAAF basic flying schools at Greenville, Mississippi, and Montgomery, Alabama. Among the members of Class SE-42-G were RAF cadets, USAAF aviation cadets and four student officers, including First Lieutenant James Strother, former photographic officer at Craig Field. The number of RAF cadets was quickly increased from ninety-five to ninety-seven by the addition of two RAF students held over from Class SE-42-F.

As the members of Class SE-42-G were learning cockpit procedure and becoming familiar with the sleek advanced trainers, the advanced flying school syllabus was modified considerably from that which had existed for earlier classes. For the first several classes, student pilots were sometimes eliminated from pilot training for low flying, but during the summer of 1942, "combat" flying was adopted, and soon instructors were leading students on low-level rat races over the lakes and forests of central Alabama. Based on recommendations by RAF Wing Commander Edward "Teddy" Donaldson, new gunnery training techniques were introduced at the advanced schools and, in addition to skeet shooting on the ground, pilots learned other techniques before being posted to Eglin Field for the fixed gunnery course.

Another innovation in the flying training syllabus proved even more exciting for the student pilots. Briefly during February and March 1942, obsolete P-35 fighters had been used at Craig Field for the final ten hours of training, but this practice was temporarily suspended, owing to maintenance problems resulting from a lack of spare parts. In July 1942, that suspension was lifted, and Craig Field then received a number of Bell P-39 and Curtiss P-40 fighters, and USAAF cadets and student officers received about ten hours of transition training on these fast aircraft. Although the RAF instructors were able to log some hours flying these fighters, RAF students completed training on AT-6As and did not receive fighter transition training.

When Class SE-42-F graduated on Friday, 3 July, Class SE-42-G became the senior class at Craig Field. Normally in attendance at graduation ceremonies were some of the parents, wives and girlfriends of USAAF graduates as well as a few American friends of the British graduates, but the July graduation was slightly different. Sub-Lieutenant B.H. Barber, RNVR, who was assigned to duty with HMS *Saker II*, the designated unit for RN personnel assigned to duty in the United States, was able to travel to Selma to attend the graduation of his brother, Eric W. Barber, at Craig Field. The two brothers, originally from Sunderland, County Durham, were able to spend a few days together before returning to their respective duties.

During Saturday afternoon, 4 July 1942, tragedy struck once more. Major Ross T. Hopkins, the popular technical executive officer at Craig Field, was killed in the crash of an AT-6A trainer some tewlve miles south of the main airfield. Hopkins had arrived at Craig Field in October 1941, following assignment as commanding officer of the primary flying training detachment at Parks Air College, East St. Louis, Illinois, and had been promoted to major just a month before his tragic death.

Exactly ten days later, staff and students at flying training stations throughout the Southeast were shocked to learn of an air collision near Madison, Florida. Four twin-engine trainers from Moody Field Advanced TE Flying School near Valdosta, Georgia, collided in mid-air and took the lives of seven members of RAF Class SE-42-G and an American flying instructor. Such tragedies brought increased pressure for improved safety and air discipline.

During much of July 1942, central Alabama suffered daily from temperatures at and above the one-hundred-degree level. The heat wave seemed to hang over the entire region and made flying bumpy and life on the ground exceedingly uncomfortable. Tuesday afternoon, 21 July, was much like any other day for the students undergoing training at Craig Field, except that flying was suspended for several hours while the student pilots were introduced to one of the massive electrical storms for which the region is noted. The storm's high winds and flood-like rains certainly cleared the air and brought relief from the stifling heat that had plagued the area. However, the high winds also brought the limbs of massive trees crashing down into streets and major highways, bringing down telephone and power lines. Until crews could complete their clearing and repair work some weeks later, many of the tree-lined streets of Selma and other nearby communities were littered with debris.

After the storm, the members of Class SE-42-G and the newly arrived Class SE-42-H resumed their normal training with the usual day and night formation flying and cross-country exercises. In addition, the young pilots occasionally gained some experience "flying the beam" and "rat racing" over the farms, woods and lakes of the region. Following the introduction of fighter tactics and considerable study of gunnery techniques, the course culminated in air and ground firing practice at one of the auxiliary airfields of the huge Eglin Field gunnery station on the Florida Gulf Coast. Each AT-6A trainer was equipped with a single machine gun and a cannister of one hundred rounds of color-coded ammunition. Since the ammunition of each aircraft was of a different color, it was relatively easy to examine the towed drogues as well as ground targets to determine a pilot's firing accuracy.

During the final days of July 1942, as members of Class SE-42-G were completing their final flying hours and excitedly making preparations for returning to the United Kingdom, a newspaper report created a stir. Simultaneous announcements from Washington and London indicated that further intakes of British aircrew trainees into USAAF flying schools would end immediately. "Definite word has not yet been received by authorities of the local school," reported the *Selma Times-Journal*, "but tentative plans call for British cadets now in this country to continue their course under the same program [the Arnold Scheme] which has been in operation for the past year." Within a few days of the announcement, Flight Lieutenant J.L. Laurillard, who had been RAFAO at Craig Field since January, departed for Canada, and Flight Lieutenant S.D. Simpson arrived to replace him.

From the beginning of the course, demerits were awarded cadets for violations of flying rules, and at the end of the course students paid five cents per point. The fund resulting from these "fines" was used to defray expenses for an end-of-course picnic or party. The party for Class SE-42-G was held during the first weekend in August. On Wednesday, 5 August 1942, the second anniversary of the opening of Craig Field, graduation ceremonies were held for Class SE-42-G graduates in the pecan grove "near the center of the field."

Of the 97 RAF student pilots enrolled in Class SE-42-G, 4 were held over to the next class, 10 were eliminated (5 for flying deficiencies, 5 for non-flying reasons) and 83 graduated. The 104 members of Class SE-42-H had arrived from Gunter and Cochran Fields on 6 June 1942. As temperatures ranged in the nineties or above one hundred degrees Fahrenheit day after day, care was taken to avoid excessive exposure on the post, but inside the barracks and classrooms, the heat was almost unbearable. As with other aircrew training at the time, schedules called for seven or eight days in training and one day off-post for relaxation. Respite from the heat could be found in the post swimming pool, but there was rarely time available to use it.

When members of the class completed their scheduled ground school work and passed all of their exams, the training staff attempted to keep them attending classes. Since Class SE-42-G contained many more mature former servicemen who had already seen service in the police and other agencies of government, they were more prone to voice their views. Moreover, Class SE-42-G had already proved to be the "hard luck" class when a number of its members had been killed in a series of disasters at Gunter and Moody Fields.

Since the RAF students wanted free time to relax and make use of the pool, the entire class apparently refused to join a ground school formation. According to some cadets who were members of the class, even after the new and relatively inexperienced RAFAO had words with them, they still refused to comply. Finally, Colonel Haddon, the post commanding officer, was drawn into the controversy; grievances were presented, and the Craig Field commander authorized a half-day off for relaxation.

Within a few days of the departure of Class SE-42-G, two fatal accidents occurred at Craig Field, one from Class SE-42-H and the other from Class SE-42-I. On Saturday, 8 August, twenty-year-old USAAF Aviation Cadet Wiley M. Dunn of Austin, Texas, was killed when his AT-6A crashed seventeen miles west of Selma. Then, less than twenty-four hours later, at 3:15 a.m., Sunday, 9 August, twenty-year-old RAF Cadet Herbert Riding Jr. of Dodsworth, Yorkshire, was killed when his trainer crashed about eight miles southwest of Craig Field. Dunn's body was shipped to his home in Texas, and Riding's remains were transported to Montgomery on Wednesday afternoon, 12 August for burial in the RAF plot in the Oakwood Cemetery Annex.

Some three weeks later, as the last few members of Class SE-42-H were completing their training, tragedy struck once more, this time to a member of the junior class. During the afternoon of Tuesday, 1 September, two aircraft in a formation of trainers bearing student pilots of Class SE-42-I collided at a point approximately fourteen miles northwest of Craig Field. Twenty-year-old RAF Cadet Frederick Shippam of Oxford bailed out of his damaged aircraft and survived, but twenty-year-old Robert John Spooner of Brundall, Norfolk, was killed in the collision. On

Wednesday, as members of Class SE-42-H were making preparations for graduation, Spooner's remains were escorted by several of his classmates to Montgomery for interment in the RAF plot alongside other RAF casualties.

On Friday evening, 4 September, a reported 360 guests joined the American and British members of Class SE-42-H in the cadet dining hall at Craig Field for a farewell buffet supper and dance. On Saturday morning at 9:00 a.m., "the largest class in the history of Craig Field" was awarded their wings at ceremonies held in the pecan grove. Of the 104 RAF students enrolled in the course, 3 were held over to the next class in order to complete their training, 1 was killed, 6 were eliminated and 98 graduated.

The RAF cadets who completed their training that day and later read the local paper describing the event were undoubtedly both homesick and amused by the publication of a letter from a Selma nurse who had just arrived at an American station in Britain. Lieutenant Agnes L. Miller, U.S. Army Nurse Corps, commented on the beauty of British towns and gardens she had seen, and described the "cutest trains" that, although they had "little bitty box cars," traveled as fast as American trains and "aren't so smoky."

On 7 August 1942, Class SE-42-I arrived at the advanced flying school, while a concert starring Louis Armstrong and Marian Anderson was being held on the stage in Craig Field's pecan grove. The new class included a large number of USAAF aviation cadets and only seventy-five RAF cadets. To that number was added the three men held over from Class SE-42-H, so the total RAF contingent was increased to seventy-eight. In the course of the next nine weeks, they followed the prescribed syllabus in learning to fly the AT-6A trainer.

At about mid-course, Class 42-H had lost LAC Spooner. Now Class SE-42-J arrived to replace Class SE-42-H, and the syllabus continued as in the past, except that students were now required to climb to about twenty thousand feet in order to gain experience using oxygen. The AT-6A was a fast aircraft, but the British cadets envied their American classmates who, near the end of the course, were able to take a transition course in order to gain a few hours flying P-39 and P-40 fighters. The larger number of RAF pilot officers assigned as flying instructors at Craig Field, and the smaller intake of RAF student pilots, made it possible for most of the RAF cadets to be assigned to one of their own countrymen for instruction.

During the final days of August and early September, the class traveled by bus to Eglin Field, Florida, for the gunnery course. At one of the gunnery station's satellite airfields, the members of Class SE-42-I spent almost ten days in the heat and humidity of the coastal area. However, nearby Fort Walton Beach provided swimming and other recreation, thus allowing an escape from the sand fleas and mosquitoes.

During the summer of 1942, while Classes SE-42-G, SE-42-H and SE-42-I were undergoing advanced flying training, major events were occurring in different parts of the world. No doubt the student pilots read about them, but they had no way of yet realizing their significance to their own future service and the course of the war. There was much happening that appeared negative for the Allied cause. On the Eastern Front in Russia, a German army was mopping up in the Crimea, while other enemy divisions were driving toward the Volga River, the city of Stalingrad and the Caucasus Mountains. In the Southwest Pacific, the Japanese paused and consolidated their gains in the Dutch East Indies, New Guinea, the Gilbert and Ellice Islands and the Solomon Islands.

While Japanese defenses were being strengthened in the Pacific islands through the building and equipping of airfields, other Japanese forces drove incessantly through Burma and Assam to the Indian frontier. There were heavy Allied losses and significant enemy gains, and several naval battles had also occurred recently. After the Battle of Midway, reports claiming that the "back of the Japanese Imperial fleet had been broken" appeared to be empty rhetoric. In North Africa, German and Italian forces were poised at a point just inside the western frontier of Egypt, and in August at Dieppe on the coast of France, brave Canadian commandos probed the German defenses of the Atlantic Wall and were repulsed with heavy losses.

On the positive side of the ledger, Malta, the lonely British outpost in the middle of the Mediterranean, still held on defiantly, and its air units regularly fought greater numbers of German and Italian aircraft. In July 1942, although enemy forces were still poised for an attack on Egypt, the British Eighth Army repulsed the invading force. Field Marshal Erwin Rommel, the German commander, steadily built up his reserve air, ground and armored strength in preparation for a decisive struggle near a tiny desert railway station called El Alamein. Allied leaders had met earlier in the year at Quebec, and they met again in Washington during the early summer. Defensive efforts gave way to plans for shifting to the offensive against enemy forces.

Closer to home, other announcements emanating from London and Washington were about to change the course of British aircrew training in the United States. On Friday, 24 July, a joint news release announced that there would be no further RAF student intakes for Arnold Scheme flying schools. A month later, Wing Commander H.A.V. Hogan, DFC, who had guided Arnold Scheme training from its beginning in June 1941, was promoted to group captain (colonel) and was designated director of UK training in the United States, replacing the recently promoted Air Commodore D.V. Carnegie, AFC. Wing Commander Kenneth J. Rampling, former officer commanding, British Flying Training School No. 5 at Clewiston, Florida, was designated to replace Hogan at Maxwell Field. However, Rampling was reassigned to the United Kingdom, evidently by request, and was quickly replaced by Squadron Leader P.F. Heppel, who presided over the final months of RAF aircrew training in the Southeastern United States.

In mid-September, as the members of Class SE-42-I were rushing to complete their flying exercises, Group Captain Hogan returned briefly from Washington to honor a large number of USAAF men who had been instrumental in making RAF Arnold Scheme training a huge success. Arnold Scheme RAF training would continue for a few more months. However, a number of USAAF officers who had contributed to the success of joint aircrew training were being transferred to other duties, so Hogan and the RAF Delegation were anxious to honor them before they departed.

The banquet was held on Friday evening, 18 September, at Montgomery's Standard Club, and the guests of honor included the commanding officers of stations where RAF men had been trained. Major General Barton K. Yount, commanding the USAAF Air Training Command; Major General Ralph Royce, commander of the Eastern Flying Training Command (formerly SEACTC); Colonel W.W. Welsh, former commander of the SEACTC; and Alabama Governor Frank Dixon were among the senior officers and civilians who were honored. Presiding over the festivities were Group Captain Hogan and Wing Commander Kenneth J. Rampling. Other officers from RAFDEL headquarters in Washington included Wing Commanders Edward M. "Teddy" Donaldson and Wilfred Oulton.

A week later, on 24 September 1942, news arrived in Selma that Colonel Julian B. Haddon, who had served as commanding officer of Craig Field since August 1941, had been nominated for promotion to brigadier general. A few days later, the promotion was confirmed. As a result of this recognition of efficiency, morale soared among staff and cadets at Craig Field, and citizens of Selma paid tribute to the newly promoted general officer.

Unfortunately, the euphoria died rather quickly in the face of yet another tragedy among members of Class SE-42-I. On Saturday, 3 October, Craig Field officers were notified by the U.S. Naval Air Station at Meridian, Mississippi, that nineteen-year-old RAF Cadet David James Calder of Edinburgh, Scotland, had been seriously injured when his advanced trainer crashed near the Alabama-Mississippi state line, two miles west of York, Alabama. The U.S. Naval air station at Meridian had been notified, and the injured RAF student was transported to the hospital in York, a town located about eighty-five miles west of Selma. Sadly, he died there on 6 October, three days after the accident. His remains were transported to Montgomery for interment in the Oakwood Cemetery Annex.

On Friday, 9 October, Class SE-42-I graduated in ceremonies held in the pecan grove near the center of Craig Field. In his address before the gathering of students, staff and guests estimated to number one thousand, Lieutenant Colonel Charles H. Anderson assured the graduates that "you have proved that you have the right stuff." Brigadier General Julian B. Haddon presented diplomas, and Major George F. Anderson, director of training, presented wings to the graduating pilots. Of the seventy-eight-man RAF enrollment, four were held over to the next class, two had been killed, three were eliminated for flying deficiencies and sixty-nine graduated with a very large class of USAAF aviation cadets and student officers.

The fifty-eight new members of Class SE-42-J arrived at Craig Field on 8 September, and when Class SE-42-I graduated, they were elevated to senior-class status and joined by the four men held over to complete training. A few days later, on 11 October, the seventy-five RAF members of Class SE-42-K arrived with their classmates as the junior class. Shortly after their arrival, Brigadier General Julian B. Haddon was transferred to the Amarillo Army Airfield in Texas, and Lieutenant Colonel Charles H. Anderson was elevated to the command of the USAAF advanced flying school at Craig Field.

Procedures remained essentially the same as in the past. The British and American student pilots of Class SE-42-J underwent the stiff Form 64 USAAF physical examination shortly after their arrival. Apparently the ground school took a more realistic bent by encompassing intelligence reports and had much practice in recognizing tanks, as well as the naval vessels of all categories and nations. The flying department still required student pilots to complete ten hours on Link Trainers, four hours of aerobatics, four day cross-country flights, three night cross-countries, ten hours of night flying and a number of hours of combat flying. After gaining oxygen experience by climbing to twenty thosuand feet, the student pilots underwent combat flying exercises or rat racing at low-level and higher altitudes as well.

On Tuesday, 10 November, Class SE-42-J completed its flying training and, owing to inclement weather, graduation exercises were held in the post chapel, and Craig Field's new commanding officer, Lieutenant Colonel Charles H. Anderson, presided. Of the gross RAF enrollment of sixty-two students, one was held over, two were eliminated for flying deficiencies and fifty-nine graduated. Class SE-43-A arrived to replace the departing graduates, and Class SE-42-K was elevated to senior-class status.

Just prior to Thanksgiving Day, Lieutenant Colonel Anderson was assigned to temporary duty at USAAF headquarters in Washington, and Colonel Earl L. Naiden, a veteran of air operations in the Philippine Islands, Java and India, replaced him as commanding officer at Craig Field. During Naiden's service in India, he was also credited with helping to organize and establish operations to airlift supplies from India to Burma and China ("flying the hump"). On 9 December, Anderson was promoted to colonel and subsequently assigned as commanding officer of the central instructors' school at Maxwell Field.

As the members of Class SE-42-K continued their training and departed for their gunnery course at Eglin Field, Florida, twenty-six-year-old Lieutenant Colonel Boyd D. Wagner, the first American fighter ace, disappeared after taking off from a Florida airfield. Wagner, who had shot down a number of Japanese aircraft over the Philippine Islands and New Guinea, was for several weeks the object of a wide search. Both students and instructors at Craig Field and other flying training stations attempted to find the aircraft in the swampy and wooded sections of south Alabama. Finally, the aircraft wreckage containing Wagner's body was found by a west Florida farmer.

The seventy-five-member Class SE-42-K, which had arrived at Craig Field on 11 October, completed its flying training during the first ten days of December 1942. A few days prior to their graduation on 12 December, USAAF Lieutenant William M. Rowe, veteran of service with the Seventeenth Fighter Squadron in the Philippine Islands, gave a lecture on air combat with Japanese pilots. Of special importance to the morale of the RAF flying instructors assigned to Craig Field was the arrival of orders promoting six RAF pilot officers to flying officer, a rank equivalent to first lieutenant in the USAAF. Of the small RAF contingent of Class SE-42-K, one student was held over, two were eliminated for flying deficiencies and seventy-three graduated.

The eighty-seven members of Class SE-43-A had arrived at Craig Field in mid-November 1942 and commenced training immediately. One RAF cadet of Class SE-42-K who had been held over to complete his training became a member of the new class, and just as his classmates departed, the ninety-four members of Class SE-43-B arrived at the advanced flying school. Ultimately, four RAF members of Class SE-43-A were transferred to the new class to complete their training, so total enrollment for that final class of RAF student pilots rose to ninety-eight.

On Friday, 18 December, as training continued for Classes SE-43-A and SE-43-B, Major General Ralph Royce, the new commanding general of the Eastern Flying Training Command, paid a brief visit to Craig Field. A few days later, Flight Lieutenant Stephen D. Simpson, who had been the RAFAO at Craig Field for about five months, was transferred to administrative duty at the headquarters of the Western Flying Training Command at Santa Ana, California. Simpson's replacement as RAFAO was Flight Lieutenant Arthur T. Grime, who since October 1941 had served tours first at the Aviation Cadet Replacement Center at Maxwell Field and then at the primary flying school at Tuscaloosa, Alabama.

As the Christmas season approached, some decorations were strung across the streets of Selma and in shop and home windows, but the Christmas lights, which were usually strung across streets, in shop windows and on the steel framework of the Edmund Pettus Bridge, were omitted that year. However, civic clubs, garden clubs and church groups made plans to use a limited amount of lighting in their efforts to entertain the men of Craig Field. Selma's approach to dealing with such numbers was unique. Plans were laid to open a dozen of the oldest and most attractive homes in the city between the hours of 5:00 and 7:00 p.m. on Christmas Day. Hospitality and entertainment would be provided in each house. In order to light the way for the guests, outside Christmas lights were to be used only for that time period at each of the houses along the "Christmas Trail."

On Wednesday, 30 December 1942 at about 5:00 p.m., twenty-five-year-old Flying Officer Philip Jones (Tuscaloosa and Gunter), a native of Wilmslow, Cheshire, and a flight instructor at Craig Field, was killed while flying one of the Curtiss P-40 fighters assigned to the advanced flying school. Jones, one of the first RAF instructors at Craig Field, had been awarded his wings with Class SE-42-B at Craig Field in February 1942. At 1:00 p.m. on Saturday, 2 January 1943, Jones's funeral was conducted in St. Paul's Episcopal Church in Selma. Six of his RAF instructor colleagues from Craig Field served as pallbearers, and a larger group of RAF cadets and instructors attended the services and accompanied the young pilot's remains to Oakwood Cemetery Annex in Montgomery for burial services.

A member of the final RAF intake at Craig Field, John McKenzie-Hall (Tuscaloosa and Gunter), a native of Tasmania, assessed his advanced flying training and recorded a traumatic landing in an AT-6A, which was common to many wartime American and British cadets:

> *Apart from an unnoticed ground loop on my first solo in England, I had never come close to having an accident and this, together with my feeling of confidence in my new-found ability, led to my one and only accident in 25 years of flying. On 13 February 1943, I carried out a cross-country flight from Craig Field to Maxwell to Dothan and returned via Maxwell to Craig. This was a 3 hour and 15 minute flight, partly following light lines, partly Dead Reckoning navigation, and partly radio beam interception. On rejoining at Craig, I was given clearance to land and made a perfect approach and touchdown. I stopped very quickly without the use of brakes and never veered from the center of the runway. The tower called me to clear the runway immediately as another aircraft was on the approach, but I couldn't.*
>
> *My log book is annotated forever with the cryptic note signed by a very irate Captain A.S. Cresswell: "Student landed wheels-up due to neglecting to lower the landing gear while making a night landing." I do not remember the undercarriage warning horn blowing as I throttled back. I do not remember the absence of the undercarriage green lights indicating wheels down and locked. I do not remember failing to carry out down-wind checks and final approach checks on undercarriage. I do, however, remember that sickening, sliding, metallic noise as propeller grinds into tarmac and flaps crumple into the trailing edge of the wing.*
>
> *Then, with a sudden complete silence under a beautiful canopy of bright stars, I do remember stepping, with great embarrassment, from the wing directly onto the ground. Awaiting the arrival of fire engines, jeeps, crash wagons, ambulance, and the prospect of making two foot-slogging circuits of the airfield next day with an aircraft tyre around my neck as punishment. To my shame, all of this [occurred] just five days before graduation. Fortunately, I was allowed to graduate and, with new flaps and prop, the aircraft was flying again in a couple of days.*
>
> *The period at Craig Field had not been all work. For the first time, I had been able to get off the field and see something of the area and those who lived around the airfield. Apart from the occasions when I was confined to camp to walk "tours," I enjoyed freedom of access to town in off-duty time. A dusty bus journey would take us to Selma, where the hospitality of the local inhabitants had to be experienced to be believed. If we wanted to sample bigger city life, we could go to Montgomery. We young strangers were an experience too to most Americans in Alabama, it seemed. I was always being asked to say "grass" and similar words, and these Anglo-American exchanges would almost inevitably bring the next round of drinks and an invitation to*

visit. I began my further education in the American way of life at this time, and being very young and immature, was fortunate in these lessons which gave me a thorough preparation for the months ahead.

In the course of training, my particular group of friends was truly international in origin. Though varying widely in backgrounds and temperamentally dissimilar, we were attracted together by a wartime situation in an alien country, and a youthful zest to live dangerously. Juan A. Adams-Langley from Chile was excitable, highly temperamental, and explosive, but since he was older and had had previous flying experience, he brought a mature character to the group. John D. Ditchburn was quiet, sometimes moody, but had a presence, which reflected a Middle East background from a family of some pre-war eminence. Hugh Owen Robinson from Jamaica was an electric character of infinite charm. His father trained race horses, and Hugh was just as frisky and unreliable as some of them must have been. Lastly, Michael Gordon Welch from Argentina was quiet, intensely religious, reliable, very determined, and a staunch friend. Though most of us were separated in the course of training, Michael remained with me as an instructor in America after graduation, but we lost touch after he was later posted to a BFTS in Florida.

Of the ninety-eight-man intake for Class SE-43-B, four cadets were held over to complete their training, one was killed in training, three were eliminated and ninety graduated. Four RAF cadets were held over to complete their pilot training, and, of those, two were eliminated for other than flying-related reasons and were posted to Canada for remustering. Two others completed their flying training with Class SE-43-C. These two RAF student pilots received their wings with a large number of USAAF cadets on 26 March 1943 and departed for the United Kingdom via Canada.

Denys Rowland Ding, who had traveled from the interior of China to Britain to join the RAF, arrived in the United States as a twenty-eight-year-old member of Class 42-D (Tuscaloosa and Gunter). Ding arrived at Craig Field in April 1942, and upon graduating he volunteered to serve as a flying instructor in the United States. This practice of interviewing graduating RAF cadets and offering them duty as flying instructors was begun with Class SE-42-A, and continued through Class SE-43-B, the final course of the Arnold Scheme. A few graduates of one of the British flying training schools also served as flying instructors until a total of more than six hundred British flight instructors were employed in American flying schools as a sort of reverse lend-lease.

Early on, most RAF instructors were assigned to USAAF basic flying schools because the need was apparently greatest there, but a fairly large number of RAF pilot officers also instructed in both single-engine and twin-engine advanced flying schools. In a few rare instances, RAF graduates were also used as check pilots in primary schools where large numbers of RAF students were being trained. In April 1942, Denys Ding became one of those few when he volunteered to serve as an instructor. After "kitting out" as a pilot officer in Toronto, Canada, and attending a flight instructors' course at Maxwell Field, he was assigned to the Alabama Institute of Aeronautics at Tuscaloosa, the primary school from which he had graduated.

Denys Ding's comments about his assignment as a flying instructor provide insight into the experience and the time:

The problem [lack of instructors] resolved itself in time, but it would be nice to think that we in some way helped in putting that look of shock on the faces of the German High Command when the USAAF appeared so rapidly on the daylight bombing scene and in such unexpectedly large numbers. My reasons for volunteering to stay and instruct were more selfish.

I was older than the average cadet and believed that age was a handicap in flying. I have since learnt very differently about that one. However, the extra 6 months of intensive flying gave me much greater confidence in my flying abilities and, who knows, may well have been the reason I got through the war in one piece.

The impact of America on some of the RAF boys was quite stunning. It was, I think, in inverse proportion to the amount of time they had spent outside their own little tight environment back home. Not unnatural, and anyway confined to a very small minority. They just wanted to get back to the U.K. A large number were shaken by the peacetime approach to training in the Army Air Corps Schools, though some of the "bull" had been worn away by previous RAF classes by the time we got to Tuscaloosa.

And we wore it away a bit more. Seriously resented by some, who knew little of local problems, was being instructed on how to treat "Negras"—no fraternizing, and just call them "John." This was too much of a challenge for some of the fellows, and the first thing they did, as a result, was to "frat" like mad. And they made some good friends as a result. In the overall picture, these things all became very minor matters. We soon settled in, and the very vast majority of us thoroughly enjoyed ourselves, and I can't overemphasize that. It was a great experience!

Our American contacts were all extremely friendly and hospitable, embarrassingly so at times and, looking back, I realize they were also very, very patient. If some resented our being in the USA they kept it to themselves, and on only one occasion did I come up against anything I would call "anti." And what timing! I had driven up to Birmingham with my girlfriend, Algie, to join her friends at the Debs Ball. A fine affair. The following day, someone threw a recovery party (milk punch) in his room at the Tutwiler Hotel.

Towards the end of the party, I was cornered and harangued at some length on the reasons why the USA would never, never, get involved in the war. It was strong isolationist stuff. Within minutes of this one-sided conversation (I had agreed with everything being said), someone burst in and announced that the Japs had bombed Pearl Harbour—an unforgettable moment.

Denys Ding untimately returned to the United Kingdom and flew DH Mosquito aircraft on operations. After the war, he returned to his tobacco company job in China for a brief period before the Communist takeover, but left and settled in the Algarve in Portugal.

The United States also experienced phenomenal change. Too many citizens of Selma and other towns and counties of the former cotton and slave states were caught up in a James McPherson Ossian-like ideal, which was more firmly embedded in the Southern psyche by the Hollywood production of *Gone With the Wind*. The effect of that film's propaganda proved to be pervasive and devastating. Great romantic myths were sometimes easier to live with than realities.

With other like-minded citizens of similar towns and counties, Selma, Alabama, remained a place filled with historic memories, a place whose citizens looked backward to an imaginary history rather than to an uncertain future. That Selma's citizens and other Southerners and their leaders failed to recognize the portents of change that two decades later would produce the greatest social revolution in American history was not their fault. During the 1960s, the reputations of many towns and cities were tarnished forever by ugly racial strife. When television cameras recorded and broadcast brutality and murder for the entire world to see, Selma and the state of Alabama made a down payment on a long-overdue debt owed to all African Americans by whites of the nation.

USAAF SINGLE-ENGINE ADVANCED FLYING SCHOOL NAPIER FIELD, DOTHAN, ALABAMA

Although the region around Mobile and Pensacola had long been settled by Spanish, French and British colonists, extensive settlement of the interior regions of southwest Georgia, west Florida and south Alabama did not come until much later. When in 1813 Creek Indians attacked Fort Mims and killed its garrison as well as the women and children seeking refuge there, war came to the region. Following the awful revenge that was taken on a band of Creeks at Horseshoe Bend in 1814, removal of the Creek Nation westward occupied the next three decades.

Much of that region was opened up to the cultivation of cotton and was settled by people from Georgia, the Carolinas, Virginia, Maryland and points north. Before the land was cleared of trees for planting crops, the Indian "old" fields and land along river and creek bottoms proved to be ideal areas for livestock to use as open range. For the five decades extending from 1836 to 1886, all of the sparsely populated counties of the region were referred to as "cow counties" because they had more cattle than human beings.

The Atlantic Coast Line Railroad penetrated the region in 1884, and during the years following 1885 capital and people moved in. Spur lines pushed on to the Gulf Coast, and huge lumber mills were put into operation cutting the vast tracts of virgin pine forests that covered the sand and clay hills of west Florida and south Alabama. In 1887, a settlement grew up along both sides of the railroad line amidst a three-square-mile plateau. The name "Dothan" was evidently adopted from Biblical references to a Canaanite town that was noted for its two wells, with the nearby Plain of Esdraelon renowned for its grazing and its pass into the hill country of Judah.

That the community's name was taken from the ancient land of Canaan may have no significance at all. However, it may well be that, given the frontier violence that prevailed when the Alabama village was the center of vast lumber operations, the label could have been administered by a fundamentalist preacher who was rebuking the "Canaanites" for "poisoning" his flock. A century later, it is impossible to determine if Dothan, Alabama, had "two wells" that were really wells or whether two widely known saloons (one on each side of the railroad tracks) were the "watering places" that attracted the lumberjacks of the region.

Whatever the reason for its peculiar name, by 1890 Dothan had a population of 247 people. Within a few years, the Central of Georgia Railroad pushed its lines into Dothan from the east. Then, with the building of the Atlanta and St. Andrews Bay Railway, a short line that linked Dothan and Panama City, the struggling and unattractive village became the major center in the region for shipping lumber and naval stores.

The village of Dothan, Alabama, also became the major market town for delivering the necessary supplies, equipment and services over unpaved roads to the people living in the scattered lumber camps of the region. Little wonder that for the ignorant and poverty-stricken people living and working in the isolation and ugliness of the scattered camps, the Biblical injunction, "For I heard them say, let us go to Dothan" should come to have special meaning. Since during that era Dothan was the only settlement within a hundred miles, there was nowhere else to go to escape the swamps, forests and dismal camps.

In 1901, when Houston County, Alabama—which contained 371,000 acres of land—was split off from Henry County, Dothan—which then had a population of slightly more than three thousand people—became the county seat. Although much timber in the immediate vicinity of Dothan had been cut by the turn of the century, the town remained a market for lumber and naval stores. Dothan was also a source of supplies for dozens of lumber camps scattered over the vast tracts of timber in west Florida. Not only did these lumber camps produce timber and naval stores but, in Jacqueline Cochran, they also produced one of the most famous aviatrixes of the twentieth century.

During the succeeding decades, Houston County, Alabama, which occupied the southeastern corner of the state, switched from cattle and lumber to farming. The stumps and roots of cut-over areas were burned and grubbed out to open the land to cotton farming. With the liberal application of fertilizers, plenty of sunshine and regular rainfall, the county began to prosper as an agricultural center. However, cotton farmers also began to encounter difficulties. The price of cotton was already inordinately low when the boll weevil scourge swept the region just after the turn of the century. Weevil infestations destroyed many cotton crops, and despite efforts made by the Alabama and United States Departments of Agriculture as well as liberal use of arsenate compounds, this plague did not end.

Finally, in desperation, many farmers of the region planted pecan trees while others began to switch from cotton row crops to peanuts. If some Houston County farmers in gratitude subscribed to the fund that erected the monument to the boll weevil at nearby Enterprise, Alabama, it would not be surprising. The boll weevil infestations were a blessing in disguise, because this insect forced farmers of the region to grow crops other than cotton, and the act of introducing diversified agriculture brought a measure of prosperity to Dothan and neighboring towns of the region.

During the 1920s, south Alabama continued to grow, despite an agricultural decline that began around 1925. By 1930, Houston County had a population of around 40,000 people, and Dothan had grown to maturity along the railroad lines. In 1930, the town had a population of 15,471, and about 30 percent were African Americans. With its network of intersecting railroads and highways, it had already become a marketing and distribution center for a corner of southwest Georgia, a wide area of southeastern Alabama and portions of west Florida. Dothan's courthouse and adjacent office buildings housed county government offices. The town's cotton and peanut warehouses, farm implement dealerships, seed and feed stores and cotton gins, cottonseed oil mills and fertilizer factories served the needs of the large agricultural community of the surrounding area.

During the 1930s, the decade of the harshest economic depression in United States history, Dothan experienced diminishing revenues and massive unemployment, as did other towns and cities. In Houston County, problems related to poverty were even worse than in the towns. Black and white tenant farmers suffered the most, but still tried to eke out a living on worn-out and eroded farmland owned by someone else. In an effort to reduce agricultural surpluses and discourage farming on depleted lands, the Department of Agriculture purchased much of the marginal land, removed it from production, assigned young men of the Civilian Conservation

Corps (CCC) to plant pine trees on it and converted it into national forests. In order to avoid further erosion, county agricultural agents sought to teach farmers how to terrace their land.

Poverty was widespread, and New Deal agencies were organized for the purpose of providing relief to the suffering and creating jobs for the unemployed. The WPA (Works Progress Administration) and PWA (Public Works Administration) employed thousands of people and allocated funds to the state governments. Counties and municipalities also received allocations of money for the purpose of putting people to work repairing and paving roads, constructing bridges and public buildings and working on other public works projects.

In the course of the 1930s, although most roads in the country remained unpaved, major highways crossing the region were being paved as rapidly as possible. Some seven state and federal highways connected Dothan with the outside world. U.S. Highway 231, which linked Chicago and Miami, passed directly through Dothan and was paved early in the decade. Soon, regularly scheduled buses joined tourists in automobiles as they passed through the town to and from Florida.

As was common practice among towns during the time, Dothan owned its own electrical distribution system. The town fathers also boasted about the availability of an excellent municipal water supply; a compact, well-lighted business district with paved streets; and a large number of paved thoroughfares radiating in all directions from the town's center. By 1938, Dothan was sprucing up its appearance. Its storefronts were being modified and repainted and azaleas, camellias and other flowering plants adorned small parks and areas around public buildings, as well as the yards of houses located along the shaded streets of the town.

In 1940, Dothan had a population of about twenty thousand people, and Camp Rucker, a huge United States Army training station, was built several miles west of the town. The military reservation further stimulated economic and social activities in Dothan. It was perceived as a progressive community, and one indication of the quality of life in the community was a country club and golf course. In cooperation with Houston County, the town was also in the process of developing a municipal airport on a 210-acre tract of land adjacent to Highway 64, some 2.7 miles west of the town.

Early in 1941, when officers of the United States Army Air Corps were seeking sites for the construction of flying schools, Dothan was recommended by the Alabama Aeronautical Commission. Civil and military officers visited the town and surveyed sites for an advanced flying school in different parts of the county. For the school site, army air corps officers approved a large peanut field located along the Dothan-to-Ozark highway near the village of Grimes, Alabama. As was standard practice in the procurement of similar sites for military installations, officials of the town of Dothan and Houston County, Alabama, purchased the approved tract of land and then leased it to the army air corps for twenty-five years at a charge of $1 per year. The 1,500-acre tract was located some eight miles northwest of Dothan and cost local authorities $130,000.

On 2 May 1941, the War Department allocated $3,100,000 for construction of a USAAC advanced flying school, and Major Earle E. Partridge was named project officer and first commanding officer. Plans called for one thousand acres of the tract to be taken up by the landing field, and the domestic site would contain 141 buildings, a 400,000-gallon water tank and a sewage treatment plant. The airfield's two hangars would be located close by a paved parking and warm-up apron 380 feet wide by 5,200 feet long, and the airfield was to have four paved runways measuring 300 feet wide by 4,500 feet long. Target butts for the firing of machine guns and small cannons were also included in the airfield plan.

The Southeastern Construction Company of Ozark, Alabama, and the Henderson, Black and Greene Company of Troy, Alabama, were awarded contracts for grading and preparing the airfield and constructing the cantonment. Since the flying school was scheduled to commence operations on 15 January 1942, site-leveling work began on 23 June 1941. Work on the landing ground and domestic site proceeded steadily; the construction of buildings commenced around 1 August 1941. Then, owing to the demand for greater advanced training capacity, the contractors were authorized to hire more men and expand work schedules so as to complete the job by 15 December 1941.

Early in October 1941, as work on the flying school was progressing, Major James L. Daniel Jr. replaced Major Earle E. Partridge Jr. as project officer and commanding officer of the new station. By the end of the month, one runway had been paved and ferry pilots had flown in ten North American AT-6A trainers from the assembly plant at Dallas, Texas. While work continued and items such as furniture, bedding, office supplies, tools, spare parts and miscellaneous equipment were being delivered and put into place, the question was raised concerning a name for the new station. Where possible, policy of the newly formed United States Army Air Forces indicated a preference for naming airfields for deceased airmen who were natives of the state in which the airfield was located.

Initially, a proposal was made to name the station after USAAC First Lieutenant Fred I. Patrick, who had been killed in an air accident in 1934. However, instead of choosing that name, responsible civil and USAAF officers named the new base after Major Edward L. Napier, MD (1883–1923), of Union Springs, Alabama, who was killed in an aircraft accident while seeking qualification as a flight surgeon in the United States Army Air Service.

In addition to Napier Field, the main airdrome, the new advanced flying school was required to develop at least three auxiliary airfields, which would be essential for proper training once the school's enrollment capacity was reached. The auxiliary airfields that were selected and prepared for use by the advanced trainers were located near Wicksburg, Alabama; at Headland, Alabama; and at the Dothan Municipal Airport, some five miles southeast of Napier Field. In addition to these auxiliary airfields, the training squadrons at Dothan shared with other training stations the use of five additional airfields for purposes of organizing day and night cross-country exercises.

During the autumn of 1941, Class SE-42-A was undergoing training at three other advanced flying schools. Classes SE-42-D and SE-42-E were reaching the final days of their primary training. And while Classes 42-B and 42-C were completing their work at two USAAF basic flying schools, some 1,500 men worked night and day to build Napier Field. Around 1 August construction had commenced and, except for some final touches to several buildings, paving roads and walks and landscaping, much of the domestic site was ready for occupancy by early December. Strangely, in an otherwise fairly straightforward military construction project, a glitch occurred in supply delivery schedules. Although the cadet skeet range had not yet been built, three train carloads of clay pigeons arrived at Napier Field. They had to be stored for some months until the flying school's skeet range could be built.

By 7 December 1941, more than one thousand officers and men had arrived in the mud of the new station and were rapidly preparing to receive student pilots. Experienced flying instructors, many of whom had taught flying at Kelly Field and other advanced flying stations, flew with recently graduated USAAF officers and trained them how to teach student pilots. Training squadrons were organized, and ground school buildings were equipped and made ready. As they awaited the arrival of the first class, the flying instructors took turns in the available aircraft and flew about the region devising and double-checking procedures that they hoped would ensure safety while everyone was compelled to use the single paved runway. In addition, they familiarized themselves with such essentials as airfield regulations, maintenance and communications procedures, records keeping, the terrain of the region and seasonal wind and weather patterns (wind rose data).

On Monday morning, 15 December 1941, at Cochran Field, Georgia, more than two hundred miles from Dothan, the members of Class SE-42-B were awakened from their slumbers at the ungodly hour of 2:30 a.m. A few days earlier, these men had completed basic flying training, and they were now preparing to be transported by coach to the advanced flying school at Napier Field. Following an early breakfast and the loading of their baggage, they boarded a bus and departed at 6:00 a.m. In Americus, Georgia, the driver made a wrong turn and was compelled to reverse the bus up a steep hill and, in doing so, ruined the already weak clutch. The coach was able to continue on to Albany, but there the men were switched to another vehicle to continue their journey southwestward to Dothan.

When the RAF student pilots arrived at the new station, they were met and welcomed by USAAF officers and Flight Lieutenant William W. Watson, who had served with the RAF during the 1939–40 debacle in France and as RAF administrative officer at Lakeland, Florida. On 12 January 1942, Flight Lieutenant Alfred G. Hill of Birmingham replaced Watson as RAFAO. Before the war, the dapper thirty-two-year-old Hill served with the RAF in Egypt, and later in northern France. While being evacuated at Dunkirk, Hill had been wounded in the knee by shrapnel and was hospitalized for three months. Since June 1941, Hill had served as RAF administrative officer at Darr Aero Tech Primary Flying School, Albany, Georgia.

Among the men under Hill's administrative care at Napier Field were fifteen prior servicemen, including nine who had served in the Royal Engineers, one who was a member of a bomb disposal team, one photographer and four others who had served in various capacities with RAF squadrons. Class SE-42-B also counted several men who had served in various police forces within the United Kingdom. One of its members, Sydney M. Kent of Cornwall, was a lay minister in the Methodist Church and was a very popular speaker at churches in each town near the flying field at which he was stationed. Two twenty-five-year-old RAF cadets, LAC Roderick Webb of Santiago, Chile, and LAC Peter Compton of Buenos Aires, Argentina, also arrived at Napier Field.

Edgar T. Castle of Canterbury, Kent (Camden and Macon), recalled that "Napier Field at Dothan, Alabama was a new base; in fact it was not completed for ages after we, the first class to undergo training there, arrived. There was mud everywhere and life was pretty basic, but the food was good." Since the base was still under construction, and these men were the first to be assigned to Napier Field, discipline was very lax temporarily, and during the days before flying began, there were greater opportunities to get away from the station than there had been in the basic flying schools. Within two days of their arrival, most of the RAF men visited a local cinema in Dothan and attended *Keep 'Em Flying*, a comedy starring Abbott and Costello, but that brief period of relative freedom was not to last.

After being issued flying helmets and radio headsets and gaining some familiarity with their new surroundings, the RAF student pilots joined their assigned squadrons on the flight line to meet their flying instructors. In addition to being warned about the necessity of adhering to regulations and maintaining good flying discipline, they were warned to avoid crash-landings in the vast snake-infested swamps of the region. Another startling announcement was that the pace of their training was being sped up, and they should expect to fly seven days per week in order to complete the advanced flying course in six or seven rather than ten weeks. Flying commenced at Napier Field on 20 December, and each student was scheduled to fly one hour per day for the first three days.

As a natural first step, they were required to familiarize themselves and then to commit to memory the complex cockpit procedures for taking off, flying and landing the classy and fast AT-6A trainers. They had to learn quickly about hydraulic flaps, as opposed to those on the BT-13s, which they were accustomed to cranking down by hand, and they found it disconcerting, to say the least, when, as the engine was cut, a horn blared to warn the pilot to lower the undercarriage. Learning to fly these "real airplanes" was exciting and demanding work, but a pleasure after weeks of experience first on biplanes, and then on under-powered BT-13s.

Although flying had become an obsession with most of the students, there were other duties to be performed. As a part of their training, the USAAF aviation cadet organization was continued, and cadet officers and noncommissioned officers were appointed for Class SE-42-B as well as for each squadron. During night hours, when most of the station's officers were not on duty, cadet officers were assigned to maintain discipline and perform other duties, such as "Officer of the Day." As Christmas drew near, many of the young men began to rearrange and trade duty schedules. If the distance was not too great, large numbers of them made plans to travel back to visit friends in their adopted hometowns where they had received primary flying training, but most such plans had to be canceled because of weather problems.

In the afternoon of 22 December, heavy rains reminiscent of a monsoon set in. On the grounds around the barracks and on the flight line at Napier Field, water and mud were everywhere. Since it was believed that the young men lacked sufficient time to be permitted to fly the advanced trainers in such rough weather, flying was halted and the students were assigned to put in some time on the Link Trainers. The rains continued much of the day on Christmas Eve, but each time it slackened, aircraft took off from the single runway. After some four to five hours of flying, several men soloed. However, since so much time had been lost for many other members of the class, First Lieutenant Cy Wilson, director of training, announced that if the scheduled graduation date was to be met, flying would have to be required on Christmas Day.

Christmas morning was dry, so flying continued, but the rains resumed in the afternoon. Flying was canceled late in the afternoon, and the men were allowed to leave the station between 5:30 p.m. and 11:30 p.m. Many of them traveled to Dothan to see a film and have a meal in Register's Cafeteria or Max's Grill. Back at Napier Field, mud around the incomplete airdrome was still about four inches deep, so the men wore their flying boots almost everywhere. During free time in their barracks rooms, they talked about girls and flying, and the *Christmas Broadcasts to the Forces* made on BBC by King George VI and Prime Minister Winston Churchill.

After all of the members of the class had soloed in the advanced trainers, the number of accidents increased. Despite the warning horns and repeated instructions to go around again, several of the cadets landed their aircraft "wheels up," and still others experienced ground loops when they applied their brakes too soon, or were learning the techniques for making cross-wind landings. Following even minor accidents, standard procedure was to send the student to the station hospital for an immediate medical examination. If the flight surgeon certified him as "cleared for flying," he resumed flying as quickly as possible. If the accident was serious and the student was judged to be unsatisfactory material for military flying, he was eliminated from training, even if he had already flown 150 hours or more.

Given the increased pace of the course, it was not surprising that by 30 December, most of the members of Class SE-42-B had completed twenty hours of flying time. Ten days had passed since their arrival; the cadets had completed almost one-third of the course, and night flying would begin within a few days. As the year 1941 came to a close, Napier Field had two hangars and one paved runway completed; its flying training department was divided into Groups I and II and four squadrons were divided between them. The advanced flying school also had on hand thirty-two North American AT-6A trainers, and was expecting Class SE-42-C within two or three weeks.

Although there were only 90 u/t (under training) pilots in that first class at Napier Field, the twelve cadet barracks, which had a capacity for 489 students, stood ready to receive additional men. Some of these billets had been built with rooms and shared baths that could accommodate about 35 men, while others that had open bays and communal toilet and shower facilities were capable of housing around 49 men. On 31 December, when the station's sewage treatment plant was finally completed and put into operation, conditions on the domestic site were significantly improved.

Before joining their squadrons for scheduled night flying, the student pilots began to learn proper procedures. Then, as night familiarization flights began and continued each night for members of the different squadrons, the young men went to bed each night to the sound of airplanes and arose at 6:30 each morning to the noise of airplanes as well as cement mixers. Since the rains had stopped, contractors were using every available dry period in efforts to pave the remaining unpaved streets and walks of the domestic site, as well as the vast apron that made up the flight line. Link Trainers provided excellent preparation for instrument flying, but since there was a shortage of the simulators, the young pilots were scheduled to put in scattered hours on them during spare daytime as well as evening hours.

Flying accidents continued, as ground loops and other normal problems occurred in the course of learning to fly the fast advanced trainers. Although clouds were building up to the southwest of Dothan, the men of at least one squadron went on their first solo cross-country flight early in the evening of Friday, 2 January. Pre-flight briefings covered such items as weather, compass settings, set speeds, beacons and identifiable landmarks. Their route was to take them from Napier Field to Crestview, Florida, to Marianna, Florida, and back to Napier Field. However, when LAC J.D. "Mac" McCarthy of Ilford, Essex, took off, set his speed and followed the compass heading he had been given, he was surprised that he saw no other aircraft. When the correct amount of time had passed and he should have sighted the first beacon, he saw none.

When he called Napier Field on the radio, he got static and indistinct words. It was a few minutes after 11:00 p.m.; he was lost, and his fuel was running low. Far below, he saw the black of vast heavy pine forests with only an occasional glimmer of light from a house or place of business. Finally, in the distance, at a point that turned out to be some fifteen miles north of Brewton, Escambia County, Alabama, he saw automobile lights cutting through the darkness along a roadway. McCarthy was afraid to parachute into a swamp and have the aircraft crash and perhaps kill someone. He was also fearful of destroying an expensive airplane and having his pilot training brought abruptly to a close.

As a result, he decided to attempt a landing in the darkness. McCarthy switched on his wing lights and began to fly low over the area, seeking a place to land. Through the filigree outlines of a thin screen of hardwood trees, he sighted what appeared to be a large open field, but as he made his approach, his aircraft brushed the treetops. Immediately, he regained altitude and began to seek another field in which to make a landing.

Approximately twelve miles north of Brewton on Highway 31, Circuit Court Clerk Reo Kirkland was driving southward when the noisy, low-flying monoplane dipped low over the highway ahead of his automobile. Recognizing that the pilot was seeking a place to make an emergency landing, Kirkland evidently signaled by flashing his lights on and off a few times as he continued southward along the highway. At a point about nine miles north of Brewton, Kirkland stopped his automobile and turned it so that its head lights illuminated a large swath of a vast open field belonging to Bart Massingale.

The circling, low-flying aircraft also attracted the attention of a number of young people who were attending a party at the Brewton Country Club. Thinking that the pilot might be in trouble, several carloads of young people drove northward along Highway 31 and arrived at Mr. Kirkland's automobile at about the time Cadet McCarthy's AT-6A was slewing and skidding across Massingale's field.

McCarthy was probably too busy concentrating on his forced landing to pay very much attention to the automobiles or anything else. With his aircraft lights on, he had circled the open field, skimmed the tops of trees as he made a long approach, put on full flaps, switched off fuel and engine and stalled into the field, wheels up. Landing gear warning horn blaring, the advanced trainer skidded across the field for several hundred feet, cut through a fence, passed under electrical lines running alongside the highway and came to rest on the edge of the highway.

McCarthy was suffering from shock and some minor cuts and bruises, but he automatically rechecked to be sure that the ignition and fuel switches were in an "off" position and, while the hot engine was ticking as it cooled, he climbed out of the aircraft. A police car arrived, and McCarthy was transported to a hotel in Brewton, where he phoned Napier Field to inform them of his experience and whereabouts. Dreading the next day and having to face his instructor and the Napier Field training staff, he apparently slept little.

The events in and around Brewton, Alabama, on Saturday, 3 January 1942, took place amid heavy rains that arrived in the early morning as a prelude to cold weather. Accompanied by two USAAF investigating officers, McCarthy rode to the crash site and back to the advanced flying school in a military staff car. Maintenance staff from Napier Field removed the trainer's wings, and the aircraft was lifted onto a huge truck and transported back to the advanced flying school.

There, the trainer's instruments were thoroughly checked, and the problem was found. In preparation for aerial gunnery exercises at Eglin Field during the following week, a .30-caliber machine gun had been mounted atop the engine before the front cockpit, and the compass had not been adjusted to compensate for the weapon. As a result, from the beginning of his cross-country flight, McCarthy's compass headings were several degrees off, and instead of flying southward to Crestview on the first leg of his cross-country flight, his flight path took him in a more southwesterly direction from Napier Field. Although he was castigated for attempting a night emergency landing in unknown territory, an action that, at the time, few experienced pilots would even attempt, his getting lost was deemed not his fault. He had survived and saved an aircraft, so he was restored to training without penalty.

On Saturday morning, 3 January, while McCarthy was returning from Brewton, his classmates at Napier Field were busy flying as much as possible during the few days left before their scheduled departure for Eglin Field and the short aerial gunnery course at that station. They also continued to put in hours on the Link Trainer in anticipation of instrument flying practice. Several of the empty barracks at Napier Field were occupied by a contingent of two hundred USAAF aviation cadets, who had been posted there for temporary duty while awaiting assignment to primary flying schools. On that same Saturday, RAF Cadet Patrick Cattrall of Ceylon (Camden and Macon) had the dubious distinction of being the first RAF cadet at Napier Field to cancel a few demerits by walking several hours on the ramp near the barracks.

For being a day late in returning from a brief leave, Cattrall, barely eighteen years old at the time, had been awarded demerits and restriction to quarters at Cochran Field, Georgia, but before departing for Napier Field, he had not had time to complete the assigned punishment. In order to keep the young cadet from being eliminated for disciplinary reasons, Flight Lieutenant J. Leonard Keith, Cochran RAFAO, arranged to transfer Cattrall's records to his Napier Field RAFAO, with the understanding that Cattrall was to discharge his demerit and restriction obligations at the advanced flying school. No doubt others at Napier Field soon joined him in walking tours for minor breaches of discipline or for sloppy quarters, beds, clothing or equipment that had been found and cited by inspecting officers.

In the meantime, training continued. In practicing instrument flying in the AT-6A trainers, it was standard practice for two students to fly together during daylight hours. As one of them completed an hour's experience flying "under the hood," he flew back to the station, exchanged places and the other student gained instrument flying experience. On 6 January a number of the student pilots completed one-hour instrument training flights during the day, and late that night they made another cross-country flight—this one solo to Tallahassee, Florida. They returned to Napier Field at 3:00 a.m.

Next day, as some of the students attended ground school classes, others continued instrument flying practice, and still others of their classmates prepared to depart on Friday, 9 January for their eight-day gunnery assignment to Eglin Field. The rush to complete training on schedule continued, and all of them had now reached that most dangerous time in flying training. They had completed slightly more than 150 hours flying time and were growing increasingly cocky about their ability to handle the sleek all-metal trainers. When out of sight of an instructor, it was perhaps normal for two students flying together to do a little low flying and "beat up" an imaginary "enemy" target, but as members of SE-42-B at Napier Field were soon to find out, it was also dangerous.

A few members of the 550-man course had already died in primary and basic flying schools, and several were known to have been killed on the single-engine advanced trainers at Craig and Maxwell Fields, but until Wednesday, 7 January 1942, Napier Field had not had a fatality. On that day, LACs Kenneth Barlass of St. Annes-on-Sea, Lancashire, and Laurence S. Bell of King's Heath, Birmingham, were flying together west of Napier Field over the Pea River State Forest between Ozark and Enterprise, Alabama, and near the Camp Rucker Military Reservation. Although the aircraft engine may have failed, it is likely that the young pilots were flying low (or diving down over the lake) when their aircraft struck a tree and crashed into Lake Tholocco.

Members of a telephone company line crew were working nearby, saw and heard the crash and rushed to the scene. Evidently Barlass, who was in the front seat, was knocked unconscious and drowned before he could be rescued. Bell, dazed and suffering a concussion, broken arm and bruised ribs, was able to get out of the aircraft, but he might not have reached the lake shore if he had not been rescued from the water by the telephone linemen. The aircraft was now under water, and apparently LAC Barlass was already dead. The telephone line crew unreeled a steel cable and ran it out into the lake from their heavy truck, attached it to the trainer and pulled the aircraft ashore. Cadet Bell was sent to the U.S. Army hospital in Atlanta, Georgia, and a few days later the body of Cadet Barlass was interred in the RAF plot in Montgomery's Oakwood Cemetery Annex.

On Friday, 9 January 1942, members of Class SE-42-B were awakened at 5:00 a.m. and made preparations to leave for Eglin Field. Some of the men flew to the field with their instructors and others departed at around 7:00 a.m. in an army van. They arrived at the Florida station at 11:00 a.m. Facilities at the aerial gunnery station included barracks and tents as well as a small post exchange canteen and movie theatre. Following orientation sessions, the men were free for a short time and made the most of it by walking the two miles through the forest and swamp to the white, sandy beaches of the Gulf Coast.

It was mid-January 1942, and it was bitterly cold even in west Florida, so while the young men awaited their turn to fly and fire their one thousand rounds of ammunition, they often built fires in the field to keep warm. On 15 January, the students of Class SE-42-B completed flying and firing their remaining ammunition and made preparations to return to Napier Field. Next day, the Napier Field trainers and a few of the instructors and men were flown back to the advanced flying school while the remaining students rode back during the afternoon in army vans and trucks.

During the brief absence of SE-42-B students at Eglin Field, several major changes had occurred at Napier Field. When they returned from Eglin on 17 January, the cadets met the members of Class SE-42-C and learned that during their few days of flying training, they had smashed several of the AT-6A trainers. As a result, one of the members of SE-42-B lamented that he hoped "they've left some for us, or else we shall never get our time in." In Class SE-42-B's cadet magazine, *Wings Aloft*, one class "wag" used the tune of the army air corps song and wrote a special stanza that commemorated for posterity a similar observation about their junior classmen:

> *Here they come out of the base leg yonder,*
> *Tearing down out of the sun,*
> *Napier Tower, clamping the same each hour*
> *Second ship, give 'er the gun.*
> *Down they come keeping their wheels up under,*
> *Hitting the deck with a helluva roar,*
> *You can easily see it's 42-C.*
> *They'll bloody soon stop the Army Air Corps.*

Members of SE-42-B might criticize junior classmen for landing "wheels up," despite the "rasping horn" and the control tower operator's frantic radio calls to "get 'em down." However, the same thing had already happened to a few members of SE-42-B and to the occasional "wool-gathering" instructor, and would happen as well to members of later classes.

On Sunday, 10 January, the members of Class SE-42-C had arrived in coaches from the USAAF basic flying school at Cochran Field, Georgia, and commenced flying on 12 January. Among that class were several men who had trained together at Americus, Georgia, including Reginald G. McCadden, James T. Jennings, Harry Hepplewhite, Joseph McKenzie and Richard F.H. Martin. In June 1941, Reginald McCadden of Belfast, Northern Ireland, had begun his flying training as a member of Class SE-42-A at Americus, Georgia. When he and several classmates were about to be eliminated from pilot training with Class SE-42-A, they had been sent to the cooler climate of Butler, Pennsylvania, where they had attended the Graham Aviation Company's Civilian Pilot Training Program School and learned to fly Piper Cubs and Waco biplanes.

McCadden and his successful colleagues had then reentered Class SE-42-C at Souther Field, Americus, and McCadden was appointed class cadet captain. Early in January 1942, having completed primary and basic flying schools, his class was divided and sent in separate contingents to three different advanced flying schools. McCadden and several of his Cochran Field classmates were posted to Napier Field.

Some forty years afterward, McCadden described an experience that indicates some of the problems he encountered within a few days of commencing the advanced flying course. The weather was changeable, even in the relatively mild climate of south Alabama:

> *I took off for night formation flying on the evening of 26 January, and minutes after takeoff, we were recalled as fog was rolling in to the airfield! I was flying on the instructor's port side, and he ordered us into line astern. He succeeded in getting down, but by the time I was due to go in, the runway was fog-bound. At least a dozen aircraft were stranded in mid-air and were eventually directed to fly to Maxwell Field near Montgomery, Alabama.*

Rapid changes in the weather were not the only changes at Napier Field in late January 1942. One change was of a more pleasant nature. A rotation policy had been announced that permitted the men of each of the eight squadrons in advanced flying training to have one day off for each seven or eight days on duty. On 18 January, the "day off" rotation policy was applied to the first of the four odd-numbered squadrons, which contained members of Class SE-42-B, the senior class. In rapid succession, beginning on 18 January, the members of Squadrons 1, 3, 5 and 7 had a day off. Then, beginning on 22 January, Squadrons 2, 4, 6 and 8 followed each other on a twenty-four-hour pass in rapid succession.

During that initial time off, the RAF students pursued their varied interests. Cadet John D. Mackie of Sutton, Surrey, and Class SE-42-C was able to examine the cultivation and processing of "ground nuts." Apparently, Mackie had worked as a buyer for Lever Brothers in London and had bought peanuts, but now got an opportunity to see firsthand how they were grown and processed for market. Although at the time farmers near Dothan were also learning how to plant kudzu, the vine of Japanese origin that was being used widely as ground cover to fight erosion, there is no indication that Mackie took an interest in that process.

Unfortunately, the day off policy could not prevent occasional fatal training accidents. On 20 January 1942, nineteen-year-old Cadet Edgar Hopkin of Gwaun-cae-Gurwen, Glamorgan, South Wales, was flying alone on a night cross-country flight to Birmingham, Alabama, and crashed. When his aircraft crashed at 4:00 a.m. some twenty-eight miles northwest of Montgomery, Hopkin may have been attempting an emergency night landing similar to one of 3 January in which Cadet McCarthy had been successful. Hopkin's remains were interred for a short time in the RAF plot of Montgomery's Oakwood Cemetery Annex.

However, by agreement with his family in Wales, his uncle and aunt, Mr. and Mrs. Lewis J. Davies, made arrangements to have Hopkin's remains moved to New Castle, Pennsylvania, for interment in the Davies plot there. In December 1941, Hopkin had spent much of a seven-day leave visiting in the home of his uncle and aunt. At 2:30 p.m. on 6 May 1942, about five months after his visit to the Pennsylvania town and slightly more than three months after his death, funeral services were conducted for Hopkin in the home of his aunt and uncle at New Castle, Pennsylvania.

A little later during that May afternoon, after a formal graveside military service was conducted by members of American Legion Post 343, Hopkin's remains were laid to rest in the Castle View Burial Park. The services included the traditional military rifle volleys fired by selected members of the Lawrence County Defense Corps (the newly formed home guard), and concluded with the sounding of "Taps."

At Napier Field, as flying continued night and day, the periods in the air were extended to as much as four hours and varied between instrument, formation and cross-country navigation flights. However, some of the young pilots took every opportunity to fly low, to buzz the occasional "target" and to "rat race" about the area. On 2 February, Cadets Raymond Payne and Robert G. Higgins, while supposedly practicing instrument flying, collided with a buzzard. Fearing heavy damage, Payne ordered Higgins to bail out as a precautionary measure, and so he did. Payne landed the aircraft safely and discovered that the only damage was a dented wing.

As the time was drawing near for the surviving members of Class SE-42-B to complete their training, Flight Lieutenant Alfred G. Hill, RAFAO, began to survey records and interview men who would be recommended to appear before the commissioning board, which was scheduled to meet within several days. The Air Ministry's official rule was that one-third of the graduates of each volunteer reserve (RAFVR) class were deemed qualified for commissions as pilot officers, while the remainder would become sergeant pilots who might later in their flying careers be eligible for commissions. Although Class SE-42-B men were being trained at three different advanced flying schools, the one-third distribution rule for commissions applied to the entire class and did not mean that each of the three schools would have an equal distribution of commissions.

When the RAF Commissioning Board met, it reviewed academic, flying and disciplinary records and interviewed several members of Class SE-42-B who had been recommended for commissions by Hill and the Napier Field training staff. In addition to meetings of that board, preparations were also made to inform the men of what would happen to them after completion of training. On 3 February, Wing Commander H.A.V. Hogan, DFC, flew to Dothan from Maxwell Field and met with the students scheduled to graduate. He urged those members of the class who were to be commissioned pilot officers to consider volunteering for an additional six months' duty in the United States as flying instructors. Hogan also gave a lecture on what the majority of them might expect during their sojourn in Canada and on return to the United Kingdom.

While many of the young men had wanted to revisit friends they had made during their primary flying training days, the increased pace of the advanced flying course had not allowed enough free time to do so. In such time that they did have away from the flying school, quite a few members of the course had availed themselves of generous hospitality offered by local citizens, and many of them had attended the "wings" ceremonies that Friday morning, 6 February 1942. LAC Stan Freestone recalled that civilian hospitality "continued at a marvelous level throughout my whole stay in the U.S."

When Class SE-42-B graduated from the USAAF advanced flying school at Napier Field on 6 February at 9:45 a.m., a march past was held as a salute to Class SE-42-B, after which they marched to the post theatre for graduation ceremonies at 10:30 a.m. Lieutenant Colonel Daniel, commanding officer, and Flight Lieutenant A.G. Hill addressed the graduating students. When the USAAF commanding officer remarked that the class had just completed the "toughest flying course in the world," none present disagreed. Daniel handed out diplomas to the graduates, and Lieutenant Cy Wilson, director of training, handed out the silver USAAF wings. Class SE-42-B had enrolled ninety students, of whom four had been held over to the next class to complete flying training, one had been eliminated, two had been killed and eighty-three graduated.

The young men were given a short end-of-course leave that extended over the weekend, and reported back to duty late on Monday, 9 February. On Tuesday evening, 10 February they boarded a train at Dothan with "tearful farewells" and began their long journey northward. Others who also departed would not be gone for very long. Pilot Officer John C. Bliss of Class SE-42-B had left a critically important job as a veteran Metropolitan Police detective inspector to volunteer for pilot training. As others returned to the United Kingdom via Canada, Bliss and several classmates also traveled to Canada to be fitted for RAF uniforms, then they returned to the United States for assignment as flying instructors. Bliss returned to Napier Field to serve his instructional tour of six months.

Class SE-42-C underwent training at Napier Field that was not significantly different from that which had been established for its first class in training. Class SE-42-B was the first RAF class to be sent from Dothan to Eglin Field, Florida, for the aerial gunnery course, but each class in its turn followed that same course. Although the advanced flying school at Dothan was equipped with single-engine North American AT-6A trainers, it had been originally intended as an advanced school for students destined to fly twin- or multi-engine aircraft.

Although the occasional instructor might vary his instruction enough to encompass some of his favorite maneuvers, such actions were soon to become the exception rather than the rule. Some fighter tactics were still taught and aerial gunnery practice continued, beginning with members of Class SE-42-C and continuing for subsequent classes, but the training staff began to de-emphasize fighter tactics and place more value on cross-country flights, instrument flying and navigation exercises.

Owing to their extensive basic training on Vultee BT-13s, most members of Class SE-42-C were able to solo with a minimum of flying time on the faster, more complex AT-6A trainers, and with experience they began rapidly to become more confident. However, because of damage to a large number of aircraft during their first week at Napier Field, some class members were able to complete little more than a thirty-minute familiarization flight in the rear cockpit of an AT-6A trainer.

"It seems that we are cracking up about 3 a day," wrote Cadet Richard F.H. Martin to his mother. "A number of them are caused by the undercarriage not being locked down, and they finish up sliding along the runway on the ship's bottom." Martin's further comment that such "wheels up" landings were "a thrill for those watching but not for the pilot" was classic understatement. Because of the shortage of advanced trainers, it was necessary for some of the instructors to be posted on temporary duty to Dallas to deliver some new aircraft from the North American factory near Love Field. Their absence also delayed the training of their assigned students, but not for long.

A few days later, Richard Martin described some of the continuing problems at Napier Field and his own experience in trying to land during another especially bad day:

> *The course is not very popular on the flight Line, as we have so far cracked up fifteen ships. One instructor and pupil landed wheels up in spite of warnings on the radio from the control*

tower. It is said that both instructor and pupil were shouting at each other so much that they forgot to put the wheels down and did not hear the warnings from the control tower.

They finished up blocking the runway, as I was waiting to land, so I lined up to land on another runway, and then the ship in front of me ground looped on landing and broke its undercarriage, so I could not land on that runway either. Finally, I landed cross wind on the one remaining runway and was OK, but someone behind me ground looped and scraped his wingtip.

It was indeed a rough day and, given the problems of other students, Martin was fortunate in not experiencing an accident. Flying the AT-6A was quite different from flying a Stearman or Vultee, and the combination of the advanced trainer's retractable and very narrow undercarriage, as well as its higher landing speed, required concentration, deft handling and extreme caution.

Although members of Class SE-42-B had had a relatively easy time during their initial days on the new station, Class SE-42-C was not permitted such freedom. Once they were settled in during a weekend, the rigorous training schedule began with a vengeance. As indicated earlier, the squadron rotation system for one day off following seven or eight days on duty was not announced until 18 January, but members of Class SE-42-C might not have known that. Some of them believed themselves justifiably unhappy over restrictions that required them to wait until 22 January to have some time off the station, while others were convinced that they had been singled out for "special" harassment owing to the number of aircraft accidents.

Both groups were at least partially correct in their assessments. The staff at Napier Field was indeed angry about the many accidents. Accident reports were watched closely by higher headquarters and were used to judge staff effectiveness. Moreover, each accident meant a significant amount of paperwork, and sometimes hours in the hangars for maintenance men to do metal repair work and check and double-check the aircraft. Many American flight instructors appeared to be in a desperate hurry to complete the training of classes earlier than scheduled and appeared to be insensitive to the needs of the students who lived under constant pressure for fear of failure.

Although temporary assignment to Eglin Field for the gunnery course provided one break, other respites from flying were much more important to cadet efficiency and morale than training officers realized at the time. Even so, it was several months later before the pace of training was eased and cadets received more time off.

Depending upon the type of flying, schedules varied considerably. Reveille was usually held at 5:30 a.m., but owing to night flying schedules, some men were not required to stand reveille. However, under normal circumstances, the cadets rose at 5:30 a.m., had breakfast at about 6 a.m., returned to their barracks at around 6:30, spent a half-hour preparing their rooms, toilets and showers for inspection and then reported either to the flight line or to ground school. Morning hours for these activities stretched between 7:00 a.m. and noon. Following lunch at 12:30, those who had attended ground school in the morning reported for flying at 1:00 p.m., while those who had flown in the morning reported to ground school classes. At around 4:00 p.m., afternoon flying and classroom instruction ended.

Then, while the aircraft were being inspected and serviced for night flying, the cadets reported for physical training at 4:15 p.m. and dinner at 5:30 p.m. Those scheduled for "early" night flying (between about 8:30 and 11:00 p.m.) reported to the flight line at about 7:40 p.m., while others either took care of housekeeping chores, studied or reported to the Link Training building for scheduled one-hour instrument training sessions. Cadets who were scheduled for "late" night flying (between about 12:00 midnight and about 4:00 a.m.) tried, but rarely succeeded, in getting sufficient rest before their scheduled flight time.

In addition to flying, regular attendance at ground school classes continued as at the primary and basic schools. Occasionally, there were also special lectures by visiting RAF officers who talked about RAF methods or about navigation or combat flying. Moreover, USAAF officers spoke to the members of Class SE-42-C about the shortage of flying instructors, indicating that a number of graduates of Classes SE-42-A and SE-42-B had been commissioned and were being assigned as flying instructors in USAAF primary, basic and advanced flying schools.

Such lectures were informative and were cause for speculation about the future, but with few exceptions, most of the men rejected the idea of serving as instructors; they were intent upon returning to the United Kingdom for an operational assignment. In the meantime, they were anxious to complete training as quickly as possible, but they also valued free time away from airplanes and military matters. Since the small town of Dothan offered little in the way of recreation for the young men, many of them sought to travel elsewhere during the little time they had off-post.

Unwilling to remain in Dothan for the entire period of his all-too-brief first open-post, Richard Martin and a 42-C classmate converted a twenty-four-hour pass into an adventure. In a letter written at the time to his family in Taunton, Devonshire, Martin described their experiences:

> I spent the evening in Dothan with one of my roommates. We went to a film (Fred Astaire in The Second Chorus) and got back to camp about 10 p.m. and slept till 8 a.m., missing breakfast, so we hitched into Dothan and had breakfast there. We then decided that we could not spend the whole day in Dothan, which is a small town with not much to do or see, and that we would hitch hike to Panama City, a port on the Gulf coast.
>
> We walked for about two miles out of Dothan, and a Ford van with seats and windows stopped and asked if we wanted a lift anywhere. They were U.S. Marines in uniform and were doing a tour of a number of towns sticking up recruiting posters. They asked if we would like to come with them, so we did.
>
> We stopped in a lot of places called towns, but often they consisted of one street and the U.S. Post Office. Some looked just like the town one sees on Cowboy films, all buildings except the Post Office were built of wood, and all that was needed was the horses and cowboys.
>
> While the Marines were sticking up posters on "Wake Island," and "Remember Pearl Harbor," and "Join the Marines," we had a quick walk around the places. Since they were small, it did not take long to see everything. Most of them had never seen a RAF uniform before, so we were subjects of great interest.
>
> The biggest town we went to was Andalusia, which was built around a main square, instead of the more usual main street; the residential area looked very pleasant with some attractive houses. We had lunch at a place called Opp; fried chicken paid for by the Marines, which was very kind of them.
>
> We came back a different way through two towns called Samson and Geneva, both nice looking places, and the country around them seemed quite fertile with some green to be seen in the fields. Maybe this is why they looked better than the others we had been through. The rest of the countryside was the usual dusty, red earth with burnt up grass and scrub, with not much growing, and the farms looked as if they were falling to bits.
>
> Oxen and mules were used for ploughing and pulling carts. It is a poor and rough country,

which, they say, is the poorest in the South, and that it has never recovered from the Civil War. The land was so uneven that we did not see a field that looked suitable for a forced landing.

When they postponed their visit to Panama City and joined the marine recruiting team, Richard Martin and his roommate probably did not realize that they were seeing more of the contrasting scenery of south Alabama than perhaps any other British cadets who were trained at Napier Field or elsewhere.

Although the prosperous farms and the poor farms that the RAF cadets saw in the region were less a product of the American Civil War and its aftermath than of geography, following the appearance of the motion picture *Gone With the Wind*, it would have been very difficult to convince many people of that fact. When the region was settled in the nineteenth century, some of the land was a rich sandy loam that continued to yield tons of cotton. However, the poorer soil brought poverty to the people who attempted to wrest a livelihood from it.

When the original forests had been cleared from many stretches of sand and red clay hills, the thin layer of rich topsoil covering this land had yielded one or two good crops. Then, the soil was virtually devoid of nutrients and was capable of growing little more than grass or pine forests. Despite its weakness, this marginal, hilly acreage continued to be farmed, mostly by tenant farmers, so that by the 1930s and 1940s, the land was eroded almost beyond redemption and was incapable of producing crops of any kind without liberal applications of fertilizer.

On the nearby flying field, as training progressed, the members of SE-42-C began their night flying. As with the system used in basic flying schools, they used a four-zone system of air traffic control, which required the young men to concentrate on a wide variety of things. As they circled their aircraft at a specified speed and altitude, awaiting orders to move to a lower tier, they had to remain alert and observe not only their own instruments but also other aircraft in the circuit. They steadily circled their aircraft, moving from the fourth tier to the third, to the second, then to the first until they were directed to land. Then they repeated the process.

In addition to practicing night circuits and landings in crowded skies, the junior classmen at Napier Field gained practice on instruments when they too were assigned to Link Trainer sessions at available hours of the day and night. In addition to formation flying and instrument flying, Napier Field continued to place great emphasis on cross-country navigation exercises.

The first daytime cross-country flight ran from Dothan to Troy to Eufala and back to Dothan. As many of the cadets had done at basic flying schools, a good highway map of the region could sometimes help immensely on daylight flights. When a town was sighted below, if in doubt, it was a relatively easy matter to let down and read the name from either the water tower or the railroad station, double-check location of the town in relation to the destination and continue in the proper direction. If, as sometimes happened, maps or charts were blown from an open cockpit, special ingenuity was called for. With a good memory, a pilot could check water towers and railway station signs. If lucky, he might discover another aircraft on the same exercise that could be followed to the destination.

However, there were other hazards. The danger of running out of fuel and being forced to either bail out or find a field in which to land was always a possibility. Occasionally, small slight scraping collisions occurred while practicing formation flying. Other accidents or unforeseen circumstances could ruin schedules and cause the aircraft to use more fuel than planned. Richard Martin cited one occasion when he was approaching an auxiliary airfield to land when the runway was blocked by a nosed-over aircraft. As a result, he was compelled to circle for some time before being cleared to land.

Every six months, all aviators flying with the USAAF or being trained by them were required to have the thoroughgoing Form 64 physical examination. On occasion, these examinations revealed serious problems and resulted in students being eliminated from training. Although there were many tension-producing events that student pilots encountered in the normal course of training, the greatest was a fear of being found lacking and being washed out of pilot training. One did not feel safe from the "washing machine" until after graduation. Although their numbers were not great, both British and American cadets were regularly eliminated from training at all of the advanced flying schools within two or three weeks of their graduation. An elimination board always reviewed the records of every student being washed out, and board confirmation was always taken reluctantly, especially late in the course. Even so, when a friend was washed out of training and left for Canada, classmates usually felt that the decision was senseless.

For recreation, most of the young men who were trained as pilots at Napier Field often wished to return to the towns where they had first learned to fly. There, they had made good and fast friends and had often been accepted as members of families. Unfortunately, the amount of free time during advanced flying training was seldom adequate to travel the distances and return on time, so they were compelled to search for other sources of off-post recreation. Since the pull of the sea has always been strong for all citizens of the British Isles, it is not surprising that many of the young men stationed in the various classes at Napier Field felt drawn to Panama City, the nearest town on the Gulf of Mexico.

However, they quickly discovered that the town and its sugar-white beaches were crowded with soldiers from nearby army camps, and that the military police enforced an 11:00 p.m. curfew. They also discovered that not only was finding a hotel room difficult, but also the nearby paper mills stank. No doubt some of the young British students made friends in Panama City, but those who were repelled by experiences there found accommodation elsewhere. The inhabitants of attractive inland towns such as Marianna, Florida, were decidedly friendly, and a number of the British students began to visit the numerous parks and lakes of the area, where they enjoyed hospitality.

On Saturday, 7 February 1942, longer cross-country flights became the order of the day for Class SE-42-C, and each squadron in its turn flew the circuit from Dothan via Blountstown to Tallahassee, then after landing at Tallahassee, they flew on to Camilla, Georgia, then back to Dothan. Unfortunately, on one such cross-country flight, twenty-one-year-old Cadet Ronald George Robbins of Horton-cum-Studley, Oxfordshire, crashed his trainer some three miles northwest of Tallahassee and became Class SE-42-C's first training fatality at Napier Field.

Despite the tragedy, flying continued, and on 9 February the members of Class SE-42-B began to return from their short leaves and prepare for departure. Following Class SE-42-B's departure on 10 February, there was a respite of ten days before the third RAF class arrived, so the training staff could concentrate on the training of Class SE-42-C. On 20 February 1942, the 150-man Class SE-42-D arrived to commence training as the junior class at Napier Field. The 6 men held over from the preceding class brought the total enrollment to 156. Flight Lieutenant Sir Anthony Lindsay-Hogg arrived at the same time and replaced Flight Lieutenant Alfred G. Hill as RAF administrative officer. Many people in Dothan were thrilled at having the tall, distinguished Etonian in Dothan, and he was sought out as a speaker at various civic clubs.

For one so young, the thirty-four-year-old baronet whose hereditary seat was Rotherfield Hall in Sussex had led a full and exciting life. For several years, he had served in the king's company of the

Grenadier Guards and as personal ensign to the late King George V. He had traveled extensively, had lived in the United States for more than a year before the war and was an accomplished horseman, automobile race driver and pilot. Declared ineligible for operational flying, he served for two years with the ATA (Air Transport Auxiliary) ferrying aircraft from factories and maintenance units to scattered airdromes in the United Kingdom. During his service as RAFAO at Napier Field, the RAF cadets of different courses perceived him differently, and mentioned being aware of his presence *only* at graduation.

In the meantime, the upper class continued their night cross-country flights, which ran from Dothan to Montgomery to Greenville, Mississippi, then back to Dothan. Winter rains also continued for several days in mid-month, and there was a sea of mud-covered walks and roadways on the air station. "There is mud everywhere," wrote Richard Martin on 22 February 1942, "so we have to wear our flying boots and, as a result, fly covered in mud." As if the rains were not enough, fog often rolled in at night and led to cancellation of night cross-country flights.

Because of bad weather and the continuing hard luck accidents of Class SE-42-C, the final ten days of training were especially difficult for the class. In a letter dated 28 February 1942, Richard Martin described conditions and how he and his classmates felt about the situation:

> This has been the worst week for work. We flew Friday, Saturday, Sunday, and Monday nights. On Friday, we flew early or at least, that is what they call it—from 1900 to 0100 hours. The other nights we were on late, that is, 2359–0430 hours. Most of us get to bed between 0500 and 0600, so you have no breakfast, as that is at 0730. Then, you have to be up by 0900 to have your room ready for inspection, so it is a little sleep and not a lot of food. The meals we do get are poor as we get fed after the American cadets, and it seems mainly to be chicken bones. It is beginning to look as if we get what's left.
>
> We are all getting fed up with being told all the time how bad a class we are, but no one says what we have done wrong, other than we have broken a number of their ships. Anyway, why worry; we are leaving here on the 10th March after getting our Wings on the 6th, and I do not think any of us will miss this camp.
>
> Outside the camp, the people have been very kind, and the hospitality tremendous, especially from the Simses at Marianna. Mr. Sims went to England with the American forces in the last war. We are hoping that they will be able to come to Dothan for our graduation parade. Once that is over, we get a few days leave, and I shall have to get to Americus to say goodbye to the Holstons before leaving for Canada...
>
> I have had a second interview with Wing Commander Hogan, and it looks as if I am going to get a commission! I shall wait until I see it in black and white before I celebrate. He said that 27 had been selected and that this class had broken more ships in a month than any class the Air Corps had ever had in training. So that is why we are unpopular with the Air Corps. He said the number we are supposed to have broken is 46.

Despite the hard work, all of the surviving members of the class were not to graduate. His classmates were shocked when Reginald McCadden experienced two aircraft accidents on successive days and was eliminated within about ten days of graduation.

As noted by Richard Martin and others, considerable resentment of the British presence in the United States was becoming more pronounced during early 1942. Having been pushed for some months by the RAF to reduce the training time from thirty to twenty-six weeks or less, USAAF training officers may have telescoped the training syllabus too much in the immediate aftermath of the Japanese attack on Pearl Harbor. Some insensitive USAAF officers and men asserted that the United States could have launched an immediate counteroffensive against the Japanese if the USAAF had the use of all trainer aircraft produced in the United States and the instructors, equipment and facilities that were used to train British aircrew.

Those who were critical of 1941 British failures in the Western Desert and 1942 ones in Burma and the Far East at Hong Kong and Singapore failed to realize that American failures at Pearl Harbor, Wake Island and in the Philippine Islands were not dissimilar. Those who made insensitive remarks about British aircrew training in the United States either did not know or forgot that timely British investments in the American aircraft and armaments industries provided the "education orders" essential for America's rapid rearmament. Moreover, the USAAF was using many British inventions in developing its own military air power and was learning much of value from the British experience in aircraft design, aircrew training and air tactics.

As Class SE-42-C's training days were drawing to a close, tragedy struck once more. Sadly, on Thursday, 5 March 1942, twenty-five-year-old Cadet Clarence Melville Johnson of Sandal, Wakefield, Yorkshire, was critically injured in an auto accident. On Friday, 6 March 1942, a graduation ceremony was held for Class SE-42-C in the post recreation hall at Napier Field, but Cadet Clarence Johnson could not join his classmates. Wing Commander Hogan made the main address to the students, and Colonel James T. Daniel and Lieutenant Cy Wilson passed out the diplomas and USAAF silver wings. Since RAF wings had not been available for the first graduates, some of the men had gotten RCAF wings and now proceeded to "remodel" them by picking out the "C" and closing the gap between the "R" and "AF."

Immediately after the ceremonies, members of the graduating class had a four-day pass, which many of them used to make fast trips to revisit old friends before departing for Canada and catching a ship back to the United Kingdom. On Saturday, 7 March, Clarence Johnson died in a Dothan hospital, and his remains were conveyed to Americus, Georgia. On 8 March 1942, Johnson's remains were interred in the Harrold family plot in the Oak Grove Cemetery. Records indicate that Johnson's death was probably not counted officially among "fatalities" for the advanced flying school at Dothan.

Not all of the cadets' time was spent flying or away from Dothan. Two members of Class SE-42-D proved to be helpful to the newly organized Houston County Defense Council, which was charged with organizing a home guard unit. Cadet Frank Keeping, a former incident officer in a British home guard unit, spoke to them about air raid organizations in Britain. Because of their interest in training people to spot enemy aircraft, Joseph Anthony "Tony" Weber, who was an expert model plane builder who had made many models that were used for the training of British aircraft spotters, also attracted the attention of the Dothan organization.

Between 28 February and 24 March 1942, without realizing it, RAF members of Class SE-42-D and perhaps a few men from Classes SE-42-C and SE-42-E may have observed some events that were to make history. Members of those three classes who flew near the Gulf of Mexico or who traveled to Eglin Field, Florida, for the gunnery course may have observed a number of twin-engine medium bombers flying about the area. If they did not see the medium bombers practicing short takeoffs from the marked runway of a closely guarded airfield, they undoubtedly saw some B-25 Mitchell bombers flying about the area at treetop level and low over the waters of the Gulf of Mexico.

Although their activities could not escape the eyes of everyone, these twenty-four aircraft and their crews were engaged in secret training exercises. Within three and a half weeks of their leaving Eglin Field, the medium bombers and their crews, which were commanded by Lieutenant Colonel James Doolittle, would become a part of the fascinating history of aviation. On 18 April 1942, sixteen of these twin-engine Mitchell bombers were flown from the deck of the aircraft carrier *Hornet* to bomb targets in Japan.

As with the two classes that preceded it, Class SE-42-D was not immune from tragedy. During a night cross-country flight that had begun shortly after midnight on Thursday morning, 9 April 1942, twenty-one-year-old LAC George Leslie Simpson of Newbiggin-by-the-Sea, Northumberland, went missing. Search planes retraced Simpson's projected route and flew search patterns over a very wide area. Finally, at 2:30 p.m., the wreckage was sighted from the air in a remote area some ten miles northeast of Troy, Alabama.

The Napier Field investigating team, led by director of training Captain Cy Young, found upon arrival by the road at a point near the crash site that the wreckage was located in such a remote hilly area that mule teams were required to reach it. Ultimately, in order to find the crash site, the searchers were guided by radio messages from aircraft flying overhead. Mules were used to transport the ground party across red clay hills, through dense undergrowth and down slippery trails. As a result, they were unable to reach the wreckage until 6:45 p.m. and, as the *Dothan Eagle* reported on 10 April, Simpson's body was found near the smashed and burned aircraft. On 11 April 1942, his remains were interred in the RAF plot of Montgomery's Oakwood Cemetery Annex.

LACs William E. Pearce and Raymond L. Rowett, two Essex County men of Class SE-42-D, met while in training and became lifelong friends. They had been classmates at Lakeland, Florida, and Cochran Field, Georgia, before arriving at Napier Field. Later, they also served together as flying instructors at Napier Field. More than forty years later, Pearce recalled their advanced flying school experiences:

> *At Napier, we had standard barrack accommodation, good food and sports facilities, and the PX was our main evening meeting place. I remember the town of Dothan as home of affluent whites and poorer blacks. Our British reaction was to feel that the blacks were disadvantaged and had not been given a fair chance.*
>
> *I remember the beginnings of the fight for equality when young blacks started to hold their place on the sidewalks rather than step aside as they were expected to do. I remember, too, being surprised at the "Poor Whites" in their fresh bib and brace on their weekly visit to town, barefoot in a Model T. Their wooden houses were very basic and did not fit my image of prosperous America.*
>
> *In town, the ladies organized dances and meeting with young Americans, mostly female, through a voluntary organization whose name escapes me. The drug store in Dothan was a regular meeting place, and I remember being impressed with the milk shakes and ice creams. Just prior to graduation came Commission Board for some of us.*
>
> *Wing Commander Hogan flew down from Maxwell Field with others to form the board. I was found suitable, and so became a pilot officer. Then it was decided that instead of returning to England immediately, I should remain and become a flight instructor. I was very unhappy about this, protested vehemently, and fought hard to be allowed home to join a squadron. However, I was tested and adjudged suitable to train as an instructor, and did that at Dothan under Captain Weaver.*

On 24 April 1942, when the graduation ceremonies were held for Class SE-42-D, Flight Lieutenant Sir Anthony Lindsay-Hogg, RAFAO, was the principal speaker. Of the net enrollment of 156 men, 2 students were held over to the next class in order to complete pilot training, 10 were washed out (including 7 for flying deficiencies and 3 for non-flying reasons), 1 was killed and 143 graduated.

On 17 March 1942, the 162-member Class SE-42-E arrived at Napier Field and was joined by 2 men held over from the preceding class. Since 3 members of Class SE-42-E were ultimately held over for further training, net intake for the class was 161. Unlike earlier classes that included only men who had received their basic flying training at Cochran Field, Georgia, Class SE-42-E included men who had completed their basic flying training at both Cochran and Gunter Fields. Those who arrived from the Georgia base traveled by coach, and those who came from Gunter Field near Montgomery traveled by army truck.

The class included among its members seven former policemen, including London "Bobbies" John Erwin, Albert Gardner, Brian Kelly and Alfred Paynter, as well as Alexander McGarvey of Glasgow, Brooklyn Harrington of Leeds and George Lawson of Dundee. Another class member who attracted local notice for an entirely different reason was Cadet Albert Williams, whose musical talent on the piano delighted Dothan's Harmony Club with "stimulating performances," including works by Bach, Chopin, Brahms and Beethoven.

Two students of the class who had particularly interesting backgrounds were Cadets Ronald Pile and Robert Henry Jacques Fernandes. Pile's British father, who had served in the Royal Flying Corps during the 1914–18 war, married and settled in France. Pile was born in Biarritz in 1921, became a British citizen in 1939 and attended Cambridge University. His mother and sister were trapped in France by the German occupation.

Fernandes, a British subject of Portuguese extraction, was born in Egypt, educated in Nimes, France, and was a student at the University of Grenoble when the Germans invaded. In June 1940, he escaped from Marseilles to Gibraltar, where he joined about five hundred passengers aboard a ship bound for Britain. Following escape from a U-boat attack, the ship managed to reach Britain on 29 June. Until he entered the RAF in October 1941, Fernandes taught French at Buckinghamshire College, Harrow, Middlesex.

Since the pace of training was still under the USAAF's wartime emergency action of December 1941, flying training began quickly, and within ten days an emergency occurred that had the fortunate result of providing experience without injury. On 31 March 1942, during a night cross-country flight, two RAF cadets evidently experienced mechanical problems and followed established procedures. At a point seven miles southeast of Brundidge, Alabama, about twenty miles north-northwest of Napier Field, Cadet J. McCallum bailed out of his AT-6 trainer. During that same night, at a point about twenty miles east-northeast of Napier Field, Cadet J.H. Bradford also bailed out. Fortunately, the two cadets were not hurt and, although Bradford's AT-6A trainer crashed in the outskirts of Blakely, Georgia, there were no civilian injuries.

Raymond Peter Grimwood (Tuscaloosa and Gunter) recalled that while his class was in training at Napier Field an expansion program was underway, and new barracks and other buildings were erected with amazing speed. He was also surprised at the new methods used to construct additional runways at Napier Field "by churning up the soil, mixing in a liquid, and then rolling them down again." In all, the USAAF expended $1.5 million more on the 1942 construction contract at Napier Field. Among the facilities built were sixty buildings, 93,000 yards of cement for the apron, 40,000 yards of street paving, as well as base engineering and ordnance buildings. As with earlier classes, the training course for Class SE-42-E was still restricted to nine weeks or less.

In addition to changes on the military airdrome, spring arrived early, and all of south Alabama and west Florida took on a new appearance, which was more noticeable from the air. The pristine beauty of the blue sky with its puffy gulf clouds was marred only occasionally at lower altitudes by gray smoke rising from the chimneys of farms and town houses and from scattered factories, but far below, the earth was beginning to warm and changes were occurring rapidly.

First, red and purple butterfly-shaped maple buds brought some brighter colors to the dull green of pines and the drab grays and browns of leafless hardwood trees. Next, the hardwood trees along creek and river bottoms began to add tiny leaves whose vivid filigree of chartreuse colors was accented by the white blossoms of dogwoods that burst into bloom underneath them, as if by some special signal. These colors contrasted sharply with the dominant browns of forest floors and newly ploughed fields, the new greens of grass and winter grain and the reds of scarred clay hills. With the rapid addition of colors from blooming daffodils, dogwoods and azaleas, Dothan and other towns also took on new beauty.

Alabama forestry officials were alarmed over the outbreak of numerous woodland fires over a wide area of south Alabama. At least sixteen huge fires were reported burning in one county, and scattered fires were also burning in five other counties. Although arson was suspected in one fire, it had long been common annual practice in that vast agricultural region for farmers to set fires and burn fields for a variety of different reasons, including the destruction of burrowing insects. Cotton fields and adjacent scrub were normally burned over to destroy boll weevil eggs in order to prevent infestations.

In other instances, fires were used to destroy crop residues and weeds, which were believed to harbor potential crop diseases. In the long term, it was believed that removal of crop residues by fire was safer than plowing them under as mulch. Sadly, too many such fires were swept out of control by winds and often reached forest areas where they fed on dry leaves and spread even more rapidly, destroying everything in their paths. For those who flew daily in the skies of the region, the fires served as reminders that for all of the new technology of war, this region was still primarily an agricultural one.

When Class SE-42-E completed the course in mid-May 1942, 18 cadets were eliminated for flying deficiencies, 3 were held over to the next class in order to continue in training and 143 graduated. The reasons why so many students were washed out of Class SE-42-E were not given in the unit history. However, probable causes included an increased number of students in training, the rapid pace in the advanced school, an increase in the number of new, inexperienced instructors and the greater complexity of the trainer aircraft used.

Whatever the final class statistics, those who were successful were happy that they had succeeded in passing the demanding course. "Wings presentation was a terrific occasion with a large parade of the whole station behind a large band when we were presented with our [USAAF silver] wings by General Stratemeyer," wrote Raymond P. Grimwood. However, since RAF wings were not issued to them, the ceremony ended for many on a sour note. "After the ceremony," Grimwood continued, "an RAF Corporal, responsible for our administration, told us, 'I think we have a few RAF wings in the stores, not more than six, so first come, first served.' I have always bought my own ever since."

On 1 May 1942, Class SE-42-F arrived at Napier Field and, beginning with that class, American aviation cadets, student officers and aviation students were assigned to Napier Field and were trained alongside the larger numbers of UK cadets. Although SE-42-F's enrollment totaled 179, the RAF contingent numbered 146, including the 3 cadets carried over from Class SE-42-E. The construction of additional buildings and the paving of roads and runways changed the physical appearance of the advanced flying school, but there were other important, but less noticeable, changes. William H.H. Grace, an American who formerly served with the RCAF, had been employed in March as a navigation instructor. Since Grace knew RAF methods, the American and British students were separated in navigation courses and the results were deemed excellent.

RAF and American cadets now had a well-supplied post exchange with a snack bar, as well as a Cadet Club, swimming pool and a recreation hall. Movies were shown and dances were held, but many of the students still regularly attended the theatres in Dothan, visited Cash's Drug Store to enjoy their milkshakes and ice cream sundaes and still patronized Max's Grill, Register's Cafeteria and occasionally the B-Line, or other places that served food.

Perhaps it was to be expected that the more reticent British students remained on station most of the time, and either could not or would not make the effort to enjoy activities away from the flying school. That they did not take advantage of opportunities to get to know people outside the military station was a sad loss for them, because for others fraternization with the civilian population brought not only hospitality, but often an extra bonus of lifelong friendships as well.

As in other towns, the people of Dothan were extremely hospitable to the British cadets, and felt that they could not do enough to make them feel welcome. As the days became warmer, outdoor activities increased. Although the British students were still drawn to Panama City and the Gulf Coast, there were attractions in Marianna and other nearby towns as well as in and near Dothan. On 30 May, Kelly Springs opened its pavilion, and American hosts took many cadets there for barbecues, picnics, swimming and dancing.

Among the Class SE-42-F students who arrived at Napier Field in the spring and thrived during their stay was Phillip G. Penfold, who had received his early flying training at Lakeland, Florida, and Macon, Georgia. As Penfold recalled his experiences,

> At Advanced Flying School at Napier Field, Dothan, Alabama, we flew AT-6s. Having got a "Below Average" grade at Basic, I fell in love with the AT-6 and finished up with an "Above Average" rating for some unknown reason. Not that it made any difference, but for the first time we had British instructors. At Napier, things were much more relaxed, and we used to fly on our solo flights down to Panama City and go up and down the coast.
>
> The hospitality of the people in Dothan was again outstanding. At the end of the course, they discovered that we were supposed to have shot so many rounds of skeet every week, which we hadn't, so, out they took us to fire off the requisite number of shots. By God, at the end of two days, did I have a black and blue shoulder!
>
> In general, the advanced course was nothing but pleasure. I think back upon it now as one of the happiest times of my life. We were now into July in Alabama and the heat and humidity was awful. We graduated on 3 July. All of the older ones such as myself who had been appointed cadet officers received commissions and were sent up to Toronto, Canada, to the No. 1 Manning Depot in order to be outfitted in officer's uniforms.

We spent two enjoyable weeks here before shipping out for three days R&R (rest and recreation) in New York City.

While Penfold was enjoying Toronto and New York, Class SE-42-E departed, and a few days later on 2 June, the 191 members of Class SE-42-G arrived on station and were shortly thereafter joined by the 5 cadets held over from Class SE-42-F.

On 3 July 1942, at 10:00 a.m., graduation ceremonies were held in the post theatre for Class SE-42-F. Of a total enrollment of 179 students (146 RAF and 33 USAAF), 5 were held over to the next class so as to complete the course, 7 were eliminated for flying deficiencies and 167 graduated. Of the 146 RAF students of that class, 2 were held over to the next class, 7 were eliminated for flying deficiencies and 137 graduated. As the class departed, so did the RAF administrative officer. Flight Lieutenant Sir Anthony Lindsay-Hogg, who had arrived in January, had completed six months on station and was reassigned as aide to the governor-general of Trinidad.

A few days later, Flight Lieutenant H. Edmund Taggart arrived to replace Lindsay-Hogg, and with Taggart came the 184-man Class SE-42-H to replace Class SE-42-F. In 1914, Taggart had been a student at the University of Glasgow. He immediately joined the infantry, was wounded three times in the course of the war and rose to the rank of captain. In March 1918, he was captured by German forces and spent the remaining months of the war in Holzminden Prisoner of War Camp. After the war, Taggart returned to Glasgow University, finished his legal training and practiced law in the city. In 1940, he entered the RAF as a flight lieutenant. Before being assigned to Napier Field, Taggart was assigned to serve first as an RAF administrative officer at the primary flying school at Camden, South Carolina, and later at the USAAF basic flying school at Cochran Field, Georgia.

As with early classes, the 191-member Class SE-42-G had arrived at Napier Field aboard buses and trucks from the two basic flying schools. After five weeks of training, 5 cadets held over from SE-42-F joined them. The 196-man intake included 125 RAF cadets and 71 Americans. As with earlier intakes from Cochran Field, the cadets rose early on Tuesday morning, 2 June, left around 7:00 a.m. and arrived in Dothan, Alabama, around noon. To the new arrivals, Napier Field was not unlike Cochran Field, except that the buildings that had been added in the spring 1942 expansion were much more noticeable.

Following lunch, assignment to squadrons and orientation, the cadets were able to look about the station during the early evening, and naturally gravitated to the flight line to observe the noisy and formidable AT-6A trainers and the busy flight line. More than forty years later, Edgar Spridgeon of Bradford (Lakeland and Macon) recalled his training at Napier Field and his aerial gunnery course at Eglin Field, Florida:

The course was extremely interesting as we built up our experience. Four-ship "tactical" formation flying, instrument flying "under the hood," high altitude flight using oxygen, gunnery instruction, and live firing on the Gulf Coast, mock combat, etc., kept us very busy. The gunnery school was based on Eglin Field, near Valparaiso, Florida. We made the journey in trucks, the aircraft already being there for the other half of the course. We flew only for half days, the rest of the time being spent swimming in the Gulf.

Although we lived in 30-bed huts, the food was the best we had anywhere, perfectly cooked and as much as we wanted cafeteria style. Typical menus were fish, fruit salad,

*and ice cream for lunch, lovely fried eggs, bacon, bananas for breakfast. Live firing at
towed targets was carried out over the sea and ground gunnery against fixed targets in
clearings in the woods. It was not as easy as it looked. It was not just a question of getting
the sights on the targets but smooth coordinated flying was very necessary as well.*

An additional feature of the course that Class SE-42-G experienced was the high-altitude
flight. The procedure was that an instructor led a squadron of about twenty aircraft up to about
twenty thousand feet. The climb to that elevation took about an hour, during which the students
were required to use oxygen. The exercise taught students that climbing to that rarified altitude
was an excellent exercise. Handling the AT-6, or any aircraft, at that altitude, and keeping it
there, required "smooth, careful flying." During the exercise, care was taken to assure that almost
an hour was also used in making the descent.

As with preceding courses, before the RAF Commissioning Board met, Flight Lieutenant
Taggart reviewed the records of RAF students and the recommendations of their instructors, got
to know the individual students and made his own recommendations. When Wing Commander
Hogan, Wing Commander Rampling and other RAF staff arrived, they interviewed graduating
cadets and decided which ones would be commissioned pilot officers (second lieutenants).

On Wednesday, 5 August 1942, the graduation ceremony took place in the post chapel. Flight
Lieutenant Taggart made a few congratulatory remarks; Colonel James L. Daniel, commanding
officer of Napier Field, presented the diplomas; and the director of training presented the cadets
with USAAF silver wings. Of the 125 UK cadets, 2 were held over to the next class, 1 was
eliminated and 122 graduated.

The 182-man Class SE-42-H intake had arrived at Napier Field around 5 July 1942. With the
addition of 2 cadets held over, the class's enrollment climbed to 184. Flight Lieutenant Taggart
and Lieutenant Colonel Daniel also conducted graduation exercises for Class SE-42-H. Of its
180 cadet graduates, 103 were from the UK intake; 2 of them were held over, 6 were eliminated
and 91 graduated.

Shortly after Class SE-42-G departed, the 202-man Class SE-42-I arrived; after about one
month, 2 additional men were added from Class SE-42-H, and total enrollment for 42-I climbed
to 204. On 9 October 1942, the graduation ceremony for Class SE-42-I was held in the post
chapel. Colonel Daniel and Flight Lieutenant Taggart again presided. Of the 204 intake, 4 were
eliminated, 1 U.S. cadet was killed, 4 were held over and 195 graduated. Of the 78-man British
intake, 4 were eliminated and 74 graduated.

Class SE-42-J arrived at Napier Field on 8 September 1942 and graduated in a ceremony at
the Napier Field Post Chapel on 10 November 1942. Of that class's 190-man intake, 3 cadets
were held over, 5 were eliminated and 182 graduated. Of the 73-man UK intake, 3 men were
eliminated and 70 graduated.

Class SE-42-K's 194-man intake arrived on 9 October and commenced training about 11
October. Added to its 194 men were 3 men who had been held over from the previous class.
Of the 197 total, 5 were held over, 3 were eliminated and 189 graduated on 13 December
1942. There were no fatalities or wastage among the 71-man UK contingent, so all of the men
graduated and received their wings.

Although cadets continued to worry about the possibility of being eliminated, training
schedules and procedures had by that time become almost commonplace. Even so, when
accidents occurred, cadets were reminded that there was danger even during training. During

the night of 16 December 1942, four aircraft went missing from Napier Field under weather conditions similar to those that had existed when the British crash occurred during the night of 20–21 May 1942 out of Gunter Field. The four missing AT-6As from Napier Field were flown by three USAAF cadets and one USAAF student officer and, within a short time, all four were found dead in the wreckage of their aircraft.

Despite such tragedies, training continued day and night. In November 1942, Cadet Joe Hitchman of South Yorkshire arrived at Napier Field with Class SE-43-A. Many years later, Hitchman recalled an amusing experience while undergoing gunnery training at Eglin Field:

> *At the end of December, we did the gunnery course over the Gulf of Mexico near Eglin Field, Florida. Whilst at Eglin, apart from the gunnery, there was little else to do to pass the time except felling some trees and letting off steam. One of the lads fancied his chances of chasing an animal, which he didn't know the identity of until it stopped, lifted its tail and stopped him in his tracks. The rest of us who shared the billet with him insisted that he strip, and bathe and bathe and bathe before allowing him inside. What a vile smell a skunk has!*

Following gunnery exercises in Florida, the cadets returned to Napier Field and rushed to complete flying and ground training on schedule. When Class SE-43-A graduated on 11 January, the eighty-seven-man UK intake had again been fortunate. The class had had no training fatalities, and only one man was eliminated from training, so eighty-six men graduated as pilots.

In mid-December 1942, the ninety-six-man RAF intake for Class SE-43-B arrived at Napier Field with their USAAF cadet classmates. Somewhat later, two RAF men who had been held over for further training were assigned to the class, so the total intake for Class SE-43-B climbed to ninety-eight. Despite the vagaries of winter weather, the class's training went smoothly, and when the class graduated on 26 February 1943, three men were held over for further training and ninety-five RAF cadets completed their pilot training successfully.

LAC Christopher Horn of Yorkshire (Americus and Macon) had logged a total of 221 hours, 15 minutes flying time when his training was completed. And although training officers at Napier Field were not overly happy about the arrangement, Horn was allowed to graduate separately in order to visit relatives in Boston before returning to the United Kingdom.

Class SE-43-B was the final RAF intake at primary flying schools, and men held over for the next class in those four schools returned to Canada to complete their training. However, several additional RAF cadets had been held over for further training at basic and advanced flying schools and, as a result, six of them joined the three men held over at Napier Field, and all nine British cadets were assigned to complete their training with Class SE-43-C. Of that nine-man RAF intake, one cadet was eliminated and, on 26 March 1943, eight RAF LACs graduated with the USAAF cadets of Class SE-43-C.

Carlstrom Field scene. *Courtesy of N. Hetherington.*

Carlstrom barracks. *Courtesy of N. Hetherington.*

The winds came, Carlstrom. *Courtesy of N. Hetherington.*

Group Captain Carnegie and civilian Instructor Jack Hunt congratulate cadet. *Courtesy of the Imperial War Museum.*

Cadets arriving at Arcadia rail station, 1941. *Courtesy of the Imperial War Museum.*

Carlstrom Field hangars and primary training aircraft. *Courtesy of the Imperial War Museum.*

Flight line preparing for flight, Carlstrom. *Courtesy of the Imperial War Museum.*

Carlstrom Field swimming pool. *Courtesy of the Imperial War Museum.*

Cadets and instructors prepare to fly, Camden, South Carolina. *Courtesy of E.N. Harrison.*

Cadets and instructor in class. *Courtesy of J.D. McCarthy.*

LAC Frederick Bradford, 42-A, Camden, South Carolina. *Courtesy of J. Moss.*

RAF cadets in civvies, Anderson, South Carolina. *Courtesy of J. Moss.*

Sergeant Pilot John Hawkes-Reed in Moncton, New Brunswick, January 1942. *Courtesy of J. Moss.*

Three RAF cadets of 42-A at Cochran Field, Georgia. *Courtesy of J. Moss.*

Damaged PT-17s awaiting repairs. *Courtesy of H. Howton.*

Cadets and instructor coming off the flight line, Camden, South Carolina. *Courtesy of J.D. McCarthy.*

Camden RAF Cadet Harry Hepplewhite. *Courtesy of H Hepplewhite.*

Battle of Britain Chapel, Westminster Abbey.
Courtesy of the Imperial War Museum.

Pilot Officer Alec Davidson of Johannesburg, South Africa. Instructor, Dothan, Alabama. *Courtesy of V. Jaynes.*

Pilot Officer J.D. "Mac" McCarthy in a 41 Squadron Spitfire, circa 1944. *Courtesy of J.D. McCarthy.*

Air Vice Marshal D.V. Carnegie with Air Vice Marshal Charlesworth. *Courtesy of Crown, IWM.*

RAF funeral procession at Oakwood Cemetery, Montgomery, Alabama. *Courtesy of J. Cunningham.*

American civilian flight instructors, Camden, South Carolina. *Courtesy of J.D. McCarthy.*

Stearman (Boeing) PT-17 primary trainer. *Courtesy of the Boeing Wichita Corporation.*

Squadron Leader R.T. Bowring of Derby (Lakeland, 42-K) and crew at Gatow, Berlin airlift. *Courtesy of R.T. Bowring.*

Stearman (Boeing) PT-17 primary trainer. *Courtesy of the Boeing Wichita Corporation.*

Lakeland RAF cadets with old automobiles destined for Miami. *Courtesy of P. Penfold.*

Six RAF cadets of Class 42-A, Camden. *Courtesy of H. Howton.*

LAC Michael Aldridge, stage and TV actor, Class 42-B, Lakeland, in North Africa. *Courtesy of T. Clayton.*

RAF Museum, Hendon, London. *Courtesy of Dr. S.H. Guinn.*

Two RAF cadets returning to Tuscaloosa, Alabama. *Courtesy of W.T. McFarlane.*

LAC Derek Sharpe after a second escape from death or injury, Tuscaloosa. *Courtesy of C. Harrison.*

LAC W.T. McFarlane later won a DFC. *Courtesy of W.T. McFarlane.*

Bomb aimer graduating class, Chatham, New Brunswick, Canada. *Courtesy of A. Maitland.*

Three RAF cadets, American family and dogs, Dothan, Alabama. *Courtesy of J. Lett.*

RAF and USAAF cadets in group hear demonstration of bagpipes. *Courtesy of J. Lett.*

Scene of Main Street, Macon, Georgia. *Courtesy of R. Tate.*

RAF cadets at Pineola Farm with Bassett girls, Fort Valley, Georgia, 1942. *Courtesy of F.N. Bate.*

Vultee BT-13 basic trainer. *Courtesy of F.N. Bate.*

Five RAF cadets on barracks beds.

RAF grave in Oakwood Cemetery Annex, Montgomery, Alabama. *Courtesy of P. Penfold.*

Five cadets standing before tent, Turner Field, Georgia. *Courtesy of J. Lett.*

RAF cadets marching at Turner Field. *Courtesy of J. Lett.*

RAF cadet standing in entrance of tent, Turner Field. *Courtesy of J. Lett.*

The Lake twins. *Courtesy of A.R. Langley.*

Sergeant Pilot Vic Dorman, 42-B/42-C (Camden, Macon, Selma). *Courtesy of A.V. Dorman.*

Seven RAF cadets in khakis, Lakeland.

Five RAF cadets and instructor studying map, Selma. *Courtesy of the Imperial War Museum.*

Headquarters, Craig Field, Selma, Alabama. *Courtesy of F. Jones.*

CLASS SE-42 G
92ⁿᵈ SCH.SQ-1ˢᵗ ECHELON
CRAIG FIELD ALA. – AUGUST 5,1942

Ninety-second School Squadron, first echelon, 42-G, Craig Field. *Courtesy of F.N. Bate.*

Vic Dorman's wings and medals. *Courtesy of A.V. Dorman.*

RAF and USAAF cadets march in Montgomery, Alabama. *Courtesy of J. Clark.*

Pilot Officer Jones with 57 Squadron Lancaster bomber crew, 1944. *Courtesy of F. Jones.*

RAF Sergeant Andrew Maitland and RCAF Sergeant Boyd. *Courtesy of A. Maitland.*

RAF Cadet Jones kneeling in grass at Craig Field. *Courtesy of F. Jones.*

Twin-Engine Advanced Flying Schools

Maxwell, Turner and Moody

USAAF ADVANCED FLYING SCHOOL
MAXWELL FIELD, MONTGOMERY, ALABAMA

The state of Alabama was admitted into the federal union on 14 December 1819, and the capital, located first at Huntsville, was moved to Cahaba in 1821 and then to Tuscaloosa in 1826. The state's capital remained in that west central Alabama town until 1846, when the legislature decided to move it to Wetumpka. On the journey to the latter village on the north side of the Alabama River, near the center of the state, the large legislative committee stopped in Montgomery and evidently was persuaded at that time to establish the capital on Goat Hill high above the town. When Montgomery became the Alabama capital, its population was barely four thousand, and it had existed as a town for only about a decade.

As early as 1814, a settlement had existed amidst the wooded high hills on the south bank of the curving Alabama River. Following the defeat of the Creek Nation and Georgia's cession of the region to the federal government, the United States Land Office in Milledgeville had auctioned off choice sites along the Alabama River. Among the men who purchased such tracts were Andrew Dexter and William W. Bibb, a man destined to become Alabama's first governor.

Meanwhile, in 1816, before Alabama was separated from it, the Mississippi Territorial Legislature encompassed the Alabama River settlements into the County of Montgomery and named the county after Major Lemuel P. Montgomery, one of General Andrew Jackson's officers who had been killed in the 1814 Battle of Horseshoe Bend. In 1819, when the newly created Alabama State Legislature met in Huntsville, it evidently reconfirmed the action of the Mississippi Territorial Government. Then, some eighteen years later, on 23 December 1837, the three contiguous and rival villages of Alabama Town, New Philadelphia and New Alabama Town in Montgomery County, Alabama, merged into the single town of Montgomery.

During the next century, Montgomery grew steadily. The business district of the town developed on the level plateau near the river. Water Street along the Alabama River connected to Commerce Street and became the town's original business district. Court Street, the original north-south thoroughfare, and Court Square had served as a dividing line between the three rival towns and remained important as the town grew. Dexter Avenue, the main east-west thoroughfare, led from the river parallel to Commerce Street, crossed Court Street and passed directly through what had been "New Philadelphia" up the long hill to Capitol Square on Goat Hill.

A series of streets named after the first five presidents of the United States ran from Court Street and Court Square eastward parallel to Dexter Avenue. Dominating the business district were a few large business establishments, and scattered along Court and adjacent streets were boardinghouses and the simple and attractive homes of citizens. Along contiguous streets were churches of every denomination, more boardinghouses and the elegant residences of planters and business leaders. Continuing north and south of Dexter Avenue and crossing the six main thoroughfares were other tree-lined residential streets. The main cemetery of the town was situated on an eminence north of the capital toward the river.

Montgomery was not only the capital of the state of Alabama, but also of Alabama's Black Belt, a broad band of very rich agricultural lands running from the Georgia border westward across Alabama, terminating in the rich Yazoo River delta of Mississippi. During the era before the American Civil War, the Alabama River acted as a barrier on the north side, but the land to the east, south and west of the town was dotted with cotton plantations.

From its emergence as the Alabama capital in 1846, Montgomery grew steadily as a government center and a market town for the rich agricultural region. Its hilly streets were paved with brick, and raised wooden walkways made it possible for pedestrians to escape walking in mud. The Alabama River, unpaved roads and a railroad connected the town with the outside world. As was the practice in so many other towns, all roads radiating out from Montgomery and leading to distant towns were named for those towns. Among others, these included the Wetumpka Road, the Mount Meigs Road, the Selma Road and the Birmingham Road.

During the decade before 1860, Montgomery grew steadily. Numerous merchants established shops; the Exchange Hotel and an opera house were built, and regular entertainment troupes visited the town. According to tradition, "Dixie" was set to music by Professor Frank Arnold at the Montgomery Opera House in 1860 so that Dan Emmett's band might play it. Although the State Capitol Building in Montgomery served for less than four months in 1861 as capitol of the Confederate States of America, that part of its history was in 1941 its greatest claim to fame.

The Civil War brought great sacrifices, and after the war ended in 1865, its effects were to linger for decades. As dozens of Alabama regiments passed through their state's capital city on the way to combat in Virginia and elsewhere, the town continued to thrive as the seat of Alabama state government. After Appomattox in April 1865, as they made their way slowly homeward, surviving veterans who traveled through the river town observed the damage wrought by General Wilson's Federal cavalry that had raided the town early in 1865.

The Southern economy collapsed, and during the years following the war the town began a long period of slow growth. Cotton did not reach its pre-war production levels again until the 1880s. During those difficult and sad postwar months, Sidney Lanier, the Georgia native and one of the most talented of Southern poets, served as a night clerk at Montgomery's Exchange Hotel. When Jefferson Davis died in 1889, his body was returned to Montgomery to lie in state in the capitol for a few days before its cortege wound its way down Dexter Avenue to the railroad station to continue its journey to Mississippi for interment.

As with other towns of the late nineteenth century, Montgomery occasionally suffered from cholera and yellow fever epidemics that caused quarantine flags to be displayed and large numbers of its citizens to flee for safety into the countryside. Despite these scourges that killed hundreds, the town continued its slow but steady growth as a seat of state government and a marketing center for a vast number of central Alabama counties.

When pre-war rail lines were restored and other competing railroads were built in the 1870s and 1880s, the town became a transportation and communications center for vast cotton and lumber industries. The huge and elegant Union Station, which handled the cars of the rail lines traversing the region, became a new symbol of the town's importance. The Jefferson Davis Hotel was built, and streetcar lines were installed. According to local tradition, the first electric streetcar in the United States was installed and operated in Montgomery in the 1890s. At the turn of the century, steamboat traffic on the Alabama River continued but, except for occasional barge traffic, that mode of transportation diminished in importance during the ensuing decades.

Around 1910, when the boll weevil began to decimate annual cotton crops, Alabama farmers began to diversify or switch completely to other crops. A vigorous lumber industry had been established in the region in the years following the war. Dairy farms and other cattle industries became more popular, but many farms and plantations did not survive the difficult years between the 1880s and 1914, and others failed during the agricultural depression that lasted from 1925 to 1940. For some of that rich agricultural land of the region, a much different destiny lay ahead.

The huge tract lying west-northwest of Montgomery and adjacent to the Alabama River evolved in the twentieth century as Maxwell Field, the largest air base in the Southeastern United States. In 1900, the land was owned by Montgomery's Mayor Warren B. Reese and was called the Reese Plantation. It contained a large two-story dwelling called the White House, which was used as a private club in which some "gentlemen of leisure" regularly played poker. Around 1899, the huge tract was purchased by Frank Kohn, and in February 1910 Kohn leased the property without charge to the Wright brothers as a winter flying field. In return, as soon as the aircraft, maintenance men and instructors arrived at the new Wright School, Frank Kohn was the first local civilian to experience an airplane ride.

Perhaps because of this early aviation experience, the U.S. War Department chose Montgomery in 1918 as the site for a pilot training school and air service repair depot. The pilot training school was located at Taylor Field on the southeastern edge of Montgomery County. On the opposite side of the town, the United States government purchased 320 acres of the Reese (Kohn) land for approximately $35,000. Construction of the air service depot was begun there on 18 April 1918 and was completed within about ninety days. The airfield that adjoined Engine and Repair Depot No. 3 was known locally as Wright Field.

Among the hundreds of servicemen who were stationed in Montgomery during 1918 was the novelist F. Scott Fitzgerald, who met and married his wife, Zelda, while stationed at Montgomery. During the Roaring Twenties, which Fitzgerald and his attractive wife came to symbolize, the novelist perfected his art, and the town of Montgomery continued to grow at such a rate that by 1927, it had become a city of 75,000 people.

During the postwar years, the air service depot became a permanent U.S. Army Air Service station. On 8 November 1922, the station's name was officially changed to Maxwell Field, in honor of a young Alabama native who had been killed in an air crash while serving with the Third Aero Squadron in the Philippine Islands. Both before and after creation of the army air corps in 1926, Maxwell Field was the main airdrome in the Southeastern United States and was home base for an observation squadron and several service squadrons. As part of their training, army air corps units were regularly on call for special duties.

On 14 March 1929, Major Walter R. Weaver, commanding officer of Maxwell Field, received a telephone call from the governor of Alabama calling for air corps units to render assistance to citizens of south Alabama who were stranded by one of the worst floods in the state's history. Weaver dispatched officers, men, vehicles and aircraft to the vicinity of Elba, Alabama, and the men rendered assistance by transporting supplies and assisting with communications. The observation squadrons aided flood victims by dropping food and other supplies from the air.

In 1931, the Air Corps Tactical School was transferred from Langley Field, Virginia, to Maxwell Field, and a new era began in the station's history. The Tactical School syllabus included administration of air units, ground, naval and air warfare, logistical support and strategy. The three types of aircraft available for the school's use were observation airplanes, fighters and bombers, and veteran flyers were encouraged to develop hypotheses and test them. While Montgomery, the state of Alabama and the nation struggled with the worst economic depression in history, air officers at Maxwell Field devised plans for wartime mobilization of the army air corps. They also developed plans for employing fighters and bombers in combat, and dreamed of the day there might be a separate United States Air Force similar to Britain's Royal Air Force.

In July 1940, when the Southeast Air Corps Training Center (SEACTC) headquarters was established at Maxwell Field, air officers and civilians alike had long been accustomed to "making do" with limited funds. Colonel Walter R. Weaver, commanding officer of the SEACTC, may have been the first American military commander to use a New Deal agency, the Works Progress Administration (WPA), to reduce the cost of building army air corps training stations. Weaver's desire to cut costs also led to his proposing that the air corps lease or purchase abandoned public school buildings, hotels or defunct textile mills that might be remodeled into useable air corps facilities. The use of brick tiles for the construction of buildings at Maxwell Field and other SEACTC stations came to be called "Weaver construction," because General Weaver concluded that the use of such materials provided attractive and durable buildings at costs comparable to those for wooden frame structures.

The building of numerous air stations provided jobs for large numbers of people of Montgomery and contiguous areas of central Alabama. The WPA and civilian building contractors prepared airfields, cut drainage ditches, installed water and sewage lines and constructed hundreds of buildings. The army air corps expansion programs of 1940–41 trained hundreds of men in new skills. Large numbers of women were also employed in secretarial and mechanical work in the dozens of offices. Although the economic impact of air corps stations on Montgomery and on other local economies was not strongly felt until about 1941, the growth had been gradual since 1939.

At first, activities at the nearby air stations did not appear to impress very many citizens of Montgomery. Although economic conditions were improving somewhat, a majority of the city's citizens were still struggling with problems brought on by the Great Depression and were not yet "air minded." In an effort to publicize air corps activities and win the support of the civilian population, Montgomery officials declared Saturday, 3 May 1941 "Flying Cadet Day." Whether, as a local newspaper reported, this was indeed "the nation's first cadet parade off a military reservation" cannot be confirmed. However, the parade of seven hundred aviation cadets down Dexter Avenue from the State Capitol Building and the showing of a new Hollywood film about flying did much to capture the public imagination and focus the attention of citizens on local and national army air corps training activities.

During 1940, American flying cadets flocked to the existing flying training schools on schedule, and with the entry of Class SE-41-H on 22 March 1941, they entered the new SEACTC primary schools in larger numbers. In May 1941, air corps headquarters in Washington and SEACTC headquarters at Maxwell Field announced that thousands of Royal Air Force pilots would commence training in the Southeastern region in early June 1941.

The civilian population undoubtedly knew from all of the separate news releases that there were plans for training British student pilots and navigators in different schools within the United States. And they also learned that the young men would arrive in civilian clothing and would have completed preliminary training in Britain. Beyond these basic points, readers of the several newspaper accounts could not have been anything but confused. Fortunately, U.S. Army Air Corps and British authorities were not.

In late May 1941, RAF Group Captain David V. Carnegie flew from Washington, D.C., to Maxwell Field and called on General Weaver. As director of UK training in the United States, Carnegie would maintain his headquarters in Washington. During the next month, he would fly about the country visiting the three army air corps geographic commands and selecting sites for schools that would train UK pilots. Around 6 June, Wing Commander Harry A.V. Hogan, DFC, arrived at Maxwell Field for assignment to General Weaver's SEACTC staff as senior RAF administrative officer (SRAFAO) and supervisor of RAF training within the SEACTC.

In mid-August 1941, RAF training at Montgomery, Alabama, began at Gunter Field and expanded to the Maxwell Field Advanced Flying School and the RAF Reception Center, and the transient quarters where numerous unhappy eliminees from pilot training were posted until transportation back to Canada could be arranged. Between October 1941 and early January 1942, other contingents of RAF students arrived every five weeks at Gunter Field and Maxwell Field. Before moving the RAF Reception Center to Turner Field, Georgia, the RAF used the Maxwell Field station for the acclimatization of Classes SE-42-E, SE-42-F and SE-42-G, as well as for advanced pilot training. Owing to a shortage of twin-engine trainers, it was necessary for the advanced school to train the pilots of the first six Arnold Scheme classes in North American AT-6s and to follow the advanced twin-engine syllabus.

Regardless of the early inaccurate or mixed information concerning the beginning of British aircrew training in the United States, once it was firmly established, ordinary citizens and servicemen recognized the merits of such international cooperation. In a 21 October 1941 editorial, the *Montgomery Advertiser* described the system of scholarships established by philanthropist Cecil Rhodes and described the training of RAF aircrew in the United States as "a different type of fellowship."

The editors had no way of knowing how prophetic their words were, but their insight was apparently inspired, for they were absolutely on target with their assertions that the British students "will learn something about this country which will influence them the rest of their lives." Anticipating by some five years the establishment of the Fulbright-Hays student and faculty exchange programs between educational institutions in the United States and other nations, the perceptive editors endorsed British flying training in the United States as "a sound investment in understanding." They called for similar student exchanges among nations in peacetime.

In a further thoughtful editorial entitled "Four Boys Talking," which appeared in early November 1941, the editors of the *Montgomery Advertiser* wrote of "the great achievement in international friendship that is going on before one's eyes." In reporting a conversation between a small-town Southern boy and several RAF students, the editors were again very perceptive. The American boy explained his country from the perspective of personal experience and life in a small Alabama town, while at the same time gaining insight into the war and life in Britain "under the guns." In the process, the American discarded his stereotyped notion of "Englishmen" that had been derived from Hollywood films and learned that, like other people of the world, the British have their own practices and traits, but are just "folks."

In assessing the value of British training in the United States, the editor asserted that the "mass intermingling of British and Americans means more than all the gestures of governments, more even than the lease-lend plan itself."

Altogether, between August 1941 and April 1943, several thousands of RAF cadets and staff personnel were stationed at Maxwell and Gunter Fields, and during that time, many friendships developed. There were also misunderstandings, but the overall effect of British students meeting Americans was indeed as good or better than it was described in editorials and news columns.

Long before the United States entered the war, the army air forces had begun to expand rapidly in order to develop sufficient air defenses for the Western Hemisphere. Until its training capacity was needed for further USAAF expansion plans, a small portion of it would be used to train British aircrew. When war came in December 1941, further expansion was ordered. During the early weeks of 1942, owing to patriotic fervor, numerous aspiring aviation cadets volunteered, and a large pool of potential aircrew was rapidly developed.

Because of such expansion, the United States Army Air Forces had not yet had time to train large numbers of commanders. In order to develop men capable of commanding the massive number of squadrons needed for global warfare, senior officers were borrowing or devising new policies governing the assignment of air corps personnel. In order to make it possible for officers to gain a wide variety of command experience, USAAF official policy in 1942 called for the promotion of effective officers and the regular transfer of experienced commanders to higher levels.

This new policy resulted in the rotation of many officers from command and instructional duties, and had an almost immediate impact on the quality of training. Within a month after the Japanese attack on Pearl Harbor, Major General Walter R. Weaver, whom Air Marshal A.G.R. Garrod had called the "Godfather of the RAF in the Southeastern United States," was transferred from Maxwell Field to Washington as acting chief of the air corps. Already one of the air corps' strongest advocates of complete and absolute cooperation with Great Britain, Weaver also strongly favored leasing private property for use by the armed forces.

After serving a few months in Washington, the energetic General Weaver was assigned to command the massive army air force Technical Training Command, with headquarters in High Point, North Carolina. On assuming that post, Weaver established dozens of USAAF schools in hotels, factories and other leased facilities, thus saving massive amounts of public money that otherwise would have been necessary for constructing training facilities. In 1944, because of ill health, Weaver retired from the USAAF and died later that same year, a casualty of the rapid expansion of the USAAF.

Colonel Albert L. Sneed replaced Weaver as commanding officer of the SEACTC, and Lieutenant Colonel E.J. Bowling assumed command of Maxwell Field. A short time later, Brigadier General George E. Stratemeyer assumed command of the Southeast Air Corps Training Center, and Sneed, subsequently promoted to major general, was posted to Australia to command USAAF units there. While some very senior officers were retained in training posts within the United States, many commanders served in training assignments a few months before being assigned to combat commands, while others returned to training assignments after leaving overseas commands. Many of the USAAF and RAF pilots who completed their training while General Stratemeyer commanded the SEACTC at Maxwell Field would encounter Stratemeyer and many of their former instructors again in India/Burma later in the war.

Hogan, a reticent professional officer, found that he had much difficulty responding to the thousands of questions, especially those raised by American women at every social function he attended. Since his duty assignment involved a large measure of diplomacy, he was able to persuade his RAF superiors to permit Mrs. Hogan to join him during his tour in the United States. The attractive "blonde with very beautiful light blue eyes" arrived in the United States by clipper and was a great hit among the Maxwell Field military family and the Montgomery social set. Through her genuine friendliness, her teas and Maxwell Field club activities with RAF and USAAF wives and Montgomery country clubs, Venetia Hogan proved to be an able and conscientious representative of Great Britain. She undoubtedly removed great pressure from the shoulders of her husband, who was already overloaded with responsibilities and labor.

During the hot days of June, July and August 1941, with a polio epidemic raging about them in the state and nation, RAF administrative officers and British cadets of the first three RAF drafts traveled to their destinations. Before the second RAF intake arrived in July, a public relations scheme began to take shape at SEACTC headquarters at Maxwell Field. Evidently, attempts were made to prevent it, but the plan was carried through anyway. On 24 July, it had been announced that five RAF students would travel to Washington and participate in an international Sunday broadcast. On 16 August, another announcement indicated that fifteen RAF students had left Maxwell Field for Washington by train and would return there by air on Sunday afternoon. Since the names of the original five students of the July announcement appeared in the August list of fifteen men, it is likely that fifteen men were perceived to be a more representative group, and only the August broadcast was transmitted.

At Montgomery, Wing Commander Hogan was receiving regular reports from RAF administrative officers at the various civil contract primary schools and was attempting to estimate pilot production levels at each stage of training. In performing his duties, he was compelled to make regular visits to numerous airfields in order to sit on commissioning boards and iron out niggling problems. By mid-August 1941, as British students began to arrive at the Gunter Field basic flying school, Hogan was able to secure the assignment of Squadron Leader Philip F. Heppel as administrative officer so as to allow him time to carry out his other duties more effectively.

Owing to the nature of RAF training in the United States and the great distances involved, Wing Commander Hogan was assigned an aircraft at Maxwell Field for use in making inspection visits to various schools. As he rushed about the region, spending long hours serving on various commissioning boards or other committees and recommending the remustering of many RAF pilots to training as observers or wireless operators/air gunners, he was no doubt enjoying his work. Since Hogan had commanded 501 "County of Gloucester" Squadron during the Battle of Britain and was credited with downing five enemy aircraft, he was very much in demand as a speaker, but he was compelled to leave most of these public relations duties to other RAF officers.

However, there were times when he was available and was prevailed upon to speak on a particular issue. On one such occasion, he addressed the Montgomery Lions Club, praising that club's national pledge to serve as spotters in the newly organized American Aircraft Warning Service, and describing the effectiveness of civilian observers during the Battle of Britain. Among Hogan's other duties was responsibility for escorting many distinguished visitors on inspection tours of RAF training within the region and dealing with the problems of RAF cadets eliminated from Arnold Scheme flying schools.

As a steady stream of RAF pilot trainees was being shipped westward via Canada and southward to the United States for training, some 40 percent of that same group was being eliminated in primary and basic flying schools and returning to Canada. The return flow to Toronto, which had begun as a trickle in late June 1941, reached flood stage in August–September and continued to increase as the numbers of RAF students in training increased. The RAF had presumed a 20 percent wastage, but 40 to 50 percent in some primary schools was believed to be simply too many.

Air Ministry officials did not believe that their selection process was as faulty as the statistics of USAAF primary flying schools indicated. In the view of officers in London, American flying instructors were unfairly eliminating well-qualified men before they had a chance to adjust to the climate, food and language differences. Shocks reverberated among Maxwell Field, Washington and London and back again, and were cause for grave concern and action.

Hogan discussed the problem with SEACTC staff officers, school commanding officers and flying instructors, and was able to persuade most of them to allow RAF men up to twelve or fifteen hours to solo in primary and up to twenty hours in more powerful basic and advanced trainers. Since Maxwell Field was such an important command and Montgomery such a huge military training center, both city and air bases attracted large numbers of visitors. Among regular RAF visitors was Group Captain David V. Carnegie, director of UK training in the United States, who was often accompanied by other staff members from the offices of the RAF Delegation (RAFDEL) and the British Air Commission in Washington. On Friday, 26 September 1941, Air Vice Marshal P.C. Maltby, air officer commanding in chief (AOCIC) Army Cooperation Command, arrived at Maxwell Field. Maltby had served as an observer and as advisor to United States Army commanders during the Louisiana maneuvers of 1941. Wing Commander Hogan had flown Maltby from Dallas, Texas, to Maxwell Field. After meeting General Weaver and his staff and before departing for Washington and the United Kingdom, Maltby visited several other stations where RAF men were undergoing training.

In early October 1941, a large group of RAF officers met with their USAAF counterparts in Washington and planned a similar inspection tour of RAF aircrew undergoing training on American stations. The visit to the United States by Air Marshal A.G.R. Garrod, air member for training (AMT), resulted from the increasing alarm in Britain that was touched off by the very high elimination rate among British Arnold Scheme student pilots. In an effort to discover reasons for such losses and work out the means for reducing the wastage, the RAF commander flew to Canada and the United States. During a period of about three weeks, Garrod spoke with RAF and RCAF officers and large numbers of eliminees in Canada. Then he traveled to Washington to meet with USAAF officers at the highest levels. With several USAAF and RAF officers, Garrod laid plans for visiting most of the schools in which British personnel were being trained in the United States.

On Tuesday afternoon, 14 October 1941, at about 4:00 p.m., Air Marshal Garrod and his party arrived at Maxwell Field and were given places of honor in reviewing a parade of some 750 RAF cadets. Brigadier General George E. Stratemeyer, assistant chief of the air corps, escorted the visitors, and he was accompanied by Air Vice Marshal Arthur T. Harris, officer commanding the British Air Mission. Other members of the British delegation in attendance were Group Captain Carnegie, director of UK training, and members of his staff, including Group Captain Lord Nigel Douglas-Hamilton and Wing Commanders G. Beck and W.E. Oulton. That evening, General Weaver and the commanders of Maxwell, Craig and Gunter Fields entertained the visiting RAF officers at the attractive Maxwell Field Officers' Club.

Following that official reception, Garrod and his party flew Wednesday morning to inspect the primary school at Tuscaloosa, then returned to the basic flying school at nearby Gunter Field. During late Wednesday afternoon, state, city and business leaders sponsored a reception for the British visitors at Montgomery's plush Beauvoir Country Club. However, all was not entertainment.

Having observed the training and listened to RAF student and staff opinions, Air Marshal Garrod had learned much about the American aircrew training system. In a conference with

General Weaver and his staff that was held in Weaver's office at 9:00 a.m., Thursday, 16 October 1941, many problems were addressed directly by both staffs. On the American side, there was a strong objection to RAF students arriving too late to begin particular courses on schedule. In order to resolve that problem, it was decided that larger numbers of RAF student pilots would be sent to the United States and held in a pool at a replacement depot, where they would be given acclimatization training.

In describing the American pre-flight training system, General Weaver emphasized the necessity for establishing an RAF supply depot so as to properly attire the RAF students, whose condition at the time was noted to be somewhat scruffy. Perhaps since the raunchy appearance of some of the RAF students might be viewed as a criticism of his own attention to detail, Air Marshal Harris was quite sensitive about discussion of this point. Regardless of the clash of strong personalities or small issues, the meeting was a cordial one, and agreement was reached that RAF manuals, instruments and instructors would be used to accommodate instruction in RAF subjects at particular schools.

In the interest of avoiding confusion as to status, it was also decided that all British trainees would hereafter officially be designated "cadets." If this conference had been held in June instead of October 1941, it might have saved much anguish and many pilots for RAF service, but that course was not followed because the two air forces knew little of each other's methods. They were learning. Another famous visitor was the short, self-effacing expert pilot, the recently promoted Brigadier General James H. Doolittle. Within three months of leading his command of sixteen B-25 medium bombers from the deck of an aircraft carrier on the Tokyo raid, Doolittle returned from China, visited friends in Montgomery and toured several air training stations.

By late 1942, many additional visitors had come and gone, and numerous changes had taken place. In early 1942, the USAAF cadet reception center was transferred to Nashville, Tennessee, and pre-flight training was expanded to meet a new USAAF goal, which aimed to produce pilots at the rate of fifty thousand annually. As a result of this change, RAF acclimatization training was shifted from Maxwell Field to Turner Field near Albany, Georgia. The advanced twin-engine flying training school at Maxwell Field was transferred to Valdosta, Georgia, and a central instructors' school was installed at Maxwell Field in its place. Such a school, which was undoubtedly borrowed from RAF experience, was deemed essential in the USAAF drive to man the expanding flying training schools and to standardize flying training. In late 1942, as the Arnold Scheme for training RAF pilots was drawing to a close, Major General Ralph Royce replaced General Stratemeyer as commander of the SEACTC, and Stratemeyer was posted to Southeast Asia.

In 1943, all previous records of visitors to Maxwell Field were broken. In late February, Lord Halifax, British ambassador to the United States, and Lady Halifax visited Montgomery, and in March 1943, General George C. Marshall, chief of staff of the United States Army, conducted some other British guests on a tour of Maxwell Field. Among the March visitors were British Foreign Secretary Anthony Eden and Field Marshal Sir John Dill, chief of the British joint mission in the United States. A few days later, on 26 March 1943, the last few RAF pilot graduates, all members of Class SE-43-C, completed their training at Craig and Napier Fields in Alabama and departed for Canada. With those March 1943 graduation ceremonies, RAF Arnold Scheme training ended in the Southeast Air Corps Training Center, now more generally referred to as the Eastern Flying Training Command.

A week later, on 4 April 1943, Maxwell Field received the president of the United States. Accompanied by Chauncey Sparks, the newly elected Alabama governor, and by Major General

Barton K. Yount, commanding general of the Air Training Command, President Franklin D. Roosevelt visited and inspected Maxwell Field.

On 5 November 1941, the men of Class SE-42-E left the cadet replacement center at Maxwell Field for primary flying schools. The 750 men of Class SE-42-F arrived the next day. In addition, a USAAF advanced flying school was opened at Maxwell Field, and small contingents of RAF student pilots began to arrive there from the basic flying schools at Gunter Field and Cochran Field, Georgia. Some of the basic flying school graduates of Class SE-42-A were also assigned to the advanced flying schools at Turner Field, Georgia, and Craig Field, near Selma, some forty-five miles west of Montgomery.

Between October 1941 and January 1942, RAF acclimatization training was conducted at Maxwell Field for Classes SE-42-E, SE-42-F and SE-42-G. Beginning in early January 1942, Class SE-42-H and subsequent RAF cadets were posted to the USAAF Replacement Center at Turner Field, Georgia. The USAAF Tactical School and Headquarters of the Eastern Flying Training Command remained at Maxwell Field. In addition, the air base was home to a very large and crowded American aviation cadet pre-flight school of ten weeks duration, Wing Commander Hogan's liaison office and student pilots of Classes SE-42-A through SE-42-F who attended the USAAF advanced flying school.

Advanced flying training for the six RAF pilot courses began early on 2 November 1941, when seventy-one RAF members of Class SE-42-A arrived at the Maxwell Field from basic flying schools at Cochran and Gunter Fields. In ten weeks of primary flying and ten weeks of basic flying, the young pilots had acquired about 130 hours of flying time and a wide variety of flying experience. They were now eager to complete their training in the sleek and fast all-metal North American AT-6A single-engine advanced trainers. As David M. Ellis of Aylesford, Kent, recalled, the Maxwell Field station "was a permanent army base and was superbly equipped with mess and recreation buildings, a good P.X., hospital, and churches, etc."

In describing advanced flying training, David Munson of Buckinghamshire was more than eloquent:

> *On to advanced at Maxwell Field, Montgomery and to real flying in military aircraft (Harvards) with full instrumentation, variable pitch propellers, and retractable undercarriages. We covered day and night cross country, instrument flying, formation, high altitude, and range firing down at Pensacola* [actually at Tyndall Field, several miles east of the complex of U.S. Naval air stations at Pensacola]. *An exciting course with excellent instruction all round.*
>
> *There were some casualties, including one nasty mid-air collision, which was very traumatic. The problems by now were few, with a low failure rate and the same marvelous families outside offering us hospitality. We were now fully integrated into the American Air Force way of life for which I shall always be grateful.*

When the class departed, Munson described "sad farewells with hosts and instructors alike."

The mid-air collision to which Munson referred occurred on Thursday, 13 November 1941, within ten days after Class SE-42-A arrived at Maxwell Field. A large formation of aircraft had moved into position southwest of the main airdrome in preparation for landing when a collision occurred, and the two RAF student pilots, Cadets Frank V. Marhoff of Boxmoor, Hertfordshire, and Richard N. Moss of Preston, Lancashire, were thrown from their aircraft and killed.

On Saturday, 15 November 1941, a British and American honor guard and many RAF and USAAC officers and cadets attended the funeral services. The two RAF men, the first of six such fatalities that occurred at Maxwell Field, were buried in the special RAF plot in the Oakwood Cemetery Annex, high on a hill overlooking the Alabama River.

Sadly, the cemetery plot in Montgomery that had been selected and purchased by Wing Commander Hogan with special funds allocated for that purpose had already been used for the burial of several training casualties from other basic and advanced training bases. Although the necessity for such a purchase had been anticipated by Air Ministry and army air corps planners, it had been assumed that all RAF men who died in training within the Southeast Air Corps Training Center region would be buried in the Montgomery cemetery. However, RAF Officials had not anticipated the generosity of American private citizens, churches and veterans' organizations.

In July 1941, a burial plot had already been provided in Georgia for the first RAF training fatality, and within three months, other plots had been provided without charge to the RAF in South Carolina and Florida towns near training stations. By the time of the first interments in Montgomery's Oakwood Cemetery Annex, at least six RAF trainee fatalities had already been buried in private cemeteries, and these sites would continue to be used for the burial of small numbers of future RAF accident victims. British casualties at the scattered British flying training schools were buried in special cemeteries; the one for BFTS No. 5 at Clewiston, Florida, was located within a larger public cemetery in Arcadia, Florida.

Owing to the need to entertain the larger numbers of RAF cadets who arrived at air stations near Montgomery, the British War Relief Society met in Montgomery and laid plans. With the support of other members of the organization, Mrs. Nash Read, president, and Mrs. John K. Danziger decided to sponsor teas for the RAF cadets every Saturday afternoon. There were a total of about one thousand RAF cadets at two air stations, including the Maxwell Field Cadet Replacement Depot and the advanced flying school, as well as the Gunter Field basic flying school, so the ladies were indeed brave to even attempt to serve such numbers.

Regardless of numbers, "tea and biscuits" were served at the St. John's Episcopal Church Parish House from 3:30 to 6:00 p.m. each Saturday, and this occasion provided a means for introducing the RAF cadets to Montgomery citizens. As long as they were in Montgomery or its vicinity, the UK student pilots always found citizens friendly and hospitable. Often, individual cadets were taken into homes as members of families. There they received absolute freedom of the household and received gifts at Christmas and birthdays.

British students in the Maxwell Field advanced flying school continued their training schedules. In early December 1941, the entire class was posted to Eglin Field, Florida, for the purpose of undergoing a ten-day gunnery course. While members of that first RAF class were in Florida undergoing gunnery training and using spare hours for an unusual December swim in the surf at nearby Gulf Coast beaches, the United States became an Ally. When Japanese naval air units attacked Pearl Harbor, American forces took immediate precautions to ensure against sabotage. Although in retrospect the events of the few days following American entry into the war may have appeared silly to the British students, the early stages of World War II had already proved that it was wise to expect the impossible.

Within a few days after the Japanese attack on Pearl Harbor, training was intensified and began to be carried out on a seven-day-per-week schedule. During the final weeks of 1941, while Class SE-42-A completed their training in aerobatics, night and cross-country flying, a number of accidents occurred. On 10 December, twenty-year-old LAC Peter Greene of Gloucester, England, was killed in an aircraft accident, and three days later, eighteen-year-old LAC William Joseph Marchant also died in an accident. These two additional deaths brought the number of Maxwell Field training fatalities to four. Although accidents were to be expected, the hurried pace of training and the long hours of flying, which often resulted in exhaustion, undoubtedly contributed to the increased number of accidents.

On 11 December, the seventy members of Class SE-42-B had arrived at Maxwell Field, and three men held over from Class SE-42-A joined them, bringing their total enrollment to seventy-three. As the new class commenced training, the Christmas season was approaching, and for the British cadet members of both the senior and junior classes at Maxwell Field, thoughts of home were much on their minds. As the men raced about grocery stores, drugstores, jewelry and department stores in Montgomery, Americans were surprised at their shopping, but those who were surprised had not yet experienced rationing and shortages of food, toys and silk stockings.

After the Japanese attack on Pearl Harbor and Germany and Italy's declarations of war on the United States, there was a new resolve among citizens and airmen alike. Thousands of American men and women were rushing into armed forces' training camps, and thousands of British subjects were arriving in Canada en route to flying training schools in Canada and the United States. At Maxwell Field and other air stations, training continued. On 3 January 1942, when a formal graduation ceremony was held at the Maxwell Field Advanced Flying School for Class SE-42-A, sixty-four RAF pilots received their wings and certificates, three men were held over for further training and four had died in accidents. The sixty-four Class SE-42-A pilot graduates constituted part of the first RAF Arnold Scheme graduating class and the first wartime pilot class to graduate from the nation's network of advanced flying schools.

As his pilot training course was drawing to a close at Maxwell Field, Arthur Prandle, who had undergone primary training at Carlstrom and Gunter Fields, wrote an article to the *Arcadian* newspaper. According to Prandle, fifty-three men completed the course and were assigned to Gunter Field for the basic flying course; one additional cadet had been eliminated at Gunter Field, another had been killed at Maxwell Field and fifty-one of the original ninety-nine-man Carlstrom Field intake graduated as pilots.

On Friday, 9 January 1942, Lieutenant General Henry H. Arnold and Air Chief Marshal Sir Charles Portal, RAF chief of air staff, visited Gunter and Maxwell Fields, inspected dining halls, flight lines and maintenance facilities and talked with officers, enlisted men and cadets. At the end of the month, staff officers of the West Coast Air Corps Training Center (WCACTC) who were en route to Washington, D.C., arrived at Maxwell Field from Moffett Field, California.

Among those accompanying them was the actor James Stewart, a recently commissioned army air corps second lieutenant/pilot. According to local reports, as the actor walked past Maxwell Field office doors, typewriters "went dead." Before joining a B-24 Liberator squadron for combat service with the Eighth Air Force in Britain, Stewart was destined to serve a tour as a flying instructor. Many years later, he would retire from the USAF Reserve with the rank of major general.

Other visitors to Montgomery and Maxwell Field included many other actors, actresses and famous fliers. In January 1942, Al Jolson presented a USO show in a Maxwell Field hangar before a crowd of approximately five thousand American and British cadets and officers. Shortly after Class SE-42-A departed for Canada, the seventy-three-member Class SE-42-C joined Class SE-42-B in training at Maxwell Field. And with the intensified training of the time, Class SE-42-B's American days were rapidly drawing to a close.

Stanley Slater of Chesterfield, England, and Class SE-42-B (Carlstrom and Gunter) completed his advanced flying training at Maxwell Field. Although one member of Class SE-42-B was eliminated for flying deficiencies, that second class suffered no training fatalities, and seventy-two men graduated as pilots in February 1942. Following graduation, some members of the class were assigned to duty as flying instructors, but Slater and most of his classmates returned to Britain as sergeant pilots. During the peak of the bomber offensive in 1943, Sergeant Pilot Stanley Slater completed a tour of operations, won a DFC and was promoted to pilot officer. Following a "rest" stint as an OTU instructor, Slater returned to Bomber Command in 1944 for a second tour of operations. During the hard-fought and costly raids on Berlin and Nuremburg, Slater won the Distinguished Service Order, a bar to his Distinguished Flying Cross and was promoted to the rank of squadron leader. During the postwar era, Slater became a career officer and retired as a group captain.

Shortly after Class SE-42-B departed in February 1942, the seventy-eight-member Class SE-42-D arrived and became junior to Class SE-42-C. Within a very short time after the new class arrived and commenced its intensified training course, all seventy-three members of Class SE-42-C successfully completed the advanced flying course and received their wings, and Class SE-42-E arrived to commence training.

Robert G. Halstead of Harrogate, Yorkshire (SE-42-C), had spent his early years in Chicago. Following completion of his advanced training at Maxwell Field, the class was granted a week's leave. Although most of the RAF pilots were drawn either to the towns where they had undergone primary training or to New Orleans for that final week, Halstead and a friend donned their RAF blues and hitchhiked to Chicago. Although they were sometimes mistaken for Wrigley's Chewing Gum salesmen, who wore uniforms of the same color, the RAF sergeant pilots spent several days with family friends and thoroughly enjoyed hospitality at every stop along the way.

Meanwhile, at Maxwell Field, Class SE-42-D was entering the final critical stage of its flying training. Joseph Crossman of Coventry, England, of Class SE-42-D (Camden and Gunter), recalled his training experiences at Maxwell Field:

> In February 1942, we completed Basic Training and moved on to Maxwell Field, Montgomery, Alabama for our Advanced flying course on the American AT-6A, Harvards. We had a week's free time, so a friend and I decide to hitch hike to Louisville to visit an uncle whom I had never met. He left England for America before I was born.
>
> It was very easy to get lifts as we were in RAF uniform and they just had to stop to see who we were; in fact, it got so easy we would stand back until we saw a nice car that we fancied riding in. We traveled through Birmingham, Alabama and Nashville, Tennessee, where we stayed overnight at a hotel, then on to Louisville, Kentucky where our final auto delivered us to the address we were looking for. We had a pleasant time with my uncle and his family, stayed the night, and started on the return journey next day.
>
> I had my first flight in the Harvard on 27 February. My instructor now was Lieutenant Brooks. The flying was very interesting, with cross country trips, landing at other airports. One such trip was to New Orleans, and we had to come in over the water to land there. Another trip was to Chattanooga, Tennessee in formation.
>
> The instructor was leading the formation and, as we were approaching Chattanooga, the inevitable happened. Down below we could see a train puffing on its way. We couldn't resist it; everyone pressed their radio buttons and sang "Pardon me, Boy, Is that the

Chattanooga Choo Choo?" The instructor told us to get off the air, but I think he had a laugh about it.

Quite a lot of the citizens came to chat with us. A reporter from the town newspaper did a write-up, and took pictures, copies of which he posted on to me. We also did night cross-countries and night formation flights. The great day came on 24 April 1942, when we were presented with our wings. The ceremony took place in a Government Building in Montgomery. In front of a gathering of friends, we each marched onto the stage to receive the Army Air Corps Diploma and Wings.

In many instances, American families, knowing that it was impossible for British family members to be present on such an important occasion, drove great distances to attend the graduation ceremonies and watch proudly as the young men received their American and RAF wings and their graduation certificates. Mr. and Mrs. John A. Davis drove from Albany, Georgia, to attend the graduation of LAC Eddie Baron of Class SE-42-D at Maxwell Field. One student from Class SE-42-D was held over for further training, and seventy-seven graduated and received their wings.

On 15 March, the Gunter Field contingent of Class SE-42-E advanced flying students traveled aboard army trucks the few miles to Maxwell Field. John Clark of Croydon, Surrey, and Sydney J.Williams, a former constable with London's Metropolitan Police, were among that intake. Following arrival of the Cochran Field contingent and the addition of one cadet from Class SE-42-D, the Class SE-42-E intake rose to eighty-one. Clark and Williams and their classmates had completed about 130 flying hours at primary and basic flying schools and now began to fly the faster North American AT-6 and BC-1 trainers.

Within a relatively short time after commencing flying, Williams ground looped twice and had to appear before an Accident Investigation Board. Despite his arguments to that body that the accidents were caused by a design fault that caused the tail wheel to wobble and lock at ninety degrees on landing, the accidents were still logged as "pilot error." Fortunately, he was not eliminated from pilot training. Within a few weeks after the hearing, Williams was pleased to learn that a special lever had been installed in the cockpit of the trainers. The new lever locked the tail wheel into the proper position for landing.

Some forty-five years afterward, Williams recalled other details of his training at Maxwell Field:

The cross-country runs became longer and longer. One cadet decided to fly too low and struck power lines, which blacked out a large area of Florida. The wings of his aircraft were split and he appeared before the usual court martial and was sent packing back to Canada. We took part in a day and night cross-country flying [exercise] for some 12 hours. We landed at several aerodromes for rest and refreshment, but on the last two legs at night a severe thunderstorm overtook us and we were flying blind.

One cadet ran straight into a cumulo-nimbus cloud, and his aircraft split and went out of control. He baled out and was going up and down inside the cloud for some twenty minutes before finally emerging and landing unhurt. Another cadet baled out and came to rest swinging in a tree for over a day until finally rescued. Two force-landed, but as far as I am aware, there was only one aircraft missing altogether and not accounted for.

The incidents Williams refers to could not be confirmed from other sources, but the storm he refers to may have occurred on 20 April 1942.

On that date, within a month of Class SE-42-E's graduation, LAC Ronald A. Parry of Annfield, Liverpool, was killed when his aircraft crashed during a solo night landing at Passmore Auxiliary Field, Autauga County, Alabama. A few days later, classmate LAC Patrick Parole was injured when he made a forced landing forty miles south of Meridian, Mississippi. Of the Class SE-42-E's eighty-one-man intake, six LACs were held over for further training, three were eliminated for reasons other than flying deficiencies, one was killed and seventy-one men graduated as pilots with slightly in excess of two hundred hours flying time.

By late June 1942, survivors of Class SE-42-F, which had begun its American tour of duty at the Maxwell Field Reception Center in November 1941, were completing their training in four USAAF advanced flying schools. The young men who had been assigned to the Maxwell Field advanced flying school decided that in celebrating their graduation, they would hold a formal dinner-dance at Montgomery's Whitley Hotel. Since their class would be the last RAF class to graduate from Maxwell Field, its members indicated a desire to "express thanks and gratitude to the people of Montgomery for the hospitality extended its members during their stay in this area." Evidently, everyone who attended the dinner dance enjoyed themselves immensely, but there were many "less than dry" eyes.

Of Class SE-42-F's enrollment of eighty-three RAF students, two were held over for further training, four were eliminated for flying deficiencies and one was killed in training. Thirty-two-year-old LAC Charles D. Eaton, an American who had joined the RAF, was killed on Tuesday night, 16–17 June 1942 in a crash that occurred northwest of Maxwell Field, some five miles north of Prattville. On 3 July 1942, the final class of British cadets graduated at Maxwell Field. The twin-engine advanced flying school was shifted to Valdosta, Georgia, and Maxwell Field became the USAAF central instructors' school and pre-flight school.

In six RAF cadet classes, the Maxwell Field advanced flying school enrolled a total of 449 British students. Of that number 2 were held over from the final class and were transferred to another advanced school to complete the course. Net intake for the six RAF classes was 447. Of the 8 students eliminated from training, 3 were eliminated for other than flying reasons and 5 were eliminated for flying deficiencies. Six RAF students died in aircraft accidents, and 433 graduated and received USAAF silver pilot's wings and RAF brevets. For a majority of the young RAF cadets and pilot officer flying instructors who served at one or more of its air training stations between 1941 and October 1943, Montgomery and its citizens continued for many years to occupy a very high place in their memories.

USAAF ADVANCED FLYING SCHOOL
TURNER FIELD, ALBANY, GEORGIA

Albany's location on the Flint River undoubtedly contributed to its early growth, but the fact that it later became a junction for seven railroad lines assured its status as a market town and distribution center. Although the Flint River's importance as a transportation route faded in the twentieth century, the river provided other benefits. The dams and generating plants built along its course in the 1930s produced immense quantities of electricity for industries and homes. By 1940, electric cooperatives formed under the aegis of the Rural Electrification Administration began to push transmission lines to farms scattered over the countryside. And the reservoirs created by the dams opened up new recreation facilities for a growing population.

If Albany residents had the faults of other natives of the Southeastern United States, it was that they accepted too many things uncritically and closed their eyes to unpleasant facts.

Although most of them thought otherwise in their somewhat closed society, they were not very well informed about the affairs of the world. However, these were not failures of the heart, but of the human will and the mediocre educational system, a regional problem.

With notable exceptions, people of the town and region were oriented to the outdoors and had little time for books or reflection. As with other Southerners, they were generous to a fault, and were imbued with strong Christian ideals, but even though most of them were hypocrites, as at least one British cadet remarked, they would never believe it. They were proud of the reputation of Southern hospitality, which had grown out of a very long rural tradition when distances between settlements were great. They tended to be active by inclination and passive by nature, too often leaving important decisions to those in positions of power.

As inveterate boosters who promoted the town and its advantages at every opportunity, they were convinced that Albany, Georgia, was a good place to rear children and that it had good local government and good schools, and the town's high school football team was second to none. They also believed that Albany was growing and provided excellent opportunities for everyone. The white majority, which articulated these views, had few complaints. For African Americans, it was an unexpressed opposite view.

During the summer of 1940, as the United States expanded its efforts to rearm, the townspeople watched with great interest as United States Army Air Corps site selection teams chose south Georgia for a number of major air stations. Officials of Albany and Dougherty County signed a contract and leased the new but unfinished municipal airport, which was located some four miles southwest of Albany on the Newton Road (Georgia State Highway 91), to Harold S. Darr of Evanston, Illinois. Darr built a primary flying school on the site and used civilian ground and flying instructors and civilian staff to train pilots for the U.S. Army Air Corps and Britain's Royal Air Force. In August 1940, the first class of American cadets arrived, and flying training commenced at the Darr primary flying school.

About six months later, army air corps site selection teams chose a site east of Albany for development as an army air corps advanced flying school. In keeping with common practice in the procurement of sites for military installations, the Albany City Commission purchased the necessary land and conveyed it to the United States government. Initially, the city commission approved purchase of a tract of 1,512 acres of land east of the Flint River, some three miles northeast of Albany. That original tract was conveyed to the United States government before construction of the advanced flying school commenced.

In March 1941, as construction was underway, the commission purchased an additional tract of 250 acres adjacent to the north side of Turner Field, and at the same time leased a 1,034-acre auxiliary field in neighboring Lee County. On 1 May 1941, the Albany City Commission approved the purchase of another 219 acres of land east of Turner Field. At that time, the City of Albany had purchased and conveyed to the United States government a total of 1,981.85 acres of land for use by army air corps advanced flying school.

The Hardaway Construction Company received the contract to build an extensive military city and an airfield with four runways on the site. Construction began immediately, and a flood of construction workers descended on the town. Skilled and unskilled workers were hired to assemble the steel hangars, build barracks, school and administrative structures and pour concrete for building and tent foundations and for the huge runways and aircraft assembly aprons along the flight line. As portions of the huge project were completed, the number of workers on the airfield dropped from 6,100 to about 4,000, but the weekly payroll climbed from an average of around $140,000 in June to $200,000 by late July. For area merchants, the long economic depression had finally ended.

The two hundred buildings under construction at the airfield were described as being formed into a giant V, the apex of which was located slightly west of the hangars. The right arm of the V extended more than one thousand yards northeast and the left arm reached about five hundred yards to the northwest. This multi-purpose training station, which was originally designed to train about nine hundred pilots and navigators annually, was commanded by Lieutenant Colonel John B. Patrick and was operated by a staff of more than three hundred officers and almost three thousand enlisted personnel.

On Thursday, 17 July 1941, twelve honor graduate navigator cadets arrived at the new airfield for the purpose of undergoing a six-week-long instructors' course before joining the navigation school's instructional staff within the new advanced flying school. Ten of these men were graduates of the USAAF civil contract navigation school that was conducted at the University of Miami by the staff of the Pan American Airways Navigation Section, and the other two had completed a similar army air corps navigation course at Barksdale Field, Louisiana. Assignment of the twelve cadet navigators as instructors at the Albany station would allow them hands-on navigational experience, which was obligatory before they could be commissioned second lieutenants. In addition to the navigator instructors, a number of experienced army air corps pilots were also assigned to the new station as flying instructors.

On 18 July 1941, the same day that Class SE-42-B students arrived at the six scattered primary flying schools, two distinguished army air corps officers visited the new station at Albany. Major General Walter R. Weaver, commanding general of the Southeast Air Corps Training Center, and Brigadier General Davenport Johnson, director of training with army air corps headquarters in Washington, arrived at Albany in a twin-engine aircraft and landed at Turner Field, the first such craft to do so. During the inspection tour, General Weaver indicated that British pilots would likely be trained at the new advanced flying school.

A few days later, the air corps announced that the new advanced flying school would be called Turner Field in honor of the late Second Lieutenant Sullins Preston Turner. Lieutenant Turner, a native of Oxford, Georgia, had been killed in an aircraft accident at Langley Field, Virginia, in May 1940. He was the son of Dr. and Mrs. E.K. Turner of Atlanta and had attended Emory University, where his father was a professor of Latin.

Although the goal of the air corps training staff was for the advanced flying school to train 280 pilots and 570 navigators simultaneously at the new school, the capability to train such numbers would be developed gradually over a period of several months. Until late December 1941, when it was hoped that essential facilities would be completed, the normal intake of navigator trainees for the fifteen-week-long course at Turner Field was expected to be 20 cadets every three weeks, rising in January 1942 to 114 every three weeks. The initial student pilot intake was to be 70 cadets every five weeks, to increase in November to 140 every five weeks.

Evidently, the first students to arrive at the new station were student navigators rather than student pilots. Until the shortage of twin-engine trainer aircraft was overcome at the new station, pilots would be trained in AT-6A single engine trainers, and the few twin-engine trainers that were scheduled to be assigned to the airfield would be used to train navigators. On 7 September, 21 flying instructors flew into Turner Field from Maxwell Field, Alabama, and in the process delivered twenty-one new North American AT-6 trainers. That same day, 81 pilot trainees arrived from basic flying schools. And on 30 September, 115 pilot trainees of the second cadet class arrived to commence training. On Friday, 31 October, Turner Field graduated its first American pilot and navigator class.

On Saturday, 1 November 1941, ninety-eight members of Class SE-42-A boarded buses at Cochran Field and were transported some sixty miles southward to Turner Field. The remainder of their Cochran Field classmates traveled to Alabama to enter advanced flying training at Maxwell and Craig Fields. The Turner Field draft was escorted by Flight Lieutenant C.C. Hirst and, on arrival, was met by Major Norris Harbold, director of training; Lieutenant Philip Von Weller, commandant of cadets; and RAF Flight Lieutenant A.G. Hill, RAFAO at nearby Darr Aero Tech. Since about seventy members of the advanced pilots' class had received their primary flying training at Darr Aero Tech, they were already familiar with Albany. Before going to Cochran Field, other class members had received their initial flying training at Americus, Georgia, and Camden, South Carolina.

Bernard V.A. Thompson of Derby, who had trained at Camden, South Carolina, remembered that the layout of Turner Field was almost exactly like the basic flying school at Cochran Field. Following dual instruction of from two to four hours, the RAF cadets soloed in the North American AT-6As. This "real airplane" possessed all of the instrumentation and characteristics of a fighter aircraft, and as Thompson soon discovered, the "noisy 650 h.p. Pratt & Whitney engine sounded very sweet in my ears and could be brought up to a beautiful whine in a dive."

Within a few days of their arrival, the Albany Lion's Club sponsored a football game at the local municipal stadium. The opposing teams included the Georgia Tech "B" Team and airmen from the Pensacola Naval Air Station. The presence in Albany of representatives from the RAF, the U.S. Army and the U.S. Navy was more than promoters could resist, so arrangements were quickly made to include RAF marching units during halftime activities. On 7 November 1941, at 3:00 p.m., the football game began, and shortly after 5:00 p.m., at halftime activities, RAF and USAAF cadets marched past a reviewing stand at the airfield. Since local newspapers gave the game and halftime activities considerable coverage, the event was deemed "one of the most popular intermission features ever staged in Albany." A few days later, on 11 November, the Turner Field RAF cadets once again dressed in their blues and this time marched through downtown Albany for an Armistice Day Parade. When they were not undergoing flying training, those RAF cadets who were not already familiar with Albany and the vicinity had time to discover the town and surrounding region. Most of them found the Lee Drug Store at the corner of Broad and Jackson Streets and several others in the city. Other stops in downtown Albany included movie theatres, cafés and restaurants, milk bars, men's shops, Spielberger's Photo Studio and Collum's Photo Shop, laundries, shoe repair shops, department stores, taxi stands, barbershops and jewelry stores. Although off-duty recreation was deemed important, when the RAF cadets reached the advanced stage of flying training, they were much more interested in completing the pilots' course and returning to the United Kingdom for combat operations.

For recreation locally, some of the cadets discovered on the occasional off-post weekend such clubs as Freddie's Office and the Cadet Club in the Gordon Hotel, while others went to the Marine Room at the New Albany Hotel. Nearby they also found the Centennial Bowling Lanes on Washington Street. During warmer months, later classes would be able to cross the Flint River and travel a few miles southward to two popular recreation centers. The Radium Springs Country Club with its hotel, swimming pool, golf course and beautiful grounds was an ideal place to walk and relax, while farther south, Riverbend Park offered similar recreation, including roller skating.

Since Albany also hosted the men of Darr Aero Tech, the largest primary flying school in the Southeast, Turner Field cadets often went elsewhere on weekends. Many of them traveled to Atlanta during occasional weekends and saw some sights associated with the American Civil War, as interpreted by the film *Gone With the Wind*. In explaining the effect of such brief weekend trips, Bernard Thompson asserted, "I gained an undying love for the 'Old South' from these trips around that area including the Civil War battlegrounds. We became 'Johnny Rebs' and said 'Damnyankee' all as one word."

Under an intensified training schedule at Turner Field, a great deal of hard work was compressed into a brief two months. In early December, USAAF pilot and navigator cadet classes arrived to enter training, but the only RAF class remained the men of Class SE-42-A. As their flying training hours in the rugged advanced trainer moved toward the magic seventy to seventy-five hours, the men absorbed much in a very short time. In ground school, they began to deal with more practical problems related to operational flying. They spent long hours studying and practicing navigation, aircraft engines and maintenance, as well as aircraft and ship identification.

In the air, the RAF cadets spent a considerable number of hours learning formation flying. On climbing high in the sky on altitude exercises, the cadets quickly learned that they could see great distances in the clear skies of southwest Georgia. When the great cumulo-nimbus clouds marched regularly across the clear afternoon skies, it was fun dodging in and out of them in the sleek single-engine craft. Since the RAF planned to assign them to operations in twin- or multi-engine aircraft, Turner Field cadets were paired for both day and night cross-country navigation training flights. The exercises began with one cadet acting as pilot, the other as navigator, and they normally switched roles halfway through the flight. These training flights could sometimes be dangerous.

At 11:15 a.m. on Monday, 17 November, an AT-6A trainer crashed near a dairy farm about five miles northeast of Turner Field, killing twenty-year-old LAC Robert S. Wilson of Newcastle-on-Tyne (Camden and Macon) and twenty-four-year-old LAC Jack Hartley of Leeds, Yorkshire (Americus and Macon). On Tuesday afternoon, 18 November, at 3:00 p.m., funeral services for the two cadets were conducted at St. Paul's Episcopal Church by the Reverend Harry S. Cobey, rector, and Chaplain Palmer Pierce of Turner Field. An honor guard of twenty RAF and twenty USAAF cadets escorted the bodies of the two cadets from the church to the Crown Hill Cemetery on Dawson Road.

On the day of the funeral for Turner Field's first two RAF training fatalities, Flight Lieutenant R. Judge arrived at Turner Field as the RAF administrative officer. Judge, a tall, red-haired advertising executive from London, had served in civil defense and as an administrative officer at an initial training wing before being posted to the United States. Within a few days of his arrival, Judge was in demand as a speaker at local civic clubs. At the rotary club, he described conditions in wartime Britain and thanked members for their hospitality to RAF cadets and to himself.

Two weeks later, the Japanese attacked Pearl Harbor and the United States entered the war. During his stay at Turner Field, Reginald Levy was among a group of RAF and USAAF cadets who were preparing on the quiet, sunny afternoon of 7 December 1941 to give a public demonstration of drill in the Albany High School football stadium. The occasion was a benefit rugby football game between the Spitfires and the Hurricanes, two RAF teams of experienced players from Darr Aero Tech and Turner Field. Rugby footballs had been obtained in Toronto and shipped to Albany via air express.

At halftime, as units of RAF and USAAF cadets prepared to march onto the field to demonstrate the drill of their armed forces, an announcement on the stadium loudspeakers alarmed the spectators. Next day, the *Albany Herald* reported the afternoon's events as follows:

> *The initial announcement read to the crowd said only: "Japan has attacked American forces at Pearl Harbo[r]." Moments later, this bulletin came through:*
> *"Airborne troops from Japan have attacked American forces at Pearl Harbor." At that instant, aviation cadets from Turner Field, local advanced flying school, took the field in a smart drill. The American Stars and Stripes and the British Union Jack flew side by side at the start of a column of British and American cadets. The drama being enacted on the field seemed to catch hold of the spectators. Soldiers of the only two great democracies left in the world were marching side by side in front of them. There was symbolism in it, and the crowd felt it.*

RAF student pilot Bernard Thompson of Derby, England, and Class SE-42-A at Turner Field recalled that "the most significant event of those days was Pearl Harbour. What a completely shattering effect it had on everyone!"

As Christmas approached, local newspapers urged citizens of Albany to invite servicemen from local stations into their homes. Because of America's entry into war, plans were made initially to omit the usual Christmas lights along city streets, and the *Albany Herald* observed that "the Christmas spirit can be kept bright by sharing generously with those who are newcomers to Albany." Although the lights may not have been used on as many nights before Christmas as in the past, they were turned on along Albany streets a few days before Christmas. From air stations scattered over the region many RAF cadets returned to Albany either by train, chartered bus or by hitchhiking to spend Christmas with friends in the town where they had trained earlier.

During the final days of December 1941, a new USAAF class of student pilots and navigators arrived at Turner Field and commenced training. The RAF students of Class SE-42-A were rushing to complete ground school examinations and the required number of flying hours. Sadly, tragedy struck once more. Early on Monday morning, 29 December 1941, LAC Edward Stanley Headington of Wandsworth Common, London, was killed when his aircraft collided with another and crashed near Sumner, Georgia. Headington, one of three sons born to a military family in India, was the second son to die in RAF service. At that time, his surviving brother was reported to be commanding a Hurricane Squadron in the Middle East. At 11:00 a.m., Tuesday, 30 December, Reverend Harry S. Cobey and Turner Field Chaplain Palmer Pierce conducted funeral services for Headington at St. Paul's Episcopal Church. An honor guard of RAF and USAAF cadets escorted the RAF cadet's remains to the Crown Hill Cemetery for burial.

After the remainder of the class completed their training, they impatiently awaited examination results. USAAF officers made recommendations as to commissions and future assignments, and a Royal Air Force Examining Board convened at Turner Field. Despite a policy prohibiting commissions to more than one-third of a graduating class, board interviews were conducted with all RAF men who had been recommended by their instructors for a commission. Finally, on 3 January 1942, all members of the graduating class marched to the post theatre for a formal graduation ceremony. Colonel John B. Patrick, commanding officer, presided, and Wing Commander H.A.V. Hogan delivered a brief message of congratulations. The ceremony was broadcast on Radio Station WALB and relayed coast to coast via the 194 stations of the Mutual Radio Network. Although RAF wings were not available, each UK cadet was handed silver USAAF pilot's wings and a certificate of graduation.

Of the ninety-seven RAF cadets who had entered advanced pilot training at Turner Field in November 1941, three were killed in training accidents, one was eliminated, five were held over for further training and eighty-eight graduated. Since the RAF section of the USAAF Replacement Center was being transferred with its staff from Maxwell to Turner Field, RAF cadets would not again be trained in the station's advanced flying school for about six months. As a result, Flight Lieutenant R. Judge, RAFAO at Turner Field, replaced Flight Lieutenant Alfred G. Hill, formerly RAFAO at Darr Aero Tech, when the latter was transferred to Napier Field at Dothan, Alabama. The five UK cadets held over from Class SE-42-A were transferred to another advanced flying school so as to be able to complete their training.

After Class SE-42-A graduated from the USAAF advanced flying school at Turner Field on 3 January 1942, a tent city was added to the available quarters in order to accommodate the RAF Aviation Cadet Replacement Center. USAAF pilot and navigator cadets continued to be trained in the advanced flying school, and RAF cadets arrived to enter a four-week-long acclimatization course in the Turner Field Replacement Center. Between October 1941 and January 1942, the thoroughgoing orientation, physical and military training course had been conducted for three RAF classes at Maxwell Field, Alabama. From 24 January to about 5 August 1942, Turner Field provided similar acclimatization training for the six additional RAF pilot intakes.

During Tuesday afternoon, 27 January 1942, high winds approaching hurricane force accompanied by lightning, heavy rain and hail swept across southwest Georgia. Although a number of primary trainers were tossed about and a few buildings lost portions of roofs, damage was considered minor. Lightning struck a building in downtown Albany, and a hangar roof was ripped at Darr Aero Tech and from a train shed at the railroad station. Apparently, no one was seriously injured in the storm, and damage was limited to broken glass and litter from limbs and other debris that was blown about by the high winds.

Within ten days, citizens of Albany received another reminder of the tornado that had struck their city exactly two years before in February 1940. On Friday, 6 February 1942, tornadoes touched down in several states, killing nineteen people and injuring many others. Although tornadoes also struck west of the Mississippi River in Oklahoma and Arkansas, the Southeastern states of Mississippi, Alabama and Georgia apparently suffered the heaviest damage.

In middle Georgia, which hundreds of RAF cadets knew well, twisters walked over the countryside and touched down in or near Dublin, Crawfordville, Eatonton, Alvaton, Montrose and Monticello, killing thirteen people and injuring many others. The greatest damage occurred when several buildings collapsed in outlying districts, but in Dublin, which many RAF cadets had visited, six buildings in the downtown district lost their roofs and forty homes were virtually destroyed. During the week of 21–29 March 1942, rains far to the north caused the Flint River to overflow its banks and flood low-lying areas in Albany. It also flooded Radium Springs resort and Riverbend Park.

Since from the beginning of army air corps expansion plans in 1939 single-engine trainer aircraft had been in short supply, heavy reliance had been placed on the North American AT-6 and AT-6A. For those men designated for assignment to twin-engine or multi-engine operational aircraft, the training syllabus had been modified so as to incorporate altitude, night and long-range cross-country navigational flights. However, by 1942, several models of twin-engine trainers had been tested and approved, and most of the defects of various models had been uncovered and corrected.

As they became available, approved twin-engine trainer aircraft included AT-7s, AT-9s, AT-12s and AT-17s, and some of them were assigned to Turner Field. For the period from January to June 1942, only USAAF student pilots of classes SE-42-B through SE-42-F and their corresponding navigator cadet classes had received their training in the USAAF advanced flying school at Turner Field.

Finally, on 3 June 1942, a number of RAF members of Class SE-42-G were assigned to the Turner Field Advanced Flying School from the basic schools at Gunter and Cochran Fields. Although the USAAF and RAF members of Class SE-42-G flew altitude and some navigation exercises in AT-6As, they were the first RAF cadets to train on twin-engine AT-9s and AT-17s. Unfortunately, at about 3:30 p.m., Monday afternoon, 15 June, USAAF Instructor Lieutenant Ellery M. Christianson of Albert Lea, Minnesota, and LAC Dennis Hope of Newcastle-on-Tyne were killed when their trainer crashed and burned near Turner Field. Lieutenant Christianson's body was shipped to his home in Minnesota for burial. At 11:00 a.m. on Wednesday, 17 June, LAC Hope's funeral service was conducted at the Turner Field Post Chapel. An honor guard of RAF and USAAF cadets accompanied Hope's remains to Albany's Crown Hill Cemetery, where the Reverend Harry S. Cobey conducted the graveside services.

Shortly after RAF training resumed at Turner Field, Squadron Leader G.M. Rothwell was assigned to that station as senior RAF officer. With his experience on thirty-seven bombing missions over Germany, he was able to provide expert advice on the training of bomber pilots and other aircrew. As was customary with newcomers, Rothwell was introduced to Albany's Kiwanis Club and spoke to that civic club of his experiences and of wartime Britain.

The citizens and business leaders of Albany were proud of the town's service as an air training center and, whenever possible, they were anxious to have military units, especially RAF ones, march during intermissions at sports contests or any other public events. The public relations value of these events had long been recognized, so participation in them was encouraged. On 16 July, such an occasion presented itself in the form of a Heroes Day Parade. Units from Turner Field, Darr Aero Tech and veterans organizations formed up at 9:45 a.m. and marched about one mile along a route extending through downtown Albany. The occasion was used to promote the sale of war bonds and commitment to the war effort. Following the morning parade, marching units returned to training and other duties as quickly as possible, but during the afternoon, the Turner Field Band presented two public concerts.

At 1:50 a.m., Tuesday, 21 July, a trainer aircraft crashed some twelve miles northeast of Turner Field. RAF Cadet Thomas Moseley, twenty-two, of Middlesborough, Yorkshire, was killed, and twenty-eight-year-old Cadet William J.D. Reynolds of St. Albans, Hertfordshire, was slightly injured. In striking the ground, the aircraft evidently caromed into a tenant farmer's cabin and damaged it without injuring anyone inside. Funeral services for LAC Moseley were conducted at the Turner Field Post Chapel at 2:30 p.m. on Wednesday, 22 July, and interment followed in Albany's Crown Hill Cemetery.

In addition to other performers, those who were featured on the regular Turner Field radio show, which was presented on Station WALB at 8:30 p.m., 22 July, included six experienced and talented cadets, two USAAF cadets and four RAF cadets. USAAF Aviation Cadet William Hook of Albany,

New York, played the trumpet, and Jason K. Goldwater of New York played the violin. The British talent included Cadets Keith Smith, pianist, of Birmingham; David Goldberg of Glasgow; John Trinder of Cambridge; and Allan Mottershead of Blackpool.

On Wednesday, 2 September 1942, at a ceremony in the Turner Field Post Theatre, the final class of USAAF navigation cadets graduated and was commissioned. Colonel John B. Patrick presented their diplomas and H.T. McIntosh, editor of the *Albany Herald*, gave the address and called on them to return to southwest Georgia after the war. The USAAF navigation school for the Southeast Army Air Forces Training Center was transferred to Selman Field, Monroe, Louisiana.

On Friday, 18 September, tragedy once more visited Turner Field. At about 1:00 p.m., a trainer plane crashed some fifteen miles northeast of the main airdrome. Flying instructor Lieutenant James H. Redding of Oil City, Pennsylvania, was killed, and RAF Cadet Harry Eckersall of Swansea, Wales, was slightly injured.

In August 1942, James Double of Class 42-H/42-I (Arcadia and Gunter) returned to Turner Field and entered into the advanced flying training program, which included day and night formation, instrument and cross-country flying. The last cross-country trip of the course was begun during daylight hours. The flight plan led the group to Brunswick, Georgia; they then flew on to Jacksonville, where they landed; then they returned to Turner at night. RAF students met hospitality at every turn, and Jacksonville, a traditional navy town, was no exception. As Jim Double described it,

> When we were parked, we were met by a large number of civilians who were waiting for us. They took us in their cars, showed us round Jacksonville and entertained us until they brought us back for briefing to night-fly back to Turner Field. We had a grand day, and this completed our flying programme. I've done 70 hours here and am now ready for graduation.

On 9 October 1942, Jim Double described in his diary how it felt on that last day at Turner Field:

> We have worked so hard for so long for this day; now it's here, and we are all relaxed and "over the moon." At 1100 hours, we are in the post cinema and graduation begins with speeches—the cinema is full of guests. One by one our names are called. I hear "L.A.C. Double" and, with clean khaki drill well pressed, I march on the stage to have those coveted wings pinned on. I'm a sergeant pilot now and ready to really start.

The observations of LAC Gordon John Cadman of Class 42-I (Tuscaloosa and Gunter) are particularly important because of the questions he posed in assessing USAAF training practices, and his comparisons of USAAF advanced flight training with similar RAF training:

> Training at advanced flying school was similar to previous courses (primary and basic) with one notable exception—one never ever really went solo! In both the AT-17 and AT-9, even after being passed by one's instructor as being competent to fly alone, one never did—day or night—always another pupil, who had reached the same stage, was in the second seat, and I never discovered why this was. Was it because it was not thought safe to allow one cadet pilot to fly on his own?
>
> In such a gentle plane as the AT-17, I cannot accept that; in the AT-9…possibly. Or was it that the trainee pilot in the second seat was thereby increasing his air experience,

and also his general knowledge of flying, by observing his fellow pupil's method of dealing with situations, his reaction (or lack of) to possible trouble and/or unexpected happenings? I make this point, because, in contrast, when we returned to the U.K. and were flying Airspeed Oxfords—another lovely training plane—when we went "solo," we went "solo"—except, of course, when flying on instruments or "under the hood."

My main recollection of my course at Turner Field is the formation flying we undertook. This is a form of flying enjoyment I had not experienced before, and in the remainder of my RAF career, did not experience again—mores the pity! It was a phase of my training, which is indelibly imprinted on my mind, for the sheer concentration that had to be brought to bear on the job at hand. I think all of my fellow pupils enjoyed this part of our advanced training above all others. We were like a school of dolphins gamboling in the air (rather trite, but true).

Another recollection of the same period is the number of cross country flights we made (eighteen total—although some were designated "time and distance" flights, but I could not say precisely what the difference was). I remember too the rather quaint and even faintly poetic names of some of the towns/turning points/flying fields we encountered on these flights—Butler, Eufala, Cochrane, LaGrange, Jackson, Alma, Jasper, Tallahassee, McRae, Opeleika, Marianna, Samson, Batesville—to name a few.

I cannot comment today on the "washout" percentage at Advanced School, but I think it was very low. Anyone who had "advanced" that far could surely fly; if he couldn't, he would have been "washed out" on the way up. My estimation of the percentage of Arnold Scheme starters (in my batch) who took the "wash-out train" was probably something like 15% to 20%, perhaps less. My own final graduation from Advanced was on 5 October 1942, and I received the wings of a USAAF pilot. (I already had a pair of RAF wings—"brevet"—in my kit, ready to sew onto my uniform just in case I had the ability and the good fortune to pass the entire flying training programme. These I immediately, and rather inexpertly, sewed above the left breast pocket of my "Blues").

As with many other British cadets of the final classes, Cadman had traveled full circle during his flight training.

Shortly after arriving in Georgia, G.G.A. Whitehead (Class 42-J, Turner, Lakeland, Gunter) also returned to Turner Field for advanced flight training:

Advance flying was at Turner Field, Albany, Georgia, where we started. We flew AT-9s and AT-17s. General conditions were similar to Gunter. The food being exceptionally good (I was underweight, so the flight surgeon prescribed an egg nog daily at mid-morning break, which meant whilst the other cadets were consuming their cokes, I went to the mess hall where I was supplied with egg, ice cream, and goodness knows what else. It was delicious and the envy of my overweight colleagues).

We did a lot of night flying, high level cross-country flights (max. 10,000 feet) and formation flying. Transition to twin-engine aircraft was fairly easy. On the other hand, the AT-9 had a much higher wing loading (and consequently a higher landing speed) and was acknowledged by instructors and pupils alike to be a difficult machine with many vices. An incident, which remains in my memory—a RAF cadet was on his first night solo in an AT-9, and was on the landing approach when an engine failed. However, he made a perfect landing, which was regarded as something of an achievement. At briefing the following morning, the Chief Flying Instructor (a former senior pilot with Eastern Airlines, and now holding the rank of Colonel), after describing the incident and complimenting the cadet on getting down safely, added, "Ah guess the good Lawd was in that ship, and he said, move over, son, I'll take this baby in!"

I don't know the "washout" rate at each school, but I believe it was nearly 50% on the whole course. Most of those washed out went back to Canada and were given other aircrew courses, e.g., as navigators, wireless operators, gunners, etc. I think the course turned out good pilots, with emphasis on precision flying. All the instructors were insistent on things being done properly, and would not tolerate sloppiness. For example, when practicing spins, one was taught to come out of the spin on exactly the same compass heading as one entered it. This was done by starting your spin lined up with a highway, and endeavouring to come out of it similarly lined up—easier said than done.

Whitehead, a keen observer of wartime American flight training, was quite serious minded. Others were less so.

On 4 December 1942, RAF officers sponsored an appreciation dinner for the USAAF staff officers of Turner Field. Group Captain H.A.V. Hogan, as a wing commander, had served for more than a year at Maxwell Field as senior RAF administrative officer for the SEACTC. He was promoted and transferred to Washington, D.C., to replace Air Commodore D.V. Carnegie as director of UK training in the United States. Hogan arrived at Turner Field for the dinner and was joined there by RAF staff officers from Maxwell Field, Turner Field and other stations. From Maxwell Field came Wing Commander Kenneth J. Rampling; Squadron Leader P. F. Heppell; Flight Lieutenant D.L. Harvey; and Flying Officer J. Gaddis. From BFTS No. 5 at Clewiston, Florida, came Wing Commander Thomas O. Prickett, DFC; from Eglin Field at Valparaiso, Florida, came Squadron Leader J.A.F. MacLachlan, DSO, DFC; and from Moody Field at Valdosta came Squadron Leader G.V. Ridpath, DFC.

Following this dinner in which appreciation was expressed to USAAF officers for their assistance and support of the RAF and its personnel, the officers returned to their respective duties. Advanced flying training for RAF cadets continued at Turner Field until February 1943, and a number of RAF flying instructors were assigned to the station. On 8 December, a trainer flown by RAF Flying Officer Douglas Crowther crashed between Fitzpatrick and Thomasville, Georgia. Crowther and a USAAF private, stationed at Turner Field and a passenger in the aircraft, were both killed.

When Class SE-42-K graduated on Sunday, 13 December 1942, Squadron Leader H.M. Young, DFC, addressed the RAF and USAAF graduates. "Leaving here is very much like leaving school and going to college," Young told the graduates, "because from now on your education is very largely teaching yourself." Drawing on his own experiences in Malta and the Western Desert, Young spoke of responsibilities to the crew and warned potential bomber pilots against "false courage and bad captaincy." A few weeks later Squadron Leader Young returned to England and joined the famous 617 Squadron. Sadly, he was killed in action during the famous "Dams Raid" of 1943, which was led by Wing Commander Guy Gibson, VC, DSO, DFC.

Robert J. Parish of Class 42-K (Turner and Americus) and 43-A (Gunter and Turner) arrived back at Turner Field on 11 November 1942. Excerpts from his diary in the vernacular of

RAF student pilots provide a detailed account of training activities, leisure travel and return to Canada:

11:11:42 **[11 November 1942]**. *Left Gunter about 8 o'clock by train. Passed Plains & Americus. Arrived Turner Field 6 O'clock. Good old Turner grub. Met all the old boys. Really good. Billeted with another RAF chap—Dick Parker & 2 nice Yankee boys. Hartman & Hawkins.*

26:11:42. *Thanksgiving Day. Really wizo dinner of Turkey & ham. Bags of vegetables. Cakes. Pies. Ice Cream. Coffee. Fruit. Nuts. cigs. & cigars. Wizo show. Sort of Xmas do. Interview with Flt/Lt. Smith re enlistment date, photography quiz.*

7:12:42 **[7 December 1942]**. *Bad weather continues, still no fly. Still catch up on back correspondence.*

18:12:42. *Get "Gen" on a 1,000 mile cross country for this week-end. Chattanooga; Blytheville, Arkansas; Columbus, Mississippi & return. Occupying complete week-end. Dinner at Chattanooga. Sleep at Columbus & take off for Turner early morning (in the dark). Just 20 British & 20 Americans, & I'm the lucky one. Bags of navigation.*

19:12:42. *Wait all morning, but bad weather en route. Snow, hail, sleet, & a cold front at Blytheville, consequently temporarily called off. Just our luck. In the afternoon eventually manage trip to Chattanooga. Laurie Carnham piloted, & took me on as Navigator. Bit off course, but main thing got there, & lobbed down OK. Flew back via Atlanta. Night flying, me as first pilot. Laurie as Co-Pilot. On Course all the way back. Nice time had by all.*

21:12:42. *Cec. comes out of hospital. Attend my second Commissioning Board. Very shakey do. Answered all the questions OK, but figure your father's occupation & salary means most to them. Consequently, have negative hopes. Not School tie—See!*

25:12:42. *Christmas Day. Merry Xmas—Like Hell!?! It isn't light enough to fly until 9 o'clock, so they promptly wake us at 6:30 a.m. & from 7:30 to 9:00, we sit in Flight Office waiting to fly—Xmas morning. Thank God, it's pouring with rain, so brainy officer decides we won't have to stay. Wonder they didn't want us to sweep up or something—& that's --- joke. But I suppose the soaking we got, walking ½ mile back to billets compensates our break. I managed last night to attend a midnight mass, but through 1 hr. Link & other various ridiculous reasons, had to attend a Catholic service. Bill Hawkins & most American boys share their Xmas parcels…damn nice chaps; if only their Army was as thoughtful.*

Very nice dinner dished up by the officers. Went to flicks with Barry Ross and Bob Woodham. Later had a few drinks at Gordon Hotel, became rather weary. Met F/Lt. Easton-Smith, who bought us all a drink, & after a chat with him, & an American officer, Smith drove us back to camp. We went round 3 a.m. testing chaps' eyes, with a chart we'd pinched. Our passes finished at 12 p.m., but I'd got hold of some blanks & stamped them, & we filled them in ourselves. Dull & unhappy sort of Christmas, but I suppose, not so bad!

31:12:42. *Barry, Cec., Laurie, Lane & I sat up to see the New Year in. Most morbid surroundings. Cec. bought a coke apiece to drink it in. Just heard clock strike 12, but if we'd missed it, could have tuned in to California station or such like to hear it since their clocks are 2 hours or so behind ours. Consequently, Yanks can celebrate about a dozen New Years' in a night.*

14:1:43 **[14 January 1943].** *Today, at long last, we were presented with our wings. Felt quite good & also very shakey, on presentation. Yankee lads looked very good in their commissioned uniforms. Loads of leg pulling. Feels good with those "elusive wings" but I figure we've earned them, on this awful bloody course. Actually, U.K. boys not pukka pilots until the 22nd, however the wings will do for the week. I should worry. About 6 more hours to go. Bet I manage to prang!*

16:1:43. *All the American boys posted. Extremely sorry to say goodbye to Hawkins, Hartman, Laurie & Lane, etc. They're damn swell fellars. Apparently getting a few days leave. Quick lecture use Useless Schlitz, then it took us 10 seconds to get out of the camp. Get bus to Atlanta with Bo and Cec. Rather amusing time with chap they called Murphy. An American ex-cadet, introduced us as 2nd Lts. & it rather shook these lads who had been talking quite ordinarily to us. Atlanta 11:30. Booked hotel room.*

During the next several days, Parish and his RAF companion had late breakfasts, toured parts of downtown Atlanta with two girls they had met, saw the Georgia evening college, the Delta Airlines office and a variety show. One afternoon, they decided to have their pants pressed and stood in a cubicle for a short time while their "trousers & tunics were pressed at 15 cents apiece." They attended the cinema on several occasions and joined others to eat "hamburgers and coffee in the car" at the Varsity Drive-In Restaurant, already an established Atlanta institution.

On the sixth day of their Atlanta visit, the RAF contingent met at the bus station for the return trip to Turner Field and departure for Canada:

21:1:43 **[21 January 1943].** *Met Cec. & the rest of the boys. Out of 90 RAF cadets, 30 were at Atlanta, & the Greyhound Company organized us a special bus back. Bags of cat calls, especially when Joe Ackerman kissed a girl goodbye. Left Station to the swells of "Auld Lang Syne." A lot of writing will have to be done, thanking these varied peoples for such a swell & hospitable time. Slept most of the returning journey to Albany.*

23:1:43. *Handed in kit bags. Polished up a bit. Dinner. Then off. Train arrived 1 hr. later. Went via Macon. Piece of coal hit a chap's hand en route, & dislocated his wrist. Diner on train. Arr. Atlanta. Mr. Cunningham was there, with a "snorter." He said, "It will be cold up North & you'll need this," as he gave us half a bottle of whiskey. Evans & Cochran got left behind there. Arr. Chattanooga about mid-night. I was "trying" to sleep. Not much of a night's rest. Overcrowded in a 12th class train. "Twas a good train with us hitched on."*

24:1:43. *Got up about 130 miles from Cincinnati; had breakfast at a "Joe's Café," place in Louisville, Kentucky. Arr. Cincinnati 12 noon. Given an hour off, so visited the joint. Very nice. Dinner on train in station. Rest of the 43-A boys met up with us here, including Sam Davidson, Ken Coulson, Bennett & Wiley. Had a good wash & shave. Dropped a postcard to Tommie Rogers, Cunninghams & Lera. Traveled on. Bags of line shooting between schools.*

Arr. Detroit midnight. Smith, Barry Ross & Stone linked up with us. Switched onto Canadian National Railway train. Bloody uncomfortable compared with USA train. Had decent meal about 1:30 a.m. First thing to eat since noon; unless one cared to buy sandwiches through the nose—poor show in Canada & America; quite a racket selling sandwiches at ridiculous prices to the troops.

Parish and his draft arrived safely at Moncton and, after a short waiting period, were assigned transportation to England.

The ninety-man RAF contingent of Class SE-43-A had arrived at Turner Field in mid-November 1942, but within a few weeks six men held over for further training, including Parish, raised the total intake to ninety-six. Of that number, three men were held over to Class SE-43-B to complete training, nine men were eliminated and eighty-four graduated on 11 January 1943.

With the addition of three men held over from SE-43-A, Class SE-43-B contained seventy-eight RAF cadets. Of that number, ten men were eliminated and the sixty-eight surviving RAF cadets were the final RAF contingent to graduate from the USAAF advanced flying school at Turner Field. Group Captain C.E. Maude, director of personnel for the RAF Delegation, briefly addressed graduates. On 28 February 1943, when the RAF pilots left Albany, Colonel John B. Patrick, commanding officer of Turner Field, and Flight Lieutenant D. Easton Smith, RAFAO, simultaneously released announcements to the newspapers. Patrick asserted that the USAAF would miss the RAF cadets, and Smith thanked USAAF officers for their help and civilians for their hospitality.

RAF pilot training at the USAAF advanced flying school, Turner Field, Georgia, had commenced in November 1941 and had stopped temporarily in January 1942, following the graduation of Class SE-42-A. RAF training resumed in June 1942 and continued until near the end of February 1943. The eight RAF intakes enrolled a total of 685 u/t pilots, and of that number, 5 were killed in training, 5 were transferred to other schools to complete training, 38 were eliminated and 637 graduated as pilots.

USAAF ADVANCED FLYING SCHOOL
MOODY FIELD, VALDOSTA, GEORGIA

The region that came to be designated south central Georgia was, in the years before American settlement, a part of the lands of the Creek Nation. In 1565, Spanish settlement at St. Augustine, Florida, led to the establishment of trading and military posts at scattered locations along the Atlantic and Gulf Coasts as well as in the interior. Following the 1821 American purchase of Florida from Spain, that territory and south Georgia were thrown open to settlement, and the Coffee Road was cut through the region from middle Georgia to what is now Jacksonville, Florida. Settlers began to arrive in south Georgia from Atlantic seaboard states to the north.

The very large Irwin County was formed early, but a large portion was carved from it, and on 23 December 1825, Lowndes County was officially created by act of the Georgia Legislature. The site of Valdosta evolved slowly from woodland to cleared farmland to village. In 1860, the route of the first Atlantic and Gulf Railroad line was built close by the village, and on 7 December 1860, Valdosta was incorporated by the Georgia Legislature. Tradition has it that the town was named Valdosta, a corruption of the "Val de Aosta" in the Italian Alps, which had inspired Governor George Troup's home in Laurens County, Georgia. The new town began to grow as a market center for south central Georgia and a portion of north Florida.

In 1864, Major Henry B. Holliday, a Civil War veteran, moved his family from Griffin, Georgia, to Lowndes County. Subsequently, Holliday established his home in Valdosta. Major Holliday's son, John Henry, was trained as a dentist and practiced for a time in Valdosta. Subsequently, "Doc" Holliday contracted tuberculosis, moved west for his health and established a reputation as a gambler and gunfighter. During the 1880s "Doc" Holliday was in Tombstone, Arizona, where he joined the Earp brothers in their bloody clash with the Clantons at the OK Corral. By that time, much of the timber of south central Georgia had been cut, and farms had been carved out of the woodlands. Except in swamps and wetlands areas, long-staple cotton became king and remained so until the scourge of the boll weevil took its toll during the first decade of the twentieth century and forced farmers to switch to the cultivation of tobacco and other crops.

In addition to the farming and lumber industries, south central Georgia attracted the attention of sportsmen early in the twentieth century. Hunt clubs were established, and quail and dove shoots became regular events. The lakes that were scattered about Lowndes County also attracted people to fishing, boating and swimming. However, when the agricultural depression enveloped the nation between 1925 and 1940, there was much suffering among the people of south central Georgia, especially the tenant farmers. In efforts to reduce agricultural production and raise prices, the Department of Agriculture purchased much marginal land in Lowndes and neighboring counties, and in order to remove it from agricultural production they converted the huge tracts into national forests.

In June 1940, when other towns in Georgia were attracting military and naval stations, it was natural that local leaders in Valdosta and Lowndes County should seek similar installations for that region. The Valdosta Chamber of Commerce contacted Georgia's congressmen, and these officials suggested that a local delegation contact Brigadier General Walter R. Weaver at Maxwell Field, Alabama. Following a December 1940 meeting with General Weaver and members of his staff in Albany, Georgia, a site selection team was sent to Valdosta to inspect potential training school sites. Within a short time, the SEACTC rejected the proposed Valdosta Municipal Airport because expanding it for training use was deemed too expensive. Since local officials were then aware of the need for an immense tract of land, they suggested that the army air corps consider the Lakeland Flatwoods Project.

The Lakeland Flatwoods Project was located some eleven miles northeast of Valdosta on land that the United States Department of Agriculture had bought during the Great Depression. Some 11,859 acres of marginal land stretching across Lowndes and neighboring Lanier Counties had been purchased in order to remove it from farming. The CCC (Civilian Conservation Corps) planted much of it in pine trees. Then, around 1938, by agreement between the U.S. Department of Agriculture and agencies of the State of Georgia, a large part of the tract had been designated the Lakeland Flatwoods Project. That project was used for experiments in forestry, grazing and soil conservation.

Once more, Valdosta and Lowndes County officials contacted Senators Richard Russell and Walter George and requested that the Department of Agriculture transfer the Lakeland Flatwoods Project to the War Department for development of an airdrome. In February 1941, following an aerial survey of the 11,800-acre tract, SEACTC officials indicated a provisional acceptance of the acreage if Valdosta and Lowndes County paved the road to the site, made use of slum clearance funds on hand and provided auxiliary airfields. Local officials agreed to provide the necessities, and during late March and early April, the Southern Engineering and Architectural Company of Jacksonville, Florida, completed a topographical survey of the site.

On 21 March 1941, just ten days after the Lend-Lease Bill became law, General Weaver initiated a formal request for transfer of the huge tract to the War Department for use as "an advanced flying school, 2-engine, and bombardier school." Originally, air corps training staff in Washington planned to establish a complete aircrew training system (pilots, navigators, bombardiers and gunners) in each of its three geographic commands, and had already begun to provide some dual training on selected air stations. In the Southeast, for example, Barksdale Field, Louisiana, and Turner Field, Georgia, trained both pilots and navigators.

An essential difference between training navigators and bombardiers was that the bombardier training required extensive tracts of land for bombing ranges. In early 1941, it appeared that the tract near Valdosta and in other areas in south Georgia might be ideal for such use. However, after consultations with other branches of the armed services, army air corps staff in Washington agreed that owing to large concentrations of army and navy stations along the Atlantic and Gulf Coasts, all air corps navigator and bombardier training schools and ranges should be located beyond the Mississippi River. As a result of this decision, the air station near Valdosta was restricted to the training of twin-engine pilots.

On 2 June 1941, it was formally announced that the army air corps would develop an air training station on a 560-acre portion of the 11,800-acre tract. Lieutenant Colonel William M. Robinson Jr., corps of engineers, was assigned to the new station to supervise construction, and Lieutenant Colonel Fred C. Nelson, air corps, was posted to Valdosta to serve as USAAF project officer. Air corps Captain Troup Miller Jr. was assigned as assistant to Colonel Nelson, and a temporary headquarters was established in a warehouse on Savannah Avenue in Valdosta.

On 8 July 1941, the War Department released a public announcement that contracts had been awarded for the construction of a twin-engine advanced flying school near Valdosta, Georgia. The engineering contract was awarded to Reynolds, Stockman and Hills Engineering Firm of Jacksonville, Florida, and the construction contract went to Artley Construction Company and the Espy Paving and Construction Company, both of Savannah, Georgia. Construction costs for completion of the flying school project were estimated at $4,820,000. Lieutenant Colonel H.D. Mendenhall, corps of engineers, was assigned to replace Colonel Robinson as supervisor of construction.

Following the award of construction contracts in July 1941, grading commenced, and within six weeks almost five thousand construction workers traveled regularly to the site. On the domestic site, frames for buildings began to rise rapidly. On Sunday, 7 September 1941, Colonel Mendenhall opened the gates of the base for a four-hour-long "open house." Although few buildings had been completed, grading was being done, and thick dust swirled over the whole area. An estimated eight hundred automobiles rolled through the air base along dusty marked routes. Occupants of the cars were able to see only dust and the frames of some of the cantonment buildings, but they appeared to be pleased to be allowed to see the scope of the huge military construction project that was being financed by tax monies.

Throughout autumn 1941 construction continued, and a military town slowly blossomed among the pine trees. In order to permit rapid delivery of fuel and other supplies, a railroad spur line was run into the tract. Two, later three, wells were punched, pumps were installed and underground as well as tower water storage tanks were installed. On the domestic site, administration buildings, classrooms, barracks, recreation facilities, an officers' club, a hospital, dining halls and BOQ (bachelor officer's quarters) rose rapidly. Post quartermaster units were accountable for food service, motor pool, storage and the issue of supplies.

Once the storm drainage system was installed, a sewage treatment plant was built and streets and sidewalks were paved, post engineer units assumed maintenance rather than construction responsibilities. These units operated Moody Field's utilities and other services such as fire protection as well as most maintenance and repair for the airfield.

While the airfield was being leveled and provided with adequate drainage, a railroad spur line was built onto the airfield. Support facilities built close by the rail line included warehouses and fuel tanks. On the flight line, service facilities included an operations room, control tower, Link Trainer building and a radio range station. Concrete aprons measuring 300 and 400 feet wide, which were paved around three sides of the airfield, gave it a U shape. Macadam taxiways connected these aprons with four huge paved runways measuring 150 feet wide by 5,000 feet long.

In addition to this construction, the army corps of engineers acquired several auxiliary airfields. Bemis Auxiliary Field was developed three miles southeast of the main airdrome within bounds of the military reservation. Four additional auxiliary fields within easy range of Valdosta and the main airfield included Rocky Ford (approximately 240 acres), New River (approximately 200 acres), Valdosta Municipal Airport (approximately 637 acres) and Lake Park (approximately 472 acres).

On 15 September 1941, Major Troup Miller Jr. was appointed director of training for the new advanced flying school, but he was replaced on 12 October by Lieutenant Colonel John W. Persons. A week later, on 19 October 1941, Lieutenant Colonel Nelson moved the training station's headquarters from the Valdosta warehouse to the recently completed administration building. In November and early December, a large number of personnel were assigned to bring service units up to normal strength. Support units and school groups and squadrons whose members had been undergoing on-the-job training at Turner Field were transported to the new school.

By 7 December, the new training base was 70 percent complete, and USAAF headquarters designated the name Moody Field in honor of Major George P. Moody, a Maxwell Field staff officer who was killed while testing twin-engine trainers. Although local officials had originally proposed naming the field after General Weaver, they were told that army regulations prevented use of the name of a living person. Within a short time, they readily accepted the naming of the field in honor of Major Moody. Within six weeks following the Japanese attack on Pearl Harbor, Lieutenant Colonel Nelson was promoted to colonel.

On 19 February 1942, Class SE-42-D became Moody Field's first class of aviation cadets, and their flying training began at 1:00 p.m. on 22 February 1942. At that time, Moody Field had a staff of forty-two USAAF officers assigned to the training department, twenty-one of whom were flying instructors. When the larger Class SE-42-E arrived in late March, the staff was increased to forty-seven flying instructors and the training department was reorganized into two groups encompassing seven squadrons. Although senior officers had considerable and varied experience, flying instructors at Moody Field averaged less than six months of instructional experience. At first, only fourteen AT-17 trainers were assigned to the station, but by March 1942 that number had climbed to forty-four. Later that same month, some eighteen AT-6As and AT-6Bs were assigned to the field for instrument training. That arrangement was only of temporary duration. The early fabric-covered AT-17s that were used for navigation and instrument training only were found to be inadequate as advanced trainers for dry regions. Owing to two fatal accidents at Moody Field, they quickly gained a reputation as "death traps" and were rejected by training staff. As a result of problems with the AT-17, AT-9s, which were of plywood construction and had been deemed inadequate for training in dry desert regions, were shifted to the damp climate of Moody Field and south Georgia.

However, owing to construction defects that limited crew visibility and made formation flying awkward, the AT-9 was restricted for flying training exercises. Its weak landing gear and poor maintenance record made it a less-than-satisfactory advanced twin-engine trainer. Finally, during the summer of 1942, AT-17s and AT-9s were withdrawn from Moody Field and replaced by AT-10s. Despite some landing gear problems, that plywood trainer quickly "proved the more popular type airplane" at Moody Field. Of the original trainers, only the AT-6s remained in use after September 1942.

Since Moody Field commenced training in February 1942, its initial training syllabus complied with existing directives and aimed to rush the training of pilots in an intensified course. Although the official training schedule indicated a seven-week-long course, it was recognized that during much of the year, weather conditions would undoubtedly create delays into an eighth or ninth week. During that intensified training program, student pilots were expected to receive in four distinct stages seventy hours of specialized day and night flying training:

Week	Transition		Formation		Navigation		Instrument	Total Hours
	Day	Night	Day	Night	Day	Night		
1	5 hours						3 hours	8 hours
2	2 hours		3½ hours				3 hours	8½ hours
3	2 hours	3 hours	1 hour		2½ hours		2 hours	10½ hours
4	2 hours	3 hours	1½ hours		2½ hours		2 hours	11 hours
5	2 hours		1 hour		2 hours	4 hours	2 hours	11 hours
6			2 hours		3 hours	4 hours	2 hours	11 hours
7			2 hours	2 hours	2 hours	3 hours	1 hour	10 hours
8	Weather caused some exercises to be delayed							
Total	13 hours	6 hours	11 hours	2 hours	12 hours	11 hours	15 hours	70 hours

Although scheduling was difficult at best, the official history indicates that each 1942 class at Moody Field lost an average of five training days owing to inclement weather.

In addition to the 70 hours of advanced flying training, student pilots underwent 112 hours of ground school, 20 hours of military training and approximately 45 hours of physical training (1 hour per day for each of five days per week during a total of eight or nine weeks). With the exception of ten former American cadets of Class SE-42-F who had commenced training in the RCAF, the first four pilot classes at Moody Field were restricted to USAAF aviation cadets of Classes SE-42-D, SE-42-E and SE-42-F.

As student pilots began to arrive at the new air station, a $40,000 USO (United Service Organization) Building was opened on Central Avenue in Valdosta. Capable of seating four hundred servicemen, the building contained a lounge, an auditorium with stage, a library, kitchen, telephones, soft drink dispensers, a telegraph office and showers.

On Thursday evening, 16 April 1942, the building was put to good use when it served for the dedication ceremonies for Moody Field. However, all were not happy occasions. Within a few hours following the dedication of the advanced flying school, four USAAF student pilots were killed when their two trainer aircraft collided in the air about four miles southeast of Moody Field. Almost a fortnight later, on 29 April, Moody Field graduated its first pilots, when all of the fifty members of Class SE-42-D were commissioned second lieutenants and received their wings.

On Saturday night, 9 May, tragedy struck once more when two trainers (one from Moody Field and the other from Spence Field near Moultrie, Georgia) collided in the air near Hahira, Georgia, and 4 American student officers were killed, 2 from each of the two advanced flying schools. In July 1942, by the time Class SE-42-F graduated, of 302 USAAF cadets enrolled in the new school, 6 had been killed in accidents and 292 graduated.

Since Moody Field had been developed later than many advanced flying schools and it specialized in twin-engine pilot training, Moody Field represented state-of-the-art design when it was dedicated in April 1942. Since the new flying training school had virtually unlimited space for expansion, USAAF training authorities continued to develop the air station during the course of the war. By 1944, more than $11 million had been spent building and expanding Moody Field. When in 1947 the United States Air Force separated from the United States Army, Moody Field's excellent facilities and location assured that it would remain a permanent USAF base.

In June 1942, as members of Class SE-42-F completed half of their advanced training, 211 student pilots of Class SE-42-G arrived at Moody Field. The class numbered 105 British cadets and 106 USAAF cadets. To meet the needs of two separate and distinct training systems, special arrangements were necessary. USAAF Major Hallie Hamilton, ground school director, and Wing Commander George Thornber, the RAF liaison officer, excused UK cadets from officer training courses and allotted that time to special training for these and other British cadets who were assigned to Moody Field.

As the RAF cadets commenced training, their syllabus varied somewhat from that of their American classmates. UK cadets received an eight-hour introduction to some of the major problems in navigation; significant time was also given to identification of aircraft and naval vessels as well as to practical training in signals, maintenance and engineering. Instructional materials were unavailable, so the Moody Field ground school staff designed and built a number of excellent training aids.

Donald A. Williamson, a Canadian who had immigrated to Scotland before the war, recalled his training experiences at Moody Field:

> At Advanced, I flew an AT-17, AT-6, and AT-9. One of them was called a Harvard, the AT-6, I think. The other two were both twin-engine planes; and all three were first-rate. My impression then and now was and is that we received a quite intensive course of training, the schedule for which was, at times, quite hectic. At one of the fields, the rule was that all planes had to be down and parked by a particular time, and this led to a really congested circuit.
>
> Our practice of flying low over some lonely farmer early in the morning and in doing so, changing propeller pitch to its noisiest, earned no lasting friendships, but seemed to be good fun. I have little recollection of any graduation ceremony, although I still have a pair of U.S. Pilot's wings together, somewhere, with a graduation certificate of some sort.

The 105-member Moody Field contingent of Class SE-42-G RAF cadets included Michael Rennie, thirty-three-year-old stage and screen actor, and Basil Bensted, fellow of the Royal

College of Organists and a licentiate of the Royal Academy.

In the advanced flying training course at Moody Field, as during basic flying training at Gunter Field, tragedy continued to plague the RAF members of Class SE-42-G. During the evening of 14 July 1942, four twin-engine trainers took off from Moody Field on night flying exercises. Lieutenant Samuel King, USAAF instructor, rode in one aircraft with a British cadet, and the three other aircraft in the flight carried two RAF cadets each. Between about 11:04 p.m. and 11:30 p.m., all four aircraft crashed in the area between Madison, Florida, and Quitman, Georgia.

Accident investigators did not reveal precisely what happened. It was speculated that a thunderstorm moved quickly into the area, and the aircraft evidently collided in the darkness and heavy clouds and crashed to earth over a broad area. A reporter indicated that she had witnessed the fiery crash of one aircraft just north of Madison, Florida, at around 11:30 p.m. Crash trucks, ambulances and training staff were dispatched from Moody Field, and with the aid of the Florida Highway Patrol and civilian observers they located first two, then all four downed aircraft.

All eight occupants had been killed. Since the watch on one pilot's arm had stopped at 11:04 p.m., it was speculated that that particular aircraft had crashed at that time and the others followed shortly thereafter. Among the dead was USAAF Flight Instructor Second Lieutenant Samuel T. King of Egypt, Mississippi. The seven RAF cadets killed in this second deadly British accident were Kenward F. Stevens, twenty-one, of High Wycombe, Buckinghamshire; Rowland W. Holmes, twenty, of Huntingdonshire; Bernard W. Howcroft, twenty-two, of Yorkshire; Philip Longbottom, twenty-eight, of Liverpool; Sidney A. Platt, nineteen, of London; Ronald B. Pinsent, twenty-one, of East Hertfordshire; and William C. Lamont, twenty, of Glasgow, Scotland.

Lieutenant King's remains were conveyed to his hometown for burial and, following a memorial service, the bodies of the 7 British cadets were escorted to Alabama for burial in the RAF plot in Montgomery's Oakwood Cemetery Annex. When that first RAF class graduated in August 1942, of the 103-man intake, 1 was held over for further training, 4 were eliminated, 7 had been killed and 91 graduated.

Early in July, Class SE-42-H, 212 strong, arrived at Moody Field. Among the 128-man RAF contingent was LAC Geoffrey Whitehall Smith, who recalled his days at Moody Field:

> *Advanced flying training lasted from 8 July 1942 to 26 August 1942. My regularly assigned instructor was Lt. D.W. Pendergrast, but I also had brief introductory trips to the various stages of training with Lieutenants Matre, Brent, Fuller, Scott, Almon, and Black. Cadets at Advanced School were treated as competent pilots doing a more mature course under a more relaxed regime.*
>
> *At one stage, all of us were becoming too slack on discipline for the Station Commander's liking, so we were "straightened out" by our flying instructor, flight commander, Commandant of Cadets, and ground instructors. We were made aware that there was still time for student pilots to wash out, although nobody did. A number of U.S. Army officers (up to the rank of Major), who had transferred from other branches and were on our course, and they, too, were given the same disciplinary "balling out" as we others had!*
>
> *I think I enjoyed my flying and lectures more at Moody Field than at any of the other schools. Twin-engine aircraft were my choice for advanced training, and I felt at home with them very quickly. I particularly enjoyed the precision flying that the system of U.S. training emphasized—formation flying, instrument flying, low level exercises, and night cross-countries. The Cessna AT-17 was my favourite. The Beechcraft AT-10, which*

handled better in formation, had the gliding qualities of a brick; this characteristic made pilots hope that only one engine ever failed.

The AT-6 "Harvard" was OK for aerobatics and formation work, but it was noisy and dirty (it was always necessary to check that the ground staff had flushed the "piss tube" and dried it out, particularly if you planned any inverted maneuvers).

We graduated on 6 September 1942 and received our wings and commissions or stripes—we had arrived! We were allowed to visit the Officer's Mess (a special closed section) at the invitation of our instructors. One rather sad thing was seeing our "old friend," 2ⁿᵈ Lt. A.B. Klopfenstein, who had been at Carlstrom Field, being made to consume excessive liquor by American graduate pilots (2ⁿᵈ Lts. and equal in rank to poor old "Klop"). He was being roundly abused for his behaviour towards us at primary school.

Following graduation and receiving a commission as pilot officer, Geoffrey Smith took a course at the central instructors' school at Maxwell Field in September–October 1942 and subsequently served for a year as an instructor in the USAAF basic flying school at Bainbridge, Georgia.

LAC Anthony V. Rippengal, who was also a member of Class SE-42-H, recalled similar experiences at Moody Field:

The story of Advanced School was much the same as Basic, more hard work. Once again, I was lucky in getting an instructor whom I liked although, unfortunately, Lt. W. Jordan was away more often than the others. The others at various stages of training included Lt. J.C. Seale, the unforgettable Lt. A.F. Cz, and Pilot Officer J.E. LeRossignol. Despite having a variety of instructors, I made it through to the end with only one minor mishap when I ran out of map on a cross-country navigation exercise!

Sadly, though, one of our cadets failed to return from a night cross-country. They found that his aircraft had crashed into some hills, but I never heard why. One minor point of interest was the AT-10, which only the instructors were allowed to land. Its peculiarity lay in the fact that there was only a range of about 20 mph between its stalling speed and its maximum speed in straight and level flight—and it stalled at about 120 mph! It was affectionately known as "the flying brick." However, it did keep us on our toes in the cockpit, and provided valuable experience handling-wise.

My social life was rejuvenated toward the end of the course when a friend of mine passed on an invitation from a family he knew in Albany to stay with them for the weekend. This proved highly successful, and I was further invited to spend my final leave with them. Thus, I enjoyed my last few days in more sight seeing and relaxed entertainment before returning to Moody Field and graduation. The ceremony took place in the theatre, and I happily pinned on my American silver wings.

I think it is fair to say that the variety of aircraft I met at advanced level gave me much additional and valuable experience, and I would not have enjoyed such a choice with the RAF. As for problems, I personally led a charmed life, and cannot remember anything that really went wrong. I have always looked back on my training in the U.S.A. with very fond memories.

The accident that Rippengal mentioned occurred on 19 September when a Moody Field trainer crashed some seven miles north of Madison, Florida. USAAF Flight Instructor Second

Lieutenant Charles W. Ferguson Jr. of Tallahassee, Florida, and twenty-three-year-old RAF Cadet Victor Holman of 42-J and Margate, Kent, were killed.

More than forty years later, Herbert Nevil Mottershead (Albany and Macon) of Derbyshire recalled his advanced flying training with Class SE-42-I and the labels applied to the advanced trainers:

> On 6 August 1942, we traveled from Cochran Field near Macon southward to Moody Field near Valdosta in high spirits, knowing this was the last stage of our U.S. training. Cadets Moran, Molyneux, Munro, and I were detailed to Lt. Thomas for instruction. Here on twin-engine aircraft we felt we were getting somewhere. We used the Curtiss AT-9 "Jeep," christened by us "the flying coke bottle," the Beechcraft AT-10 "Wichita," the Cessna AT-17 "Bobcat" and the North American AT-6 "Harvard."
>
> After going solo on the AT-6 at 4 hours, 45 minutes, there was no looking back. Instrument flying, day and night cross-country exercises, and formation flying passed the days away, until all too soon came our graduation on 8 October 1942, when we received the silver wings of the USAAF. It had been a wonderful 2 months and was not without incidents.
>
> On one occasion, I took off with Lt. Thomas alongside, when at 200 feet, I realized my right wing was low and what was more I could not bring it up. Fortunately, I had the presence of mind to realize that I had not removed the aileron lock pin before take off.
>
> Removing the pin immediately put the fault to right. Lt. Thomas simply said, "I wouldn't do that again if I were you!" Only the day before, two American students had taken off when their plane went into a vertical climb, stalled, then crashed into the runway killing both occupants. Needless to say, I never forgot my pre-takeoff drill again.
>
> Amongst our class were a few ex-London Policemen, and one of these, Dick Cheek, was elected as class leader for parades, etc. He was a well-liked and respected cadet with a wonderful physique to go with it. At Moody Field, whenever Dick was called upon to march us, especially to the flight area, he would say, "Now lads, I want a good show today. We'll show these Yanks how marching should be done." We never let him down, as with arms swinging back and forth at shoulder height, and everyone in step, we would put on a "Guards" Exhibition.
>
> Irrespective of what our U.S. hosts were doing at the time, all work would stop, while they watched us. When it came to the "halt," it was like a bomb blast, as all feet came down together. We were British and proud of it. [First Officer Richard L.W. Cheek, DSO, became a brilliant bomber pilot, but was unfortunately killed in a flying accident in the western desert in 1944.]
>
> I believe it was at Advanced that we used in daytime an auxiliary field close to a field of watermelons, and a nighttime auxiliary field near a peach orchard. In both fields, it was amazing how many would touch down and park, while the occupants would have their fill of melon or raid the peach trees, and the funny thing was, I never recall anyone saying they had been chased off by the owner.
>
> On the day of graduation, we were assembled in the Camp theatre to be presented

with our silver wings and our Diploma. That evening, we held a party in a Valdosta Hotel where some of our boys "pushed the boat out a little too far." Being in a sober state, I removed my jacket in order to help one or two of them, only to find later that my wallet, which I had left in my jacket, had been stolen. This incident marred for me what had been a wonderful experience covering more than 7 months, for my wallet contained money I had saved and earmarked to buy my Mother a watch from the station PX.

The accident that Mottershead described as involving two American student pilots resulted in the death of two USAAF members of Class SE-42-J. Following graduation, Mottershead returned to Britain, and his service as a bomber captain on active operations brought him a DFC.

Oliver V. Brooks also recalled pilot training at Moody Field. "There were no check rides as such in advanced," he wrote, "but I did a cross-country with Squadron Leader A.D. Frank, DFC, but I think he was an RAF Liaison Officer satisfying himself on the standard, and just came along for the ride." On one occasion, in an effort to render aid to possible survivors, Squadron Leader Frank requested permission to be allowed to crash-land beside a crashed aircraft in the Okefenokee Swamp, but that request was denied.

Another member of Class SE-42-I who later built a reputation as a superb bomber pilot was Douglas A. Boards. Many years after the war, Boards recalled his training experiences at Moody Field:

Advanced flying school lasted from 6 August 1942 to 9 October 1942 and took place at Moody Field, 12 miles Northeast of Valdosta. By now, all adjustments to the U.S. way of life had been made, and we were quite "Americanized." Discipline at the school was similar to basic, being a USAAF station, but was a little more relaxed—no tours to walk! However, there was an unusual punishment for breaches of flying discipline.

On parade, cadets who had committed infractions such as "failing to overshoot when approaching to land, because another aircraft in front was too close," would be called out and fitted with an arm sling and a card saying in large letters "paralyzed throttle arm." He had to wear it at all times except when flying. Another, for staying in the air too long, was an alarm clock slung around the neck with a card saying "I must get to know and understand this very complicated instrument." It may seem childish, but it worked—ridicule was a good deterrent! I was not caught out.

The quality of instruction was very good, both in the air and on the ground. Both British and American cadets attended the advanced course, and we were now doing much more complicated flying. The aircraft were also more advanced in number (three types).

Our recreational arrangements were the same as those at primary and basic. Together, with two or three other cadets, we were well entertained by friends we had made while we were at primary, and who lived in Thomasville, about 50 miles away. They took us horseback riding, swimming, to barbecues, visiting people and sight-seeing, including a weekend at Jacksonville Beach at the end of the course. Immediately after the graduation exercise, which was held in the Post Chapel at 0930 on 9 October

1942, we were put into trucks and taken to the railway station, where we left for
Canada at noon.

Although the RAF cadets apparently enjoyed whatever sports events were available during free time, Basil Wood and a number of his classmates attended a local football game and committed the ultimate sin. As Wood described it some forty-five years later,

At Valdosta we were invited to attend a college football match against an "away" team
(from some 200 miles away). They had NO supporters, and we felt very sorry for them,
especially as they were much smaller than the Valdosta team. So, about 60–70 of us sat in
the center of the home supporters and cheered for the visitors.

The end result was that the cheerleaders concentrated on us, and their leader (a little
redhead, realizing that we were only going to cheer for the visitors), finally threw her
megaphone on the ground, jumped on it, and exclaimed: "My God, How I hate you all!"
and stormed off.

Early in October 1942, Class SE-42-I completed its training and, following a short leave, returned to Moody Field for the graduation ceremony and the award of wings on 8 October 1942. Of the eighty-one-man RAF intake, one was held over, two were eliminated and seventy-eight graduated.

Earlier, in September 1942, when Class SE-42-I had completed only half of the advanced flying course, the 225-member Class SE-42-J arrived at Moody Field. As with all of the earlier classes, the enrollment was divided between American and British student pilots and included 92 RAF cadets and 133 USAAF student officers, cadets and aviation students. Training commenced around 12 September and continued to graduation on 10 November.

The RAF cadets of Class SE-42-J had undergone an acclimatization course at Turner Field before being posted to Albany or Americus for their primary flying training, and subsequently to Cochran Field for their basic flying course. As a result, all of their flying training took place in the state of Georgia. Each of these men who trained alongside American student pilots had the same anxieties about failure as others before them. LAC Alexander Ricketts was concerned about possibly missing roll call, so he bought an alarm clock at the post exchange. When he did so, he had no idea that such a simple purchase would ultimately lead to his being promoted to cadet sergeant. He described the events as follows:

One morning, the duty cadet in the guard room, whose job it was to ring an electric bell,
which sounded in all of the barracks, overslept. However, my alarm clock went off as usual
& could be heard in my barrack block & we all turned out, the only barracks to do so. A
minor panic ensued & the duty officer & sergeant had to rouse the guard room & ring the
bell. At the subsequent inquiry, my name and alarm clock came out, and as a result I was
promoted.

Shortly after Class SE-42-J entered advanced training, USAAF headquarters ordered each class to undergo twelve hours of transition flying on AT-6s, then a fixed gunnery course at Eglin Field, Florida, but the program was canceled after about 120 men completed the gunnery course in Florida.

On 9 November 1942, following ceremonies in the post theatre, the USAAF and RAF members of Class SE-42-J graduated and received their wings. Of the original ninety-two-man RAF enrollment, one was held over for further training, one was killed in a flying accident, six were eliminated from training and eighty-four graduated.

On 10 October 1942, the 217-man Class SE-42-K arrived at Moody Field, 86 of whom were British cadets. As with previous RAF drafts, the members of Class SE-42-K came from every part of the United Kingdom and the Empire-Commonwealth. Most of them had completed a flight grading course and many of them had been permitted to fly more than thirty hours solo in the United Kingdom before arriving in the United States.

Among the members of that class was John Lilley of Nottinghamshire (Albany and Macon), who recalled his training at Moody Field some forty years later:

> We moved to Moody Field on 10 October 1942, and the first two days or so were given to settling in. We did not have to report to the flight line until the third day, when I had a look over the AT-10, our new aircraft, for the first time. This was a Beechcraft, fitted with twin Lycoming engines R/680/9 developing 295 hp, and a cruising speed of 150.
>
> The following day I met my instructor, an American named Lieutenant F.P. Seignious. The initial impression of the aircraft was that it was far more complicated than previous ones, as there were more gadgets to master. Still, this only took a few days, and I soon reached a reasonable level of proficiency. Flying was interspersed with Link Trainer, Radio School, and Ground School.
>
> Initially, we flew as second pilots, and after about two week's instrument and formation training, I was checked out as first pilot. I have only hazy recollections of the local town of Valdosta. It was a sleepy place with very little to do there other than the cinema. In fact, often when we had Open Post, we would stay on the camp, because there was little point in going into Valdosta.
>
> Night and cross-country flying entered the curriculum. These were usually undertaken with another student, and were very enjoyable. I can't now remember the distances involved, for although they seemed lengthy, I don't think they were really very far. They were about 3 hours duration, so they must have been about 400 miles. Examples of such flights are Moody to Alma to Americus and back to Moody or Moody to Jasper to Tallahassee and back to Moody. Whilst at Moody Field, in the second part of the course, I was called before two Commissioning Boards, at which I seemed to do well, and it was then that the possibility of remaining in the U.S.A. as an instructor after graduation was first raised.
>
> I completed the course successfully, and on 8 December 1942, I was called into the office of Flight Lieutenant Callaghan the Senior RAF Administrative Officer on the base, and informed that I had been commissioned a Pilot Officer. The graduation day was 13 December 1942, and immediately afterwards we split up with the RAF men heading for Canada, and the American second lieutenants going on leave and then to their new assignments.

Other members of the course had similar feelings about Valdosta but were excited about flying twin-engine aircraft.

George W. Childs of London completed his primary training at Tuscaloosa, Alabama. Many years later, he recalled that the sulphur water at Moody Field created problems, and he recalled how astounded he and his classmates were at the reception accorded them when they arrived on that training station:

> *Moody was wonderful after Cochran. I have never known another service unit where one was given such a welcome. Instead of a grumble, and "we weren't expecting you; the cookhouse is closed, etc.," we were met by a captain who apologized for the C.O. The C.O. was apologizing to us, because he couldn't be there to meet us! A meal was ready. No bullshit.*
>
> *Rooms had 3 cadets apiece, & the Americans outnumbered the British 2 to 1, so we had 2 Americans and 1 Brit per room. The only place they did that, & it did break down barriers. If I remember rightly, the C.O.'s name was Colonel Nelson, & he wore riding boots, with spurs, under his uniform trousers. It was rumoured [that] he often wore a Stetson with his uniform too.*

As with many other cadets who served on airfields scattered throughout the Southeastern United States, Childs also expressed concern about alligators and snakes, but his concern was valid, since Moody Field was located on the edge of the Okefenokee Swamp.

As retired RAF Wing Commander Colin Armstrong recalled, although flying was virtually everything to cadets at Moody Field, he and some of his classmates were able to find some off-post recreation:

> *By this time, we had all fairly well settled down to military flying. The only novel thing was a new type of aircraft. I personally was disappointed that I hadn't been selected for single-engine aircraft, but that soon disappeared, as one got involved in the different techniques required for twin-engine aircraft and a more stable activity. Lots of instrument flying, beam flying, formation, navigation, etc.—no aerobatics.*
>
> *My main instructor was Pilot Officer Norman, but I was also instructed by Lieutenants Low and Jackson and Pilot Officer Saunders. During this phase of training, I flew 25 hours dual, 45 hours solo, including 27 hours at night. It took me 6 hours, 10 minutes to go solo. During Open Post, I seem to remember we spent a lot of time at the local open air swimming pool, which was called Silver Springs, and seemed to be a natural pool cut out of rock. I don't have any vivid memories of this phase of my training. Maybe it was because we were near the end of the course, and I was beginning to concentrate on the impending homeward journey.*
>
> *As I had relations in Boston, Massachusetts, I had requested that I be permitted to return to Canada via Boston, and the RAF magnanimously agreed. However, it was to be only a short weekend visit, and I had to miss the passing out parade. Nevertheless, it was worth it, as I was able to see New York and all of the country between Georgia and Massachusetts on the eastern seaboard.*
>
> *It was in Boston that I received my first military salute. Because I had been handed my American wings before leaving Georgia, I was wearing them on my enlisted men's uniform. When out walking with a relation and passing through the Harvard gates, I was extremely surprised to be thrown a salute. The guard hadn't recognized the uniform, but had recognized the wings, and assumed that I must be an officer. After a short but enjoyable time in Boston, I caught the train to Moncton in Canada.*

On 13 December 1942, the Class SE-42-K graduation exercises that Armstrong missed were held in the post theatre. Of the eighty-six RAF members of the class, six were eliminated for flying deficiencies and eighty graduated.

Although some Arnold Scheme advanced course washouts successfully completed pilot training after returning to Canada, Norman A. Tranter, who was eliminated at Moody Field after having logged 156 hours' flying time, opted for training as an air bomber. Tranter completed the required courses in Canada and went on to survive thirty-three combat operations with 106 Squadron, 5 Group, Bomber Command.

The 224 members of Class SE-43-A arrived at Moody Field on 12 November 1942. During the early morning hours of 29 December, while a number of cadets were flying night exercises, a twin-engine trainer crashed and both student pilots were killed. Killed were USAAF Aviation Cadet William M. Reid Jr. of Asbury Park, New Jersey, and RAF Cadet Leslie H. Carter of Winchester, England. Cadet Reid's body was shipped to his home for burial, and Cadet Carter was interred in the RAF plot in Montgomery's Oakwood Cemetery Annex. When the class completed the advanced flying course, 215 pilots received their wings. Of the 91 RAF cadets on the course, 3 were eliminated for flying deficiencies, 1 was killed in an aircraft accident and 87 graduated on 11 January 1943.

A month earlier, on 13 December 1942, following the departure of Class SE-2-K, the 251-man Class SE-43-B arrived at the advanced flying school. The 93-man RAF contingent within that class constituted the final RAF Arnold Scheme students to be trained at Moody Field. Of that number, 4 men were eliminated from pilot training and 89 graduated on 23 February 1943.

As Ronald A.E. Allen of London reacted to his American experiences, "I would not have missed the experience of training in the USA for all the tea in China! I have acknowledged, and will always do so, the tremendous hospitality and warmth shown to the U.K. trainees by the American people. We were welcomed virtually everywhere."

Moody Field was an important twin-engine flying school that had on its staff many officers with ability and drive; the quality of training in ground school and in the flying department was superb. Since the USAAF profited from design problems in its earlier aircrew training schools as well as from RAF combat training experience, Moody Field was better designed and equipped than most advanced flying schools of the time.

Between 3 June 1942 and 23 February 1943, a period of slightly more than eight months, 668 RAF student pilots were trained at Moody Field alongside about 1,170 USAAF student officers, aviation cadets and aviation students. Of the RAF cadets, 25 were eliminated, 9 were killed in aircraft accidents and 634 graduated and received their wings.

CHAPTER FIFTEEN

THE TRAINING OF RAF NAVIGATORS

PAN AMERICAN AIRWAYS NAVIGATION SECTION
UNIVERSITY OF MIAMI, CORAL GABLES, FLORIDA

Between March 1941 and October 1942, some 1,200 British cadets were assigned to the Pan American Airways Navigation Section at the University of Miami in Coral Gables, Florida. They were to be trained as aerial navigators. The young men who arrived in sunny south Florida ranged in age from eighteen to thirty-two, and most of them had never traveled outside Great Britain. The aircrew training, and virtually everything they experienced and saw, was new and different. Since most of them had only recently completed a relatively slow voyage across the submarine-infested North Atlantic and two separate rail journeys—one across much of eastern Canada to Toronto or a shorter journey from Halifax, Nova Scotia, to Moncton, New Brunswick, and the second southward to Miami, Florida—they were well aware of distances and discomfort.

Some of the British students were told that during the economic depression of the 1930s, the Public Works Administration (PWA), the Works Progress Administration (WPA) and other New Deal agencies created jobs for thousands of people in south Florida and spent millions of dollars building public buildings, draining swamplands, assisting in the paving, widening and resurfacing of major highways and rebuilding many miles of bridges and causeways linking Key West in the Florida Keys to the mainland. With federal aid, Miami also developed canals, yacht basins and numerous bridges linking the city with surrounding beaches and islands. Pan American Airways (PAA) established its headquarters in downtown Miami and its flying boat base at nearby Dinner Key.

Pan American Airways began to develop passenger routes and fueling stations serving Central and South America, and had gained substantial experience in navigating its aircraft over jungles, lakes, mountains and seas. Originally called avigation, aerial navigation was in its infancy when the European war broke out in September 1939. When Pan American Airways began to establish passenger routes to Europe and the Orient in competition with Britain's Imperial Airways, its navigation system was in place, and Pan American flying boats were the fastest means for travel about the world. The introduction of improved charts and radio stations made airfields easier to locate and served as check points, fueling stations and sources of in-flight meteorological reports.

The company's long over-water routes had dictated the development of dependable systems of navigation, and the safest and most accurate system that emerged joined together radio, navigation tables and improved charts. A large number of airports were established at key points along airline routes, and many of them were equipped with radios, beacons and landing lights. In the months before the United States went to war, numerous American and British military and civilian observers and technical experts flew as passengers aboard clipper flying boats along the great U-shaped route from Britain to New York or Baltimore.

Return flights from the United States were routed via Brazil and West Africa to Lisbon, Portugal. There, passengers awaited a flight to the United Kingdom or elsewhere, usually on Dutch KLM Airlines flights that used American-built Douglas DC-2 or DC-3 airliners. With this expansion of air service, Miami, Florida, became an ideal location for the training of Pan American Airways aircrew and service staffs.

By 1940, Miami's population had reached about 190,000, and Miami Beach was well developed with hotels, parks, beaches, promenades and canals. The Miami metropolitan area had become a winter vacationland as well as a prosperous commercial link with Caribbean islands and South America. Agriculture in south Florida was also expanding rapidly. Major highways had been paved and rail stations and airports had been improved. Railroads, airlines and buses transported large numbers of passengers and vast cargoes to and from south Florida on regular schedules. At that time, Coral Gables was perceived as a separate town containing lush tropical flora, golf courses, palatial homes, country clubs, swimming pools, a Veterans' Administration hospital and the University of Miami. Nearby Dinner Key was the Pan American Airways Flying Boat Training Station.

The requirements of the emerging "air age" transformed Florida. Since 1914, Pensacola in west Florida had been the United States Navy's major air training center. During the late 1930s and early 1940s, as the United States War and Navy Departments clamored for more sites on which to build airdromes and year-round training stations, representatives of these two air services met with officials of the Civil Aeronautics Authority (CAA). It was agreed that the state of Florida would be divided into distinct regions that would be used in planning and developing training and coastal defense air stations. Commercial aircraft would be restricted to airways beams and higher altitudes. For its international operations, Pan American Airways began to train more personnel at Coral Gables, and John Paul Riddle of the Embry-Riddle Company began to offer flying instruction in land-planes and seaplanes, in addition to courses in aircraft and engine maintenance. Established airlines also began to serve the tourist industry of south Florida.

After France fell in June 1940, the United States embarked upon a rearmament program that stimulated further change in Florida. In 1941, the United States Navy built vast air training centers by developing several more huge airfields around Pensacola, Miami and Jacksonville and extended satellite air stations along the Florida east coast from Opa-locka to Brunswick, Georgia. The navy also established a large supply depot and an advanced flying training station at Opa-locka, and a dirigible station at Richmond, south of Miami. In addition, the navy established operational and training air stations at Fort Lauderdale, Vero Beach, Jacksonville and Key West.

Although USAAF crews would later ferry hundreds of aircraft through east Florida bases such as Sebring and Homestead, most wartime USAAF training and operational stations were located in the interior and along the west coast of the Florida peninsula. USAAF bases were established at Fort Myers, Arcadia, Lakeland and Tampa northward to Orlando, Ocala and Tallahassee and westward to Tyndall Field and Marianna, east of Pensacola. In addition, the USAAF trained American aviation cadets alongside the British students, as well as in separate flight schools. The USAAF leased several hotels along Florida's east coast extending from Boca Raton to Miami Beach. A USAAF officer candidate school was established at Miami Beach and a radar school at Boca Raton.

Beginning in 1941, several thousands of Royal Air Force student pilots were being trained by civilian contract flying school operators at Arcadia, Lakeland and Clewiston, and some members of virtually every course were drawn to Miami. Many of them pooled resources, bought automobiles and drove long distances to that fabled city, known to most of them from magazines and cinema travelogues. When automobile owners were posted elsewhere to continue their flight training, their cars were usually sold to newly arrived students, even though the wartime rubber shortage made tires hard to find.

Not only was Miami a training center for service personnel, but it was also a major supply and equipment center for overseas units. As the war progressed, huge U.S. Army, U.S. Army Air Forces and U.S. Navy depots and airfields near Miami were either established or enlarged for the purpose of servicing aircraft arriving from or destined for the several theatres of war. These airdromes served as departure points on the South Atlantic ferry route for American and Allied aircrews who regularly flew land-based tactical aircraft and transports loaded with supplies and replacement parts to Africa and the Middle East.

After Pearl Harbor, American civil airlines joined the war effort, and many experienced personnel were commissioned in the USAAF. In addition to its other activities, Pan American Airways operated a ferry pilot school in Miami and trained hundreds of older experienced pilots to fly cargoes from American depots around Miami to war zones. Pilots and other aircrew flew across the Caribbean to Puerto Rico, Trinidad, British Guiana and on to Natal, Brazil. From Natal, hundreds of air transports loaded with critical materials flew eastward via Ascension Island to Takoradi on the West African coast.

USAAF officers, formerly employees of Pan American Airways and other airlines, assumed control over the Takoradi complex on the West African coast from RAF staff. From that base, aircraft were assembled, and pilots flew them eastward across central Africa to Sudan, Egypt, Iraq, India-Burma and China. In 1943, a later route led from the United States via Ascension Island to Fisherman's Lake or Monrovia, Liberia, then northward to war zones in North Africa and the Mediterranean theatre of operations.

Although the military services had for many years trained small numbers of pilots as aerial navigators, the emergence of new and larger multi-engine flying boats, bombers and transports emphasized the importance of establishing the aerial navigator as a regular member of aircrews. The large-scale training of aerial navigators for service with the army air corps began in 1940 on the campus of the University of Miami at Coral Gables, Florida.

According to an oft-repeated story, army air corps Brigadier General Delos Emmons, while on an April 1940 flight to Lisbon and London, observed thirty-four-year-old Florida native Charles J. Lunn at work as navigator of the Pan American Clipper and was impressed with his accuracy. Using astronavigation, dead reckoning and regular meteorological reports by radio, Lunn was able to calculate wind drift, to maintain knowledge of the precise location of the flying boat and to provide accurate estimates as to the estimated time of arrival (ETA) at particular passenger stops and refueling stations along the route.

General Emmons was amazed, and when he asked Lunn if navigators could be trained to do as he did, Lunn replied that he could train as many as desired. Emmons, a career officer and commanding general of GHQ Air Force, then recommended that a contract be negotiated with Pan American Airways to train air corps navigators. Since during the preceding three years Emmons had commanded bomber group exercises that flew over vast stretches of water and land, he was well aware of the state of air corps aerial navigation. He already recognized the need to train many more navigators than the handful of pilots who had been performing that duty. From earlier experience, the general knew that accurate navigation had been necessary for a bomber crew to locate the battleship USS *Utah* at sea off the California coast, and he also acknowledged the need for accuracy when the course was plotted for the flight of several four-engine B-17 bombers to and from Rio de Janiero, Brazil.

Since the army air corps had succeeded in its 1939 campaign to persuade civilian flying schools to enter into contracts to provide introductory pilot training for its flying cadets, Emmons and other air corps officers were convinced of the necessity to seek a contract for navigation training from Pan American Airways, the most experienced civilian airline. In July 1940, President Juan Trippe agreed that PAA should train air corps navigators. On 18 July 1940, in a letter to the adjutant general, the chief of the air corps requested authority from the war department to negotiate a contract with Pan American Airways. On 7 August 1940, Captain Norris B. Harbold, an experienced army air corps navigator, arrived in Coral Gables and spent a few days inspecting the equipment and facilities that Pan American Airways would use.

Since the company planned to expand its own aircrew training program for its growing fleet of flying boats, it had already negotiated a contract with the University of Miami for classroom, office and housing space for students. If the army air corps was unable to lease adequate classrooms, billets and meals for a large numbers of trainees, it would be compelled to build barracks and other facilities. Captain Harbold inspected the airline's leased facilities on the university campus and at the Pan American Airways flying station at Dinner Key. But for the University of Miami and its recent acquisition of the San Sebastian Hotel, the army air corps would have been compelled to build or negotiate a lease for classrooms and barracks near Dinner Key, and the training of army air corps navigators by Pan American Airways would likely have been delayed for months.

Captain Harbold was authorized to negotiate a contract as quickly as possible and, once he inspected and approved the facilities and equipment, he entered into a verbal agreement with Pan American Airways. The San Sebastian Hotel close by the University of Miami campus, as well as the airline's single four-engine Sikorsky S-40 flying boat and its four twin-engine Consolidated Commodore flying boats, were deemed adequate for training, and the final arrangements were negotiated. University facilities were to be leased to Pan American Airways for instruction, for air corps administration, supply, cadet billets, food service and recreation. The University of Miami agreed to award academic credit to cadets who successfully completed the airline's courses of instruction.

Harbold's verbal agreement was followed by a War Department contract with Pan American Airways that stipulated the precise terms and the fees to be paid to the airline for the instruction of army air corps personnel—space, equipment, supplies and manpower. By agreement, the air corps was supposed to furnish most of the instructional materials and equipment, handle the discipline and pay of air corps cadets and regularly withdraw the food ($1 per day or $30 a month) and housing allowance ($0.75 per day or $22.50 a month) from each cadet's pay and transmit it to Pan American Airways. By agreement, Pan American Airways then paid the University of Miami for food, housing and use of classroom and office space.

A prime reason for the contract that was signed between the War Department and Pan American Airways, and which failed to include the University of Miami as one of the contractors, is that the university was a private, church-related institution. Before the advent of significant direct federal aid to education in 1958, such institutions closely guarded their independence. Although the trustees, administration, faculty and staff of such private and church-related universities were anxious to serve the nation in any way possible, their charters, unless recently changed, prohibited legal or financial obligations to government at any level.

The arrangements between Pan American Airways and the University of Miami worked exceedingly well for both parties, but because of the prohibitions required by the university's charter, it was impossible to shift such charges over to Lend-Lease (U.S. government) funding. As a result, both the British Treasury and the United States Army Air Corps were compelled to continue to pay Pan American Airways for instructional costs (including per-hour charges for use of the flying boats), utilities, classrooms and offices, and the airline continued to pay the University of Miami. Instead of being able to rely on Lend-Lease funds to meet such expenses, the British Treasury was compelled to use some of its own dwindling supply of dollars to pay for training RAF navigators at Coral Gables. That provision was one of several reasons the British government withdrew its men from the Pan American Airways Training Section in October 1942.

Around 10 August 1940, First Lieutenant Thomas B. Carnahan arrived at the University of Miami and established the Army Air Corps Training Detachment. Within a few days, Captain Francis H. Goodrich, who was to remain in that post for more than a year, replaced Carnahan as detachment commanding officer. Carnahan continued to serve at the school, as did the medical officer, First Lieutenant James M. Marshall, MD. On 12 August 1940, fifty army air corps navigation cadets of Class 41-A reported to detachment headquarters and commenced the twelve-week-long navigation course.

Pan American Airways Chief Instructor Charles J. Lunn walked out for at least a month to protest the air corps' failure to deliver instructional equipment. Since classrooms and other facilities were crowded and instruments and other instructional materials were not available, the first class of American navigation cadets stayed at the Coral Gables school for sixteen weeks, instead of twelve, in order to complete every phase of the curriculum. Arrival of the second class of fifty cadets was understandably delayed.

Since the air corps planned to enlarge its own class enrollments at the school, and its officers were anxious to benefit from British air combat experience, a proposal was made to the Air Ministry that the RAF enter ten students in each of the next three classes beginning 1 February, 22 March and 3 May 1941. On 5 November 1940, in response to that offer, RAF Group Captain Mackworth of the British Air Mission paid an "unofficial" visit to the Coral Gables school. The Royal Air Force had laid down training requirements for the observer brevet many years before, but the outbreak of war led them to revise qualifications. The practice of qualifying pilots as observers was abandoned, and candidates for observer training were sought for the newly established No. 1 Air Observer School at Eastbourne, Sussex. The RAF also laid down training requirements for the observer brevet, but the requirements were changing as new and larger aircraft were introduced to active operations.

In November 1940, Class 41-A, the first fifty-man army air corps navigator course, was nearing completion of the Pan American Airways course. Once they completed their training at Coral Gables, they were scheduled to undergo an additional six months of training in armaments, gunnery and practical navigation at a newly established air corps navigation school at Barksdale Army Air Field near Shreveport, Louisiana. Owing to low budgets, armaments training was severely limited, but for experience in practical navigation, the early PAA navigator graduates were assigned to work alongside civilian navigators aboard airliners before being assigned to an army air corps squadron.

Following a tour of the school, a critical examination of the curriculum and discussion with army air corps and Pan American Airways staff, Group Captain Mackworth argued against RAF participation in the school's aerial navigation courses. Mackworth's objections were legion, but his primary concern was that the twelve-week-long course was too short and did not include armaments training, enough personal attention or sufficient flying experience to measure up to the RAF's standard qualifications for aerial observer. When Pan American Airways responded to Mackworth's objections by employing additional instructors, modifying the school's curriculum and lengthening the course from twelve to fifteen weeks, the Air Ministry examined the issue and approved an "experiment" in international aircrew training.

Air Commodore George C. Pirie, air attaché at the British Embassy, was directed to make the necessary arrangements for the training of RAF observers at the Florida school. Following correspondence and telephone calls, Pirie traveled to Coral Gables and met with officials of the University of Miami and Captain Goodrich. Goodrich recommended that the RAF students be supplied with khaki uniforms similar to those worn by American cadets, and arrangements were completed for future contingents of British student observers to be admitted to the university and trained alongside American navigation cadets. Entry into the course was set for February 1941, but problems developed. Despite British agreement in January to send ten students to Florida for the February intake, the acceptance message from air corps headquarters was delayed.

Pirie expressed the opinion that the British failure to approve a Pan American Airways request for "landing facilities at Singapore" strained relations with the company and might have accounted for what was perceived as a lack of cooperation in Miami. Although the air attaché's statement concerning his government's handling of the Singapore issue may well have been a cause for friction, it is likely that Group Captain Mackworth's criticisms also alienated Pan American Airways personnel and set the stage for later conflict. Early on, Captain Carl F. Dewey, director of the school, and Chief Instructor Charles J. Lunn adopted the view that there would be no British "takeover" of either the syllabus or the instructional methods of what was now called the Pan American Airways Navigation Section of the University of Miami.

For the next intake, plans were advanced to expand the training syllabus from twelve to fifteen weeks and to increase student enrollment to one hundred cadets per class. The entire course would last fourteen weeks and two days, or seventy-two instructional days, and would include sixty hours of meteorology. The first forty-two days of the course would be spent on the ground in classrooms, and the students would be assigned about three hours of homework daily. During the next twelve days, the class would be split into two sections, and while one section reviewed everything it had studied, groups of ten students from the other section would practice navigational exercises in six four-hour daytime flights and six four-hour nighttime flights. The policy of enrolling overlapping classes continued, and each future fifteen-week course would alternate its arrival time first after seven weeks, the next after eight weeks and then repeat.

The addition of fifteen navigation instructors and four meteorology instructors to the staff undoubtedly improved instruction and permitted more individual attention to students. Heaton B. Owsley, experienced meteorolgist who had served as PAA weather forecaster in Lisbon, Portugal, was brought to Miami as the chief meteorology instructor. The University of Miami also began to award 15 semester hours of academic credit for students successfully completing the course. The navigation course consisted of 290 hours of classroom work and practical navigation, and the meteorology course consisted of 60 hours of instruction.

Pan American Airways staff were naturally sensitive to criticism of what they perceived as their own pioneering efforts in aerial navigation. For more than a century, Britons had made many valuable contributions to the science of maritime navigation, but Pan American Airways had developed its own system of aerial navigation and its staff were proud of the company's achievements. Pride in their system and resentment of any criticism of it may have led to defensive attitudes among PAA staff that may well have sprung from competition between Pan American Airways and Britain's Imperial Airways. In the absence of specific evidence of an anti-British sentiment or an isolationist point of view among airline officials, problems that developed may well have stemmed from such a clash of interests.

Another reason for some disagreement may have stemmed from Major General Davenport Johnson, army air corps director of training. Johnson apparently did not like the prospect of a British incursion at Miami and may have attempted to block the RAF intake. Since the air corps was planning to further increase its pilot output, a program that always included a proportional increase in navigators, bombardiers and aerial gunners, Johnson wanted failed American student pilots to have an opportunity to be trained as navigators. From his perspective, washed out pilots would possess the best qualifications for training as navigators, but unless there were places for them, these excellent aircrew candidates were likely to be discharged from the air corps (one of their options at that time) and lost to the navy or some other service.

Evidently General Arnold agreed with linking pilot and navigator training, but felt that there was more to be gained than lost from training British navigators. Just as Group Captain Mackworth's objections to navigator training by Pan American Airways were overridden by the Air Ministry, Arnold overrode Johnson's objections to training British aircrew. Air corps staff also began to develop plans whereby navigators would be training alongside pilots at selected advanced flying schools (TE), such as the one at Turner Field, Georgia. In the meantime, the Pan American Airways contract was revised and the school's training capacity was doubled.

It is known that the first ten-man draft of RAF student observers was handpicked for training in the United States at the No. 1 Navigation School at Eastbourne, Sussex, and it is assumed the second ten-man draft was selected in the same way and followed the same route to North America, as did other drafts. They departed Eastbourne, Sussex, and, following a brief leave, they reported to RAF Wilmslow, Cheshire, to be issued civilian suits and await assignment to a larger draft destined for training in North America. After about a week, the enlarged aircrew draft was assembled and scheduled for departure. That night, they boarded blacked-out train cars and traveled northward to Glasgow, Scotland. The next day they boarded a troop transport at Gourock on the Firth of Clyde bound for Canada. Crossing the cold and forbidding North Atlantic to Halifax, Nova Scotia, or to Montreal took between ten and fifteen days. After Halifax was designated the major port for arriving and departing British aircrew, the students disembarked at Halifax and immediately boarded a train for the thirty-hour trip across eastern Canada to Toronto and the RCAF No. 1 Manning Depot.

On completion of documentation at the RCAF No. 1 Manning Depot, the RAF aircrew trainees, dressed in the civilian suits they had been issued at RAF Wilmslow, boarded cars on a rail siding within the grounds of the Canadian National Exhibition and departed. Most contingents were escorted by RCAF officers on assignment from the No. 1 Movements Group (Montreal) to handle administrative details including travel requisitions, meal and luggage vouchers, physical checks by American immigration officers and delivery of the men and accurate nominal rolls to the appropriate U.S. Army Air Corps and RAF staff officers at their respective destinations. An RCAF pilot officer accompanied the first small ten-man draft destined for Coral Gables, Florida, but the escort for the second small draft is unknown.

The brief period at Toronto had been one of relative relaxation. Now, before the harsh and demanding grind of flying training, came long train journeys for the different drafts. The earlier run from Halifax to Toronto had been good training. The rail trips on the huge Canadian and American trains would convey the young British passengers southward to Florida. American music and the Hollywood cinema had given them a particular view of the United States, but even these impressions could not convey the excitement at really glimpsing for oneself many of the places only vaguely seen before in films or learned of from magazines, books or music.

That next stage in the odyssey of the British aircrew students, actual entry into the United States, was a first for most of them. The early drafts were properly "disguised" for entry into the neutral United States as civilians. Their civilian uniforms made them look like a "convention of insurance salesmen" and consisted of gray flannel or worsted suits, RAF-issue black shoes, blue shirts and black ties. As they boarded Canadian Pacific Railway cars standing on the siding at the National Exhibition, the temporary "civilians" were issued two blankets and, if they did not already have one, they were joined by an escort officer.

The train departed the exhibition grounds, sped across western Ontario and crossed the river into Detroit. Before arrival there, the men were fed lunch aboard the train. At Detroit, as they filed off the Canadian Pacific Train and into coaches of the Louisville and Nashville Railway, their two baggage cars were shunted onto nearby tracks to be joined with the train for the trip southward. Some hours later, the train rolled into Cincinnati, Ohio, and the men changed from coaches to Southern Railway Pullman sleeping cars and continued their journey southward to Chattanooga and Atlanta. After changing trains at Atlanta, their Central of Georgia coaches carried them via Albany and Waycross to Jacksonville, where they changed to coaches of the Florida East Coast Railway and continued southward to Miami.

At 7:00 a.m., 22 March 1941, the first RAF students, including Pilot Officer Edward W. Anderson and nine leading aircraftsmen (LACs), arrived at the railway station in Miami and were met by Air Commodore George C. Pirie. The u/t observers strode out of the train cars in woolen civilian suits that were much too heavy for the south Florida climate. Arrangements were quickly made to purchase khaki drill outfits for them, so after they had walked to the nearby Columbus Hotel for breakfast, they were taken to "the shop of Donald S. Lavigne, 114 N.E. Second Avenue, Miami, and all our men were fitted for tropical kit of trousers, three shirts, two ties, one belt, one cap, all of khaki colour; total cost in each case being about $17." On arrival at the University of Miami, that first ten-man draft of RAF students joined the ninety American cadets of Class 41-E.

Air Commodore Pirie's notes about his inspection of the navigation school are important for the light they shed on details of administration. Pirie found Captain Carl Dewey and Charles J. Lunn of Pan American Airways; Dr. Bowman F. Ashe, president of the University of Miami and distinguished geographer; and the air corps staff anxious to be of assistance. When the British officer met Captain Francis H. Goodrich, commanding officer of the air corps detachment and supervisor of the army contract, Pirie asked that the RAF cadets be treated the same way American cadets were. Pirie was anxious that there be no complaints by "the Nyes or Wheelers [isolationist United States Senators Gerald P. Nye and Burton K. Wheeler] that our men were being trained in military subjects or were merely 'tourists' after the Nazi fashion."

In addition to his inspection, Pirie made arrangements for Mr. Oates, the elderly British vice-consul in Miami, to handle pay for the British cadets. Each month, Oates would be billed by the university for board and lodging for the RAF students and would mail a check to the university bursar. On Friday of each week, the vice-consul would also post a check in the amount of $141.75 to the senior RAF student at the university to cover the weekly pay (less allotments) for all ten RAF students for the preceding week. Whereas the rate of pay for army air corps cadets was $75 per month (after deductions), the pay of British LACs ranged from approximately $50 to $63.30 per month, depending upon income tax deductions and dependents' allotments.

Following assignment to billets on the third floor of the San Sebastian Hotel, a comfortable building that normally housed university faculty and staff members, the men underwent a cursory physical exam (FFI) before having lunch in the university cafeteria. Later, during 22 March, Pirie inspected the quarters and facilities of the university. He saw and was impressed with the four rooms on the third floor of the San Sebastian Hotel that served as quarters for the ten RAF students (two or three men to a room). He was also pleased that the RAF contingent was readily accepted by the American cadets and by the "extremely well turned out" girls at the university. Pirie observed the RAF students as they received their course supplies and equipment and was glad to see the Miami press "unexpectedly friendly" in contrast with their apparent anti-British views in 1939–40.

That afternoon, the RAF students were welcomed to the school by its director, Captain Dewey, were issued manuals and other materials and sat an examination in trigonometry. The RAF men were readily accepted by their American classmates and by students of the coeducational University of Miami. Female student editors and reporters for student publications were anxious to meet and write about the British arrivals. That easy acceptance into the school and community surprised RAF officers who expected isolationist reactions, but that friendliness appeared to be one-sided.

Regardless of the former tone of the Miami press, the most important elements in this mixture of human beings were the attitudes of the British students themselves. Although rank was not recognized, the ten picked RAF students proved to be very aloof, much to the chagrin of friendlier Americans. Distressed by the British reserve, Mrs. Bessie Bailey, secretary in the army air corps detachment office, described them as follows: "They went their way and, although quartered and messed with our cadets, they were not of us." Miss Beatrice Bretzfield, office manager for the PAA Navigation Section, described the first class of ten RAF students of Class 41-E as "cold." When that first PAA class completed the course on 27 June, an American cadet won highest honors, and LAC Alfred B. Marsh of Leicester placed second.

After the first course completed its training and departed, Flight Lieutenant Norman C.K. Dibble was assigned to the Coral Gables school as RAF administrative officer. Not only did Dibble provide instruction in RAF procedures during spare hours from the normal schedule of activities, but he also assumed responsibility for pay and other administrative details formerly handled from the office of the British vice-consul in Miami. At first, Dibble was reserved, but he soon adjusted to his new duties and to the Americans. According to Miss Bretzfield, "Dibble, we thought, was a typical Englishman—arrogant, snobbish, and smug. We were wrong!" Just as Flight Lieutenant Dibble overcame his initial reserve, the second course of ten RAF students did as well.

That second ten-man RAF intake arrived on 5 May 1941 and joined ninety-five air corps cadets of Class 41-F. The RAF students seemed more relaxed than the members of Class 41-E and were much more friendly and open. Alan Bartlett, former first violinist with the London Symphony, was a member of Class 41-F, and he charmed everyone with his talent and personality. As the months passed, the air war increased in intensity, and when Bartlett was reported killed on operations in May 1942, sadness prevailed among school and detachment staff members. Describing Alan Bartlett, Miss Bretzfield said, "The force of his personality and his genius remain as a constant reminder of a great spirit we were privileged to have with us for a little while." Bartlett was not the only PAA-trained RAF navigator to die on Bomber Command operations.

Almost exactly five years after that first RAF class arrived in Miami, Charles Lunn wrote a letter to Dr. Bowman F. Ashe, president of the University of Miami, and provided him with "a few highlights of the RAF Cadet Training Program" at the university. Lunn's notes were evidently intended as a brief for the university president as he prepared for the ceremony awarding former Prime Minister Winston Churchill an honorary degree. Lunn proudly reported that RAF Cadet William Charles Wallace had averaged 98.6 percent, "the highest grade in the history of the school." In referring to the first RAF class at the school, Lunn's description was both sad and proud. "Eight of the first class of ten gave their lives for their country. One of the two surviving classmates is Wing Commander Edward William Anderson, who has played a major role in polar navigation. He was awarded the DFC."

By April 1941, the army air corps had decided to establish military navigation schools in each of its three separate geographic flying training commands, but owing to a shortage of instructors and a lack of sufficient numbers of twin-engine trainer aircraft, that objective could not be met. Until sufficient cadre and appropriate aircraft were available to equip and staff these schools, army air corps officers launched joint training, a plan that had been much talked about the year before. In order to make maximum use of available aircraft, navigators were trained in advanced flying schools alongside pilots of twin-engine aircraft. In the SEACTC, such combined pilot and navigator training was carried out at the USAAC advanced flying school at Turner Field near Albany, Georgia. When this plan was implemented, General Arnold was able to offer a larger number of training spaces for RAF navigators at the Coral Gables school.

Apparently, some RAF staff officers of the Air Ministry's directorate of training believed that the American general had ulterior motives when he offered the RAF 75 percent of the capacity of the Pan American Airways School. General Arnold made the generous offer in an April 1941 visit to London. Some of them expressed the view that the real reason for relinquishing the extra navigation training spaces to the RAF was that USAAF officers could do nothing with Charles Lunn and the navigation school's management. Although some of the USAAC officers may have been put off by Lunn's bluntness and his intentionally delaying the first class of air corps navigators, they recognized his expertise in the field and apparently respected him and his work.

It is doubtful that General Arnold was even aware of the operational details of the Pan American Airways school. Instead of wishing to rid the USAAC of a problem, Arnold was sincere when he helped Britain to establish its various training schemes in the United States. Arnold's generosity was designed for the express purpose of rendering aid to Britain and removing the grip of an exasperated president of the United States from his own neck and to gain rapid expansion of the American aircraft industry. No doubt, he also agreed with many of his subordinate staff that air corps officers could learn much from British wartime operational and training experience.

It was undoutedly difficult for Arnold to hide his feelings that he would prefer to retain a significant number of trainers and operational aircraft in order to meet the defense needs of the United States, so it was probably natural that the British should have been suspicious of such generosity. Proof that the air corps chief had no intention of dumping the Pan American Airways contract school as a nuisance lies in the fact that after the RAF voluntarily withdrew from the school on 17 October 1942, American navigator cadets filled all classes to capacity until the school closed in 1944.

In November 1940, Group Captain Mackworth had inspected the Pan American Airways Section. In April 1941, General Arnold offered to increase the number of places for RAF u/t observers in each class, and by 5 June 1941, British student pilots had begun to arrive in the United States in large numbers. This was evidently cause of yet another inspection. On 9–10 June 1941, Wing Commander Wilfred E. Oulton (later air vice-marshal), director of navigation training for all UK flying schools in the United States, visited and assessed navigation training in Arnold Scheme primary flying schools as well as the Pan American Airways School at Coral Gables. Oulton's report of this survey provides insight into RAF staff attitudes as training began.

In describing his visit to Coral Gables on 9–10 June, Oulton was evidently prepared to be more critical, but he conceded that following "a careful examination of the syllabus and instructional methods, it was agreed that the ground instruction given is very thorough. The staff of 17 instructors is rather less than the RAF uses for a school of 400 pupils, but should be adequate." Oulton was not yet content, however, because he correctly insisted to school officials that there were vital differences between training navigators for peacetime flying and for war service.

Evidently, Oulton had studied the curriculum of the Pan American Airways Navigation Section and was visiting the Florida school "with a view to effecting some improvement" in the course syllabus. He had not yet seen the report that Pilot Officer Anderson would write when that first RAF draft completed the bombing and gunnery school (B&GS) in Canada. Moreover, Flight Lieutenant Dibble had not been present at Coral Gables long enough to submit reports through channels. Lacking evidence to support any negative assessment, Oulton faced a complicated task that required a high order of tact and diplomacy. Although the RAF officer was necessarily critical of the PAA navigation curriculum, which he viewed as unsuited for modern war, it was necessary for him to tread lightly so as not to alienate school staff.

If the RAF intended to assign PAA-trained observers (navigators) to serve exclusively with Coastal Command and to fly over vast stretches of water on convoy escort duties or anti-submarine patrols, their navigational and meteorological training was superb. However, while performing such active duty as navigators, they would have to use British charts, radio frequencies and terminology. Although their navigational and meteorological training at Coral Gables qualified them for assignment to Coastal Command, they might not so easily fit into other RAF commands. If they were to be effective crew members, they needed more air experience as first navigators, and they also needed to become proficient wireless operators. In addition, Oulton felt that they ought to be well-grounded in bombs, aerial gunnery, aircraft and ship identification, RAF procedures and hundreds of other details.

If, on the other hand, PAA-trained navigators were slated to serve in Bomber Command or in the Army Cooperation Command, they would not be expected to use astronavigation very much and would be required to learn more dead (deduced) reckoning navigational methods. Moreover, for any of these assignments, navigators would use RAF charts and would need RAF terminology, aircraft and ship identification and wireless (radio) procedures. In order to learn these things, Bomber Command and Army Cooperation Command navigators needed to complete a portion of the syllabus of an RAF air observer and navigation school (AONS) and of a bombing and gunnery school (B&GS). Instead of anticipating flights over vast stretches of water, they would have to gain experience flying over urban areas in the haze and murky weather of Britain and northwestern Europe.

Given the potential tasks to which the young navigators might be assigned and the understanding that RAF officers had of the Pan American Airways Navigation Course, it is little wonder that in June 1941 they were concerned that much of the training received by the RAF cadets might prove to be relatively useless. The small number of hours aboard flying boats and the limited amount of hands-on navigation experience was insufficient to prepare for combat assignments. During their pre-flight initial training wing (ITW) course, all aircrew candidates had studied navigation intensively, learned British terminology and used British maps and charts, and were now being asked to learn to use American maps and charts that they would probably never see again after training. To some of the RAF students, the differences in terminology and in maps, charts and procedures may have been confusing.

While the first RAF intake was undergoing training, PAA school staff demonstrated their desire to modify their aerial navigation course wherever necessary. "The eagerness of the School to find better ways is very noticeable," wrote Pilot Officer Edward W. Anderson, officer in charge of that first RAF intake, "and the ready acceptance of R.A.F. ideas is a sign of the quality of Captain Dewey (in charge of the school) and Mr. Charles Lunn (Chief Instructor) and also a compliment to those who presented the ideas." The PAA staff was indeed enthusiastic about its program and was anxious to improve it, but Pilot Officer Anderson's assertion that RAF ideas were readily accepted appears to have been at least partially a product of wishful thinking.

A stormy portion of Wing Commander Oulton's June visit occurred when he suggested to Lunn and Captain Dewey that the RAF supervise the school as a British air observer navigation school (AONS). Oulton's proposal was bluntly rejected because "the Company has its own ideas on navigation training, and rather than deviate one jot from their present syllabus, they would very gladly close down the school altogether." Both Captain Dewey and Mr. Lunn indicated a desire to cooperate, but it "was tacitly understood that they would not, as yet, accept advice on how to teach *navigation*, and on what subjects a navigator should know. They are insistent that any graduate of their school shall measure up to *their* standard of theoretical knowledge."

There was no shootout at Coral Gables or at Dinner Key; instead there was grudging agreement that "one or more R.A.F. instructors, with extensive operational experience" would be posted immediately to the Pan American Airways Navigation Section, and that these instructors would use daily periods and Saturday mornings that were not used by PAA instructors "to deal with A.O.N.S. subjects not in the Pan American syllabus, and thereby give the course a warlike and operational bias which it lacks at present."

In addition, and certainly more important in the long term, there was further agreement to use "British instruments, maps, charts, publications, navigator's logs, and technical terms" instead of American ones. Course notes would also be rewritten to refer to British publications, and ground flights on the Grope simulator would be redesigned to cover European operations. Oulton believed that if he was able to persuade Charles Lunn to visit the United Kingdom, Lunn would learn firsthand the vital importance of RAF wartime experience in navigation.

Despite these concessions that the RAF wing commander had gained, he was still not completely satisfied with the PAA course at Coral Gables. Since of the fifty hours of scheduled flying time, each RAF student flew only four hours as first navigator, Oulton was anxious to increase that time. In order to do so, he proposed that the Air Ministry increase the number of aircraft there by diverting six Lockheed Hudsons from an RAF contract for temporary use at the school. "Owing to P.A.A. expansion to cover all ex-German lines in S. America," Oulton argued, "it would appear impossible to get more aircraft and crews out of the firm; and impossible to get more than the present amount of flying out of the aircraft now available." That proposal was rejected in London, and RAF navigation pupils continued to gain minimal air time.

Only on 7 July 1941, after Arnold Scheme pilot training had been operating for a month, did the RAF increase its student navigator load at Miami. The RAF proposed enrolling 190 u/t observers, but compromised for 150 in order that 50 USAAF cadet navigators could be enrolled in each class. With the enlarged intake of 150 RAF students being posted to Miami and the increasing heat of summer 1941, Oulton suggested posting a disciplinary sergeant to assist the recently assigned RAF administrative officer, and he favored providing RAF staff and students with standard British-issue tropical uniforms, including short-sleeved shirts, shorts and sun helmets. Oulton was also anxious to test the results of the PAA training against products of the RAF's established air observer navigation schools (AONSs), and his suggestion was to have tragic consequences.

The RAF navigation officer suggested that the entire first output of ten navigators might be assigned to Bomber Command so as to allow follow-up on their effectiveness. There was no explanation as to why there could not also have been follow-up reports on navigators assigned to other commands. Perhaps a prime reason for the proposal was encompassed in the view that if the men were assigned to Bomber Command and flights were made over land areas, perhaps it might be easier to argue for the introduction of more RAF procedures and specific changes in the Pan American Airways curriculum. Since eight of that first ten-man PAA navigation class died on operations, it may well be that Oulton's advice was followed.

Evidently several follow-up surveys were done in an effort to assess the quality of training these Pan American Airways graduates had received in the United States and in Canada, and these reports were undoubtedly valuable references for Oulton and others, but such assessments could not be found in existing files. Whether or not a similar follow-up was made on men assigned to Coastal Command is also unknown.

Even with a second course under training by mid-May 1941, Air Ministry staff were unsure as to how long the RAF might continue to send men to the PAA school. Although RAF officers were not completely satisfied with the quality of training being offered in the Pan American Airways Navigation Section, they suddenly found themselves placed in a position that compelled them to accept it. American political leaders had been told that Britain needed pilots, navigators and other aircrew. Since during his April 1941 visit to the United Kingdom General Arnold had offered training space for 150 RAF observer students and Air Ministry staff were seeking other aircrew training in the United States, they could hardly refuse the offer.

In early June 1941, while the first 650 students pilots were en route from Canada to flying schools in the United States, arrangements were underway in Britain to prepare and transport 750 more u/t pilots and 150 student observers for the July 1941 intakes. The July and September drafts of 150 student observers would be transported by way of Toronto to Coral Gables in civilian clothing. After October 1941, as with other British aircrew contingents, all future drafts traveling to the United States would wear British service uniforms. Most of them would enter Canada via Moncton, New Brunswick, and would travel by rail directly southward to Miami via Boston, New York and Washington, D.C.

On 27 June 1941, within three weeks of Wing Commander Oulton's visit to south Florida, members of the first RAF class of ten students completed their training at Coral Gables and were posted to Canada. After considerable delay, the United Kingdom Air Liaison Mission in Ottawa finally persuaded Canadian officials to admit the ten British students to RCAF No. 2

Bombing and Gunnery School at Moss Bank, Saskatchewan. From Moss Bank on the Canadian prairie, Pilot Officer E.W. Anderson forwarded through Air Vice Marshal L.D.D. McKean, CBE, commanding the United Kingdom Air Liaison Mission in Ottawa, to the Air Ministry in London a "Report on the 5th Pan American Airways Navigation Course [the first four classes had enrolled American cadets] at Miami University, Miami, Florida." Anderson's report is of historical interest because it provides insight into a practice that later became Air Ministry policy.

Since Anderson had been commissioned before leaving Britain, he had evidently completed the RAF navigation course at Eastbourne. If Pilot Officer Anderson had already qualified as a navigator in England, he would not be the last qualified RAF officer to undergo American aircrew training in order to assess its quality and report his findings to superior officers. As the only officer on the draft, Anderson had been designated officer-in-charge of that first ten-man group of RAF student observers sent to the United States for training.

Anderson's report was very thorough and positive, covering such topics as instruction, syllabus, flying, social activities and student discipline. The young RAF officer was complimentary concerning Captain Dewey and Mr. Lunn, whose "dynamic personality and infectious enthusiasm" outweighed any slackness in teaching or in marking papers. The young pilot officer cited the long hours of private study necessary for success in the course and proposed a few minor changes.

The Anderson report from Mossbank, Saskatchewan, stirred questions that could only be determined by the Air Ministry. Would the nine observer graduates be commissioned as promised, or would the RAF policy be enforced and only one-third of them receive commissions? Would the trained observers be assigned to navigate aircraft from Canada to the United Kingdom? The agile Air Ministry officer who examined these queries quickly passed the buck and directed that commission recommendations would be made by bombing and gunnery school staff, and that decisions about PAA-trained men navigating aircraft to England would also be made in Canada. When the men returned to England, a commission board would conduct the required interviews for RAF commissions.

In referring to the nine LACs who were on the course with him, Anderson pointed out that "under conditions both trying and demoralising they put their backs into everything both in and out of working hours, and more than justified their selection." It was a different world, and "it took a little time to get acclimatised to the very hot sun and the very cold Coco [sic] Colas." Anderson also indicated that "comparisons between the U.S. Army Air Corps and the R.A.F. are dangerous." In mid-August 1941, the ten RAF observers of Class 41-E graduated from No. 2 Bombing and Gunnery School in Canada. Although no records could be found to either confirm or deny it, ample reason exists to suspect that most of the first group of ten PAA-trained navigators served aboard aircraft being ferried from Dorval, Quebec, to England.

Anxious to evaluate Pan American Airways and Canadian navigator training, RAF training officers in North America also asked the Air Ministry to assign the first graduates of the Pan American Airways Section to duty with Bomber Command. That only eight of the ten RAF members of Class 41-E, the first RAF draft enrolled at Coral Gables, survived the war indicates that the request was granted. Apparently the second RAF ten-man contingent followed in the footsteps of the first graduates and also reported for duty with Bomber Command.

Records obtained by Owen Morgan indicate that the only members of the initial PAA class who survived the war were Pilot Officer (later wing commander) Edward William Anderson, OBE, DFC, AFC; and Peter H. Waterkeyn (rank unknown). Evidently all of the navigators were commissioned shortly after arriving back in the United Kingdom. Those men who were killed in action in 1942 included Flying Officer John A.S. Banting of 218 Squadron; Pilot Officer Leon R. Goad of 101 Squadron; Pilot Officer Norman E. Myring of 101 Squadron; Pilot Officer Edward Sharman of 12 Squadron; Pilot Officer Leonard Treppass of 214 Squadron; and Pilot Officer Thomas W.W. Woodford of 9 Squadron. Five of the eight casualties among PAA Class 41-E were killed within six months of being commissioned. The two class members who were killed in action in 1943 were evidently in their second tour of operations. They included Flying Officer Alfred B. Marsh, DFC, of 156 Squadron and Flight Lieutenant James Bannon of 7 Squadron.

During the early evening of 3 July 1941, the first 150-man RAF draft arrived in Miami and joined 53 American cadets to form Class 41-G. With the arrival of the new intake, the Pan American Airways Navigation School became a predominantly Royal Air Force School and was to remain so for another eighteen months. Representative RAF members included LAC John E. "Ted" Lake of County Durham; LAC J.S.V. "Mac" McAllister of Carrickfergus, Northern Ireland; LAC Owen D. Morgan of Palmer's Green, London; LAC Arthur R. Morris of Kidderminster, Worcestershire; LAC Francis "Frank" O'Neill of Lanarkshire, Scotland; LAC Gerald W. Powell of South Harrow, Middlesex; and LAC John H. Pughe-Jones of Lancashire. The men had joined the RAF earlier and had completed an ITW course.

At the RAF embarkation depot at Wilmslow, Cheshire, they had been issued RAF summer kit including topees, gray woolen suits and a small suitcase. However, their departure from that depot was delayed owing to the presence of the *Bismarck* in the North Atlantic. One evening near the end of May, they joined hundreds of other RAF men and boarded a train at Wilmslow, Cheshire, and were delivered at dockside in Glasgow, Scotland, the following morning. Among those men accompanying the PAA draft was a one-hundred-man contingent destined to fill No. 1 Course at BFTS No. 3, Miami, Oklahoma; and No. 1 Course at BFTS No. 4, Mesa, Arizona. On 3 June, the *Windsor Castle* embarked on its voyage across the North Atlantic, and on 10 June the ship docked at Halifax, Nova Scotia.

On 12 June, following the normal thirty-hour train ride, the men arrived at the RCAF No. 1 Manning Depot in Toronto. On 1 July, following a stay of almost three weeks at the Toronto camp, 149 of 150 observers dressed in their gray woolen suits and boarded train cars bound for Miami, Florida. Some forty hours later, just after midnight on 2–3 July 1941, the members of Class 41-G arrived at Miami and were transported by buses to the San Sebastian Hotel on the edge of the University of Miami campus.

When his comrades departed, LAC Gerald W. Powell was in sick quarters at the RCAF Manning Depot but, as in other similar cases, Powell was provided with vouchers that permitted him to travel alone to Miami. He did so, and joined his classmates in time to attend a party on the Fourth of July. Powell and Dick Hornby, a classmate, discovered that by showing their RAF ID cards, they could go to the movies for only twenty cents. Some of them also discovered the Cromwell Hotel on Miami Beach and spent many Saturday afternoons there. The summer of 1941 was hot, but there was swimming and hospitality. Through Bob Ingersoll, a Coral Gables police officer, Powell and Hornby met the Hubbell family and visited them regularly during their Miami days. Most of the members of Class 41-G were "adopted" by American families.

Since 1937, army air corps pilot training classes had been designated by year and alphabet letters designating year and month of graduation (40-A, etc.). New aircrew ratings—navigators, bombardiers and aerial gunners—underwent shorter training periods than that of pilots. Since PAA trained seven navigation courses during each year and USAAF advanced flying schools graduated nine to eleven pilot courses each year, similar class designations and different graduating dates began to create confusion. Within a month after 20 June 1941, when the army air corps (USAAC) was redesignated the United States Army Air Forces (USAAF), all aircrew training class designations were standardized. Once the alphabet designation for navigation classes was gone, new drafts of students were labeled by numbers, according to the month of arrival rather than the month of graduation.

That Class 41-G received "a motorcycle police escort with sirens blaring from the railway station to Miami University" had nothing to do with their being the final class designated under the old system. They were simply a new course of British cadets that enrolled 150 cadets. During the summer heat, RAF students still wore khaki uniforms on campus. Off campus, many still wore gray flannel suits until they could obtain lighter civilian clothing. Since their RAF-issue suits had been worn often and for long periods, the garments were virtually shapeless, and local store clerks often referred to the British cadets as "fluffy pants" or "baggy pants." When away from the university, the cadets walked about a great deal and spent considerable time in parks and on the beaches. As in other towns, young ladies were intrigued by the cadets' British accents, and they were regularly asked to talk about anything so their admirers could listen to the accents.

Without exception, the men who trained on Course 41-G enjoyed the hospitality, food, sunshine and recreation facilities. As Owen Morgan recalled,

> We were made very welcome by families in Coral Gables or Miami, and the Coral Gables Methodist Church gave a homely welcome to cadets who attended the church. Also the Cromwell Hotel, Miami Beach, opened the pool and beach facilities to U.K. cadets at weekends, and many took the opportunity to relax and enjoy the sun and sea.
>
> It was interesting later to see a film in the U.K. called Moon Over Miami in which one of the opening shots was the Cromwell Hotel and pool. When our course graduated, we were the guests of the president of the university, Dr. Bowman F. Ashe, one evening at his home.

President and Mrs. Ashe held receptions for most of the graduating navigation classes, and some PAA classes were entertained at a graduation dance at a country club in Coral Gables.

In the dormitory portion of the hotel, the cadets lived four to a room and suffered only the occasional inspection of quarters and equipment. Infractions brought demerits and occasional tours of walking around the hotel. They wore USAAF khaki uniforms to class and during other school activities. Normal class hours lasted from 7:00 a.m. to 3:00 p.m., and buses regularly carried the cadets to and from the beach at Matheson's Hammock for a daily swim. However, there was always considerable homework to be completed before the next day. On weekends, the British cadets usually attended local churches, and those who did so were "adopted" by American families who picked them up in their automobiles and drove them about south Florida showing them the sights.

On 12 August 1941, the second ten-man RAF intake graduated as a small increment of Navigation Class 41-F and departed by rail for Canada and the RAF bombing and gunnery school (B&GS) at Mossbank, Saskatchewan, Canada. Then, on 25 August, Class 41-7, the second large observer intake consisting of 150 men, arrived at Coral Gables. Apparently, they sailed across the North Atlantic with Arnold Scheme Class 42-C from Gourock to Canada aboard the *Stratheden*, and had spent two weeks at RCAF No. 1 Y Depot in Halifax, Nova Scotia, before being transported on to Toronto. From Toronto, they traveled by rail via Detroit, Cincinnati, Atlanta, Albany, Jacksonville and Miami. After they arrived, a formal schedule of physical training, including swimming, calisthenics and competitive sports, was introduced as part of the PAA training syllabus. Richard Chapman, national golf champion, was appointed the first physical education director at the school.

Among the members of Class 41-7 were thirty-year-old Fred Higson from Stockport, Lancashire; Eric Overbury from Lewes, Sussex; and Edward J. "Ted" King of London. Holdovers added to the normal Class 41-7 intake brought the totals to 205 students, 53 USAAF and 152 RAF cadets. Most members of Class 41-7 were in their twenties, but older, married students, led by thirty-year-old Fred Higson, shared other interests. They enjoyed fruit and avocado salad, pancakes and other American foods, and they spent off-duty afternoons at Matheson's Hammock beach and weekends "either at Miami Beach, where some of the smaller luxury hotels charged us 1 dollar 20 cents for a bed for Friday or Saturday nights; or northwards around Palm Beach." In Miami, the over-thirties group found that once they were recognized as RAF students, patrons of Casey's Oasis and Jack Dempsey's Bar would not let them pay for anything.

Since during their time at Coral Gables the members of Class 41-G were the senior class, and those of Class 41-7 constituted the junior class, they had a variety of common experiences to remember in the years ahead. On 21 September, there was a considerable stir at Miami and Coral Gables. His Royal Highness the Duke of Windsor, governor of the Bahamas, flew into Miami and reviewed the Pan American Airways navigation students on the University of Miami campus. A fortnight later, a hurricane warning was issued by the U.S. Weather Bureau, and preparations were made for the storm.

Although the wind was said to have gusted to about 125 miles per hour in the vicinity of Miami, the storm quickly swept across the southern tip of Florida, turned northward in the Gulf of Mexico, picked up speed over water and rammed into the Florida panhandle before it turned northeastward, drenching that region and much of Florida, Alabama and Georgia with torrential rains before it reentered the Atlantic Ocean near Savannah, Georgia. Except to halt flying for two days, the storm had little effect on navigation training at Coral Gables and Dinner Key.

Occasionally British cadets in training at Coral Gables encountered British student pilots in Miami on end-of-course leaves from flying schools at Opa-locka, Lakeland, Arcadia and Clewiston. That awareness of other British aircrew students caused them to take notice of newspaper reports concerning these men. They read that windows and doors of buildings had been battened down at all Florida airfields during the storm, and that aircraft used at these schools that could not be put into hangars were flown to distant airfields to prevent damage or destruction. Evidently, property damage was minimal, but a few people who were struck by flying debris lost their lives. Florida's leaders had developed a means of using commercial radio stations to warn people, and cities had enforced more rigid building codes. The British cadets under training in the region had yet another weather experience to relate.

With Classes 41-G and 41-7 in residence in the university's San Sebastian dormitory, the Pan American Airways Navigation Section reached its maximum enrollment of four hundred students, approximately three hundred RAF cadets and about one hundred USAAF cadets. Around 15 October 1941, as Class 41-G completed its training, another hurricane swept ashore near Jacksonville and again dumped heavy rains on north Florida and Georgia, but had little effect on Miami and extreme south Florida.

Meanwhile, the weather was calm in Coral Gables; graduation exercises were held, and Wing Commander Fleming congratulated the graduates and recognized LAC Roy Leafe, the class honor graduate, who had achieved a 95.8 percent academic average. "Class 41-G has departed in a blaze of glory," wrote American cadet R.O. Kenyon in the student newspaper, "leaving behind a string of broken hearts, regulations, octants, bottles, etc." Of the original Class 41-G intake of 150 men, 146 graduated, 2 were held over for further training and 2 were evidently washed out for academic failure and returned to Canada for remustering. Class 41-7 became the senior class and received occasional reminders that they were still in a branch of the armed services.

Ted King recalled room inspections and penalties:

> On occasions, officers of the USAAC descended on our rooms looking for breaches of regulations such as dust, failure to have a 45 degree angle on the bed sheet fold, etc. Although there were staff who maintained the room, this did not prevent the USAAC [officers] from giving us "demerits"; the punishment given for demerits usually an hour's walking around the hotel. We thought this farcical as it was very pleasant to stroll around the building in the gentle warmth of a Florida autumn!

On Thanksgiving Day, 1941, the class marched in RAF dress blue uniforms through downtown Miami, and on another occasion they dressed for a formal inspection by the Duke of Windsor, at that time governor of the Bahamas.

On 27 November 1941, newspapers reported that thirty-six British cadets from Pan American Airways Navigation Section at the University of Miami would introduce the game of rugby at a charity game in Miami's Orange Bowl. Dressed in "jerseys and knee length blue shorts," the Royal Air Force team would play a team from Nassau, Bahamas. A week before the scheduled game, players ranging in age from nineteen to thirty-two were "engaged in hard, rough-and-tumble practice sessions." Fans were warned that they would be introduced to British terms such as "scrum" and "pack."

On 4 December 1941, Class 41-7 graduated. Of the class's total enrollment of 205, 4 cadets (3 USAAF and 1 RAF) were held over to complete training, 11 were eliminated (9 RAF and 2 USAAF) and 190 navigators graduated (48 USAAF and 142 RAF). This was the highest number of RAF eliminees thus far at Coral Gables, but since the numbers remained fairly consistent for later intakes, the screening and selection process may well have faltered because a thorough grounding in mathematics was essential to survive the course. On 3 December 1941, the graduated navigators boarded the *Silver Meteor* in Miami for the long return journey to Canada.

Wing Commander Oulton's work in trying to persuade Pan American Airways authorities to modify their syllabus to approximate that of the RAF did not go unappreciated, nor did Oulton fail in his efforts to persuade Chief Instructor Charles J. Lunn to visit Britain in order to observe British methods. Lunn's visit produced mixed results. On 25 August 1941, Oulton received a report from Squadron Leader J.H. Burnett of the navigation staff, Headquarters, 25 Group, RAF Flying Training Command, which indicated that the RAF had not been as successful as had been assumed:

> Mr. Lunn arrived on August 9th and a comprehensive program has been arranged for him, including visits to units in Bomber, Coastal, and Flying Training Commands. Mr. Lunn has expressed the greatest possible enthusiasm for our navigational methods and

for the high morale of our aircrews, and from the point of view of indicating to him the various problems with which we are faced in this country, the tour has been of the greatest value.

Unfortunately, although a great deal of trouble was taken to arrange for Mr. Lunn to take part in operational flights in Bomber and Coastal Command aircraft, we were not able to persuade him to do so. This was, of course, rather disappointing as such flights would have given practical proof of the importance of our methods of training and were understood to be the main object of his visit—for training only, he could have visited units in Canada.

Burnett was obviously disturbed by Lunn's point of view and much preferred eliminating some of the theory from the PAA syllabus in favor of more practical training.

Squadron Leader Burnett accompanied Lunn on his visit to Air Observers School No. 9 at Penrhos, South Wales. Burnett was apparently flabbergasted when he learned of Lunn's objective in visiting the United Kingdom. Even so, he observed that the American had learned much, but apparently not quite enough:

Although Royal Air Force u/t (under training) observers are now being trained, there is still no modification to the syllabus, but the object of the Principal of the School, Mr. C.J. Lunn's visit to this country, is to find out what our problems are.

As a result of his visit, he intends to introduce map reading, and more D.R. into his flying syllabus, but he does not intend to cut out any theory from his ground training, his contention being that if a navigator is sufficiently versed in theory, he will never have any doubts in the air, whereas a rule of thumb navigator often gets, say, an astro fix which, if it does not agree with his D.R. position, leaves him in doubt as to whether to believe it, or carry on with his D.R.

Whether Lunn misunderstood the purpose of his visit and thought that he was to be a trouble shooter for the RAF is unknown. That he held very strong views about teaching navigation, there was no doubt.

Following his encounter with Lunn's very strong personality, Squadron Leader Burnett expressed the view that the course of instruction at the Pan American Airways School was not suitable for air observer training. "The navigators turned out by this school will be capable of navigating across the Atlantic but will be liable to get lost on a 200-mile cross country…No Reconnaissance, Photography, Signals, or Aircraft Identification, is included in the syllabus. A radical change will have to be made to the syllabus to suit the requirements of the Royal Air Force."

What Burnett and a small number of RAF officers apparently overlooked was that the quality of Pan American Airways training in navigation and meteorology was superb. The RAF officers failed to recognize that this proven system of theory and applied navigation that had worked well for training men for an American commercial airline was not and never could be a course that encompassed all of the wartime training objectives of both American and British air forces. Moreover, wartime navigation was changing rapidly, and new techniques and instruments were being developed to meet combat needs. Whether the RAF really needed Pan American Airways navigation training was of no consequence to USAAF officers, but the British needed to decide.

Even with all of the failures to convince Lunn to make the desired changes in the syllabus of the PAA School of Navigation, Oulton continued his efforts to help improve navigational training in the United States.

Major John Egan, one of the USAAF's leading military navigators, was director of navigational training at Mather Field, Sacramento, California, one of three large USAAF navigation training schools that had been established by 1 July 1941. Unlike Lunn, when Egan arrived in the United Kingdom in September 1941, he did not hesitate to absorb as much new experience as he possibly could. Not only did Egan visit RAF Flying Training Command schools, but he also visited operational training units of various commands. When he flew an operational sortie to Nuremburg with a crew from Bomber Command and on an anti-submarine patrol with a Coastal Command aircrew, Major Egan impressed RAF officers.

From the time of Egan's visit, USAAF navigational training began to emphasize British methods, but Egan's discovery of "a new series of altitude and azimuth tables, later published by the Hydrographic Office as H.O. 218," was deemed "his most important find." As the months passed, the United States Army Air Forces would enlarge and perfect its huge navigation schools at Monroe, Louisiana; Hondo, Texas; and Sacramento, California. At these three schools, USAAF cadets would modify the Grope simulator and adopt it for use. They would also use astrographs and other instruments developed by British and American scientists to aid aircrew in navigation, blind flying, bombardment and communication training.

Dressed in their gray flannel woolen suits, Class 42-1 arrived in Miami at 2:00 p.m. on Friday, 17 October 1941 in almost ninety-degree heat. Among the class's 150-man RAF contingent were Kenneth J. Bailey of Basingstoke, Hampshire; John A. "Jack" Cook of Folkestone, Kent; Maurice W. Griffin of Somerset; Robert Harvey of Cromford, Derbyshire; and John A. Thomas of Mansfield, Nottinghamshire. Apparently, all members of the draft had been selected for observer training in the United Kingdom during August 1941. On 5 September, they had boarded the *Pasteur* in Scotland, traveled across the North Atlantic and arrived in Halifax on 15 September. The RAF draft then boarded train cars and traveled to Toronto, where they were billeted for almost a month in crowded conditions at the Canadian National Exhibition Building. The observer draft then traveled by rail via Detroit, Cincinnati, Chattanooga, Atlanta and Jacksonville to Miami.

Following assignment to rooms in the San Sebastian Hotel, they were able to spend the weekend getting adjusted to their new surroundings. Assigned three or four to a room, they found the billets very comfortable and the unexpected maid service a bonus. Meals were served in the university cafeteria and waiters attended to the needs of the cadets. Their training began on Monday, 20 October, and the very tough schedule of classes required some adjustment. The cadets had reveille at 5:30 a.m., and the almost frantic pace continued until "lights out" at 9:30 p.m. Although the schedule was fairly rigid in the beginning, students adjusted quickly and, upon discovering spare time, used it well.

During that same month when eastbound and westbound RAF cadets jammed the facilities at Toronto, the RCAF advised the Air Ministry that it no longer had sufficient vacancies at Mossbank or in its other (AONS and B&GS) schools to provide PAA graduates with bombing and gunnery training. As a result, a formal request was made for the establishment of an operational training unit (OTU) in the United States that would provide the necessary bombing and gunnery training for PAA graduates. Since USAAF officers were reluctant to consider such training at a civilian contract facility and were at the time busy expanding their own training facilities, the Air Ministry proposal could not be acted upon immediately.

Since the Pan American Airways school did not fully meet the training requirements for observers laid down by the Air Ministry, RAF graduates of the large Pan American Airways drafts were officially deemed unqualified to serve as navigators in the British Isles or Europe until they had undergone refresher courses at an air observer and navigation school (AONS) and armaments training at a bombing and gunnery school (B&GS). The harshest blow to Pan American Airways graduates came when they were told that official policy prevented award of the brevet or their promotion in rank until they underwent further training in the United Kingdom. Normally, graduates received observer badges and were promoted (one-third to receive commissions and remainder sergeant's stripes), but the new policy required PAA-trained navigators to return to the United Kingdom as leading aircraftsmen (LACs) without brevets or promotions in rank. The students deemed Pan American Airways's thorough training in astronavigation a poor substitute for more substantial rewards such as increases in rank and pay.

Until after 7 December 1941, military training at the University of Miami was limited to sporadic sessions of close order drill. In October 1941, after Wing Commander Oulton's recommendation to that effect, the RAF had sent Wing Commander C.N. Fleming to Coral Gables as RAF commanding officer. A short time later, RAF Sergeant L.A. Bailey was assigned to assist Fleming as the disciplinary and drill sergeant. As Sergeant Bailey put the RAF cadets through their paces, Charles Lunn and others of the PAA staff were amused by the RAF sergeant's cockney accent and his regular reminder to the cadets that "yer pawkets are for yer pennies—not yer 'ands."

Even if military details were of limited concern until Sergeant Bailey's arrival, it was clearly understood at the Coral Gables school that several hours had to be devoted to home study in navigation and meteorology, the two most difficult subjects. However, life was made somewhat easier by use of the free time that was written into the schedule or granted when flying was canceled owing to weather conditions. On Saturdays, reveille was delayed an hour, and after breakfast the remainder of the morning was taken up with lectures by RAF officers. Following lunch, the cadets were free until l:00 a.m. Sunday morning, and large numbers of them usually took advantage of the Saturday afternoon buses that the university provided for transporting swimming parties to and from Miami Beach.

The quality of PAA training and the large number of eliminees from pilot training schools operating under the Arnold Scheme brought a number of distinguished airmen to the Southeastern United States for a training conference. Air Marshal A.G.R. Garrod, who represented the Air Ministry in London; RAF Delegation staff members Group Captains D.V. Carnegie and Lord Nigel Douglas-Hamilton; and Wing Commander W.E. Oulton visited the several schools where RAF aircrew were undergoing training. American general officers who acted as hosts and escorted them included Brigadier General George E. Stratemeyer, deputy chief of the air corps, and Brigadier General Clarence L. Tinker, commanding general of the Third Air Force, headquarters at Tampa's McDill Field. After inspecting the school and talking with many students, the RAF officers commended the University of Miami, Pan American Airways and local citizens for their assistance to Britain.

On Saturday afternoons and Sundays, even during the autumn and winter months, citizens of the area still picked up the RAF cadets at the curb outside the San Sebastian Hotel. Being "adopted" by an American family usually meant attendance at church, Sunday dinner (lunch) at the host family's home, picnics, swimming parties and sightseeing trips in and around Miami. Host families were anxious to show the British students the Everglades, the Tamiami Trail, the Seminole Indian village near Dania and dozens of other local attractions.

To the original 150-man RAF intake for Class 42-1, 1 cadet who had been held over from the preceding class was added, bringing the total enrollment to 151. Of that number, 1 student was held over to the subsequent class, 8 were eliminated and on 30 January 1942, 142 graduated and boarded the *Silver Meteor* for the return journey northward. Back in the United Kingdom, the members of Class 42-2 had been selected, documented and provided with their preliminary training by late September 1941, and during early November they too traveled from Glasgow to Halifax, Nova Scotia, across the storm-tossed North Atlantic aboard the *Pasteur*.

When the draft arrived in Canada in early October, it was the first westbound draft to be processed through the incomplete, but new, RAF No. 31 Personnel Dispersal Center outside Moncton, New Brunswick. The new arrivals were assigned to sleep in unfinished, windowless barracks. Before they were moved to heated accommodation after two nights in the cold, they "went out in the night and collected empty cement sacks to pile on top of all the clothing and coverings" they had been able to find. They also used blankets or other materials to block the open window spaces.

During their stay of about two weeks in Moncton's cold autumn weather, they regularly walked the several blocks into the town where they attended the cinema, used the facilities of the YMCA and shopped for wives, parents and sweethearts in the many shops and department stores. They also regularly patronized local cafés and restaurants where they found excellent food at bargain prices. After completing their documentation and assignment to a training school, the PAA draft boarded a train and traveled by what had already become the standard route from Moncton via Mont Joli, Montreal, and Toronto to Detroit, Cincinnati, Chattanooga, Atlanta and Jacksonville, then down the Florida east coast to Miami.

Among the members of Class 42-2 who arrived in sunny and warm Coral Gables on 5 December 1941 were Charles Brameld of Yorkshire; Alan Budinger, Edward Foster and Ronald Leavers of Nottingham; and R.H. Mason and Edgar C. "Ed" Smith. Instead of the standard RAF-issue gray woolen suits, men of this draft were dressed in the heavy blue woolen uniforms of the RAF. Civilian suits were not issued to RAF students after PAA Class 41-7 or to members of Arnold Scheme Class SE-42-F and their equivalents at other schools. Effective mid-October 1941, primarily because of cold weather, U.S. Army regulations required men in the various branches to switch to winter uniforms, and PAA Class 42-2, Arnold Scheme Class 42-F and others arriving after that time traveled from Canada to American flying schools in RAF blue uniforms.

More than forty years after the war, in providing details about the changes in organization and administration of the navigation school following Pearl Harbor and the American declaration of war, Charles Brameld of Yorkshire paid grateful tribute to the Pan American Airways Navigation Section:

> *We were cordially received at the San Sebastian Hotel, near the University of Miami. I was surprised to learn that there was a small permanent staff of R.A.F. officers & N.C.O.s in charge of us as well as P.A.A. people. We were called together on arrival and told that we were confined to camp, i.e., the hotel, the University, and the short stretch of road between the two, until such time that we bought civilian clothing. In Miami's warmth, we need not buy more than shirt & trousers. The intent was that we were to give money & our measurements to someone on the senior course (42-1) who would do the shopping for us.*

This was because the U.S.A. was then a neutral country, and we were not allowed to drift around in the military uniform of a country at war (Mind you, for all aspects of the course, flying or ground, we had to wear uniform). Next day, we were paraded again and told that the previous instruction was cancelled. We had to wear uniform, and uniform only, at all times that we were out and about. The reason? Overnight, Pearl Harbour had crashed into the news.

Our accommodation at the San Sebastian was very good. So were the meals at the University of Miami. We needed perhaps to develop a taste for a few dishes to which we were unaccustomed, but, after wartime rationing in Britain, the food was marvellous. The damp heat, night and day, was trying for a few days, but we soon acclimatised. After all, we were fit young men, mostly in the age range of eighteen to twenty or twenty-one years; the few past that were considered old. All P.A.A. people with whom I had dealings over the next few months were delightful—helpful, courteous, a pleasure to know. I recollect no trouble at all due to accents from first day to last.

Our reception by the people of the district at large was also very good, almost overwhelming. We were inundated with invitations to parties, to meals and for tours round Florida. My own and a friend's enjoyment of the simple pleasure of walking was an embarrassment: every few yards a car would draw up alongside us. "Do you want a lift?" "Would you like to go to Key West?" "Where would you like us to take you?" It was non-stop. Add to the foregoing that we had free dancing lessons at Madame Bellasco's Academy, the best seats in Miami cinemas at nominal prices, free admission to "Francis Ott's Water Spectacles" at the Biltmore Hotel pool, and, I'm sure, lists of other perks that I have ungraciously forgotten, and you may begin to gain an impression of our treatment.

I remember particularly one invitation. Fifty R.A.F. cadets (or was it a hundred?) were invited by Colonel and Mrs. Stehlin to a party at their home, transport there and return being laid on for us. The transport turned out to be a fleet of limousines, enough to allow one car to each couple of us. And there was an escort of motor-cycled policemen, sirens blowing, two in front of the convoy, two behind, and others in turn chasing ahead to hold up the traffic at junctions and allow us non-stop progress. The party was superb. Transport was, as promised, available to take us back to the San Sebastian Hotel, but the police escort was absent—a touch of diplomacy, perhaps, in view of the condition of a few of the group.

As long as British cadets were assigned to training stations in south Florida, the citizens of Miami, Miami Beach, Coral Gables and Palm Beach provided ongoing hospitality.

Since Charles Brameld became a teacher and headmaster following extensive wartime service as an RAF navigator, his responses to questions concerning Pan American Airways training in navigation answer most standard British criticisms of the PAA syllabus. Brameld also views developments in aerial navigation from a historical perspective:

Our course, 42-2, consisted of one flight of American cadets (fifty, I think) and three flights each of fifty R.A.F. cadets. I was in "A" Flight. Our Navigation Instructor was Mr. Pat Reynolds for most of the time. For the first week or two, it had been Mr. Lapine (Lepine?), but he joined the U.S. Army Air Forces (Navy?). Both were excellent teachers, patient, helpful, friendly, always ready to give extra help to anyone who found any topic difficult.

Chief Navigation Instructor over the whole school was Mr. Charlie Lunn who introduced us to that imaginary paragon of everything virtuous in a navigator, Navigator Pinpoint. I do not know if P.A.A. still utilise the incomparable "Pinpoint" in their training, but I certainly should like to think so. The ground/classroom instruction was very, very thorough, both in the navigation theory course and in the meteorology course. The course had a strong mathematical basis and particularly to the underlying maths of astro-navigation that we were required to learn. Well, certainly there were topics we covered that might be considered not completely essential (overlooking for the moment that in a situation where competence is vital, no extra information or skill can be considered unessential).

Strictly speaking, in order to become effective, practical navigators for wartime purposes, we didn't need to know how to make our own Mercator charts by use of the Table of Meridianal Parts (I can still, over forty years later, quote a definition of a meridianal part). We didn't need to learn the Mercator Sailing formulae for finding rhumb line track and distance by trigonometry. We didn't need to cover the haversine formula for solving the "spherical triangle" in astro-navigation, as use of Air-Navigation Tables was at the time the standard method of plotting position from astro sights.

We even looked briefly at earlier solutions such as Admiral Wemyss' Star Curves and Napier's Laws of Spherical Parts which had been outmoded and made to look clumsy first by the haversine formula and then by the Air-Navigation Tables. (I think I can still quote Napier's Laws correctly, too.) We were very, very well drilled in use of the Air-Navigation Tables, which, as I say, were then standard procedure.

I myself readily accepted that, in that era, the Pan American Airways experience of astro-navigation was the world's best, that so was their training in this area of the navigator's job. They were trying their hardest to make us as good navigators as they would try with their own trainees. I also accepted, and still feel this is right, that it was better by far to plan a course that some might see as over-ambitious than to risk omitting anything that might later appear to be vital.

I will mention in passing that a couple or so years later, say 1943 or 1944, I met up with another P.A.A.-trained man who argued that the whole time we spent learning "astro" was wasted, in that it was soon largely superceded in bomber operations by the use of radar navigational aids, especially "GEE." My counter arguments to this were that this was arguing from hindsight; that at the time astro-navigation was an essential tool for navigators; that I myself used it on numbers of occasions while on bomber operations in Wellington aircraft both in Europe and in Africa.

I did not use astro later in Mosquito aircraft, but that was for special technical reasons; and that in any case, although the great majority of navigators being trained were needed to replace the constant losses in Bomber Command where use of astro was drastically reduced by the arrival of GEE, some of the navigators trained did go to Coastal Command where competence in astro remained highly important throughout the war. And P.A.A.-trained men, in my view, finished with a greater competence than most.

In any final analysis, I feel that the aforementioned "not completely necessary" topics were but a small proportion of the total course and of its final examination. I would stress again and again that we were given a really thorough grounding in the trade of air-navigator, in deduced-reckoning navigation, in plotting, in fixing position by various methods, in determining wind speed and direction, in "dry swims" and in all the many other ploys of the complete navigator. I personally enjoyed every bit of it and would not have wished any of the content omitted. From the start, I made up my mind that I should learn all aspects of navigation, as if my life depended on it. Perhaps it did.

In the event, I was one of the three or four members of Course 42-2 who, in the final theory examination, obtained full marks. On our certificates (mine still proudly stuck in my Flying Log Book) it says, "Navigation Theory, Excellent, 99.5%." We were told the deduction of .5% was to establish the principle that no one is perfect. At the end of the course, we needed more air practice, but I received that on two later, supposedly more advanced courses given to us by the R.A.F.

But on those courses, I learned nothing new in basic theory (although we did need to cover some specific aspects of bomber operational procedure). Indeed, on one occasion, two or three of us, ex-P.A.A., were able to help our [RAF] instructor over a wooly patch in his own knowledge of astro-navigation.

On one of the earlier courses [at Coral Gables], I think the first one where British cadets were concerned, one young trainee told his instructor he had found a flaw in the maths on which all astro-navigation was built, a flaw that had been there all the time, through Napier's Laws, Haversine formula, A.N.T.s, the lot. P.A.A. was unable to disprove his contention, but, since in the Pentagon there was a V.I.P. whose role was "Senior Scientific Adviser to the U.S. Air Corps" or some such title, the young man was taken by P.A.A. officials to see him.

The great man at first was inclined to suggest (problem unseen) that such a slip was so unlikely that perhaps the youth might like to go back and think about it again. On the young man's assertion that he already had re-thought it, but could not see where he was wrong, the Senior Scientific Adviser looked at the matter and quickly agreed that the point was valid, there was indeed a basic flaw, but that, after a little calculation, any error because of this was so minute as to be not worth considering.

The flaw? Astro theory uses the simple geometric theorem that every tangent to the earth's surface is at right angles to the radius at the point of the circle touched by the said tangent. But the earth is not a perfect circle, so there are occasions where this theorem is not accurately valid. The Senior Scientific Adviser I understood to be one Albert Einstein.

We began flying training early in the course. I do not remember the date but think it would be in January 1942. We had both day and night flights, these being interspersed with the ground instruction, to a total of fifty hours for each cadet. A night flight brought no remission of the following day's programme, and, incidentally, we were required to rise at some unearthly hour, 5:30 a.m., my memory says, for an early start to the day's lectures, etc., at about 6:30 a.m.

The P.A.A. plan was for a good proportion of the day's labours to be done early, before the heat of the day, plus considerable "assignments" (we called it "homework") to be done in the evening. Unfortunately for us, the afternoons, which were left free by P.A.A., were sometimes taken up by the RAF permanent staff to instruct us in the mysteries of RAF machine guns, bombs, gas drills, and the like.

As I understood matters at the time, much of the training of British pilots being done in U.S. flying schools came under "lend lease" or some sort of financially easy arrangement, but our P.A.A. Navigator's course had to be paid for in full by the British government, and for this reason, the fifty hours specification for our flying time was tightly adhered to. We flew in Commodore flying boats, top speed rather less than 80 knots, from Dinner Key. Some groups flew in Sikorskis [Sikorsky S-40 flying boats], but my group's aircraft was always a Commodore.

Most of the flights were of five hours duration. I soon found I had a tendency to airsickness, perhaps reason to pack up flying, but decided to keep quiet and put up with it; I'm glad now I did. We frequently used the "radius of action" navigational procedure or "radius of action to a moving base," with a set time of five hours. I imagine this was a deliberate ploy to regulate the flying time and arrive at the fifty hour total.

I remember that most of my flying time was with Captain Camp or Captain Gray or Captain Elsasser as pilot, but, alas, cannot remember the names of the navigational instructors who kept check on us in the air. I remember grumbles at the time about the frequency of using the radius of action technique, but, since this added an extra navigational complication to a trip, I reckon it was good practice.

Subsequent training flights on later courses of the type: go from Base to Point A, to Point B and so on, back to Base, seemed that much the easier. Not such good practice was that we flew as a bunch of, I believe, ten trainee-navigators in one aircraft, plus, of course, the experienced P.A.A. Nav.-Instructor. One of the ten, in turn, was first-navigator for that trip, doing his plotting, fixing of position, wind finding and being responsible for alterations of course. The other trainees also did their own plot but using the first-nav's courses, did their own position fixing and wind determination, but had no responsibility for changing course.

In the event, I did one five-hour flight only as first navigator, which was not a great deal on which to build the confidence to take on the responsibility as navigator in a bomber crew. At the end of the course, I felt I needed more air time as sole navigator and was glad we had two more training courses to come in U.K. But, can this be considered a valid criticism of P.A.A.? I think not. If the British Government/R.A.F. agreed to the course as given, i.e., fifty hours flying but ten trainee navigators per aircraft, then P.A.A. delivered the goods and there can be no grumble. My reasoning says that the R.A.F. must surely have known in advance what the provision was to be.

I have no accurate memory of how many of the 150 RAF cadets on Course 42-2 did not complete the course satisfactorily, but do not think it was many. One or two were chronically air-sick and packed in. One or two "disappeared" quietly, presumably having been found not up to the standard needed and asked to leave. And I do remember rightly that an odd one stayed over to join Course 42-3 or 42-4 to give it another go? I've a general vague idea that the total failure rate could scarcely have been as high as twenty or even have topped ten. Anyway, whatever the number who failed, I do feel quite sure that the substantial majority of the 150 hopefuls who started the course did, in fact, pass satisfactorily, and that a body of very well trained people went back to England in April 1942 to swell the aircrew ranks at a time when this was a pressing need.

On arrival back in the United Kingdom, observer graduates reported to an aircrew pool and awaited assignment to further training.

To the 150-man intake of Class 42-2 was added 1 man who had been held over from the preceding class, and the total enrollment rose to 151. Of that number that commenced training on 8 December, 2 were held over to a subsequent class, 6 were eliminated and 143 graduated on 18 March 1942. On arrival at Moncton, the graduates joined other trained aircrew awaiting transportation to the United Kingdom. After a few days, the best students were directed to report to Dorval Airport at Montreal, and they gained practical experience in flying back aboard a bomber being ferried to the United Kingdom. Some graduates were assigned to a larger draft that boarded a transport in Halifax, and still other members of the graduating class were sent by rail to Norfolk, Virginia, and were assigned to an eastbound transport.

Before they graduated in December 1941, the RAF and USAAF cadets of Class 41-7 jointly published a cadet magazine entitled *On Course*. That practice of issuing a joint publication was continued by Class 42-1 and included a group picture of 42-2 class members. The next issue of *On Course* was devoted exclusively to USAAF cadet activities for Class 42-6, a class that included the final RAF draft. What precisely led to this divergence is unknown, but it is suspected that the RAF's assumption of more of the navigation training of RAF cadets separated the USAAF and RAF cadets more than usual. Beginning wih 42-2, RAF students issued course books entitled *The Log*.

On 30 January 1942, a few days after Class 42-1 departed, the 150 RAF cadets of Class 42-3 arrived in Miami from RAF No. 31 Personnel Depot at Moncton, New Brunswick. LAC Stanley Dale, an experienced radio broadcaster, had arrived at Coral Gables in October with Class 42-1, and after a short period under training had been reassigned temporarily to radio broadcasting duties. Dale's absence while he was on assignment to do radio shows in New York during much of December 1941 and January 1942 did not disrupt his navigational training too much. On 2 February, he returned from the public relations assignment and reentered navigation training at Coral Gables as a member of Class 42-3. As would be expected of a talented individual who served as master of ceremonies on numerous occasions, Dale was swept up in campus life and in writing for various student publications.

In the Class 42-2 issue of *The Log*, RAF LAC W. Allan Marsden produced a poem that perhaps best captured the mood of the times:

> *Some future day when what is now is not,*
> *When all our faults and follies are forgot,*
> *And thoughts of difference passed like dreams away,*
> *We'll meet again, upon some future day.*
> *When we have proved, each on his course alone,*
> *The wider world and learnt what now unknown*
> *Have made life clear and worked out each a way,*
> *We'll meet again, we shall have much to say.*
>
> *With happier mood, and feelings born anew*
> *Our boyhood's bygone fancies we'll review,*
> *Talk O-er old talks, play as we used to play,*
> *And meet again, on many a future day.*
>
> *Some day, which oft our hearts will yearn to see,*
> *In some far year, Tho' distant yet to be,*

Shall we indeed—ye winds and waters say!
Meet yet again, upon some future day?

Among others writing for that issue of *The Log* were LACs Stanley "Scruffy" Dale and Eric Harrison.

During his short fifteen weeks at the University of Miami, Harrison gained a reputation as an eccentric "campus character" and a superb musician. Harrison, who had studied at the Royal College of Music and was a fellow of the Royal College of Organists, had been a guest soloist with the London Philharmonic Orchestra and the BBC. On Monday evening, 11 May, Harrison presented a farewell piano concert in Granada Workshop of the university's School of Music. His brilliant renditions captivated his audience, and his performance was deemed "the most exceptional concert of the year."

Another member of Class 42-3 at Coral Gables was LAC William Gordon Bailey. As with other PAA students, Bailey was much impressed by Chief Instructor Charles Lunn and Instructor Charles Howell. In recalling his training experiences four decades later, Bailey provided an excellent description of training that encompassed RAF influence on modifications to the curriculum:

> *We commenced work in earnest on Monday, 2 February 1942—maths, meteorology, and navigation. The hours were long. We regularly worked in the evenings, but normally had Sundays free, except when the flying details commenced later in the course. My first flight took place on 9 March 1942 and the final flight at Miami on 2 May 1942. The course requirement was a total of 50 hours (25 day + 25 night). All flights took place in P.A.A. "Commodore" Flying Boats, numbers 667, 668, 669, & 670, from the P.A.A. Boat Base at Dinner Key.*
>
> *From what little information I have been able to gather since 1942, I believe those Consolidated Commodores may have been derivations of Curtiss boats, but I am fairly certain they were NOT Sikorsky. The boats were re-furbished as "flying classrooms" with individual chart tables for approximately 12 pupils at a time. The Navigation School was a joint venture, inasmuch as there were USAAF pupils undergoing training at the same time. You will readily understand there was intense (friendly, of course) rivalry between the two air forces concerned. Although the Flying and Nav. instruction took place separately, we did share common Met. lectures.*

Bailey's comments are important because they confirm that by early 1942, the Pan American Airways Navigation Section had sufficiently modified its curriculum to provide separate instruction for RAF and USAAF students.

Early on, there had been a considerable dispute between Chief Instructor Charles J. Lunn and RAF officers concerning modifications essential to the conduct of air operations over Britain and Western Europe. As early as late June 1941, Wing Commander Wilfred E. Oulton (later Air Vice Marshal W.E. Oulton, CB, CBE, DSO, DFC) had attempted to persuade Lunn that, owing to weather conditions and the topography of the British Isles and Europe, the RAF's wartime needs were different from those of a peacetime international airline.

Learning to fly safely in crowded airspace over Britain's vast urban areas, scattered villages and complex of rivers, peaks, valleys, rail, electrical and telephone service lines required special training that could not be provided outside that environment. As a result, the RAF preferred that their students first have a thorough grounding in map reading and dead reckoning navigation before undertaking study of the theory and practice of astronavigation. As far as it went, the practice of using flying boats for group navigational exercises over water was excellent, but in practice individual students spent much too little time serving as responsible navigators in charge of plotting the various day and night exercises.

The training essential for flying over vast stretches of ocean out of sight of land, mostly along latitudes of more temperate zones, required a knowledge of astronavigation first and dead reckoning second. Delivering bomb loads to specific targets in compact urban environments and bringing crews and aircraft back safely to home stations were made more complex by night operations, combat conditions, cloud cover, rapidly changing weather conditions and industrial haze. Such conditions called for deduced (dead) reckoning navigation and chart reading abilities of a high order.

On clear nights, bomber crews had to worry about enemy night fighters, searchlights, blackout conditions, anti-aircraft fire and changing weather conditions. On nights when clouds obscured the target area, when smoke, fog and industrial haze prevailed, navigators had to rely heavily on guesswork. Until sophisticated navigational instruments and target marking techniques were perfected, charts and deduced reckoning (DR) navigation were relied upon to deliver the bomber within the vicinity of the target.

Since the University of Miami was a private institution and had only recently been accredited by the Southern Association of Colleges and Schools, officers of the institution were undoubtedly concerned about the clash between the RAF and PAA officers. The navigation course was listed in the university's official catalogue and carried fifteen semester hours of academic credit. Since about 1970, curricula in American colleges and universities have been much more flexible and innovative, but since disagreements over the navigation course occurred in an era when institutional accreditation was threatened by efforts on the part of any outside interests to tamper with the curriculum, the concern of university officers was understandable, as was Chief Instructor Lunn's reaction to British requests for change.

A partial solution to the disagreement over what aspects of the course should be emphasized was found by assigning an RAF navigator with combat experience to the Pan American Airways Navigation Section. From June 1941, Flight Lieutenant N.C.K. Dibble served as RAF administrative officer, and around August 1941 Flying Officer W.H. Trewin, an RAF navigational officer, arrived at the Coral Gables school. During any spare hours in weekly schedules, Trewin instructed the British students in RAF methods and procedures, the use of RAF charts and DR navigation.

Since Trewin was a staff member, he was able to continue efforts to persuade the Pan American Airways staff to upgrade their navigation course, but Lunn was unbending and bluntly insisted that the syllabus of the Pan American Airways Navigation Course would remain unaltered. However, as indicated earlier, Lunn traveled to the United Kingdom during August 1941, and although official RAF reports indicate that he was quite argumentive and appeared to discount much that he saw, Lunn undoubtedly absorbed much more than either he or his RAF hosts credited him with at the time.

In December 1941, when the United States entered the war, changes had already been rapidly implemented. On 17 December, Wing Commander C.N. Fleming, a distinguished RAF aerial navigator, arrived and assumed his post as commanding officer of RAF students and staff at the University of Miami. Flight Lieutenant N.C.K. Dibble remained RAF administrative officer, and the recently promoted Flight Lieutenant W.H. Trewin continued in his instructional capacity, as did RAF Disciplinary Sergeant Major L.A. Bailey. By December, four additional experienced RAF navigation officers—Flying Officers C.L. Turner, R.E.W. Pemberton, G.O. Faulkner and T. Lupton—had adjusted and assumed their duties.

Evidently, these RAF officers had brought with them to Coral Gables a number of Britain's special training aids and ideas for others. Particularly valuable for simulating wartime conditions under which navigators worked was the Grope, a training device similar to the Link Instrument Trainer, but which simulated combat conditions aboard bombers, including searchlights and anti-aircraft fire. This and other training aids necessitated special aptitudes and undoubtedly helped navigation school graduates to adjust more quickly to the new technology that was emerging in their field.

Although a few eliminees from pilot training had undoubtedly been included in at least two of the most recent classes that entered the Pan American Airways Navigation Section, the number of such trainees increased during the final intakes. However, eliminated pilots from American and Canadian schools did not completely displace men specifically selected by the RAF for navigation training. Such men continued to arrive in Canada and to be posted to Miami to fill in the required numbers for each intake at Miami.

During the spring of 1942, as weather conditions improved, the Miami area became more crowded with military personnel. By the time Class 42-3 completed the navigation course on 13 May, the U.S. Navy and USAAF had constructed numerous new airfields and taken over control of many of the hotels of Miami Beach for military training programs, including an officer candidate school (OCS). Of the 152 RAF students in the Class 42-3 (the extra 2 men beyond normal enrollment were apparently LAC Dale and 1 other who had been held over from preceding courses), 9 men were eliminated and 143 navigators graduated.

Beginning with Class 42-4, which commenced training in March 1942, the remaining three courses contained many pilot eliminees, mostly from Arnold Scheme schools. In January 1942, Harry E.V. Pinnell was eliminated from Arnold Scheme pilot training Class SE-42-F at the Graham Aviation School, Americus, Georgia. Following a brief stay at RCAF Trenton, Ontario, for remustering, Pinnell was assigned to Coral Gables for navigation training. In his spare time, Pinnell recalled with fondness dating coeds at the University of Miami and spending a great deal of time with classmates swimming and sunbathing at nearby Matheson Hammock. "We led a marvellous social life at Miami," Pinnell wrote forty years later, "and when we graduated, the Coral Gables Country Club staged a graduation dance for us."

David Logan Howell, who had been eliminated from pilot Class SE-42-G at Tuscaloosa, Alabama, also entered navigation training with PAA Class 42-4. The following excerpts from letters to his parents trace part of that experience:

> *16 May 1942. Coral Gables, Florida. As you can guess, it gets hotter & hotter here as Summer approaches. Tonight, we are having our first night flight—it should be fun finding (or losing myself) by way of the stars. I am beginning to learn something about them now which is a help. The names are easy enough to remember—"Beetle juice" for Betelgeux, etc. They call the Plough the "Dipper" over here. A few others have different names…On the verandah where I'm sitting, shaded from the sun by thick stone walls, there is a fine cool breeze blowing. "I must go back to the Isles again—to the rolling sea and the sands—and all I ask is a 4-engined ship and a star to steer her by…"*

I am writing very confusedly this a.m. No: I was not on a party last night. I feel 100%…Prime Minister Churchill has had a good reception again in Washington. His photo is in today's Miami Daily News with Halifax and the others (F.D.R. and MacKenzie King) on the Pacific War Council. He is a great warrior. Churchill is much thought of over here.

25 May 1942. *Charles Pitchford, a new-found friend (ex-Pensacola, F.A.A. draft and Newport, Mon.) and I spent a most pleasant week-end at the races. We swam Saturday & Sunday at the Venetian swimming pool with the result that we both got a good sunning. Sunday afternoon, I was in flight. Our first night flight is to be tonight (it has been cancelled twice) and I am to be Navigator in Chief!…One shipload* [flying boat from the PAA school] *of British cadets came down on Nassau the other night, and the Duke* [of Windsor] *sent his personal secretary to see that they were entertained properly, and they were put up in one of the best hotels! We flew over the Bahamas the other day, and I must say they are lovely, with their reefs and sand & swamps.*

I am taking great delight in re-writing some of my more useful notes in a beautiful note book which I got for 75 cents at the University Book-Store here. Particularly formulae which I want to refer to from time to time and notes on Compass Swinging and Radio (Loop Bearings, etc.) and Photography. Also a smattering of Bomb-Aiming which I may need at Bombing and Gunnery School. I have a snappy index at the beginning.

I have now put in 25 hours flying at Miami (including 5 hours night). I was Navigator on that occasion and we had rather a bad time as regards weather. A cold front was situated over Nassau and was registering severe thunderstorms to our port on our journey out and to starboard on the way back. Running into clouds, the sky became overcast and astro-navigation impossible. However, we had our radio loop O.K. and got "fixes" from Station WIOD. As things turned out, we made good a track right up the Florida coast and were soon within sight of the lights of Miami. It is fun, this night flying—we have a good little instructor from P.A.A.

31 May 1942. *Sunday. The Duke & Duchess are here on an official visit in connection with Defense and are going North to the Capitol today, so it is possible I may see them. They were over in Key West yesterday, I know…Charles Pitchford and I paid a visit to Miami Beach yesterday and had a good walk around the sands and the elegant hotels now housing the army. The beach is filled with soldiers. The question people ask us constantly is: "How do you like America?" Our answer, of course, is "Plenty!" (or words to that effect).*

9 June 1942. *Three R.A.F. pilots under training* [evidently at 5 BFTS near Clewiston] *did meet the Duke of Windsor in the Roney-Plaza, Miami Beach the week-end he & the Duchess were here. They came in for the week-end from a nearby town and just "dropped in" to the Roney Plaza, and bumped into the Duke himself, who was entertaining high Naval & Military officers & diplomats. So he asked them to stay on & join the party. Which they did—and got themselves & the other RAF some publicity on the front page of the Miami Daily News.*

David Howell's letters to his parents indicate an acute sense of history and an intelligent awareness of everything going on around him.

During the first week in June, Howell participated in two radio broadcasts. On the Blue Network from Radio Station WKAT, Miami Beach, with a Mr. Hanson serving as master of ceremonies, the program focused on the history of the Pan American Airways Section at the University of Miami. Guests interviewed on the program included Chief Instructor Charles Lunn, Wing Commander C.N. Fleming, LAC Howell and an American cadet (possibly Goodall). On 8 June 1942, the second program was broadcast from Radio Station WIOD and dealt primarily with Great Britain. Again Lunn and Fleming spoke, as did students Howell and Goodall.

Since the time he was in training at Tuscaloosa, Alabama, David Howell had been sending packages through the Red Cross to his brother, Edward, whom David had learned was in a German POW camp. However, during June 1942, David Howell received some good news in a cable from his father in Scotland. David's brother, Edward A. Howell, an RAF fighter pilot with 33 Squadron, had escaped to safety after having been a prisoner of the Germans since his capture on Crete. Edward Howell, later wing commander, had escaped over the mountains in northern Greece and made his way via Turkey to Egypt.

In letters to his parents acknowledging the good news about his brother, Howell mentioned former Tuscaloosa classmates with whom he maintained contact and compared flying as a student pilot in a biplane with the more staid flying in a multi-engine flying boat. His descriptions of daily and nightly training routine provide excellent insights into the activities of PAA navigation students in contrast with the pace of student pilots during the summer of 1942:

> *17 June 1942. Ron MacKenzie is now at Advanced School (Fighters). He has flying born in him. The flying we do is very different from the old days of hedge-hopping in Moths over Worcestershire & Gloucestershire and spinning in Stearmans over the woods of Alabama. We fly along at a slow, steady pace, frantically poring over our charts, taking celestial "fixes" with octant, peering out into the black night over a dark sea onto the "target."*
>
> *At cast-off, you settle down and the old ship gathers momentum and soon is battling through the waters…swish…swish…swish…swish…on & on and then, all of a sudden—no swish, and you are airborne. The long, slow climb over Base and take-off at a given height at a certain spot. So starts the night flight. Home at 2.00 in the morning to sandwich & milk & bed. Up at 6.00 for a full day's work next day.*
>
> *28 June 1942. This will be my last letter to you from Coral Gables. It has been a very wonderful time here, on the whole—rough at times, the going, but, looking back—it has been an excellent course. I am deeply grateful to P.A.A. for all I have learnt about Navigation—which is only the fundamental knowledge necessary to equip the navigator with the rudiments of the game. But to me, it is a lot.*
>
> *The instruction has been admirable in every respect, both on the ground at the University here and in the air (thanks to Messrs. Benham, Powell & Howell). "Benny" is our ground (classroom) instructor—graduate of the Naval Academy & a 100% bloke in every way. He is writing a book on Navigation. Powell & Howell are the two flight instructors I have had. Both good men…This week we shall be gone. It is sad; most of us hate going, but are anxious to get cracking too.*

Howell's praise of his instructors and the PAA navigation course is typical of the feelings with which most RAF cadets departed Coral Gables.

Robert H.B. Condie of Glasgow, Scotland, was also a member of Class 42-4. Unlike many of his classmates who had been eliminated from pilot training, Condie had been graded in the United Kingdom for navigation training and had completed an extended ITW course while attending Glasgow University. In assessing his training at Coral Gables, Condie wrote some forty years later,

> *The quality of instruction was very high, as one would expect from a major international airline. Some of the ground theory, for example, in astro (celestial) navigation, was carried to what in the circumstances was a fairly advanced level. However, considering the distance we had come, flying time was rather limited—only 55 hours in my case. Apart from acquiring the basics, my other gain from exposure to these long-distance Clipper Captains was the realization that air navigation is as much an art as a science. Ability to calculate accurately at high speed and under stress was vitally necessary for operational flying, but the development of "intuition" or a sixth sense helped to avoid major navigational blunders.*

Class 42-4 of the Pan American Airways Navigation Section had enrolled a total of 149 RAF students. Of that number, 7 men were eliminated from training and 142 graduated on 3 July 1942.

At 7:00 a.m. on Friday, 15 May 1942, the 150 members of Class 42-5 arrived at the University of Miami and were immediately assigned to their quarters. Among their numbers were John C. Sampson of Kent, Thomas Nelson of Surrey and Joseph Saxon of Lutterworth, Leicestershire. Sampson and Saxon had originally applied for RAF service as observers and had undergone an ITW course before being assigned to Elementary Air Observers School No. 1 at Eastbourne, and probably crossed the North Atlantic from Glasgow aboard the *Rangitiki* in late March–early April 1942. From Moncton, they traveled directly southward through the New England states to Miami. Since Nelson was initially a student pilot, he completed a flight grading course and sailed in January 1942 from Gourock to Halifax aboard the *Montcalm*. After a few days at Moncton, his draft entrained for Turner Field, Georgia. Eliminated from Class 42-H at Carlstrom Field, he was remustered to PAA at RCAF Trenton, Ontario.

During the weekend, the new class was able to settle in and find their way around the school. The intensified navigation course commenced on Monday, 18 May. The slightly modified daily schedule began with reveille at 6:00 a.m., breakfast at 7:00 a.m. and then lectures until 10:30 a.m. Following the morning session, the cadets were permitted a break until 1:00 p.m., at which time lunch was served. Classes recommenced at 1:45 p.m. and lasted until 6:00 p.m. Following the evening meal, the cadets were expected to study until about 9:00 p.m. They were then free but were expected to be in bed when "lights out" was ordered at 10:00 p.m.

In a series of letters to his wife, Joe Saxon described his experiences at the Coral Gables School. After indicating that the university was coeducational, "just as you have seen it on the screen," Saxon indicated that he believed "little work and a hell of a lot of play" went on at the Coral Gables institution. Saxon found that RAF students were also prone to laxity owing to the deadly heat. "It's a bit of a bind doing trigonometry in this heat, and the afternoon session seems to last forever, quite half the class fall asleep at intervals." Despite the anxiety about heat, Saxon and his classmates found the outdoors very enticing provided one avoided sunburn, "a punishable offence."

Thomas Nelson was surprised that there was so little contact between the American and British cadets. In contrasting the differences in their training schedules, he described how more free time helped the RAF cadets to develop a busier social life:

The Americans seemed to be held on a much tighter leash and were given only a minimum of time off, being expected to "crack the books" every evening they were not flying or "star gazing." On the other hand, there was almost no restriction on the British cadets and as soon as school was over, we could come and go as we pleased. And we all did…almost every night!

Every one of us had a girl friend and without exception, we were accepted as "family" by their parents. We went swimming at the Venetian Pool in Coral Gables almost every evening, then to a movie or a soda fountain or occasionally a trip to a night club. We had to be back at the San Sebastian by 11 p.m. At the weekends, we made trips to Miami Beach and the surrounding countryside, even getting as far as Tampa. After all this time, I still marvel at the hospitality and friendliness that was extended to us.

Despite the free time and social activities, two students of Class 42-5 had the first perfect flight records in the history of the school, and the class as a whole recorded the best scholastic record of all RAF classes trained at Coral Gables.

Regardless of friendliness and hospitality, adjustments were always necessary. When during the early part of June 1942 Miami suffered from the effects of a tropical storm that brought with it thunder and lightning and four days of virtually continuous rain, the British cadets received a rude awakening. These aerial displays and the thunderclaps at night brought back memories to many of the cadets of enemy air raids. This heavy weather was depressing, but the aftermath was even worse. Following the storm, the winds reversed their normal flow and began to blow from the direction of the Everglades (west-southwest) bringing into Coral Gables, Miami and other coastal towns clouds of mosquitoes. Newcomers to the region, especially the British cadets, suffered a great deal from insect bites.

There were a few more pleasant occurrences that were reminders of home. The Duke and Duchess of Windsor passed through Miami again at the end of May, and a fortnight later an RAF staff navigator at the PAA school was married. Flying Officer C.L. Turner had proposed to his fiancée by sending an expensive cablegram, and she had accepted. In June, Turner's fiancée gained passage from Britain via Lisbon to the United States aboard a Pan American Clipper, and the young couple was married in a local church on 13 June. For Class 42-5, the most pleasant set of events came after they had been attending lectures and studying hard for a month. When flying began at Dinner Key on 26 June, schedules became more flexible, but there was still little time for anything but hard work.

On 2 July, Class 42-4 boarded the *Silver Meteor* and departed for Canada, and the next day Class 42-6 arrived. On 4 July, in celebration of Independence Day, a large parade was formed and marched down Ponce de Leon Boulevard in Coral Gables. The two formations marching at the end of the parade were 100 USAAF cadets and 150 RAF cadets from the PAA Navigation School. The temperature hovered around one hundred degrees, and the RAF cadets were dressed in their heavy woolen blue uniforms. In describing the progress of the parade, Tom Nelson of Class 42-5 wrote that it was "Ten steps, Halt, Wait…Ten Steps, Halt, Wait. We received very warm applause but maybe it was for the perspiration we were scattering or our dogged determination!" From his vantage point at the rear of the formation, LAC Saxon thought that the RAF unit "looked as if 150 spiders were marching."

During the ensuing weeks, there was less free time as the members of PAA Class 42-5 continued their schedule of day and night flying, lectures, sessions on the Grope simulator and examinations. Finally, on 25 August examination results were published, and next day the surviving 145 members of the class boarded the *Silver Meteor* for the long rail journey up the East Coast to Canada.

Class 42-6 was the final RAF class to complete its training with the Pan American Airways Navigation Section at the University of Miami. Among class members were Peter Bellamy Smith, formerly of BFTS No. 2, Lancaster, California; John A. Lobban of Hertfordshire; and Arthur G. Clarke of Devon. Smith had been eliminated from pilot training with 5 Course at British Flying Training School No. 2, Lancaster, California, and traveled to Coral Gables with several other washed out pilots who had been remustered to navigation training. Clarke had volunteered for service as an observer, and Lobban had entered pilot training at Carlstrom Field, Florida, and had washed out of pilot training at Gunter Field, Alabama.

LAC Arthur Clarke praised the Pan American Airways navigation training that he received at the University of Miami. His description of personal experience in air combat provides insight into the value of astro navigation, even in Bomber Command operations. Clarke wrote that "professionally, the emphasis on astro navigation training was invaluable. When compasses were shattered by cannon shell over Berlin, it enabled us to return, using Dead Reckoning, astro compass polaris shots for latitude, etc., to land at our own base, Lakenheath [Suffolk], August 1943." Other PAA graduate navigators praised the teaching of astro navigation.

Several class members had begun their navigation training at Eastbourne, Sussex, and in June 1942 had crossed the North Atlantic from Gourock to New York aboard the United States Army transport *Thomas H. Barry*. Formerly the *Oriente*, the 25,000-ton *Barry* had brought six thousand United States Army troops to Northern Ireland, and was now bound for New York with returning Canadians and large contingents of RAF and Fleet Air Arm aircrew trainees. On 27 June, after the ship docked at New York, the RAF aircrew boarded a smaller vessel and was transported up the Hudson River to Fort Slocum.

Documentation, which took several days, was undoubtedly carried out by a port transit unit sent to the American military base from RAF No. 31 Personnel Depot at Moncton. The RAF navigation cadets boarded the *Silver Meteor* in New York City and arrived in Miami during the evening of 3 July 1942. They commenced training on 6 July. Forty years later, Peter Smith recalled his Coral Gables training days:

> *All my flying was done in Commodore twin-engined boats which I understood were the civilian version of the Consolidated PBY-1 which first flew in 1929. Most of the training flights were of 5 hours duration over the Caribbean at an airspeed of 82 knots! There was also a four-engined Sikorsky Flying Boat, although I never actually flew in that one. The Chief Instructor was Charlie Lunn, who, I believe, was navigator on P.A.A.'s first transatlantic flights. He was greatly respected by the pupils and when it came to our departure, it was evident that he was in tears.*

Of the 150 RAF students enrolled in Class 42-6, the final RAF intake at the Pan American Airways Navigation Section, 3 were eliminated and 147 graduated on 17 October 1942.

Retrospective views of wartime navigation training at Coral Gables are of interest primarily because many RAF officers were never quite satisfied with the course syllabus. On being queried as to whether being trained in the United States made a difference, responding graduates who were assigned to Bomber Command for European operations were critical of having been taught astronavigation, and at least one felt that "only the general experience was useful." Others who were assigned elsewhere were more positive about how they applied their PAA training in their wartime assignments.

Arthur R. Morris of Class 41-G described how "Astro Navigation proved invaluable during a 1942 Wellington flight from Malta to Egypt." And in describing some of his thirty-seven bombing missions with 148 Squadron over the Mediterranean, at Tobruk and in the El Alamein campaign, Morris described his use of astronavigation, indicating that his "navigation log was picked out as best for Astro and sent to Group Hq. at M.E.F." When asked whether American training helped in his later career, former teacher and headmaster Charles Brameld asserted that travel is always a broadening experience, and paid tribute to his Pan American Airways instructors "because the thorough and conscientious help I was given at P.A.A. percolated into my own attitude to teaching over 36 years in the job."

In 1945, Thomas Nelson wrote to Charles Lunn, and Lunn recommended him for a job with Pan American Airways, which was at that time beginning the airline's service in Britain and Europe. Nelson became the first British employee hired by Pan American, and he continued with them until 1950. In a 4 November 1991 letter, Nelson described the feelings of scores of British and American PAA graduates and airline passengers when he wrote, "Pan Am's last flight left Europe this week, and now the airline only has its Caribbean routes and is not even as big as it was in 1941. It breaks my heart in many ways."

On 26 February 1946, slightly more than three years after the last class left Coral Gables, Sir Winston Churchill visited the University of Miami and spoke briefly at a special convocation. The purpose of the convocation was for the university to confer upon the former prime minister an honorary doctor of laws degree. During the course of the ceremonies, the great statesman thanked the university for training Royal Air Force cadets:

> Upwards of twelve hundred cadets of the Royal Air Force received here a very high quality of technical, navigational, and meteorological training. They flew five and one-half million miles over Florida upon instructional courses, and the majority gave their lives for their country and for our common cause. It is a consolation to learn that they left so many pleasant memories behind them among the two thousand Miami households who received them with true American hospitality, and afterwards followed their fortunes and their fate almost as if they were sons of the soil. Kindred hearts will beat in Britain on this account when they read of our ceremony here today.

During the sixty years since World War II, many former cadets have made nostalgic return visits to Coral Gables, Miami Beach and the University of Miami, where they made so many friends while undergoing training in the Pan American Airways Navigation Section.

Charles Brameld vigorously countered an implied criticism of PAA training and, in the process, undoubtedly described what many graduates of the Coral Gables school must have felt and still feel about their training days during the third and fourth years of World War II:

> For me, those five to six months between setting sail from Greenoch and returning to Liverpool are still a highlight in my life, one to look back on nostalgically. A shot on our T.V. news...of a building in Washington reminds me of a quick view of it, floodlit,

December 1941, in the middle of the night through the blinds of the train window after a hefty dig in my ribs from someone determined to wake me up so as not to miss it.

I go out on a clear winter night, look up at the sky, and my mind immediately begins to click over, Sirius, Procyon, Pollux, Castor, Capella or Dubhe, Merak, Phecda, Magrez, Alioth, Mizar, Benatnasch. A phrase from "Chattanooga Choo Choo" takes me back. It was a fairly new hit while we were there, and a friend of mine nearly drove me mad singing it over and over and over…I'm not a pop music fan, in fact I actively detest pop music; [but] I shall remember the words of "Ch. Ch. Ch." for ever. It all left its mark. I wouldn't have missed any of it.

Aircrew training in the United States and the dozens of American tunes the students listened to while in training made an indelible mark on the minds and emotions of the British student navigators. And those same British cadets left behind memories of cheerful, dedicated young men from a foreign land preparing to defend their homeland and, if necessary, to give their all in doing so.

WHERE HAVE ALL THE RAF CADETS GONE?

41-7. FREDERICK GEORGE HIGSON, thirty, of Stockport, Cheshire, served as a teacher before he joined the Royal Air Force and volunteered for observer training. With other RAF students, he traveled directly from Toronto to Coral Gables. On completion of his training, he returned to Britain via Moncton and Halifax. Following a radar course at RAF Prestwick, Scotland, he was assigned to 151 Squadron on DH Mosquitoes in Britain. Subsequently, Flight Lieutenant F.G. Higsdon served in North Africa and Southeast Asia as navigator on Bristol Beaufighter VIs in 89 Squadron. He was demobilized in December 1945, and later served as a university lecturer at Loughborough.

41-G. J.S. VICTOR MCALLISTER, of Carrickfergus, County Antrim, Northern Ireland, was a graduate in agriculture at Queen's University (1936–40). Initially, he tried to join the North Irish Horse, but there were no vacancies. In 1940, he volunteered for the Royal Air Force. At RAF Swanton Morley, where he was assigned for ground defense duties, he discovered that the station armament officer, Flight Lieutenant Charlton, defused unexploded bombs, continued in UXB work and was awarded George Cross for defusing more than 200 UXBs. After ITW training in Wales, he boarded the *Windsor Castle* for Halifax. He traveled directly from Toronto to Coral Gables, Florida, and his training ended on 15 October 1941. Back in Britain, McAllister volunteered for air radar training for service on night fighters. He was trained at Prestwick, and later crewed with Sergeant A. J. "Red" Owen and was posted to 600 Squadron at Predannack, Cornwall, on Beaufighter IIs, equipped with Mrk IV AI radar. In November 1942, he was transferred to Blida, Algeria, and continued operational flying from North Africa. After Salerno, he was transferred back to Britain, where he joined 85 Squadron on DH Mosquitoes. He and his pilot were credited with destroying two V-1s and some ten enemy aircraft. Flight Lieutenant J.S.V. McAllister, BA, PhD, OBE, DFC, DFM, was demobilized in June 1946, married and subsequently was appointed to the faculty of agriculture for Northern Ireland.

41-G. ARTHUR R. MORRIS, twenty-one, of Kidderminster, Warwickshire, served as a teacher on deferred service when he volunteered for aircrew duties with the RAF. Following temporary service on ground defense duties, he was posted to ITW at Newquay, Cornwall. Subsequently Morris joined other u/t aircrew and boarded *Windsor Castle* for Halifax. He and his course mates traveled by rail directly from Toronto to Coral Gables, Florida, arriving on 3 July 1941. Navigation training was completed by December 1941, and he and his classmates returned to Britain via Moncton and Halifax. Although the second PAA course arrived back in Britain as sergeants with brevets, 41-G was not promoted until 9 March 1942, when the bombing and gunnery course was completed. Following OTU at Moreton in Marsh, Morris was posted to a ferry flight at Portreath, Cornwall. Assigned to Wellington bombers flying to Egypt via Gibraltar and Malta, the flight "from Malta to Kasfreet, Egypt was at night and astro-navigation proved invaluable." After joining 37 Squadron, a crash-landing led to hospitalization for a week. Morris later joined 148 Squadron on Wellingtons in the Middle Eastern Air Force (MEAF), and flew thirty-seven sorties on shipping and harbors. During the Alamein Campaign, the only navigational aids were star shots to check ground speed,and drift was obtained by the rear gunner with a gunsight and a four-pound incendiary bomb. "We flew at 7,000 ft over desert and climbed up to 12,000 ft for the bombing run," Morris wrote. On returning to Britain, Morris served at 26 OTU before undergoing GEE training at RAF Wyton, Huntingdonshire, a Mosquito training unit. Morris then joined 139 Squadron PFF for night flying unit training before being assigned to 608 Squadron, PFF, on DH Mosquitoes at Downham Market, Norfolk. Flight Lieutenant A.R. Morris, DFC with bar, flew 590 sorties before 28 February 1945, and 87 sorties afterward, logging 925 flying hours. He returned to the classroom and continued there to retirement in 1982.

42-2. CHARLES BRAMELD, twenty, of Rawmarsh, South Yorkshire, graduated from St. John's College in York and volunteered for observer aircrew in March 1941. Following ITW at Paignton, Devon, he joined his classmates on a voyage aboard the *Pasteur* to Halifax in mid-November 1941. From Moncton, New Brunswick, they traveled by rail to Coral Gables, Florida. On completion of their navigation training, they again traveled by rail northward to Moncton, only to be sent by rail to Norfolk, Virginia, for transport to Liverpool. Following training at AFU (O), RAF Wigtown, Scotland, on Ansons, he and some of his classmates were assigned to an OTU at RAF Lossiemouth, Scotland, after which they were posted to 142 Squadron on Wellingtons at Waltham, Lincolnshire, where they learned the use of GEE. Following a first tour of thirty-two operational trips, Brameld was mentioned in despatches (MiD), then he became an instructor in OTU for nine months. Brameld's second tour with the Pathfinder forces (PFF) began at RAF Warboys, where he learned OBOE, a radar-controlled bombing device. Subsequently, he was posted to 109 Squadron, RAF Little Staughton on Mosquito aircraft. Duties there included dropping colored markers to guide four-engine bombers on day and night raids. Flight Lieutenant Charles Brameld, DFC with three bars, had flown thirty-two sorties on Wellingtons; now with 109 Squadron, he flew eighty-five additional sorties. Brameld was demobilized on 6 February 1946, and continued service as a teacher and headmaster for thirty-six years.

42-3. JOHN CHARLES SAMPSON, twenty-one, of Kent gained early fame when he captured a German Bf109 pilot who parachuted to safety during the Battle of Britain. In February 1941, he volunteered for RAF aircrew service. Following ITW at Babbacombe, Devon, he was posted to the elementary air observer's school at Eastbourne, Sussex. After traveling aboard the *Rangitiki* to Halifax, he and his course mates traveled to Moncton, then to Coral Gables for navigation training. On completion of training, he returned to Britain and further training. Subsequently, Sampson flew twenty sorties on Stirling bombers. After December 1943, he served as an instructor for a few months, and then, after additional training, he was assigned to serve on DH

Mosquitoes. Sampson joined 105 Squadron PFF on Mosquitoes and flew another seventy-three sorties. Flight Lieutenant J.C. Sampson, DFC with bar, continued flying with 162 Squadron, delivering diplomatic mail and newspapers around Europe. In all his flying, he logged 963 hours of flying time.

42-4. DAVID LOGAN HOWELL, twenty-six, of St. Andrews, Scotland, was a horticulturist before joining the RAF. He completed a flight grading course in October 1941 and hoped to be trained as a pilot, but that was not to be. He washed out of pilot training at Tuscaloosa, Alabama, in February 1942. In Canada, he was reassigned to navigator training at the Pan American Airways School in Coral Gables, Florida. On successful completion of that course, he returned to Britain aboard the *Letitia* between 19 and 29 July 1942. After further training, Howell was assigned to 218 Squadron on Stirling bombers, where he served until December 1943. During his break from combat operations, he served as an instructor. After further training and work in a Lancaster Finishing School (LFS), Howell joined 15 Squadron on a Lancaster bomber crew. On 7 February 1945, his aircraft was shot down over the Ruhr; he baled out and became a POW until 10 May 1945. Flight Lieutenant D.L. Howell, DFC, survived the war and became active internationally in the Moral Majority.

EPILOGUE

In May 1940, the office of the chief of the United States Army Air Corps had designated the fifteen states of the region south of the thirty-seventh parallel latitude as the preferred air training zone within the continental United States. The original reason for so designating that southernmost belt of states was that the climate there permitted year-round flying, thereby assuring consistent production of fairly precise numbers of aircrew. Although there were well-defined periods during the war when the Sunbelt states experienced high winds, rain and extreme cold, it was true that most months of the year were relatively clear, calm and sunny, if not always warm.

The training pipelines that connected British and Canadian training and transient stations with the United States also had a dramatic impact on the United States. British aircrew training was carried out from airdromes in eighteen of the forty-eight wartime states. Although most flying training occurred in nine of the fifteen southernmost states, a region regarded by many as the best flying training region in the world, aircrew training also took place within nine additional states. With the expansion of the American armed services and the establishment of dozens of training bases, American and British trainees began to influence the development of the American Sunbelt.

However, since many servicemen saw winter snows and sometimes suffered from intense cold at scattered military stations in the southernmost states, it would be inaccurate to assert that the thirty-seventh parallel latitude separated colder regions from warmer ones. More to the point, the line reflected real estate values in the 1940s. North of the line, urban areas were more numerous and land was comparatively more expensive than elsewhere in the nation. South of the thirty-seventh parallel latitude, many tracts of land were already classified as public domain or could be purchased at low cost because of the devastating economic depression. Such lands became available for building large airfields and training camps and for dispersing munitions and other defense plants.

Just as the training of British fliers served as an important adjunct of the wartime Anglo-American alliance, British, American and other Allied training and wartime defense spending defined and stimulated development of the American Sunbelt, an agricultural region that grew at a phenomenal rate during and after the war. Even so, American flight training was both a success and a failure. Too many British pilots washed out of pilot training and were remustered to other duties. In some instances, washouts were restored to pilot training in Canada or elsewhere. Unfortunately, many who failed were embittered and blamed the American training system for their failure. An examination of the Arnold Scheme failure rate in each of the thirteen classes at the six primary flying schools reveals why.

Numbers and Percentages of Royal Air Force Washouts in Arnold Scheme Primary Schools

Class	Albany	Americus	Arcadia	Camden	Lakeland	Tuscaloosa	Average
42-A	86	21	44	36	32	19	39.6
42-B	77	31	27	26	35	24	36.6
42-C	55	18	40	30	38	35	35.8
42-D	73	35	32	18	44	38	40.0
42-E	60	20	59	22	41	64	44.3
42-F	90	37	80		49	57	62.5
42-G	71	26	68		40	37	48.4
42-H	74	36	72		27	43	50.4
42-I	63	18			42	49	43
42-J	63	26			41	42	43
42-K	35	38			30	33	34
43-A	32	43			24	35	33.5
43-B	37	33			8	21	24.8

Concern of the Air Ministry over excessive wastage in British operational training units of overseas-trained aircrew caused them to establish pre-OTU advanced flying units (AFUs) so as to accustom pilots and navigators to British terrain, weather and RAF policies and procedures before sending them on to fly tactical aircraft. The AFUs made use of excess airfields, aircraft and aircrew. A further change a few months later was even more drastic. In March 1942, Air Vice Marshal Arthur Harris, officer commanding in chief, Bomber Command, announced that henceforth only one pilot would fly British bombers instead of two. This policy created an immediate pilot surplus and led to a reduction in training.

In the United States, a Royal Air Force depot was established at Maxwell Field, Alabama, in the form of a four-week-long acclimatization or pre-flight course. This new and unpopular addition to RAF pilot training in the United States was designed to prepare British student pilots (now referred to as cadets) for success in the rigorous U.S. Army Air Forces flight training program. Since the British cadets would be training alongside U.S. Army Air Corps aviation cadets, American training officers preferred that all cadets (American and British) drill American style (132 steps per minute with rifles on the right shoulder). It was believed that American military drill, regular hours, physical exercise, outstanding food and the discipline imposed by the U.S. Army Air Corps Aviation Cadet Handbook would assure success.

The idea of an acclimatization course was excellent, but for too many British cadets it failed. It was far too "American orientated," and it failed to take into account British cultural taboos, military traditions and practices. Many British cadets accepted the course and enjoyed it. Others, especially older men who had served in the British armed forces, rejected many aspects of the acclimatization course. They were proud of British drill (140 steps per minute with arms swinging shoulder high; rifles on the left shoulder instead of the right) and viewed American drill as sloppy. They rejected American aviation cadet discipline as expressed in the handbook and refused to report each other's breaches of discipline. They also resented restrictions that kept them on-post except on weekends. After three RAF classes, 42-E, 42-F and 42-G, were trained at Maxwell Field, the RAF Reception Depot was shifted to Turner Field, Georgia.

Before embarking for the return voyage to Britain, the October 1941 graduates of Pan American Airways Navigation School at Miami, Florida, and almost two hundred newly graduated RAF sergeant pilots boarded rail cars in the United States and traveled north to Moncton, New Brunswick, rather than to Toronto, Ontario. By December 1941, ice and snow covered the Canadian Maritime Provinces following several arctic storms. As more RAF pilots and other aircrew arrived from warmer regions of the United States, Canadian temperatures dropped to record lows of twenty to twenty-two degrees below zero. Those under training (u/t) westward-bound aircrew who arrived in October 1941 from Britain wore woolen RAF blue uniforms.

Early in January 1942, Class SE 42-A arrived at RAF No. 31 Personnel Dispersal Center (PDC) at Moncton, New Brunswick, Canada. They had departed from three USAAF advanced flying schools: Turner Field, Albany, Georgia; Craig Field, Selma, Alabama; and Maxwell Field, Montgomery, Alabama. Mid-winter at these American advanced flying schools was pleasant; there was sunshine almost every day, days were relatively warm and nights ranged between cool and downright cold. Since members of the first five classes had entered the United States in civilian suits, their RAF uniforms, including greatcoats, had been stored at RCAF No. 1 Manning Depot at Toronto. The original plan was for the British students to retrieve their uniforms in Toronto when their training was completed.

The problem of left luggage in Toronto was solved for future arrivals from warmer regions, but members of the early graduating aircrew classes suffered from the intense cold without greatcoats. Train schedules were disrupted, and cases of frostbite became all too common. Most entertainment for RAF aircrew had to be provided indoors, so YMCA attendance at Moncton climbed by about 200 per day and by the end of the month reached a record of almost 30,000 men served, 23,850 of them from the RAF. On Wednesday evenings at the YMCA, "English style" dance steps such as the "Palais glide" were being taught by anxious RAF airmen to groups of young ladies from Moncton and vicinity.

For more rugged souls who preferred outdoor recreation, many institutions, including the Salvation Army's Red Shield Hostel on Moncton's Church Street extension, operated outdoor ice rinks in winter and other sports in season. The Salvation Army ice rink was located to the rear of the hostel, and that large facility also maintained two hundred beds and provided meals and snacks in its canteen. Its large reading room held books, magazines, games, writing materials and tables. Other less well-organized civic and religious organizations did their bit as well. Raw weather continued, and the depot's population fluctuated.

On arrival back in Canada en route to England, Sergeant Pilot Stan Slater of SE-42-B (Arcadia, Gunter, Maxwell) recalled that "any euphoria from gaining our wings was soon dispelled at Moncton in Canada. We were greeted by a RAF Flight Sergeant, whose first words were 'You can take them tin things down,' referring to our hard earned U.S. Army Air Corps [sterling silver] wings." Slater could not recall his transport, but he felt that "it was much more comfortable than the outward journey."

In early March 1942, Class SE-42-C graduates from the USAAF advanced flying schools at Dothan, Selma and Montgomery, Alabama, entrained at Montgomery for Moncton. Graduates of that third RAF class spent a short period at RAF No. 31 Personnel Depot at Moncton before embarking for Britain at Halifax aboard the *Stirling Castle*.

On 22 May 1942, when Class SE-42-E graduates arrived at Moncton from American flight schools, they encountered large quantities of mud produced by the melting winter snow and ice. Many of the new pilots viewed it as a "miserable place," especially after RAF officers deprived them of the "leather shoes, silk shirts, fawn pants, etc. of USAAC uniforms [gabardine dress uniforms] which nearly everyone kept & wanted to pay the RAF for 'losing them.'" The equipment branch at Moncton evidently wanted to issue the USAAC uniforms to the next draft destined for training in the United States. As one sergeant pilot described the incident, "Only after threat of mass court martial did we 'find' the missing items. (Would they really have court martialed 200 pilots for the sake of shirts & shoes? Anyhow, we wanted to get on with the war, so we produced the goods.)"

Following a brief stay at Moncton and a short railway journey to Halifax, Class SE-42-G boarded the *Awatea*, which collided with a destroyer escort. The destroyer escort, the USS *Ingraham*, sank with a heavy loss of life. *Awatea* returned to Halifax with its crushed bow, and, the RAF aircrew, after a brief delay, were sent by rail to New York City, where they boarded HMS *Queen Elizabeth*. With the tragic British crashes that killed fourteen RAF cadets, Class SE-42-G had been the hard luck class at Gunter Field, Alabama, and Moody Field, Georgia, and that luck followed them to Moncton and then left them.

Before entering the RAF, David Logan Howell of St. Andrews, Scotland, and Pan American Airways Navigation Class 42-4 had been a market gardener or horticulturist, and he was also a highly intelligent observer. In a July 1942 letter to his parents shortly after he arrived back in Moncton, he described what he saw:

> *It is delightfully cool and fresh up here—in the evenings and early mornings, in contrast to the intense humidity of S.E. Florida. It gets quite hot during the day though…Moncton is really getting quite spruce & gay! Flowerbeds have sprung up outside some of the buildings (I mean in "31" [the RAF depot]), and there is a colossal food-production campaign underway. Tomatoes have been grown & are ready. Staked potatoes & other vegetables also are sprouting. Everywhere men are at work, digging, hoeing, raking, levelling. They might put us on that if we are here long enough!!*

Class 42-4 navigators left shortly thereafter for Halifax, but other aircrew may have been put to work gardening.

A Class 42-I graduate had been commissioned and assigned as a flight instructor at a USAAF flight school at Bainbridge, Georgia. In spring 1943, he and other RAF instructors arrived at the Moncton RAF depot. They had completed their tours of duty, thereby adding experience and about four hundred additional hours of flying time. At Moncton, they encountered a "bombastic, silly little man" (an RAF officer) who enjoyed keeping the pilots in formation for long periods.

The officious PDC officer had erected a podium for himself in the center of one of the large drill halls, so the payback for his authoritarian actions was the mysterious, almost complete, sawing through of the podium legs. At the next scheduled formation, the podium collapsed, and the officer fell and broke a wrist. As a result, the station commander restricted everyone to the base until "the culprit owns up." "Nobody did, because the entire group was responsible. Anyway, there was a hole in the fence and it was easy to make one's way to town."

In Halifax, Class 42-I's sergeant pilot graduates were told that they were supposed to have embarked for the voyage to Britain aboard the *Queen Mary*, instead of the *Queen Elizabeth*. The reason for the change was that the *Queen Mary* had been involved in a collision in the Firth of Clyde that cut the cruiser *Curacao* in half. As a result, the huge liner was in Norfolk, Virginia, undergoing repairs to damages caused by her deadly collision with the RN cruiser. As the RAF pilots boarded the *Queen Elizabeth* in Halifax, they were amazed at its size and even more shocked about the number of passengers that it would be carrying across the Atlantic to England.

Sergeant Pilot Gordon J. Cadman (Tuscaloosa, 42-I) described the eastbound voyage:

> *The voyage home on board the QEI was an adventure in itself—there were, we were told,*
> *19,000 of us on board…We had our meals at 12-hour intervals. A card, which we*
> *received as we went on board, gave our meal-times (as I recall, my own case was 8 a.m.*
> *and 8 p.m.). The mess deck in our case, one of the swimming pools, was in use virtually*
> *on a 24-hour basis. We slept in 3-tiered bunks in a tiny triangular cabin (9 of us) right*
> *at the stern of the ship—smack over one of the propeller shafts.*

Although shaken by the vibrations caused by the ship's powerful engines, the occupants of that particular stern cabin and the other British aircrew aboard enjoyed the voyage; they were going home!

During the relatively brief trip across the North Atlantic, they laughed a great deal at some of the remarks made by American soldiers on board. National pride and ignorance caused many of them to assume that the huge British liner and British Spitfires and British Hurricanes were American-built under the Lend-Lease program. By the time Class 42-I graduate pilots disembarked in Glasgow, British aircrew trained overseas were being sent first to Pilot Reception Center (PRC) No. 7 at Harrogate, Yorkshire, where they underwent health checks. The pilots were then sent to PRC No. 3 at Bournemouth on the south coast. Only then were they allowed to go home on leave for two weeks before reporting to an AFU.

On arrival at one AFU, the American-trained pilots were incensed when their RAF commander told them that "as American trained pilots we were probably amongst the best 'circus' pilots in the world—we were now going to learn exactly how to fly in combat, and how not to make a gift of our lives and our aircraft to the enemy—we were going to be taught how to survive. Quite an unnecessary speech I felt then, and am even more convinced today."

During the war, American-trained British fliers served in virtually every capacity from aircraftsman second class to wing commander and carried out assignments in every part of the world in every conceivable duty assignment. American-trained British aircrew were also among the men who served as instructors, flew the bombers and fighters, reconnaissance, attack (ground support) and air-sea rescue (ASR) craft, as well as long-range Coastal Command and Air Transport Command aircraft and gliders. Many of these American-trained fliers won high honors during air combat operations.

Several American-trained RAF pilots won the Victoria Cross (VC). Dozens of American-trained RAF aircrew also won the Distinguished Service Order (DSO)—Britain's second-highest award for valor—the Distinguished Service Cross (DSC), the Distinguished Flying Cross (DFC), the Distinguished Flying Medal (DFM) and the Air Force Cross (AFC), while many more were Mentioned in Despatches(MiD).

Arnold Scheme schools also produced a number of distinguished high-ranking airmen, including several officers of air (general officer) rank. Air Vice Marshal John Moss, who became deputy chief of staff of the Royal Rhodesian Air Force, received his pilot training as a member of Class SE-42-A (Camden, Macon, Albany). Air Chief Marshal Sir Douglas C. Lowe, GCB, DFC, AFC, received his pilot training as a member of Arnold Scheme Class SE-42-B (Americus, Macon, Dothan). Other Arnold Scheme graduates included Air Commodores Thomas H. Blackham, DFC, MBE of Class SE-42-A (Carlstrom, Macon, Selma); Patrick A. Kennedy, CBE, DSO, DFC, AFC of Class SE-42-C (Camden, Macon, Dothan); David C. Saunders,

CBE, AFC of Class 42-D (Camden, Gunter, Maxwell); John Frost, CBE, DFC, DL of Class SE-42-E (Lakeland, Gunter, Selma); John Miller, CBE, DFC, AFC of Class SE-42-F (Americus, Macon, Dothan); and Robert H.G. Weighill, CBE, DFC of Class SE-42-D (Tuscaloosa, Gunter, Maxwell). Marshal of the Royal Air Force Sir Michael Beetham, GCB, CBE, DFC, AFC, DL who retired as chief of air staff in 1982, received his training as a member of Arnold Scheme Class SE-42-K (Lakeland, Macon, Albany). Beetham was the highest ranking American-trained British pilot, and his career provided a direct link between the RAF and the USAF that stretched from 1942 to the Falklands War of 1982.

Many more American-trained aircrew eventually moved from military to civil aviation. Many of them remained in the RAF, and dozens of others flew as airline captains. Some of them pioneered in the development of modern navigation and air traffic control methods. Hundreds enrolled in universities to be trained as architects, teachers, doctors, lawyers, dentists and engineers, and many others returned to their pre-war positions with the police forces and British industries. Over the years, great numbers of the former aircrew made nostalgic return visits to the United States.

Within Britain, other wartime British graduates of American flying schools rose to responsible posts in local and national government (including several members of the House of Lords and the House of Commons), in professions such as law, medicine, dentistry, architecture, engineering, finance, commerce and industry, as well as in literature, theatre, motion pictures, television and the arts. And whether they ever acknowledged it or not, their wartime travels and experiences in the United States prepared them to adjust to the dramatic changes that occurred before and after 1945.

ARNOLD SCHEME STATISTICS

Classes that Were Posted Directly from Toronto to USAAF Primary Flying Schools

Class	Date of Arrival	Net Intake	Elim. Before Solo	Elim. After Solo	# of Fatalities	# of Grads	Date Posted
SE-42-A	9 June 1941	549	6	241	1	301	23 Aug. 1941
SE-42-B	17 July 1941	555	10	218	1	326	30 Sep. 1941
SE-42-C	30 Aug. 1941	632	12	215	2	403	27 Oct. 1941
SE-42-D	1 Oct. 1941	651	12	237	3	399	19 Dec. 1941
Total		2,387	40	911	7	1,429	

Acclimatization Classes at Maxwell Field; Sent from Maxwell Field to Primary Flying Schools

Class	Dates	Original Intake	Held Over Previously	Held Over to Next	Net Intake	Elim.	# of Fatalities	# of Grads
42-E	17 Oct. 1941 to 5 Nov. 1941	749	0	3	746	0	0	746
42-F	6 Nov. 1941 to 17 Dec. 1941	750	3	3	750	2	1*	747
42-G	18 Dec. 1941 to 17 Jan. 1942	746	3	8**	741	3	0	738
Total		2,245	6	6	2,237	5	1	2,231

*One fatality in Class SE-42-F on 10 December 1941: LAC Stanley Holden, North Harrow, Middlesex. He was thirty years old.

**Eight men held over from Class SE-42-G were transferred to the RAF replacement center at Turner Field, Albany, Georgia.

Acclimatization Classes at Turner Field; Sent from Turner Field to Primary Flying Schools

Class	Date	Intake	Held Over	Elim. Before Solo	Elim. After Solo	# of Fatalities	# of Grads	Date Posted
SE-42-H	24 Jan. 1942	758	10	0	0	0	748	21 Feb. 1942
SE-42-I	18 Feb. 1942	519	12	0	0	0	507	29 March 1942
SE-42-J	30 March 1942	507	12	2	0	0	493	30 Apr. 1942
SE-42-K	1 May 1942	518	11	1	0	0	506	2 June 1942
SE-43-A	3 June 1942	518	4	0	0	0	514	6 July 1942
SE-43-B	8 July 1942	518	1	14*	0	0	503	6 Aug. 1942
Total		3,338	50	17	0	0	3,271	

*Fourteen RAF cadets were posted to Canada to complete training.

RAF Pilots Trained at Southern Aviation School, Camden, South Carolina

Class	Intake	Held Over Prev.	Held Over to Next	Net Intake	Elim. for Non-flying	Elim. for Flying Deficiency	# of Fatalities	# of Grads	% Grad.	% Elim.
42-A	66	0	2	64	0	36	0	28	43.8	56.3
42-B	66	2	2	66	2	24	0	40	60.6	39.4
42-C	76	2	1	77	4	26	0	47	61.0	39.0
42-D	50	1	5	46	3	15	1	27	58.7	41.3
42-E	40	5	1	44	1	21	0	22	50.0	50.0
Total	298	10	11	297	10	122	1	164	55.22	44.78

RAF Pilots Trained at Alabama Institute of Aeronautics, Tuscaloosa, Alabama

Class	RAF Intake	Held Over Prev.	Held Over to Next	Net Intake	Elim. for Non-flying	Elim. for Flying Deficiency	# of Fatalities	# of Grads	% Grad.	% Elim.
42-A	70	0	3	67	0	19	0	48	71.6	28.4
42-B	70	3	2	71	5	19	0	47	66.2	33.8
42-C	91	2	3	90	4	31	0	55	61.1	38.9
42-D	95	3	3	95	1	37	0	57	60.0	40.0
42-E	120	3	4	119	10	54	0	55	46.2	53.8
42-F	124	4	3	125	9	48	0	68	54.4	45.6
42-G	123	3	5	121	3	34	0	84	69.4	30.6
42-H	129	5	8	126	1	42	0	83	65.9	34.1
42-I	112	8	5	115	2	47	0	66	57.4	42.6
42-J	104	5	5	104	2	40	0	62	59.6	40.4
42-K	78	5	2	81	1	32	0	48	59.3	40.7
43-A	73	2	4	71	4	31	0	36	50.7	49.3
43-B	65	4	0	69	4	16	1*	48	69.6	30.4
Total	1,254	47	47	1,254	46	450	1	757	60.37	39.63

*There was one RAF fatality at the Alabama Institute of Aeronautics on 4 October 1942: LAC Kenneth McGregor of Londonderry, Northern Ireland, age twenty-six.

RAF Pilots Trained at Souther Field, Americus, Georgia

Class	Original Intake	Held Over Prev.	Held Over to Next	Net Intake	Elim. for Non-flying	Elim. for Flying Deficiency	# of Fatalities	# of Grads	% Grad.	% Elim.
42-A	53	0	2	51	1	20	0	30	58.8	41.2
42-B	53	2	3	52	1	30	0	21	40.4	59.6
42-C	50	3	2	51	14	2	2*	33	64.7	35.3
42-D	90	2	1	91	4	31	0	56	61.5	38.5
42-E	100	1	2	99	3	17	0	79	79.8	20.2
42-F	103	3	3	103	4	33	0	66	64.1	35.9
42-G	101	3	5	99	2	24	0	73	73.7	26.3
42-H	98	5	5	98	2	34	0	62	63.3	36.7
42-I	99	5	4	100	0	18	0	82	82.0	18.0
42-J	100	4	7	97	0	26	0	71	73.2	26.8
42-K	175	6	5	176	1	36	1**	138	78.4	21.2
43-A	200	5	2	203	2	40	1***	160	78.1	21.9
43-B	197	2	0	199	5	28	0	166	83.4	16.6
Total	1,419	41	41	1,419	39	339	4	1,037	73.08	26.92

*On 2 November 1941, nineteen-year-old LAC Harold Norman Evans of Wolverhampton, Staffordshire, and nineteen-year-old LAC Peter George Hills of Faversham, Kent, both of Class 42-C, were drowned.

**On 29 June 1942, twenty-year-old LAC Maurice Hislop of Bournbrook, Birmingham, 42-K, was killed.

***On 17 August 1942, nineteen-year-old LAC Douglas Warren Flatau, of Flax Burton, Somerset, 43-A, was killed.

RAF Pilots Trained at Darr Aero Tech, Albany, Georgia

Class	Original Intake	Held Over Prev.	Held Over to Next	Net Intake	Elim. for Non-flying	Elim. for Flying Deficiency	# of Fatalities	# of Grads	% Grad.	% Elim.
SE-42-A	172	0	0	172	1	84	1*	86	50	50
SE-42-B	171	0	5	166	2	75	0	89	53.6	46.4
SE-42-C	170	5	1	174	2	53	0	119	68.4	31.6
SE-42-D	165	1	3	163	7	65	1**	90	55.2	44.8
SE-42-E	172	3	4	171	4	56	0	111	64.9	35.1
SE-42-F	173	4	5	172	7	83	0	82	47.7	52.3
SE-42-G	173	5	6	172	3	68	0	101	58.7	41.3
SE-42-H	175	6	7	174	4	70	0	100	57.5	42.5
SE-42-I	168	7	7	168	3	60	0	105	62.5	37.5
SE-41-J	167	7	6	168	10	53	0	105	62.5	37.5
SE-42-K	173	6	8	171	0	35	0	136	79.5	20.5
SE-43-A	168	8	11	165	2	30	0	133	80.6	19.4
SE-43-B	172	11	11	172	3	34	0	135	78.5	21.5
Total	2,219	63	74	2,208	48	766	2	1,392	63.04	36.96

*On 25 July 1941, nineteen-year-old LAC D'Arcy Harry Michael Wilson of Windermere, Westmoreland, was killed.

**On 30 October 1941, nineteen-year-old LAC Eric Nepean George Newberry Furze of Plympton, Devon, was killed.

RAF Pilots Trained at Lakeland School of Aeronautics, Lakeland, Florida

Class	Original Intake	Held Over Prev.	Held Over to Next	Net Intake	Elim. for Non-flying	Elim. for Flying Deficiency	# of Fatalities	# of Grads	% Grad.	% Elim.
42-A	90	0	1	89	0	32	0	57	64	36
42-B	90	1	0	91	5	29	1*	56	61.5	38.5
42-C	100	0	0	100	0	38	0	62	62	38
42-D	100	0	0	100	2	42	0	56	56	44
42-E	115	0	0	115	1	40	0	74	64.3	35.7
42-F	119	0	0	119	0	49	0	70	58.8	41.2
42-G	118	0	2	116	0	40	0	76	65.5	34.5
42-H	122	2	1	123	0	27	0	96	78	22
42-I	122	7**	2	127	1	41	0	85	66.9	33.1
42-J	122	2	2	122	0	41	0	81	66.4	33.6
42-K	79	3	1	81	0	30	0	51	63	37
43-A	74	1	0	75	0	24	0	51	68	32
43-B	68	0	0	68	1	7	0	60	88.2	11.8
Total	1,319	16	9	1,326	10	440	1	875	65.99	34.01

*One student from Class SE-42-B, twenty-year-old LAC Robert Arthur Gordon Cleave of New Malden, Surrey, went missing in the Gulf of Mexico on 2 September 1941 and was later officially declared dead.

**Six members of Class SE-42-H students at Carlstrom Field were transferred into Lakeland's Class SE-42-I when the Riddle Aeronautical Institute at Carlstrom Field, Florida, discontinued RAF training.

RAF Pilots Trained at Carlstrom Field, Arcadia, Florida

Class	Original Intake	Held Over Prev.	Held Over to Next	Net Intake	Elim. for Non-flying	Elim. for Flying Deficiency	# of Fatalities	# of Grads	% Grad.	% Elim.
42-A	99	0	2	97	0	44	0	53	54.6	45.4
42-B	99	2	0	101	1	26	0	74	73.3	26.7
42-C	133	0	6	127	4	36	0	87	68.5	31.5
42-D	140	6	1	145	2	30	0	113	77.9	22.1
42-E	198	1	5	194	5	54	0	135	69.6	30.4
42-F	228	5	3	230	4	75	1*	150	65.2	34.8
42-G	224	3	3	224	5	63	0	156	69.6	30.4
42-H	230	3	6	227	1	71	0	155	68.3	31.7
Total	1,351	20	26	1,345	22	399	1	923	68.62	31.38

*On 5 January 1942, nineteen-year-old LAC Alfred Thomas Lloyd of New Radnor, Wales, apparently drowned.

RAF Primary Flying Training Graduates Posted to Basic Flying Schools

Class	Date	Intake	Held Over	Eliminated Before Solo	Eliminated After Solo	# of Fatalities	# of Grads	Date Posted
SE-42-A	9 June 1941	550	6	182	59	1	302	23 Aug. 1941
SE-42-B	9 June 1941	555	10	160	58	0	327	30 Sep. 1941
SE-42-C	30 Aug. 1941	632	12	153	62	2	403	27 Oct. 1941
SE-42-D	1 Oct. 1941	651	12	161	76	3	399	19 Dec. 1941
SE-42-E	5 Nov. 1941	756	12	168	100	0	476	10 Jan. 1942
SE-42-F	17 Dec. 1941	760	13	219	91	1	436	21 Feb. 1942
SE-42-G	17 Jan. 1942	751	19	133	109	0	490	29 March 1942
SE-42-H	21 Feb. 1942	772	22	146	107	0	497	30 April 1942
SE-42-I	29 March 1942	527	17	107	65	0	438	2 June 1942
SE-42-J	30 April 1942	510	19	119	53	0	338	3 July 1942
SE-42-K	1 May 1942	525	16	86	49	1	373	6 Aug. 1942
SE-43-A	6 July 1942	530	17	74	58	1	380	7 Sep. 1942
SE-43-B	6 Aug.1942	520	17	57	35	1	410	10 Oct. 1942
Total		8,039	192	1,765	922	10	5,150	

RAF Pilots Trained at Gunter Field, Montgomery, Alabama

Class	Original Intake	Held Over Prev.	Held Over to Next	Net Intake	Elim. for Non-flying	Elim. for Flying Deficiency	# of Fatalities	# of Grads	% Grad.	% Elim.
42-A	158	0	2	156	1	6	0	149	95.5	4.5
42-B	155	2	1	156	0	6	1	149	95.5	4.5
42-C	204	1	0	205	1	18	0	186	90.7	9.3
42-D	197	0	5	192	0	36	0	156	81.3	18.7
42-E	240	5	4	241	0	41	2	198	82.2	17.8
42-F	175	4	10	169	2	19	3	145	85.8	14.2
42-G	205	10	7	208	2	29	8	169	82.4	18.8
42-H	209	7	3	213	0	25	3	185	86.9	13.1
42-I	148	3	0	151	1	23	0	127	84.1	15.9
42-J	143	0	0	143	1	9	2	131	91.6	8.4
42-K	189	0	8	181	1	14	3	163	90.1	9.9
43-A	184	8	1	191	1	13	0	177	92.7	7.3
43-B	184	1	3	182	4	9	0	169	92.9	7.1
43-C	6*	0	0	6	0	0	0	6	100	0
Total	2,397	41	44	2,394	14	248	22**	2,110	88.1	11.9

*Of the six-man RAF intake for Class 43-C, three had been held over at Gunter Field and three were transferred from Cochran Field.

**There were twenty-two fatalities at Gunter Field during the training of British personnel, as follows:

Class SE-42-B

9 December 1941, LAC Louis Wells of Bootham, York, age nineteen. Died in an auto accident in Florida while on his end-of-course leave. Interred in the Oak Ridge Cemetery at Arcadia, Florida.

Class SE-42-E

9 February 1942, Corporal Reginald Arthur Price of Slough, Buckinghamshire, age twenty-two.
9 February 1942 LAC Charles William Wadkinson of Millhouses, Sheffield, age nineteen.

Class SE-42-F

7 April 1942, LAC Reginald Arthur John Shotbolt of Luton, Bedfordshire, age twenty.
10 April 1942, LAC Thomas Walpole Atkin of Acklam, Middlesbrough, Yorkshire, age twenty-three.
10 April 1942, LAC Frederick Nash of Dover, Kent, age twenty-four.

Class SE 42-G

7 May 1942, LAC Oswald Hendrie McDonald of Edinburgh, Scotland, age twenty.
21 May 1942, LAC Victor William Lear of Radstock, Somerset, age nineteen.
21 May 1942, LAC Arthur Vernon Lowe of Sheffield, Yorkshire, age twenty-two.
21 May 1942, LAC James Edward Maddick of Dundee, Scotland, age twenty-one.
21 May 1942, LAC Patrick Geoffrey Marshall Overton of Porthcawl, Glamorgan, Wales, age twenty-two.
21 May 1942, LAC Michael Ernest Peachell of Broadway, Dorset, age twenty-two.
21 May 1942, LAC David Stanley Peattie of Knock, Belfast, Northern Ireland, age nineteen.
21 May 1942, LAC Ronald Edward Randall of Birmingham, age twenty-six.

Class SE-42-H

28 May 1942, LAC Frank Rogers of Pontardulais, Glamorgan, Wales, age twenty-three.

13 June 1942, LAC James Arthur Barnes of Preston, Lancashire, age twenty-one.

13 June 1942, LAC Walter Samuel Bowden of Exeter, Devon, age twenty.

Class SE-42-J

10 August 1942, LAC Albert Edgar Ayling of Cowplain, Hampshire, age nineteen.

10 August 1942, LAC Cecil Evan Gray of Sanderstead, Surrey, age twenty-six.

Class SE-42-K

14 September 1942, LAC Douglas Albert Gell of Ilford, Essex, age nineteen.

24 September 1942, LAC Charles Norman Frederick Downs of Palmer's Green, London, age twenty.

25 November 1942, LAC Gordon Grieve Warner of Oulton Broad, Lowestoft, Suffolk, age twenty-four.

RAF Pilots Trained at Cochran Field, Macon, Georgia

Class	Original Intake	Held Over Prev.	Held Over to Next	Net Intake	Elim. for Non-flying	Elim. for Flying Deficiency	# of Fatalities	# of Grads	% Grad.	% Elim.
42-A	144	0	2	142	0	4	0	138	97.2	2.8
42-B	172	2	3	171	0	5	0	166	97.1	2.9
42-C	199	3	9	193	0	7	0	186	96.4	3.6
42-D	202	9	6	205	2	9	2	192	93.7	6.3
42-E	236	6	9	233	1	18	0	214	91.8	8.2
42-F	260	9	14	255	3	19	5	228	89.4	10.6
42-G	286	14	14	286	7	34	1	244	85.3	14.7
42-H	288	14	14	288	5	40	1	242	84.0	16.0
42-I	190	14	10	194	0	13	2	179	92.3	7.7
42-J	176	10	10	176	1	10	0	165	93.8	6.2
42-K	184	10	13	181	0	25	0	156	86.2	13.8
43-A	196	13	8	201	1	22	0	178	88.6	11.4
43-B	226	8	5	229	9	32	0	188	82.1	17.9
Total	2,759	112	117	2,754	29	238	11*	2,476	89.9	10.1

*There were eleven fatalities at Cochran Field during the training of British personnel, as follows:

Class SE-42-D

26 December 1941, LAC John Keith Briers of Alvaston, Derby, age twenty-one.

8 January 1942, LAC Kenneth Neil Thomson of Edinburgh, Scotland, age twenty-seven.

Class SE-42-F

18 March 1942, LAC John Ferrior Latta, Bombay, India, and Ayrshire, Scotland, age twenty-five.

28 March 1942, LAC Thomas Henry Hedger of Sunderland, County Durham, age twenty.

28 March 1942, LAC Richard Edward Davies of Kenilworth, Warwickshire, age twenty-three.

11 April 1942, LAC Philip Walter Winter of Gowerton, Glamorgan, Wales, age twenty.

11 April 1942, LAC Wilfred John Hawes of Woodham Ferrers, Essex, age thirty.

Class SE-42-G

6 May 1942, LAC Geoffrey Holmes of Wakefield, Yorkshire, age twenty.

<u>Class SE-42-H</u>
3 June 1942, LAC Arthur William Wakeley of Winton, Bournemouth, age twenty.
<u>Class SE-42-I</u>
18 July 1942, LAC Eric William Frederick Charrosin of Upper Norwood, Surrey, age twenty-one.
22 July 1942, LAC Leonard Alfred Carter of Lewisham, London, age twenty-one.
<u>Cochran Field RAF Flying Instructor</u>
13 January 1943, Pilot Officer Anthony Guy Mole of Clifton, Bristol, age twenty-six.

RAF Classes Enrolled in Basic Flying Training and Posted to an Advanced Flying School

Class	Dates	Intake		Held Over		Elim. Before Solo		Elim. After Solo		# of Fatalities		# of Grads		Date Posted to Advanced
		C	G	C	G	C	G	C	G	C	G			
SE-42-A	23 Aug. 1941	144	158	3	5	3	1	5	2	0	0	138	149	3 Nov. 1941
SE-42-B	30 Sep. 1941	174	157	3	1	3	1	2	6	0	1	166	148	10 Dec. 1941
SE-42-C	27 Oct. 1941	202	205	9	0	4	3	10	9	0	0	186	186	9 Jan. 1942
SE-42-D	19 Dec. 1941	211	197	6	4	4	7	29	5	2	0	192	159	20 Feb. 1942
SE-42-E	10 Jan. 1942	242	244	8	3	6	4	29	12	0	2	214	198	27 Mar. 1942
SE-42-F	21 Feb. 1942	269	179	14	10	11	11	18	3	5	3	228	145	27 Apr. 1942
SE-42-G	29 Mar. 1942	300	215	15	13	26	15	18	13	1	8	244	169	20 Jun. 1942
SE-42-H	30 Apr. 1942	302	216	34	11	17	1	3	3	1	3	242	184	4 Jul. 1942
SE-42-I	2 Jun. 1942	204	151	10	0	9	4	16	8	2	0	179	127	6 Aug. 1942
SE-42-J	3 Jul. 1942	186	143	10	0	10	1	9	1	0	2	165	131	3 Sep. 1942
SE-42-K	6 Aug. 1942	194	189	13	8	17	9	12	3	0	3	155	163	10 Oct. 1942
SE-43-A	7 Sep. 1942	209	192	8	1	14	9	12	2	0	0	178	177	11 Nov. 1942
SE-43-B	10 Oct. 1942	234	185	3*	3	20	19	6	4	0	1	188	169	14 Dec. 1942
Total		2,871	2,431	136	59	144	85	169	71	11	23	2,475	2,105	

C = Cochran, G = Gunter

RAF Pilots Trained at Craig Field, Selma, Alabama

Class	Original Intake	Held Over Prev.	Held Over to Next	Net Intake	Elim. for Non-flying	Elim. for Flying Deficiency	# of Fatalities	# of Grads	% Grad.	% Elim.
42-A	122	0	2	120	0	1	1	118	95.7	4.3
42-B	155	2	4	153	3	2	3	145	94.8	5.2
42-C	150	4	7	147	1	2	3	141	95.9	4.1
42-D	120	7	1	126	1	3	0	122	92.9	7.1
42-E	170	1	4	167	1	6	0	160	95.8	4.2
42-F	153	4	2	155	0	3	1	151	97.4	2.6
42-G	95	2	4	93	5	5	0	83	89.2	10.8
42-H	104	4	3	105	0	6	1	98	93.3	6.7
42-I	75	3	4	74	0	3	2	69	93.2	6.8
42-J	58	4	1	61	0	2	0	59	96.7	3.3
42-K	75	1	1	75	0	2	0	73	97.3	1.7
43-A	87	1	4	84	0	3	0	81	96.4	3.6
43-B	94	4	4	94	0	3	1	90	95.7	4.3
43-C	0	4	0	4	2	0	0	2	50	50
Total	1,458	41	41	1,458	13	41	12*	1,392	95.5	4.5

*There were twelve fatalities (and one instructor fatality) at Craig Field during the training of British personnel, as follows:

Class SE-42-A

27 December 1941, LAC Douglas Fairer Leman of Cartmel, Lancashire, age twenty.

Class SE-42-B

13 January 1942, LAC John Feldon Rimer of Southgate, London, age nineteen.

14 January 1942, LAC George Benson Whigham of Falkirk, Stirlingshire, Scotland, age twenty-one.

20 January 1942, LAC Alfred Bolton Kinnear of Caerlon, Monmouthshire, age twenty.

Class SE-42-C

3 February 1942, LAC David William Turner of Reading, Berkshire, age nineteen.

3 February 1942, LAC Paul Derek Underwood of West Ewell, Surrey, age twenty.

5 February 1942, LAC George William Rowley of Dodsworth, Yorkshire, age nineteen.

Class SE-42-F

9 May 1942, LAC Ernest George Gulliver of Knaphill, Woking, Surrey, age twenty.

Class SE-42-H

9 August 1942, LAC Herbert Riding of Barnsley, Yorkshire, age twenty-one.

Class SE-42-I

1 September 1942, LAC Ernest Robert John Spooner of Brundall, Norfolk, age twenty.

6 October 1942, LAC David James Calder of Edinburgh, Scotland, age nineteen.

Class SE-43-B

7 February 1943, LAC Felix Quinn of Stockton-on-Tees, County Durham, age twenty.

RAF Flying Instructors

30 December 1942, Flying Officer Philip Jones of Wilmslow, Cheshire, age twenty-five.

RAF Pilots Trained at Napier Field, Dothan, Alabama

Class	Original Intake	Held Over Prev.	Held Over to Next	Net Intake	Elim. for Non-flying	Elim. for Flying Deficiency	# of Fatalities	# of Grads	% Grad.	% Elim.
42-B	90	0	4	86	0	1	2	83	96.5	3.5
42-C	149	4	6	147	3	1	1 (2)	142	96.6	3.4
42-D	150	6	2	154	3	7	1	143	92.9	7.1
42-E	162	2	3	161	0	18	0	143	88.8	11.2
42-F	143	3	2	144	0	7	0	137	95.1	4.9
42-G	123	2	2	123	0	1	0	122	99.2	.8
42-H	103	2	2	103	3	3	0	97	94.2	5.8
42-I	75	2	2	75	2	2	0	71	94.7	5.3
42-J	73	2	2	73	1	2	0	70	95.9	4.1
42-K	71	2	2	71	0	0	0	71	100.0	
43-A	87	2	2	87	0	1	0	86	98.9	1.1
43-B	96	2	3	95	0	0	0	95	100.0	
43-C	6	3	0	9	1	0	0	8	88.9	11.1
Total	1,328	32	32	1,328	13	43	4 (5)*	1,268	95.5	4.5

*There were five fatalities (only four recorded) at Napier Field during the training of British personnel, as follows:

Class SE-42-B

7 January 1942, twenty-one-year-old LAC Kenneth Barlass of St. Annes-on-Sea, Lancashire, crashed into Lake Tholocco between Ozark and Enterprise, Alabama. LAC Lawrence S. Bell survived with a broken arm after he crashed twenty-eight miles north of Montgomery at 4:00 a.m. and was pulled from the lake by linesmen.

20 January 1942, nineteen-year-old LAC Edgar Hopkin of Gwaun-cae-Gurwen, Glamorgan, Wales. Buried in Montgomery, later moved to Castle View Burial Park, New Castle, Pennsylvania.

Class SE-42-C

7 February 1942, twenty-one-year-old LAC Ronald George Robbins of Horton-cum-Studley, Oxfordshire. Crashed three miles northwest of Tallahassee, Florida.

7 March 1942, twenty-five-year-old LAC Clarence Melville Johnson of Sandal, Wakefield, Yorkshire, was injured in an auto accident near Dothan, Alabama, on 5 March. His class graduated on Friday, 6 March, but CMJ died on Saturday, 7 March, and was buried in Americus on 8 March. Statistics above do not indicate that Johnson was counted among training "fatalities" for Napier Field.

Class SE-42-D

9 April 1942, twenty-one-year-old LAC George Leslie Simpson of Newbiggin-by-the-Sea, Northumberland, crashed in heavily wooded, hilly area near Troy, Alabama.

RAF Pilots Trained at Maxwell Field, Montgomery, Alabama

Class	Original Intake	Held Over Prev.	Held Over to Next	Net Intake	Elim. for Non-flying	Elim. for Flying Deficiency	# of Fatalities	# of Grads	% Grad.	% Elim.
42-A	71	0	3	68	0	0	4	64	94.1	5.9
42-B	70	3	0	73	0	1	0	72	98.6	1.4
42-C	73	0	0	73	0	0	0	73	100.0	0.0
42-D	78	0	1	77	0	0	0	77	100.0	0.0
42-E	80	1	6	75	3	0	1	71	94.7	5.3
42-F	77	6	2*	81	0	4	1	76	93.8	6.2
Total	449	10	10	447	3	5	6**	433	96.9	3.1

*Two members of Class SE-42-F transferred to another advanced school to complete training.

**There were six fatalities at Maxwell Field during the training of British personnel, as follows:

Class SE-42-A

13 November 1941, LAC Frank Victor Marhoff of Bedmond, Hertfordshire, age twenty-nine.

13 November 1941, LAC Richard Norman Moss of Preston, Lancashire, age twenty.

10 December 1941, LAC Peter Greene of Gloucester, age twenty.

13 December 1941, LAC William Joseph Marchant of Shirley, Warwickshire, age eighteen.

Class SE-42-E

20 April 1942, LAC Ronald Arthur Parry of Anfield, Liverpool, age twenty.

Class SE-42-F

17 June 1942, LAC Charles Dean Eaton (U.S. citizen in RAF) of Kirkwood, Missouri, age thirty-two.

RAF Pilots Trained at Turner Field, Albany, Georgia

Class	Original Intake	Held Over Prev.	Held Over to Next	Net Intake	Elim. for Non-flying	Elim. for Flying Deficiency	# of Fatalities	# of Grads	% Grad.	% Elim.
42-A	97	0	5	92	1	0	3	88	95.7	4.3
42-G	89	0	4	85	0	3	2	80	94.1	5.9
42-H	95	4	2	97	3	3	0	91	93.8	6.2
42-I	78	2	2	78	2	2	0	74	94.9	5.1
42-J	73	2	4	71	1	2	0	68	95.8	4.2
42-K	88	4	6	86	0	2	0	84	97.7	2.3
43-A	90	6	3	93	5	4	0	84	90.3	9.7
43-B	75	3	0	78	1	9	0	68	87.2	12.8
Total	685	21	26	680	13	25	5*	637	93.7	6.3

*There were five fatalities at Turner Field during the training of British personnel who were buried in a plot in Crown Hill Cemetery, Albany, Georgia, which was provided by the American Legion. These fatalities are as follows:

Class SE-42-A

17 November 1941, LAC Robert Seymour Wilson of Newcastle-on-Tyne, age twenty.

17 November 1941, LAC Jack Hartley of Woodlesford, Yorkshire, age twenty-four.

29 December 1941, LAC Edward Stanley Headington of Wandsworth Common, London.

Class SE-42-G

15 June 1942, LAC Dennis Hope of Newcastle-on-Tyne, age nineteen.

21 July 1942, LAC Thomas Moseley of Middlesbrough, Yorkshire.

RAF Pilots Trained at Moody Field, Valdosta, Georgia

Class	Original Intake	Held Over Prev.	Held Over to Next	Net Intake	Elim. for Non-flying	Elim. for Flying Deficiency	# of Fatalities	# of Grads	% Grad.	% Elim.
42-G	105	0	3	102	1	3	7	91	89.2	10.8
42-H	125	3	3	125	0	0	0	125	100	0
42-I	78	3	1	80	2	0	0	78	97.5	2.5
42-J	91	1	1	91	3	3	1	84	92.3	7.7
42-K	85	1	0	86	0	6	0	80	93.0	7.0
43-A	91	0	0	91	1	2	1	87	95.6	4.4
43-B	93	0	0	93	1	3	0	89	95.7	4.3
Total	668	8	8	668	8	17	9*	634	94.9	5.1

*There were nine fatalities at Moody Field during the training of British personnel, as follows:

Class SE-42-G

14 July 1942, Cadet Rowland William Holmes of Stonley, Huntingdonshire, age twenty.

14 July 1942, Cadet Bernard Walter Howcroft of Doncaster, Yorkshire, age twenty-two.

14 July 1942, Cadet William Gibson Lamont of Glasgow, Scotland, age twenty.

14 July 1942, Cadet Phillip W. Longbottom of Liverpool and London, age twenty-eight.

14 July 1942, Cadet Sidney Arthur Platt of Leytonstone, London, age nineteen.

14 July 1942, Cadet Ronald Bertram Pinsent of Southgate, London, age twenty-one.

14 July 1942, Cadet Kenward Frederick Stevens of High Wycombe, Bucks, age twenty-one.

Class SE-42-J

19 September 1942, LAC Victor Holman of Margate, Kent, age twenty-three.

Class SE-43-A

29 December 1942, LAC Leslie Herbert Carter of Winchester, Hampshire, age nineteen.

Cumulative Arnold Scheme Statistics

Total Intake: 7,885

Eliminated at Acclimatization Centers: 9

Eliminated at Primary Schools: 2,687

Eliminated at Basic Schools: 526

Eliminated at Advanced Schools: 170

Eliminated Before Solo: 2,187

Eliminated After Solo: 1,205

RAF Cadets Eliminated or Washed Out: 3,392

Posted to Canada to Complete Training: 42

Commissioned: 1,070

Percentage Commissioned: 24.5 percent

RAF Arnold Scheme Pilot Officers Assigned to Duty as Flying Instructors: 577

Arnold Scheme RAF Cadets Killed in Training: 81

Arnold Scheme RAF Instructors Killed: 17 (EFTC: 10, CFTC: 3, WFTC: 4)

RAF Classes that Underwent Advanced Flying Training and Either Returned to the United Kingdom or Were Retained as Instructors

Class		42-A	42-B	42-C	42-D	42-E	42-F	42-G	42-H	42-I	42-J	42-K	43-A	43-B	43-C
Date		3 Nov. 1941	11 Dec. 1941	9 Jan. 1942	20 Feb. 1942	17 March 1942	27 April 1942	20 June 1942	4 July 1942	6 Aug. 1942	3 Sep. 1942	10 Oct. 1942	11 Nov. 1942	14 Dec. 1942	21 Jan. 1943
Intake	T	97						89	99	79	74	92	97	78	
	S	122	157	152	127	171	157	97	108	78	62	76	88	98	4
	M	68	73	73	78	81	83								
	D		90	153	156	164	146	125	105	77	75	73	89	98	9
	V							105	128	81	92	86	91	93	
Held Over	T	5						4	2	1	3	6	4	1	
	S	2	10	6	1	4	2	4	3	4	1	1	4	4	0
	M	0	0	0	1	6	2								
	D			6	2	3	2	2	2	2	2	2	2	3	0
	V							3	3						
Eliminated Before Solo	T	0	1	0	0	0		0	2	0	2	0	3	6	0
	S	0	0	0	0	0	2	0	2	2	2	0	1	1	
	M	0	0	0	0	0	2								
	D		1	1	0	11	1	1	0	2	1	0	1	0	
	V							0	0	0	6	6	0	3	
Eliminated After Solo	T	1	3	3	4	7	1	3	4	4	1	2	6	3	2
	S	1	1	0	0	3	2	0	4	1	0	2	2	2	1
	M	0	1	0	0	3	2								
	D		0	3	10	7	6	4	2	0	2	0	0	0	0
	V							0	0	2	0	0	3	1	1

															Total
Died	T	3						2	0	0	0	0	0	0	5
	S	1	4	2	0	0	1	0	1	2	0	0	0	0	11
	M	4	0	0	1	1	0								6
	D		4	1	1	0	0	0	0	1	0	1	0	0	8
	V							7	0	1	1	0	1	0	10
Graduated	T	88						80	91	74	68	84	84	68	
	S	118	145	141	122	160	151	83	98	69	59	73	81	90	
	M	64	72	73	77	71	76								
	D		83	142	143	143	137	122	101	73	70	71	86	95	
	V							91	125	78	84	80	87	89	
Total Graduated		270	300	356	342	374	364	376	415	294	281	308	338	342	

T=Turner; S=Selma, M=Maxwell, D=Dothan, V=Valdosta

Between June 1941 and July 1942, thirteen courses of Royal Air Force cadets underwent flight training in six Arnold Scheme primary flying schools. Though the training period in each of the schools did not exceed ten weeks, the British cadets made friends easily and were treated like royalty by local citizens. They found a warm welcome in churches of all denominations, and although a majority of them favored Episcopal (Church of England) and Roman Catholic services, they early discovered that the easiest way to meet girls and their families was immediately after church services. Looking lost and lonely, they were invariably invited to Sunday dinner (lunch) and were "adopted" by American families, often for the duration of their training.

The British cadets discovered that their American families enjoyed hearing them talk and were aware of the Battle of Britain, the London Blitz, of Winston Churchill's inspiring addresses, of the brave young pilots who helped to save Britain from invasion by Nazi forces and of the international Bundles for Britain drives. The American families asked questions, encouraged their British friends to talk, showed them around popular local sites, arranged to pick them up at the school entrance during their next time-off period and returned them to the flight school on time. The Camden, South Carolina school enrolled five classes containing RAF cadets; Carlstrom Field at Arcadia, Florida, enrolled eight such classes; and the remaining primary flight schools at Americus and Albany, Georgia, Lakeland, Florida, and Tuscaloosa, Alabama, enrolled thirteen classes each. A total of 7,885 RAF student pilots enrolled in six Arnold Scheme primary flying schools.

The two USAAF basic flying schools that trained British student pilots, Cochran and Gunter Fields, were located near the cities of Macon, Georgia, and Montgomery, Alabama. Each of these larger cities also contained other military bases. Although military uniforms were common in these garrison towns, the polite and gentlemanly conduct of the RAF cadets made them popular with the local citizens. As their schedules permitted, many British cadets made new friends in or near Montgomery or Macon and, as often as possible, they also returned to visit friends in the towns near their primary flight schools. The thirteen RAF classes underwent basic military flying training between August 1941 and October 1942. As an adjunct to their instrument, navigation and night flying experience, British cadets were required to undergo numerous hours in Link Trainer simulators in both basic and advanced flying schools.

The USAAF advanced flying schools were more specialized than either the primary or basic courses, and were designed to provide day, night, formation and instrument flying in either single- or twin-engine aircraft. Single-engine RAF pilot training schools were located in Alabama and included Craig Field near Selma and Napier Field near Dothan. As an important part of their syllabus, pilots in single-engine advanced flying training were posted to Florida to undergo gunnery training.

Owing to a shortage of twin-engine trainers, the six courses trained at Maxwell Field near Montgomery, Alabama, and one course at Turner Field near Albany, Georgia, trained on single-engine aircraft. Maxwell Field was converted to USAAF pre-flight training. Twin-engine schools at Turner Field, Albany, Georgia, and Moody Field at Valdosta, Georgia, were equipped with both single-engine and twin-engine trainers. Following dual flights with an instructor, student pilots in advanced training flew night and day in pairs; that is, one pilot flew as navigator while the other served as pilot, then they changed places as they flew long cross-country and formation flights. Each pilot trainee also spent many hours in the Link Trainer simulator practicing navigation exercises for night flights.

By 1 April 1943, the twenty-fifth anniversary of the founding of the Royal Air Force, 4,370 RAF pilots had graduated from the USAAF advanced flying schools and received certificates and silver USAAF wings. Air Ministry regulations stipulated that one-third of each class could be commissioned as pilot officers (second lieutenants), and the remainder would be graduated as sergeant pilots. As commissions were awarded, RAF officers asked the new pilot officers to volunteer for duty as flight instructors in American flying schools. As a form of reverse Lend-Lease, more than 600 newly commissioned RAF officers served in virtually every USAAF basic and advanced flying school in the United States, and a few pilots served in civil contract primary flying schools.

Commissioned RAF pilots who agreed to serve as instructors for six months first traveled to Toronto, Canada, where they obtained proper dress uniforms and were granted brief leaves in New York before reporting to a USAAF instructors' school. During the six months of their own training and the six to eight months in which they served as flying instructors, many RAF instructors were once more "adopted" by American families, and some of them married American women.

In August 1941, after having completed ten weeks of primary flight training, the first RAF cadets arrived at Cochran Field, Georgia, and Gunter Field, Alabama. They soon found that local citizens were as friendly and hospitable as citizens of towns where they had completed a primary course. In January 1942, Pilot Officer Wallace F. Freshwater (Camden, Macon, Turner) and eighty other members of Class SE-42-A of his class were commissioned pilot officers (second lieutenants), and thirty-four of them agreed to remain in the United States for assignment as flight instructors. In March 1942, following an instructors' course, Freshwater and twenty-five of his classmates returned to Cochran Field as instructors. As officers and flight instructors, they enjoyed the hospitality of Macon and the small town of Fort Valley, Georgia.

Fort Valley, governmental seat of Peach County, is located approximately twenty-eight miles south-southwest of Macon and about fifteen miles southwest of Cochran Field. During 1941–45, Harris Field, one of the auxiliary airfields developed by the basic flying school, was located east of the town. Another auxiliary field lay close to Byron, a tiny community located between Fort Valley and Macon. When RAF instructors were assigned to Cochran Field during the months following March 1942, the city of Macon was crowded with military families from Camp Wheeler and Cochran Field, so accommodation was difficult to find. As a result, many of these young RAF flying instructors found lodgings in Fort Valley.

During late summer and autumn 1941 and the entire year of 1942, Macon and Fort Valley citizens adopted many of the British students and instructors from Cochran Field. During the 1941 Labor Day weekend, two weeks after Class SE-42-A arrived at the basic flying school, a number of Fort Valley ladies invited several RAF cadets to the town. Numerous local families acted as hosts. Between August 1941 and December 1942, Ralph and Henriette Bassett, Jonas and Louise Hillyer and Dr. and Mrs. Frank Vinson "adopted" cadets from each of the thirteen RAF classes and came to know many of the RAF instructors assigned to Cochran Field.

The Bassett family of Pineola Farm, some three miles northwest of Fort Valley, sought out numerous British cadets in order to welcome and entertain them during their stay in Georgia. Ralph P. Bassett, a graduate of the University of Georgia, had served in France as an officer in the United States Army during 1917–19. While stationed in France, he met and married Henriette Bourdier. After the war, Ralph returned with his bride to Fort Valley, where he was an agent of the Metropolitan Life Insurance Company. Ralph was also a partner with his brother, Noble, in the operations of Pineola Farm. Henriette had grown up near Bourges and attended schools there and in Paris. Although she considered herself a Parisienne, she had also attended the Arnold School on Regents Road in Leicester, England, where she learned English.

Other French war brides came to the United States and scattered to a number of different states, pledging to keep in touch with each other. In Georgia, Henriette and Ralph began to convert a rambling old farmhouse into a home. A part of Henriette's natural loneliness was absorbed in homemaking and in giving birth to five daughters. She also maintained contact with several of her "war bride" friends and new friends she developed in her adoptive hometown in Georgia.

Originally named Fox Valley because of the presence of so many foxes in the rolling hills and woodlands of the region, the town reportedly became Fort Valley by accident of misinterpretation of someone's handwriting. During the post–Civil War era, a post office and State Normal School and Mechanical Institute for Negroes were established in the village.

By 1900, Samuel H. Rumph had moved from his native South Carolina to establish Willow Lake Farm at nearby Marshallville where, following lots of hard work and experimentation, he began to produce excellent freestone peaches commercially. He gave the new peach strain his wife's unusual name, Elberta. Rumph's pioneering efforts encouraged others to develop large orchards and new varieties of peaches. From these efforts came the creation of Peach County, with tiny Fort Valley as its governmental seat.

However, since peaches were not selling well, peach trees were replaced by cotton. Then the boll weevil destroyed the cotton and peaches came back again. New strains of peaches, such as R.H. Hiley's Hiley Belle, were developed, and pecan groves were also planted as a supplement to fruit culture. Even though many trainloads of peaches and other crops were shipped out of the county during the 1920s and 1930s, the town and county still did not prosper. These were depression years for American farmers, and small towns dependent on farm populations could not support many businesses, so vacant stores became a standard feature of the community during the lean years extending from 1925 to 1938.

During that latter year and succeeding ones, many changes came to middle Georgia and elsewhere in the nation. The economy shifted, more peaches were being sold at better prices and new businesses moved into vacant shop buildings. The Blue Bird Bus Body Company, builder of school buses, was expanded, a huge milling operation that processed both wheat and corn was established and several new public and commercial buildings were built. In addition, the State Normal School and Mechanical Institute for Negroes was renamed Fort Valley State College. In early March of every year, that institution continued to celebrate a Ham and Egg Festival in conjunction with a Negro Folk Music Festival that was usually presided over by the great W.C. Handy.

In June 1941, Cochran Field and Camp Wheeler military bases opened near Macon, and the gigantic USAAF air depot at Warner Robins Field followed soon thereafter. The number of aircraft flying over the area increased phenomenally and, as these defense installations expanded, many new people sought houses and apartments in Fort Valley. Between August 1941 and December 1942, Royal Air Force student pilots arrived at Cochran Field every five weeks. Since Henriette Bassett knew loneliness and the problems of adjusting to a different culture, her heart went out to the British boys who came to the airfield some eighteen miles away. She was prominent among the group of ladies who invited the first group of RAF cadets to Fort Valley for the Labor Day weekend. And when they arrived in small groups aboard the huge army trucks, it was she who always asked to meet any young men from Leicester, where she had attended school many years before.

Pineola Farm, the Bassett family home, was an enchanting place to the RAF boys, especially to those who had grown up in an urban environment. The Bassett daughters were young and attractive flirts, and the rambling old L-shaped house was comfortable and homey. One entered from a driveway with pine trees scattered about. Porches virtually surrounded the house, at least across the front and halfway down each side. At ground level, shrubbery and flowers were cultivated in a broad band along the porch, and in one section vines climbed a trellis to ward off the direct rays of the sun.

The continuous porch was under a roof and contained a number of rocking chairs, and on one end a porch swing was supported by chains attached to the ceiling. Other contiguous screened porches completed the outside of the huge house. Pineola Farm encompassed more than one thousand acres of land and was almost completely self-sufficient. For home use, the farm produced vegetables, chickens and eggs, pork, grain for flour and cornmeal, pear and fig trees and many pecan trees. Its fields produced hay, oats, corn and other feed for farm animals.

Life was good at Pineola Farm and in the nearby small town, and the added six hundred hours of flying were not only valuable additional experience for the RAF instructors, but were fun as well. Royal Air Force student pilots and flight instructors at USAAF basic and advanced flying schools were fascinated with the beauty and the soft, lovely drawls of Southern girls, and some RAF men married American girls from Georgia and Alabama.

On 15 August 1942, a year after he first arrived at Cochran Field as a student pilot, Pilot Officer Wallace F. Freshwater of Brewood, Staffordshire, and Class SE-42-A (Camden, Macon, Turner) and Virginia Wright were married in the Fort Valley Methodist Church. Following a day of flying instruction, Wally and other RAF instructors who lived in Fort Valley often persuaded colleagues or students to drop them off at Harris Auxiliary Field, where their wives or girlfriends would meet them and drive them home. For the remainder of his instructional assignment, Wally and Virginia lived in an apartment on Church Street.

In spring 1943, when Wallace completed his instructional assignment at Cochran Field, Virginia followed him to Moncton, New Brunswick, Canada. Later, Virginia boarded the *Tamaroa* in New York and traveled to Britain with seven other American war brides. While in the United Kingdom, Virginia and the other brides were compelled to take some kind of employment or serve in the forces. Some of them joined the Women's Auxiliary Air Force (WAAF) while others took office jobs or employment with the Red Cross or war industries. Virginia lived at Wally's home in Brewood, Staffordshire, and worked as a cost accountant in a nearby munitions plant. Following duty assignments in RAF squadrons in Britain, Wally Freshwater was posted to India-

Burma, and in 1946, Virginia returned to Fort Valley to await his release from the Royal Air Force. In 1947, Squadron Leader (Major) Freshwater rejoined his wife in Fort Valley, where they made their home until Virginia's death in 1983. Ultimately, Wallace Freshwater returned to England and made his home in Staffordshire.

In September 1942, Jeanne Cousins of Macon married Pilot Officer Terence Parry of London and Class SE-42-B (Camden, Macon, Selma). Terence served as a flight instructor at Cochran and Turner Fields. Jeanne traveled to Britain aboard the *Tamaroa* and remained there until her husband completed his military service. The young couple came back to Atlanta, Georgia, and engaged in the antique business. Ultimately, they divorced; Jeanne returned to Macon, Georgia, and Terence moved back to England.

On 12 May 1943, Helen Florence Whiting of Camilla, Georgia, married George Allan Findley of Comrie, Perthshire, Scotland, and USAAF flying base at Bainbridge, Georgia. Following service in Australia and the United Kingdom, George Findlay completed his military obligation and immigrated to Georgia in 1946. Engaged in business in Albany, the couple eventually moved to Atlanta, Georgia.

On 23 October 1942, Elizabeth Shaw of Madison, Florida, married Pilot Officer John H. Bracewell of Lancashire and Class SE-42-C (Camden, Macon, Dothan). Bracewell instructed at Cochran and Turner Fields. On returning to the United Kingdom, Bracewell served in Bomber Command with distinction. Sadly, he and his crew were killed in action in 1944 over Berlin and were buried in the British War Cemetery in Berlin's Charlottenburg District. Elizabeth traveled to the United Kingdom aboard the *Tamaroa*, served in the WAAF during the war and returned to the United States in 1946. Elizabeth ultimately remarried.

Jean Ridgely of Lakeland, Florida, married Pilot Officer Kenneth R. Waugh of Sao Paulo, Brazil, and Class SE-42-C (Lakeland, Gunter, Maxwell). Waugh served as a check pilot at the primary flying school at Lakeland, Florida. Jean, an attractive brunette, traveled to England aboard the *Tamaroa* with other RAF wives and joined the WAAF. When Kenneth was killed in action during a March 1944 Bomber Command raid on Munich, Jean was expecting their first child, so she was discharged from the WAAF and returned to the United States in 1944.

Eleanor Anne Hotchkiss of Hawkinsville, Georgia, married Pilot Officer Eric John Holman of Essex, England, on 28 October 1942 in New York City. Holman, who had served as a flight instructor at Cochran Field, had been posted to Canada, so the wedding took place in New York.

Rosa Wadley of Macon, Georgia, married Pilot Officer Francis W. Savage of Birmingham, England, and Class SE-42-E (Americus, Macon, Maxwell). Frank served as an instructor at Cochran Field, and on returning to the United Kingdom he built a distinguished record with RAF Bomber Command. During the postwar period, Frank immigrated to the United States and the young couple made their home in Macon for a time, but ultimately relocated to Atlanta. Frank worked for the Amoco Oil Company.

Emma Jean Harmon of Wetumpka, Alabama, married John Clark of Thornton Heath, Croydon, Surrey, and Class SE-42-E (Albany, Gunter, Maxwell) on 30 October 1942. John served as a flight instructor at Gunter Field and Jean worked as a bookkeeper in the engineer's office at Maxwell Field. John's abilities as a flight instructor brought assignment in that same capacity back in the United Kingdom. Jean sailed to Britain aboard the *Tamaroa* and joined John. She served with the American Red Cross at a number of locations.

Adele Hall, a tall, attractive brunette of Montgomery, Alabama, married Pilot Officer Alan Paul Garsed of Argentina and Class SE-42-E (Lakeland, Gunter, Maxwell) on 9 August 1942 at St. Peter's Roman Catholic Church in Montgomery. Garsed served as a flight instructor at Gunter Field, and returned to the United Kingdom for war service. Adele H. Garsed traveled to Britain with seven other American war brides aboard the *Tamaroa*. Subsequently, Garsed immigrated to the United States, and the couple made their home in Mobile, Alabama, until Paul's death in 1981. Nothing further is known.

Louise Pound married Pilot Officer Walter Ronald Bloor of Litchfield, Staffordshire, and Class SE-42-F (Carlstrom, Macon, Dothan). Bloor served as a flight instructor at Cochran Field. Louise traveled to the United Kingdom aboard the *Tamaroa*, served for a while in the WAAF and returned to the United States. Following his RAF service, Ron immigrated to the United States and the family made their home in Macon, Georgia.

Mary Clemon Daniel of Manchester, Tennessee, married Pilot Officer Denis Harry Payne of Aldershot, Hampshire, and Class SE-42-E (Americus, Macon, Dothan). Payne had attended the RAF Technical College at Halton before enrolling in flight training, and after graduating at Dothan he served as a flight instructor at Cochran Field. Mary C. Payne traveled to Britain with seven other American war brides aboard the *Tamaroa*. On returning to the United Kingdom, Denis flew numerous missions from Britain and Southeast Asia. When his term of service ended, he immigrated to the United States and he and his family made their home in Atlanta. Payne served in the British Foreign Service.

On 6 December 1942, Frances M. Duncan married Pilot Officer John Bryce Paterson of Lanarkshire, Scotland, and Moody Field, Georgia. Frances traveled to the United Kingdom aboard the *Tamaroa*. Nothing further is known.

Geraldene Frances Montgomery of Nashville, Tennessee, married Pilot Officer John Clay Stedman of Carlisle, England, and Turner Field. Their engagement and marriage announcement were in the news. Nothing further is known.

Eve Madeleine Strickland was engaged to marry Pilot Offiver Stanley E. Miller of London and Shaw Field, South Carolina. Their engagement announcement appeared in news. Nothing further is known.

Philip G. Penfold of London and Class SE-42-F (Lakeland, Macon, Dothan) served as an instructor at Cochran Field. Later, he married a girl from upstate New York and Clearwater, Florida. Following wartime RAF service, Philip immigrated to the United States and made his home in New York state.

In September 1945, Mary Elizabeth Quinn of Mississippi arrived in the United Kingdom aboard the *Mauretania* to marry Flight Lieutenant Gibson of Rathmines, Dublin, Eire.

Peggy Green of Montgomery, Alabama, formerly of New Jersey, married Ronald Slade-Betts of Bromley, Kent, and Class SE-42F (Tuscaloosa, Gunter, Selma). Slade-Betts served as a flight instructor at Craig Field, Selma, Alabama.

Margaret Sloss of Birmingham, Alabama, married Ian W. Sturrock of Kilmarnock, Scotland, and Class SE-42-D (Tuscaloosa, Gunter, Selma). Sturrock served as a flight instructor at Gunter Field.

Erwin Joseph Lischke of Czechoslovakia and Class SE-42-C (Lakeland, Gunter, Selma) married a girl from Montgomery. Lischke served as a flight instructor at Gunter Field.

Victor E. Hewes of Leicester and Class SE-42-H (Carlstrom, Macon, Dothan) served as a flight instructor at Cochran Field and married a girl from Fort Valley, Georgia.

Lucy Moore of Sumter, South Carolina, married Peter C. Aspinall of Purley, Surrey, and Class SE-42-I (Lakeland, Gunter, Selma). Peter served as a flight instructor at Shaw Field, South Carolina.

Richard N. Goodwin of Class SE-42-I served as a flight instructor at Greenville, Mississippi, and married a Mississippi girl. He returned to Greenville postwar.

Alfred Massheder of Rawdon, Leeds, England, and Class SE-42-H served as a flight instructor at Greenville, Mississippi, and married a Mississippi girl, Frances Burton, on 27 February 1943. In July 1943, Frances sailed to Britain aboard the SS *Erin*. While her husband continued service in the RAF, Frances lived with him. In late 1945 or early 1946, their first child was born, and in April 1946 she sailed back to the United States aboard SS *Bayano*. Alfred later returned to the United States, and the family made their home in McKinney, Texas, later Richardson, Texas.

William A. Woodruff of London and Class SE-42-I (Tuscaloosa, Gunter, Selma) served as a flight instructor at Bainbridge, Georgia. He married a girl from Birmingham, Alabama, in 1963 and was a professor of psychiatry (Emeritus) at the University of Vermont.

Victor H. "Johnny" Johnson of Birmingham and Class SE-42H (Tuscaloosa, Gunter, Selma) married a girl from Birmingham, Alabama.

Ian Trotter of Class SE-42-H married a girl from Montgomery, Alabama.

On 29 October 1945, Edith Winsper of Fairfield, Alabama, married Lionel Harry Smart (Albany, Gunter, Selma) of Harrow Weald, Middlesex, England. Smart, of 41 Squadron, had lost a leg in a 1945 crash of his Spitfire and was demobilized with disability. Harry was trained as a teacher and served at a number of schools. The young couple immigrated to Canada for a time, but ultimately returned to England.

In 1946, Sue Stripling of Macon, Georgia, married George T. Shaw. Pilot Officer Shaw served as a flight instructor at Cochran Field. Back in the United Kingdom, he underwent further training and served in North Africa and Italy. After the war, George immigrated to the United States and the young couple made their home in Macon, Georgia.

Sallie Burns Deese of Camden, South Carolina, married Herbert John Patrick Cattrall of Kandy, Ceylon, and Class SE-42-B (Camden, Macon, Dothan) in the early 1990s.

Lucy Laney of Arikton, Alabama, married Ronald Raffels of Class SE-42-F (Tuscaloosa). Raffels washed out of pilot training and was trained as a bomb aimer in Canada. Before returning to the United Kingdom, he and Lucy were married. Lucy traveled to Britain in 1944 and worked there until Ronald was demobilized. The young couple returned to the United States in 1946 and made their home in Alabama. Ronald died circa 1984.

William Webber of Class SE-42-I returned to the United States after the war, married and later became an architect in Tampa, Florida.

Paul Weiss of Class SE-42-I returned to Montgomery, Alabama, married and made his home there.

Al Bernens of Class SE-42-I returned to Montgomery, Alabama, married and made his home there.

Thomas Nelson of Class 42-5, Pan American Airways Navigation Section, University of Miami, Coral Gables, Florida, and Patricia Ann Moss of Columbus, Ohio, were married in September 1953.

JEAN HARMON CLARK
AN AMERICAN WAR BRIDE IN ENGLAND

Between 7 June 1941 and 26 March 1943, Arnold Scheme primary flying schools enrolled 7,885 British cadets and graduated 4,370 pilots from five USAAF advanced flying schools. The citizens of each American town or city treated RAF cadets like royalty. The fabled Southern hospitality knew no bounds; friendliness, kindness, generosity and hospitality to the young fliers were common attributes of American citizens who encountered RAF cadets. And the young Brits recalled their American experiences as the best times in their lives.

John Clark of Thornton Heath near Croydon, Surrey, was a member of Class SE-42-E, the fifth of thirteen RAF classes in the Arnold Scheme. The first four classes had been transported across the North Atlantic to Halifax, Nova Scotia, and entrained there for a thirty-hour train ride through the beautiful Maritime provinces to Toronto, Ontario. After processing and being issued temporary U.S. visas, they were divided into six separate drafts and entrained for direct rail travel to their assigned primary schools. John Clark's huge draft of about 1,100 men also traveled by ship to Halifax, Nova Scotia, and by train to Toronto, Ontario, but after being processed the entire draft boarded rail cars once more. Their train traveled through Detroit, Cincinnati, Nashville and Chattanooga to Montgomery, Alabama.

There at Maxwell Field they underwent four weeks of acclimatization training, the purpose of which was to prepare them for the long and rugged schedules in the flying training program. The American system of pilot training emphasized military, academic, physical and flight training. British cadets in each phase of flight training were fed extremely well, underwent calisthenics and other physical exercises, drilled American style, attended classes in American history and aircraft and ship identification and played games. Most of the RAF cadets were anxious to get on with their main purpose—flying training—and John was not an exception.

After the four weeks at Maxwell Field, the large RAF draft was divided and shipped to six primary flying schools. With more than one hundred other RAF leading aircraftsmen (LACs), John was posted to Darr Aero Tech at Albany, Georgia, and there he underwent sixty hours of flying instruction in a Stearman (Boeing) PT-17 biplane. After ten weeks at Albany, John and most of his fellow successful cadets were posted to Gunter Field near Montgomery, Alabama. At that crowded station, they flew Vultee BT-13 aircraft—a low-wing monoplane with fixed undercarriage, radio, a 450-horsepower radial engine and a dual-pitch propeller. John enjoyed flying that more demanding aircraft, and he successfully completed the course on schedule, despite flying seven days per week, a regimen that was introduced after the Japanese attack on Pearl Harbor and U.S. active entry into the war.

Upon graduation from basic flying, John was posted to nearby Maxwell Field for his advanced flying training course on North American AT-6A aircraft. The Harvard, as the British called it, was a superb metal-clad monoplane trainer that was equipped with a 650-horsepower radial engine, variable pitch propeller, radio and retractable landing gear. The Harvard, despite engine noise, was a dream to fly—just like a fighter plane. In March 1942, while undergoing the nine-week flying course at Maxwell Field, John met Emma Jean Harmon, a civil service employee. On 16 May 1942, John completed advanced flying training at Maxwell Field and was commissioned pilot officer (second lieutenant).

After a brief rail journey to Toronto, Canada, where he received properly tailored RAF uniforms, John returned to Montgomery for an instructors' course before reporting to nearby Gunter Field for a nine-month-long flying instructor assignment. John and Jean saw each other regularly during the following months, and on receipt of parental and RAF permission, John and Jean married on 30 October 1942 at the Cloverdale Baptist Church in Montgomery, Alabama.

Shortly after the new year, the young couple learned that Jean, as the wife of a British serviceman, could travel to Britain under the guidelines that had been devised by the Ministry of Labor and National Service for the Overseas Manpower Committee. In April 1943, John completed his tour of instructional duty and was posted to RAF No. 31 Personnel Dispersal

Center (PDC) at Moncton, New Brunswick, to await assignment to a transport from Halifax, Nova Scotia, to Great Britain. In the meantime, Jean's application unexpectedly moved swiftly through channels.

Instead of having to wait four to six months, as she had been told earlier, Jean received a telegram on Saturday, 17 April, telling her to report to the British Volunteer Movement Group in New York on Wednesday, 21 April. On Monday, Jean resigned her job and got an income tax clearance. She said farewell to her parents on Tuesday and, with a friend who had married another RAF officer, departed on a rail coach for New York on Wednesday. After an eighteen-hour journey, they arrived at Pennsylvania Station in New York City and, with their required limited amount of luggage, checked in at the Spelman Hall YWCA. Major Montgomery, a British army officer in charge of the volunteer group, was very helpful and informed them that there were eight war brides en route to Britain.

Jean Harmon Clark's narrative follows:

> The 8 of us were given instructions and were assigned to His Majesty's Armed Merchant Cruiser (AMC) Tamaroa, a 12,275-ton cargo ship, which had transported goods to and from New Zealand. We were informed that the vessel was scheduled to embark from New York's Pier 97 on Friday, 23 April 1943. We two brides from Alabama sent our husbands in Canada a telegram telling them when we were leaving, only to have the telegrams returned with the message that the addressees were en route to New York. For security reasons, we had to be careful not to discuss with anyone where we were going. As advised, we put the address of the pier and a note in a sealed envelope, took it to Grand Central Station, asked a porter to deliver the envelope to two RAF officers, tipped him generously, and prayed that we would get to see our husbands before sailing.
>
> When we returned from Grand Central Station, Pier 97 was extremely busy. Stevedores were rushing about, hundreds of troops and other passengers were lined up and boarding the ship. Major Montgomery was anxious to get us aboard, and finally, after much concern, our husbands arrived, and we were able to spend about 35 minutes with them before being rushed aboard the Tamaroa to our assigned 4-person cabins. Among the passengers were a large number of American officers and men, a few British and Canadian citizens, 5 or 6 Canadian women transport pilots, and several Dutch airmen who had been trained in the United States. Guy Della-Ciappa, who later produced the Red Skelton Show, was one passenger known to have gained fame.
>
> The Tamaroa, a 12,375-ton ship of the Shaw, Saville, and Albion Line, normally carried cargoes of food and a complement of passengers between New Zealand and Britain. Between 20 April and 29 May 1941, Captain W. Dawson commanded the Tamaroa, and it crossed the North Atlantic eastbound from Auckland, New Zealand via the Panama Canal to Britain. The Tamaroa shared the good fortune of a westbound ship, the HMS Britannic. Both ships carried aircrew ultimately destined to undergo training in the United States, and both managed to avoid being caught up in the clash between the Royal Navy and the German warship, Bismark. HMS Britannic later disembarked several hundred RAF aircrew volunteers in Halifax, Nova Scotia, destined for pilot training in the United States and Canada.
>
> The Tamaroa delivered 70 Royal New Zealand Fleet Air Arm aircrew volunteers and tons of much needed meat, butter, and cheese. The New Zealand aircrew volunteers

would be later transported to the United States for training in the U.S. Navy's Towers Scheme. Aware that the British Admiralty would seize the Tamaroa *and convert it into a transport, Captain Dawson hosted a farewell dinner on 28 May 1941, before his ship docked and the passengers disembarked. The menu was one of the most imaginative to appear aboard any ship during World War II, and was provided by New Zealand student pilots, Gordon Waite and John Sisley of the Royal New Zealand Fleet Air Arm, who were destined to be trained in the United States under the Towers Scheme.*

Under the listing of soups, diners read a quotation from Alice in Wonderland, *"Soup of the evening, beautiful soup"; The fish generated a quotation from Shakespeare's* Timon of Athens, *"there's no meat like them; I could wish my best friend at such a feast"; Sweetbreads and braised onions elicited a quotation from Shakespeare's* Henry IV, *"The daintiest that they taste"; The meat course of roast beef, ham, veal, and turkey prompted a quotation from Shakespeare's* Romeo and Juliet, *"Look to the baked meats, good Angelica; spare not the cost"; The cold buffet brought forth a quotation from Milton's* Paradise Lost, *"A table richly spread in regal modes, with dishes piled, and meats of noblest sort and savour"; Sweets generated an appropriate "a surfeit of the sweetest things" from Shakespeare's* A Midsummer Night's Dream; *and finally, the poetic steward ended with coffee and dessert and a quotation from Alexander Pope, "Coffee which makes the politician wise, and see through all things with half-closed eyes."*

After the Tamaroa *was unloaded, its refrigerated holds were removed, and it was re-fitted as a full-fledged troop transport, classified as an armed merchant cruiser. The* Tamaroa, *her crew British merchant seamen, and her deck guns manned by Royal Navy gunners, continued her wartime service. On Saturday, 24 April 1943, early in the morning, she sailed out of the New York harbor and joined a large convoy of 40 or 50 ships. As we sailed past the Statue of Liberty, passengers came out of their cabins to view the symbolic monument. The American war brides were told that the army colonel in charge of the troops did not like having women aboard ship, so we tried to stay out of his way. We did as we were instructed, wearing our life jackets constantly and practicing lifeboat drills. Since I was very seasick, I stayed on deck a good bit.*

After a few days, the passengers were called together and told to be alert as the ship was entering very dangerous waters. One day, at an unusual time, the gunnery crews began firing their guns. When we peeped out of our cabin, the destroyers and cutters serving as escort ships were dashing around, and the whole convoy was in a straight line. Normally, they would be scattered far ahead and to the right and left. Later, we were told that our convoy moved into single file so that, if a Nazi U-boat fired a torpedo and missed one ship, it would not hit another. That period at sea was scary, but we didn't lose any ships.

On 8 May 1943 at midnight, 16 days out of New York, we docked at Avonmouth in the Bristol Channel. Everyone remained aboard ship for the night and disembarked the next day onto the docks of Bristol. We told our friends, good-bye. It was sad to see the American troops leave. It was good to be on land once more; the date was 9 May 1943, Mothers Day, and we were assigned to a hostel in Bristol. After settling in with our luggage, we went to use the telephone. Since we had never met, I was very nervous about calling John's father, so I let several people use the phone ahead of me. Finally, I got the courage and asked the operator to connect me with Thornton Heath 2646.

When John's father answered, I told him "this is Jean; is John there?" He was as shocked as I was scared. He said "no" and asked me where I was. I told him that we were in Bristol and would leave the next morning. He very kindly sent telegrams to my parents and to John that we had arrived safely. Since it was light until about 10 p.m., we walked around Bristol and saw lots of signs of bomb damage—vacant lots covered in rubble, bombed out churches and shops. Next morning, we boarded a train for London. We enjoyed the scenery, the changes in the countryside, hedgerows, lovely villages, trees, green grass, shrubbery, barrage balloons over towns, and the different architecture. Even from the windows of the train, the ancient city of Bath was enchanting.

We had been told to look for a woman with a WVS (Women's Volunteer Service) arm badge when we arrived in London. All of us were looking for the woman when one of the girls pointed out, "There is someone looking at us." When I looked, Dad came near us and said "Jean." I said, "I am" because John looked so much like him, and there were 3 Jeans in our group. He got permission from the lady in charge for me to ride with him in a taxi to the Ministry of Labor where I could complete some documents and obtain an identity card. I was also issued a gas mask, a metal helmet, a fire-watcher's badge, and food and clothing ration books.

John's father got permission for me to go home with him and his wife to Thornton Heath, about 10 miles south of London near Croydon, and come back next day. (John's mother died while he was in America, and his father had remarried; his new wife was so nice and helpful to me when I first got there.) As we got off the bus in Thornton Heath, the all-clear sirens were going. The first thing we did was to put up the blackout curtains. Before dark, houses had to be blacked-out. The curtains ensured that lights could not be seen by enemy aircraft or passersby. Air raid wardens would always check every house from the outside to be sure no light was showing. If going out at night, we used pencil flashlights always held straight down.

Next day, a very cold 11 May, we were back in London getting all of my documentation completed. The only clothing I had was a lightweight spring suit, so Dad, who was a tailor, said he would make me a heavier costume (suit). We saw the girls and after tearful "good byes," we parted. All of the other girls' husbands were already in England, most of them flying missions. Two of my friends joined the WAAFs (Women's Auxiliary Air Force). Sadly, I never saw some of them again.

I reported to offices of the Croydon Ministry of Labor and was told that I would not have to worry about a job until after my husband arrived. Dad took me to meet friends and John's mother's family. They had a butcher shop, and the practice of openly hanging meat up inside the shop was strange to me. Every night, the Germans came. At first, we could hear the guns firing and bombs exploding. When the shrapnel became heavy, we usually got under the stairs. If we had fire-watching duty, we had to go outside. Dad usually took my turn.

Everyone was anxious for John's arrival. The first night I was home, one of John's school friends came by and appeared shocked to meet John's wife. On 24 May, John's transport docked in Liverpool, and we were all delighted that he had arrived safely. He reported to the Aircrew Receiving Center at Harrogate, North Yorkshire and finally arrived home on 28 May. Seven days leave time passed much too rapidly, and John left for an assigned Advance Flying Unit to complete familiarization and conversion training to fly twin-engine aircraft. He told me that on completion of that course, he would be assigned as an instructor for 6 months.

The Thornton Heath village greens and parks had anti-aircraft gun emplacements, usually manned by women gunnery crews. At night, we could go out and see the German aircraft in the searchlights. For a time, it was a nightly ordeal, and when all guns were firing tracer shells, it would look like sheets of flame. The noise was frightening! Finally, the all clear would sound and we would go back to bed. My first job assignment was in the office of the nearby Redwing Aircraft Company. I enjoyed working with the 3 other women there, even though they laughed at my accent. One afternoon, I heard a loud bell ringing; everyone picked up their purses and started out. I asked, "What's wrong?" They said, "Enemy aircraft overhead," so I grabbed my purse and followed.

The guns were firing, and a plane came in under cloud cover and dropped several bombs on the neighborhood. As soon as the "all clear" sounded, we started home. I met Dad as he was coming to get me. He knew I was going to be scared, so he was going in and out of doorways to miss the shrapnel as he was coming to escort me home. Since John would soon finish his AFU course, I decided to seek employment that would allow me to move from place to place with him. On 3 August, I went to the American Red Cross Personnel Office in London's Grosvenor Square and applied for a job with them.

On 15 September, I went to work as a civilian in the Office of Home Service and Communication. We handled cables to and from American families and American servicemen. I found it easy to travel by train from Thornton Heath to Victoria Station. In the fall, our office moved to 3 Princess Gate in Knightsbridge, and I would ride a bus there from Victoria Station. Getting home after dark presented special problems. At that latitude, it began to get dark at about 4:00 p.m. All street lights had cap covers on them with only a dim cross of light showing, and all buses and trains had very small hooded lights. Aboard the trains, the blackout curtains were closed and porters would call out the stations, so passengers quickly learned to recognize their stops. Everyone rushed on and off trains and buses, and there was very little talking.

Until his unit moved to the continent after D-Day, my brother, Tom, who was serving with the 130th Station Hospital in Wiltshire, was able to get a pass to visit me in Thornton Heath. Just before Christmas 1943 John moved to RAF Weston-on-the-Green, near Oxford. On learning that, I discovered that the Red Cross could transfer me to the 2nd General Hospital in Headington, Oxfordshire; I also learned that I could eat lunch daily in the officer's mess. Americans made up the hospital's Red Cross staff, and they did not understand about food rations in Britain.

Although rations changed slightly during the war, as a British subject, my normal weekly ration was: sweets (candy) 12 oz.; lard 4 oz.; butter 2 oz.; sugar 8 oz.; egg 1; bacon or ham 4 oz.; cheese 2 oz.; milk 2 pints; and tea 2 oz. Depending on the cut you got, meat was so many pence, but you could get cheese instead of meat. Kidneys, hearts, etc. were not rationed, nor were potatoes, vegetables, and bread. Coal used for heat, clothing and furniture were sold by use of coupons, if you could find any.

John got us rooms in Islip, a lovely old village about 5 miles from Oxford. Islip was listed in the Domesday Book, and our cottage was called "The Barn." In the 17th century, it had been a barn, and had been made into a nice two-story cottage with old beams in the ceiling. We had a very happy time there—no air raids. Rupert ("Ru") was in the Observer Corps, and had to go once a week at night to chart air raids. I think we had one alert. In our spare time, we would hunt mushrooms and firewood (sticks, dead limbs, etc.) to supplement our coal ration. The baker and milkman delivered their goods to the house regularly.

Living in the house with us were Rupert and Elizabeth Crisp, and their 3-year-old son Anthony. John and I had a bedroom, sitting room, and shared the kitchen and bath. After I had used my whole week's ration of butter right away, Elizabeth tried to teach me to manage my cooking. We ate together lots of times. I would ride to Oxford with "Ru" when he went to work, catch a bus to the hospital, and ride the train home to Islip. Everyone had apple and plum trees in their gardens (yards) and plots of land (allotments) usually located elsewhere in which to grow vegetables. We went to live with them on 1 January 1944, and they remained wonderful friends until they passed away in the 1980s and 1990s.

From Oxford, John transferred to RAF Wymeswold near Loughborough, Leicestershire as an instructor on a B.A.T. Flight (training pilots on instruments for blind flying). I stayed with Elizabeth and continued to work with the Red Cross. In preparation for the invasion, D-Day, 6 June 1944, the 2nd General Hospital was transferred and replaced by the 91st General Hospital, and I continued to work with their Red Cross staff at Headington. By May 1944, John found accommodations with an elderly lady in Loughborough. Through the Ministry of Labor, I transferred with the Red Cross and was assigned with Evelyn Stevens to the 505th Airborne Infantry Regiment of the 82nd Airborne Division at Quorn, an estate nearby.

Evelyn and I were doughnut girls, and had an office in what had been the Quorn Hunt Stables from which the estate had launched fox hunts. Many of the paratroopers had seen action in North Africa, Sicily, Italy, and Normandy. When I went to work there, some of them were just returning from Normandy. Injured paratroopers who could no longer jump from aircraft cooked the doughnuts. The paratroopers were good to us and called Evelyn "Steve" and me "Bama."

Finally, during the summer of 1944, John and I were able to have a holiday at St. Arvans in Monmouthshire. We had a wonderful week, visiting ruins (Tintern Abbey) and the hills and valleys of the River Wye. After so many months with limited food, we didn't mind the same food every day—fresh salmon, English peas, and new potatoes. Too soon, we returned to our jobs in Loughborough. In the meantime, two of the girls with whom I had traveled to England had lost their husbands on air operations. Jean [Ridgely Waugh], whose husband was a pathfinder, went missing in a bombing raid on Munich, and Elizabeth's husband went missing in a bomber raid on Berlin. Since Jean found out that she was expecting a baby, she was allowed to return to her home in Florida. We hoped that both pilots had been taken prisoners of war, but later reports indicated that both of them had been killed. Elizabeth [Shaw Bracewell] had to stay in Britain until after the war.

In September, the 82nd Airborne Division was alerted for "Operation Market Garden." One morning, Evelyn and I watched our paratroopers leave in full gear. We had gotten to know so many of them. It was so sad to see them go, knowing that they were jumping in Holland and that some would be killed. With their departure, our job at Quorn ended.

John and I moved into the home of Violet Graves and her 9-year-old daughter, Ann. Violet's husband was a prisoner of war in Germany. We lived with them 2 months, and *it was pleasant living with a young girl and her mother. In November 1944, John was transferred to Little Rissington and was assigned to fly from RAF Windrush, an airfield located between Burford and Northleach, Gloucestershire. John obtained rooms for us in a cottage with the White family in the village of Eastington. When we were moving to Eastington from Loughborough, we met Flight Lieutenant Jack Frost in the rail station at Derby. Jack, who had trained and instructed at Gunter with John, was en route home on leave. That very morning he had flown a fighter sweep over Holland and had witnessed the death of John Heap, one of John's schoolmates. Heap was killed when his damaged aircraft overshot the runway and crashed. We were very upset.*

The Whites were farmers, and they had a row cottage of stone with stone floors and very thick walls, no electricity, no running water, oil stove and lighting by candles and oil lamps. Water came from the village pump. The nearest shop was 2 miles away, the bus stop was one mile. Each day, John cycled 7 miles to and from his flying duties. Louise and Ron Bloor lived in the same village, and it was great to be with one of the girls who came over with me. She had been in the WAAF and had a baby girl, so she was discharged. We had many laughs about our trips to the shops to buy our rations, walking the 2 miles there and back with our small baskets of groceries. The Whites had cows and chickens, so we got a little extra milk and vegetables. We had moved to Eastington in winter with lots of snow and very cold weather.

Adele and Alan Garsed were living in another village close by, so we could visit each other. This area was in the Cotswolds, beautiful country, stone walls around everything, and lots of sheep. Alan was also a flight instructor. Adele was from Montgomery, and we had traveled from there to Bristol. She and Alan had a baby girl. We spent Christmas 1944 in Eastington, and John's Dad and Violet spent the holiday with us. He was surprised at our primitive place, but we all had a very good time.

At that point the war was really bad. The "Battle of the Bulge" was under way, and fighting in Europe was heavy. Allied bombers escorted by long range fighters continued to attack enemy factories, rail lines, military targets, and cities in Europe. We followed the war closely and felt that the Allies were winning the war, so we were happy. I worried about my brother, Tom, whose hospital unit moved through France and Germany, as Allied forces advanced. In the spring of 1945, the war appeared to be coming slowly to an end, and we listened to our battery radio faithfully. V.E. Day came in May 1945, and we waited for news of my friend, Elizabeth's missing husband, but he did not come home. After several months, Elizabeth returned to Georgia to rebuild her life.

Even before the Japanese surrendered in August 1945, RAF officials recognized that they had too many pilots. In July 1945 John was declared redundant and on his final RAF flight, he buzzed our little village and frightened some of our neighbors. In August 1945, we left Eastington and while John attended RAF Accounting School in Hereford, I lived with Elizabeth and Rupert Crisp at Islip, Oxfordshire. Elizabeth had a baby girl, Clare, and her son, Anthony, was 5, so I was a big help to her. In late November, when John's accounting course was finished, he was transferred to RAF Earl's Colne near Colchester, Essex. We were able to obtain rooms in Colchester with the Cranmers and their 5-year-old daughter, Susan. We enjoyed our time with them.

When John got leave, we would visit Dad, and our aunt and uncle in Streatham, Cambridgeshire. I spent lots of time with them, and we had lots of fun. Uncle Geof and

Aunt Dorie had a shop, village post office, and telephone exchange. I would often help in the post office and telephone exchange, but I'm afraid that some of the customers had problems with my southern accent. When I said, "the line is busy" they didn't know what I meant. They were accustomed to "the line is engaged." Uncle Geof would laugh and say that it was his American niece.

Just as we were celebrating VE Day, we learned that our uncle and aunt's only child, Richard, had been killed two days after VE Day. Richard was serving in the RAF Medical Corps and had spent 3 years in North Africa and Italy. He had flown to Venice with a pilot in order to get medical supplies, and while they were taking pictures, they crashed into a canal. Richard had married just before he left and was due home in August. His wife, Olive, came to stay with us at Eastington shortly afterward.

We also spent a good bit of time with Kitty and Percy Hewitt in Norwood, Surrey. They were like my parents. Kitty and I loved to go to London looking; we didn't do much shopping as everything was still rationed. Just before Christmas 1945, I went to Elizabeth and Rupert's. John came later. We were worried as I was supposed to get a hen from the Whites in Eastington for Christmas dinner, but they were all stolen. Our Christmas feast looked dim, but Rupert was able to get a hen, and someone in the RAF flew to Ireland and brought back a large number of frozen turkeys. John called from Oxford and said that he had obtained a turkey weighing 16 pounds.

Since John did not want to bring the turkey to Islip on public transportation, Rupert, despite petrol rationing, drove to Oxford and returned with John and the turkey. Not only did we have a turkey we also had a real English Christmas pudding with holly on top. On Christmas Eve 1945, the women went to church while Rupert and John decorated the Christmas tree. After we went to bed, 5-year-old Anthony awakened and asked if Father Christmas had been there. It was a wonderful Christmas! We spent New Year's with Kitty and Percy. Germany and Japan had been defeated; World War II was over, so it was indeed a happy New Year.

John knew he would be eligible for demobilization at the end of June 1946, so in January we contacted the Movements Group in London. Problems intervened. I began to have severe pains in my side and had to see a doctor. In February 1946, I was admitted in the Colchester Hospital. The diagnosis was that I had appendicitis and was two months pregnant. The appendix was removed, but the doctors kept me in hospital for 10 days. John immediately made arrangements to take me to Streatham to stay with Uncle Geof and Aunt Dorie for 2 weeks.

Before long periods of travel might be a threat to my health and that of our baby, John made final arrangements for me to travel home. As we traveled about England saying our good-byes, we observed the changes from wartime. It was still a time of great sadness for all those who had lost loved ones in the war. The ruined buildings and torn-up greens and parks were still there, but gone were the hated blackout curtains, the barrage balloons, searchlights, and anti-aircraft artillery. The golden green of England was spreading rapidly. On March 23, 1946 I boarded the S.S. Bayano in Liverpool. Even though I was seasick, the trip westward to America was far different from the voyage eastward to war torn Britain.

On 5 April 1946, I arrived safe and sound in Montgomery and was met by my family. John was released from the Royal Air Force and arrived in Montgomery on 1

July 1946. Even though we missed our family and friends in England, it was wonderful for John and me to be able to make a home together. Back in Alabama, I knew what a southern accent sounded like.

The forces that brought two twenty-year-olds together as husband and wife came at a time of the most devastating war in human history. He had traveled four thousand miles to train as a pilot, and he met an amazingly beautiful Alabama girl. No doubt, he felt that he simply did not wish to live without that lovely girl with the beautiful Southern accent, so he didn't. Their marriage and their tolerance of each other's differences led them to a successful marriage amid death and destruction in war-torn Britain. Back in the postwar United States, they survived, succeeded and raised a family. John and Jean's experience was not unique, but it proved to be one of the better results of the Arnold Scheme.

Almost eight thousand British aircrew candidates came to America to receive training by American instructors alongside American cadets, and those who completed training successfully departed with a better understanding of each other. Both groups were witnesses to one of the greatest wartime cooperative ventures ever undertaken. In addition to the value of aircrew training, the British presence in the United States promoted understanding between the peoples and air forces of both countries. Personal relationships that developed on both sides of the Atlantic Ocean during wartime transcended national interests and still endure more than six decades later.

SOURCES

The following individuals supplied information crucial for the writing of this book. Special thanks to all.

INTERVIEWS AND CORRESPONDENCE

CWO George F. Auman, assistant operations Officer
Cadet John Boaden of Helston, Cornwall, and Class SE-42-E
RAF Cadet Gordon John Cadman of Sussex and Class SE-42-I
H.J.P. Cattrall
John and Jean H. Clark
RAF Cadet William Andrew Coffee, Class SE-42-C
RAF Cadet George A. Ebner of Glasgow and Class SE-42-G
Cadet Robert R. Farrow of Sussex and Class SE-42-H
Captain and RAF Cadet Raymond Peter Grimwood, Class SE-42-E
RAF Cadet John McKenzie Hall
Flight Lieutenant and RAF Cadet Christopher Harrison of Derby and Class SE-42-F
Flight Lieutenant and RAF Cadet David Howell of Glasgow and Class SE-42-G
Flight Lieutenant and RAF Cadet Harry Leng of Dawlish, Devonshire, and Class SE-42-E
Air Chief Marshal Sir Douglas Lowe
Mrs. Audrie Manning, wife of Pilot Officer C.J.C. Manning, RAF check pilot at Tuscaloosa
A. Massheder
Tom Nelson
RAF Cadet Thomas C. Overend of Ayr, Scotland, and Class SE-42-H
Denis and Mary Payne
Philip Penfold
George Shaw
Edith Smart
RAF Cadet Anthony Vidler of Class SE-42-J
Dr. William Woodruff
RAF Cadet George A.C. Wright of Surrey and Class SE-42-G

LETTERS

LAC Norman Bate, Arcadia 42-F, 26 October 1941
Charles Brameld
R.E. Chandler to Stan Vossler, 16 October 1942
Brian Davies, Arcadia, 42-G
Woody Forrest, 42-A, to author
J.A. Mason to Instructor Stan Vossler, 2 February 1942
McCarthy to L.C. Martin, 4 September 1984
Arthur Morris
Thomas Nelson to C.J. Lunn
Air Vice-Marshal Wilfred E. Oulton to author
Peter Smith
LAC George A. Stone, Lakeland, 42-G

Visit us at
historypress.net